FRANK
O'HARA
POET
AMONG
PAINTERS

FRANK
O'HARA
POET AMONG PAINTERS

Marjorie Perloff

University of Texas Press, Austin and London

To
MAUREEN GRANVILLE-SMITH
and DONALD ALLEN

Note: Since the original publication of this book, all manuscripts cited on pages 36–38, 41–42, 44–45, 52–53 and in
notes 1, 3, 4, 8, 17, 18, and 20 for Chapter Two have been
published in two volumes edited by Donald Allen: *Early
Writing* and *Poems Retrieved* by Frank O'Hara (Bolinas,
Calif.: Grey Fox Press, 1977). Copyright © 1977 by Maureen Granville-Smith, Administratrix of the Estate of Frank
O'Hara. I am grateful to Donald Allen and Grey Fox Press
for permission to include material published in these two
books.

International Standard Book Number 0-292-72429-2
Library of Congress Catalog Card Number 78-71567

Copyright © 1977 by Marjorie Perloff; copyright © 1979 by the
    University of Texas Press

Designed by MaryJane DiMassi
Typeset by York Graphic Services, Inc.
Printed in the United States of America

First Paperback Edition, 1979

THE CRITIC

I cannot possibly think of you
other than you are: the assassin

of my orchards. You lurk there
in the shadows, meting out

conversation like Eve's first
confusion between penises and

snakes. Oh be droll, be jolly
and be temperate! Do not

frighten me more than you
have to! I must live forever.

—FRANK O'HARA
(1951)

CONTENTS

ACKNOWLEDGEMENTS

For permission to include material published by them, grateful acknowledgement is made to the following:

Alfred A. Knopf, Inc., for permission to quote from *The Collected Poems of Frank O'Hara*, edited by Donald Allen. Copyright © 1971 by Maureen Granville-Smith, Administratrix of the Estate of Frank O'Hara.

City Lights Books, for permission to quote from *Lunch Poems* by Frank O'Hara. Copyright © 1964 by Frank O'Hara; for permission to quote from *Planet News* by Allen Ginsberg. Copyright © 1968 by Allen Ginsberg.

Corinth Books, Inc., for Permission to quote from *Second Avenue* by Frank O'Hara. Copyright © 1960 by Frank O'Hara.

Grove Press, Inc., for permission to quote from *Meditations in an Emergency* by Frank O'Hara. Copyright © 1957 by Frank O'Hara; for permission to quote from *The Sonnets* by Ted Berrigan. Copyright © 1964 by Ted Berrigan and "*C*," a Journal of Poetry.

Donald Allen and Grey Fox Press, for permission to quote from *Standing Still* and *Walking in New York* by Frank O'Hara. Copyright © 1975 by Maureen Granville-Smith, Adminstratrix of the Estate of Frank O'Hara.

New Directions Publishing Corporation, for permission to quote from *Collected Earlier Poems* by William Carlos Williams. Copyright © 1938 by New Directions Publishing Corporation; Copyright © 1951 by William Carlos Williams; and to Faber and Faber Ltd, for permission to quote from *The Cantos* by Ezra Pound. Copyright © 1948 by Ezra Pound; for permission to quote from *Selected Writings* by Guillaume Apollinaire. Copyright © 1971 by Roger Shattuck. All Rights Reserved.

Harper & Row, Publishers, and to Weidenfeld & Nicholson, Publishers, for permission to quote from *The Bedbug and Selected Poetry* by Vladimir Mayakovsky. Copyright © 1960 by Patricia Blake and Max Hayward. Originally published by World Publishing Company.

Doubleday and Company, Inc., for permission to quote from *Freely Espousing* by James Schuyler. Copyright © 1969 by James Schuyler.

Ron Padgett, for permission to quote from *Great Balls of Fire.* Copyright © 1965, 1967, 1968, 1969 by Ron Padgett.

George Wittenborn, Inc. for permission to quote from *Dada Painters and Poets,* edited by Robert Motherwell. Copyright © 1951 by Robert Motherwell.

Wesleyan University Press, for permission to quote from *The Tennis Court Oath* by John Ashbery. Copyright © 1959 by John Ashbery.

Georges Borchardt, Inc., for permission to quote from *Rivers and Mountains.* Copyright © 1962, 1963, 1964, 1966, 1977 by John Ashbery.

Anne Waldman, for permission to quote from *Another World* (New York: Bobbs-Merrill Co., Inc. 1971). Copyright © 1971 by Anne Waldman.

PREFACE

A DECADE AFTER HIS death, Frank O'Hara remains a controversial
figure. Among New York poets and artists, he has been well-known
since the mid-fifties, and by the early sixties he had become a kind of
culture hero. Yet precisely because of his close association with the
"New York School," O'Hara was—and continues to be—considered
an "art world" figure rather than a serious poet. Because he wrote his
poems very quickly—often on the run and during his lunch hour at the
Museum of Modern Art—it has been assumed that his poetry is trivial
and frivolous. Because his life was so colorful and his accidental death
on Fire Island when he was only forty such a dramatic, indeed a tragic
event, interest has centered on the man rather than on the work.

The purpose of my book is to right this balance. Like many students
of contemporary poetry, I first read Frank O'Hara in Donald Allen's
pivotal anthology, *The New American Poetry* (New York: Grove,
1960), but it was not until 1972, when the editors of *Contemporary
Literature* asked me to write a review essay on the volumes of poetry
that had appeared within the preceding two years, that I began to
understand O'Hara's poetic world. The occasion was the publication

of Ron Padgett and David Shapiro's *Anthology of New York Poets* (New York: Random House, 1970). This anthology was dedicated to Frank O'Hara; the preface pays special tribute to him and reprints the entire text of "Personism: A Manifesto," written in 1959. There are twenty-two pages of poems by O'Hara and an interesting biographi-cal/bibliographical note.

The more O'Hara I read, the more enthusiastic I became about his work. Here, I felt, was a writer who made poetry look like a delightful game but who also had an uncanny way of getting what John Ashbery has called, with reference to Picabia, "the perishable fragrance of tra-dition" into his work, a tradition he sometimes extended, sometimes subverted. It was this combination of seeming artlessness and an acute awareness of poetic tradition that aroused my interest and curiosity, and when I came to write my review-essay, O'Hara became its center.

The present study thus reflects my growing conviction that O'Hara is one of the central poets of the postwar period, and that his influence will continue to grow in the years to come. He is also an important art critic, his improvisatory but incisive essays and reviews recalling those of an earlier poet-art critic whom he loved—Apollinaire. And his col-laborations with painters, composers, playwrights, and film-makers have given us some of the most delightful mixed-media works of the fifties and sixties.

The chapters that follow treat O'Hara's poetry chronologically. The focus is critical rather than biographical, but whenever it seems useful, I relate the poetry to the life. I begin with the poetry scene of the early fifties as a context for O'Hara's poetic, as that poetic can be deduced from his practical criticism and casual commentary, for O'Hara dis-liked theory for its own sake. The second chapter deals with the early period (1946–53), when O'Hara was beginning to invent a style. Access to the unpublished manuscripts of the Harvard years (1946–50) has shown me how learned and sophisticated this "playful" poet really was, and in discussing the early New York period I try to demonstrate how O'Hara's interest in Dada and Surrealist poetry, in Abstract Ex-pressionist painting, and in the colloquial speech of poets like William Carlos Williams came together to produce a body of exciting experi-mental poetry, quite unlike the established neo-Symbolist verse of the fifties.

The third chapter breaks the chronological development and takes up O'Hara's relationship to the visual artists of his time, including the various ways in which painting affected his poetry, his collaborations with Larry Rivers and Norman Bluhm, and his prolific art criticism. Chapter Four is the longest and perhaps the central chapter. Here I submit the poems of the "great period" (1954–61) to close inspection, discussing their style, genre, and use of convention. The problem of influence is a major topic, for O'Hara assimilated an astonishing variety of styles. His best poems fuse what he called the "charming artifice" of Apollinaire (and of a host of other French poets from Rimbaud to the Surrealists) with the bardic voice of Mayakovsky, the colloquial speech of Williams or the late Auden, the documentary precision of Pound's *Cantos,* and the Rilkean notion of being "needed by things." O'Hara's equivocal response to the English Romantics is especially interesting. Generically, his major poems follow Romantic models, but he almost always injects a note of parody, turning the conventions he uses inside out. Aside from literary models, O'Hara's poetry also incorporates specific film techniques, phonetic and rhythmic devices modeled on the music of John Cage and Eric Satie, and such concepts of Action Painting as "push and pull," the "all-over," and the notion of the canvas as a field which the artist enters. The result of assimilating such varied influences is the creation of a new kind of lyric poem.

Model + Technique

The final chapter considers the work of the sixties—smaller in output and rather different in kind—and takes up the difficult question of O'Hara's role as a New York poet. After discussing some of the astonishing elegies written for him by his friends and followers (a whole book could be compiled of these), I consider the relationship of O'Hara's poetry to that of John Ashbery and Allen Ginsberg, the two poets perhaps most immediately comparable, although in very different ways. I conclude that these poets have taken the contemporary lyric down parallel courses that never quite meet. And this is only natural: "schools" or movements always recede into the background as the permanently interesting artists emerge from their ranks.

Throughout this book I have tried to keep in mind O'Hara's own strictures on literary criticism, so charmingly put forward in the little poem, "The Critic" (1951), cited at the beginning of the Preface. I hope that if O'Hara were alive today, he would not consider me "the assassin of [his] orchards." I have tried, on the contrary, to respect his wish: "Do not / frighten me more than you / have to! I must live forever."

Many people have helped me to write this book. The following granted interviews: Joe LeSueur, John Ashbery, Grace Hartigan, Norman Bluhm, David Shapiro, and Patsy Southgate. These writers and artists helped to make the poetry milieu of the fifties and sixties come alive. They provided indispensable information about specific poems, collaborations, and events in O'Hara's life. They also persuaded me, I might add, that the time is not yet ripe for a biography, because their versions of specific incidents did not always coincide. I have had helpful conversation and/or correspondence about O'Hara with Bill Berkson, Paul Schmidt, and Allen Ginsberg. Kenneth Koch offered his assistance by mail but could not be interviewed because he was out of the country during the year in which this book was written.

I have profited from discussion of O'Hara's poetry with the following persons: Charles Altieri, James Breslin, Gerda Blumenthal, Stuart Curran, Frederick Garber, Lawrence Kramer, William McPherson, Diane Middlebrook, Norma Procopiow, David St. John, and Catharine R. Stimpson. Emily Mitchell Wallace deserves special mention: friend and fellow scholar, she was always ready to take up a difficult point, to help me track down a possible influence or reference, or to advise me on handling controversial biographical material tactfully. Doris Grumbach invited me, in January 1975, to review *Art Chronicles* for the *New Republic;* it was this review (1 March 1975) that brought my work on O'Hara to the attention of Michael Braziller of George Braziller, Inc., and initiated what has been a happy association between author and publisher, especially with my patient and discerning editor, James Hoekema. I should also like to thank Julia Strand for helping to bring the manuscript to completion. I owe a particular debt to the students in my seminar, "The Poetics of the Contemporary Lyric," given at the University of Maryland in the fall of 1975, especially to Douglas Messerli and Donald Duncan.

The following persons read portions of the manuscript and gave sound advice: Joe LeSueur, Sandra Earl Mintz, Claude Rawson, David Shapiro, William Spanos, Minda Tessler, and my two college-age daughters, Nancy and Carey—both keen O'Hara fans. My husband, Joseph K. Perloff, took time off from his heavy schedule at the

Hospital of the University of Pennsylvania, and time away from his own writings, to read every page (at every stage) and to help me organize the material and present it as clearly as possible. His suggestions—the suggestions of someone outside "the field"—were especially helpful. I am happy to add that, unlike many spouses, he had nothing to do with typing the manuscript; that unpleasant task was entirely my own.

I come finally to the two people to whom this book is dedicated and without whom it could not have been written. Frank O'Hara's sister, Maureen O'Hara Granville-Smith, the executrix of the Frank O'Hara Estate, has made available to me many unpublished manuscripts and letters as well as published items I might have missed: newspaper clippings, articles, photographs, reproductions of art works, recordings, etc. More important, she has encouraged the project from its inception, discussing the book with me at every stage of development and helping me to make crucial decisions. She has made me feel that I too "knew" Frank O'Hara. Her generosity and kindness can never be repaid.

Donald Allen, O'Hara's literary executor, has provided me with many copies of the manuscripts—letters, poems, essays, journals—he is currently editing. He has read my book from an editorial standpoint, providing missing or additional information, correcting errors of fact, expression, or taste, and detailing the necessary background. In conversation and correspondence, he has led me to many important sources I might otherwise have missed. I feel very fortunate to have had the help of the person who probably knows more about Frank O'Hara's poetry than anyone else.

Marjorie G. Perloff

University of Southern California
Los Angeles, California

1

THE AESTHETIC OF ATTENTION

—Don't be bored, don't be lazy, don't be trivial, and don't be proud. The slightest loss of attention leads to death. [1]

MYTHOLOGIES

IN THE FALL OF 1975, at the Frumkin Gallery on 57th Street, Alfred Leslie exhibited a startling group of neo-realist—or as he calls them, "confrontational"—paintings, consciously modeled on the art of David, Caravaggio, and Rubens, and "meant to influence the conduct of people." [2] The most controversial, if not the best, painting in the Leslie show was a large (9-by-6-foot) canvas called *The Killing of Frank O'Hara*. O'Hara was only forty years old when he was fatally injured, having been struck by a beach buggy on Fire Island in the early morning hours of 24 July 1966; he died the next evening in Bayview Hospital at Mastic Beach, Long Island. Leslie chose to dismiss the facts, which I shall detail in a moment, and depicted the accident as if it were an heroic myth. The dead poet, dressed in a plain white T-shirt and tan trousers, lies serenely on a rectangular plank, his body showing no signs of injury. Four teen-age girls, wearing cut-off jeans and bathing suits, are carefully lowering the body from a raised platform, which floats ambiguously in midair against an empty background painted in thick browns and blacks. A young bearded man, standing toward the rear of the platform, is pulling a rope, his movements suggesting the tolling of a mourning bell. "The painting," wrote

David Bourdon in the *Village Voice,* "is in effect a modern-dress apotheosis which Leslie paints with as much drama as Renaissance painters gave to the lowering of Christ from the cross."[3] Another reviewer, John Perreault, commented, "This painting redeems Frank O'Hara from the sordidness of his death."[4]

But why should Frank O'Hara be depicted as Christ descending from the Cross? Why the teen-age girls (Perreault calls them the "furies") as if O'Hara had been some sort of pop idol or rock star? And why the title, which implies that the poet was somehow tracked down and murdered by his enemies? It is, to say the least, a strange conception of the accident,[5] and O'Hara himself, who disliked all forms of apotheosis, hero worship, the making of "monuments," who loved to debunk those he called "the farters of our country," whose own poetry leans heavily toward parody, would surely have been amused and embarrassed by the painting's implications.

Yet we cannot simply dismiss *The Killing of Frank O'Hara* as a bad mistake or a piece of hackwork. Leslie is a highly accomplished, intelligent artist; he and O'Hara were friends and collaborated on films together; he had, moreover, thought about the subject for a long time, having already painted two versions—both more realistic images of the accident itself—in 1968 and 1972.[6] What Leslie's painting suggests to me is that, within a decade of the poet's death, an elaborate myth had been built up, a myth centering on O'Hara as the "laureate of the New York art scene"—the minor artist, memorable less for his actual achievement than for his colorful life and his influence on others. "From his posts as critic for *Art News* and curator at the Museum of Modern Art," writes Herbert A. Leibowitz, "he moved as a mercurial presence through the galleries and the studios of such painters as de Kooning and Larry Rivers, writing monographs about the new masters, encouraging the young, amusing with his talk—and dashing off his poems at odd moments with an insouciance that was legendary."[7]

It is easy to see how this legend of O'Hara as "aesthetic courtier" arose. In the course of his brief career, he experimented with every literary genre as well as with mixed-media works—poem-paintings, musical comedies, films, ballets, operas. His wide circle of devoted friends seems to have adored him for his great personal charm, his humor, his startling insight, and his extraordinary generosity. A poet who could refer to himself jestingly as having been "made in the image of a sissy truck-driver" (*CP,* 338), he had romantic attachments to any number of artist friends. He was a tireless partygoer, a heavy drinker, a restless, inexhaustible, eclectic, and wildly energetic genius. Pater's famous credo: "To burn always with this hard, gemlike flame, to maintain this ecstasy, is success in life," might well have been his motto.[8] Accordingly, his premature death—a death caused by such a freak accident—was quickly mythologized. "The loss of the man," wrote the young Ted Berrigan in his obituary essay, "makes the air more difficult to breathe in."[9] And Allen Ginsberg, in an elegy written just four days after O'Hara's death, declared:

> Deep philosophical terms dear Edwin Denby serious as Herbert Read
>   with silvery hair   announcing your dead gift
> to the grave crowd   whose historic op art   frisson was
>   the new sculpture your big blue wounded body made in the
>   Universe. . . .[10]

The artist, in short, became a work of art, and attention was deflected from O'Hara's real achievement, which was his poetry. The myth has two variants. The first, seen in Leslie's painting, is that of the artist as victim of a cruel, uncaring society, a man too good for this world. The second also views the artist as outsider but stresses his self-destructive bent. According to this myth, the poet who lives too hard and fast, burning the candle at both ends, finds his fulfillment only in death.[11] Thus, in an essay called "The New York School," written for the San Francisco *Advocate,* James M. Saslow writes: "Many of the lives [of the New York artists] tell us as much or more about their real purpose as did their paintings and poems. By their own admission, many remained frustrated in their work, and turned to other parts of their lives for fulfillment. Booze, fast cars and a feverish creativity took their toll. Many, like Jackson Pollock, Mark Rothko, and Frank O'Hara died violently or committed suicide." After describing, with dubious accuracy, the wild drinking parties of the New York artists, Saslow writes: "The pivotal figure in the cross-fertilization [between the poets and the painters] was the still unsung gay poet Frank O'Hara. Frail, thin, with a capacity for alcohol described as 'truly monumental,' O'Hara was at once poet laureate, guru, art critic and associate curator of painting at the Museum of Modern Art." The heavy drinking of O'Hara and his friends, Saslow explains, reflected "an overriding group obsession with *machismo*" at a time when Gay Liberation had not yet occurred. Drinking was a show of prowess, "a way of parodying Western movies." Within this false "macho framework," "the artists chose the most violent and extreme aspects of life, as if to dramatize their credo that *all* feeling, *all* experience is precious—regardless of its place in traditional good and evil. And ultimately, they deliberately courted death—at once the most taboo and most sublime experience."

Here is where the myth becomes dangerous: "When Frank O'Hara died it was officially termed an accident. But Elaine de Kooning felt deeper, more primeval forces were at work:

> And Frank O'Hara, getting killed on Fire Island, standing next to a beach buggy at three in the morning with 30 people standing around, and a car was coming with headlights on. Everyone saw it. How can you be hit by a car with headlights which everyone saw?

"The whole New York art scene," Saslow concludes, "was shattered by this mystery, which seemed to touch so many chords in their collective struggle." [12]

But the "mystery" Saslow speaks of so ominously has very little to do with what really happened on Fire Island on the evening in question. The facts, very briefly, are these. On Saturday, 23 July 1966, O'Hara and his friend J. J. Mitchell were houseguests at the home of Morris Golde on Water Island, Fire Island. That evening, O'Hara and Mitchell went to the Fire Island Pines, a bar-discotheque. At approximately 2 A.M., they set out to return to Golde's house in a beach taxi. About seven other people, who were also at the discotheque, but whom they did not know, were fellow passengers. A few minutes after reaching the beach, the taxi (a covered jeep) damaged a rear wheel and stopped. All the passengers descended and assembled near the left side of the taxi, away from the ocean, while the driver tried to repair the wheel. The headlights remained on because there was no other source of illumination; the beach was very dark. The driver radioed for another taxi, and the passengers milled about, waiting. O'Hara, who had been standing next to Mitchell, wandered toward the rear of the taxi. After a few minutes, another beach buggy came from the opposite direction. This buggy (an open jeep) appeared to be coming quite close to the disabled car at a speed of 15-20 m.p.h. The passengers standing in front of the taxi got out of the way, and Mitchell shouted "Frank!" At that moment, O'Hara emerged from the rear of the taxi, facing the headlights of the oncoming jeep. The young driver said he was blinded by the headlights of the stalled taxi, shining up into the air. O'Hara was struck by the right front fender, evidently in the abdomen; the jeep continued on for another ten feet or so and came to a stop. A policeman was on the scene within four or five minutes and a doctor was called. Arrangements were made to take O'Hara by ambulance and police launch to Bayview General Hospital in Mastic Beach. Mitchell accompanied O'Hara, who was in great pain. Later that day, July 24, he underwent exploratory abdominal surgery, but he died on the evening of July 25, of traumatic internal abdominal injury. According to a friend who was at his bedside, even during these last terrible days of his life, O'Hara "had the courtesy to notice his nurse's accent, and he insisted on speaking to her in French. He even made jokes for her." [13]

I cite these facts only to show how careful we must be not to mythologize the death of the poet. No one can know, of course, what was going on inside O'Hara's mind during the night of July 24, but it seems safe to say that if he had wanted to commit suicide, if he had "courted death" as the myth has it, there would have been a much surer way of doing it. Being hit by a beach buggy is hardly a guarantee of instant—or certain—death, and indeed, as we have seen, O'Hara did not die immediately and remained conscious until the end. I cannot even regard the poet's act as an unconscious death wish—what Yeats called "a lonely impulse of delight." The circumstances were too trivial, too fortuitous—one might say, too ridiculous. Who would think that one could be killed by a beach buggy? If, moreover, O'Hara had somehow survived the accident, what shape would the myth take then?

I think, accordingly, that it is time to forget all about Fire Island and the so-called "killing"—or instinctive suicide—of Frank O'Hara. For what really matters is not the myth of the *poète maudit* but his work. As his friend, the composer Morton Feldman, recalls: "I know if Frank could give me one message from the grave as I write he would say, 'Don't tell them the kind of man I was. *Did I do it?* Never mind the rest.'"[14]

"Did I do it?" A decade after O'Hara's death this question remains largely unanswered, partly because interest in the legend—our inveterate love of gossip—has deflected attention from the poet's accomplishment. By the early sixties, O'Hara had acquired a large underground reputation, appearing in such avant-garde periodicals as *Evergreen Review, Kulchur, Big Table, Floating Bear,* and *Locus Solus,* as well as in Donald Allen's pivotal anthology *The New American Poetry* (1960).[15] But the more established Little Magazines—*Poetry,* the *Kenyon Review,* the *Hudson*—regarded O'Hara as little more than a New York dilettante, an art-world figure who dashed off occasional poems mainly to amuse his friends. In a typical response Marius Bewley, reviewing *Love Poems* (1965) for the *New York Review of Books,* called O'Hara's lyrics "amiable and gay, like streamers of crêpe paper, fluttering before an electric fan."[16]

The posthumous publication in 1971 of the *Collected Poems,* meticulously edited by Donald Allen and beautifully produced by Alfred A. Knopf, should have exploded this image. For one thing, no one suspected that O'Hara had written so much: as John Ashbery says in his Introduction, "That *The Collected Poems of Frank O'Hara* should turn out to be a volume of the present dimensions will surprise those who knew him, and would have surprised Frank even more" (*CP,* vii). But although the *Collected Poems* won the National Book Award, its amazing size (over five hundred pages) turned out to be something of a handicap. Critics immediately complained that the book was too monumental. Thus William Dickey remarks that it is "pretentious" to "enshrine" a poet as delicate, charming, and evanescent as O'Hara "in a volume that rivals the Variorum Yeats, in size if not in seriousness. Surely that solemnity would have amused Frank."[17] And Helen Vendler begins her review by saying: "Now that Knopf has given us O'Hara's *Collected Poems,* they had better rapidly produce a *Selected Poems,* a book that wouldn't drown O'Hara in his own fluency. For the record, we need this new edition; for the sake of fame and poetry, we need a massively reduced version, showing O'Hara at his best. His charms are inseparable from his overproduction."[18]

In theory, Vendler is quite right. Many of the poems in the volume are negligible—impromptu notes to friends, in-jokes, birthday or Christmas greetings—and it may well be the case that O'Hara himself would not have reproduced them all in a *Collected Poems*. Yet the editor of a posthumous collection is in a difficult position, especially when the poet in question is, as Donald Allen points out in his Editor's Note, both "diffident and tentative" about the publication of his work. O'Hara always found it difficult to assemble poems for a volume, to meet deadlines or editorial demands. Indeed, he used to stuff some of his best poems into desk drawers or coat pockets and then forget all about them. Since the poet's precise wishes were thus impossible to determine, Allen decided "to provide a reliable text for all the poems Frank O'Hara published during his lifetime—in individual volumes and in anthologies and periodicals—together with all the unpublished poems he conceivably would have wanted to see in print."[19]

There are, I think, two justifications for this procedure. First, it can be argued that no editor can determine, especially so soon after a poet's death, which of his poems are important, which expendable. The burden of choice is too great, and so Allen rightly includes all those poems that O'Hara would have been willing to publish separately. Secondly, and more important, as both Allen and Ashbery note, O'Hara did tend to think of his work as a whole, an ongoing record of his life. The sum of the *Collected Poems* is, in fact, much greater than its parts, and the more one reads even the slight poems, the more one sees their place in the total pattern. Future readers will not, I think, be satisfied with an abbreviated text. Indeed, although the *Selected Poems,* issued in 1973, is still a large volume (over two hundred pages), I find that, despite my concurrence with most of Allen's choices, there are too many poems missing. In his review of the *Collected Poems* for *The New Republic,* Kenneth Koch explains why this is the case:

> It is a great experience to read it all. I have known Frank O'Hara's work for about twenty years, and I had read a great many of the poems before. One reaction I had to this book, though, was astonishment. All those "moments," all the momentary enthusiasms and despairs which I had been moved by when I first read them when they were here altogether made something I had never imagined. It is not all one great poem, but something in some ways better: a collection of created moments that illuminate a whole life.[20]

Others were less convinced that "this huge tombstone of a book," as Thomas Shapcott calls the *Collected Poems* in his review for *Poetry,* represents an important poetic achievement. Neither the major anthologies nor the standard surveys of the poetry of the fifties and sixties have paid much attention to O'Hara. M. L. Rosenthal's well-known *The Modern Poets, American and British Poetry After World War II,* published in 1967, still provides the norm. Rosenthal devotes two long chapters to the Confessional Poets, Robert Lowell having the place of honor, followed by Sylvia Plath, John Berryman, W. D. Snodgrass, Anne Sexton, and, rather oddly, Theodore Roethke and Allen Ginsberg. Another chapter called "The 'Projectivist' Movement" discusses Charles Olson, Robert Creeley, and Robert Duncan, with briefer commentary on Denise Levertov, Paul Blackburn, and LeRoi Jones (now Imamu Baraka). The epilogue, "American Crosscurrents," refers briefly to such diverse poets as Theodore Weiss, Paul Goodman, Galway Kinnell, Louis Simpson, Robert Bly, and James Wright. O'Hara is not mentioned a single time; neither, it is only fair to say, are such other New York poets as John Ashbery and Kenneth Koch, or West Coast poets like Edward Dorn and Philip Whalen.[21]

A slightly later survey, *Salmagundi's* special double issue devoted to Contemporary Poetry (Spring–Summer 1973), adds to the names in Rosenthal's book those of Adrienne Rich, A. R. Ammons, and John Ashbery. Each of these poets is the subject of a long sympathetic essay; O'Hara is mentioned only in passing in Paul Zweig's essay on "The New Surrealism." Again, *The Norton Introduction to Literature: Poetry* (1973) includes poems by Lowell, Plath, Olson, Ginsberg, Kinnell, Ammons, and Baraka, as well as a special thirty-page section on Adrienne Rich as a representative contemporary poet. The *Norton* contains one poem by Ashbery and one by Koch—there are no poems by O'Hara.[22]

This, then, is the current situation. On the one side, we have O'Hara's devoted admirers, generally themselves artists, who regard the poet as their Lost Leader. On the other, there is the Academy, which remains largely indifferent to the poetry. There are now signs that the gap is narrowing as a new generation of students and younger poet-critics are discovering O'Hara's poetry.[23] But O'Hara continues to be a controversial figure, a poet who elicits curiously contradictory responses from readers who otherwise tend to agree about the poetry they admire. To understand why this is the case, we must begin by looking at the poetry climate of the early fifties, when O'Hara first arrived in New York, fresh from a year of study at Ann Arbor (1950–51), and got a job at the front desk of the Museum of Modern Art. It was a chance move that turned out to be decisive in shaping his aesthetic.

THE "RAW" AND THE "COOKED"

In *The Poem in its Skin* (1968), which contains one of the first useful discussions of O'Hara's poetry, Paul Carroll writes:

> To a young poet the scene in American verse in the late 1940s and early 1950s seemed much like walking down 59th Street in New York for the first time. Elegant and sturdy hotels and apartment buildings stand in the enveloping dusk, mysterious in their power, sophistication, wealth and inaccessibility. One of the most magnificent buildings houses Eliot, his heirs and their sons; other tall, graceful buildings contain e.e. cummings, Marianne Moore, Ezra Pound, Wallace Stevens, William Carlos Williams. The doormen look past you but you are noted if you walk too near. No Admission.
>
> Civilized, verbally excellent, ironic, cerebral and clearly bearers of the Tradition, the poems admired as models included: the Eliot of "The Love Song of J. Alfred Prufrock" and *Poems 1920* and "The Waste Land," the Ransom of "The Equilibrists" and "Bells for John Whiteside's Daughter," the Tate of "Sonnets at Christmas," . . . the Warren of "Bearded Oaks," and of course the Auden of "In Memory of W. B. Yeats," "September 1, 1939," and "Musée des Beaux Arts." Then came the sons: the Lowell of *Lord Weary's Castle,* the Delmore Schwartz of "For Rhoda" and "In the Naked Bed, in Plato's Cave," the Shapiro of *Person, Place and Thing* and *V-Letter,* the Wilbur of "A Black November Turkey" and "Love Calls us to the Things of This World."[24]

Or, as O'Hara himself was to sum it up in *US,* the first of the lithograph stones he made with Larry Rivers,[25] "poetry was declining / Painting advancing / we were complaining / it was '50." Eliot, he declared in 1952, had had a "deadening and obscuring and precious effect" on his "respective followers."[26] It is important to note that the Eliot described by O'Hara is not at all the *real* poet, the self-doubting, struggling revolutionary of the early twenties. Rather, the Eliot vener-ated by the generation brought up on Brooks and Warren's *Under-standing Poetry* was the magisterial Elder Statesman, no longer writing lyric poetry (*Four Quartets* was published in 1944) but making impor-tant public pronouncements about its nature and function. James Breslin points out, quite rightly I think, that Williams's well-known attack on "The Waste Land" in his *Autobiography* (a book O'Hara knew well) as the poem that "returned us to the classroom just at the moment when . . . we were on the point of escape . . . to the essence of a new art form" reflects Eliot's position at the time the statement was made (1951) rather than the time about which it was ostensibly made (1922).[27]

What troubled Williams, in short, was less "The Waste Land" itself than that Eliot had become, in the words of Delmore Schwartz, an "international hero," the age's "literary dictator," at a time when Williams's own poetry was not yet widely appreciated.[28] Wallace Ste-vens represents a related case. By 1950, Stevens had many admirers, but he was still considered something of a coterie poet whose later work seemed to defy the New Critical demand for precision and com-plexity. In *Poetry and the Age* (1953), for example, Randall Jarrell complained of Stevens's tendency to use philosophical abstractions, declaring: "But surely a poet *has* to treat the concrete as primary. . . . for him it is always the generalization whose life is derived."[29] As for Pound, although the *Pisan Cantos* won the Bollingen Prize for 1949, the poet who wrote those Cantos was, after all, a mental patient at St. Elizabeth's until 1958, and thus relatively inaccessible to most younger poets.

Eliot thus reigned supreme, and the prevailing mode was that of neo-Symbolism—a poetry, in Paul Carroll's words, "civilized, verbally excellent, ironic, cerebral"—and traditional. Even *Lord Weary's Castle* (1947), a book thoroughly disliked by O'Hara and his circle, was, of course, still squarely in the Eliot tradition that Lowell had absorbed from Tate, Ransom, and Jarrell at Kenyon College. Although every-one called it a "difficult" book, full of recondite symbols, *Lord Weary's Castle* was an instant success. Eliot himself, who rarely commended younger poets, singled out Lowell for praise.[30] The reason for the book's success is quite simple: whereas *Prufrock and Other Observa-*

tions, published in a limited edition of five hundred copies, was at first wholly misunderstood, and Eliot had to create his own audience, Lowell, as Breslin notes, "received [an audience] ready-made—the one created (in the main) by Eliot."[31]

It is a nice irony. Looking back at *Lord Weary's Castle* some ten years later, Lowell admitted that he now found its formalism oppressive, that he longed for a more "open," less "Alexandrian" poetry. "Any number of people," he said, "are guilty of writing a complicated poem that has a certain amount of Symbolism in it and really difficult meaning, a wonderful poem to teach. Then you unwind it and you feel that the intelligence, the experience, whatever goes into it, is skin deep."[32] And W. D. Snodgrass similarly recalls:

> . . . in school, we had been taught to write a very difficult and very intellectual poem. We tried to achieve the obscure and dense texture of the French Symbolists (very intuitive and often deranged poets), but by using methods similar to those of the very intellectual and conscious poets of the English Renaissance, especially the Metaphysical poets. . . .[33]

This demand for the tightly structured lyric, distinguished by its complex network of symbols, its metaphysical wit, and its adaptation of traditional meters, lasted well into the sixties. A perfect emblem of the time is Anthony Ostroff's *The Contemporary Poet as Artist and Critic* (1964), a popular collection of symposia in each of which three poets comment on a poem by a fourth poet who then comments on their comments. Thus Richard Wilbur's "Love Calls Us to the Things of this World" is submitted to close analysis by Richard Eberhart, May Swenson, and Robert Horan. The three poet-critics concur on Wilbur's central theme but disagree about such details as the use of Biblical allusions—for example, the line "Let there be clean linen for the backs of thieves." In his reply, Wilbur notes that, given his natural bent toward indirection and ambiguity, "it is good to be so thoroughly understood."[34] It is as if the dismemberment of Orpheus had become, by a curious inversion, the favorite pastime of Orpheus himself.

Yet all this time, as Carroll puts it, "the barbarians were already inside the gates of the city." By "barbarian," Carroll means simply "the alien or enemy of prevailing contemporary standards of correctness or purity of taste." More specifically, the "barbarians" were those who "shared a concern with trying to write types of poems either alien or hostile to the poem as defined and explored by Eliot and his heirs" (pp. 206–07). And Carroll suggests that one might appropriately date "the invasion of the barbarians" as taking place in 1956 "when Lawrence Ferlinghetti published in his City Lights Pocket Poet Series the small hardboiled-looking, funeral-black bordered edition of *Howl and Other Poems* by young Allen Ginsberg."

The challenge Ginsberg and the Beats presented to the Establishment has often been chronicled, as has the parallel revolt of the Black Mountain poets.[35] O'Hara's role in the ongoing battle between Redskin and Paleface, between the "raw" and the "cooked," is more difficult to assess. Indeed, as Ashbery argues in a remarkable obituary essay,[36] O'Hara was caught between "opposing power blocs":

> "Too hip for the squares and too square for the hips" is a category of oblivion which increasingly threatens any artist who dares to take his own way, regardless of mass public and journalistic approval. And how could it be otherwise in a supremely tribal civilization like ours, where even artists feel compelled to band together in marauding packs, where the loyalty-oath mentality has pervaded outer Bohemia, and where Grove Press subway posters invite the lumpenproletariat to "join the Underground Generation" as though this were as simple a matter as joining the Pepsi Generation which it probably is.

In such a setting, O'Hara's "Lunch Poems," with their recreation of everyday experience, could only confound their audience. For

> O'Hara's poetry has no program and therefore cannot be joined. It does not advocate sex and dope as a panacea for the ills of modern society; it does not speak out against the war in Viet Nam or in favor of civil rights; it does not paint gothic vignettes of the post-Atomic Age: in a word, it does not attack the establishment. It merely ignores its right to exist, and is thus a source of annoyance for partisans of every stripe.

Here Ashbery seems to be thinking not only of O'Hara's poetry but of his own. He too had no "program," and his highly original lyric mode did not gain wide recognition until the seventies. In a sense, Ashbery speaks for the whole New York School—Kenneth Koch,

James Schuyler, Barbara Guest, Edwin Denby, and their followers—although, as I shall argue later, the differences between these poets finally make the group label (derived from their shared allegiance to the New York painters) largely irrelevant. O'Hara's sense of what a poem should be, for that matter, turns out to be rather different from Ashbery's poetic.

But it is quite right to point out, as Ashbery does, that O'Hara was caught between the "opposing power blocs" of "hip" and "square." On the one hand, although his own poetry stems directly from his personal experience, he disliked Confessionalism, the baring of the recesses of the soul. Of Lowell's famed "Skunk Hour," he remarked:

> I don't think that anyone has to get themselves to go and watch lovers in a parking lot necking in order to write a poem, and I don't see why it's admirable if they feel guilty about it. They should feel guilty. Why are they snooping? What's so wonderful about a Peeping Tom? And then if you liken them to skunks putting their noses into garbage pails, you've just done something perfectly revolting. No matter what the metrics are. And the metrics aren't all that unusual. Every other person in any university in the United States could put that thing into metrics.

Lowell's "confessional manner," O'Hara feels, lets him "get away with things that are just plain bad but you're supposed to be interested because he's supposed to be so upset." [37]

Such severe judgment is unusual for O'Hara, who generally refused to attack other poets, because, as he put it, "It'll slip into oblivion without my help." But Lowell's poetic sensibility was peculiarly alien to his. Joe LeSueur, one of O'Hara's closest friends, tells an amusing anecdote about a poetry reading given by O'Hara and Lowell at Wagner College on Staten Island in 1962. O'Hara, who read first, introduced his work by saying, "On the ferry coming over here, I wrote a poem," and proceeded to read "Lana Turner has collapsed!" (*CP*, 449), much to the amusement of the audience. When it was Lowell's turn, he said something to the effect: "Well, I'm sorry *I* didn't write a poem on the way over here," the implication being that poetry is a *serious* business and that O'Hara was trivializing it and camping it up. [38]

From then on, the two poets kept their distance. But O'Hara had his reasons for rejecting the Lowell mode. When he says of "Skunk Hour": "I really dislike dishonesty [more] than bad lines" (*SS,* 13), he means, I think, that the reputed "openness" of *Life Studies* is only a surface gesture; that "Skunk Hour" is still a conventional poem in its reliance on Biblical and literary allusions (e.g., John of the Cross's "One dark night," Satan's "I myself am hell"), its double meanings ("the chalk-dry and spar spire / of the Trinitarian Church"), and its pervasive symbolism. Rightly or wrongly, O'Hara regarded such poetry as extending the New Critical, academic tradition.[39]

O'Hara's attitude to what Lucie-Smith calls "the raw" (*SS,* 12) is more complicated. Allen Ginsberg, who wrote one of the first elegies for O'Hara, was a good friend, and O'Hara always spoke of his poetry with love and admiration. There are frequent references to Ginsberg in the poems, for example:

> so they repair the street in the middle of the night
> and Allen and Peter can once again walk forth to visit friends
>
> (*CP,* 346)

or

> . . . and Allen and I getting depressed and angry
> becoming again the male version of wallflower or wallpaper
>
> (*CP,* 400)

He was also very fond of Gregory Corso's *Gasoline* and *Bomb* (both 1958), calling the latter a "superb and praiseful poem."[40] Between 1958 and 1962, in the pages of *Yūgen, Kulchur,* and the *Evergreen Review,* O'Hara's work appeared side by side with that of Ginsberg, Corso, Michael McClure, Gary Snyder, and Philip Whalen—all poets whose work he praised.[41] During these years he was especially close—both personally and in his attitudes toward poetry—to LeRoi Jones (Imamu Baraka), who edited first *Yūgen* and was later one of the editors of *Kulchur.*

Yet O'Hara had none of the revolutionary fervor, the prophetic zeal of the Beats. Unlike Ginsberg, he neither attacked "the narcotic / tobacco haze of Capitalism" nor believed that poetry was closely related to mysticism and could *change* one's life. Unlike Jack Kerouac, whose prose style he admired,[42] he cared nothing for the mystique of "saintly motorcyclists" on the Open Road. Unlike Gary Snyder, he was not enchanted by Zen or Japanese culture. While others journeyed to the Himalayas, Kyoto, or Tangier, O'Hara preferred to walk the streets of Manhattan with its rush-hour frenzy and warring taxicabs, the "luminous humidity" of the Seagram Building, the "gusts of water" spraying in the Plaza fountain.

O'Hara's relationship to the Black Mountain poets was more remote. Like the Beats, these poets appeared side by side with him in the Little Magazines: *Yūgen* 6 (1960), for example, contains O'Hara's "Personal Poem" and Charles Olson's famed "The Distances." But O'Hara had few personal ties to Black Mountain, the main connection being John Wieners, who was a devoted student and friend of Olson's but was never really considered a member of the Black Mountain group. O'Hara first met Wieners in Cambridge in 1956, and the two remained friends, often exchanging poems. When Wieners's *Hotel Wentley Poems* appeared in 1958, O'Hara called it "a beautiful sequence of things,"[43] and in "Les Luths" (1959), he remarks: "everybody here is running around after dull pleasantries and / wondering if *The Hotel Wentley Poems* is as great as I say it is" (*CP*, 343). From the vantage point of the mid-seventies, one can see many similarities between Wieners and O'Hara. Both loved to parody established genres; both wrote bittersweet lyrics, at once formal and colloquial, about homosexual love; both regarded all Movements and Manifestos with some suspicion.

Such instinctive distrust of dogma must have colored O'Hara's view of Charles Olson. When he gave Jasper Johns a list of the "poets [who] interested [him] most," he said, "I don't know if you like Charles Olson but I always find him interesting if sometimes rather cold and echoey of Ezra Pound, but I like the Maximus poems and IN COLD HELL IN THICKET . . . very much."[44] "Olson," he told Lucie-Smith, "is—a great spirit. I don't think that he is willing to be as delicate as his sensibility may be emotionally and he's extremely conscious of the Pound heritage and of saying the important utterance, which one cannot always summon up and indeed is not particularly desirable most of the time" (*SS*, 13).

What O'Hara implies here is that Olson's poetry is perhaps too *willed,* too consciously "significant." Poetry need not have palpable design on us; the "important utterance," indeed, "is not particularly desirable most of the time." Again, O'Hara was skeptical about Olson's epic ambitions (his allegiance to the form of the *Cantos*) even though Pound was, as we shall see, one of O'Hara's own models. As for Creeley and Levertov, O'Hara told Lucie-Smith that their limitation was "making *control* practically the subject matter of the poem": "*control* of the language . . . *control* of the experiences and . . . *control* of your thought." "The amazing thing," he added, "is that where they've pared down the diction so that the experience presumably will come through as strongly as possible, it's the experience of their paring it down that comes through . . . and not the experience that is the subject (*SS*, 23).

This is another way of saying that the Black Mountain poets were too theoretical, too self-consciously programmatic—one might even say, despite their protests to the contrary, too "academic." Or at least so it would appear to O'Hara who, as Bill Berkson observes in one of the best essays on the poet, regarded "ideas as inseparable from the people who had them. Theory and experience had to jell, and the varieties of experience around made dogma appear pointless."[45] Indeed, O'Hara's now notorious "Personism: a Manifesto," first written for Donald Allen's *New American Poetry* (1960), but then retracted and published in *Yūgen*,[46] is probably a sly parody of Black Mountain manifestos, particularly Olson's "Projective Verse," that Sacred Text of 1950, revered by Creeley, Duncan, Levertov, Dorn, and a score of other poets.[47] For Olson's complex network of "principles" and "rules"—his talk of kinetics, energy discharges, field composition, and logos—O'Hara substitutes an air of innocent bonhommie about versecraft:

> Everything is in the poems. . . . I don't believe in god, so I don't have to make elaborately sounded structures. I hate Vachel Lindsay, always have; I don't even like rhythm, assonance, all that stuff. You just go on your nerve. If someone's chasing you down the street with a knife you just run, you don't turn around and shout, "Give it up! I was a track star for Mineola Prep." (*CP*, 498)

The witty insouciance displayed in this passage is, of course, something of a pose. For, as we shall see, O'Hara cared very much indeed about the creation of "elaborately sounded structures." In a lecture on "Design" given at The Club in 1952, he discussed, with great insight, the relative merits of the stanza forms and linear patterns of such poets as George Herbert, Apollinaire, and e.e. cummings.[48] Thus, the insistence that "You just go on your nerve" must be seen as O'Hara's reaction to the endless pompensities of the poetry manifestos of the fifties and sixties. In 1961, for example, when the Paterson Society asked him to submit a statement on his poetic, O'Hara wrote a letter explaining why he couldn't formulate such a statement—and then never sent the letter. Reprinted at the back of the *Collected Poems,* this letter expresses O'Hara's life-long conviction that one cannot theorize about poetry, at least not in a formal way:

> I don't want to make up a lot of prose about something that is perfectly clear in the poems. If you cover someone with earth and grass grows, you don't know what they looked like any more. Critical prose makes too much grass grow, and I don't want to help hide my own poems, much less kill them. (*CP,* 510)

To understand O'Hara's conviction that "critical prose makes too much grass grow," we need merely read the first few "Statements on Poetics" at the back of Donald Allen's *New American Poetry.* Olson's "Projective Verse" is followed by his "Letter to Elaine Feinstein," which contains commentary like the following:

> Image, therefore, is vector. It carries the trinity via the double to the single form which one makes oneself able, if so, to issue from the "content" (multiplicity: originally, and repetitively, chaos—Tiamat: wot the Hindo-Europeans knocked out by giving the Old Man (Juice himself) all the lightning. (p. 399)

Or take this passage from Robert Duncan's "Pages from a Notebook" in the same anthology: "I study what I write as I study out any mystery. A poem, mine or anothers, is an occult document, a body awaiting vivisection, analysis, X-rays" (p. 400).

In the same period, Robert Bly and his followers were publishing manifestos in *The Fifties* (later *The Sixties*), advocating the liberation of the unconscious and the use of "deep images,"[49] while the Objectivists, dormant for a few decades, were being recalled to life and reformulating their doctrines. In an interview for *Contemporary Literature,* George Oppen explains the meaning of *Discrete Series,* the title of a book of poems he had published in 1934, as follows:

> That's a phrase in mathematics. A pure mathematical series would be one in which each term is derived from the preceding term by a rule. A discrete series is a series of terms each of which is empirically derived, each of which is empirically true. And this is the reason for the fragmentary character of those poems. I was attempting to construct a meaning by empirical statements, by imagist statements.[50]

O'Hara's response to what must have seemed to him unnecessarily labored accounts of the poetic process was to assume the role of Poetic Innocent:

> . . . how can you really care if anybody gets it, or gets what it means, or if it improves them? Improves them for what? For death? Why hurry them along? Too many poets act like a middle-aged mother trying to get her kids to eat too much cooked meat, and potatoes with drippings (tears). I don't give a damn whether they eat or not. Forced feeding leads to excessive thinness (effete). Nobody should experience anything they don't need to, if they don't need poetry bully for them. I like the movies too. And after all, only Whitman and Crane and Williams, of the American poets, are better than the movies. (*CP,* 498)

If these comments sound unnecessarily frivolous, we should remember that O'Hara consistently rebelled against the notion of poetry as an Institution precisely because he personally cared about it so much. In a 1957 letter to John Ashbery, he wrote: "It seems that my life has been very empty due to work [i.e., at the Museum of Modern Art] and that I am padding this letter with all sorts of boring things. I've been very depressed lately but now that I've done a few poems, however bad, I feel much better. Sometimes when I don't have the chance to spill the beans into a few deaf lines I think I'm losing my mind."[51] And a few years later, he wrote to Bill Berkson, "poetry is the highest art, everything else, however gratifying . . . moving, and grand, is less demanding, more indulgent, more casual, more gratuitous, more instantly apprehensible, which I assume is not exactly what we are after."[52]

What, then, was O'Hara after? If none of the existing movements of the fifties could provide a model for what he considered *poetry,* what were its roots? In one of his rare formal statements on aesthetics, written at the request of Donald Allen for the appendix of *The New American Poetry,* O'Hara said: "It may be that poetry makes life's nebulous events tangible to me and restores their detail; or conversely, that poetry brings forth the intangible quality of incidents which are all too concrete and circumstantial."[53] Here the poet oddly echoes the great Russian Formalist critic Viktor Shklovsky, who said in a famous essay of 1917: "Art exists that one may recover the sensation of life; it exists to make one feel things, to make the stone *stony*—art removes objects from the automatism of perception." It *defamiliarizes* objects by presenting them as if seen for the first time or by distorting their form "so as to make the act of perception more difficult and to prolong its duration."[54]

In his drive to "defamiliarize" the ordinary—even the "sheer ugliness in America"[55]—the artist must be as *attentive* as possible to the world around him. As O'Hara puts it in "Meditations in an Emergency":

> My eyes are vague blue, like the sky, and change all the time; they are indiscriminate but fleeting, entirely specific and disloyal, so that no one trusts me. I am always looking away. Or again at something after it has given me up. It makes me restless and that makes me unhappy, but I cannot keep them still. . . . It's not that I'm curious. On the contrary, I am bored but it's my duty to be attentive, I am needed by things as the sky must be above the earth. And lately so great has *their* anxiety become, I can spare myself little sleep. (*CP,* 197)

The notion of being "needed by things," playful as O'Hara makes it sound in this context, is a central feature of his poetic. It derives, quite possibly, from Rilke, whose poetry O'Hara knew well and loved.[56] In the first of the *Duino Elegies,* the poet reminds himself:

> Yes, the seasons of spring needed you. Some of the stars
> made claims on you, so that you would feel them. In the past,
> a wave rose up to reach you, or

as you walked by an open window
a violin gave itself to you. All this was your task.[57]

For both Rilke and O'Hara, it is the artist's "duty to be attentive" to the world of process in which he finds himself. And such attention requires a peculiar self-discipline, the ability to look at something and, paraphrasing Ezra Pound, to "See It New!" In the interview with Lucie-Smith, O'Hara explains de Kooning's attitude to the great painters of the past in this way: "if de Kooning says that what he really is interested in is Poussin; that's his way of not being bored with Kandinsky when all the world is looking at Kandinsky. That attitude may only work for two years, but that doesn't matter in the life of the artist as long as it energizes him to produce more works that are beautiful" (*SS*, 35).

To be "influenced" by another artist, then, is to find new means of evading monotony, boredom, sameness—to force oneself to "see" in new ways, to *defamiliarize* the object. The painting of Larry Rivers, says O'Hara, "has taught me to be more keenly interested while I'm still alive. And perhaps this is the most important thing art can say."[58]

One way of avoiding boredom, of keeping oneself and one's reader "more keenly interested," is to create a poetic structure that is always changing, shifting, becoming. In an early lyric called "Poetry" (1951), O'Hara declares:

> The only way to be quiet
> is to be quick, so I scare
> you clumsily, or surprise
> you with a stab.
>
> (*CP*, 49)

The poet's desire is "to deepen you by my quickness," or, as he puts it in "My Heart" (1955):

> I'm not going to cry all the time
> nor shall I laugh all the time,
> I don't prefer one "strain" to another.
> I'd have the immediacy of a bad movie,
> not just a sleeper, but also the big,
> over-produced first-run kind. I want to be
> at least as alive as the vulgar.
>
> (*CP*, 231)

And he concludes: "you can't plan on the heart, but / the better part of it, my poetry, is open."

Openness, quickening, immediacy—these are the qualities O'Hara wants to capture in his poetry. In "Music" (1954), for example, the poet-speaker is "naked as a tablecloth," and his door "is *open* to the evenings of midwinter's / lightly falling snow." Or again, in "Digression on Number 1, 1948," the poet says:

> I am ill today, but I am not
> too ill. I am not ill at all.
> It is a perfect day, warm
> for winter, cold for fall.
>
> A fine day for seeing.   (*CP*, 260)

"A fine day for seeing" is thus a quirky day, "warm / for winter, cold for fall." Contradiction becomes the proper condition for "seeing." Sameness, monotony, evenness of surface—these create boredom. This is why the poet exclaims in "To Hell With It":

> (How I hate subject matter! melancholy,
>   intruding on the vigorous heart,
>   the soul telling itself
> you haven't suffered enough ((Hyalomiel))
>   and all things that don't change,
> photographs,
>   monuments,
>   memories of Bunny and Gregory and me in /
>   costume. . . .
>   (*CP*, 275)

Photographs, monuments, static memories—"all things that don't change"—these have no place in the poet's world. We can now understand why O'Hara loves the *motion* picture, *action* painting, and all forms of dance—art forms that capture the *present* rather than the past, the present in all its chaotic splendor. And New York is therefore the very center of being, quite simply because it is the place where more is happening at once than anywhere else in the world: "I can't even enjoy a blade of grass unless I know there's a subway handy, or a record store or some other sign that people do not totally *regret* life" (*CP*, 197).

But how does one create a poetic structure that has immediacy, openness, "quickness," a structure that avoids the monotony and stasis of monuments and photographs? An important hint is provided in a letter O'Hara wrote to Larry Rivers in 1957, enclosing a group of poems, a letter Rivers then incorporated into a collage:[59]

> Now please tell me if you think these poems are filled with disgusting self-pity, if there are "holes" in them, if the surface isn't kept "up," if there are recognizable images, if they show nostalgia for the avant-garde, or if they don't have "push" and "pull," and I'll keep working on them until each is a foot high.
>
> Yours in action art,
> Frank

Although O'Hara is partly joking here, teasing Rivers who had accused his poems of being filled with "gorgeous self-pity," this letter is surely a key document for any student of O'Hara's work. The notion that, as in the case of abstract painting, the "surface" must be kept "up," is a recurrent theme in his writings. In "Notes on *Second Avenue*" (1953), for example, he talks of wanting "to keep the surface of the poem high and dry, not wet, reflective and self-conscious. . . . I hope the poem to *be* the subject, not just about it."[60] Again, the terms "push" and "pull" derive from theoretical discussions of Abstract Expressionism, specifically to Hans Hofmann's discussion of the successful relationship of planes in Cubist and abstract art. "Pictorial space," wrote Hofmann, "exists two-dimensionally. . . . Depth . . . is not created by the arrangement of objects, one after another, toward a vanishing point, in the sense of Renaissance perspective, but on the contrary . . . by the creation of forces in the sense of *push and pull*."[61]

O'Hara's understanding of Jackson Pollock's sense of *scale* sheds further light on the terminology used in the letter to Larry Rivers:

> In the past, an artist by means of scale could create a vast panorama on a few feet of canvas or wall, relating this scale both to the visual reality of known images . . . and to the real setting. . . . Pollock, choosing to use no images with real visual equivalents . . . struck upon a use of scale which was to have a revolutionary effect on contemporary painting and sculpture. The scale of the painting became that of the painter's body, not the image of a body, and the setting for the scale, which would include all

referents, would be the canvas surface itself. Upon this field the physical energies of the artist operate in actual detail, in full scale. . . . It is the physical reality of the artist and his activity of expressing it, united with the spiritual reality of the artist in a oneness which has no need for the mediation of metaphor or symbol. It is Action Painting.[62]

The *surface* of the painting, and by analogy the *surface* of the poem, must, then, be regarded as a field upon which the physical energies of the artist can operate, without mediation of metaphor or symbol. The poet's images—for example, the "hum-colored / cabs," the "yellow helmets" worn by the laborers, or the "glass of papaya juice" in "A Step Away From Them" (*CP*, 257–58)—are not symbolic properties; there is nothing *behind* these surfaces. Rather, their positioning in the poet's field, their *push and pull* interaction, function metonymically to create a microcosm of the poet's New York world—a world verifiable on any city map yet also fictive in its fantastic configurations:

> now it is dark on 2d Street near the abattoir
> and a smell as of hair comes up the dovecotes
> as the gentleman poles a pounce of pigeons
> in the lower East Sideness rippling river. . . .   (*CP*, 324)

This distrust of symbolism is a central tenet of O'Hara's poetic. In a 1962 essay on Philip Guston, he praises the late oils and gouaches in which there is "no symbolic aura. . . . There are no figures, the images are material presences like Druidic spirits." In works like *North* and *The Scale,* "the marvelous burgeoning into life of their surfaces [note again the stress on surface], the visual velocity of the painter's unerring hand make of Guston's self-imposed demands simultaneous triumphs."[63] Again, in his first "Art Chronicle" for *Kulchur* (Summer 1962), O'Hara admires Jasper Johns's "meticulously and sensually painted rituals of imagery" which "express a profound boredom, in the Baudelairean sense, with the symbols of an over-symbolic society."[64] Similarly, he writes enthusiastically of the "found objects" in Claes Oldenburg's first exhibit at *The Store* (1962) where "you find cakes your mother never baked, letters you never received, jackets you never stole when you broke into that apartment." Oldenburg succeeds because he manages to "transform his materials into something magical and strange."[65] The following year, O'Hara again praises Olden-burg's ability to make "the very objects and symbols themselves, with the help of papiêr-maché, cloth, wood, glue, paint and whatever other mysterious materials are inside and on them, *into* art. . . . There is no hint of mysticism, no 'significance,' no commentary, in the work."[66]

The aesthetic of *presence* rather than transcendence is formulated with particular force in O'Hara's first essay on David Smith, which appeared in *Art News* in 1961. The stainless steel and painted sculptures standing on the lawn at Bolton's Landing, New York, near Smith's house, are not so much formal constructs as they are live presences. They remind the poet of "people who are awaiting admittance to a formal reception and, while they wait, are thinking about their roles when they join the rest of the guests already in the meadow."[67] Smith's sculptures, O'Hara argues, defy all our traditional notions of organic oneness and unity. "This is no longer the Constructivist intersection of colored planes, nor is the color used as a means of unifying the surface. Unification is approached by inviting the eye to travel over the complicated surface exhaustively, rather than inviting it to settle on the whole first and then explore details. It is the esthetic of culmination rather than examination."

The esthetic of culmination rather than examination—this formulation applies nicely to O'Hara's own poetry. As in the case of Smith's sculptures, O'Hara's poems reject the dense network of symbolic images one finds in, say, Richard Wilbur's "Love Calls Us To The Things Of This World" or John Crowe Ransom's "The Equilibrists." Rather, the reader's eye and ear must "travel over the complicated surface exhaustively," participating in the ongoing process of discovery and continually revising his sense of what the poem is "saying." The observer can no longer be detached. "The best of the current sculptures," says O'Hara, "didn't make me feel I wanted to *have* one, they made me feel I wanted to *be* one" (p. 125). If the art work has *presence* and if the beholder is as *attentive* as possible, the process of identification thus becomes complete.

I have drawn the above examples from O'Hara's art criticism rather than from his commentary on poetry simply because it is so much more plentiful. But in his rare literary essays, he makes precisely the same points. In his review of John Rechy's *City of Night,* for example, he argues that the novel's real forte is its naturalistic surface, its con-crete embodiment of scenes and moods. "What comes out in the *Mardi Gras* section of the book is that atrocious fanfare which Rimbaud celebrated; it is to my mind the finest and most compelling prose realization of derangement through social confrontation in American letters . . . since *Day of the Locust*." In such explorations of "the dis-tinctive and odd quality of a city or a quarter or a milieu," Rechy follows William Carlos Williams's prescription that "the objective in writing is to reveal. It is not to teach, not to advertise, not to see, not even to communicate . . . but to reveal." Rechy's book is a "quest novel," an attempt to escape from Hell, but "it is no paradigm of Dante. It would be boring if it were . . . since that aspect of the Joycean-Eliotean idea . . . has been pretty much exhausted by Harvard and Yale students. (Lord! spare us from any more Fisher kings!)."[68]

Here, as generally in O'Hara's criticism, Williams clearly takes precedence over Eliot as a model; indeed, as we shall see, Williams's influence is seminal.[69] As always for O'Hara, the Enemy is the Great Insight or the Mythic-Symbolic Analogue—being excessively solemn about oneself. "Life," as he says in his essay on Pasternak, "is not a landscape before which the poet postures, but the very condition of his inspiration in a deeply personal way: 'My sister, life, is in flood today. . . .' This is not the nineteenth-century Romantic identification, but a recognition."[70]

The notion that *recognition* is central to art is the cornerstone of O'Hara's "Personism." The background of this "manifesto" is inter-esting. Allen Ginsberg had argued in an essay called "Abstraction in Poetry" that poems like O'Hara's *Second Avenue* were experiments in writing "long meaningless poems," "bulling along page after page" so as to learn "freedom of composition," and that from such "freedom of composition," in which the poet tries to avoid personal considerations, a new poetry comparable to abstract art would emerge.[71]

O'Hara found Ginsberg's argument "intriguing" but felt that it didn't quite define what he was trying to do:

> Personism, a movement which I recently founded and which nobody knows about, interests me a great deal, being so totally opposed to this kind of abstract removal [i.e., the kind Ginsberg describes] that it is verging on true abstraction for the first time, really, in the history of

poetry. . . . Personism has nothing to do with philosophy, it's all art. It does not have to do with personality or intimacy, far from it! But to give you a vague idea, one of its minimal aspects is to address itself to one person (other than the poet himself), thus evoking overtones of love without destroying love's life-giving vulgarity, and sustaining the poet's feelings toward the poem while preventing love from distracting him into feeling about the person. That's part of Personism. It was founded by me after lunch with LeRoi Jones on August 27, 1959, a day in which I was in love with someone (not Roy, by the way, a blond). I went back to work and wrote a poem for this person. While I was writing it I was realizing that if I wanted to I could use the telephone instead of writing the poem, and so Personism was born. It's a very exciting movement which will undoubtedly have lots of adherents. It puts the poem squarely between the poet and the person, Lucky Pierre style, and the poem is correspondingly gratified. The poem is at last between two persons instead of two pages. (*CP,* 498–99)

Much of this "manifesto" is, of course tongue-in-cheek: the reference to the "founding" of the movement, its arcane quality (nobody knows about it!), the comical reference to Lucky Pierre, the insistence that he could have used the telephone "instead of writing the poem"—an insistence most reviewers have taken all too seriously.

But beneath the bravado, O'Hara is quite serious. He implies, for example, that the dramatic monologue has become a dead convention, its use assuming that the poet can penetrate the experience of a fictional narrator, can distance himself from that experience and define its meaning.[72] Always a skeptic, O'Hara recognizes that the only mind he can wholly penetrate is his own, but he sees that this need not be a loss if he can project a lyric "I" engaged in what looks like live talk—intimate, familiar, expressive; "real" conversation that seems purely personal and yet avoids what he calls in the letter to Larry Rivers "disgusting self-pity."

"Personism," says O'Hara, "does not have to do with personality, or intimacy, far from it!" What he means is that the poet does not use the poem as a vehicle to lay bare his soul, to reveal his secret anxieties or provide autobiographical information. Indeed, O'Hara's personal pronouns shift so disarmingly and confusingly that we are never quite sure who's who, and accordingly, we don't take the text as a personal testament. Rather, "Personism" means the *illusion* of intimate talk between an "I" and a "you" (or sometimes "we," "he," "they," or "one"), giving us the sense that we are eavesdropping on an ongoing conversation, that we are *present*. But this is not to say, as critics often have, that an O'Hara poem is just good casual talk. Here is a passage from a letter to Joe LeSueur from Belgrade in 1963:

> As for the smokey dark lights of Belgrade, I do hope that Prague isn't *more* like Kafka than this! In the daytime it's very nice and pleasant and even rather pretty in a wrong-headed sort of way (the parks don't fit right somehow, and the squares appear to be in the wrong places, and there is all of a sudden a hill or an abutment where there shouldn't be—as if the building of the city had stubbornly resisted taking cognizance of the site), but as soon as dusk falls, about 5:30 it is really quite dark, these peculiar ghostly iridescent lightings come on here and there making very bright places and leaving very dark ominous ones, and a dry smokey mist appears, like in the back of a pool hall . . . and all the places (or Trgs, as they're called here) fill with people and many of the streets too, all of them looking dark and sort of ominous in the light, strolling and windowshopping and realshopping and talking, and the cars disappear entirely from whole streets in the center of the city (they couldn't get through them anyway), and it is all rather subduedly noisy and noncheerful, as if Orson Welles in one of his more malevolent moments had taken over the Galleria Umberta from the Milanese.[73]

Compare this description of Belgrade to the image of New York found in "Rhapsody" (1959), a poem which begins:

> 515 Madison Avenue
> door to heaven? portal
> stopped realities and eternal licentiousness
> or at least the jungle of impossible eagerness
> your marble is bronze and your lianas elevator cables
> swinging from the myth of ascending
> I would join
> or declining the challenge of racial attractions
> they zing on (into the lynch, dear friends)
> while everywhere love is breathing draftily
> like a doorway linking 53rd with 54th
> the east-bound with the west-bound traffic by 8,000,000s
> o midtown tunnels and the tunnels, too, of Holland[74]

The letter, although charming, witty, and graphic, is perfectly straightforward, its syntax loosely paratactic, with a piling up of qualifiers, parenthetical clauses, and prepositional phrases like "from whole streets in the center of the city" or "like in the back of the pool hall." Everything is given more or less the same emphasis: this is what I saw (or did), and then this and then this. The description of Belgrade is highly subjective but still essentially realistic: this is how the city looks to the poet at different times of day. In "Rhapsody," on the other hand, we begin with juxtaposition and ellipsis:

> 515 Madison Avenue
> door to heaven? portal
> stopped realities and eternal licentiousness

Here phrases and clauses are much shorter, and the connectives are often missing or confusing. The "eternal licentiousness" of the "portal" of 515 Madison Avenue immediately modulates into the fantasy of the jungle, the elevator cables turning into lianas and the elevator ride itself into a wonderful journey to *Schlaraffenland,* and then into an East-West joyride through "midtown tunnels and the tunnels, too, of Holland" so that the whole world is absorbed into the fabric of the voyage. Thus, although the letter is allusive—note the references to Kafka and Orson Welles—it does not transform names into something wholly other, as O'Hara does in the case of the dreary Holland Tunnel.

Lineation, of course, is a major factor in making the poem seem so different from the letter. For when word groups are set off in line units, we respond to them quite differently than we would if we met them in a paragraph. The words "I would join," for example, stand out as particularly emphatic, as if the poet were *joining* the "Rhapsody" (the title alludes to an Elizabeth Taylor movie) of the elevator trip. And the three monosyllabic words seem to float in space, suspended between the preceding line ("swinging from the myth of ascending") and the following one ("or declining the challenge of racial attractions"). Between "ascending" and "declining," the poet's consciousness floats for a brief moment at heaven's gate.

The letter from Belgrade is much less structured; it has none of the defamiliarization we meet everywhere in the poem. In terms of O'Hara's own aesthetic, it has too many "holes" in it, too many phrases and sentences that are entertaining but could obviously be eliminated (for example, "it is all rather subduedly noisy and non-cheerful"). It lacks the "push and pull" of "Rhapsody," whose "surface" is "kept up" and peculiarly tight. Despite its air of casual talk, the poem displays careful sound patterning: take the short i's in "impossible," "lianas," "swinging from the myth of ascending," "they zing on (into the lynch, dear friends)." Again, the witty reverberations of "the challenge of racial attractions," a phrase that originally refers to the jungle imagery of the elevator cables, is transformed, in stanza after stanza, as we shift from the anecdote in which "the Negro driver tells me about a $120 apartment / where you can't walk across the floor after 10 at night / not even to pee, cause it keeps them awake downstairs," to the "Niger" which "joins the Gulf of Guinea near the Menemsha Bar," and then to the "hammock on St. Mark's Place . . . in the rancid nourishment of this mountain island"—Manhattan. The poem, moreover, shifts back and forth from present to past in a series of rapid dissolves, thus creating "push and pull," and, by shifting address regularly (the "you" is alternately "515 Madison Avenue" and the "you who were there always," the "you [who] know[s] all about these things"), O'Hara distances his emotions, thus avoiding "disgusting self-pity."

There is, therefore, a real difference between the "verse letter" or "verse telephone call" we find in the *Collected Poems* and an actual letter or phone call. The letter moves from one item to another just as we all put down our thoughts (even if we don't all write such charming and amusing letters); the poem *looks* improvisatory but invites "the eye [or ear] to travel over the complicated surface exhaustively," tracing the process whereby the poet's consciousness moves from perception to perception until he comes to the awareness that he belongs "to the enormous bliss of American death." Only when we reach the last line of "Rhapsody" do we understand how its seemingly unrelated images have led up to this conclusion. Here, then, is what O'Hara called "the esthetic of culmination."

In the poetry of postwar America, it is difficult to find precise models or analogues for an "action poem" like "Rhapsody." Painting, sculpture, film, music—these provide much more useful analogues, and I shall discuss the role they play in O'Hara's development. But for literary models we must turn to France—to the poetry of Rimbaud and Apollinaire, to Tristan Tzara and the Dadaists, to such Surrealists as Robert Desnos and Benjamin Péret. Indeed, much of what O'Hara admired in the visual arts of his own time came out of this tradition.

Russian literature—the poetry of Mayakovsky and the prose of Pasternak—also finds its way into the *Collected Poems,* as does, in a more oblique way, the poetry and poetic of Rilke. But it is the French influence that sets O'Hara apart from Black Mountain and the Beats, not to speak of the Confessional Poets like Lowell and Berryman, or the oracular "deep image" school associated with Robert Bly, James Wright, and Galway Kinnell.

How that French influence was gradually adapted to an American idiom, how O'Hara came to fuse the "charming artifice" of Apollinaire with the vernacular toughness he admired in the poetry of Williams, Pound, and the later Auden, and in the prose of Joyce and Gertrude Stein, is a central concern of the chapters that follow. It is a fascinating study in "tradition and the individual talent." In that insistently documentary New York poem, "A Step Away from Them" (1957), O'Hara declares:

> My heart is in my
> pocket. It is Poems by Pierre Reverdy.   (*CP,* 258)

2
THE EARLY
YEARS (1946-53)

The poet who was to declare in "Personism" (1959) that "Nobody should experience anything they don't need to, if they don't need poetry bully for them" (*CP*, 498), began his writing career with a very different point of view. In a journal kept during his junior year at Harvard (from October 1948 through January 1949), O'Hara writes: "No matter what, I am romantic enough or sentimental enough to wish to contribute something to life's fabric, to the world's beauty. . . . Simply to live does not justify existence, for life is a mere gesture on the surface of the earth, and death a return to that from which we had never been wholly separated; but oh to leave a trace, no matter how faint, of that brief gesture! For someone, some day, may find it beautiful!" [1]

These words recall Stephen Dedalus in Joyce's *Portrait of the Artist*, longing to forge "out of the sluggish matter of the earth a new soaring impalpable being," [2] and indeed the young Frank O'Hara regarded Joyce as his hero. In "Lament and Chastisement," an account of his Navy days (1944–46), written for Albert Guérard's Advanced Composition course in 1948, O'Hara notes that during the trying days of basic training at Key West, "I carried *Ulysses* with me for luck. I read it in high school because a friend who was preping [*sic*] for West Point sent it to me because it was so dirty. Then I read it from beginning and it was about something else entirely. In my locker: *Ulysses* for luck, and oh my god didn't *Portrait of the Artist as a Young Man* say everything? Should I send it to all my friends so they'd understand me?" Later, during heavy fighting in the Pacific, he recalls that "I reread *Ulysses,* needing to throw up my sensibility and Joyce's art into the face of my surroundings; I found that Joyce was more than a match. I was reassured that what was important to me would always be important to me. . . . I found that I myself was my life."[3]

O'Hara's juvenilia are particularly interesting because they immediately dispel the myth of the poet as charming pop artist or spontaneous scribbler, which grew up in his later years. Surely he was one of the best read and most learned poets of his time. In this respect—and in this respect only—he recalls his Harvard predecessor T. S. Eliot. Even before he entered college, as "Lament and Chastisement" makes clear, O'Hara was quite familiar with Whitman and Stevens, with *Swann's Way* and *The Counterfeiters,* as well as with the music of Stravinsky and Schoenberg.

At Harvard, O'Hara took the standard courses required of English majors between 1946 and 1950.[4] Aside from six courses in English Composition (some of these were, in fact, advanced writing courses), he took Chaucer, a one-year survey of "English Literature from the Beginning to 1700," and period courses on the Renaissance, the Restoration, the Eighteenth Century, and the Romantics. Only in his senior year could he "branch out" somewhat: he elected to take John Ciardi's "Poetry Workshop," Albert Guérard's "Forms of the Modern Novel," Edwin Honig's "Allegory," Walter Jackson Bate's "English Critics," and—perhaps most important for his future development—Renato Poggioli's "The Symbolist Movement."

Yet the Commonplace Book that O'Hara kept during these years reveals a breadth of reading that goes far beyond the classroom. Interestingly, the writers he cites least frequently are the great English classics: Shakespeare, Spenser, Milton, Wordsworth, Keats, Tennyson, Browning, and, among novelists, Richardson, Austen, Eliot, Dickens, James, and Lawrence. From the first, then, his literary predilections reflect a highly personal note. Thus he prefers Anglo-Saxon charms and *Beowulf* to Chaucer; the Jacobean dramatists, especially Webster, to Shakespeare; he considers Donne's sermons and the *Devotions upon Emergent Occasions* superior to the lyric poems; he admires the plays of Dryden and Otway, the poems of the Earl of Rochester and Christopher Smart;[5] Fielding's *Jonathan Wild* (*Tom Jones* and *Joseph Andrews* are not mentioned), and Gothic Romances, especially Maturin's *Melmoth the Wanderer*.

The Commonplace Book frequently cites Dostoyevsky, Strindberg, and Kierkegaard, but never mentions Tolstoy or Chekhov, perhaps because these writers were too "realistic" for O'Hara's taste. Again, although his amusing accounts of Manhattan cocktail parties have been compared to those of Scott Fitzgerald, O'Hara makes no mention of Fitzgerald's novels and disparages Hemingway. "I can learn little from him [Hemingway]," he writes in the Harvard Journal, "I'm tired of the current fad for short stories which clack along like a sewing machine dispensing pertinent information in stitches and stopping only when the garment is finished. . . . I want to move toward a complexity which makes life within the work and which does not resemble life as most people seem to think it is lived. . . ."[6]

Because his imagination was essentially lyric rather than narrative, O'Hara was always drawn to novels that are nonmimetic and stylized, novels that subordinate plot and characterization to linguistic innovation: Djuna Barnes's *Nightwood,* Virginia Woolf's *Between the Acts* and *The Waves,* Ronald Firbank's *Vainglory* and *The Flower beneath the Foot,* Beckett's *Murphy* and *More Pricks than Kicks,* the fiction of Gertrude Stein and Jean Rhys. Yet despite his love for these writers, it is no exaggeration to say that O'Hara's heart was, from the very beginning, French. Baudelaire and Rimbaud were early favorites. In his moving memoir of the writer Bunny Lang, one of his closest friends in Cambridge, who was to die tragically of cancer in 1956 at the age of thirty-two, O'Hara typically recalls: "We both loved Rimbaud and Auden: she thought I loved Rimbaud too much and I thought the same about Auden and her."[7]

In the Harvard Journal, he talks enthusiastically of Camus, Cocteau, and Stendhal's *Red and the Black* in the Scott-Moncrieff translation. In 1948–49, his command of the French language was evidently still limited; in the Commonplace Book, he cites Corneille and Racine, Voltaire and Laclos, Baudelaire and Nerval, Rimbaud and Lautréamont (a particular favorite) in translation. Yet in the same notebook, he copies out whole sonnets by Ronsard and Desportes and begins to write playful French poems of his own, for example, "L'Ennui," which ends with the lines:

> notre pain quotidien
> de l'angoisse s'efface.
> Quelle mélasse.[8]

A reading list compiled toward the end of the Harvard period[9] adds the names of later French poets from Villiers de l'Isle Adam and Mallarmé to Breton and Char, this time referring to all titles in French. Here Dada and Surrealist texts begin to assume importance: the list contains ten poems by Apollinaire, Reverdy's *Les Epaves du ciel,* Jarry's *Les Minutes de sable mémorial,* Aragon's *Le Paysan de Paris,* Desnos's *Deuil pour deuil,* Max Ernst's *La Femme 100 têtes,* and Péret's *Le Grand jeu.* Whether or not O'Hara knew enough French to read these texts with relative ease,[10] it is remarkable that he turned to these poets rather than to what were then the "acceptable" models—Yeats, Hopkins, Eliot, Frost, Tate, Ransom—for inspiration. For that matter, despite all his later travels abroad in connection with Museum of Modern Art traveling exhibitions, O'Hara never visited England and never expressed any particular desire to see London.[11] With the exception of Auden, whom he considered an American poet anyway,[12] and the early Dylan Thomas, the poetic landscape of modern Britain struck O'Hara as excessively conventional and tame; it could not, in any case, compete with the Germany of Rilke, the Russia of Mayakovksy and Pasternak, the Spain of Lorca—and certainly not with France.

From the first, then, O'Hara emerges as a highly sophisticated poet with strong tastes of his own. Having studied music all his life—he originally wanted to be a concert pianist—he could relate poetry to developments in contemporary music: it was he who was to introduce Ashbery to the work of Schoenberg and Cage.[13] Yet, as in the case of literature, his musical tastes were eclectic: if he admired Cage, he also loved Rachmaninoff, *La Bohème* and the Weill-Brecht operas. John Ciardi, whose Freshman Composition course O'Hara took in 1946–47, and who recalls that "aside from picking and probing at his papers I could teach him nothing but only hope to stir him a little closer to his questions," comments in a letter to Donald Allen:

> His talent was obvious, even when he was a Freshman. He also had a lovely sardonic sense of fun. When my wife and I were fixing an attic apartment in Medford, Frank and Ted Gorey [Edward St. John Gorey]—they were inseparable in college and took all my courses together—and George Rinehart (who showed high promise in his short stories but who left Harvard in disgust at the end of his junior year and who never went on to write)—these three, as students needing some extra money made a crew to steam the weird wall paper from the apartment. They were at it for days as they played a game of killing insults. They were beautiful and bright and I have never come on three students as a group who seemed to have such unlimited prospects.[14]

Yet the winter of 1948–49 seems to have been a time of crisis in O'Hara's life. "I often wish," he writes in a journal entry of 17 October, "I had the strength to commit suicide, but on the other hand, if I had, I probably wouldn't feel the need." Here we already see the poet's characteristic self-deprecatory humor, his refusal to take himself too seriously. And despite these moments of despair, near the end of the journal the tone changes: "If life were merely a habit, I should commit suicide; but even now, more or less desperate, I cannot but think, 'Something wonderful may happen.' It is not optimism, it is a rejection of self-pity (I hope) which leaves a loophole for life. . . . I merely choose to remain living out of respect for possibility. And possibility is the great good."[15]

These words turned out to be oddly prophetic. A few months after he made this journal entry, O'Hara met John Ashbery, who was to become a life-long poet friend and fellow art critic, and who later wrote so movingly about O'Hara's poetry.[16] Ashbery was then an editor of the *Advocate;* he admired a group of poems O'Hara submitted and sent them on to Kenneth Koch who had recently graduated and was living in New York. A friendship between O'Hara and Koch was thus formed. Within the next year, O'Hara was to achieve what he probably most longed for at this point in his life—a circle of exciting artist friends, among them Bunny Lang and George Montgomery, whom he knew at Harvard, and three painters whom he met on visits to New York: Fairfield Porter, Jane Freilicher, and Larry Rivers. All would play an important part in his life and his poetry.

What sort of poetry was O'Hara writing as an undergraduate? The first surviving poems, dating from the fall of 1946, are generally imitations or parodies—what Ashbery has aptly called, with reference to the early work in general, "muscle-flexing" (*CP,* viii). Thus "Portrait of James Joyce" plays with the diction and themes of *Finnegans Wake:*

> riverrun, said jute, oh why the enterrential
> faggus?
> discolum in ionic, doric or sabbatic
> juicecum?[17]

The same poem alludes to Leopold Bloom ("remind people to go to church. / does em good.") as well as to Molly ("syncopated menstruation"). A related poem from this period, "Dialogue for man, woman & chorus of frogs," is a Joycean parody of pastoral comedy, in which "george" and "mary" exchange obscenities in high style ("I sat, forzando / And william's lips, fructose / pursed levulously") and poke fun at the Church in Joycean tones: "Kiss the foot of the papal chamberpot," or "In nomine papyrus / Ab altare dei. / Hocus in hodie. Pocus in anus."[18]

O'Hara's interest in Gertrude Stein is reflected in the following imitation:

> He rode and rode continuously, inexpressibly continuously, and stopped for rest every now and then. Too often then and not often now but just often enough. Yes, sometimes. Yes, sometimes he fell off now and then when he had ridden too long but it was not serious it was gay yes it was not serious because it was him if it had not been him or if it had ceased to be him it would have become serious. . . .
>
> "Portrait of J. Charles Kiefe" (PR, 4)

"A Procession of Peacocks" is an example of a Wallace Stevens imitation, generally rare in O'Hara's early work:

> At night they carry me
> in a palanquin of twigs
> as if I were a bruisable pear,
> soft as the sunrise. . . .   (PR, 9)

And in "The Muse Considered as a Demon Lover," O'Hara parodies both Baudelaire and Rimbaud:

> The light went
>
> out. "Que manges-tu, belle sphinx?"
> came roaring through the dark; beau!
>
> I muttered and hid my head, but a
> wrenching kiss woke me again with a
>
> "Suis-je belle, ô nausée?" ...
>
> The angel's voice called gaily: "There
> are faith, hope, and charity, and
>
> the greatest of these is homily. I
> am an angel. Trouvez Hortense!" [19]

Not only does O'Hara imitate and parody the styles of his early masters; he also experiments with a wide variety of verse forms. There are, for example, a number of early nature poems written in quatrains:

> Stars nod without
> they show their light
> glimmer about
> keep dark the night. . . .
>
> ("Solstice," Notebook A, p. 5)

"Portrait of Jean Marais" has both end-rhyme and internal rhyme:

> Coursing blood is all the flood
> The heart espies and then decries
> as flowing in the winter night
> it searches for a spring surmise.   (Notebook A, p. 26)

The early manuscripts contain parody ballads like the erotic "Hell-shaft":

> Really, said the red-faced axe-layer
> you have such lovely hair.
> Janus, said the red-faced axe-layer
> your skin is so fair.

Really, said the red-faced axe-layer
you have flanks like a mare.
Janus, said the red-faced axe-layer
even clothed you look bare. . . .   (PR, 12)

Or heroic couplets are used for parody effect as in "Virtú":

Marble niches frame a virgin's grey decay
as casually as rain clouds fill the day
with not quite black foreboding. As the sun
beams sickly on the desecrated fun.   (Notebook A, p. 24)

The influence of music, so important throughout O'Hara's career, is evident in "Quintet for Quasimodo" (Notebook A, pp. 14–15), "Triolet" (p. 33), and especially the charming "Gavotte," which begins:

Alack alack alay
my ministrante has come to me
to lead the dark away.
Meetly she
embraces me
coolly, drily, tenderly.   (Notebook A, p. 28)

I cite these texts, not because they are "finished" poems in their own right, but to emphasize O'Hara's familiarity with poetic convention. However "unformed" his later poetry may look, we should bear in mind that he tried his hand at sonnets, songs, ballads, eclogues, litanies, and dirges: "Marian's Mortality" (Notebook A, pp. 42–44) is a good example of a conventional dirge with strophe, antistrophe, and epode.

In 1949 (O'Hara's senior year), these imitations, parodies, and exercises in adapting traditional verse forms give way to two kinds of poems that will continue to appear side by side until 1954 or so. One is the clotted, somewhat mannered Surrealist mode of *Oranges: 12 Pastorals* (*CP*, 5); the other, the natural, colloquial, whimsical, light-hearted mode of "Les Etiquettes Jaunes" (*CP*, 21), a mode clearly derived from William Carlos Williams. I shall argue later that not until O'Hara learned to fuse these two modes—to adapt Surrealist images and forms to an American idiom—was he able to write the poems that we think of as his central achievements.

John Ashbery speaks quite rightly of the "posturing that mars 'Oranges'" (*CP,* ix), but it is still a very interesting sequence. In its first version, written in 1948, it contained nineteen pastorals. When O'Hara gave the series to Grace Hartigan in 1952, he reduced the nineteen to twelve, and it is these twelve poems that were published in 1953 by the Tibor de Nagy Gallery on the occasion of an exhibition of Hartigan's series of twelve paintings called *Oranges,* which incorporates O'Hara's pastorals.[20] If we compare the two versions, we note that O'Hara eliminated passages of three kinds: (1) those that attempt to describe heterosexual love in conventional terms, for example: "Walking by water, at the harp's disgrace / we shuddered; the young girl wrapped / in her yielding but echoed faintly / across our hearts' dawn-bandaged tremors" (Part 3); (2) those that are realistic and matter-of-fact: "I was twelve. / She was my first whore and I was too young" (Part 12); and those with anti-Catholic references like the attack on the "nada litany" of Franco's Spain (Part 12) or Part 15, which ends with the words, "Hail to our Savior! I bathe His feet in my tears and rest Them on my head. Let us each place a corn-flake on the center of his tongue and ejaculate!"[21]

In its final version, *Oranges* is a series of prose poems in which the poet never mentions or so much as alludes to the title word, thus endowing it with an aura of Dada inconsequentiality. O'Hara gives us a witty account of its composition in his famous poem, "Why I Am Not a Painter," written in 1956:

> One day I am thinking of
> a color: orange. I write a line
> about orange. Pretty soon it is a
> whole page of words, not lines.
> Then another page. There should be
> so much more, not of orange, of
> words, of how terrible orange is
> and life. Days go by. It is even in
> prose. I am a real poet. My poem
> is finished and I haven't mentioned
> orange yet. It's twelve poems, I call
> it ORANGES.   (*CP,* 262)

The twelve prose poems are essentially antipastorals in which the usual conventions are slyly inverted, but which, nevertheless, celebrate erotic love in "pastoral" settings. Thus the poem begins with the line, "Black crows in the burnt mauve grass, as intimate as rotting rice, snot on a white linen field" (*CP*, 5). The polarity of images in this sentence—"mauve grass" / "rotting rice"; "snot" / "white linen field"— can be traced back at least to Rimbaud's "Ce qu'on dit au poète à propos des fleurs," but more immediately to collections of prose poems like Tristan Tzara's *Cher ami, l'Antitête,* Louis Aragon's *Pur Jeudi,* or André Breton's *Poisson soluble.* Throughout, O'Hara juxtaposes the beautiful and the ugly, the elegant and the "low" or obscene, to create new angles of vision: "O pastures dotted with excremental discs, wheeling in interplanetary green" (p. 5); "There is a little pile of excrement at my nape like a Japanese pillow" (p. 5); "the sun seemed empty, a counterfeit coin hung round the blue throat patched with leprosy" (p. 6); or "Gregorian frogs belch and masturbate" (p. 9).

Such juxtapositions could easily become tedious, but *Oranges* subsumes them into a larger design. The poem begins with images of "Tess amidst the thorny hay, her new-born shredded by the ravenous cutter-bar" (a snide reference to Hardy's Tess of the d'Urbervilles and her illegitimate child), and of the "village Ophelia," "floating by," who "loved none but the everyday lotus, and slept with none but the bull on the hill," and ends with the view of "the body of a blue girl, hair floating weedy in the room" (p. 8). Between these derogatory images of floating female corpses, the poet as seer appears, invoking *his* gods— Pan and Orpheus. In Part II, he declares, "Pan, your flesh alone has escaped. Promise me, god of the attainable and always perfecting fruit, when I lie . . . play into my rain-sweet canals your notes of love!" (p. 5). His erotic ecstasy reaches its climax in Part 7:

> Then in other fields I saw people walking dreamily in the black hay and golden cockleburs; from the firmament streamed the music of Orpheus! and on earth Pan made vivid the pink and white hunger of my senses!
> Snakes twined about my limbs to cool them, and springs cold and light sucked my tongue; bees brushed sweet from my eyelids; clouds

washed my skin; at the end of the day a horse squandered his love. The sun replenishes, mirror and magnifier, of my own beauty! and at night through dreams reminds me, moaning, of my daytime self. (p. 7)

And now, in Part 8, the figures of Pan, Orpheus, and the poet himself merge in a frenzied pagan dance. After this crescendo, the poet comes back down to earth; in Part 11 he says: "I make my passport / dossier: a portrait of the poet wrapped in jungle leaves airy on vines, skin tender to the tough wind. . . . Standing in the photograph, then, filthy and verminous but for my lavender shaving lotion, I must confess that the poor have me always with them, and I love no god. My food is caviar, I love only music, and my bed is sin" (p. 8).

But although the poet now regresses, saying petulantly: "Bring me my doll: I must make contact with something dead" (an echo from Rilke),[22] the memory of the vision remains, and *Oranges* ends on a Paterian note: "O my posterity! This is the miracle: that our elegant invention the natural world redeems by filth" (p. 9). These exclamatory phrases provide artful closure, for the poet *has,* all along, tried to submit his powers of "elegant invention" to the "filth" of actual experience, of the "natural world": his inverted pastoral is a subtly veiled paean to homosexual love. The corpses of legendary women float downstream; other women drop dead in laundry yards (see Part 5), leaving the poet-as-Pan, or as Orpheus, dancing in the sunlight on the crest of rocky mountains.

If *Oranges* strikes us as unnecessarily long and repetitious, it is probably because its central polarity between beauty and ugliness, landscape and machine, the masculine and the feminine, is rendered in excessively abstract, amorphous terms. The poem also suffers from certain coy intrusions like "I forgot to post your letter yesterday. What shall we have for lunch?" or "We are all brothers. You do not have tuberculosis. Kiss me" (p. 7). But O'Hara's pastoral sequence remains an important early attempt to inject a Surrealist note into the neo-Symbolist poetic landscape of postwar America.

O'Hara's other long Surrealist poem of this period is "Meditations on Max Ernst's *Histoire Naturelle*," a set of seven prose poems written in 1949 (PR, 15–24). Ernst's series of collages (1926) exploits the techniques of *frottage* and *decalcomania*, that is, "the production of images in the first case by rubbing a chalk or some other medium across a rough or textured surface, in the second by blotting images onto paper from wet paint." "From the random forms Ernst produced," writes Kenneth Coutts-Smith, "he read and isolated images that his conscious mind was too inhibited or preconditioned to discover; he tried to create an irrational, or unconditional landscape of images."[23]

One can argue that O'Hara's prose poems do create a verbal equivalent of Ernst's "frottage" landscapes. If *Oranges* stressed the juxtaposition of polar images, which is one of the central characteristics of Surrealist poetry,[24] "Meditations" concentrates on a slightly different aspect of Surrealism: the attempt to render subconscious states, the psychic automatism defined in Breton's First Manifesto.[25] The Introduction to "Meditations" presents the reader with "ferocious lions" who "scent succulence lasciviously," while "lime trees grow tractably, especially on the boarded plains" (p. 15). This dream landscape, rather like a canvas by Henri Rousseau, gives way, in the second paragraph, to "washing-machines (those mirrors of apple blossoms) and looms (the progenitors of nudes) and airplanes (memorials to our fathers). In the same way the films have taught us how beautiful we really are from the anguish of our shadows and the accuracy of objects (the heart of Charlie Chaplin). All machines, similarly, enliven us" (p. 15).

This conjunction of opposites—nature versus the machine—is, of course, typically Surrealist; like *Oranges,* the above passage is perhaps too pure an imitation. The six prose poems that follow remain opaque. We can say that they are clearly love poems of some sort; there are references to a passionate affair, as well as to the fear of a mother who asks the poet, "Are you a cannibal?" (p. 18), and of a father who "warned of the consequences / how passion wells up like a tornado of spiralling blood so that the tongue barely can move its thickness into the mouth of another" (p. 19). But too many references in these prose poems remain wholly private; there is a kind of veil between poet and reader so that the experience of the former remains largely inaccessible. Perhaps O'Hara wanted to create this blurred effect in keeping with the notion of *frottage,* but since words inevitably have meanings, it is doubtful whether one can ultimately "translate" Ernst's visual effects into poetry. *Meditations* remains an interesting experiment rather than a finished poem.

The short Surrealist poems of the Harvard period are generally merely clever. Take "Homage to Rrose Sélavy," based on Duchamp and Desnos:

> Towards you like amphibious airplanes
> peacocks and pigeons seem to scoot![26]

Or "Today":

> Oh! kangaroos, sequins, chocolate sodas!
> You really are beautiful! Pearls,
> harmonicas, jujubes, aspirins! all
> the stuff they've always talked about
>
> still makes a poem a surprise!   (*CP*, 15)

Or "Concert Champêtre":

> The cow belched and invited me
> to breakfast. "Ah" I said "I
> haven't written a pastoral for
>
> ages! . . ."   (*CP*, 15)

Or "A Scene":

> Pie, tomatoes, eggs, coffee, spaghetti
> clobbered the dusty kitchen toward
> Mrs. Bennett Smith, teacher of pianoforte.   (*CP*, 19)

These poems seem to be modeled closely on those of Péret. Take the following examples, translated by Michael Benedikt in his anthology, *The Poetry of Surrealism:*[27]

> Who Is It (*Qui est-ce*)
>
> I term tobacco that which is ear
> and so maggots take advantage of this opportunity to
> throw themselves on ham   (p. 224)

It Keeps Going On (*Ça continue*)

An old suitcase a sock and an endive
have arranged for a rendezvous between two blades of grass
sprouting on an altar draped in drooping bowels   (p. 225)

A Thousand Times (*Mille fois*)

Among the gilded debris of the gasworks
You will come upon a bar of chocolate which flies off as
      you approach
If you run as fast as an aspirin-bottle
you will find yourself somewhere far beyond the chocolate
which upsets the landscape so
Just like an open-toed sandal. . . .   (p. 226)

Péret develops these images according to a peculiar inner logic appropriate to a given poem. His use of pseudo *if-then* clauses, and of false analogies using the word "like" (*comme*), leads inexorably to the poem's conclusion. "A Thousand Times," for example, converts the kaleidoscopic landscape of chocolate bars and aspirin bottles into one where the poet is alone and happy "at the bottom of the sea," where "there would be a telephone-booth / from which nobody could ever complete a call" (p. 226). In such later Surrealist poems as "Easter," O'Hara manages the same feat, but in the poems cited above, he all too often merely piles up bizarre disjunctive images in exclamatory line units; the poem could start or stop almost anywhere. Then too, the third-person mode used in "Concert Champêtre" or "A Scene" is essentially alien to O'Hara's sensibility; he needs always to *be* in the poem.

Indeed, even while he was writing fanciful lyrics about chocolate sodas and jujubes, O'Hara was, as I noted above, experimenting with the more personal, direct style of Williams. From the first, he accepted Williams as a master, no doubt because he identified with Williams's struggle against convention, pretentiousness, conformity—the "going thing."[28] Thus, in an amusing little poem of 1952 called "WHAT SLEDGEHAMMER? Or W. C. WILLIAMS'S BEEN ATTACKED!" (PR, 111), O'Hara writes:

Yester the heat I walked my tiglon "Charles F"
around the Park, as three nuns in a stationwagon

(au Zoo) robbed the Elizabeth Arden Building.
In the University pistols were not shot off

because they aren't "clean precise expression." Ho
ho ho, kra, chuh chuh, tssk tssk tssk, tereu. . . .

And there's going to be a wedding! there's going to be a
We-Know-What-To-Do-In-The-Fall (a Ball!) between
the Metatheosophists with Italian bedbugs
swinging from their woolly nipples and *The Hudson Review*

(that Organ) . . .

This is obviously an attack on the school of Eliot and the New Critical orthodoxy that made "The Waste Land" with its scenes of Philo-
mela's rape ("tereu") its sacred text. O'Hara admires Williams's "liberation of language," his "attempt to find an honest, tough, hard,
beautiful thing."[29] He follows Williams in believing that "The objective in writing is to reveal," and in a letter to Jasper Johns, listing his
favorite poets, he says: "you said you liked PATERSON; all the books of
WCW have great great great things in them, I don't believe he ever
wrote an uninteresting poem; the prose poems KORA IN HELL have
recently been reprinted and are very good, interesting because very
early and ambitious."[30]

Yet O'Hara also recognized that Williams often had an unfortunate
influence on lesser poets. In his lecture on "The New Poets," given at
The Club on 14 May 1952, he refers disparagingly to the "WC Wil-
liams-ites" with their "I am the man your father was Americanism,"
their "Cleanness thinned down to jingoism," their cult of the "He-
Man."[31] His own debt to Williams, for that matter, is less to the complex epic poem *Paterson* than to the Dadesque prose poems of *Kora,*
and especially to the early shorter poems, whose unrhymed tercets or
quatrains are distinguished by their very short lines, broken at odd
junctures, and their use of colloquial speech.

The charming "Autobiographia Literaria," for example, with its
parody-Coleridge title, uses the four-line stanza of such famous Williams poems as "The Catholic Bells" and "The Last Words of my
English Grandmother" to invert, very delicately, the Romantic notion
of the child as blessed seer, "trailing clouds of glory" before "Shades of
the prison-house begin to close" upon him. O'Hara's child, unlike

Wordsworth's, is a pathetic little misfit, unloved, unwanted, un-friendly. Even the animals "were / not friendly and birds / flew away." But, by a humorous twist, this child grows up to be, of all things, a happy poet:

> And here I am, the
> center of all beauty!
> writing these poems!
> Imagine! (*CP,* 11)

Here the exclamatory tone, the colloquial manner, the transforma-tion theme, the sense of immediacy (we *witness* the writing of "these poems"), and the final humorous twist are reminiscent of Williams's "Invocation and Conclusion" (1935):

> January!
> The beginning of all things!
> Spring from the old burning nest
> upward in the flame!
>
> I was married at thirteen
> My parents had nine kids
> and we were on the street
> That's why the old bugger—
>
> He was twenty-six
> and I hadn't even had
> my changes yet. Now look at me![32]

Williams's conclusion is more equivocal than O'Hara's; we can take the final "Now look at me!" as an exclamation of resignation rather than hope. But in style and structure, the two poems are certainly similar.

"Les Etiquettes Jaunes," written shortly after O'Hara graduated from Harvard, is an even better example of his Williams mode:

> I picked up a leaf
> today from the sidewalk.
> This seems childish.
>
> Leaf! you are so big!
> How can you change your
> color, then just fall!

As if there were no
such thing as integrity!

You are too relaxed
to answer me. I am too
frightened to insist.

Leaf! don't be neurotic
like the small chameleon.   (*CP*, 21)

This playful poem brings to mind two poems by Williams about trees:

Trees [1917]

Crooked, black tree
on your little grey-black hillock,
ridiculously raised one step toward
the infinite summits of the night. . . .

       you alone
warp yourself passionately to one side
in your eagerness.   (*Collected Earlier Poems*, p. 142)

The Trees [1934]

The trees—being trees
thrash and scream
guffaw and curse—
wholly abandoned
damning the race of men—

Christ, the bastards
haven't even sense enough
to stay out of the rain. . . .
(*Collected Earlier Poems*, p. 66)

The poetic device of all these poems is to personify a plant form and then rebuke it for possessing certain human follies. But O'Hara's is more comically absurd than the two Williams poems; its title is in itself quite different from "Trees," implying that leaves choose to turn yellow and fall according to some sort of Emily Post code, the French language adding a note of mock elegance. The conversation between poet and leaf enlarges on this humorous notion: it is fickle of the leaf to change color and then, what's worse, just to "fall" (double entendre),

"As if there were no / such thing as integrity!" Both literally and figuratively, the leaf is "too relaxed / to answer" the poet, who is, in an absurd reversal, so amazed by its transformation that he is "too frightened to insist." Thus a simple thing like a wet autumn leaf, found on one's path, becomes comically emblematic of neurotic behavior. The poet begs the leaf not to be "like the small chameleon."

Unlike the Surrealist poems I discussed earlier, there is not a word in this poem that cannot be readily understood; the diction is childlike, monosyllabic, purposely flat; the sentences short and exclamatory; the line breaks quirky as in "too / frightened" or "no / such thing." "Les Etiquettes Jaunes" is no more than a charming slight poem, but we can already see O'Hara's own aesthetic emerging: even the falling of a single leaf, the poem implies, is worthy of notice. "Don't be bored, don't be lazy, don't be trivial, and don't be proud. The slightest loss of attention leads to death."

There are a number of other poems in the Williams mode dating from the Harvard period, beginning with "Gamin" on the opening page of the *Collected Poems* and including "God" (PR, 11), "First Night" (PR, 26), and "A Walk on Sunday Afternoon" (*CP,* 20). But the outstanding poem of the Harvard years—and one of O'Hara's first great poems—is "Memorial Day 1950" (*CP,* 17), written in the spring of that year and not published during O'Hara's lifetime. The poet was, as his friends attest,[33] an uncertain judge of his own work, often preferring a slight poem which happened to allude to something that interested him at the moment to one that would later be considered on aesthetic grounds an important poem. Indeed, "Memorial Day 1950" survived purely by accident: John Ashbery copied it out and sent it in a letter to Kenneth Koch, who fortunately saved the letter.[34]

"Memorial Day 1950" is O'Hara's version of Rimbaud's "Les Poètes de sept ans," part autobiographical memoir, part artistic manifesto—a portrait of the young artist escaping from the restrictions of his narrowly bourgeois childhood world. But whereas Rimbaud's poem still observes the unities of time (the terrible long Sundays) and place (the poet's stifling childhood home with its polished mahogany break fronts), and relates stimulus (the smell of latrines) to response (the longing for succulent grass) in what is still an essentially realistic mode, O'Hara's poem is the verbal equivalent of a Dada collage—a bright, colorful, exuberant poem that juxtaposes disparate images in dreamlike sequences.

Whereas O'Hara's first Surrealist experiments like *Oranges* are partial failures because they present a hothouse world under glass, a world cleverly organized around a particular set of images but too remote from the reader, "Memorial Day" succeeds because it fuses the colloquialism and natural speech rhythms of Williams with the dialectic of polarized images characteristic of Dada and Surrealism. It is a fusion O'Hara would not quite achieve again for some years to come.

The poem's language is dynamic and immediate: "Picasso made me tough and quick," "Once he got his axe going everyone was upset," "Through all that surgery I thought / I had a lot to say, and named several last things Gertrude Stein hadn't had time for," "Guernica hollered look out!" "those of us who thought poetry / was crap were throttled by Auden or Rimbaud," "you must look things / in the belly, not in the eye," and so on. Such racy diction is very different from the frequently ornate style of *Oranges:* "My feet, tender with sight, wander the yellow grass in search of love" (*CP,* 7).

But, more important, "Memorial Day 1950" is one of O'Hara's first poems to resemble film, with its dissolves, cuts, its images at once concrete and hallucinatory, bleeding into one another. Take the opening:

> Picasso made me tough and quick, and the world;
> just as in a minute plane trees are knocked down
> outside my window by a crew of creators.
> Once he got his axe going everyone was upset
> enough to fight for the last ditch and heap
> of rubbish.

Here Picasso appears as dream surgeon, chopping through the debris of dead art ("the last ditch and heap / of rubbish") with his axe, as if he were a human bulldozer chopping down plane trees outside the poet's window.[35] Similarly, the scene in which the poet's parents take exception to their son's vocation is presented in Surrealistic terms:

> How many trees and frying pans
> I loved and lost! Guernica hollered look out!

but we were all busy hoping our eyes were talking
to Paul Klee. My mother and father asked me and
I told them from my tight blue pants we should
love only the stones, the sea, and heroic figures.
Wasted child! I'll club you on the shins! I
wasn't surprised when the older people entered
my cheap hotel room and broke my guitar and my can
of blue paint.

This passage is enormously suggestive: the tight blue pants and blue paint, logically quite unrelated, merge as emblems of the rebellious creative imagination. The reproof, "Wasted child! I'll club you on the shins," is not only spoken by the parents but, it seems, by the whole community of "older people—those "older people" who enter the poet's cheap hotel room and break his guitar and can of paint.

But the guitar cannot be broken. In the final sequence its strings are used to hold up pictures in the poet's atelier. And if the paintcan breaks, all the better for it must be spilled to be explored:

> At that time all of us began to think
> with our bare hands and even with blood all over
> them we knew vertical from horizontal, we never
> smeared anything except to find out how it lived.

This elliptical statement is an important reference to the doctrine of Action Painting (and, by implication, Action Poetry)—the belief that the materials used by the artist exist in their own right; they are not merely means to the creation of mimetic illusion. From his masters— Picasso, Stein, Ernst, Auden, Rimbaud, Apollinaire—the poet learns that "art is no dictionary"—that the Symbolist doctrine of correspondences between external world and higher reality is meaningless although one's stance toward art can "tell" one certain things: "Poetry didn't tell me not to play with toys / but alone I could never have figured out that dolls meant death."[36]

Rather, the poet learns that art is the creation of new patterns out of disparate objects; he invokes the "Fathers of Dada!": "You carried shining erector sets / in your rough bony pockets, you were generous / and they were lovely as chewing gum or flowers!" His predilection is for "collages or sprechstimme," for "airplanes," those "perfect mobiles . . . crashing in flames" and showing us "how to be prodigal" (*CP*, 18). For the new artist, all change, flux—the celebrated *vertige* of the Surrealists[37]—is valuable, even "the sewage singing / underneath my bright white toilet seat" which will eventually "reach the sea," where "gulls and swordfishes will find it richer than a river."

In the final verse paragraph, the supposedly "wasted child," pitied by his parents, has become a real poet. All broken objects are now reassembled:

> Look at my room.
> Guitar strings hold up pictures. I don't need
> a piano to sing, and naming things is only the intention
> to make things. A locomotive is more melodious
> than a cello. I dress in oilcloth and read music
> by Guillaume Apollinaire's clay candelabra. Now
> my father is dead and has found you must look things
> in the belly, not in the eye. If only he had listened
> to the men who made us, hollering like stuck pigs!

In this landscape of guitar strings and locomotives, the poet practices his craft. "Naming things is only the intention / to make things"; the key is to recognize things for what they are, to "look things in the belly, not in the eye"—a lesson the poet's father evidently never learned.

"Memorial Day 1950" thus ends on what looks like a harsh note, but in the context of the poem, even this image of the father takes on an unreal quality. Once dead, he too can become part of the landscape of erector sets and airplanes, the locomotive, the white toilet seat, and the can of blue paint. The poem is, in short, a memorial to the great artists who were O'Hara's early models—Apollinaire and Rilke, Picasso and Stein, Max Ernst and Rimbaud. It is a poem of great vitality and joy, a poem that shrewdly and humorously assesses what it means to make oneself an artist in a world that distrusts art.

ANN ARBOR INTERLUDE

After his graduation from Harvard, O'Hara spent a year at Ann Arbor and received an M.A. in English from the University of Michigan in the summer of 1951. It is during this year that he won the Hopwood

Award in Creative Writing (thus winning a contest that John Ciardi had urged him to enter)[38] for *A Byzantine Place,* a manuscript that contained such early poems as "Les Etiquettes Jaunes" and "The Muse Considered as a Demon Lover."

O'Hara wrote a good deal of poetry during his Michigan year, but it is a poetry of consolidation rather than of notable innovation. One senses that, his student apprenticeship behind him, the poet now needed a city—specifically New York City—just as much as, say, Wordsworth needed the Lake District or Van Gogh the landscape of Provençe as a source of inspiration. Away from the excitement, the violence, the whirlwind social scene of New York, he languished. Thus he writes in "Ann Arbor Variations" (*CP*, 65):

> The wind blows towards us particularly
> the sobbing of our dear friends on both
> coasts. We are sick of living and afraid
> that death will not be by water, o sea.

And in "A Pathetic Note," he writes to a New York friend:[39] "When you go down West / Fourteenth Street think of Africa and me. . . . Keep photographing the instant, / so that in my hysteria I will know what / it is like there" (PR, 50).

The Christmas holidays of 1950, spent in the magical city, prompted the following light-hearted, Cole Porter-type song:

> I'm going to New York!
> (what a lark! what a song!)
> where the tough Rocky's eaves
> hit the sea. Where th'Acro-
> polis is functional, the trains
> that run and shout! the books
> that have trousers and sleeves!
>
> I'm going to New York!
> (quel voyage! jamais plus!)
> far from Ypsilanti and Flint!
> where Goodman rules the Empire
> and the sunlight's eschato-
> logy upon the wizard's bridges
> and the galleries of print!

I'm going to New York!
(to my friends! mes semblables!)
I suppose I'll walk back West.
But for now I'm gone forever!
The city's hung with flashlights!
the Ferry's unbuttoning its vest!   (PR, 49)

Back in Ann Arbor, away from "the trains / that run and shout!,"
"the books / that have trousers and sleeves," "the galleries of print,"
and especially from "my friends! mes semblables," O'Hara continued
to write parodies and imitations. Thus he mocks Eliot in "Mr. O'Hara's
Sunday Morning Service," which begins: "There is this to be said / for
Sunday morning: that if / I have been very bad the night / before . . .
Dick will pop into my room / and invite me out to the / high abandoned airfield" (PR, 66). He tries his hand at a Drydenesque "Ode on
Saint Cecelia's Day" (*CP*, 27–29), and at Petrarchan sonnets like
"Boston," "The Satyr," and "The Tomb of Arnold Schoenberg." These
experiments are generally merely playful; "After Wyatt" (*CP*, 68), for
example, has a first quatrain that rhymes "semen" with "simoon,"
"parachute" with "boot." A more interesting poem is the charming
"Variations on a Theme by Shelley," which opens with the lines:

We live in an opal or
crystal ball. The sun's
an eye, against it clouds
crowd like Spanish castles
on a mountain.   (PR, 46)

This is an allusion to the "Hymn to Apollo" ("I am the eye with which
the universe / Beholds itself and knows itself divine"), but O'Hara
now inverts Shelley's theme, concluding that "we become the eye and
defy / questions with our beauty."

The Surrealist poems of the Ann Arbor period are mostly negligible.
There are experimental *calligrammes* in the Apollinaire tradition—
"WHEEWHEE" (*CP*, 25) is a forerunner of concrete poems, its words and
letters spread all over the page—and coy presentations of the poet as

"Dada / baby," as in "Night Thoughts in Greenwich Village," which begins:

> O my coevals! embarrassing
> memories! pastiches! jokes!
> All your pleasaunces and
> the vividness of your ills
> are only fertilizer for
> the kids.

and ends on a bathetic note, with echoes of Hart Crane's "Chaplin-esque":

> O my coevals! we cannot die
> too soon. Art is sad and
> life is vapid. Can we thumb
> our nose at the very sea?   (*CP*, 38)

The best poems of the Ann Arbor year are those in the Williams mode; indeed, some of O'Hara's finest short poems date from 1950-51, even if these are less complex, less interesting than "Memorial Day 1950" or than the longer poems that were to be written just a few years later. "A Pleasant Thought from Whitehead," for example, is a witty Ars Poetica poem that brilliantly debunks the convention itself—witness Dylan Thomas's famed "In my Craft or Sullen Art," which appeared just five years earlier. Unlike Thomas's posturing speaker who "labour[s] by singing light / Not for ambition or bread. . . . But for the lovers, their arms / Round the griefs of the ages, / Who pay no praise or wages / Nor heed my craft or art,"[40] O'Hara's "I" is droll and self-deprecating:

> Here I am at my desk. The
> light is bright enough
> to read by it is a warm
> friendly day I am feeling
> assertive. I slip a few
> poems into the pelican's
> bill and he is off! out
> the window into the blue!   (*CP*, 23-24)

The notion of the pelican as carrier pigeon, delivering poems to an editor who is immediately "delighted," is wonderfully absurd, as is the idea that only an "assertive" person would risk the action described. But the poem is more than funny because O'Hara does such interesting things with lineation. By breaking lines where he does, he creates verbal patterns whose meaning runs counter to the literal sense of the poem as a continuous statement. For example "friendly day I am feeling" becomes a semantic unit in its own right, running counter to "I am feeling / assertive." In the second stanza, we have the following lines:

> Ah!
> reader! you open the page
> my poems stare at you you
> stare back, do you not? my
> poems speak on the silver
> of your eyes your eyes repeat
> them to your lover's this
> very night.   (*CP*, 24)

Here form *is* meaning in a very real sense: the placement of "my," framing lines 3 and 4 and thus enclosing the word "you" (repeated three times) and "stare" (used twice), serves to draw the reader into the poet's situation. The same effect is created in the next line with "your eyes your eyes repeat / them to your lover's this / very night." Having established a kind of love union with his reader, the poet is momentarily ecstatic. Even the "improving stars" seem to be reading his poems over his reader's (or lover's) "naked / shoulder" and then "flash / them onward to a friend."

Fred Moramarco has argued that the verbal positioning used in this passage is a technique derived from Abstract Expressionist painting.[41] This may well be the case, although O'Hara could have learned the same thing from Williams, whose short poems—"As the cat . . . " or "Nantucket" or "The Red Wheelbarrow"—hammer words into what Hugh Kenner has called "an audio-visual counterpoint, a kind of "suspension system."[42] The bravado of "improving stars" certainly recalls Williams, but the last three lines strike me as pure O'Hara:

> The eyes the poems of the
> world are changed! Pelican!
> you will read them too!   (*CP*, 24)

This coda picks up the key words—*eyes, poems*—of the preceding section, and the final comic twist has an inexorably absurd logic all its own: the pelican has done all the dirty work, what with carrying those poems to the editor, so now he gets his reward—he may read them too! And we can further relate this conclusion to the comic title of the poem. Whitehead, after all, insisted that all forms of human inquiry and experience are interrelated, and that the gulf between man and nature, value and fact, must be bridged. So the "pleasant thought from Whitehead" is the comic notion that in our "organicist" universe, the gulf between poet and pelican has been bridged. One can take this theme in two opposite ways: as a kind of triumph or as an admission of failure—an invention of a poetry fit only for pelicans.

"Morning" (*CP,* 30) is one of O'Hara's first important love poems. Its model may well be Williams's famous "Love Song" in its first version of 1915, especially the stanza:

> I am alone
> The weight of love
> Has buoyed me up
> Till my head
> Knocks against the sky.[43]

O'Hara's poem, with its flat four-line stanzas characterized by short choppy lines, monosyllabic diction, and repeated *i* and *o* sounds, begins in low key:

> I've got to tell you
> how I love you always
> I think of it on grey
> mornings with death
>
> in my mouth the tea
> is never hot enough
> then and the cigarette
> dry the maroon robe
>
> chills me I need you

What makes this disarmingly simple declaration of love a poem? Chiefly, I think, its innovative lineation and syntax. "Morning" is one of O'Hara's first poems to contain what I call "floating modifiers"—

that is, word groups that point two ways. Thus, "in my mouth" literally refers back to "death," but the lineation forces us to relate it to "the tea" as well. The position of "dry" has the same effect—it looks back to "cigarette" but also forward to "maroon robe."

The syntactic ambiguity of these ordinary words and phrases as well as the consistent enjambment, which makes one read on without pausing all the way to the end, give the poem its "push and pull"— the reader is kept busy trying to bring its shifting surfaces to a point of rest. Moreover, O'Hara chooses his images very carefully: "I miss you always / when I go to the beach / the sand is wet with / tears that seem mine" seems banal enough until one realizes that the poet has here carried the pathetic fallacy to an absurd extreme—even the wetness of the sand is a projection of his sorrow. Or again, in the case of the stanza, "the parking lot is / crowded and I stand / rattling my keys the car / is empty as a bicycle," the effect is gained by setting off "crowded and I stand" in one line and by the odd reference to the car as being "empty as a bicycle" (room for one person only!) while the keys, disconcertingly, rattle.

"Morning" reaches a crescendo of anxiety in the eighth stanza: "What are you doing now / where did you eat your lunch . . . ," and then decelerates again, ending on a note of nice understatement:

> if there is a
> place further from me
> I beg you do not go   *(CP,* 32)

These lines have a Chaplinesque quality, a mixture of drollness and abject self-distrust: clearly the poet has no hope of recapturing the past but if he can just prevent his lover from going to "a place further from me," he will have won a Pyrrhic victory.[44]

The charm, wry humor, and technical mastery of O'Hara's quatrain poems is impressive, but he could only go so far in this vein. To get beyond the Williams mode as well as the rather frozen Surrealism of "Dido" *(CP,* 74) and "Jane Awake" (p. 72), he had to make contact with the artistic milieu of New York. In the fall of 1951, he settled permanently in Manhattan, and within the year, he had met Joe Le-Sueur, James Schuyler, Barbara Guest, Helen Frankenthaler, Grace

Hartigan, Franz Kline, Elaine and Willem de Kooning, Jackson Pollock, and Ned Rorem. He began his career at the Museum of Modern Art by working in the lobby at the front desk, ostensibly so that he could see Alfred Barr's monumental retrospective of Matisse. He also began to review for *Art News* and published his first book of poems, *A City Winter* (1952), as well as the pamphlet *Oranges* (1953). His play *Try! Try!* was produced by the Artists' Theatre, and he acted in the Living Theatre's production of Picasso's *Desire Caught by the Tail* at the Cherry Lane. The time of apprenticeship was over.

THE CITY "HUNG WITH FLASHLIGHTS"

In "Four Apartments," Joe LeSueur recalls his first meeting with O'Hara: "We met on New Year's Eve, 1951, at a party John Ashbery gave in a one-room apartment in the Village. Paul Goodman said: 'There's a poet named Frank O'Hara I think you'll like,' and led me across the room to him. Tchaikowsky's Third Piano Concerto was playing full-volume on John's portable phonograph, and almost immediately Frank and I began dreaming up a frivolous ballet scenario" (p. 287).

A "frivolous ballet scenario" inspired by Tchaikowsky's Third Piano Concerto, composed in a crowded room at a New Year's Eve party— here, in a nutshell, is a portrait of the artist during his early New York years, years in which O'Hara was, as LeSueur recalls, "in high [gear] all the time, high on himself, and his every waking minute, regardless of what he was doing, was vital, supercharged, never boring if he could help it" (p. 289). And James Schuyler confirms this image of the poet: "The first time I dropped by to see him [at the Museum] I found him in the admissions booth, waiting to sell tickets to visitors and meanwhile, writing a poem on a yellow lined pad called 'It's the Blue!' He also had beside him a translation of André Breton's *Young Cherry Trees Secured Against Hares. . . .*"[45]

O'Hara himself has described "the milieu of those days" in his memoir of Larry Rivers:

> We were all in our early twenties. John Ashbery, Barbara Guest, Kenneth Koch and I, being poets, divided our time between the literary bar, the

San Remo, and the artists' bar, the Cedar Tavern. In the San Remo, we argued and gossiped: in the Cedar we often wrote poems while listening to the painters argue and gossip. . . . An interesting sidelight to these social activities was that for most of us non-Academic and indeed non-literary poets in the sense of the American scene at the time, the painters were the only generous audience for our poetry, and most of us read first publicly in art galleries or at The Club. The literary establishment cared about as much for our work as the Frick cared for Pollock and de Kooning, not that we cared any more about establishments than they did, all the disinterested parties being honorable men. (*CP,* 512)

While it is no doubt true that the painters were "the only generous audience" for O'Hara's poetry in the early New York years, his reference to himself as a "non-literary poet" must, like many of his self-deprecatory remarks, be taken with a grain of salt. We have seen throughout this chapter that O'Hara was very literary indeed, even if his models were not the usual ones. At The Club (the 39 East 8th Street Club), which O'Hara mentions above as the meeting place for poets and artists, he gave, for that matter, some surprisingly "literary" lectures.

In a valuable essay for *Artforum*,[46] Irving Sandler gives a brief history of The Club: its founding in 1949 when the young Abstract Expressionists needed a meeting place more private and comfortable than their wartime haunt, The Waldorf Cafeteria on 6th Avenue; its lecture series and panel discussions, its styles of debate and aesthetic principles, and its ultimate demise in the mid-fifties after the leading painters of the group had become more established and came to prefer the informality of the Cedar Street Tavern (whose neutral, colorless decor typified what de Kooning called a "no-environment") to the organized panel discussions of The Club (p. 31). Sandler lists a selection of events held at The Club in 1951–52; let me cite those in which O'Hara participated as well as a few others which provide a backdrop for his activities and interests at this time:

November 9: An evening with Max Ernst, introduced by Robert Motherwell.

January 18: The first of three Symposia on Abstract Expressionism, promoted by the publication of Thomas Hess's *Abstract Painting*. The first panel, entitled "Expressionism," consisted of Harold Rosenberg (moderator), William Baziotes, Philip Guston, Thomas Hess, Franz Kline, Ad Reinhardt, and Jack Tworkov.

February 20: A conversation between Philip Guston, Franz Kline, Willem de Kooning, George McNeil, and Jack Tworkov.

March 7: A group of younger artists: Jane Freilicher, Grace Hartigan, Alfred Leslie, Joan Mitchell, Frank O'Hara, and Larry Rivers, moderated by John Meyers, continuing their discussion of Abstract Expressionism.

March 14: John Cage speaking on "Contemporary Music."

April 11: "The Image in Poetry and Painting": Nicholas Calas (moderator), Edwin Denby, David Gascoyne, Frank O'Hara, Ruthven Todd.

May 14: "New Poets": Larry Rivers (chairman), John Ashbery, Barbara Guest, Frank O'Hara, James Schuyler.

O'Hara's lecture notes for the April 11 panel are surprisingly formal. He begins with a dictionary definition of *design* and proceeds to contrast *design* to *form:* "design" is the "exterior aspect" of poetry, "form" its "interior structure." Thus the *design* of a devotional poem by George Herbert may be a chalice or a diamond, but its *form* is "the traditional rhymed metaphysical meditation, with the favorite metaphysical rhetorical characteristics including the far-fetched images called 'conceits.'" The poet, O'Hara argues, must steer clear of the Scylla of conventional design and form on the one hand, and the Charybdis of his own private ideas and emotions on the other. Excessive reliance on the design of earlier poets breeds dullness and deadness; too little design, on the other hand, produces "muddy rantings."[47]

This is, of course, a perfectly traditional argument; O'Hara might be T. S. Eliot talking about the delicate balance between fixity and flux.[48] But in judging the poets of his own time, O'Hara reveals his own biases. Yeats and Hopkins, he suggests, while obviously poets of the Great Tradition, are too remote to influence writers of his own generation. He praises Dylan Thomas's early poetry for its "directness and intensity, a richness and compulsive passion which is akin to that of Lautréamont and Rimbaud in French," but remarks shrewdly that "unfortunately his growing public demanded an image of the poet as stormbattered heather-kicking bard from the wilds, and Thomas' latest poetry shows to my mind that his over-emotional and semi-hysterical readings have led his own diction to the verge of sentimentality and verbosity."[49]

O'Hara's view of Wallace Stevens is respectful but somewhat distant. "Stevens . . . has had very little influence when one considers his stature. More than any other living poet he has maintained poetry as high art. Never making concessions to styles or public sentiments he has remained austere without becoming cold or finicky; his work has grown steadily in beauty and wisdom while never thickening into mere fuss and elegance nor hardening into theory. The sensibility his poems reveal is one which other ages [may] well envy us for possessing" (p. 3).

A great poet, in short, but one who looks to the past rather than to the future and who is, in any case, inimitable, *sui generis.* Interestingly, O'Hara here anticipates a controversial distinction Hugh Kenner has recently made in *A Homemade World* (1975) between Stevens's still traditional, Symbolist language and Williams's bold experimentation with audio-visual structures.[50]

The April 11 lecture contains one of O'Hara's first references to Ezra Pound, whom he calls "the father of modern poets in English." "His influence is pervasive and especially so now: his influence is almost invariably healthy in that it seldom detracts from the individuality of the poet who admires him; rather, it points up, clarifies it" (p. 4). This is, I think, a very perceptive comment for it is quite true that poets as otherwise dissimilar as Lowell and Zukovsky, Berryman and Ginsberg, or O'Hara himself and Olson, all felt a special debt to the style and structure of the *Cantos.*

A second new favorite (not quite new since his name is already invoked in "Memorial Day 1950") is Auden. According to O'Hara, Auden is "an American poet" in "his use of the vernacular," just as Eliot's style characterizes him as insistently English. "Auden extended our ideas of what poetry could be; his poems saw clearly into obscure areas of modern life and they provided us with obscure and complex insights into areas which had hitherto been banal." O'Hara praises Auden's poetry for being "intimately based on . . . experiences and expressions of what had been looked down upon by the pretentious estheticism and mysticism of the Eliot school" (p. 2).

So far as I know, O'Hara never reversed these estimates. Of modern English and American poets, Williams, Pound, and Auden remained his favorites, and certainly he never came to trust the school of Eliot, or to have much interest in Yeats, Hopkins, or Stevens. But despite his advocacy of the poetry of immediate experience, of concrete particulars and contemporary vernacular, his theory remained ahead of his practice for another few years. The choice of poems for inclusion in *A City Winter* (1952) is itself indicative. O'Hara's first published book contains fourteen poems: "Poem (At night Chinamen jump . . .)," "Early Mondrian," "Poem (Let's take a walk . . .)," "The Argonauts," "The Lover," "The Young Christ," "Yet Another Fan," "A Pastoral Dialogue," "A Terrestial Cuckoo," "A Mexican Guitar," "Jane Awake," "Gli Amanti," "Jove," and the title poem, which is a sonnet cycle based on specific sonnets by Wyatt, Petrarch, and Shakespeare. Reading "At night Chinamen jump / on Asia with a thump" (*CP*, 13) or most of the other poems in the volume one would never guess that O'Hara had already written such wonderful lyrics as "A Pleasant Thought from Whitehead," or "Memorial Day 1950." Take the octave of the second sonnet in "A City Winter":

> My ship is flung upon the gutter's wrist
> and cries for help of storm to violate
> that flesh your curiosity too late
> has flushed. The stem your garter tongue would twist
> has sunk upon the waveless bosom's mist,
> thigh of the city, apparition, hate,
> and the tower whose doves have, delicate,
> fled into my blood where they are not kissed.   (*CP*, 76)

This version of Wyatt's "The Lover Compareth His State to a Ship in Perilous Storm at Sea" is neither a full-fledged parody, nor a reasonably good imitation, nor an interesting poem in its own right. The game becomes tiresome as when, in the third sonnet, O'Hara concludes with the Shakesperean couplet: "you are not how the gods refused to die, / and I am scarred forever neath the eye." Auden, reading these and related Surrealist poems of the early fifties, wrote to O'Hara: "I think you . . . must watch what is always the great danger with any 'surrealistic' style, namely of confusing authentic non-logical relations which arouse wonder with accidental ones which arouse mere surprise and in the end fatigue."[51]

This is an interesting observation. For curiously, the major poems of

O'Hara's early New York period—"Chez Jane," "Easter," and "Second Avenue"—are not vernacular poems in the Pound-Williams-Auden tradition but Surrealist lyrics that carry the mode of the earlier *Oranges* to what is probably a point of no return. These are the poems of what John Ashbery has aptly called Frank's "French Zen period" (*CP,* ix)—fascinating, if not always successful, experiments.

"Chez Jane" (September 1952), for example, could be considered—to paraphrase Henry James's famous comment on Ford Madox Ford's *The Good Soldier*—one of the best French Surrealist poems in English. "Much surrealist poetry," writes Mary Ann Caws, "instantly brings to mind the art of film, since both are above all concerned with the changing moment, with the metamorphosis of the instant." Thus in the "game called *l'un dans l'autre* . . . one thing is seen as potentially within the other (for instance a lion's mane within the flame of a match), opposites are joined, and the distance between the present and the future is annihilated. The presence of one element is in some way seen as predictive of the opposite element[s] by a deliberate and yet spontaneous stretching of vision." The poem becomes a "collage in motion," holding "within itself the opposition of poles."[52]

These principles are entirely applicable to "Chez Jane," which is one of O'Hara's first "painterly" poems, a kind of Surrealist still life, depending upon intense visualization.

> The white chocolate jar full of petals
> swills odds and ends around in a dizzying eye
> of four o'clocks now and to come. The tiger,
> marvellously striped and irritable, leaps
> on the table and without disturbing a hair
> of the flowers' breathless attention, pisses
> into the pot, right down its delicate spout. (*CP,* 102)

On one level, this passage is quite literal. The scene is Jane Freilicher's living room; the "white chocolate jar" is evidently one of those white Dutch cocoa jars commonly used as vases; "four o'clocks" are little flowers of variegated colors, and Jane Freilicher recalls that on this particular occasion, her cat did piss down the spout of her teapot. Near the end of the poem, when O'Hara talks of "dropped aspirin / into this sunset of roses," the reference is again to the common practice of putting aspirin in water so that the roses in the vase will last longer.[53]

But although "Chez Jane" may be read as an occasional poem, its particular conjunction of images is wholly fanciful, exemplifying the game of *l'un dans l'autre*. The "white chocolate jar" immediately brings together opposites—light and dark; it is further juxtaposed to the "petals swill[ing] odds and ends around in a dizzying eye," so that stasis is opposed to movement. Again, it is a particular moment in time—four o'clock (I take the phrase in its primary sense here)—but also the "four o'clocks now and to come," so that the distance between present and future is annihilated. The static world of the white chocolate jar is now transformed by the appearance of the tiger cat, leaping on the table and pissing "into the pot, right down its delicate spout," without so much as "disturbing a hair / of the flowers' breathless attention." Here again, polar opposites—motion and stasis, delicacy and crudity—are reconciled; the absurd contrast between tiger piss and the delicate teapot spout is especially effective.

These polarities now yield to the metamorphosis of the instant. "A whisper of steam goes up from that porcelain / urethra. 'Saint-Saëns!' it seems to be whispering." So tiger-cat piss becomes steam becomes the sound of the composer's name and, by implication, his music. And this *vertige* delights the poet; he declares playfully: "Ah be with me always, spirit of noisy / contemplation in the studio, the Garden / of Zoos, the eternally fixed afternoons!" Here sound is pitted against silence, flux against eternity. Finally, the "brute beast" rests, "caressing his fangs," subdued by the "exact peril" (his mistress, Jane), which "only a moment before dropped aspirin / in this sunset of roses and now throws a chair / in the air to aggravate the truly menacing." The poem's ending is like a whirlpool: the tongue of the tiger-cat, the aspirin, sunsets, roses, chair thrown into the air—all these disparate images come together to create a dizzying, "truly menacing" vortex.

It is interesting to compare "Chez Jane" to Stevens's "Earthy Anecdote" or his "Anecdote of a Jar."[54] In the former, Stevens uses the "bucks . . . clattering / Over Oklahoma" and the firecat as symbols of two opposing sets of values: the bucks represent chaos, mindlessness, brute strength, the masculine principle, while the firecat stands for order, imaginative transformation, vitality, the feminine. At the end, the firecat, having won the day, "closed his bright eyes / And slept."

Again, in "Anecdote of a Jar," the round jar which the poet places in Tennessee transforms the "slovenly wilderness" which "sprawled around, no longer wild"; it functions as an ordering principle.

But in a Surrealist poem like "Chez Jane," the dialectic of opposites has no "meaning" beyond itself. The "white chocolate jar" and tiger cat do not stand for any particular set of values; rather, the poet is interested in capturing the moment of metamorphosis itself, the moment when tiger piss turns into the sound of "Saint-Saëns." Unlike Stevens's jar, O'Hara's is sometimes agent, sometimes acted upon. Everything is potentially something else, and the game is to record these changes.

In "Chez Jane," O'Hara was therefore doing something rather new in American poetry which was, despite the influx of French Surrealism during the war years, still essentially the poetry of Symbolism. Some readers may find O'Hara's poem excessively cold and intellectual; the poet himself is not yet present *in* the poem as mediator of polarities. But, taken on its own terms, "Chez Jane" has a kind of perfection and finish not yet found in the more prolix *Oranges,* written three years earlier. It is also quite free of the coyness—what we might call the "Dada giggle"—of such poems as "Night Thoughts in Greenwich Village" or "Tarquin," written at Ann Arbor.

A more personal vision of Surrealism is found in the long experimental poem "Easter" (1952), which O'Hara did not choose to publish during his lifetime. Critics have generally been unreceptive to this poem, calling it "messy," "strident," "bombastic," and "formless."[55] But when we read "Easter" in the context of its probable models, the long catalogue poems of Tzara and Péret, its form, so oddly reminiscent of a Walt Disney film like *Fantasia,* becomes more comprehensible. Here is a passage from Tzara's "Drugstore Conscience" (*Droguerie-conscience*) in Michael Benedikt's translation:

> the lamp of a lily will give birth to so great a prince
> that fountainheads will flourish in factories
> and the leech transform itself into a sickness-tree
> I'm searching for the roots of things my immovable lord. . . .
>
> wet parrot
> lignite cactus swell yourself up between a black cow's horns . . .
>
> (*Poetry of Surrealism,* p. 89)

"Easter" contains many passages that similarly juxtapose natural and mechanistic items in a dream landscape wholly devoid of logic:

> an army of young married couples' vanilla hemorrhages
> a spine-tingling detonation nested in leaves
> alfalfa blowing against sisters in a hanky of shade
> and the tea ship crushes an army of hair
> in rampant jaws those streets whose officer deploys a day of
> hairs strutting the rosy municipal ruts. . . .
>
> birdie, birdie
> on the uptown train. . . . (CP, 98)

An even closer model for "Easter" is found in Péret: "Nebulous" (*Nebuleuse*), also translated by Michael Benedikt, begins:

> When the night of butter just emerged from the churn
> inundates the moles of railway stations announced by the
>   trumpets of eyes
> and enlarges like a subway platform coming closer and closer
> only to obliterate your image
> which revolves in my brains like a heliotrope in the grip
>   of a bad case of seasickness
> then collar buttons leap into the air like lambkins formerly
>   perched upon a powder keg. . . .
>
> (*Poetry of Surrealism*, p. 237)

This passage is echoed by the following lines in "Easter":

> When the world strips down and rouges up
> like a mattress's teeth brushed by love's bristling sun
> a marvelous heart tiresomely got up in brisk bold stares
> when those trappings fart at the feet of the stars
> a self-coral serpent wrapped round an arm with no jujubes . . .
>
> (CP, 97)

O'Hara has now mastered Péret's style. In both cases, "when . . ." clauses and similes ("like a heliotrope," "like a mattress's teeth") are purposely designed as verbal traps, making us look for a logic that doesn't exist. Causality and analogy are consistently subverted; disparate images juxtaposed so as to create an antilandscape that no longer "refers" to a recognizable world.

Another important source for "Easter" is the poetry of Rimbaud, particularly the long, obscene, purposely outrageous "Ce qu'on dit au poète," in which Rimbaud inverts all values, treating the conventionally beautiful as if it were ugly and vice-versa. Lilies become enema syringes; the "sea of Sorrento" is filled "With the dung of a thousand swans"; "bright butterflies . . . Leave droppings all over The Pansy"; and at one point the poet asks:

> In brief: is any flower, weed
> Or lily, alive or dead
> Worth a sea gull turd?
> Worth a candle flame?[56]

O'Hara similarly debunks the "beautiful" and elevates the obscene to poetic status: "the glassy towns are fucked by yaks"; there are "floods of crocodile piss" and "shadows of prairie pricks dancing"; the poem refers to "a hardon a sequoia a toilet tissue," to "your deflowered eyeballs," "the pubic foliage of precarious hazard," "the ship sawed up by the biting asses of stars," the "orchids of the testicles," the "Boom of pregnant hillsides / awash with urine," and so on.

An interesting commentary on these images, and on the poem in general, is provided by Kenneth Koch:

Another of his works which burst on us all like a bomb then [1952] was "Easter," a wonderful, energetic, and rather obscene poem of four or five pages, which consisted mainly of a procession of various bodily parts and other objects across a vast landscape. It was like Lorca and Whitman in some ways, but very original. I remember two things about it which were new: one was the phrase "the roses of Pennsylvania" and the other was the line in the middle of the poem which began "It is Easter!" (Easter, though it was the title, had not been mentioned before in the poem and apparently had nothing to do with it.) What I saw in these lines was 1) inspired irrelevance which turns out to be relevant (once Frank had said "It is Easter!" the whole poem was obviously about death and resurrection); 2) the use of movie techniques in poetry (in this case coming down hard on the title in the middle of the work); 3) the detachment of beautiful words from traditional contexts and putting them in curious new American ones ("roses of Pennsylvania").[57]

This is a very acute reading. The claim for Lorca and Whitman may be somewhat exaggerated because "Easter" is still predominantly a third-person impersonal poem, lacking the bardic intensity of these two poets. But Koch quite rightly notes that O'Hara's technique is to detach beautiful words from traditional contexts, that the poem centers around a procession of bodily parts across a vast landscape, and that at the word "Easter," the tone and mood of the poem undergo a definite shift, death giving way to resurrection, separation to union. Thus images like "the ship sawed up by the biting asses of stars" and "sins of sex and kisses of birds at the end of the penis" give way, after "the balm of Easter floods, my tongue's host / a rivulet of purple blood" to positive references: "the ship shoves off into the heady ocean of love," or "The day passes into the powdery light of your embrace." Indeed, the poem ends on a note of joy:

> the Sun sings in the stones of the savage
> when the world booms its seven cunts
> like a river plunged upon and perishing
> Sun, to the feast!
> to be pelted by the shit of the stars at last in flood
> like a breath.   (*CP*, 100)

Despite the references here to "cunts" and "shit," the poet is presenting a vision of new beauty. Sexual ecstasy is the keynote: the Sun activates the stones; the "seven cunts" open up the floodgates and rivers shoot out, meeting "the shit of the stars" in a marvelous "feast"—a "flood / like a breath." This is in sharp contrast to the opening of "Easter," in which "The perforated mountains of my saliva leave cities awash." The dry mouth of the poet is finally infused with new "breath"; the "perforated mountains" turn into the sunlit "seven cunts."

"Easter" does, then, display a sense of form. Its consistent use of high-low polarities, its anaphoric "When the world ... " clauses—clauses that are regularly left suspended but that nicely tie lines together—and the elaboration of its central Easter theme (here, of course, a secular, even a blasphemous Easter) make this a very exciting, innovative poem.

Yet the cataloguing technique of "Easter"—the endless piling up of polarized images in exclamatory phrases—is not without its dangers. Six months or so after he completed "Easter," O'Hara tried to carry its form one step further and the result is his most Byzantine and difficult poem, *Second Avenue*, written in the spring of 1953 and first published in book form by Totem Press in 1960.

Kenneth Koch was enthusiastic about *Second Avenue*. He describes it as "a poem in eleven parts," whose "chief persona is a sort of Whitmanian I, though other voices appear and disappear as they do for example in the *Cantos* and *Paterson*. . . . Mr. O'Hara is the best writer about New York alive . . . he succeeds in conveying the city's atmosphere not by writing directly about it but by writing about his emotions, all of them somehow filtered through its paint supply stores and its inspiring April smog." The language, Koch adds, resembles that of Williams in being "convincing and natural." "To speak historically," he concludes, "I think *Second Avenue* is evidence that the avant-garde style of French poetry from Baudelaire to Reverdy has now infiltrated American consciousness to such an extent that it is possible for an American poet to write lyrically in it with perfect ease."[58]

This would be a good description of O'Hara's later poems, but I wonder if it accurately describes *Second Avenue*. John Ashbery speaks of "the obfuscation that makes reading 'Second Avenue' such a difficult pleasure" (*CP*, ix), and O'Hara himself seems to be somewhat defensive about this particular poem. In "Notes on *Second Avenue*," apparently sent to the editor of a literary magazine in 1953,[59] he insists that the "philosophical reduction of reality to a dealable-with system . . . distorts life," that the "meaning" of the poem can't be paraphrased, but then, evidently recognizing the obstacles in the reader's path, he does an about-face and proceeds to "explain" certain passages.

"There are," O'Hara points out, "several scenes in the poem with characters," for instance, "a flier in his plane over the ocean" (*CP*, 143); "a little Western story" (*CP*, 144); "a newspaper clipping report of Bunny Lang's trip in the Caribbean" (*CP*, 144); "a true description of not being able to continue this poem and meeting Kenneth Koch for a sandwich while waiting for the poem to start again" (*CP*, 146); "a talk with a sculptor (Larry Rivers, who also sculpts) about a piece in progress" (*CP*, 147); "a description of a poetry critic and teacher: (tirade?)" (*CP*, 148); "a description of Grace Hartigan painting" (*CP*, 149); and finally, "a little description of a de Kooning WOMAN which I'd seen recently at his studio" (*CP*, 147).

O'Hara admits that the poem may "seem very jumbled, while actually everything in it either happened to me or I felt happening (saw, imagined) on Second Avenue." The "verbal elements," he concludes, "are not too interesting to discuss although they are intended consciously to keep the surface of the poem high and dry, not wet, reflective and self-conscious. Perhaps the obscurity comes in here, in the relation between surface and meaning, but I like it that way since the one is the other (you have to use words) and I hope the poem to *be* the subject, not just about it" (*CP*, 495–97).

This last statement affords some interesting clues as to the strengths and weaknesses of *Second Avenue*. It is perhaps too painterly a poem, O'Hara's most ambitious attempt to do with *words* ("you have to use words") what the Abstract Expressionists were doing with paint. Surely it is not coincidental that Grace Hartigan considers *Second Avenue* "Frank's greatest poem, one of the great epic poems of our time." She loves the poem's endless transformations: "It has everything art should have. It has imagery, emotional content, leaps of imagination, displacements of time and place going back and forth, flashings of modern life and inner feelings. Name it, name anything, and it's got it."[60]

O'Hara does indeed include "everything," and yet the question remains whether a poem, especially such a long poem, can "*be* the subject, not just about it," whether verbal structure can be so insistently nonmimetic. For the mode of *Second Avenue* seems to be one of intentional displacement and disorientation. Take the opening passage, whose bardic intensity and aureate diction recall Hart Crane:

> Quips and players, seeming to vend astringency off-hours,
> celebrate diced excesses and sardonics, mixing pleasures,
> as if proximity were staring at the margin of a plea . . .
>> (*CP*, 139; spaced dots, O'Hara's)

No sooner does O'Hara provide us with this lyric model than he undercuts it:

> This thoroughness whose traditions have become so reflective,
> your distinction is merely a quill at the bottom of the sea. . . .

Lines 4 and 5 prick the balloon, as if to say, "Oh, so you thought I was going to be *poetic*, did you? But why be poetic when our 'traditions have become so reflective? And what, after all, is the poet's pen but 'a quill at the bottom of the sea'?"

Grace Hartigan has pointed out to me that the use of pronouns in these lines is especially artful. The poem moves from "*This* thoroughness" (what thoroughness?) to "*your* violet dinginess" and "*your* distinction," to "*One* distinguishes," and finally to "*I* must bitterly . . ." These constantly shifting pronouns and referents create a fantasy landscape in which one cannot distinguish subject from object, interior from exterior, past from present or future, time from space. The reader is, so to speak, lost in the funhouse.

For Grace Hartigan, the inclusion of such varied references to person, place, and time within the space of ten lines is an amazing feat, making *Second Avenue* a ground-breaking poem, a kind of lyric *Who's Who*. I myself am less convinced that the principle of disorientation can keep a poem going for some six hundred lines without boring the reader a little. For one thing, O'Hara's range of styles in *Second Avenue* is perhaps too variable. There are, for example, a number of documentary-realistic passages, like the opening of Part 9, where the poet is discussing art and literature with Larry Rivers in the latter's studio:

> Now in November, by Josephine Johnson. The Heroes,
> by John Ashbery. Topper's Roumanian Broilings. The Swimmer.
> Your feet are more beautiful than your father's, I think.
> does that upset you? admire, I admire youth above age, yes,
> in the infancy of the race when we were very upset we wrote,
> "O toe!" and it took months to "get" those feet. Render. Rent.
> Now more features of our days have become popular, the nose
> broken, the head bald, the body beautiful. Marilyn Monroe.

> (*CP*, 147)

As this "conversation" continues, the poet remembers all sorts of unrelated incidents:

> As I walked into the Dairy B & H Lunch, I couldn't remember
> your other eye, I puked.

Or this memory of his father's admonition:

> My father said, "Do what you want but don't get hurt,
> I'm warning you. Leave the men alone, they'll only tease you.

When your aunt comes I want you to get down off that horse
And speak like a gentleman, or I'll take it away from you.
Don't grit your teeth at me." (*CP*, 148)

And this memory is, in turn, followed by the satiric portrait of the
literary critic as "chicken . . . pecking and dribbling," and "grinning
Simian fart, poseur among idiots / and dilettantes and pederasts."

These passages, introducing a new note of harsh realism, immediacy, and "Personism," look ahead to the later poems, but they don't
quite seem to belong in the same poem that contains the following
description of a de Kooning portrait of a woman:

You remained for me a green Buick of sighs, o Gladstone!
and your wife Trina, how like a yellow pillow on a sill
in the many-windowed dusk where the air is compartmented!
her red lips of Hollywood, soft as a Titian and as tender,
her grey face which refrains from thrusting aside the mane
of your languorous black smells, the hand crushed by her chin,
and that slumberland of dark cutaneous lines which reels
under the burden of her many-darkly-hued corpulence of linen
and satin bushes, is like a lone rose with the sky behind it.
(*CP*, 147)

Here the coy and rather labored metaphors look back to O'Hara's
earlier style.

One is, in short, hard put to find any line of development in *Second
Avenue;* individual sections appear in no particular sequence; scenes
and images are juxtaposed without a view of their place in the larger
scheme. Perhaps O'Hara wanted it that way, wanted to stun us by his
insistent dislocations, as in "I hold all of night in my one eye. You," or
"are you myself, / indifferent as a drunkard sponging off a car window?" (p. 142), but such *vertige* ultimately cannot sustain the poem,
and I would agree with Helen Vendler that, at least in this case, there is
too little design, although the poem's meanderings are less those of a
diary than those of a catalogue of insufficiently related items.[61]

Yet in many ways *Second Avenue* represents a real stylistic advance.
It is, for instance, one of the first poems to invoke O'Hara's friends by
name.[62] I have already referred to John Ashbery, Grace Hartigan, and

Bunny Lang; here is a portrait of Joe LeSueur:

> I met Joe, his hair pale as the eyes of the fields of maize
> in August, at the gallery, he said you're the first Creon
> of 1953, congrats. Your costume, he said, was hand
> over fist. If you worked harder you could remake
> old Barrymore movies, you're that statuesque, he said.   (*CP,* 143)

And Kenneth Koch:

> Kenneth in an abandoned storeway on Sunday cutting ever more
> insinuating lobotomies of a yet-to-be-more yielding world
> of ears, of a soprano rallying at night in a cadenza. . . .   (*CP,* 146)

And there are many lines and passages throughout *Second Avenue* that have the immediacy, excitement, and sense of *presence* that characterizes the later poetry. Here, for example, is the opening of the eleventh and final section:

> My hands are Massimo Plaster, called "White Pin in the Arm of the Sea"
> and I'm blazoned and scorch like a fleet of windbells down the /
>   Pulaski Skyway
> tabletops of Vienna carrying their bundles of cellophane to the laundry,
> ear to the tongue. . . .
> I emulate the black which is a cry but is not voluptuary like a warning,
> which has lines, cuts, drips, aspirates, trembles with horror. . . .
>   (*CP,* 150)

Here the poet's sense of personal energy, fluidity, vitality is rendered in terms of the everyday things in his life—the Massimo plaster, carefully designated by its precise name, "White Pin in the Arm of the Sea," the "fleet of windbells down the Pulaski Skyway," the black paint, cutting, dripping, aspirating.

By late 1953, then, all the necessary ingredients were present: the passages of casual, colloquial diction capturing actual speech or actual events, the unique O'Hara syntax with its ambiguous verbal positioning, its odd line breaks and consistent enjambement—all working together to give the reader a sense of tautness and breakneck speed; the versions of painting rendered "poetically"; the vignettes of artists, friends, enemies, people in the street; the images of the city; the art world, the private world. But after *Second Avenue,* O'Hara learns to relate individual elements more intricately, to forge them into a coherent whole. And he now begins to put what we might call "straight Surrealism" behind him. In the poems of 1954-61, O'Hara's great period, we can no longer identify the echoes of Péret or Tzara or Desnos as readily; Surrealism has now been assimilated into an American idiom.

Nevertheless, when one looks at the *oeuvre* of these early years— years of testing—one is astonished by the poet's range, his daring, his willingness to experiment—and his frequent successes. If we replaced *A City Winter* with a more representative collection of early poems—a collection that would include "Autobiographia Literaria," "A Pleasant Thought from Whitehead," "The Critic," "An Image of Leda," "A Postcard from John Ashbery," "Les Etiquettes Jaunes," "Poem (I've got to tell you"), "Memorial Day 1950," "Easter," *Second Avenue,* and "Chez Jane"—O'Hara's central place in the literary scene of the early fifties would already be assured.

3
POET
AMONG
PAINTERS

—Sometimes I think I'm "in love" with painting.
(*CP,* 329)

IN 1965, FRANCINE DU PLESSIX, who was editing a special issue on the relationship of poetry to painting for *Art in America,* asked twenty-two painters to choose a contemporary poem they especially liked and "make for it a work in black and white in the medium of their choice." "To avoid duplications," she explains, "I set a 'first come, first served' system of choice. Three New York painters who asked to illustrate Frank O'Hara, for instance, had to take a second choice because Jasper Johns had been the first to reply to our project, and had asked to interpret the work of this particular poet."[1]

O'Hara's popularity among the leading artists of his day is by now legendary. As René d'Harnoncourt, then director of the Museum of Modern Art, explained it in his preface to *In Memory of My Feelings* (the deluxe memorial volume published in 1967, in which thirty O'Hara poems are illustrated by artists with whom the poet had been closely associated): "Frank was so sure of his own reactions toward works of art that he did not need to be aggressive. He had absolute integrity without self-righteousness. . . . many of us, because of Frank's presence, learned to see better."[2] The thirty illustrations in the book naturally vary in quality, style, and appropriateness to the poem in question, but, taken as a whole, they provide an eloquent testimony to O'Hara's extraordinary rapport with painters as diverse as Larry Rivers, Robert Motherwell, Jasper Johns, Grace Hartigan, Barnett Newman, Robert Rauschenberg, Alfred Leslie, Norman Bluhm, Joe Brainard, Helen Frankenthaler, and Willem de Kooning. From the early fifties, when he sold Christmas cards at the front desk of the museum, to the year of his death when, as curator, he had begun work on a major retrospective of Jackson Pollock and had at last secured de Kooning's agreement to organize a large retrospective of his paintings, O'Hara worked closely with many of these artists, organizing their exhibitions, visiting their studios, interviewing them, and writing about their work. The collaborations ("poem-paintings" and related mixed-media performances) that grew out of these associations are often important art works in their own right although literary people have tended to dismiss them. I shall discuss these collaborations later in the chapter.

It is often argued that the visual arts took up too much of O'Hara's time and prevented him from devoting himself to his real vocation— poetry. John Ashbery, for example, remarks: "I sometimes wish he had not been so fruitfully involved with the Museum and with the art world. Due to the economics of art, Frank, unlike most of the artists who illustrated his book, could not support himself from his work although he was an internationally acclaimed poet. This meant that he could never devote more than a fraction of his time to his poetry."[3]

Practically speaking, this is quite true: dashing off poems during one's lunch hour or at a crowded party as O'Hara regularly did would not seem to be the best way of polishing one's craft. But like Williams, whom he resembles in so many ways, O'Hara used—and indeed needed—his other role as a source of inspiration. Joe LeSueur recalls that O'Hara's only leave of absence from the Museum (January–June 1956), when he accepted a grant from the Poets' Theatre in Cambridge, Mass., turned out to be "sheer hell for him":

> . . . he hated being away from New York and all of his friends and re-turning to the scene of his college years, and while he was up there he wrote no play and only a few poems. When he could manage it he stormed back to New York, drank more than I ever saw him drink, and talked about how provincial Cambridge was. . . . Frank clearly wasn't cut

out for grants, which he never applied for, or for places like Yaddo, where he never went; they created what I think he viewed as artificial writing situations. But the museum set-up worked for him, it seems to me. Not that he liked the routine and paper work, which in fact frequently drove him to the point of despair; it was simply that he must have needed the reality and discipline of the workaday world. . . . And finally, he believed in what he was doing. It wasn't just a job to him, it was a vital part of his life's work.[4]

The Museum thus served O'Hara as a *point de repère,* a fixed and stable center whose nine-to-five routine could offset his otherwise freewheeling and disorganized mode of living. But then, even Frank's fabled all-night drinking and talking sessions, whether at the Cedar Bar or at parties on Long Island, served an important function. As LeSueur remarks:

> . . . he seemed to be inspired and exhilarated by all of his painter friends, from Bill de Kooning, whom he idolized, to certain painters who appeared in the sixties, such as Alan d'Arcangelo. He devoted so much time to looking and thinking about their work you'd have thought he had a vested interest in their development as artists. But I don't entirely go along with the idea, suggested by several of Frank's friends, that his generosity took him away from his own work. That wasn't exactly what happened. He offered them encouragement, inspired them with his insights and his passion; they impinged upon and entered his poetry, which wouldn't have been the same and probably not as good without them.
>
> ("Four Apartments," p. 292)

The poetry certainly wouldn't have been the same. In the first place, painters and painting provided O'Hara with one of his central subjects. Consider the role that Grace Hartigan, whose life was closely bound up with Frank's from the early fifties to 1960,[5] plays in the poems. By her account, painter and poet would often use the same image as starting point. Thus, when Grace Hartigan painted *Oranges,* the series that corresponds to O'Hara's twelve pastorals by that name written some years earlier, she used the poet's words in the most ingenious ways, sometimes crowding a whole poem onto a corner of the canvas, sometimes spreading just a few words of text across the surface so as to create patterns of great tension and excitement. Words are played off against semiabstract, suggestive shapes of dazzling bright color, as in *What Fire Murmurs Its Sedition,* in which the entire text of the third prose poem, partly in script and partly in large and small block print, is scattered across and around the reclining nude figure of the poet (Fig. 1). Interestingly, poet and painter treat the word "oranges" in similar ways: O'Hara never mentions it except in the title; Hartigan uses the color occasionally, but it is by no means prominent in her series.

Here, then, we have a case of poetry inspiring painting. The converse is equally true. Grace (the name has, of course, endless possibilities) appears in poem after poem, beginning with the early love sonnet, "Poem for a Painter," in which the speaker exclaims: "Grace, / you are the flowergirl on the candled plain / with fingers smelled of turpentine" (*CP*, 80). In her painting, O'Hara evidently found a visual confirmation of his own aesthetic; consider the remarks he makes in the 1954 essay "Nature and the New Painting":

> She began as an abstract painter. . . . her early work shows the influence of Hans Hofmann's teachings and Jackson Pollock's free, iconoclastic spirit. She is said to have awakened one morning to the decision that she could paint abstractly no longer. . . . She put behind her the exclusively esthetic concerns of her abstractions, her new canvases erupting with images and influences hitherto repressed: fantastic nudes and costumed figures, loaded still lifes like rock quarries, overt references to the monumental bathers of Cezanne and Matisse. . . . Essentially a painter of *heterogeneous pictures* which bring together *wildly discordant images* through insight into their functional relationship . . . her method is seen in bold relief next an abstract painter like Philip Guston, for instance, whose varied periods and explorations culminate in the pure, unified and perfect silence of his present work. (*SS,* 44–45, my italics)

What O'Hara calls Hartigan's "progress of inclusion" is beautifully conveyed in the following passage from *Second Avenue,* which is, the poet tells us, "a description of Grace Hartigan painting."[6]

Grace destroys

the whirling faces in their dissonant gaiety where it's anxious,
lifted nasally to the heavens which is a carrousel grinning
and spasmodically obliterated with loaves of greasy white paint
and this becomes like love to her, is what I desire
and what you, to be able to throw something away without yawning

"Oh Leaves of Grass! o Sylvette! oh Basket Weavers' Conference!"
and thus make good our promise to destroy something but not us.

(*CP,* 149)

Notice how O'Hara's heterogeneous images and syntactic dislocations "imitate" the process of painting itself. The pronoun "it" ("It's
anxious") has no antecedent, the relative clause "which is..." no
specific referent, and yet we are told that "this" (the "dissonant gaiety"? the "heavens" seen as a "carrousel"? the "loaves of greasy white
paint"? or all these things taken together?) becomes "like love to her"
and is also "what I [the poet] desire." The shorthand phrase "and what
you" in line 6 again shifts perspective: "you" is now Grace herself; her
painting is all she desires it to be—a structure of "wildly discordant
images" that manages to avoid all bombast ("Oh Leaves of Grass! o
Sylvette! oh Basket Weavers' Conference!"), that can *deconstruct*
("throw away without yawning") pure abstraction in favor of hetero-
geneity ("Images ... hitherto repressed," "chaotic brushwork and
whirling impasto," *SS,* 45), that is charged with personal *passion* ("and
thus make good our promise to destroy something but not us").

In such bittersweet love poems as "Christmas Card for Grace Hartigan" (*CP,* 212) and "For Grace after a Party" (p. 214), O'Hara lets one
image "bleed" into another even as Hartigan does in her painting.
"Put out your hand," he says in the latter, "Isn't there / an ashtray
suddenly, there? beside / the bed?" Or again, in the famous "In Memory of My Feelings" (1956), dedicated to Grace Hartigan, the aphoris-
tic phrase, "Grace / to be born and live as variously as possible" (*CP,*
256), is embedded in a long meditation on the nature of identity, the
ability to assume roles, to have "sordid identifications." The painter
herself has pointed out to me that this reference to "Grace" relates
back to the preceding lines:

> One of me is standing in the waves, an ocean bather.
> or I am naked with a plate of devils at my hip.

Here O'Hara alludes to two Hartigan nudes.[7] He seems to identify
even with the figures in Grace's paintings, entering, so to speak, the
world of her canvas.

Perhaps the best example of the personal role Grace Hartigan plays
in the poems is found in "'L'Amour Avait Passé Par Là'" (1950). Here

the poet appears as a Pierrot figure, lamenting the loss of his love, and
his shift in mood from a gently self-mocking sorrow to consolation is
rendered chiefly in art images. The poem begins:

> Yes
> like the still center of a book on Joan Miró
> blue red green and white . . .
> and the huge mirror behind me blinking, paint-flecked
> they have painted the ceiling of my heart
> and put in a new light fixture
> and Arte Contemporáneo by Juan Eduardo Cirlot
> and the Petit Guide to the Musée National Russe. . . .

The poet is about to turn into a blank page in an art book. But then he
recalls that he must "get to the Cedar to meet Grace," and he declares
with a wonderful flaunting of logic:

> I must tighten my moccasins
> and forget the minute bibliographies of disappointment
> anguish and power
> for unrelaxed honesty. . . .

And the "unrelaxed honesty" of his tête-à-tête with Grace may lead to
new thresholds:

a candle held to the window has two flames
and perhaps a horde of followers in the rain of youth
as under the arch you find a heart of lipstick or a condom
left by the parade
of a generalized intuition
it is the great period of Italian art when everyone imitates Picasso
afraid to mean anything
as the second flame in its happy reflecting ignores the candle and the wind
(CP, 333)

Here the "second flame" with its "happy reflecting" is associated with
Grace and counters the bleak "light fixture" earlier suspended from
the poet's heart.

A second strategy found in O'Hara's poems about art is to use an
allusion to artists or works of art as a touchstone for grounding and
authenticating a particular mood. This occurs in "Having a Coke with
You" (1960), where the object of the poet's love (Vincent Warren) is

comically compared and found superior to Rembrandt's *Polish Rider,*
Duchamp's *Nude Descending a Staircase,* and the equestrian figures of
Marino Marini, who (in what I find a penetrating insight) fails some-
how to "pick the rider as carefully as the horse" (*CP,* 360). In "A Warm
Day for December" (*CP,* 375), the poet makes the round of the 57th
Street galleries and notes that he is "Isolated by my new haircut / and
look more Brancusi than usual." Or take "Radio," written in 1955:

> Why do you play such dreary music
> on Saturday afternoon, when tired
> mortally tired I long for a little
> reminder of immortal energy?
>
> > > All
> week long while I trudge fatiguingly
> from desk to desk in the museum
> you spill your miracles of Grieg
> and Honegger on shut-ins.
>
> > > Am I not
> shut in too, and after a week
> of work don't I deserve Prokofieff?
>
> Well, I have my beautiful de Kooning
> to aspire to. I think it has an orange
> bed in it, more than the ear can hold.   (*CP,* 234)

The charm of this poem depends upon the comic inversion of the
last three lines, the seemingly absurd logic that the poet doesn't need
music because his "beautiful de Kooning" gives him "more than the
ear can hold." But of course O'Hara is perfectly serious: being "shut
in" at the museum, far from making him "shut out" from the pleasures
of music, has taught him to "listen" to paintings. All the arts—visual,
aural, verbal—are interdependent. Perfect one, the poem suggests,
and you will come closer to the others. What is especially interesting is
that O'Hara's reference to the de Kooning, far from being an offhand
remark, is based on actual fact. Indeed, one of O'Hara's peculiar
strengths is the loving attention he bestows on the documentary detail
that provides authenticity. Kenneth Koch makes this point in a letter
to Frank, dated 22 March 1956:

RADIO is perfect. I was in the Cedar Tavern last night and Bill de Kooning
was there, so I asked him if he'd seen your poem about his picture. He

said, Yeah . . . but how can I be sure it's about my picture, is it just about a picture? I quoted him "I have my beautiful de Kooning / to aspire to. I think it has an orange / bed in it . . . " He said "It's a couch. But then it really is my picture, that's wonderful." Then he told me how he had always been interested in mattresses because they were pulled together at certain points and puffed out at others, "like the earth." (*CP,* 536)

Another group of poems inspired by art can be classified as meditations on particular paintings with the intent of "translating" the tone of the painting into a verbal medium. These are poems that, unlike the passages from *Second Avenue* and "In Memory of My Feelings" discussed above, treat the painting as an independent object, without reference to the artist. "Poem (The eyelid has its storms . . .)," for example, tries to capture what O'Hara calls, in his monograph on Jackson Pollock, "the tragedy of a linear violence" (*AC,* 33). It begins:

> The eyelid has its storms. There is the opaque fish-
> scale green of it after swimming in the sea and then sud-
> denly wrenching violence, strangled lashes, and a barbed
> wire of sand falls to the shore.   (*CP,* 223)

As a commentary on one of Pollock's "all-over" paintings, this is an effective poem, but I wonder if it can be said to lead a life of its own. I have similar reservations about "Blue Territory," a poem "about" Helen Frankenthaler's painting by that name.[8] Again, if one knows this abstract painting, whose curvilinear shapes, vibrant colors, and shimmering surfaces carry minimal suggestions of an ocean landscape, O'Hara's rendition is interesting:

> Big bags of sand   until they came,
>   the flattering end
> of the world
>   the gulls were swooping and gulping and filling
> the bags
>   as helpful creatures everywhere were helping
> to end
>   the world
>   so we could be alone together at last, one by one
>   Who needs an ark? . . .   (*CP,* 270)

But if we take this impressionistic "tone poem" on its own terms, its "picture" fails to come into focus.

A more interesting "translation" of painting into poetry is "Joseph Cornell," written in 1955. Cornell was a master of the Surrealist assemblage; his intriguing shadow boxes combine exotic words and images with ordinary materials—thimbles, eggshells, mirrors, and maps—to create strange fables of the unconscious. "Taglioni's Jewel Casket" (1940), which is owned by the Museum of Modern Art, is a good example. A box made of wood, velvet, glass, and plastic, it contains four rows of glass cubes. On the inside of the cover, which is made of blue velvet, we find the following "message" on white paper: "On a moonlight night in the winter of 1835 the carriage of Maria Taglioni was halted by a Russian highwayman, and that enchanting creature commanded to dance for this audience of one upon a panther's skin spread over the snow beneath the stars." Such a box, as William Rubin points out,[9] becomes a kind of "spatial theatre," combining three-dimensional space and scenic illusion. The stilted narrative about Madame Taglioni is wittily juxtaposed to the prosaic plain box with its arithmetically precise rows of glass blocks.

In his poem, O'Hara gives us the equivalent of Cornell's boxes:

> Into a sweeping meticulously-
> detailed disaster the violet
> light pours. It's not a sky,
> it's a room. And in the open
> field a glass of absinthe is
> fluttering its song of India.
> Prairie winds circle mosques.
>
> You are always a little too
> young to understand. He is
> bored with his sense of the
> past the artist. Out of the
> prescient rock in his heart
> he has spread a land without
> flowers of near distances.   (*CP*, 237)

Here the verbal experience closely approximates the visual. In the first "box," the poet gives his version of a Cornell "message," an exotic and stylized description reminiscent of the passage about Maria Taglioni. The second box abruptly shifts to the response of the viewer, the "You" (all of us) who is "always a little too / young to understand" that the artist must, like Cornell, create new forms because "He is / bored with his sense of the / past." The third sentence aphoristically conveys the very spirit of Cornell's art: "the land without / flowers of near distances" (even the line break here emphasizes the deprivation), the bare "thing itself," as Wallace Stevens would say, made "Out of the / prescient rock in his heart."

Even here, of course, we need to know something about Cornell's work in order to understand O'Hara's poem. But in certain cases, when O'Hara worked very closely with a particular painter, the poem absorbed the spirit of the painting thoroughly enough to become independent. This is true, I think, of "On Seeing Larry Rivers' *Washington Crossing The Delaware* at the Museum of Modern Art" (*CP,* 233). Rivers explains what he was trying to do in this particular painting in an interview with O'Hara for *Horizon* (1959):

> . . . what could be dopier than a painting dedicated to a national cliché—Washington Crossing the Delaware. The last painting that dealt with George and the rebels is hanging in the Met and was painted by a coarse German nineteenth-century academician who really loved Napoleon more than anyone and thought crossing a river on a late December afternoon was just another excuse for a general to assume a heroic, slightly tragic pose. . . . What I saw in the crossing was quite different. I saw the moment as nerve-wracking and uncomfortable. I couldn't picture anyone getting into a chilly river around Christmas time with anything resembling hand-on-chest heroics. (*AC,* 112)

"What was the reaction when George was shown?" O'Hara asks. "About the same reaction," Rivers replies, "as when the Dadaists introduced a toilet seat as a piece of sculpture in a Dada show in Zurich. Except that the public wasn't upset—the *painters* were. One painter, Gandy Brodie, who was quite forceful, called me a phony. In the bar where I can usually be found, a lot of painters laughed" (*AC,* 113).

O'Hara himself, however, understood the Rivers painting perfectly. His poem, written in 1955, treats Washington's Crossing of the Delaware with similar irreverence and amused contempt:

> Now that our hero has come back to us
> in his white pants and we know his nose

trembling like a flag under fire,
we see the calm cold river is supporting
our forces, the beautiful history.   (*CP,* 233)

The next four stanzas continue to stress the absurdity of what O'Hara,
like Rivers, presumably regards as a nonevent, the "crossing by water
in winter to a shore / other than that the bridge reaches for." Here the
silly rhyme underscores the bathos of what is meant by our "beautiful
history" (note that the crossing takes place in a "misty glare"); and the
poem ends with a satiric address to George, culminating in the pun on
"general":

Don't shoot until, the white of freedom glinting
on your gun barrel, you see the general fear.   (*CP,* 234)

Although O'Hara's poem is especially witty if read in conjunction
with Rivers's painting, it can be read quite independently as a pastiche
on a Major Event in American History, an ironic vision of the "Dear
father of our country," with "his nose / trembling like a flag under
fire."

O'Hara's poetic response to the painting of Larry Rivers, like his
lyric celebrations of Grace Hartigan, suggests that he was really more
at home with painting that retains at least some figuration than with
pure abstraction. Pollock, Kline, and Motherwell may well have been
O'Hara's Gods, but, practically speaking, it was difficult to carry over
into poetry the total abstraction of, say, Frankenthaler's "Blue Territory." Words, after all, have meanings, and thematic implications thus
have a way of coming in by the back door. When, in the next chapter,
we consider O'Hara's major poems, we shall see that he did, of course,
make use of such major concepts of Abstract Expressionism as "push
and pull," "all-over painting" (composition as continuum with no
beginning or end), and Harold Rosenberg's famous observation that
in Action Painting the canvas becomes an arena upon which to *act*
rather than a space in which to reproduce. But as a poet, O'Hara
displays a certain ambivalence to the great Abstract Expressionists, an
ambivalence that creates interesting tensions in his art criticism to
which I now turn.

"SITTING IN A CORNER OF THE GALLERY"

—I dress in oil cloth and read music
by Guillaume Apollinaire's clay candelabra.   (*CP*, 18)

O'Hara's criticism reveals striking parallels with that of his life-long hero, Guillaume Apollinaire.[10] In his introduction to the French poet's collected art criticism, LeRoy Breunig writes: "Apollinaire possessed a gift that most professional critics will envy, and that was his flair. He knew how to recognize greatness. His innate taste and his faith in the 'nobility' of art permitted him to choose from among the mass of unknown painters swarming in the salons and the galleries of the period those who were destined to survive."[11] A good example of Apollinaire's unorthodox approach to art criticism may be found in his review of the *Salon d'Automne* of 1911, the first Salon in which the Cubists were included. "In a tiny room, Room 8," Apollinaire begins, "are the works of a few painters known by the name of cubists. Cubism is not, as is generally thought, the art of painting everything in the form of cubes." After giving some background about Picasso's earliest Cubist paintings and the relationship between Cubists and Fauves, Apollinaire comments acutely:

> However, the public, accustomed as it is to the brilliant but practically formless daubs of the impressionists, refused to recognize at first glance the greatness of the formal conceptions of our cubists. People were shocked to see contrasts between dark forms and lighted segments, because they were used to seeing only painting without shadows. In the monumental appearance of compositions that go beyond the frivolities of contemporary art, the public has refused to see what is really there: a noble and restrained art ready to undertake the vast subjects for which impressionism had left painters totally unprepared. Cubism is a necessary reaction that will give rise to great works, whether people like it or not. (p. 183)

With hindsight, we know what a prophetic statement this was in 1911, even though Apollinaire provides us neither with a theory of Cubist painting nor with practical analyses of individual works. In O'Hara's art criticism, we find the very same qualities: an absence of theoretical discourse and, except in rare cases, close technical analysis, counterbalanced by an astonishing ability to recognize greatness, to distinguish between the first-rate and the second-best. Like Apollinaire, O'Hara had the innate gift of entering a gallery in which a large group show was installed and immediately spotting *the* important painting or paintings.

This peculiar genius is nowhere more evident than in the three "Art Chronicles" O'Hara wrote while art editor for *Kulchur* in 1962 and 1963. In the third "Chronicle," O'Hara reviews the Museum of Modern Art retrospective of Mark Tobey and concludes: "Tobey has done fine things in his own way . . . but they will never be major, any more than Redon will ever challenge Renoir. . . . Not while Willem de Kooning and Barnett Newman are about."[12] This is a judgment time has certainly borne out. Today we hear little about Tobey while de Kooning, still at the height of his powers, is increasingly recognized as perhaps the greatest painter of the period. In the same "Chronicle," O'Hara distinguishes between Pop artists like Andy Warhol or Robert Indiana, who "tend to make their art *out of* vulgar (in the sense of everyday) objects, images, and emblems," and Claes Oldenburg, who "makes the very objects and symbols themselves, with the help of papier-mâché, cloth, wood, glue, paint and whatever other mysterious materials are inside and on them, *into* art" (*SS,* 141). This distinction between what we might call commercial Pop Art and the brilliant illusionism of Oldenburg's "seven-foot pistachio icecream cone" or his "monstrous wedge of chocolate and vanilla layer cake" seems increasingly valuable as we look back at Pop Art from the vantage point of the later seventies.

The "Art Chronicles" are chiefly concerned with the great abstract painters, but because O'Hara always cared more for individuals than for movements, he was one of the first critics to recognize the genius of Alex Katz, whose realistic "flat sculptures" were painted, so to speak, against the grain. Katz's "large free-standing figures," O'Hara notes, "are modern in ethos, emphasizing almost inadvertently the spatial absence which surrounds them. . . . They have an air of watchfulness, without ever being silhouettes" (*SS,* 136). This account of Katz's work in the Summer 1962 "Art Chronicle" is amplified in one of O'Hara's best critical essays, "Alex Katz," written for *Art and Literature* shortly before his death. Here he defines Katz's pictorial world as "a 'void' of smoothly painted color . . . where the fairly realistic figure existed (but did not rest) in a space which had no floor, no walls, no source of light, no viewpoint. . . . Katz's people simply existed somewhere. They stayed in the picture as solutions of a formal problem, neither existential nor lost. . . . They were completely mysterious pictorially, because there seemed to be no apparent intent of effect. They knew they were there" (*AC*, 145–46). Certainly, Katz's "flat" sculptural portrait of O'Hara himself (see *AC*, 146) testifies to that sense of peculiar *presence*, of being *there* that the poet speaks of.

Perhaps O'Hara is at his most trenchant in the "Art Chronicles" when he discusses the reception of *Art* in these exciting years. In 1962, for example, the Guggenheim mounted a show called *Abstract Expressionists and Imagists,* which was evidently a mixed bag, reflecting, in O'Hara's view, "a living situation," whose "free-wheeling accuracy" "keeps you fresh for looking" (*SS*, 128). But the art audience, longing for certainties, was evidently indignant. "Unfortunately," says O'Hara, "many people wanted to see a justification, packaged in a new Sherry's container, with a card saying, 'Because of this show you are entitled to keep on admiring abstract expressionism.' Hence the criticism the Guggenheim has gotten about the quality of the show, some of it near hysteria: "A WEAK HOFMANN! HOW COULD THEY!" None of the reviewers seems to have thought, "How could he!" (*SS*, 128).

Such witty deflation is typical of O'Hara. And his conclusion acts as the perfect squelch: "A lot of people would like to see art dead and sure, but you don't see them up at the Cloisters reading Latin." Here, and in his hilarious, if admittedly bitchy attack on two leading art reviewers of his day, John Canaday and Emily Genauer,[13] O'Hara recalls the Apollinaire of "Watch Out for the Paint!," the droll essay in which the poet tells the anecdote about the bourgeois lady who came to Mallarmé when the latter was a lycée teacher and begged him to excuse her son from after-school detention because she wanted to take him to the Manet exhibit. "All Paris," said the lady, "is going to it to laugh at his paintings. I will never forgive myself if my child is deprived of this unique amusement, which, furthermore, will help to educate his taste." Whereupon Mallarmé doubled the punishment. "How prudently," Apollinaire concludes, "one must refrain from pronouncing hasty judgments. It is so easy to be wrong; and there is not always a Mallarmé around to double the punishment called for by sacrilegious laughter."[14]

Like Apollinaire, O'Hara was always fighting "sacrilegious laughter," exposing narrow-minded reviewers and obtuse critics. And it is especially useful to read his art criticism against the background of Apollinaire's because it helps us to understand what O'Hara was *not,* what demands we cannot make on his reviews, essays, and museum catalogues. When *Art Chronicles* was published in 1974, a number of reviewers complained that O'Hara was too "subjective" and "impressionistic" a critic, and that he merely adopted the going view of such theorists as Harold Rosenberg on Abstract Expressionism, providing no original insights into the movement.[15]

There is some truth to these strictures. O'Hara is at his weakest when he tries to generalize about such abstractions as Art, Beauty, Reality, or Nature. The early essay, "Nature and the New Painting" (1954) is particularly interesting in this connection because it illustrates both the poet's strengths and his weaknesses as a critic. Much of this essay contains specific description of the work of Grace Hartigan (quoted earlier in this chapter), Robert di Niro, and Larry Rivers, and what O'Hara says of their art is consistently useful. Yet it is never clear what he means by "nature." He says, for example, "In past times there was nature and there was human nature; because of the ferocity of modern life, man and nature have become one. . . . In the abstractions of Willem de Kooning and in his female figures, we perceive structures of classical severity: the implacable identifications of man with nature. This is not symbolized. It is painted" (*SS,* 42). The implication is that in Abstract Expressionist art, "nature" is absorbed into painting so fully that the canvas presents a perfect union of the two. Yet a page or so later, O'Hara explains that Grace Hartigan rejected abstraction in order to "return to nature"—that is, to figurative images—a change in style that "introduced a passion which was only implied in the early work" (p. 45). But if this is the case, what happens to the perfect fusion of art and nature in the abstractions of de Kooning?

Similarly questionable generalizations are found in the pioneering and frequently brilliant monograph on Jackson Pollock. Contrasting Cubism and Surrealism ("Surrealism destroyed where Cubism only undermined. . . ."; "Cubism was an innovation, Surrealism an evolution"), O'Hara declares: "Surrealism enjoined the duty, along with the liberation, of saying what you mean and meaning what you say, above and beyond any fondness for saying or meaning" (*AC,* 18). This sounds profound but what is O'Hara actually saying? He seems to imply that Surrealism is somehow more literal than other schools of art, and yet the Surrealists themselves thought of their work as precisely the opposite: the embodiment of dreams, hallucination, unconscious thought—the art of free association and hidden erotic meanings.

O'Hara's importance as an art critic does not, then, emerge from his formal essays or set pieces: the introductions he wrote for the catalogues of the exhibitions he organized at the Museum, *New Spanish Painting and Sculpture* (1960); *Franz Kline* (1960); *Motherwell* (1962); *Nakian* (1964); or *David Smith* (1966). These essays are full of brilliant aperçus about individual works, but too often we find sentences like the following: "If the motto of American art in recent years can be said to be 'Make it new,' for the Spanish it is 'Make it over.'"[16] Or: "Underlying, and indeed burgeoning within, every great work of the Abstract Expressionists ... exists the traumatic consciousness of emergency and crisis experienced as personal event" (*AC,* 67). Or: "Stylization was the order of the day, whether the archaistic stylization of a Manship, a kind of mock-heroic idealization of the proletariat, or a belated Art Nouveau stylization of human and animal forms ..." (*AC,* 82).

But if we look at O'Hara's occasional criticism—his reviews in *Art News* and *Kulchur,* his interviews and memoirs—a very different critical intelligence emerges. The early reviews (1953–54) are curiously literary; the young Harvard graduate is not yet wearing his learning lightly. Thus he says of the figures in Kenneth Callahan's painting: "Their anatomy is that of El Greco, but their habitat comes from Romantic poetry, not painting, and they appear through the pearly mists of Shelley—which on canvas is sometimes just grey."[17] Kees Van Dongen's women have bosoms that "rise and fall as in a revelatory chapter of Proust."[18] Helen Frankenthaler's "heavily-painted pictures" have "the compact sordidness of one of those 'unspeakable' chapters in Henry James."[19] Yet at the same time, reviewing Adolph Gottlieb's April 1954 show at the Kootz Gallery, O'Hara comments acutely on "the multiplicity of grids and events in space both between and behind these grids" and notes that "often the thick surface strokes are not so much signs of specific meaning as signals of that speed which results from force as well as felicity."[20]

In 1955, O'Hara joined the Museum of Modern Art as a special assistant in the International Program, and for the next few years, the organization of traveling exhibitions kept him so busy that he produced relatively little art criticism. But these were the years of intense exposure to the world of contemporary painting and sculpture, and by the late fifties, when O'Hara was at the height of his poetic powers, he was also writing much more casually and spontaneously, and yet more seriously, about art. Between 1958 and 1960 alone, O'Hara published the following: the book on Jackson Pollock for the Braziller "Great American Artist" series, the important interviews with Franz Kline and Larry Rivers, a witty and penetrating essay on the latter's *Next to Last Confederate Soldier,* and a number of interesting short pieces on Pollock, Cavallon, Norman Bluhm, or, again, on such topics as American versus non-American Art.

When *Jackson Pollock* appeared in 1959, Hilton Kramer called it an example of "the 'poetical' school of criticism," and a number of art critics objected to the poet's purple prose and intensely personal response to the painter.[21] Yet the book turned out to be immensely popular, and despite the lapses cited earlier, it was and continues to be an important assessment of Pollock's work. The general principles put forward about Action Painting may be no more than a restatement of Harold Rosenberg's (e.g., the conception of "wall" as opposed to "easel"; the painting as field of force which the poet enters; the rejection of metaphor and symbol in favor of the thing itself—paint as paint, wire mesh as wire mesh). Nevertheless, O'Hara's Paterian comments on particular paintings are often very valuable in that they force the reader to take another look at the canvas, to *see* it as if for the first time.

Pollock's *White Light,* for example, "has a blazing, acrid, and dangerous glamor of a legendary kind, not unlike those volcanoes which are said to lure the native to the lip of the crater, and by the beauty of their writhings and the strength of their fumes cause him to fall in" (*AC,* 29). *Number 1, 1948,* on the other hand, derives its strength from a very different strategy: it replaces the brooding languor of *White Light* with "an ecstatic, irritable, demanding force, an incredible speed and nervous legibility in its draftsmanship; and the seemingly blood-stained hands of the painter, proceeding across the top just beyond the main area of drawing, are like a postscript to a terrible experience" (*AC*, 31).

It is interesting to turn from the formal, distant, somewhat man-nered style of the Pollock monograph—a style dictated, at least in part, by the conventions governing the writing of an "art book"—to the very different essays on Larry Rivers. O'Hara seems to have been happiest as a critic when he could write about a painter who was also a close personal friend, and his pieces on Rivers constitute a kind of prose counterpart to his "I do this, I do that" poems like "A Step Away From Them" or "Joe's Jacket."

The interview "Larry Rivers: Why I Paint as I Do" is, like all of O'Hara's interviews, notable for the poet's self-effacement.[22] His questions are brief and pointed; he obviously knows the work thor-oughly but is not anxious to parade his knowledge. On the other hand, the Rivers presented in this interview consistently sounds like O'Hara himself, so that, in a second, more devious way, the poet is present after all. Interestingly, the interview thus embodies the doctrine of "Personism"; the words are squarely between two people; poet and painter become one.

The dialogue is prefaced by a graphic picture of Rivers's studio:

> In the daytime, the light pours in from three skylights, but at night it is a vast, dim place, lit by seven naked light bulbs hanging high up near the ceiling. At night the studio looks very much like the set for Samuel Beck-ett's *Endgame;* it's hard to believe you can find out anything about the outside world without using a ladder; the windows are way up.
>
> (*AC*, 106)

After describing the members of the Rivers household, including "a friendly, frantic shepherd dog named Amy," and mentioning the paintings currently on the studio walls, O'Hara adds:

> Another wall has the huge *Journey* of 1956, a painting which looks small in the space of the studio; lurking under a nearby potted plant is a plaster

commercial figure of Psyche or Aphrodite which Rivers rescued from a night club; she is holding an orange light bulb in her uplifted hand and Rivers uses her as a night light. (p. 107)

This note of comic eclecticism sets the scene for the dialogue that follows.

Rivers's aesthetic turns out to be remarkably close to O'Hara's despite their very different backgrounds. Rivers came from a poor Jewish family and grew up "in the streets of . . . the Bronx" (p. 109). He started out as a jazz musician, worked for a time as delivery boy for an art-supply house, and only then turned to the study of painting, working with Hans Hofmann and attending N.Y.U. at night, while his former mother-in-law, the Mrs. Bertha Burger who acted as one of his main models, kept house for him and his two sons and helped to support him.[23] His world was thus quite unlike the provincial Catholic milieu of Baltimore and Grafton, Mass., in which Frank was raised, or the Harvard of John Ashbery and Kenneth Koch, or even the sophisticated world of the Museum of Modern Art.

Nevertheless, Rivers's view of art is immediately familiar to anyone who has read O'Hara. He rejects the primacy of subject matter in painting, insisting that the *how* supercedes the *what*. Like O'Hara, he stresses the importance of "the immediate situation" (p. 108), of energy, of the role of "accident" in art (p. 117), and of the need to evade "the discomforts of *boredom*." "One of my theories," he says, sounding just like O'Hara, "about the art of the last hundred years is that more alterations to the image of painting have been brought about by the boredom and dissatisfaction of the artist and his perversity than anything else" (p. 113). Like O'Hara, he has a predilection for campy humor, as in the George Washington painting which fuses, in Sam Hunter's words, "history, nostalgic sentiment, the world of common-place objects and emblems," assimilating "popular folklore to the high style of advanced art."[24]

A painting, says Rivers, is best defined as "a smorgasbord of the recognizable":

> I may see something—a ribbon, say, and I'll use it to enliven a three-inch area of the canvas. Eventually it may turn into a milk container, a snake, or a rectangle. . . . I may even have private associations with that piece of

ribbon, but I don't want to *interpret* that association. . . . I feel free to use the appearance of a thing—that piece of ribbon—without assigning any specific meaning to it as an object. (*AC,* 118)

And when Frank asks him to apply these principles to the recently painted *Second Avenue with THE,* Rivers explains:

> What you see is the view from a studio on Second Avenue—a top-floor studio—looking across at the buildings opposite. The canvas shows a selected few of the multitude of objects I could see from where I stood. The rectangles are reflections from glass windows across the street. The dark vertical lines are the studio floor boards. I looked down, saw them, and painted them. The horizontal lines are the window sills. The semi-circles on the right are the rims of a drum. The line of little white squares are the white keys of a piano I had there in the studio. And the rocket-woman figure, she was in the studio too, a statue which was in my field of vision. That little shape up there by the letters THE—just to the left—that's a woman leaning out of a window opposite. I should have had the letters ALPINE up there too. That was the title—a chic one, don't you think—some builder had given one of those buildings. (*AC,* 118)

"What about those letters THE?" Frank asks. "Those letters were pasted on the studio window by some movie director who photographed them for THE END of his picture. The END part of it had disappeared" (*AC,* 118).

I cite this passage at length because it makes clear the close affinities between Rivers's painting and O'Hara's poem *Second Avenue,* written a few years earlier in Rivers's studio.[25] Just as Rivers takes recognizable objects (the studio floor boards and window sill, the woman, and the lettering on the window) and displaces them, creating a new tension between illusionistic detail and abstract configurations, so O'Hara takes his images from Second Avenue street scenes, cutting, distorting, and reassembling them so that his finished composition retains no more than "traces" of that which is being represented:

> Candidly. The past, the sensations of the past. Now!
> in cuneiform, of umbrella satrap square-carts with hotdogs
> and onions of red syrup blended, of sand bejewelling the prepuce
> in tank suits, of Majestic Camera Stores and Schuster's,
> of Kenneth in an abandoned storeway on Sunday cutting even more

insinuating lobotomies of a yet-to-be-more-yielding world
of ears, of a soprano rallying at night in a cadenza, Bill, of
"Fornications, la! garumph! tereu! lala la! vertigo! Weevy! Hah!",
of a limp hand larger than the knee which seems to say "Addio"
and is capable of resigning from the disaster it summoned ashore.
Acres of glass don't make the sign clearer of the landscape
less blue than prehistorically, yet less distant, eager, dead!

(*CP*, 146–47)

The isolation of the adverb "Candidly," creating ambiguity of reference, the shift from "The past" to "now!", the images of storefronts and pushcarts "dissolving" into thoughts of Kenneth Koch, memories of a concert, and the ridiculous allusions to *The Waste Land* in line 8, the final contradictory image of a blue landscape "less distant, eager, dead!"—all these features find their way into the poem as if by random penetration of the artist's consciousness, just as Rivers describes the entry of similar elements into his painting.

O'Hara is thus the ideal interpreter of Rivers's work for, like Grace Hartigan, Rivers is a painter who rejects pure abstraction on the one hand and "straight" representational painting—what Rivers calls "cornball realism" (*AC,* 119)—on the other. Both artists explore the expressive potential of commonplace objects; the white piano keys and window sills of Rivers's *Second Avenue with THE* correspond to images like the "old Roman coin," the "bolt-head," or "the construction workers with silver hats on" in O'Hara's "Personal Poem" (*CP,* 235).

In the 1965 memoir "Larry Rivers," O'Hara recapitulates the qualities that link poet and painter. Rivers's arrival on the New York painting scene is comically compared to the appearance of "a demented telephone. Nobody knew whether they wanted it in the library, the kitchen or the toilet, but it was electric" (*CP,* 512). Like O'Hara himself, Rivers was "restless, impulsive and compulsive"; he could not abide an aesthetic that separated the visual arts from his other two loves, jazz and poetry. "His work," says O'Hara, "is very much a diary of his experience.... Where much of the art of our time has been involved with direct conceptual or ethical considerations, Rivers has chosen to mirror his preoccupations and enthusiasms in an unprogrammatic way" (p. 514). What O'Hara means here, I think, is that at a certain moment in our history, when Abstract Expressionism was in danger of moving toward standardization and mere repetition, Rivers, following de Kooning, who had always retained certain figurative elements (outlines of his own fingers, written letters, the silhouette of a woman's face, and other illusionistic gestures), deflected the course of New York painting. His art is thus particularly close to the lyric mode of O'Hara. And accordingly, the collaboration of two such cognate sensibilities was bound to produce interesting results.

POEM-PAINTINGS

Collaboration between poets and painters is largely a twentieth-century phenomenon. Genuine collaboration—as opposed to *illustration* which is something quite different, being, by definition, *ex post facto*—is rare at any time because it is so hard to strike a balance between two such seemingly inimical arts. A so-called *poem-painting,* whether done by a single artist or as a collaboration, tends to be either a painting with a few words of text used as part of the visual scheme, or, conversely, an illustrated poem in which visual images are subordinated to verbal meaning. Under the right circumstances, however, the poem-painting, done as a collaboration, has enormous potential. Like opera, ballet, the masque, or the animated film, it can provide the special pleasure created by the interaction of seemingly unrelated media.

As in the case of his art criticism, O'Hara's concept of the poem-painting can be traced back to Apollinaire, who wrote poems "after" paintings (pasting "Les Fenêtres" on the back of Delaunay's work of the same name so as to create a kind of double image), and whose *Calligrammes* contain fascinating experiments with verbal-visual composition. In "Il Plêut," for example, the words float down the page from left to right like rain drops; in "La Cravate et La Montre," the arrangement of words imitates the two objects named in the title; and in "Visée" ("Aim"), the variations in position of the lines correspond to the shifting attitudes of the poet.[26]

But these are not, strictly speaking, poem-paintings. A closer model for O'Hara's collaborations is found in Dada and Surrealist art, although the *peinture-poésie* of Picabia, Schwitters, Magritte, or Ernst is almost never the result of collaboration. A painting like Picabia's famous *M'Amenez-Y* (1919–20) is a good example of Dada experimentation with verbal-visual patterning.[27] Its banal mechanical shapes (two half-circles, a cylinder, a screw) are juxtaposed to the title which is based on one of Marcel Duchamp's verbal "readymades": "M'amenez-y" ("bring me there") is a substitution for the correct "Amenez-y-moi"; it is also a play on the word "amnésie." Across the top of the canvas, Picabia has comically announced that this is a portrait painted in castor oil ("l'huile de ricin"), and within the circles, we find the words "peinture crocodile" and "ratelier [dentures] d'artiste"—an amusing word play. The artist's signature is prominently placed in the bottom right-hand corner, the pointless reference to "Pont-L'Evêque" (a small town in Normandy where cheese is made) as the place where *M'Amenez-Y* was painted, in the bottom left. Picabia's words do not, of course, make a poem, but his composition does depend upon a particular conjunction of verbal and visual images.

Kurt Schwitters's collages of the same period are poem-paintings of a rather different type. In his essay *Merz* (1920), Schwitters declares: "It was my desire not to be a specialist in one branch of art but an artist. My aim is the Merz [a play on *merde*] composite art work. . . . First I combined individual categories of art. I pasted words and sentences into poems in such a way as to produce a rhythmic design. Reversing the process, I pasted up pictures and drawings so that sentences could be read in them."[28] These two processes may be illustrated by *Collage* (1920) and *Sonata* (1923), both of which are reproduced in Motherwell's *The Dada Painters and Poets,* a book O'Hara knew and loved.[29] *Sonata* is primarily verbal; short nonsense words are arranged in columns in various phonetic configurations, and the small rectangular collage in the bottom right-hand corner plays a subordinate role. This is an early example of Concrete Poetry. *Collage,* on the other hand, cuts up newspapers and posters and then reassembles them, so that bits of headlines, words, phrases, and parts of phrases are scattered across the surface, right side up and upside down. These two collages are interesting experiments, but the relationship between word and visual image seems largely arbitrary.

René Magritte's *peinture poésie* looks ahead to Pop Art. A painting like *The Wind and the Song* (1928–29) contains what seems to be a realistic replica of a large pipe against a blank background. Across the bottom of the canvas is the legend "Ceci n'est pas une pipe."[30] But, as William Rubin argues, the painting is not as simplistic as it first appears, for "merely reproducing any three-dimensional object on a delimited flat surface—that is, picturing it—automatically engenders a set of aesthetic rapports that have no necessary relation to the meaning of the object qua object" (p. 94). The image of the pipe is not, in other words, equivalent to a real pipe. The didactic legend "Ceci n'est pas une pipe" further complicates the scheme, for the word "pipe" releases different signals than either the painted image of the pipe or a real pipe. A resonance, albeit a limited one, is thus set up between verbal and visual images.

The most interesting Surrealist poem-paintings are, however, those of Max Ernst, in whose work word and image are not merely juxtaposed as in the collages of Magritte or Picabia, but fused so as to form what Lucy Lippard has called "a genuinely 'intermediary' statement."[31] In an essay called "Beyond Painting," written in the mid-thirties, Ernst defines *collage* as an "alchemical composition of two or more heterogenous elements resulting from their unexpected reconciliation . . . toward systematic confusion and 'disorder of the senses' (Rimbaud), or to chance, or to a will to chance."[32] Ernst's own favorite "collage word" (e.g., the key word governing the form the collage will take) is *phallustrade,* which he defined as "an alchemical product composed of the following elements: an *autostrada,* a balustrade, and certain amounts of phallus." Thus, the Dada collage, *The Hat Makes the Man* (Fig. 2), is, as Lippard says, "a *phallustrade* in every sense, the visual pun [being] extended by the verbal puns in the accompanying inscription: '*Bedecktsamiger stapelmensch nacktsamiger wasserformer* ('*edelformer*') *kleidsame nervatur auch UMPRESS NERVEN! (C'est le chapeau qui fait l'homme, le style c'est le tailleur).*'"[33]

It is impossible to translate this into literal English because every word is a pun or double-entendre: "*Bedecktsamiger*" means "covered" plus "seeded" ("covered with seed"?); "*edelformer*" combines the meaning of "edel" (lofty, noble, precious, aristocratic) with erotic connotations because "edle Teile" are private parts, and so "edelformer" may connote "one who has elegant private parts" or merely a person who observes the forms or who creates elegance. The collage itself is a page from a hat catalogue, transformed by means of watercolor, pencil, scissors, and glue into a series of sculpted vignettes with mechanistic, organic, cartoonlike, even narrative characteristics. In this witty and intricate *phallustrade,* "Words and forms begin to bounce on and off each other in a trans-disciplinary, cross-referential action that continues to provide surprises long after the initial decoding." (Lippard, p. 13).

Ernst carried this form of "literary art" (note that it is not at all an illustration in the conventional sense) even further in *La Femme 100 têtes,* a "collage novel" in which the artist took a series of perfectly ordinary nineteenth-century wood engravings found in magazines and cut them up so as to discover a new figurative "reality" brought about by the chance encounter of previously unrelated images. Each resulting picture was given a poetic caption. Neither the picture nor the caption carries the "plot" alone; rather, in Lippard's words, they offer "a double viewpoint that forms a stereophonic unity. The reader must literally read between the lines provided by the verbal-visual interaction and project himself into that intermediary space." The collage-novel has, moreover, important analogues to film: "The pictorial dislocation of action and sequence juxtaposed against the ambiguous captions, apparently out of sync, suggest a silent movie with subtitles in a foreign language. The mixing is done, impressionistically, in the mind" (Lippard, p. 13).

Ernst's use of the "collage-novel" and the *phallustrade* thus looks ahead to the poem-paintings of our own time. But it is important to remember that he was primarily a visual artist, that even his so-called collaborations with Paul Eluard on *Repétitions* (1921) and *Les Malheurs des Immortels* (1922) are not true collaborations, for in these books, Ernst takes an Eluard poem already written and then proceeds to illustrate it. The next step was for poet and painter to work simultaneously on the same spatial area, playing off words against visual images so as to create new forms. This is what happens in *Stones,* the series of lithographs made by O'Hara and Rivers between 1957 and 1960.

In a very amusing essay called "Life Among the Stones" (1963),[34] Rivers describes the genesis of these lithographs. "It started," he recalls, "with this Siberian lady Tanya who came to my house in the summer of 1957. Her life at the time called for an activity. She found it and dedicated herself with gentle fury to the production of lithographs. . . . She wanted me to work on lithograph stones with a poet. She had the devotion, the press, and she would print" (p. 91).

"The Siberian lady Tanya," as Rivers jokingly calls her here, was Tatyana Grossman, whose print workshop in West Islip, Long Island, is now world famous. "Both technically and aesthetically," writes Calvin Tompkins in his study of contemporary printmaking, "the prints published by Tatyana Grossman's Universal Limited Art Editions [they include more than a hundred lithographs by Jasper Johns, and Robert Rauschenberg's intriguing *Shades,* a series of lithographs on Plexiglas] are·generally acknowledged to be equal or superior to anything being done in Europe or anywhere else." [35]

Tatyana Grossman's choice of Frank O'Hara as Rivers's collaborator was the result of a series of fortunate coincidences. She recalls:

> I went to see . . . Barney Rosset of the Grove Press to ask if he could perhaps suggest a poet for such a book [i.e., of lithograph stones], and he suggested Frank O'Hara. Well, I read some of O'Hara's poems, but I didn't really understand them very well, they were so abstract. But then a few days later . . . I drove out to Larry Rivers' studio in Southampton. . . . I talked to Larry about this idea of a book that would be a real fusion of poetry and art, a real collaboration, not just drawings to illustrate poems, and Larry listened, and then he called out, "Hey, Frank!" And down the stairs came a young man in blue jeans. It was Frank O'Hara.[36]

Rivers was delighted that "This Siberian lady didn't just find some painter and some poet who would work together. She asked two men who really knew each other's work and life backwards." [37] Despite their "super-serious, monstrously developed egos," Rivers and O'Hara saw what had to be done: "Frank O'Hara wasn't going to write a poem that I would set a groovy little image to. Nor were we going to assume the world was waiting for his poetry and my drawing which is what the past 'collaborations' now seem to have been" (p. 93).

Working on the lithograph stone proved to be a new challenge for O'Hara and Rivers, who saw themselves as carrying on the tradition of "Picasso, Matisse, Miro, Apollinaire, Eluard, and Aragon" (p. 92).

Rivers describes the difficulties posed by the medium as follows:

> The lithograph stone surface is very smooth. The marks going on it can be made with a rather difficult to handle almost rubbery crayon or with a dark liquid called Touche. . . . Whatever you do comes out the opposite to the way you put it down. In order for the writing to be read it must be done backwards. It is almost impossible to erase, one of my more important crutches. Technically it was really a cumbersome task. One needed the patience of another age, but our ignorance and enthusiasm allowed us to jump into it without thinking about the details and difficulties.
>
> (p. 93)

The first of the twelve *Stones* was called *US* (Fig. 3). Rivers's detailed account of its genesis will help us to understand the actual process of collaboration:

> Each time we got together we decided to choose some very definite subject and since there was nothing we had more access to than ourselves the first stone was going to be called "us." Oh yes, the title always came first. It was the only way we could get started. U and S were written on the top center of the stone backwards. I don't know if he wrote it. I remember decorating the letters to resemble some kind of flag and made it seem like the letters for our country. Then I put something down to do with his broken nose and bumpy forehead and stopped. From a round hand-mirror I eked out a few scratches to represent my face. The combination of the decorated U and S, his face and mine [see top left], made Frank write ". . . they call us the farters of our country. . . ." I did something, whatever I could, which related in some way to the title of the stone and he either commented on what I had done or took it somewhere else. . . . Sometimes I would designate an area that I was sure I was going to leave empty. He might write there or if I did put something down I would direct him to write whatever he wished but ask that it start at a specific place and end up a square or rectangular thin or fat shape of words over or around my images. (pp. 93–94)

Here Rivers stresses the *improvisational* character of the collaboration, its status as an event or happening rather than as a predetermined, planned "work of art." This is not to say, however, that anything goes; the account makes quite clear that, at each step of the way, the two artists depended upon one another's response. It is therefore misleading to call *Stones,* as does one reviewer, "no more than props to support an avant-garde party game of two addressed to those who can recognize names, allusions, and events and the spirit of exclusiveness they exalt."[38] For although *US* is not one of the best lithographs in the series (the surface is perhaps too cluttered, and O'Hara has not yet mastered the technique of lettering, writing backwards being extremely cumbersome unless one uses a mirror), it has a definite structure.

The predominant visual motif is Frank's face in profile with its broken nose. It appears in the upper left-hand corner, next to the sketch of Rivers himself seen frontally; then again in reverse (an enlarged mirror image) in the upper right, this time shaded in and superimposed on other shapes; again in the lower left, where the head is turned upside down and attached to a contorted torso, the whole pose reminiscent of Picasso's *Guernica* figures; and finally, in the lower right-hand corner, we find, embedded in a sort of valentine, the poet's face, cheek-to-cheek with Rivers's face, again seen frontally. These faces are placed against a background of doodles, some resembling hands, legs, phalluses, and animal shapes; others reminiscent of Chinese ideograms.

O'Hara's verbal images are intimately related to this landscape of stance and gesture. The pun on the word US is not just a local joke ("They call US the Farters of our Country") but the theme of the whole poem-painting, which portrays heroism and anti-heroism in various guises. Thus at the very center, O'Hara places a letter from James Dean (the Hollywood hero as victim) to Jane (the painter Jane Freilicher); the foolishly empty letter: "It's swell out here. How are you?" is viewed upside down and almost bumps into the sign: "A HERO of the '50's is arriving in Hollywood." The artists themselves are seen as comically out of step with the times:

> poetry was declining
> > > > Painting advancing
> > > we were complaining
> > it was '50

The immediate postwar years, as every literary historian has noted, were lean ones for American poetry. The tone of the period is conveyed by O'Hara's references to the petty bickering ("Poetry belongs to Me, LARRY, and *Painting* to you") and innuendo: "THAT'S what G said to P, and . . ." (evidently Gertrude Stein to Picasso),[39] a line leading straight into the bubble, "Look where it got them." The young artists are, moreover, a bit precious: "Parties were 'given' / we 'went'" is ironically placed right under what I have called the *Guernica* figure. At bottom center, O'Hara places the lines:

> A very soft rain
> we were sitting on the stairs

The absolute simplicity of these words in which poet and painter become two ordinary human beings, sharing a moment of love, forms an effective contrast to the bravado of the opening lines. So, too, the "valentine scene" in the lower right, next to the lines just cited, is juxtaposed to the two rather formal, sharply etched portraits of O'Hara and Rivers in the upper left.

The composition of *US* is thus both complex and ingenious, words and pictures fusing so as to create interesting spatial tensions. An even more effective poem-painting is number 3, entitled *Rimbaud & Verlaine* (Fig. 4). The lettering is now much surer than in *US*, O'Hara having mastered the art of "mirror-writing." Rivers's account of the composition of this particular lithograph is especially valuable:

> There was a photo of Rimbaud and his depressed friend Verlaine in the studio. I began to make a drawing looking at it. We then remembered a ballet night at the City Center. During an intermission we were making our way down the wide staircase from the cheap seats to the mezzanine when our mutual friend and my dealer John Myers thinking he was being funny screamed out for general use "there they are all covered with blood and semen." This is a reference to something said about Rimbaud and Verlaine that Verlaine's wife hounded him with for his whole life. After recalling this Frank decided to use it and in a delicate two-line series he began writing. . . . His first two lines had to do with the poetry of Rimbaud and Verlaine. He brought the lines up to my drawing and stopped. . . . He then went on about the staircase and something about the ballet. I waited till he was through and in the spaces left (I directed the space between the lines and the general distribution) I tried a staircase . . . no good. Here I found out how hard it was to get rid of anything—in order to erase you must scrape with a razor. Finally I began making bullets that were also penises with legs. Simple Simon's response to what Frank had written about the corps de ballet. If there is "art" somewhere in this lithograph its presence remains a mystery. (p. 94)

There is, of course, plenty of "art" here. The sketch of Rimbaud and Verlaine, a contrast of lights and darks, is brilliantly rendered: a light-haired, handsome Rimbaud with strange visionary eyes is contrasted to the small, somewhat petty, dark Oriental figure of Verlaine. Rimbaud clearly dominates the scene as he did in the real affair. O'Hara's lines, "The end of all existences / is a pint of blood on a / windowsill," an allusion to the terrible Brussels drama in which Verlaine shot Rimbaud, provide a nice ironic commentary on Rivers's static, understated portrait of the two poets. The blood motif then returns in the reference to Myers's snide remark made at the ballet, a remark that relates O'Hara and Rivers to Rimbaud and Verlaine. The image of the bullets (penises with legs) is especially effective: these shapes are related not only to the "beats / of the corps de ballet," and the movements of poet and painter descending the City Center staircase, but also the relationship of Rimbaud and Verlaine, culminating in the shooting. There are other ingenious visual details: note the chairlike shape at the left, suggesting a balcony seat, and the silhouette of a person sitting in the audience near it. The black spots scattered across the surface, moreover, resemble drops of blood. Relatively little of the available space is used in this lithograph so that whiteness predominates, in keeping with O'Hara's reference to "white air" in the last line. *Rimbaud & Verlaine* is a poem-painting in the full sense of the word.

Love (Fig. 5), one of the finest plates in the series, relates word to picture in a rather different way. "We decided," Rivers recalls, "to do a LOVE stone. I distributed male and female over the surface with a few genitalia for the sex of it. He wrote in between and on the drawing and never even mentioned man or woman or bodies or sex" (p. 97).

This is quite accurate. In the spaces between Rivers's silhouettes of athletic males and phallic shapes, O'Hara places the words of a poem whose tone wholly undercuts the visual impression:

LOVE
To be lost
the stars go out a broken chair
is red in the dark a faint lust
stirs like a plant in the creased rain

Here O'Hara typically cuts at odd junctures so that "a faint lust" belongs to "in the dark" rather than to its complement: "stirs like a plant. . . ." The tone is wistful, sad, resigned. This stanza, in turn, modulates into two passages written in parody-nineties diction: "where the gloom / swells into odour / like earth in the moon," and "lightless the arrow wears its sigh of depth and its sorrows of snow." The strange tension between the verbal ("pretty" images, rhymes, sonorous vowel sounds) and the visual (broad-shouldered supermen, giant genitalia, a top hat) creates a delicately ambiguous vision of *Love.* The reader-viewer is confronted by contradictory signals that arrest the attention.

Not all the *Stones* are as interesting as the three I have discussed. *Springtemps,* their second plate, consists of a self-contained O'Hara poem to Joseph Rivers on the left, and blurred, semiabstract images of flowers, butterflies, and human bodies on the right; neither the picture nor the poem seems to gain much from this juxtaposition. Again, *Music,* the sixth plate (Fig. 6), is strictly speaking an illustrated poem rather than a poem-painting. The lower half of this lithograph reproduces O'Hara's poem "Students" (*CP,* 290); above the text, Rivers places what he calls his "own version of Batman. Violinman." The painter himself remarks shrewdly that this *Stone* "is a little more old-fashioned: our unintegrated style." In this case, Frank had already written the poem and asked Larry to respond. "A good poem," says Rivers, "but for the kind of mind I have, useless" (p. 96).

The point here is not so much whether Rivers liked the poem as that it was a finished product, a condition which leaves the painter with no role but that of illustrator. True artistic collaboration must, however, involve simultaneity. One of the loveliest *Stones* is *Melancholy Break-fast* (Fig. 7), which contains semiabstract images of such breakfast items as eggs, toasters, gas burners, griddles, and a table. These images are distorted as if seen through the blur of half-sleep or a hangover. Everything in the scene is disconnected: in O'Hara's words, "the silent egg thinks / and the toaster's electrical ear waits." And the bottom line sums it up: "The elements of disbelief are very strong in the morning." Here poet and painter seem to be on the very same wavelength.

To turn from *Stones* to *Poem-Paintings,* the collaborations made by O'Hara and Norman Bluhm in 1960,[40] is to move into a much more lyrical, delicate, evanescent, but equally interesting pictorial world. Bill Berkson describes the genesis of *Poem-Paintings* as follows:

> One dreary Sunday midday in October 1960, the painter Norman Bluhm and Frank O'Hara, poet and self-confessed *balayeur des artistes,* met at Bluhm's studio in the old Tiffany Building on Park Avenue South, and, as the inclement weather wasn't helping either's mood or conversation, they decided to get on with a collaboration project they had talked about weeks before. A few hours later, they had made these twenty-six poem-paintings.[41]

And John Perreault, reviewing *Poem-Paintings* for *Art News,* suggests that the two artists put together the series "all in one short frenzy of creativity that must have been like two collaborating Zen monks in a zany dance of the seasons."[42]

It didn't quite happen in this romantic way. Norman Bluhm told me in an interview that it took many Sundays (not just a few hours!) to complete *Poem-Paintings.* Here is his account:

> Frank and I enjoyed music. We used to meet Sunday mornings at my studio, listen to music and talk and look at the paintings, and then go to my house and listen to records. One time, listening to opera (Toti del Monte, the famous 300-pound soprano, singing *Madame Butterfly*), I said to Frank: "I have all this paper, let's put it on the wall." And we decided we'd like listening to the music and playing around with words and paint. But it wasn't a serious art project. We just wanted to do something while the music was going on. For instance, if we were listening to a Prokofiev symphony, you could feel the boots in my painting.[43]

Music, Bluhm insists, was the driving force behind the collaboration. An Italian on his mother's side, Bluhm had, as a child, longed to be an opera singer; Frank, of course, had longed to be a concert pianist. For both artists, music was terribly important, and both believed that all the arts are interrelated, that the modern compartmentalization of the arts is hopelessly limiting.

The work on *Poem-Paintings,* Bluhm recalls, "was a terrific event, a Happening—a way of amusing ourselves. They were done as an event by two people who had this special feeling for each other and for art, music, and literature." As for technique, "the words are more important than gesture. Basically, we tried to keep the art as just a gesture [hence the decision to use only black and white paint], not an illustration of the poem. The idea was to make the gesture relate, in an abstract way, to the idea of the poem. Only rarely did we do a thing à la Dali where you pick up the drip and throw it into the word."

Sometimes Bluhm would do a drawing and O'Hara would invent an appropriate set of words; sometimes the procedure was reversed. But each poem-painting, Bluhm told me, "grew out of some hilarious relationship with people we knew, out of a particular situation. The tone was comic or satiric—a kind of operatic buffo. We thought of our collaboration as a theatrical event, an amusement. We did it for fun, forgetting our miseries, our love affairs—our more serious problems."

Take, for example, *Homage to Kenneth Koch* (Fig. 8). This picture displays a large abstract shape, etched in black, with a thick white drip running through it, and on the right side, in O'Hara's beautiful writing, the following poem:

> I was standing
> outside your window
> how lucky I was
> you had just washed it
>
> and later I thought of you
> in the car barn,
> my head was inside the hood
> and I felt very hot
>
> are you inside the hood too?

This charmingly absurd poem in which lovers hope for a rendezvous inside the boiling hood of a car was inspired, according to Bluhm, by the following incident: "One time, we (Kenneth Koch and I) picked up two girls at a cocktail party. He ended up with the better-looking one but she did have big feet. I told Frank about it and drew the shape of a foot (the big black abstract form)." Frank responded by writing an appropriately foolish love poem.

Or again, *Welcome to Kitty Hawk* (Fig. 9) evidently grew out of a conversation about airplanes. "My father," Bluhm recalls, "was a flyer, and I told Frank a story about a mechanic who built his own airplane and as it reached 200 feet, the engine split off and the plane crashed." This is not exactly a happy story, but Bluhm's black shape (he calls it a "bad airplane") looks like a chicken hawk and so O'Hara's caption is very amusing.

Few of the *Poem-Paintings* contain real poems. Number 3 boasts the single word *Bust;* number 6, the letters B-A-N-G in the four corners, surrounding a shape that looks like a comical furry phallus. Many are no more than in-jokes: number 19 refers to Chicago because it was Bluhm's birthplace; number 13 contains the phrase "sale morbidité," which is, as Bill Berkson says, "a *Gabin-erie* picked up during his [Bluhm's] decade in Paris." Number 5, which contains no visual images, is a more or less direct transcript of O'Hara's conversation: the words "I'm so tired of all the parties, it's like January and the hangovers on the beach" are scrawled across the surface of the picture.

Individually, these poem-paintings may be quite negligible—a stroke or two of paint, a few curved lines and drips, and a phrase like "reaping and sowing / sowing and reaping . . . Skylark," as in number 1. But John Perreault is surely right when he compares these collaborations to "footprints of a wild ballet."[44] Like Chinese ink drawings, they have a lyric charm quite different from the more complex and subtle *Stones.* For one thing, O'Hara has a chance to display his beautiful handwriting which looks like calligraphy. The technique of making lithographs made this impossible in *Stones,* where the poet uses block print. The combination of O'Hara's rounded letters and Bluhm's curling horseshoe shapes, his thick white paint flecks, and suggestive, fleeting gestures, make *Poem-Paintings* real works of art even if their verbal messages hardly qualify as "poems." Take *Hand* (Fig. 10), which presents the shape of a clenched fist, outlined in thick black paint, with a splash of white across its center. The word HAND appears in the upper left; within each of the five "fingers," there is delicate small writing:

> You eat all the time
> you even know how to use
> chopsticks
> so why don't you write me
> a letter
> forget it

The final "forget it" is placed inside the thumb; so, as we come to the last finger, we also come to the end of O'Hara's little Dada poem with its naive address to someone's hand. In itself, the poem is trivial, but the placement of words and phrases within the thick black outlines of finger-shapes, and the further contrast of black and white create a lovely spatial configuration. Indeed, the twenty-six collaborations should be seen as an integral whole, a total event, rather than as separate paintings. Their inventiveness, wit, and charm become increasingly apparent as we study the relation of gesture to gesture, footmark to handprint, lyric phrase to four-letter word, proverb to sexy innuendo, white drop to black letter, and so on.

The "collaborations" of the sixties with such artists as Joe Brainard and Jasper Johns are no longer, strictly speaking, poem-paintings. The untitled ink-and-paper collage below (Fig. 11), for example, is one of a series of twenty-odd Pop cartoons O'Hara made with Joe Brainard between 1963 and 1966.[45] It combines tacky blue-and-white flowered wallpaper with bits of a dollar bill bearing George Washington's picture, a ticket for the Paris metro, a piece of memo pad, the letters of "9th Street," and, at dead center, a page from *Nancy* comics with the bubble caption: "Would you like a coke?" These juxtapositions are entertaining but fairly obvious; one misses the intricate verbal-visual counterpoint of *Stones* or the fragile lyricism of the O'Hara–Bluhm *Poem-Paintings*. In these cartoons, we are back in the world of Picabia and Schwitters; the "Nancy Collage" is an amusing assemblage, but it attempts—and achieves—less than O'Hara's earlier collaborations.

Jasper Johns's well-known *Skin with O'Hara Poem* (1963–65) takes us out of the realm of poem-paintings altogether (Fig. 12). The lithograph contains two large imprints of hands on either side. In the center are two blurred black shapes suggesting facial outlines; black smudges move across the surface connecting the hands to these facial shapes. Above the right hand, Johns has reproduced the text of "The Clouds Go Soft" (*CP*, 474), typed to scale. The bottom lines of the poem are slightly covered by black smudges. The poem thus becomes part of a game of lost-and-found; now we see it (although at first the viewer barely notices its existence), now we don't. It is an exciting composition, combining realistic figuration and Dada game-playing, but *Skin with O'Hara Poem* is *by* Jasper Johns; it is not a collaboration. The poem, an already completed work, is used as part of a spatial structure.[46]

We may conclude that the poem-painting, in the sense of a genuine collaboration, presents unusual challenges but also difficulties to the artist. Peter Schjeldahl calls it an "exotic hybrid of the two loneliest and traditionally 'highest' arts";[47] and Bill Berkson notes: "Collaboration between serious artists (even in the best of spirits . . .) involves always a brisk atmosphere of competition. Strategy may amount to a step-by-step oneupmanship: by painting a wide black line down the middle of the sheet, artist A lets artist B know that he knows what B's muse is up to and 'pardon my dust.'"[48]

This chapter has concentrated on O'Hara as a "poet among painters," and I have, accordingly, neglected his perhaps equally important collaborations with composers, choreographers, and film-makers. Certainly films like Alfred Leslie's *The Last Clean Shirt,* for which O'Hara wrote subtitles to create a double-scenario, or the text he provided for Ned Rorem's *Four Dialogues* would repay study. But painting had a special place in O'Hara's poetic universe, and so I have stressed its place in O'Hara's artistic development. The poet himself made the crucial distinctions in a letter written to Gregory Corso in 1958:

> Several people you know are around lately, Kerouac whom I've only seen once or twice but liked a lot, Howard Hart and [Philip] Lamantia who are reading with a French hornist as the Jazz Poetry Trio. . . .
> I don't really get their jazz stimulus but it is probably what I get from painting . . . that is, you can't be inside all the time it gets too boring and you can't afford to be bored with poetry so you take a secondary enthusiasm as the symbol of the first—for instance, I've noticed that what Kerouac and "they" feel as the content of jazz in relation to their own work (aspirations), I feel about painting with the corresponding difference in aspiration, that is where one takes Bird for inspiration I would take Bill de Kooning: partly because I feel that jazz is beautiful enough or too, but not fierce enough, and where jazz is fleeting (in time) and therefore poignant, de K is final and therefore tragic. . . . Then also, I don't have to see what I admire while I'm writing and would rather not hear it, which seems unavoidable in the jazz milieu since even if they don't whistle while they work they read with it. Maybe I should try to give a reading somewhere in front of a Pollock or a de K. . . . I guess my point is that painting doesn't intrude on poetry.[49]

To give a poetry reading in front of a de Kooning—this is the kind of aspiration we expect from O'Hara. But note that he doesn't want painting to "intrude on poetry," that it remains his "secondary enthusiasm." When asked by Lucie-Smith whether he had ever wanted to be a painter, O'Hara replied that he had not, although he admitted to "fooling around" with painting whenever he happened to be waiting around a studio for someone. "I might do some little thing, you know. But I never really did it seriously because . . . it seems to me that painting and sculpture take so much concentration over such a period of time that I'm not sure I can do it. Whereas one *can* write relatively fast" (*SS*, 21).

This amounts to no more than saying that his own particular genius was not for painting; surely the statement that painting is more difficult and time-consuming than writing poetry is tongue-in-cheek, for many abstractionists and Pop Artists of O'Hara's day hardly excercised the "concentration" over long periods of time that he talks of here. And in any case, the question, "Why are you not a painter?" must have struck O'Hara as wonderfully absurd. His pseudo-answer to this pointless question became the subject of one of his greatest poems:

WHY I AM NOT A PAINTER

I am not a painter, I am a poet.
Why? I think I would rather be
a painter, but I am not. Well,

for instance, Mike Goldberg
is starting a painting. I drop in.
"Sit down and have a drink" he
says. I drink; we drink. I look
up. "You have SARDINES in it."
"Yes, it needed something there."
"Oh." I go and the days go by
and I drop in again. The painting
is going on, and I go, and the days
go by. I drop in. The painting is
finished. "Where's SARDINES?"
All that's left is just
letters, "It was too much," Mike says.

But me? One day I am thinking of
a color: orange. I write a line
about orange. Pretty soon it is

a whole page of words, not lines.
Then another page. There should be
so much more, not of orange, of
words, of how terrible orange is
and life. Days go by. It is even in
prose, I am a real poet. My poem
is finished and I haven't mentioned
orange yet. It's twelve poems, I call
it ORANGES. And one day in a gallery
I see Mike's painting, called SARDINES.   (*CP*, 261–62)

Readers often assume that O'Hara is stressing differences: the painter like Mike Goldberg is constantly "taking out," and finally nothing remains of SARDINES but the letters, whereas the poet keeps "putting in" and "putting in." But on a second reading, it becomes clear that the poem is a profound jest. If someone asks a stupid question, O'Hara implies, he deserves a stupid answer. For in fact, Frank's art turns out to be just like Mike's. If Mike's painting finally contains no sardines, so Frank's "Oranges" never mentions the word "orange." In both cases, the original word or image merely triggers a chain of associations that ultimately leads straight to its demise. O'Hara is a poet not a painter for no better reason than that is what he *is*. But of course the poem is also saying that poetry and painting are part of the same spectrum, that in the final analysis SARDINES and ORANGES are one. This is why the rhetorical device governing the poem is repetition ("I drink; we drink"; "I go and the days go by"; "I drop in; I drop in again"). Art does not tolerate divisions; it must be viewed as process, not product.

1. Grace Hartigan. What Fire Murmurs Its Sedition. *1952. Oil on paper, 48 x 38½″. No. 3 of* Oranges. *Collection Mr. and Mrs. Leonard Kasle. Reproduced with permission of the artist.*

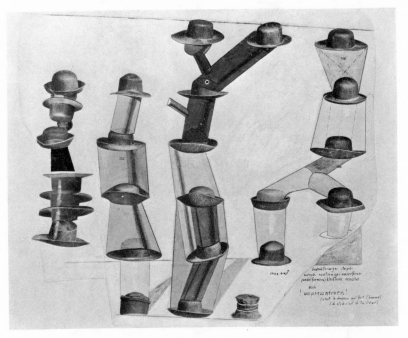

2. *Max Ernst*. The Hat Makes the Man. *1920. Collage with pencil, ink and watercolor, 14 x 18″. Museum of Modern Art, New York.*

4. *Larry Rivers and Frank O'Hara.* Rimbaud & Verlaine. *Plate 3 of* Stones, *1957–60. Lithograph, 19 x 23¼″. Museum of Modern Art, New York (Gift of Mr. and Mrs. E. Powis Jones).*

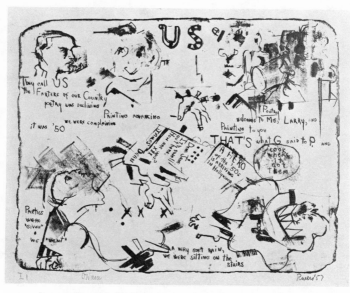

3. *Larry Rivers and Frank O'Hara.* US, *Plate 1 of* Stones, *1957–60. Lithograph, 19 x 23¼". Museum of Modern Art, New York (Gift of Mr. and Mrs. E. Powis Jones).*

5. *Larry Rivers and Frank O'Hara.* Love. *Plate 4 of Stones, 1957–60. Lithograph, 19 x 23¼". Museum of Modern Art, New York (Gift of Mr. and Mrs. E. Powis Jones).*

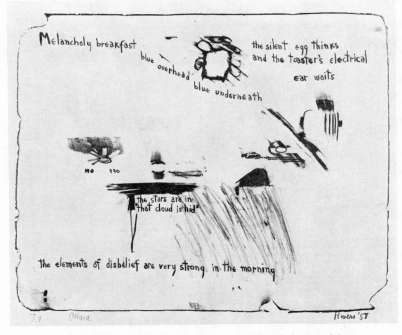

Melancholy breakfast
blue overhead
blue underneath
the silent egg thinks
and the toaster's electrical
ear waits

HO 170

"the stars are in
that cloud is hid"

the elements of disbelief are very strong in the morning

7. *Larry Rivers and Frank O'Hara.* Melancholy Breakfast.
Plate 8 of Stones, *1957-60. Museum of Modern Art, New York
(Gift of Mr. and Mrs. E. Powis Jones).*

6. *Larry Rivers and Frank O'Hara.*
Music. *Plate 6 of* Stones, *1957-60.
Lithograph, 19 x 23¼". Museum of
Modern Art, New York (Gift of Mr. and
Mrs. E. Powis Jones).*

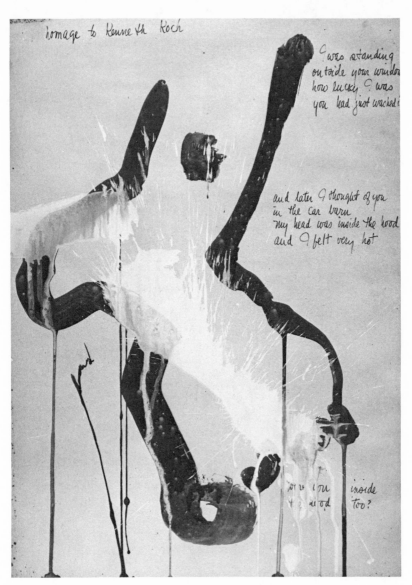

8. *Norman Bluhm and Frank O'Hara.* Homage to Kenneth Koch. *1960. Gouache and ink, 19¼ x 14". New York University Art Collection.*

9. *Norman Bluhm and Frank O'Hara.* Welcome to Kitty Hawk. *1960. Gouache and ink,* 19¼ x 14". *New York University Art Collection.*

10. *Norman Bluhm and Frank O'Hara.* Hand. *1960. Gouache and ink,* 19¼ x 14". *New York University Art Collection.*

11. Joe Brainard and Frank O'Hara. Untitled. 1964. Collage with ink on paper, 10 x 8''. Collection Frank O'Hara Estate.

12. Jasper Johns. Skin with O'Hara Poem. *1963–65. Lithograph, printed in black, 22 x 34''. Museum of Modern Art, New York (Gift of the Celeste and Armand Bartos Foundation).*

4
IN FAVOR
OF ONE'S TIME
(1954-61)

—and it was given to me
as the soul is given the hands
to hold the ribbons of life!
as miles streak by beneath the moon's sharp hooves
and I have mastered the speed and strength which is the armor of the world.
                    ("There I Could Never Be A Boy," CP, 216)

IN 1954, FRANK O'HARA was twenty-eight. Within the seven "green and turbulent" years that followed, he produced his finest poems and collaborations as well as his best art criticism. It was, both personally and artistically, the golden period of his life. During the summer of 1955, for example, he wrote to Fairfield Porter that he had written a new batch of poems, "so summery I don't know how they'll make the difficult transition to fall. Perhaps just shrivel up, turn brown and blow away. That would make me feel very grand. After all, if we can't make leaves, neither can god poems." [1]

By the late fifties, O'Hara was at the center of a circle of artists that included not only the painters discussed in the last chapter, but the poets John Ashbery (then living in Paris but in close communication),

James Schuyler, Barbara Guest, Kenneth Koch, Edwin Denby, Allen Ginsberg, John Wieners, and LeRoi Jones; the composers Ned Rorem, Ben Weber, and Virgil Thompson; the dancers Merce Cunningham, Paul Taylor, Vincent Warren, and Merle Marsicano. I do not mean to imply that all these artists belonged to one circle. There were, of course, many related circles, and diversity was O'Hara's special gift: the composers he knew, for example, ranged from the conservative Samuel Barber to the avant-garde Morton Feldman and Lucia Dlugoszewski. Or again, moving out into a wider circle, he was friendly with Leonard Bernstein and Tennessee Williams.

The poet's closest personal friendships—with Joe LeSueur, with whom he shared four apartments between 1955 and 1965, with Vincent Warren, the object of his most tender love poems, and with Grace Hartigan and Patsy Southgate—took place during this period.[2] And although he was now assistant curator at the Museum of Modern Art, organizing important exhibitions, his duties were not yet so extensive that there wasn't plenty of time for movies, concerts, operas, ballet, late evenings at the Cedar, parties all over town, and weekends at Southampton. In a letter to John Ashbery, characteristically dashed off in spare moments over a four-day period (1–4 February 1961), O'Hara lists a dizzying series of gallery openings and plays attended, new Balanchine ballets, and even his and Vincent's "assiduous TVing"; the following paragraph gives a good idea of his daily life:

> Hello, it is now February 4th, Friday thank heaven, and I think I am going to paint my bedroom this weekend. I veer between orange and blue, though Mario says the latter is the brightest color and would be very nerve-wracking. (That might be quite appropriate.) The opera [Aaron Copland's *The Second Hurricane*] was a lot of fun and afterwards we went to Donald Droll's for supper where were Elaine de Kooning, Edwin, John Button, Edward Bagaline (who is very nice and is supposed to have a great collection—as I said above; we couldn't accept his invitation to see it as it was 2:00 when he issued it), and Beatrice Monti, who is Joan and Jean-Paul's dealer in Milano. She was very interesting and the quiche lorraine was divine.[3]

"It's lucky," Joe LeSueur has commented wryly, "that he didn't become famous because it would have intruded upon his working hours and the way he lived."[4]

O'Hara certainly didn't work at becoming a famous poet. All his friends agree that he was reluctant to submit poems for publication or to assemble them in a volume. The selection for *Meditations in an Emergency* (1957) was largely the work of James Schuyler and Kenneth Koch; later when O'Hara was supposedly putting together *Lunch Poems* for City Lights Books at the request of Lawrence Ferlinghetti, he kept procrastinating so that Ferlinghetti had to send him constant reminders like "How about LUNCH? I'm hungry," to which O'Hara would respond "Cooking" or something similar.[5] Thus the "lunch poem" project, initiated at least as early as 1959, did not come to fruition until 1964, and when O'Hara supplied a biographical note for the dust jacket, he adopted the playful stance of "Personism":

> Often this poet, strolling through the noisy splintered glare of a Manhattan noon, has paused at a sample Olivetti to type up thirty or forty lines of ruminations, or pondering more deeply has withdrawn to a darkened ware- or fire-house, to limn his computed misunderstandings of the eternal questions of life, co-existence and depth, while never forgetting to eat Lunch his favorite meal.[6]

Many of the important poems of this period—for example, "A True Account of Talking to the Sun at Fire Island" (1958)—remained unpublished during O'Hara's lifetime. And those that did get into print often did so by chance. Diane di Prima, whose *Floating Bear* published such major O'Hara poems as "Mary Desti's Ass" and "For the Chinese New Year and Bill Berkson,"[7] has given an amusing account of how she acquired the poet's manuscripts:

> I would go over to Frank O'Hara's house pretty often. He used to keep a typewriter on the table in the kitchen, and he would type away, make poems all the time, when company was there and when it wasn't, when he was eating, all kinds of times. There would be an unfinished poem in his typewriter and he would do a few lines on it now and again, and he kept losing all these poems. They would wind up all over the house. . . . The poems would get into everything and I would come over and go through, like, his dresser drawers. There would be poems in with the towels, and I'd say, "Oh, hey, I like this one," and he'd say, "OK, take it." Very often it would be the only copy. My guess is that huge collected Frank O'Hara has only about one-third of his actual work.[8]

O'Hara's attitude toward his poetry thus struck most people as casual, if not downright careless. "As far as I could tell," Joe LeSueur recalls, "writing poetry was something Frank did in his spare time. He didn't make a big deal about it, he just sat down and wrote when the spirit moved him." He didn't need much time "because he usually got what he was after in one draft, and could type very fast, hunt-and-peck fashion. And from the very beginning it seemed to me that he never tried to get a poem going, never forced himself to write; he either had an idea or he didn't, and that was all there was to it" ("Four Apartments," pp. 288–89).

Because speed and spontaneity were of the essence, the typewriter was the essential instrument. LeSueur recalls only two non-typewriter works: "his poem about James Dean, 'written in the sand at Water Island and remembered' and his 'Lana Turner has collapsed' poem, which he wrote on the Staten Island Ferry on the way out to a reading at Wagner College" (p. 290). And indeed, during Frank's six months' leave of absence from the Museum in the winter of 1956 when he accepted a grant from the Poets' Theatre in Cambridge, he wrote to Mike Goldberg: "There were a couple of weeks of foul depression, gnashing teeth, pacing and boredom, when I felt that I would never, NEVER . . . be able to play the typewriter again. But the presence of this Steinway you all gave me [a Royal portable donated by his friends after Frank lost his own typewriter in Penn Station] has finally asserted itself, and I now stagger from bed, stride to the desk, and begin my scales each morning, or almost each."[9]

"Playing the typewriter" rather than writing in longhand inevitably leads the poet to emphasize visual prosody. For example, O'Hara used long lines frequently, evidently because he liked their appearance on the page—their ability to convey sensuality and strength.[10] When spoken, however, these lines tend to break down into groups of twos or threes, as in the following example:

Now the violets are all gone, // the rhinoceroses, // the cymbals
(*CP*, 346)

What is heard does not, then, reflect what is seen. O'Hara was not, for that matter, a particularly good reader of his own poetry. Like Williams, he wrote primarily for the eye rather than the ear; like Williams, he placed special emphasis on speed and spontaneity, only rarely revising more than a phrase or two of a poem. But this is not to say that he didn't take his poetry very seriously. As Joe LeSueur remarks with great insight: "I didn't realize right away that if you took poetry so much for granted as you did breathing it might mean you felt it was essential to your life" (p. 288).

Poetry and life—O'Hara refused, at least consciously, to make a distinction between the two. He regarded both as part of the same vital process, living every moment as if it were his last, forcing himself to go without sleep so as not to miss anything. "There's nothing so spiritual about being happy," O'Hara says in a poem of 1956 (*CP*, 244), "but you can't miss a day of it, because it doesn't last." We are now in a better position to understand why O'Hara was so reluctant to judge or to rank his own poetry. Given his intense relationships with people, he naturally tended to prefer whatever poem he had just written because it could remind him of a particular person or incident. All his best poems grow out of personal relationships. I have already talked of the "Grace Hartigan" poems; other important figures in the lyrics of the later fifties are Mike Goldberg, Kenneth Koch, Joan Mitchell, and of course Joe LeSueur and Vincent Warren. It is interesting that the poems written for Joe LeSueur—"Joe's Jacket," "Waking Early Sunday," "Adieu to Norman, Bonjour to Jean-Paul"—are written in the realistic, documentary "I do this, I do that" mode which LeSueur himself admires most,[11] whereas the love poems to Vincent Warren, whom O'Hara met in 1959, tend to be less factual, more emotional, direct, Romantic. And the lyrics addressed to Bill Berkson or directly concerned with him have a very different quality again—they are more elusive, detached, abstract.

To understand O'Hara's method of composition in this period, we might begin by looking at a specific poem whose genesis has been amusingly described by LeSueur in "Four Apartments":

> Sometimes . . . the details in a poem will remind me of a day I would otherwise have forgotten. Mother's Day, 1958, for example. Frank was struck by the title of a *Times* book review, "The Arrow That Flieth by Day," and said he'd like to appropriate it for a poem. I agreed that the phrase had a nice ring and asked him for the second time what I should

do about Mother's Day, which I'd forgotten all about. "Oh, send your mother a telegram," he said. But I couldn't hit upon a combination of words that didn't revolt me and Western Union's prepared messages sounded too maudlin even for my mother. "You think of a message for my mother and I'll think of one for yours," I suggested. We then proceeded to try to top each other with apposite messages that would have made Philip Wylie applaud. Then it was time to go hear a performance of Aaron Copland's *Piano Fantasy* by Noel Lee. "It's raining, I don't want to go," Frank said. So he stayed home and wrote "Ode on the Arrow That Flieth by Day," which refers to the Fantasy, Western Union, the rain, and Mother's Day. (rpt. *CP,* 541).

The Ode does indeed "refer" to these seemingly unrelated items but in a very oblique way. The key to O'Hara's transformation of the materials LeSueur describes is the poem's title, taken from Psalm 91:5: "Thou shalt not be afraid of the terror by night; nor the arrow that flieth by day." How *not* to be afraid—this is the theme of the poem. To capture the mood of deepening anxiety, O'Hara eliminates all narrative, giving us instead snatches of his conversation, both spoken and unspoken. The opening note is one of deceptively light-hearted banter:

> To humble yourself before a radio on a Sunday
> it's amusing, like dying after a party
> "click" / and you're dead from fall-out, hang-over
>   or something hyphenated   (*CP,* 300)

One might note that the awareness of death is introduced right away, however comically, but it is then deflected by the wonderfully absurd distillation of pseudo-Mother's Day Greetings invented by Frank and Joe on this occasion:

(hello, Western Union? send a Mother's Day message to Russia: SORRY NOT TO BE WITH YOU ON YOUR DAY LOVE AND KISSES TELL THE CZAR /
LA GRANDE JATTE WASN'T DAMAGED IN THE MUSEUM OF MODERN ART FIRE / S / FRANK)

David Shapiro has suggested that this kind of parenthetical injection, the mimetic representation of sending a telegram, corresponds to the introduction of noise in the "musique concrète" of Satie, one of

O'Hara's favorite composers.[12] It creates a discontinuity of texture, forcing the reader to shift gears, as it were, and commanding our attention. Such attention is important, for, despite the playful fantasy of the telegram, its "message" has serious implications in that the very thought that this *is* Mother's Day introduces a note of irritation and malaise.

> the unrecapturable nostalgia for nostalgia
> for a life I might have hated, thus mourned
>
> but do we really need anything more to be sorry about
> wouldn't it be extra, as all pain is extra

The poet tries to comfort himself with this last thought but he knows only too well that he will never "WIN A DREAM TRIP . . . somehow." And indeed, in the next passage he must confront "the arrow that flieth by day" directly:

> for God's sake, fly the other way
> leave me standing alone crumbling in the new sky of the Wide World
> without passage, without breath
>
> a spatial representative of emptiness
>
> if Joan says I'm wounded, then I'm wounded

The cause of his "wound" cannot be named. Neither tortured at the stake like Joan of Arc nor reviled by hostile critics like André Gide, he cannot put the blame on "moral issues or the intercontinental ballistics missile / or the Seer of Prague" [Kafka]. Indeed, the poet's anxiety has no cause. And this is precisely why it is so devastating:

> (you're right to go to Aaron's PIANO FANTASY, but I'm not up to it this
> time, too important a piece not to punish me
>   and it's raining)

It is a nice irony that the poet's original joke comes true: he does, after all, die from "something hyphenated"; he is gunned down by a nameless source, turning him, at least momentarily, into the "death of a nation / henceforth to be called small."

What the "Ode" does, then—and this is entirely absent from Le-

Sueur's narrative of the incident—is to reenact the mental process whereby amusement and horseplay gradually give way to anxiety and ultimately to withdrawal. But O'Hara's comic self-depreciation precludes sentimentality. The implication is that under other circumstances (if only it weren't Mother's Day and weren't raining to boot!) he could and does resist "the arrow that flieth by day." "All pain," as he puts it, "is extra." Something amusing, distracting, challenging is sure to turn up. Maybe the air will once again "salute" him as he stands "leaning on the prow."

The poem's mode reflects O'Hara's gradual shift from the Tzara-Péret model of his earlier years to the more open, flexible forms of Apollinaire and Reverdy, the laconic informality of the later Auden, the brutal and personal intensity of Mayakovsky. Williams continues to be a central influence, but Pound now becomes equally important. I shall return to the question of influence later in this chapter. But first I want to look at the poetic signature, the particular style that identifies a given lyric as a "Frank O'Hara poem," the sort of poem that has been so widely imitated, if never quite reproduced, during the past decade.

"WHATEVER ENERGY I BURN FOR ART"

"Music," the opening poem of *Lunch Poems,* written in 1954, contains most of the stylistic devices I wish to discuss.

> If I rest for a moment near The Equestrian
> pausing for a liver sausage sandwich in the Mayflower Shoppe,
> that angel seems to be leading the horse into Bergdorf's
> and I am naked as a table cloth, my nerves humming.
> Close to the fear of war and the stars which have disappeared.
> I have in my hands only 35¢, it's so meaningless to eat!
> and gusts of water spray over the basins of leaves
> like the hammers of a glass pianoforte. If I seem to you
> to have lavender lips under the leaves of the world,
>> I must tighten my belt.
> It's like a locomotive on the march, the season
>> of distress and clarity
> and my door is open to the evenings of midwinter's
> lightly falling snow over the newspapers.
> Clasp me in your handkerchief like a tear, trumpet
> of early afternoon! in the foggy autumn.

As they're putting up the Christmas trees on Park Avenue
I shall see my daydreams walking by with dogs in blankets,
put to some use before all those coloured lights come on!
But no more fountains and no more rain,
and the stores stay open terribly late.   (*CP*, 210)

This is at once an "easier" and a "more difficult" poem than such earlier lyrics as "Chez Jane," "Easter," or "Memorial Day 1950." As in the case of "Ode (to Joseph LeSueur), "one's first impression is that "Music" is no more than a record of daily trivia; it recounts an uneventful lunch hour spent in the former Mayflower Donut Shoppe on Fifth and 59th, detailing Frank's random thoughts about the Plaza fountain across the way, the equestrian statue nearby, Bergdorf Goodman's down the street, the thirty-five cents in his pocket, the liver sausage sandwich he has ordered, and the impending Christmas season with its giant trees on Park Avenue, colored lights, and long shopping hours.

But the real strategy of the poem is to remove objects from what Viktor Shklovsky has called "the automatism of perception," [13] by adapting the techniques of film and action painting to a verbal medium. For one thing, the poem is framed as a series of cuts and dissolves, whether spatial, temporal, or referential. Thus in line 3, the highly concrete setting—the Mayflower Shoppe on the Plaza—dissolves into a comic fantasy scene, created by the optical illusion of staring into the Plaza fountain on a rainy day: "that angel seems to be leading the horse into Bergdorf's." Or again, the poem suddenly cuts from Fifth Avenue to Park, where the giant Christmas trees are being put up, and one's "daydreams," whoever they are, emerge with their "dogs in blankets."

Temporal dissolves work the same way. The "real" time of the poem is "early afternoon! in the foggy autumn" (line 16), a rainy day in that in-between time of the year after the leaves have fallen and before the Christmas lights come on, a time of half-light and shadow in "this season / of distress and clarity." Yet in line 13, the poet says "and my door is open to the evenings of midwinter's / lightly falling snow over the newspapers," and the end of the poem presents the Christmas season itself: "But no more fountains and no more rain, / and the stores stay open terribly late."

Time shifts are not, of course, anything new in poetry, but it is one of O'Hara's trademarks to maintain the present tense (or conditional present as in "If I rest . . .") regardless, and to supply no adverbial pointers (e.g., "when," "after," "before," "during") that signal a shift. The concept of person is similarly fluid. The "I"—a very familiar, intimate, *open* "I"—is omnipresent but whom is he addressing? If the first "you" (line 8) is a close friend or lover, the second, to whom the poet says rapturously, "Clasp me in your handkerchief like a tear, trumpet / of early afternoon!" is clearly a larger "you"—perhaps the Manhattan traffic, the rising moon, the sky, or indeed the whole universe as if to say, "You out there!" While the poet's self thus remains a constant center, anything or anyone that comes within its field of vision can be addressed or called by name. The repetition of definite articles and demonstratives reinforces this sense of intimate conversation and invites the reader's participation: "*The* Equestrian" (note the ellipsis of the noun here), "*the* Mayflower Shoppe," "*that* angel," "*the* Christmas trees on Park Avenue"—all these references suggest that the reader is familiar with the scene, indeed that he is part of it.

The syntax of "Music" may be described as a system of non-sequiturs. "If I rest for a moment . . ." the poet begins, but no "then" clause ever follows, and the conditional clause dissolves into the parenthesis of line 3. The second "If I seem to you" clause in line 8 is completed by "I must tighten my belt," a clause that follows grammatically but makes no sense. Appositives and parallel nouns similarly turn out to be pseudo-appositives and pseudo-parallels: "It's like a locomotive on the march, the season / of distress and clarity"; or "the fear of war and the stars which have disappeared." In what sense is a "season" a "locomotive on the march"? And why "distress *and* clarity," or "the fear of war *and* the stars"? The use of "and" to introduce coordinate clauses is similarly illogical: "That angel seems to be leading the horse into Bergdorf's / *and* I am naked as a table cloth," or "it's so meaningless to eat! / *and* gusts of water spray . . ." and so on.

The syntactic dislocations of "Music" are by no means as radical as those found in such earlier poems as "Second Avenue," with its all but impenetrable verbal surface, its total ambiguity of reference. But the repeated nonsequiturs act to undercut the documentary realism of the poem's scene and introduce the opposing note: an element of fantasy, of imaginative transformation. Not "I rest," but "*If* I rest"; not "I have lavender lips," but "*If* I *seem* to you to have lavender lips." Or again, "I *must* tighten my belt," and "It's *like* a locomotive on the march." Nothing really *happens* to the poet; it is all potential, conditional, projected into a possible future ("I *shall see* my daydreams"). And individual images and metaphors are often comically or grotesquely far-fetched, reinforcing the fantasy note: "and I am naked as a table cloth"; "Clasp me in your handkerchief like a tear / trumpet of early afternoon!"; "If I seem to you to have lavender lips"; "I shall see my daydreams walking by with dogs in blankets."

How do all these elements work together? Again, the title gives us a clue, for the poem is like a melodic graph of the poet's perceptions. The varied sound images—some documentary and realistic, some fanciful and surreal—fuse to create a pattern that brings to mind modern dance (another favorite O'Hara art form) rather than a "poem" in the traditional sense of the word. "Music" begins on a note of suspended animation: the poet rests "for a moment near The Equestrian / pausing" for his sandwich. But immediately his imagination begins to transform the external scene: "that angel seems to be leading the horse into Bergdorf's," and "gusts of water spray over the basin of leaves / like hammers of a glass pianoforte." The tempo now accelerates as the poet's self increasingly *opens* to experience. It merges with the landscape of the coffee shop, becoming as "naked as a table cloth," and his door is "open to the evenings of . . . snow over the newspapers." A sense of anticipation, of excitement, of brinkmanship pervades the poem: nerves hum, the speaker is "Close to the fear of war and the stars which have disappeared," he finds it "so meaningless to eat!" The leaves in the Plaza fountain become, in a truly filmlike dissolve, "the leaves of the world," and underneath them, the poet's lips, with a hint of impending doom, turn lavender. The initial "pause" gives way, precisely at the midpoint of the poem, to the urgency of the "locomotive on the march," the mood of yearning and ecstasy coming to a head with the imperative "Clasp me . . . !" But the vision of the pre-Christmas season with its "dogs in blankets" doesn't last. The moment gives way to stasis: "no more fountains and no more rain."

"Music" thus captures the sense of magic, urgency, and confusion of the modern cityscape in its "season of distress and clarity." It presents an impression of total fluidity, conveyed by the repeated use of present participles: "pausing," "leading," "humming," "falling," "putting," "walking." And the deliberate indeterminacy of the long verse lines is offset and heightened by repetitive internal sound patterning: "*rest*" / "Eque*str*ian"; "*p*a*us*ing" / "*s*a*us*age"; "*s*eems to be *l*ea*d*ing," "*l*avender *l*ips under the *l*eaves of the wor*l*d," "*Cl*asp me in your h*a*ndkerchief," and so on. The effect of all these devices is to create an aura of intense animation.

Like an action painting, "Music" presents the poet's act of coming to awareness rather than the results of that act. Accordingly, it traces the shift from calm to the crescendo of anticipation and excitement associated with "gusts of water" spraying over the leaves and the rapturous imperative, "Clasp me . . . !" After this crescendo, the mood gradually darkens as time, which has haunted the poet from the beginning, freezes. He can, after all, rest only "for a moment," "pausing" to take in a scene so animated ("my nerves humming") that there is hardly time to eat lunch. And in the course of the poem, lunchtime imperceptibly modulates into the foggy "early afternoon" and finally into darkness, when the fountains and rain are no longer visible and "the stores stay open terribly late." By the time the colored lights come on, the poet's "daydreams" will have vanished.

To recapitulate, let us consider "Music" in the broader context of O'Hara's poetry.

1. Imagery

"Music" fuses realism and surrealism, the literal and the fanciful. In so doing, it marks a clear-cut rejection of the Symbolist mode that had dominated American poetry for the first half of the century. Unlike Prufrock's "sawdust restaurants with oyster shells," with their symbolic connotations of aridity, sterility, and decay, O'Hara's Mayflower Shoppe points to nothing beyond itself; it has no underlying significance that demands interpretation. The name "Mayflower," for example, does not, in this context, call to mind our Founding Fathers or the innocence of an Early America; the coffee shop is simply *there,* an authentic presence we can all locate and recognize. Or again, whereas

Prufrock's fear of eating a peach reflects his fear of ripeness and fertility, O'Hara's "liver sausage sandwich" has no particular symbolic properties; it could, for that matter, be a salami or cheese sandwich just as easily.

Like the landscapes of Williams, of Reverdy, or of Apollinaire, O'Hara's is thus what Charles Altieri has called a "landscape without depth,"[14] a presence stripped of its "ontological vestments." Aerial perspective, three-dimensionality give way to a world of surfaces. In poem after poem of this period, what looks like a flat literalism predominates:

> It is 12:20 in New York a Friday
> three days after Bastille day, yes
> it is 1959 and I go get a shoeshine
> because I will get off the 4:19 in Easthampton
> at 7:15 and then go straight to dinner
> and I don't know the people who will feed me   (*CP*, 325)

> It's my lunch hour, so I go
> for a walk among the hum-colored
> cabs. First, down the sidewalk
> where laborers feed their dirty
> glistening torsos sandwiches
> and Coca-Cola. . . .   (*CP*, 257)

> I cough a lot (sinus?) so I
> get up and have some tea with cognac
> it is dawn
>   the light flows evenly along the lawn
> in chilly Southampton and I smoke
> and hours and hours go by I read
> Van Vechten's SPIDER BOY then a short
> story by Patsy Southgate and a poem
> by myself. . . .   (*CP*, 341)

The matter-of-fact realism of these passages has been widely imitated: "It is 12:20 in New York a Friday" (the first line of "The Day Lady Died") has become a kind of formula for New York poets. But whereas any number of minor poets can offer us such a *catalogue raisonné*,[15] O'Hara's empiricism is deceptive for it modulates easily and surprisingly into fantasy and artifice. The lessons of Dada and

Surrealism have, after all, been learned; even the most casual personal poems retain the witty modulations and sudden polarization of images found in the poetry of Tzara, Péret, and Breton, or, for that matter, in the poetry of Apollinaire, which is one of the dominant influences on O'Hara's poetry of this period. Take the following passage from "Rhapsody":

> I am getting into a cab at 9th Street and 1st Avenue
> and the Negro driver tells me about a $120 apartment
> "where you can't walk across the floor after 10 at night
> not even to pee, cause it keeps them awake downstairs"
> no I don't like that "well I didn't take it"   (*CP*, 326)

This bit of "supper-club conversation for the mill of the gods" strikes the poet as "perfect in the hot humid morning on my way to work," and he realizes that

> it isn't enough to smile when you run the gauntlet
> you've got to spit like Niagara Falls on everybody or
> Victoria Falls or at least the beautiful urban fountains of Madrid
> as the Niger joins the Gulf of Guinea near the Menemsha Bar. . . .

By the time we come to this last line, the *real* New York scene has dissolved, the Menemsha Bar becoming part of an exotic tropical landscape, an imaginary "jungle of impossible eagerness."

"Naphtha" (*CP*, 337–38) displays a similar development:

> Ah Jean Dubuffet
> when you think of him
> doing his military service in the Eiffel Tower
> as a meteorologist
> in 1922
> you know how wonderful the 20th Century
> can be
> and the gaited Iroquois on the girders
> fierce and unflinching-footed
> nude as they should be
> slightly empty
> like a Sonia Delaunay
> there is a parable of speed

> somewhere behind the Indians' eyes
> they invented the century with their horses
> and their fragile backs
> which are dark

Lines 1–7 are perfectly straightforward, but the "and" at the beginning of line 8 is a false connective, for who are these "gaited Iroquois" who appear "on the girders"? Construction workers who are not afraid of heights? Statues? The Indian as primitive life source? Or what? And then the whole tableau turns into a Sonia Delaunay painting which is "slightly empty." Emptiness, and the concomitant need to maintain one's "fragile," precarious balance is the keynote here, and so we can forget all about the Eiffel Tower and shift to the intimate conversation of the third verse paragraph:

> how are you feeling in ancient September
> I am feeling like a truck on a wet highway. . . .
> apart from love (don't say it)
> I am ashamed of my century
> for being so entertaining
> but I have to smile

Such surprising conjunctions of literal reference and comic fantasy are typical of O'Hara; he shifts from *real* to *surreal* and back again with astonishing speed. And this is why his poetry is ultimately so difficult to imitate. It is easy enough to begin a poem with "It is 12:23 in New York, a rainy Monday," or "I am walking up Broadway and I meet Ernie," but without O'Hara's Dada or fantasy context, such empiricism (the literalism of simple Pop Art) becomes monotonous.

2. Proper Names

O'Hara's poetry is, as everyone has remarked, one of constant name-dropping. Interestingly, proper names are not used very frequently in the early work. "Easter," with its "razzle-dazzle maggots," "glassy towns," and "yaks," is a poem of wholly imaginary landscapes, but "Music" refers to "The Equestrian," "the Mayflower Shoppe," "Berg-dorf's," "Park Avenue"—authentic New York settings. By the late

fifties, O'Hara had established an elaborate network of cross-refer-
ences to close personal friends, artists, film stars, city streets, bars,
exotic places, titles of books, movies, operas, and ballets—in short, the
name of anyone or anything that happens to come across the poet's
path. The following are typical:

Richard Barthelmess as the "tol'able" boy barefoot and in pants,
Jeanette MacDonald of the flaming hair and lips and long, long neck,
Sue Carroll as she sits for eternity on the damaged fender of a car
and smiles, Ginger Rogers, with her pageboy bob like a sausage
on her shuffling shoulders, peach-melba-voiced Fred Astaire of the feet,
Eric von Stroheim, the seducer of mountain-climbers' gasping spouses. . . .
                                                                              (*CP*, 232)

Where is Mike Goldberg? I don't know
he may be in the Village, far below
or lounging on Tenth Street with the gang. . . .   (*CP*, 301)

Shirley Goldfarb continues to be Shirley Goldfarb
and Jane Hazan continues to be Jane Freilicher (I think!)
and Irving Sandler continues to be the balayeur des artistes
and so do I (sometimes I think I'm "in love" with painting)
and surely the Piscine Deligny continues to have water in it
and the Flore continues to have tables and newspapers   and people under them
and surely we shall not continue to be unhappy
we shall be happy
but we shall continue to be ourselves everything continues to be possible
René Char, Pierre Reverdy, Samuel Beckett it is possible isn't it
I love Reverdy for saying yes, though I don't believe it   (*CP*, 329)

One's first response to these endless allusions is that they are part of
a tiresome in-joke. Why should we know who Shirley Goldfarb is, or
whether Jane Hazan has retained her married name (Freilicher) or
where Mike Goldberg is "lounging"? And don't these very private
allusions make excessive demands on readers, especially future readers who will need extensive annotation in order to understand a given
O'Hara poem?

Perhaps we can answer these questions by looking at some possible
sources for this naming technique. Paul Carroll suggests that O'Hara
may have been influenced by the Dada poems of Pierre Albert-Birot,[16]

translations of which appear in Motherwell's *Dada Painters and Poets* (1951), one of the central source books for the New York poets. "At the Paul Guillaume Gallery," for example, begins:

> The 13th day of November this year of 1917
> We were at Paul Guillaume the negrophile's place
> 108 Faubourg St. Honoré at 8 o'clock
> A short time after we were there
> Along came Apollinaire
> He sat down on a leather chair
> And spoke first of a new art that one day he had implied
> To be a sort of "technepheism"
> To use a very simple term. . . .

Another Albert-Birot poem, "Openings," begins:

> The 1st of March 1919 I was
> at Rosenberg's where Herbin the painter
> Was showing his pictures
> Rue de la Beaume
> It's a street
> Where one sees nothing but stone
> And you ask yourself as you go in
> Are there people there
> You push the little half open door
> And you find some
> Here's Cendrars Hello
> And Soupeault   (you arrive)
> How are you   (I depart)
> Fine Hello Severini
> Good day my friend
> Good day Max Jacob. . . .[17]

   How important is it to recognize the names and addresses in these poems? The references to Severini, Apollinaire, and Jacob surely count for something because their conversations, gestures, and manners conjure up the artistic milieu of the time and give the poem an air of authenticity: this *really* happened at a *real* show! The day (1 March 1918) and place (Rosenberg's) are immortalized. But we cannot press much further, for the proper names in these Dada poems do not resonate with meaning. A similar process occurs in Pound's more personal Cantos. In Canto 80, we read:

> which is what I suppose he, Fordie, wanted me to be able to picture
> when he took me to Miss Braddon's
>   (I mean the setting) at Richmond
> But that New York I have found at Périgeux
>   *si com' ad Arli*
> in wake of the sarascen
>   As the "Surrender of Breda" (Velásquez)
> was preceded in fresco at Avignon[18]

O'Hara is squarely in the Pound as well as in the Dada tradition. In the passage cited from "To the Film Industry in Crisis," we do miss a lot of the fun if we aren't familiar with Ginger Rogers–Fred Astaire movies or have never seen an Eric von Stroheim film, and the allusions to Reverdy, Char, and Beckett in "Adieu to Norman" serve to ground the poet's experience even as the reference to "Fordie" (Ford Madox Ford) and Velásquez's *Surrender of Breda* authenticate Pound's artistic world. But in most cases (as in "Where is Mike Goldberg?"), the referential quality of the names is purposely undercut. As Charles Altieri remarks:

> His [O'Hara's] texture of proper names gives each person and detail an identity, but in no way do the names help the reader understand anything about what has been named. To know a lunch counter is called Juliet's Corner or a person O'Hara expects to meet is named Norman is rather a reminder for the reader that the specific details of another's life can appear only as momentary fragments, insisting through their particularity on his alienation from any inner reality they might possess.[19]

This seems to me precisely the point. To give another instance: when one says, "It is 12:20 in New York," one is recognizing that numbers no longer have any mystical significance. In this respect, O'Hara goes one step further than Pound, who still uses historical, literary, and mythological figures as touchstones. In O'Hara's poetry, such touchstones have largely disappeared; only the arts continue to be endowed with a certain value. His poetic world is thus one of immanence rather than transcendence; persons and places, books and films are named because they are central to O'Hara's particular consciousness, but they have no "inner reality." Compare O'Hara's treatment of, say, Jane Freilicher to Yeats's mythologizing portraits of Lionel Johnson or Lady Gregory, and the difference will become clear.

3. Syntactic Ambiguity

One of the central features of O'Hara's style is what Eric Sellin has called, with reference to Reverdy's poetry, "syntactic ambiguity." As we have seen in the case of "Music," O'Hara's poetic structure is a system of nonsequiturs, making use of false connectives and demonstratives, pronouns with shifting referents, dangling conditional clauses, incomplete declarative sentences, confusing temporal and spatial relationships, and so on. Sellin quite rightly calls such ambiguity "irreducible" (as distinguished from the semantic ambiguities discussed by William Empson and his followers), because its effect is "to render two or several contextual meanings simultaneously possible for a given passage."[20] Or, as Ernst Gombrich puts it in a brilliant short discussion of Cubism, "If illusion is due to the interaction of clues and the absence of contradictory evidence, the only way to fight its transforming influence is to make the clues contradict each other and to prevent a coherent image of reality from destroying the pattern in the plane." A Cubist painting resists all our attempts to apply "the test of consistency." "Try as we may to see the guitar or the jug suggested to us as a three-dimensional object and thereby to transform it, we will always come across a contradiction somewhere which compels us to start afresh." By intentionally scrambling his representational clues, the Cubist painter thus forces us "to accept the flat surface with all its tensions."[21] The ambiguity cannot, in other words, be resolved.

This is precisely what happens in O'Hara's poetry which carries on what Sellin calls "the cubist-surrealist esthetic [of] simultaneity" (p. 112). Indeed, if the Surrealists taught O'Hara how to mix semantic spheres, moving from literal to hallucinatory, it is the Cubist or proto-Cubist poets who provide the model for his syntax. Take the following example from Apollinaire's "Zone":

> Today you walk through Paris the women are blood-stained
> It was and I would prefer not to remember it was during beauty's decline

Surrounded by fervent flames Notre Dame looked at me in Chartres
The blood of your Sacred Heart flooded me in the Montmartre
I am ill from hearing happy words
The love from which I suffer is a shameful sickness
And the image which possesses you makes you survive /
in sleeplessness and anguish
It is always near you this passing image[22]

In this nine-line passage, the present dissolves into the past and vice-versa without explanation. More important, the "you" of line 1 and "I" of line 2 both refer to the poet, a pattern repeated in lines 6–7. To further complicate things, the familiar you ("tu") of the opening lines gives way, in line 4, to the formal "your Sacred Heart" ("votre Sacré-Coeur"), referring to Christ. Clausal relationships are also obscure: in the first line we have simple juxtaposition of two declarative sentences without punctuation ("Today you walk through Paris," and "the women are blood-stained"). These present-tense observations are now followed by the gnomic "It was" ("Cétait") and a confusing conjunction: "*and* I would prefer not to remember it."

Reverdy's poetry, which O'Hara especially loved,[23] furnishes similar examples. "Trace de Pas" has, as Sellin notes, an interesting example of a "bridge phrase" or, as I prefer to call it, a "floating modifier."

Five branches have lit up
The trees hold back their tongues
By the window
A head still stuck out
A new star was going to appear
Above
The airplane competed
With the stars for quickness . . .[24]

Here lines 5–7 are syntactically ambiguous. Does "above" ("Là-haut") belong with the line that precedes it ("A new star was going to appear above") or the one that follows ("Above, the airplane competed with the stars")? The syntax forces us to consider both possibilities.

O'Hara's poetry abounds in such "Cubist" syntax. A few examples must suffice here.

From First to Second Person:

> yet *I* always loved Baltimore
> the porches which hurt *your* ass
> no, they were the steps
> well, *you* have a wet ass anyway
> if they'd only stop scrubbing   (*CP*, 402)

From First to Third Person:

> I stop for a cheeseburger at JULIET'S
> CORNER. . . .
> and *one* has eaten and *one* walks
> past the magazines with nudes
> and the posters for BULLFIGHT and
> the Manhattan Storage Warehouse
> which they'll soon tear down. *I*
> used to think they had the Armory
> Show there.   (*CP*, 258)

Second-Person Shifts:

> How funny *you* are today New York
> like Ginger Rogers in *Swingtime*
> and St. Bridget's steeple leaning a little to the left
>
> here I have just jumped out of a bed full of V-days
> (I got tired of D-days) and blue *you* there still
> accepts me foolish and free
> all I want is a room up there
> and *you* in it.   (*CP*, 370)

AMBIGUOUS REFERENCE

> *There* I could never be a boy,
> though I rode like a god when the horse reared
> At a cry from mother I fell to my knees!
> *there* I fell, clumsy and sick and good. . . .   (*CP*, 216)

PSEUDO-CONNECTIVES

>   this country
> has everything but *politesse,* a Puerto Rican cab driver says
> *and* five different girls I see
>   look like Piedie Gimbel
> with her blonde hair tossing too   (*CP*, 340)

so the weight
>   of the rain drifting amiably is like a sentimental breeze
and seems to have been invented by a collapsed Kim Novak balloon

yet Janice is helping Kenneth appeal to The Ford Foundation. . . .

(*CP*, 346)

>   considering
>   my growingly more perpetual state *and* how
>   can one say that angel in the Frick's wings
>   are "attached" if it's a real angel?   (*CP*, 393)

FLOATING MODIFIERS

>   the warm walking night
>   *wandering*

>   amusement of darkness. . . .   (*CP*, 269)

>   First, down the sidewalk
>   where laborers feed their dirty
>   glistening torsos sandwiches
>   and Coca-Cola, *with yellow helmets
>   on.* They protect them from falling
>   bricks, I guess.   (*CP*, 257)

normally I don't think of sounds as colored unless I'm feeling *corrupt*
concrete Rimbaud obscurity of emotion which is simple and very definite
even lasting. . . .   (*CP*, 331)

>   Someone else's Leica sitting on the table
>   the black kitchen table *I am painting*
>   the floor yellow, Bill is painting it. . . .   (*CP*, 393)

SPATIAL AND TEMPORAL DISSOLVES

>   now it is dark on 2d Street near the abbatoir
>   and a smell as of hair comes up the dovecotes
>   as the gentleman poles a pounce of pigeons
>   in the lower East Sideness rippling river
>   where have you gone, Ashes, and up and out
>   where the Sorbonne commissions frigidaires
>   from Butor and Buffet and Alechinsky storages
>   Beauty! said Vera Prentiss-Simpson to Pal Joe
>   and the hideaway was made secure against the hares   (*CP*, 324)

> I walk through the luminous humidity
> passing the House of Seagram with its wet
> and its loungers and the construction to
> the left that closed the sidewalk if
> I ever get to be a construction worker
> I'd like to have a silver hat please   (*CP,* 335)

When these syntactic and prosodic devices are used in conjunction, we get a poetry of great speed, openness, flexibility, and defiance of expectations. Like the "all-over" painting, an O'Hara lyric often seems intentionally deprived of a beginning, middle, and end; it is an instantaneous performance. Syntactic energy is thus equivalent to the painter's "push and pull"—the spatial tensions that keep a surface alive and moving. The rapid cuts from one spatial or temporal zone to another, moreover, give the poetry its peculiar sense of immediacy: everything is absorbed into the NOW.

4. *The Engaged Self: Personism in Action*

"Personism ... does not have anything to do with personality or intimacy, far from it." What does O'Hara mean by this enigmatic statement in the Manifesto? And what is the meaning of his frequent slurs on confessional poetry?[25] Let us try to sort out these distinctions.

In O'Hara's major poems, as is surely apparent to even the most casual reader, the first person is ubiquitous. In "Music," the pronoun "I" and its cognates appear ten times in the space of twenty-one lines. Yet, unlike the typical autobiographical poem with its circular structure (present–past–return to the present with renewed insight), "Music" does not explore the speaker's past so as to determine what has made him the person he is; it does not, for that matter, "confess" or "reveal" anything about his inner psychic life. The role of the "I" is to respond rather than to confess—to observe, to watch, to be attentive to things. The poet's ruminations are "Meditations in an Emergency" not "*on* an Emergency"—an important distinction for it suggests that the self, no longer able to detach itself from the objects it perceives, dissolves and becomes part of the external landscape. As in Pasternak's

Safe Conduct, one of O'Hara's favorite books,[26] the "I" fragments into the surfaces it contemplates. Hence the poet can only tell us what he *does* (what books he buys, what he eats, where he is walking, what he is saying and to whom); how he *responds* to external stimuli, whether traffic jams, headlines, nasty remarks made by friends, or a visit to an art gallery; and what he *recalls* (fragments from the past in the form of sharply visualized scenes float up into his conscious mind). But he makes no attempt to reflect upon the larger human condition, to derive meaning from a series of past incidents, or to make judgments upon his former self, as Robert Lowell does in the *Life Studies* poems. Indeed, the past is often so immediate that it becomes the present, as we shall see when we consider some of O'Hara's great memory poems. In this connection, it is interesting to note that O'Hara substitutes titles like "In Memory of My Feelings" for Yeats's "In Memory of Major Robert Gregory" or Lowell's "My Last Afternoon with Uncle Devereux Winslow." It is a matter of reifying a feeling rather than remembering another person or a particular event; in so doing, that feeling becomes part of the poet's present.

Here the shift in pronouns, discussed in the preceding section, is relevant. When O'Hara switches from "I" to "one" in "A Step Away From Them," he enlarges the poem's horizons, making the seemingly personal situation (going for a walk during lunch hour) fictive, theatrical. Rimbaud's "Je est un autre" ("I is somebody else") provides a key to O'Hara's Personism. The poet's "I" is distanced by various devices: self-deprecatory humor, long-angle shots, fantasy—"If I seem to you / to have lavender lips under the leaves of the world. . . ." Again, the confusing second-person references extend the range of the poem, drawing the reader into the situation. "Clasp me in your handkerchief like a tear!" the poet exclaims, and immediately we are drawn into the magic circle. We are *there.*

Kenneth Koch has called the *Collected Poems* "a collection of created moments that illuminate a whole life," and many readers have agreed that the volume is in essence one long poem, that once they began to read O'Hara, they could not put the book down.[27] This suggests to me that "Personism" works in a special way. In the course of the *Collected Poems,* we come to know the speaker very much as we know a friend; we see him in all his moods—exuberant, sensual, ecstatic, playful, interested, attentive, remote, bored, depressed, despairing, alternately loving and bitchy. The more one reads the poems, the more one longs to know how "Frank" will react to a particular event, whether it is a headline, a lovers' quarrel, or a traffic jam. The "aesthetic of attention" invites our response so that ultimately the poet's experience becomes ours.

Perhaps the closest model I can find for O'Hara's lyric voice is that of Mayakovksy, whose poetry O'Hara had been reading avidly since the early fifties.[28] Here is a section from the famous "I Love" of 1922 in the George Reavy translation:

> Adults have much to do.
> Their pockets are stuffed with rubles.
> Love?
> Certainly!
> For about a hundred rubles.
> But I,
> homeless,
> thrust
> my hands
> into my torn pockets
> and slouch about, goggle-eyed.
> Night.
> You put on your best dress.
> You relax with wives and widows.
> Moscow,
> with the ring of its endless Sadovayas
> choked me in its embraces.
> The hearts
> of amorous women
> go tic-toc.
> On a bed of love the partners feel ecstatic.
> Stretched out like Passion Square
> I caught the wild heartbeat of capital cities.[29]

Despite Mayakovsky's straightforward syntax and short lines, his tone looks ahead to O'Hara's. Thus he shifts from flat statement ("Adults have much to do") to an unexpected question and answer ("Love? / Certainly!"), from first person ("But I, / homeless") to second ("You put on your best dress. / You relax with wives and widows"), from present tense (lines 1–14) to past (lines 15–17) and back to the present. The last three lines juxtapose third-person observation (it is not clear whether the poet is himself one of the partners "On a bed of love") to personal recollection, as "Stretched out like Passion Square / I caught the wild heartbeat of capital cities."

The mood of the poem is buoyant, exclamatory, highly emotional. Gradually, Mayakovsky draws the reader into his personal circle so that we too catch "the wild heartbeat of capital cities." And yet "I Love" skirts sentimentality because the poet knows how foolish he is; in the second stanza, we read, "I know where lodges the heart in others. / In the breast—as everyone knows! / But with me / anatomy has gone mad: / nothing but heart / roaring everywhere" (p. 161).

Such rapid transitions from lyricism to buffoonery characterize many of O'Hara's best poems, for example: "Adieu to Norman, Bon Jour to Joan and Jean-Paul," "Poem (Khrushchev is coming on the right day!)," "Mary Desti's Ass," and especially "A True Account of Talking to the Sun at Fire Island," which is O'Hara's adaptation of Mayakovsky's "An Extraordinary Adventure which befell Vladimir Mayakovsky in a Summer Cottage."[30]

To recapitulate: O'Hara's poetry is characterized by a remarkable confluence of styles. Aside from the influence of painting, discussed in the last chapter, and the close bonds between O'Hara's lyric and the arts of film and music, the poems reflect an unusual combination of literary influences. Dada and Surrealism continue to stand behind O'Hara's distinctive imagery—an imagery inclining toward artifice and the landscape of dream. The colloquialism and celebration of ordinary experience recall Williams and, to a lesser extent, the later Auden; but the use of proper names and documentary "evidence" seems to derive from Pound rather than Williams. I have also noted that O'Hara's syntactic structures were influenced by Apollinaire and Reverdy, while his peculiar brand of Personism can be traced back to Mayakovsky, Pasternak, and Rimbaud.[31]

The *Collected Poems* is, in short, a very learned (detractors would say, an eclectic) book. O'Hara's reputation as casual improvisator, unschooled doodler, could hardly miss the mark more completely. Indeed, he used to call aspiring poets who wanted to "tell it like it is," to throw convention to the winds, the "Campfire Boys."[32] His own sense of poetic form was very different. As he once wrote to Bill Berkson with reference to musical composition, "you don't know whether it's a piece or not unless some convention is at least referred to." "There is," he adds, "about as much freedom in the composition of music as there is in a prison recreation yard."[33] Surely "freedom" in poetry has similar limitations.

RESHAPING THE GENRES

One of the special pleasures of reading O'Hara's poetry is to see how the poet reanimates traditional genres. Ode, elegy, pastoral, autobiographical poem, occasional verse, love song, litany—all these turn up in O'Hara's poetry, although his tendency is to parody the model or at least to subvert its "normal" conventions. Let us look at some of the poet's most interesting generic transformations.

1. The "Surreal-Autobiographical" Poem

This group, which includes such poems as "There I Could Never Be a Boy," "In Memory of My Feelings," "Ode to Michael Goldberg ('s Birth and Other Births)," "Crow Hill," and "A Short History of Bill Berkson" has its source in the Romantic tradition. "There I Could Never Be a Boy," for example, with its allusions to Keats's "Endymion" and its echoes of Dylan Thomas's "Fern Hill," is a kind of Wordsworthian portrait of the poet as imaginative child, whose heightened sensibility can create its own worlds ("I rode like a god when the horse reared"; "in the billowing air I was fleet and green / riding blackly through the ethereal night / toward men's words which I gracefully understood"), but who suffers from the terrible repression of adults: "At a cry from mother I fell to my knees!" and "All things are tragic / when a mother watches!" (*CP*, 216–17). This last note is Rimbaldian, recalling "Les poètes de sept ans," and gives a slightly ironic edge to the poet's Romantic vision.

"Ode to Michael Goldberg" similarly presents Wordsworthian moments of vision, but its structure offers a more complex network of variations and oppositions. The mood is alternately somber and light-hearted; events are viewed seriously only to be parodied a moment later. Thus the mowing scene, during which the boy has his first glimpse of sex:

> Yellow morning
> 　　　　　silent, wet
> 　　　　　　　　　　blackness under the trees over stone walls
> hay smelling faintly of semen. . . . 　　　　　　　　　　(*CP*, 291)

is juxtaposed to short, staccato quatrains, comically recalling Frank's first experiences at the movies:

> 　　　　　Karen Morley got shot
> 　　　　　in the back by an arrow
> 　　　　　I think she was an heiress
> 　　　　　it came through her bathroom door. . . .

This scene now modulates into a momentary return to a realistic present: "I'd like to stay / in this field forever / and think of nothing / but these sounds, / these smells and the tickling grasses / "up your ass, Sport," and then dissolves, in turn, into the touching account of the poet's first intimations of his future vocation:

> 　　　　　Up on the mountainous hill
> 　　　　　behind the confusing house
> 　　　　　where I lived, I went each
> 　　　　　day after school and some nights
> 　　　　　with my various dogs. . . .
>
> 　　　　　the wind sounded exactly like
> 　　　　　Stravinsky
> 　　　　　　　　　　I first recognized art
> 　　　　　as wildness, and it seemed right,
> 　　　　　　　　　　I mean rite, to me
>
> 　　　　　climbing the water tower I'd
> 　　　　　look out for hours in wind
> 　　　　　and the world seemed rounder
> 　　　　　and fiercer and I was happier
> 　　　　　because I wasn't scared of falling off
>
> 　　　　　nor off the horses, the horses!
> 　　　　　to hell with the horses, bay and black 　　　　(*CP*, 292)

Here the wind is very much a Romantic image, and lines 12–13 recall Wallace Stevens's "The World is Larger in Summer." Yet the punning (a slightly coy device) on "right" (*Rites of Spring*) parodies the Romantic theme as does the final "to hell with the horses." And the next passage moves away from Romantic heightened consciousness to a Rimbaldian scatological vision of adolescent masturbation:

> what one must do is done in a red twilight
> on colossally old and dirty furniture with knobs,
> and on Sunday afternoons you meet in a high place
> watching the Sunday drivers and the symphonic sadness
> stopped, a man in a convertible put his hand up a girl's skirt
> and again the twitching odor of hay, like a minor irritation
> that gives you a hardon, and again the roundness of horse noises
>
> (*CP*, 292)

The poem continues to shift ground in this way, passages that detail concrete particulars being foregrounded against a backdrop of more abstract ruminations. The overall structure is reminiscent of *Me II*, Larry Rivers's "painted autobiography," which is, according to Sam Hunter, "composed of small, scattered vignettes of family life from babyhood to full maturity. First family snapshots and then special aspects of illustrated journalism offered Rivers a sense of continuity with the movement of life, while putting the necessary distance between him and events."[34] So too O'Hara absorbs the family snapshot into the larger movement of life so as to create a dynamic composition.

"Ode to Michael Goldberg" is a charming poem, but I myself prefer the enigmatic, elliptical "In Memory of My Feelings" (1956)—in my opinion not only O'Hara's best autobiographical poem, but one of the great poems of our time. Its central theme, the fragmentation and reintegration of the inner self—a self that threatens continually to dissipate under the assault of outer forces—is a familiar Romantic topos, but O'Hara turns the autobiographical convention inside out, fusing fantasy and realism in a painterly collage-poem, whose form is at one with its meaning. Grace Hartigan, to whom "In Memory" is dedicated, suggests that O'Hara's aim in this poem is to define "inner containment"—"how to be *open* but not violated, how *not to panic*."[35] The structure of the poem embodies this theme; it is an extremely

"open" lyric sequence that nevertheless never gives way to formlessness, never "panics."

O'Hara's actual biography plays a part in the poem, but it is subordinated to a series of hallucinatory visions and memories. The implication all along is that what matters is not what happened but how one
felt or feels about it; the poet writes, after all, in memory of his "feelings." And evanescent as these feelings are, O'Hara unifies his kaleidoscopic visions by repeating certain key images: the hunt (a hunt for
what or for whom?), nautical references (from the gondola of the
opening to the "German prisoners on the *Prinz Eugen*" of Part 4), and
a procession of circus animals, exotic locales (Borneo, Ramadan,
Venice's Grand Canal, the sands of Arabia, Persia, the mountains of
Greece), and Romantic characters (Manfred, the gondolier, Lord
Nelson, Shanghai Lil, a Hittite, an African prince, a "Chinaman
climbing a mountain," "an Indian / sleeping on a scalp.") In the
"midst" of all "these ruses" is the serpent, who stands here for the
poet's true self—the self that must triumph if he is to become an artist.

Part 1 begins:

> My quietness has a man in it, he is transparent
> and he carries me quietly, like a gondola, through the streets.
> He has several likenesses, like stars and years, like numerals.
>
> (*CP*, 252)

This enigmatic passage is best understood in terms of Rimbaud's concept of the "dédoublement du moi," the split between the ordinary,
empirical ego and the poet's created self. Rimbaud, for that matter,
stands squarely behind the poem, Part 4 echoing the catalogue of
assumed selves in Part IV of "Enfance." [36] Another probable source is
Apollinaire's "Cortège," in which the self is painfully assembled from
bits and pieces of the poet's past identities. At the outset, then, Frank
O'Hara the "poet" is still dominated by Frank O'Hara the man who
carries him "quietly, like a gondola, through the streets." He has not
yet articulated poetic speech; it is only a "quietness," containing "a
number of naked selves," longing to emerge but kept in check by "so
many pistols I have borrowed to protect myselves / from creatures
who too readily recognize my weapons / and have murder in their
heart!"

The "I" thus regards himself as victim but of whom or of what? The would-be murderers are especially frightening because they are wholly disguised: "in winter / they are warm as roses, in the desert / taste of chilled anisette." When the poet tries to escape his condition by assuming the role of Byron's Manfred, climbing to the mountain top "into the cool skies," he is attacked from all sides:

> An elephant takes up his trumpet
> money flutters from the windows of cries, silk stretching its mirror
> across shoulder blades. A gun is "fired."   (*CP,* 253)

And now, in a passage reminiscent of the "Circe" episode in *Ulysses,* the poet remembers moments of unspecified but terrible humiliation:

> One of me rushes
> to window #13 and one of me raises his whip and one of me
> flutters up from the center of the track amidst the pink flamingoes
> and underneath their hooves as they round the last turn my lips
> are scarred and brown, brushed by tails, masked in dirt's lust,
> definition, open mouths gasping for the cries of the bettors for the lungs
> of earth.
> So many of my transparencies could not resist the race!

After this nightmare scene, with its strong overtones of sexual fear, there is only emptiness, a self in fragments: "dried mushrooms, pink feathers, tickets, / a flaking moon drifting across the muddied teeth." The image of the serpent appears for the first time, and the "I" identifies with it, but this serpent does not yet have power. A victim of "the hunter," its eyes "redden at sight of those thorny fingernails," and "My transparent selves / flail about like vipers in a pail, writhing and hissing." Finally, the "acquiline serpent comes to resemble the Medusa." Part 1 ends on a note of death; the poet's old self must die if it is to be reborn.

In the poem's opening movement, memory thus appears in the guise of surrealistic fantasy, frightening in its very indeterminacy. The perspective of Part 2 is, by contrast, that of more straightforward autobiography, the connecting link between the two occurring in the opening lines: "The dead hunting / and the alive, ahunted."

> My father, my uncle,
> my grand-uncle and the several aunts. My
> grand-aunt dying for me, like a talisman, in the war,
> before I had even gone to Borneo. . . .   (*CP*, 253)

The irony, of course, is that these relatives did not die "for" the poet at all, but that their death was supposed to pain and trouble him whereas his recollection of the group merely resembles "the coolness of a mind / like a shuttered suite in the Grand Hotel / where mail arrives for my incognito." "Trying desperately to count them as they die" becomes a meaningless exercise: this is the way memory does not, indeed cannot operate.

But how to transcend "these numbers"? In Part 3, the speaker chooses one option: he assumes the role of hero. Like the "moi" of Rimbaud's *Saison en enfer,* he reappears as noble savage in the deserts of Arabia ("The most arid stretch is often the richest"), swallows "the stench of the camel's spit," and then reappears in a series of guises: French Revolutionary, Napoleonic platoon leader, and finally as "meek subaltern . . . violating an insane mistress." These various roles merge in a hallucinatory sequence, the mistress now following the poet "across the desert / like a goat, towards a mirage . . . and lying in an oasis one day, / playing catch with coconuts, they suddenly smell oil."

Absorption in history is one way of escaping the empirical self: "Beneath these lives / the ardent lover of history hides." But the moment doesn't last and in Part 4, we switch, once again, to the real Frank O'Hara visiting Chicago with Jane Freilicher ("the fountains! the Art Institute, the Y / for both sexes, absent Christianity"), a Frank who is enchanted by an early morning vision (before Jane is up) of a Norwegian freighter on the "copper lake," "on the deck a few dirty men . . . Beards growing, and the constant anxiety over looks." Remembering Grace Hartigan's portraits of himself,[37] he now merges his identity with that of the seamen. And out of this fusion, the poet achieves the breakthrough he has longed for all along:

> Grace
> to be born and live as variously as possible. The conception
> of the masque barely suggests the sordid identifications.
> I am a Hittite in love with a horse I don't know what blood's

in me I feel like an African prince I am a girl walking downstairs
in a red pleated dress with heels I am a champion taking a fall
I am a jockey with a sprained ass-hole I am the light mist
                              in which a face appears
and it is another face of blonde I am a baboon eating a banana
I am a dictator looking at his wife I am a doctor eating a child
and the child's mother smiling I am a Chinaman climbing a mountain
I am a child smelling his father's underwear I am an Indian
sleeping on a scalp
                    and my pony is stamping in the birches,
and I've just caught sight of the *Niña*, the *Pinta* and the *Santa Maria*.
                    What land is this, so free?   (*CP*, 256)

In the first version (1955) of this passage, O'Hara arranged these
images in four 4-line stanzas, each having the refrain "What land is
this, so free?" which appears only once in the final draft. The first
stanza, for instance, went like this:

> I don't know what blood's in me
> I feel like an African prince
> I am a girl walking downstairs
> in a red pleated dress with heels
>   what land is this, so free?

(See Notes to the *CP*, 538)

By running together two clauses in one line on the one hand, and
breaking a clause in half at a line-end, on the other, O'Hara stresses the
multiplicity of selves, the chaos and plenitude of life which cannot be
presented in the orderly little ballad stanzas of the original. In a moment of heightened consciousness, the poet is able to assume all roles:
he turns Indian, catching sight of the *Niña, Pinta,* and *Santa Maria,*
and watching the white men arrive (again an echo of Rimbaud's "Les
blancs débarquent" ["the white men are landing!"] in the *Saison*). And
these white men bring him, not a real horse (no more camels, goats, or
elephants!) but "the horse I fell in love with on the frieze"—in short, a
work of art.

In this moment of ecstasy, the fragmented self, victimized by nameless attackers, is reborn: "And now it is the serpent's turn. / I am not
quite you, but almost, the opposite of visionary." So begins Part 5. The

"visionary" is no longer needed, for what the poet has learned is that to be an artist is to come to terms with life itself: "When you turn your head / can you feel your heels, undulating? that's what it is / to be a serpent." Now "the heart . . . bubbles with red ghosts, since to move is to love." The poet can now reject the hero figure of Part 3: "The hero, trying to unhitch his parachute, / stumbles over me. It is our last embrace." Out of the body comes the "cancerous statue" which is the poet's real self, which "against my will / against my love" has "become art." And the poem concludes triumphantly:

> and I have lost what is always and everywhere
> present, the scene of my selves, the occasion of these ruses,
> which I myself and singly must now kill
> and save the serpent in their midst.
>
> (*CP*, 257)

Few poets of our time, I would posit, could manage the difficult structural and textural modulations of this poem, its swift and sudden transitions from long flowing line to short choppy one, from romantic melody to jazz syncopation, from fact to fantasy, past to present, self to other, nightmare landscape to the direct presentation of things. The French influence is as important as ever, but it is now thoroughly domesticated, absorbed into the fabric of colloquial American idiom: "My / 12 years since they all died, philosophically speaking" or "I'm looking for my Shanghai Lil." And on every rereading, some new marvelous detail strikes our attention. Notice how the "barrage balloon" of Part One's hunting scene reappears, quite unexpectedly, as the hero's parachute in Part 5. The poem ends on what Grace Hartigan has called a note of "inner containment"; the "serpent self" triumphs over "the occasion of these ruses."

2. Poems for Emergent Occasions: The "I do this, I do that" Poem

What are probably O'Hara's best known poems—"Adieu to Norman, Bon Jour to Joan and Jean-Paul," "A Step Away from Them," "Personal Poem," "Lana Turner has Collapsed!"—all belong to the genre of the occasional poem, although with rare exception, the occasion is not an important public one (or even a pivotal private event like a wedding or a *bon voyage* party), but an ordinary incident like a luncheon date or a weekend beach party.

Such occasional poetry gave O'Hara a chance to display his wonderful sense of humor. "Khrushchev is coming on the right day!", for example, explores the essential absurdity of our responses to the latest news. The poem is not really about Khrushchev at all; rather, it pokes fun at the American desire to make foreign dignitaries, especially from an alien country like Russia, feel "at home" in the United States. Even a dour leader like Khrushchev, a person who probably mistrusts all things American, the poem implies, will have to be pleased with New York on such a marvelous September day, a day on which "the cool graced light / is pushed off the enormous glass piers by hard wind / and everything is tossing, hurrying on up" (*CP,* 340). The irony, of course, is that Khrushchev himself couldn't care less; he has hardly come to America in order to savor the fall weather. But the poet's own mood is one of such buoyancy, such *joie de vivre,* that he wants even Khrushchev to enjoy his visit, and so, when the Puerto Rican cab driver complains to him that "this country / has everything but *politesse,*" the poet thinks, in a marvelously silly nonsequitur, that "Khrushchev was probably being carped at / in Washington, no *politesse.*" Ultimately, the poem implies, none of it matters; what matters is that it is one of those rare New York mornings when one actually loves walking to work because "the light seems to be eternal / and joy seems to be inexorable." And so the train that "bears Khrushchev on to Pennsylvania Station" becomes part of the "tossing," "blowing" life of the city, ultimately merging with the "hard wind."

Yet O'Hara's own attitude to his improvisatory occasional poems is curiously equivocal. In a letter to Fairfield Porter, he contrasts his own work to John Ashbery's with reference to the two sons (the "bad" one played by Frank's idol, James Dean) in the film *East of Eden:*

> I think one of the things about *East of Eden* is that I am very materialistic and John is very spiritual, in our work especially. As an example, the one boy gives the father $5000 he has earned by war-profiteering in beans for a birthday present, but the good boy gives him the announcement of his engagement which symbolizes the good life the father wants for both

sons. John's work is full of dreams and a kind of moral excellence and kind sentiments. Mine is full of objects for their own sake, spleen and ironically intimate observation which may be truthfulness (in the lyrical sense) but is more likely to be egotistical cynicism masquerading as honesty.[38]

This is unnecessarily harsh self-criticism, although the distinction O'Hara makes between his own mode and Ashbery's is not entirely beside the point. I shall return to this distinction in the next chapter. In any case, although some of O'Hara's lesser poems may suffer from what he calls "egotistical cynicism masquerading as honesty," his "ironically intimate observation" usually transforms life into art, preventing "objects" from being treated merely "for their own sake." Certainly this is the case in the witty Khrushchev poem.

My personal favorite among O'Hara's occasional poems is "Joe's Jacket," which was published in *Big Table* in 1960 but was not included in *Lunch Poems*. This poem was written during the summer of 1959 when Frank lived with Joe LeSueur at 441 East 9th Street. It was the summer he met and fell in love with Vincent Warren. This is the background of the poem which is "about" a weekend houseparty in Southampton and alludes obliquely to the complex set of relationships between Frank, Vincent, and Joe, as well as to Frank's long-standing literary friendship with Kenneth Koch and his wife Janice.

On the surface, "Joe's Jacket" is like a Scott Fitzgerald short story in miniature: the summer weekend parlor-car ride to Southampton, the drunken party, the morning after the night before, the return to the hot city, the Monday morning hangover. But these incidents are presented in a series of separate "shots," reminiscent less of Fitzgerald than of a film like Godard's *Weekend*. In this connection, the poem's metrics are especially ingenious. The whole "story" is told as if in one long breath. The poem's long (13-20-syllable) lines are almost wholly unpunctuated and almost all run-on; there is not a single full stop in the space of fifty-two lines. Once we have "entrained" with Frank, Jap, and Vincent, therefore, we cannot really stop until the whirlwind weekend is over. Yet this "action poem" simulates speed and acceleration by careful structural means; it is a good example of the "push and pull" technique O'Hara alludes to in his letter to Larry Rivers.

The poem opens on a note of pleasurable anticipation:

> Entraining to Southampton in the parlor car with Jap and Vincent, I
> see life as a penetrable landscape lit from above
> like it was in my Barbizonian kiddy days when automobiles
> were owned by the same people for years and the Alfa Romeo
> was only a rumor under the leaves beside the viaduct and I
> pretending to be adult felt the blue within me and the light up there
> no central figure me, I was some sort of cloud or a gust of wind
> at the station a crowd of drunken fishermen on a picnic Kenneth
> is hard to find but we find, through all the singing, Kenneth smiling
> it is off to Janice's bluefish and the incessant talk of affection
> expressed as excitability and spleen to be recent and strong
> and not unbearably right in attitude, full of confidences
> now I will say it, thank god, I knew you would   (*CP*, 329)

En route in the train with Jap (Jasper Johns) and Vincent, the poet feels euphoric and light-hearted; his is, at least for the moment, a stable and secure world. Like a painting of the Barbizon school, whose source of light comes from a definite point, his "landscape" seems "penetrable" as he recalls the orderly days of his childhood "when automobiles / were owned by the same people for years," and he "felt the blue" within himself. Blue is O'Hara's favorite color; a whole essay could be devoted to its appearances and uses in the *Collected Poems*. To feel "the blue within" oneself is to be free, happy, imaginative; to become, further, "some sort of cloud or gust of wind" is again a Romantic image of creative fulfillment. And even the dinner Janice has prepared is "bluefish."

It is interesting to note how different this whole passage is from the poems of O'Hara's mentors and contemporaries. The phrase "life as penetrable landscape" immediately recalls "Life changed to landscape" in Robert Lowell's "Beyond the Alps," but Frank's train ride is not a symbolic journey from the old world to the new; it is merely a trip on the Long Island Railroad. Again, "Joe's Jacket" marks a certain withdrawal from the Williams mode of O'Hara's earlier poems; for, whereas Williams would have captured the sense of the permanent moment in all its perceptual immediacy, O'Hara rapidly shifts from the present to the past and, later in the poem, to the future, absorbing both past and future into what happens *now*. And finally, despite its air of documentary realism, the opening scene of "Joe's Jacket" is some-how fantastic, with its dreamlike image of the Alfa Romeo, "only a rumor under the leaves beside the viaduct," and its condensed, amus-ingly devious account of the dinner conversation, where it is never clear who says what, the whole tone of the exchange being captured by the running together of verbal snatches: "now I will say it, thank god, I knew you would."

The "excitability and spleen" which begin to surface toward the end of this section come into the foreground in Part 2, which depicts "an enormous party mesmerizing comers in the disgathering light." Notice that the "light," previously coming from a known source, is now "disgathering." And Frank's memories of his "Barbizonian kiddy days" now give way to a drinking marathon:

> I drink to smother my sensitivity for a while so I won't stare away
> I drink to kill the fear of boredom, the mounting panic of it
> I drink to reduce my seriousness so a certain spurious charm
> can appear and win its flickering little victory over noise
> I drink to die a little and increase the contrast of this questionable moment
> and then I am going home, purged of everything except anxiety and selfdistrust
> now I will say it, thank god, I knew you would

When this last line is repeated, it no longer sounds good-humored or light-hearted. Something nasty and unexplained has happened, but we never learn what it is. A lovers' quarrel? An insult? A misunder-standing? A general feeling of malaise, of being unloved? In any case, it appropriately begins to rain.

Now this scene dissolves in its turn, giving way to the hour before dawn; the "enormous party" gives way to "an enormous window morning." The wind returns but the poet now views its force with total despair: "the beautiful desperation of a tree / fighting off strangula-tion." His bed has "an ugly calm"; the book he reaches for contains D. H. Lawrence's "The Ship of Death"; in the next line, ship and bed merge as the poet begins "slowly to drift and then to sink." Just as he reaches this low point, "the car horn mysteriously starts to honk, no one is there / and Kenneth comes out and stops it in the soft green lightless stare." This last phrase recalls Wallace Stevens's Green Night: it is the time of creativity and before we know it, Frank and Kenneth are working away on the latter's libretto, totally absorbed in their task. Frank's anxiety is temporarily dispelled: "I did not drift / away I did not die I am there with Haussmann and the rue de Rivoli / and the spirits of beauty, art and progress, pertinent and mobile / in their worldly way, and musical and strange the sun comes out."

The beauty of "Joe's Jacket" is that the poem refuses to end on this high Romantic note. Sunrise is all very well, but "Entraining" invariably means "returning," and so the fourth stanza begins:

> returning by car the forceful histories of myself and Vincent loom
> like the city hour after hour closer and closer to the future I am here

"I am here" counterpointed to the words "I am there," four lines above, is especially poignant. The poet realizes that he is not part of the exciting Paris art world; he is *here*. There is no escape. But returning to Joe (nothing is said of Vincent's departure or subsequent movements) has its comforts: "Joe is still up and we talk / only of the immediate present." At 4 A.M., the "sleeping city" is "bathed in an unobtrusive light which lends things / coherence and an absolute." This "unobtrusive light" replaces the earlier extremes; it is the light of common day, of neutrality, of things as they are in our normal, everyday lives. As such, it does lend things a kind of "coherence."

And so, in Part 5, the poet, now all alone after Joe has finally gone to bed, prepares "for the less than average" working day. The word "calm" is repeated three times within two lines, but this is not the pleasant tranquility of the parlor car; it is the calm of empty routine, dead ritual. Frank can only face the day by wearing Joe's seersucker jacket, a jacket he last wore on a European holiday:

> there it was on my Spanish plaza back
> and hid my shoulders from San Marco's pigeons was jostled on the /
> Kurfürstendamm
> and sat opposite Ashes in an enormous leather chair in the Continental
> (*CP*, 330)

Rome, Venice, Berlin, Paris with John Ashbery—Joe's jacket has seen him through all these places:

> it is all enormity and life it has protected me and kept me here on
> many occasions as a symbol does when the heart is full and risks no speech
> a precaution I loathe as the pheasant loathes the season and is preserved
> it will not be need, it will be just what it is and just what happens

Only now do we understand the title of the poem. "Joe's Jacket" is the talisman that protects Frank from daily misfortunes; as a synecdoche, it stands, of course, for Joe's love. But Frank also resents its protection ("a precaution I loathe"), and in a second, ironic sense, Joe's jacket is his straitjacket: "Entraining" with Vincent, he ultimately returns to Joe. The jacket is, then, an ordering principle which the poet alternately needs and resents.

"In Memory of My Feelings" explores the artist's need to protect his "naked selves" from external chaos. "Joe's Jacket" has a related theme: how to order one's life somehow, how to ward off anxiety in favor of some kind of coherence. But because this is a poem about the life of an artist, "order" is always to be distinguished from mere routine. The poet goes through the routine of "rising for the less than average day," and having his coffee, but he must fight routine just as he previously fought "anxiety and self-distrust." Happiness comes in those moments when life and art are one, when Frank and Kenneth work in harmony on the opera libretto while the rest of the household is asleep. Such moments of "soft green lightless[ness]" redeem life, but they are rare. Most of the time, one can only cope by accepting "just what it is and just what happens." And "what happens" is that Frank pursues Vincent, quarrels with Kenneth and his friends, and returns, worn out, to Joe. The tension between *just what is* and what one yearns for ("I am here"—"I am there") is beautifully dramatized in this most seemingly spontaneous but most carefully structured "I do this, I do that" poem.

3. Odes

In a reading given at Buffalo on 25 September 1964, O'Hara prefaced his rendition of "Ode on Lust" with the remark, "I wrote it because the ode is so formidable to write. I thought if I call it an ode it will work out."[39] This comment, facetious though it is, sheds some light on the group of long poems written in 1957–58 and published by the Tiber Press in 1960 under the title *Odes*. There are, of course, earlier as well as later odes scattered throughout the *Collected Poems* (and such long litanies as "To the Film Industry in Crisis" and "Ave Maria" also properly belong to this class); the term "ode," moreover, is used fairly loosely. "Ode to Michael Goldberg" is, as I have argued, an autobiographical poem on the Wordsworthian model; "Ode (to Joseph Le-Sueur) on the Arrow that Flieth by Day" resembles such occasional poems as "A Step Away from Them" and "Adieu to Norman." Nevertheless, most of the "odes" in the Tiber Press book do have certain common characteristics that merit discussion.

Such poems as "Ode to Joy," "Ode on Lust," and "Ode to Willem de Kooning" reveal a very different side of O'Hara from the one we have considered so far. Their tone is more oracular, impersonal, and exclamatory, their syntax insistently paratactic (the "and" clauses piling up to create an almost unbearable intensity), their prosody more formal and elaborate than is typical of O'Hara. "Ode to Joy" (*CP*, 281), for example, has traces of the Greater or Pindaric Ode. Not that its three stanzas resemble the Pindaric model (strophe—antistrophe—epode), but the subject is "elevated" (the triumph of love over time), the tone sublime, and the three "strophes" have an intricate and elaborate prosodic scheme. Each strophe has thirteen lines, longer lines alternating with somewhat shorter ones in a fixed pattern, with the final line invariably having only four or five syllables and two stresses. In each strophe, lines 2, 4, 7, 8, 12, and 13 are indented. The phrase "no more dying," which appears in the opening line, becomes the refrain, reappearing after the first strophe and again at the end of the ode. Thus, although O'Hara's strophes contain neither rhyme nor meter, and although enjambment is used so consistently that the integrity of the individual line is somewhat obscured, the overall pattern is considerably more formal than that of, say, "The Arrow that Flieth by Day." Certainly, its visual appearance on the page is very tidy, the three strophes looking exactly alike.

"Ode on Lust" (*CP*, 282) has a similarly structured visual pattern. Three boxlike stanzas whose lines have six to eight syllables are juxtaposed to two long, snakelike couplets, in which the lines range from seventeen to twenty-three syllables; the third "box" is followed by a kind of coda, made up of five such long lines. The effect is to create what looks like a composition for solo voice and chorus, the "long line" sections responding to the short, abrupt ones.

Thematically, these odes are curious for their avoidance of Personism; they are perhaps closer to such earlier long poems as "Second Avenue" and "Easter." "Ode to Joy" is a celebration of erotic love, of sexual bliss as a way of defying death. This theme is insistently Romantic but O'Hara's imagery is often surrealistic:

> and the streets will be filled with racing forms
> and the photographs of murderers and narcissists and movie stars
>   will swell from the walls and books alive in steaming rooms
>   to press against our burning flesh not once but interminably
> as water flows down hill into the full-lipped basin
> and the adder dives for the ultimate ostrich egg
> and the feather cushion preens beneath a reclining monolith
>   that's sweating with post-exertion visibility and sweetness
>   near the grave of love
>   No more dying

The "reclining monolith / that's sweating with post-exertion visibility and sweetness" is a sly sexual image reminiscent of a Miró painting; the poem contains many such comic-erotic images, thus undercutting its own high Romanticism:

> in the sky a feeling of intemperate fondness will excite the birds
> to swoop and veer like flies crawling across absorbèd limbs
> that weep a pearly perspiration on the sheets of brief attention
> and the hairs dry out that summon anxious declaration of the organs
> as they rise like buildings to the needs of temporary neighbors
> pouring hunger through the heart to feed desire in intravenous ways

Yet despite this injection of parody, "Ode to Joy" is essentially quite serious about its theme: only the ecstasy of loving, the "lava flow[ing]" of sexual consummation has the power to make "Buildings . . . go up in the dizzy air," to "ride . . . heroes through the dark to found / great cities where all life is possible to maintain as long as time," to turn even "the grave of love" into "a lovely sight." "No more dying."

The finest of the 1957–58 odes is, I think, the "Ode on Causality" (*CP*, 302–03). This poem begins on an ironic note with the aphorism, "There is the sense of neurotic coherence," and we soon learn that there is no sense of any kind of coherence, the notion of causality being comically deflated in the last strophe: "what goes up must / come down, what dooms must do, standing still and walking in New York."

After the opening series of witty, seemingly unrelated aphorisms, there is an abrupt shift to a scene at the grave of Jackson Pollock. (In an earlier version, the poem was called "Ode at the Grave of Jackson Pollock," and Donald Allen notes that lines 8–9, in which the little girl Maude shows the poet Pollock's grave, refer to its actual location at the Springs near Easthampton, Long Island [*CP*, 542]). The sight of the grave and the child's comment that "'he isn't under there, he's out in the woods'" leads to a moment of transcendence as the poet prays for his own artistic powers:

and like that child at your grave make me be distant and imaginative
make my lines thin as ice, then swell like pythons
the color of Aurora when she first brought fire to the Arctic in a sled
a sexual bliss inscribe upon the page of whatever energy I burn for art
and do not watch over my life, but read and read through copper earth

not to fall at all, but disappear or burn! seizing a grave by throat
which is the look of earth, its ambiguity of light and sound. . . .

(*CP*, 302)

After rejecting the usual trappings of funeral rites ("for Old Romance was draping dolors on a scarlet mound"), O'Hara concludes by celebrating the great painter in terms of his own art:

let us walk in that nearby forest, staring into the growling trees
in which an era of pompous frivolity or two is dangling /
                                                its knobby knees
and reaching for an audience
                            over the pillar of our deaths a cloud
heaves
          pushed, steaming and blasted
                                        love-propelled and tangled /
                                                        glitteringly
                            has earned himself the title *Bird in Flight*.

The oracular, exclamatory mode of "Ode on Causality" and "Ode to Joy" ("make me be distant and imaginative / make my lines thin as ice, then swell like pythons") recalls neither Wordsworth nor Keats but the Shelley of "Ode to the West Wind" or perhaps the Collins of "Ode on the Poetical Character." But to be perfectly accurate, we would have to say that O'Hara's model is Shelley-cum-Dada, for the "Ode on Causality," like the "Ode to Joy," frequently injects comic burlesque elements like the following:

> sweet scripts to obfuscate the tender subjects of their future lays
> to be layed at all! romanticized, elaborated, fucked, sung, put to "rest"
> is worse than the mild apprehension of a Buddhist type caught halfway up
> the tea-rose trellis with his sickle banging on the Monk's lead window. . . .

Here the pun on "lays," the four-letter words, and the absurd image of the Buddhist and the Monk deflate the lyric intensity of the earlier passage. But in ending his ode with the rhapsodic reference to the painter's apotheosis (he becomes a work of art),[40] the poet recaptures his original ecstasy.

"Ode on Causality" thus provides us with an interesting example of the fusion between disparate modes and conventions. The basic structure of the ode is the "free Pindaric" of Cowley as adapted by Collins and Shelley, but such imagistic passages as "Maude lays down her doll" derive from quite different sources—in this case, Rimbaud's "Enfance, Part II," which begins: "That's she, the little dead girl, behind the rose bushes." At the same time, the aphorisms ("suddenly everyone's supposed to be veined, like marble" or "the rock is the least living of the forms man has fucked"), as well as the passage punning on *lays* which I cited above, introduce a Dada note; they recall Tzara or Apollinaire. The total effect of the poem is that of a Brahms or Schumann *lied,* interrupted at certain junctures by "noise" passages in the vein of Satie or Cage. Such conjunctions are wholly characteristic of O'Hara's lyricism.

4. Love Poems

Finally, I wish to say something about the remarkable series of love poems written for Vincent Warren between 1959 and 1961. O'Hara had been writing love poems ever since his Harvard days, but it was not until he fell in love with the beautiful dancer in 1959 that what he himself called "my delicate and caressing poems" (*CP,* 356) were perfected. These forty-odd erotic lyrics should be read in sequence, although they are not found that way in the chronologically arranged *Collected Poems.*[41] The range of moods from sexual excitement, joy, and hope, to loneliness, delusion, despair, and cynicism, and finally to the stoical acceptance of the way things are is extraordinary. Even such seemingly trivial little songs as "Did you see me walking by the Buick Repairs" (*CP,* 367) repay study. This particular short lyric, with its intricate repetition ("I was thinking of you") and foreshortened last line—"and right now"—recalls Yeats's famed "A Deep-sworn Vow."

The risk of the intimate erotic lyric is that the poet is too close to his own experience to objectify it; in O'Hara's words, "sentiment is always intruding on form" (*CP,* 276). And we do find cases in the Vincent Warren sequence where the sentiment is stated too flatly:

> When I am feeling depressed or anxious sullen
> all you have to do is take your clothes off
> and all is wiped away revealing life's tenderness. . . .
>
> when I am in your presence I feel life is strong
> and will defeat all its enemies and all of mine
> and all of yours and yours in you and mine in me. . . .
>
> (*CP,* 349)

Or again, the poem may succumb to triviality:

> I want some bourbon / you want some oranges / I love the leather
>   jacket Norman gave me
>   and the corduroy coat David
>   gave you, it is more mysterious than spring. . . .   (*CP,* 356)

And occasionally, there is an irritating note of campy cuteness:

> everything
>
> seems slow suddenly and boring except
> for my insatiable thinking towards you
> as you lie asleep completely plotzed and
> gracious as a hillock in the mist. . . .   (*CP,* 354)

But for the most part, the Vincent Warren poems do work because O'Hara defines his sexual longing or sexual pleasure in terms of witty and fantastic hyperbole. He rarely resorts to that stock-in-trade of what I have elsewhere called "corn-porn" poetry[42]—that is, the elaborate metaphor in which the lover's penis is compared to a firehose on a burning deck, the vagina to a cave full of roses, and so on. Rather, his analogies are intentionally absurd; witness the following epigrammatic lyric:

> Some days I feel that I exude a fine dust
> like that attributed to Pylades in the famous
> *Chronica nera areopagitica* when it was found
>
> and it's because an excavationist has
> reached the inner chamber of my heart
> and rustled the paper bearing your name
>
> I don't like that stranger sneezing over our love   (*CP,* 366)

Here the pseudo-learned reference to the recently excavated Greek statue, still "exud[ing] a fine dust," provides the poet with a playful twist on a very familiar theme: the longing to keep one's love all to oneself.

Or again, "To You" (*CP,* 342), which begins as a very conventional love poem with the lines, "What is more beautiful than night / and someone in your arms," shifts ground in the third line to an entirely different frame of reference, the poet now burlesquing his romantic overture:

> that's what we love about art
> it seems to prefer us and stays
>
> if the moon or a gasping candle
> sheds a little light or even dark
> you become a landscape in a landscape
> with rocks and craggy mountains
>
> and valleys full of sweaty ferns
> breathing and lifting into the clouds. . . .

So the landscape of love is defamiliarized, becoming a valley "full of sweaty ferns."

The ability to transform ordinary experience in this way is nowhere more evident than in "You are Gorgeous and I'm Coming" (*CP*, 331), an acrostic poem in which the first letters of successive lines spell out the name Vincent Warren. Here is the first or "Vincent" half:

Vaguely I hear the purple roar of the torn-down Third Avenue El
it sways slightly but firmly like a hand or a golden-downed thigh
normally I don't think of sounds as colored unless I'm feeling corrupt
concrete Rimbaud obscurity of emotion which is simple and very definite
even lasting, yes it may be that dark and purifying wave, /
                          the death of boredom
nearing the heights themselves may destroy you in the pure air
to be further complicated, confused, empty but refilling, exposed to light

Here the love scene becomes a fantastic blend of real and imaginary objects, noises, colors, and movements; such images as "the purple roar of the torn-down Third Avenue El" which "sways lightly but firmly like a hand or a golden-downed thigh" have intensely erotic overtones, but the poet's orgasm is never described overtly. Rather, the long, unpunctuated, sinewy lines with their run-on clauses and condensed catalogues of nouns and adjectives ("corrupt / concrete Rimbaud obscurity of emotion") convey the lover's passion ("empty but refilling," "thundering and shaking") as it moves toward a final crescendo in the poem's last line, which is distinguished by its eleven monosyllables, its repetition of words and sounds (especially voiceless stops), and its internal rhyme (st*ar*s, *are*, f*or*, *our*), to create a stunning cadenza:

newly the heavens stars all out we are all for the captured time of our being

The same technique informs "Poem (Twin spheres full of fur and noise)," although this one begins with a graphic (and some would say, distasteful) description:

          Twin spheres full of fur and noise
          rolling softly up my belly beddening on my chest
          and then my mouth is full of suns
          that softness seems so anterior to that hardness. . . .   (*CP*, 405)

If the piece continued in this vein, it would be just another self-indulgent poem, elaborating unnecessarily on what the poet does in bed. But O'Hara rapidly transforms the "Twin spheres" into celestial bodies, and what began as a description of fellatio becomes a parody Sun God myth:

> jetting I commit the immortal spark jetting
> you give that form to my life the Ancients loved
> those suns are smiling as they move across the sky
> and as your chariot I soon become a myth
> which heaven is it that we inhabit for so long a time
> it must be discovered soon and disappear   (*CP*, 406)

The poet knows he is no Helios driving his golden chariot across the sky; he is not even the golden chariot. But it's nice to think that love confers immortality upon himself and Vincent, even if "the immortal spark" lasts only a moment.

The sense of tentativeness introduced in the poem's last line ("it must be discovered soon and disappear") is found again and again in these love poems, the ecstatic tone of "You are Gorgeous and I'm Coming" giving way, more often than not, to a rueful, self-deprecatory one. "Present," for example, is a kind of parody version of Donne's "The Good Morrow" or "The Extasie"; images of celestial spheres and heavenly bodies are again used as points of reference, but the poet knows he and Vincent are, at best, sublunary lovers, and even then, all too often their paths don't cross, although Frank likes to imagine that they can and do:

>   even now I can lean
> forward across the square and see
> your surprised grey look become greener
> as I wipe the city's moisture from
> your face
>   and you shake the snow
> off onto my shoulder, light as a breath. . . .   (*CP*, 353)

The longing to be with the beloved affords "some peculiar insight," but when the poet supplicates the heavens, he is greeted only by "the mixed-up air."

Perhaps the most moving of the Vincent Warren poems is "St. Paul and All That" (*CP*, 406). It concerns the brief reunion of the lovers at a time when Frank already knows that their love is doomed, that his love is greater than Vincent's. The poem traces the graph of the poet's shifting emotions as he unexpectedly finds Vincent in his room:

> Totally abashed and smiling
>
>   I walk in
>   sit down and
>   face the frigidaire
>
>   it's April
>   no May
>   it's May
>
>   such little things have to be established in morning
>   after the big things of night
>   do you want me to come?

"Totally abashed and smiling" (a phrase picked up later in the poem in the line "full of anxious pleasures and pleasurable anxiety"), Frank tries to act normal: "I walk in / sit down and / face the frigidaire" (the reception is evidently cold!), but he is so excited that he can't remember "little things" like whether it's April or May. He goes over in his mind all the meaningful statements he was going to make when this longed-for moment finally occurred, statements like "life in Birmingham is hell" or "you will miss me / but that's good," or allusions to "this various dream of living," but at the same time he understands the futility of it all. O'Hara successfully distances himself from the "Frank" who exists in the poem:

> when the tears of a whole generation are assembled
> they will only fill a coffee cup
>   just because they evaporate
> doesn't mean life has heat. . . .

In the bittersweet passage that follows, the poet recognizes that his love is now met with some measure of indifference:

> I am alive with you
>   full of anxious pleasures and pleasurable anxiety
> hardness and softness
>   listening while you talk and talking while you read

I read what you read
            you do not read what I read
which is right, I am the one with the curiosity. . . .
            when you're not here someone walks in and says
                                                            "hey,
there's no dancer in that bed"

Recognition of the truth is one thing. But now the poet suddenly recalls the heyday of love, exclaiming with the rapt lyricism of his beloved Rachmaninoff:

O the Polish summers! those drafts!
those black and white teeth!

But this bravura passage is punctuated immediately by the clear-headed acceptance of the fact that "you never come when you say you'll come but on the other hand you do come."

What role does the title of the poem play? Vincent Warren has noted that "St. Paul" is a play on his middle name.[43] But it is also a nice irony to bring St. Paul into the picture, for the allusion points up Vincent's delinquency. No faithful apostle, responding to the Call and always "coming" when he is needed, this "St. Paul" fails to bring his disciple a New Dispensation. And yet, the Pauline doctrine of Reversal, of a love that will turn the world upside down and which redeems suffering, is central to the poem, for the "I" who speaks still believes in it. When he finds the dancer in his room, he experiences such a moment of reversal. But the reversal is, of course, temporary and illusory, and the poet is shown as accepting the inevitable: "the sun doesn't necessarily set, sometimes it just disappears."

In the summer of 1961, the love poems to Vincent Warren come to an abrupt end, and the poetry written after this date is recognizably different. The center of O'Hara's world was shifting somewhat. As the Museum took up more of his energies, he spent more time uptown, away from Second Avenue. He was also meeting a whole group of younger poets, whose conversation and work influenced his style. The most notable of these was Bill Berkson ("Golden Bill," as Frank called him in a letter to John Ashbery),[44] who worked with O'Hara at the

Museum and became an especially close friend. The letters to Bill Berkson are full of intellectual excitement and discussion, and the "Bill Berkson" poems, written in the early sixties, are correspondingly less emotional and more abstract than those written for, say, Grace Hartigan or Joe LeSueur or Vincent Warren. But surely age also played a part in the increasing detachment of the "I do this, I do that" poems written for various occasions. For in June of 1961, Frank O'Hara turned thirty-five. And that month he began a poem with the lines:

> April is over is May too June
> and thundershowers tomorrow
> you wouldn't want those tears to
> stick to your cheeks long. . . .   (*CP*, 408)

5
THE PILLAR OF OUR DEATHS

—*I don't think I want to win anything I think I want to die unadorned*

("Biotherm," CP, 438)

THE LAST YEARS

DURING THE LAST five years of his short life, O'Hara wrote relatively little poetry.[1] After the enormous productivity of the late fifties, a lull was perhaps inevitable, and, in any case, the Museum now took up much of his time and energy. Between 1961 and 1963, the poet seems to have suffered periodic bouts of depression. Emptiness, despair, and death now become frequent themes:

> Darkness and white hair
> everything empty, nothing there,
> but thoughts how awful
> image is, image errrgh
> all day long to sit in a window
> and see nothing but the past
> the serpent is coiled thrice
> around her she is dead. . . .

(CP, 419)

> The light presses down
> in an empty head the trees
> and bushes flop like
> a little girl imitating
> The Dying Swan the stone
> is hot the church is a
> Russian oven. . . .
> it is all suffocating. . . .   (*CP*, 475)

A number of poems contain references to suicide, although O'Hara usually treats this subject with self-deprecatory humor:

> I see the cobwebs collecting already
> and later those other webs, those awful predatory webs
> if I stay right here I will eventually get into the newspapers
> like Robert Frost
> willow trees, willow trees they remind me of Desdemona
> I'm so damned literary
> and at the same time the waters rushing past me remind me of nothing
> I'm so damned empty. . . .   (*CP*, 429)

> can I borrow your forty-five
> I only need one bullet preferably silver
> if you can't be interesting at least you can be a legend. . . .
>   (*CP*, 430)

> where am I what is it
> I can't even find a pond small enough
> to drown in without being ostentatious. . . .   (*CP*, 434)

> Soon I will fall drunken off the train into
> the arms of Patsy and Mike and the greenish pain.
> Obliterate everything, Neapolitan seventh!
> It will be a long hard way to the railway station,
>
> and Anna Karenina never wore dungarees.   (*CP*, 474)

Perhaps the most poignant of these "dark poems" is "The Clouds Go Soft" (1963), which Jasper Johns used in his collage-painting *Skin with O'Hara poem.* This meditative lyric, whose muted, subdued tone immediately sets it apart from most of the poet's work, is surely O'Hara's Dejection Ode. Change, motion, vitality, openness—these had always been his lifeblood: recall "To Hell With It" (1957), with its exclamation: "how I hate subject matter! melancholy intruding on the vigorous heart . . . and all things that don't change" (*CP*, 275). But now only the external landscape is capable of transformation, and even then, the movement is, in Wallace Stevens's phrase, "downward to darkness":

> The clouds go soft
>
>   change color and so many kinds
>
>   puff up, disperse
>
>   sink into the sea

It is the time of Sputnik, when the very heavens "go out of kilter" as "an insane remark greets / the monkey on the moon." But "here on earth," in the poet's mental landscape, all seems frozen, static:

>   at 16 you weigh 144 pounds and at 36
>
>   the shirts change, endless procession
>   but they are all neck 14 sleeve 33
>
>   and holes appear and are filled
>   the same holes   anonymous filler
>   no more conversion, no more conversation
>   the sand inevitably seeks the eye
>
>   and it is the same eye
>   (*CP*, 475)

O'Hara has rarely been so conscious of the inexorability of fate, the sense that he can escape neither his shirt size nor the sand that gets in his eye ("the same eye"). In the context, the "holes" are, of course, not armholes but graves. Even the verse form of "The Clouds Go Soft," with its ominous blank spaces and its lines that trail off, never quite meeting the next line, conveys the poet's sense of inner emptiness. Struggle, this particular poem tells us, is simply not worth it.

But one must be careful not to generalize about the later poems, for the same Frank O'Hara who wrote "The Clouds Go Soft" also wrote the wonderfully droll "Poem (Lana Turner has collapsed!)":

> Lana Turner has collapsed!
> I was trotting along and suddenly

it started raining and snowing
and you said it was hailing
but hailing hits you on the head
hard so it was really snowing and
raining and I was in such a hurry
to meet you but the traffic
was acting exactly like the sky
and suddenly I see a headline
LANA TURNER HAS COLLAPSED!
there is no snow in Hollywood
there is no rain in California
I have been to lots of parties
and acted perfectly disgraceful
but I never actually collapsed
oh Lana Turner we love you get up

(February 1962; *CP*, 449)

Certainly, O'Hara himself consistently rejected "collapse" as an easy way out. Indeed, during the five-year span under consideration, the variety of his accomplishments and the range of his activities continued to be as astonishing as ever. Collaboration became especially important in these years, as O'Hara worked on collages with Joe Brainard and Jasper Johns, and with Alfred Leslie on films. In 1961–62, he was art critic for *Kulchur;* the three important *Art Chronicles* date from this period, as do the NETA interviews with David Smith and Barnett Newman, and the Larry Rivers memoir. Within the next three years, he organized three major shows for the Museum: *Motherwell, Nakian,* and *Smith.* The catalogues for these exhibitions are now collector's items, the poet's introductions reflecting, once again, his uncanny ability to make the important discriminations about the art of his day. At the time of his death, O'Hara was working on a major retrospective of Jackson Pollock and had begun to make plans for the first major exhibition of de Kooning's painting at the museum.

As Associate Curator (he was to be named Curator in late 1966 when his death intervened), he now traveled abroad a good deal. In the fall of 1963, for example, he was in Europe for the opening of the Franz Kline exhibition at the Stedelijk Museum in Amsterdam and its second showing at the Museo Civico in Turin. On this particular trip, he also visited Rome, Milan, Paris, Antwerp, Copenhagen, Stockholm,

Zagreb, Belgrade, Prague, and Vienna. The letter from Belgrade to Joe LeSueur (quoted in Chapter 1) is full of wit, good humor, and high spirits; certainly the Frank who parties in Rome, visits nightclubs in Prague, and makes friends with local artists everywhere, does not sound like the despairing poet of "The Light Presses Down."

What is probably O'Hara's best play, *The General Returns from One Place to Another,* a parodistic fantasy about General MacArthur's return to the Pacific theater in peacetime—a general in search of a war—was produced at the Writer's Stage Theatre in 1964 and published the following year in *Art and Literature.* This comedy, evidently inspired by a production of Brecht's *In the Jungle of Cities,*[2] exploits some wonderfully absurd devices: in Scene 1, for example, the General enters "almost nude, but wearing galoshes and a toupee." In each subsequent scene, according to the stage directions, "he enters with one more article of clothing added, decorations, etc."[3] Since the General's power declines by a notch or two at each step of the way, we are finally confronted by a four-star general in full regalia—and no army to command—a general despised by the greedy natives and even by that predatory American camp follower, the cocktail-swilling Mrs. Forbes. Unlike some of the early plays like *Try! Try!,* which are merely silly, *The General Returns* has shrewd and funny things to say about East–West relations.

In this period, O'Hara was also teaching for the first time. In the spring of 1963, he gave a poetry workshop at the New School. Joe LeSueur recalls that it turned out to be a very *expensive* course, not for the class but for its instructor, because Frank invariably brought eager students round for drinks after class, and the liquor supply at 791 Broadway needed constant replenishment. Frank was, for that matter, now becoming something of an underground celebrity; young poets began to besiege him with letters and phone calls, and LeSueur remembers that when Ted Berrigan, one of O'Hara's most ardent disciples, first arrived in New York fresh from the Midwest, he would stand patiently on Avenue A near their apartment, hoping to catch a glimpse of his idol.[4] O'Hara, LeSueur notes, was "generous to a fault"; he couldn't turn down any of the writers who sought his help, always finding time for a long talk at the Cedar or a word of advice. The following excerpts from a letter (6 February 1963), written to the poet

Frank Lima at a time when the latter had a drug problem and couldn't bring himself to seek help, is typical:

> . . . no matter how much anyone likes you, you are the only one who can really do anything about things. . . . You've got to think of yourself first, because nobody else will. Everybody who likes and tries to help you is thinking of themselves first and you at least second: that's the way life is. . . .
>
> Think of your book with John Myers, think of going to Spain, think of going to France, think of the other books you'll write. All these things can happen, and each more easily than the last, if you can just get over these first difficulties. If it's not one psychiatrist it can be another, if not one job another, but you've got to want to, and right now you've got to want to very hard, in order to make it happen. And you do want to so come on. Rome wasn't built in a day and neither are individual lives or careers, you know that. The end.
>
> Boy, I bet this letter makes you mad.
>
> Love,
Frank[5]

O'Hara would have been happy to know that Lima *did* "make it happen"; he has since won a number of poetry awards and, at this writing, his new collection *Angel* is receiving enthusiastic reviews.[6]

Edwin Denby, whose poetry and dance criticism O'Hara consistently admired, sums up what many artist-friends felt about O'Hara's generosity: "Frank was so wonderful about the book [*In Public, In Private*[7]] and wrote a review in *Poetry* and had the marvelous gift of saying nice things. He would make compliments and then quote lines from the poems and in some instinctive way he managed to prepare the ear for what was interesting about the quotations." Yet there were all too many hangers-on ready to take advantage of Frank's "marvelous gift." "He had started giving parties at his loft on Broadway after he started making enough money working very hard at the Museum of Modern Art. No one was grateful for it. He was writing less and working hard. He really wanted to establish the painters he liked."[8]

One concludes that O'Hara wrote fewer poems during the sixties than he had in preceding years primarily because he was too busy doing other things. Indeed, it is a particularly bitter irony that the very summer O'Hara died was a time of special promise, both personal and literary. In his *Panjandrum* memoir of 1973, Vincent Warren recalls: "In the spring of 1966 Frank and I came together again. I decided to return to N.Y. We had one beautiful weekend at Patsy Southgate's on Long Island in June and Frank was planning to come to Montreal in August to see what would have been my last performance here when his life was interrupted."[9]

A new writing project was also under way: the collaboration with John Ashbery and Kenneth Koch on a play the three poets had begun in 1953. Ashbery remarks: "We wrote the second act in about June of 1966 and were planning to write a third act the following week, but Kenneth couldn't make it, and very shortly thereafter Frank was killed. His collaboration on Act II is therefore one of the last things he ever wrote, although unfortunately I am unable to recall now which of us wrote what."[10]

Throughout the sixties, even when he himself was writing little, O'Hara regarded poetry as his first love. In a long letter to Bill Berkson (12 August 1962), in which he contrasts the formal qualities of music to those of poetry, O'Hara urges his friend to make poetry—rather than fiction or any other kind of writing—his first priority, for "Poetry is the highest art, everything else, however gratifying . . . moving and grand, is less demanding, more indulgent, more casual, more gratuitous, more instantly apprehensible, which I assume is not exactly what we are after. . . ."[11]

This rejection of the "casual," the "gratuitous," the "instantly apprehensible" is nothing if not sound, but it is only fair to say that many of O'Hara's own poems written in the sixties suffer from precisely these faults. Take "The Lunch Hour FYI," written in the summer of 1961:

Plank plank   tons of it
                        plank plank
marching   the streets
                  up and down
                                              and it's all ours
2
what we all want is a consistent musical development heh heh
                  tappety-tap drrrrrrrrrrp!

Just as aloha means goodbye in Swahili

so it is 9:05

and I must go to work   roll OVER dammit

(see previous FYI)

hip? I haven't even coughed yet this morning

The poem goes on in this way for three more sections, ending with the lines:

coughcough

coughcoughcoughcough

good morning,

darling,

how do you like the first snow of summer?

your

plant in   your window

(*CP*, 421–22)

"The Lunch Hour" is one of a series of "For Your Information" poems written for Bill Berkson. Their background is related in the following letter from Berkson to Donald Allen (12 August 1970):

> The F.Y.I. works were written as correspondence between Frank & me & mostly by Frank—he would write the poems, like *Lunch Poems,* at his desk at the Museum of Modern Art. Together, they were supposed to form "The Collected Memorandums of Angelicus & Fidelio Fobb"—2 brothers (Frank was Angelicus, I was Fidelio) who wrote poems, letters, postcards (all "memorandums") to each other. The poems, however, don't seem to involve this brother-act too much—they have to do with what our lives in New York were like at the time (1960–61). "F.Y.I." comes from the typical heading for office memorandums—"For Your Information"—which was also the title of *Newsweek* magazine's "house organ," a little offset journal of employee gossip distributed weekly. I had worked at *Newsweek* the summers 1956–57 and told Frank about it & he picked up on "F.Y.I." He was also inspired to ring a lot of changes on the original in titles like "F.M.I." ("For My Information"), etc.   (*CP*, 551)

Since the "For Your Information" poems were written, like *Hymns of St. Bridget* (on which O'Hara and Berkson collaborated between 1960 and 1962) and "The Letters of Angelicus & Fidelio Fobb,"[12] mostly for the poets' own diversion, it may be unfair to judge them too stringently on aesthetic grounds. Nevertheless, I would argue that there *is* a falling off in the FYI poems, that "Lunch Hour" replaces the Personism of *Lunch Poems* with a somewhat self-conscious games-manship. Modulation now gives way to simple repetition ("Plank plank"); the language is usually that of ordinary talk ("roll OVER dammit") and simplistic sound imitation ("tappety-tap drrrrrrrrrrp!"). These new lyrics are much more loosely articulated: words tend to be spread all over the page, the blank space becoming an important prosodic element as a sort of musical rest. The three-step (or modified two-step) line of Williams's late poems is used frequently as is the device of placing verse paragraphs alternately on the left and right sides of the page as in "For a Dolphin" (*CP,* 407). Often, as in the case of "Lunch Hour," one is hard put to find a *raison d'être* for the particular prosodic shape used; sheer randomness seems to be the rule. These are poems that can start or stop anywhere, that accommodate almost anything the poet happens to want to record. Their tone, moreover, is curiously detached; O'Hara's former emotional vibrancy—a vibrancy that linked him to Mayakovsky—is absent.

But perhaps these "For Your Information" poems are best considered as bits of muscle flexing, exercises that prepare the way for that great Bill Berkson poem, "Biotherm." This long (464 lines) lyric sequence was written over a five-month period (26 August 1961–23 January 1962). In a letter to Donald Allen (20 September 1961), O'Hara provides an important background statement about the poem:

I've been going on with a thing I started to be a little birthday poem for BB and then it went along a little and then I remembered that was how Mike's Ode [*Ode to Michael Goldberg ('s Birth and Other Births)*] got done so I kept on and I am still going day by day (middle of 8th page this morning). I don't know anything about what it is or will be but am enjoying trying to keep going and seem to have something. Some days I feel very happy about it, because I seem to have been able to keep it "open" and so there are lots of possibilities, air and such. For example, it's been called *M.L.F.Y., Whereby Shall Seace* (from Wyatt), *Biotherm,* and back and forth, probably ending up as *M.L.F.Y.* The Wyatt passage is very beautiful: "This dedelie stroke, wherebye shall seace / The harborid sighis within my herte. . . ." *M.L.F.Y.,* I hasten to add, is not like that at all though, so don't get your hopes too high. . . . Biotherm is a marvelous sunburn preparation full of attar of roses, lanolin and plankton ($12 the

tube) which Bill's mother fortunately left around and it hurts terribly
when gotten into one's eyes. Plankton it says on it is practically the most
health-giving substance ever rubbed into one's skin.[13]

How much openness can a poem bear? This is a tricky question, of
course, and for a long time I regarded "Biotherm" as just another FYI
(or rather MLFY) poem—a witty improvisation, a transcript of the
charming if jumbled talk of a marvelous raconteur. Its endless puns,
in-jokes, phonetic games, allusions, cataloguing, journalistic parodies,
and irrelevant anecdotes may seem, on a first or even a later reading,
merely tiresome.[14] Interestingly, "Biotherm" also seems to have much
less relationship to painting than do the earlier poems. Film is now the
dominant sister art; the poem is full of references to movie stars, Hollywood films, and invented scenarios, and its structure often resembles
the film technique of crosscutting at accelerated speed, a technique
particularly common in the silent film comedies of the twenties, for
example those of Buster Keaton.

If we study O'Hara's crosscutting, we find that everything in this
seemingly wild talk-poem relates to everything else. The setting is the
beach: the first line of "Biotherm" invokes the magic suntan lotion
("The best thing in the world"); and twelve pages later, O'Hara concludes with the lines:

yes always though you said it first
you the quicksand and sand and grass
as I wave toward you freely
the ego-ridden sea
there is a light there that neither
of us will obscure
rubbing it all white
saving ships from fucking up on the rocks
on the infinite waves of skin smelly and crushed and light and absorbed
(*CP*, 448)

Although the beach setting is never formally introduced or presented
in realistic detail, sand, sea, and cloud images, as well as larger beach
scenes, fade in and out at fairly regular intervals:

or what's the use the sky
the endless clouds trailing we leading them by the bandanna, red
(*CP*, 436)

after "hitting" the beach at Endzoay we drank up the liebfraumilch
                    and pushed on up the Plata to the pampas   (*CP*, 437)

bent on his knees the Old Mariner said where the fuck
        is that motel you told me about mister I aint come here for no clams
I want swimmingpool mudpacks the works carbonateddrugstorewater /
                                                                    hiccups
from a nice sissy under me clean and whistling a donkey to ride rocks
                                                        (*CP*, 437)

                the dulcet waves are
                sweeping along in their purplish
                way and a little girl is
                beginning to cry and I know
                her but I can't help because
                she has just found her first brick
                what can you do what   (*CP*, 438)

One day   you are posing in your checkerboard bathing trunks (*CP*, 440)

                on the beach we stood on our heads
                I held your legs it was summer and hot
                the Bloody Marys were spilling on our trunks
                but the crocodiles didn't pull them
                it was a charmed life full of
                innuendos and desirable hostilities   (*CP*, 444)

These brief flashes of real and fantastic beach locales provide a sense
of continuity rather like that of a Godard film; they are brief reminders that the poem's variations radiate from a center which is the loving
relationship between Frank and Bill, and which is epitomized by the
line "pretty rose preserved in biotherm" on the same page as the Wyatt
love poem (439). What the poet preserves in "biotherm" in order to
entertain his friend is a dazzling array of memories and inventions.
There are fantastically absurd menus, alluding to French dishes and
American friends:

Hors-d'oeuvre abstrait-expressionistes, américain-styles, bord-durs, etc.
Soupe Samedi Soir à la Strawberry-Blonde
Poisson Pas de Dix au style Patricia
Histoire de contrefilet, sauce Angelicus Fobb
La réunion des fins de thon à la boue
Chapon ouvert brûlé à l'Hoban, sauce Fidelio Fobb
Poèmes 1960–61 en salade   (*CP*, 445)

Or burlesque film scenarios:

"Practically Yours"
> with June Vincent, Lionello Venturi and Casper Citron
> a Universal-International release produced by G. Mennen Williams
> directed by Florine Stettheimer
> continuity by the Third Reich
>
> *(CP, 437)*

Or comic word substitutions:

> you meet the Ambassador "a year and a half of trying to make him"
>   he is dressed in red, he has a red ribbon down his chest he
>   has   7   gold decorations pinned to his gash   *(CP, 436)*

Or bastard foreign language, in this case German:

> "vass hass der mensch geplooped
> that there is sunk in the battlefield a stately grunt
> and the idle fluice still playing on the hill
> because of this this this this slunt"   *(CP, 440)*

Or bittersweet memories of actual events:

> then too, the other day I was walking through a train
> with my suitcase and I overheard someone say "speaking of faggots"
> now isn't life difficult enough without that
> and why am I always carrying something
> well it was a shitty looking person anyway
> better a faggot than a farthead   *(CP, 441)*

Or catalogues containing unexpected items:

> favorites: vichyssoise, capers, bandannas, fudge-nut-ice, collapsibility,
>   the bar of the Winslow, 5:30 and 12:30, leather sweaters, tuna fish,
>   cinzano and soda, Marjorie Rambeau in *Inspiration*
>   whatdoyoumeanandhowdoyoumeanit
>
> *(CP, 445)*

> favorites: going to parties with you, being in corners with you,
>   being in gloomy pubs with you smiling, poking you at /
>   parties when

you're "down," coming on like South Pacific with you at them,
shrimping with you into the Russian dressing, leaving /
                                                    parties with
you alone to go and eat a piece of cloud   (*CP,* 447)

Or literary parodies, in this case of Pound's famous *Usura* Canto:

> I am talking about the color of money
> the dime so red and the 100 dollar bill so orchid
> the sickly fuchsia of a 1 the optimistic
> orange of a 5 the useless penny like a seed
> the magnificent yellow zinnia of a 10
> especially a roll of them the airy blue of a
> 50 how pretty a house is when it's filled with them
> that's not a villa that's a bank
> where's the ocean
> now this is not a tract against usury it's just putting two and two together
> and getting five (thank you, Mae)
> (*CP,* 446)

Individually, such passages may seem to be pure slapstick, but the
remarkable thing about "Biotherm" is that, as in a sophisticated or-
chestral composition, everything mentioned casually is picked up
somewhere later in the poem in an altered context. Thus the "bandanna" of line 6 reappears nine pages later in the catalogue quoted
above. Or again, the reference to "Swan Lake Allegra Kent / those
Ten Steps of Patricia Wilde" reappears in the "(MENU) / Déjeuner
Bill Berkson," first as "Poisson Pas de Dix au Style Patricia" and then
as "Café ivesianien 'Plongez au fond du lac glacé'". One remembered
lunch dissolves into another; and the film-menu-poetry-party parodies
are regularly juxtaposed to sudden expressions of deep affection:

> we are alone no one is talking it feels good
> we have our usual contest about claustrophobia
> it doesn't matter much
> doing without each other is much more insane   (*CP,* 441)

or

> you were there I was here you were here I was there where are /
>   you I miss you. . . .

when you went I stayed and then I went and we were both lost /
                                                    and then I died
                                                        (*CP*, 442)

Like Godard's *La Chinoise* or *Weekend,* "Biotherm" consistently
plays off the intensities of personal emotion against the vagaries of
everyday conversation. It is an extremely difficult poem because the
reader enters the "frame" only gradually, overhearing snatches of
conversation between Frank, Bill, Patsy, and John, and only gradually realizing that "Biotherm" is something of a rock opera, partly
playful but also full of anxiety, alternating percussive passages with
lyrical tunes, an extravaganza celebrating the poet's great love for his
friend and memorializing their careless summer beach days of "infinite waves of skin smelly and crushed and absorbed." Another way of
putting it is that O'Hara's long lyric sequence is an elegy for "Biotherm," that magic potion that preserves roses—a potion interchangeable with "kickapoo joyjuice halvah Canton cheese / in thimbles" (*CP*,
437) or "marinated duck saddle with foot sauce and a tumbler of
vodka" (*CP*, 448). Food and liquor images are especially prominent in
this poem because the poet's imagination transforms them into *Plankton,* the "health-giving substance" that makes Biotherm so special.
Thus when the poet says in one expansive moment:

> I am sitting on top of Mauna Loa seeing thinking feeling
> the breeze rustles through the mountains gently trusts me
> I am guarding it from mess and measure   (*CP*, 444)

he is describing not only his guardianship of Mauna Loa but the creative act as well. "Biotherm" is a poem dangerous to imitate for it implies that anything goes, that all you have to do is "merely continue."
But in fact O'Hara does succeed here in "guarding it from mess and
measure"—that is, from total formlessness on one hand, and from a
more traditional rhetorical and prosodic organization on the other. It
is his last great poem and one of the important poems of the sixties.

THE DAY FRANK O'HARA DIED

By 1964 or so, O'Hara's style, especially the style of the "I do this, I do
that" poems, was beginning to have a marked influence. Ted Berrigan

wrote a series of "Sonnets," one of which, subtitled "After Frank O'Hara," begins:

> It's 8:54 in Brooklyn it's the 28th of July and
> it's probably 8:54 in Manhattan but I'm
> in Brooklyn I'm eating English muffins and drinking
> pepsi and I'm thinking of how Brooklyn is New
> York city too how odd I usually think of it as
> something all its own like Bellows Falls like Little
> Chute like Uijongbu. . . .[15]

And Ron Padgett wrote a poem called "16 November 1964," whose opening recalls O'Hara's "Personal Poem" ("Now when I walk around at lunchtime . . ."):

> As this morning seemed special when I woke up
> I decided as is my custom, to go for a refreshing walk
> in the street. Preparing myself for the unexpected, I
> Combed my hair and generally made ready. I was ready.
> In the hall outside my door the lady from down the hall
> Shouted my name to get my attention.[16]

Such early imitations were, of course, merely derivative; in these poems, Berrigan and Padgett capture the O'Hara manner without the substance. Their model is quite obviously the occasional mode of "A Step Away from Them," "Adieu to Norman, Bon Jour to Joan and Jean-Paul," and especially O'Hara's celebrated elegy for Billie Holiday:

THE DAY LADY DIED

> It is 12:20 in New York a Friday
> three days after Bastille day, yes
> it is 1959 and I go get a shoeshine
> because I will get off the 4:19 in Easthampton
> at 7:15 and then go straight to dinner
> and I don't know the people who will feed me
>
> I walk up the muggy street beginning to sun
> and have a hamburger and a malted and buy
> an ugly NEW WORLD WRITING to see what the poets
> in Ghana are doing these days
>
> > I go on to the bank

and Miss Stillwagon (first name Linda I once heard)
doesn't even look up my balance for once in her life
and in the GOLDEN GRIFFIN I get a little Verlaine
for Patsy with drawings by Bonnard although I do
think of Hesiod, trans. Richmond Lattimore or
Brendan Behan's new play or *Le Balcon* or *Les Nègres*
of Genet, but I don't, I stick with Verlaine
after practically going to sleep with quandariness

and for Mike I just stroll into the PARK LANE
Liquor Store and ask for a bottle of Strega and
then I go back where I came from to 6th Avenue
and the tobacconist in the Ziegfield Theatre and
casually ask for a carton of Gauloises and a carton
of Picayunes, and a NEW YORK POST with her face on it

and I am sweating a lot by now and thinking of
leaning on the john door in the 5 SPOT
while she whispered a song along the keyboard
to Mal Waldron and everyone and I stopped breathing

(*CP,* 325)

"In one brief poem," Ted Berrigan said in his obituary essay on
O'Hara, "he seemed to create a whole new kind of awareness of feeling, and by this a whole new kind of poetry, in which everything could
be itself and still be poetry."[17] What Berrigan means here, I think, is
that O'Hara dispenses with all the traditional props of elegy—the
statement of lament, the consolation motif, the procession of mourn-
ers, the pathetic fallacy, and so on—and still manages to pay an intensely moving tribute to the great jazz singer. It is not an easy feat. In
his own earlier elegies, for example the four poems prompted by the
sudden tragic death of the young James Dean in 1955,[18] O'Hara often
makes a straightforward statement of lament and complaint, thus
risking sentimentality, much as William Carlos Williams does in his
"Elegy for D. H. Lawrence," which begins:

> Green points on the shrub
> and poor Lawrence dead
> the night damp and misty
> and Lawrence no more in the world
> to answer April's promise
> with a fury of labor

                    against waste, waste and life's
                    coldness.

(Collected Earlier Poems, 361)

O'Hara avoids the bathos inherent in such a frontal attack by making no reference at all to Lady Day until the twenty-fifth line of his
poem, and then only obliquely: the poet catches a glimpse of "a NEW
YORK POST with her face on it." The title leads us to expect an elegy or
at least an account of Billie Holiday's death; instead, O'Hara traces the
process whereby he comes across the news of that death, a process so
immediate, so authentic that when we come to the last four lines, we
participate in his poignant memory of Lady Day's performance.
Reading the last six words of the poem, "and everyone and I stopped
breathing" (reminiscent of the arresting ending of Yeats's "In Memory
of Major Robert Gregory": "but a thought / Of that late death took all
my heart for speech"), we too stop breathing. For a moment, however
brief, memory and art enable us to transcend the ordinary particulars
of existence.

How does the poet accomplish this? If we look at the details that
make up the first twenty-five lines of the poem, we see that they are
not, after all, as random as they appear to be. As Charles Altieri has
observed: "The actual particulars by which the poem captures the
vitality of life at the same time constantly call attention to their own
contingency and perpetual hovering on the brink of disconnection."[19]
O'Hara knows exactly that he will get off the train at 7:15 and go to
dinner, but he doesn't know the people who will feed him. He goes to
the bank where the barely familiar teller "Miss Stillwagon (first name
Linda I once heard)" disproves his expectations by not looking up his
"balance for once in her life." He cannot decide what book to buy for
Patsy Southgate and practically goes to sleep "with quandariness."
This is a particularly odd detail: when one is in a quandary, one may
well suffer from insomnia but hardly from sleepiness!

A similar disconnection characterizes the network of proper names
and place references in the poem. On the one hand, the poet's consciousness is drawn to the foreign or exotic: Ghana, the Golden Griffin, Verlaine, Bonnard, Hesiod, trans. Richmond Lattimore, Brendan
Behan, *Le Balcon, Les Négres,* Genet, Strega, Gauloises, Picayunes.[20]
On the other, the poem contains a set of native American references:

"shoeshine," "the muggy street beginning to sun," "a hamburger and a malted," "an ugly NEW WORLD WRITING," "6th Avenue," "a NEW YORK POST," "the 5 SPOT," "the john door," and the reference to Billie's accompanist, Mal Waldron.

Why does O'Hara introduce Verlaine and Genet, Gauloises and the Golden Griffin into a poem about Billie Holiday? I think because he wants to make us see—and this is his great tribute to Lady Day—that she embodies both the foreign-exotic and the native American. As a person, Billie Holiday was, of course, quintessentially American: a southern Black who had experienced typical hardships on the road to success, a woman of great passions who finally succumbed to her terrible drug addiction, a victim of FBI agents and police raids. In this sense, hers is the world of muggy streets, hamburgers and malteds, the john door, the "5 SPOT." But her great voice transcends what she is in life, linking her to the poets, dramatists, and artists cited in the first part, to *Le Balcon* and *Les Nègres,* to Gauloises and Strega. Even the name Lady Day (ingeniously reversed in the elegy's title) reconciles these opposites.

Disconnections which turn out to be connections, isolated moments in time which lead to one moment transcending time—everything in the elegy works in this way. The syntax is particularly interesting in this regard. The paratactic structure (and ... and ... and), linking short declarative statements sequentially rather than causally, calls attention to what seems to be the meaningless flux of time. One moment is succeeded by another as Frank moves back and forth from street to street, from store to store. But then it seems as if he is virtually running out of steam. The conjunctions become increasingly insistent (eleven of the poem's nineteen *and*'s occur in the last ten lines), and the pace slows down until finally the sequence of meaningless moments is replaced by the *one* moment of memory when Lady Day enchanted her audience by the power of her art. Time suddenly stops.

O'Hara does not have to say here, as he did in "For James Dean," "For a young actor I am begging / peace, Gods.... I speak as one whose filth / is like his own" (*CP,* 228), or as Williams says in the Lawrence elegy, "Sorrow for the young / that Lawrence has passed / unwanted from England." "The Day Lady Died" moves surely and swiftly to its understated climax; it establishes the singer as an authentic presence even though the poem never mentions her by name and seems to be "about" the poet's own activities, his trivial preweekend errands on a typical July Friday in muggy Manhattan.

In their imitations of O'Hara's mode, Berrigan and Padgett use the poet's particulars—the time signals, the place names, the random re-counting of activities—but theirs tend to be simple empiricism, a cata-loguing of "this is what happened to me today," in which the particu-lars don't add up. Comparing the model to its offshoots, one can appreciate, more than ever, O'Hara's exquisite modulations of tone, his split-second dissolves, his time shifts, syntactic displacements, and emotional resonances, especially when one realizes that, in the best poems, each small detail, like the bottle of Strega which Frank buys for Mike, plays its part in the larger network.

Yet, whatever the faults of their early versions of "Personism," young poets like Berrigan and Padgett played an important role; they were the first to recognize that O'Hara had struck a new chord, that a new poetry was in the making. And after his death in 1966, the literary response was astonishing. Almost immediately, elegies for O'Hara began to appear in the little magazines. If none of these elegies is as brilliant as "The Day Lady Died," many are poignant and arresting; indeed, a whole anthology could be compiled of poems written for Frank O'Hara in the five years or so following his death. A short list would begin with Allen Ginsberg's "City Midnight Junk Strains," written four days after the poet's death, and include, in order of publi-cation: Patsy Southgate's "Nobody Operates Like an IBM Machine: For Frank O'Hara," George Montgomery's "The Death of Frank O'Hara," Tony Towle's "Sunrise: Ode to Frank O'Hara," James Schuyler's "Buried at Springs," David Shapiro's "Ode (Permit me to take this sleeping man . . .)," Gerard Malanga's "In Memory of the Poet Frank O'Hara 1926–1966," Ron Padgett's "Strawberries in Mex-ico," John Wieners's "After Reading *Second Avenue:* For Frank O'Hara," and Diane di Prima's "From Kerhonson, July 28, 1966" and "Inverness, Cape Breton Island."[21]

One should note that this list is not limited to the so-called New York poets. John Wieners, originally a student at Black Mountain College, later a resident of Boston and briefly of San Francisco, stands apart from the New York group, an important poet in his own right.

And Ginsberg, of course, was never considered primarily a New York poet, having much closer ties to the Beats—Kerouac, Corso, Snyder, Whalen—than to the poets and painters originally associated with the Eighth Street Club, although the two groups did overlap.

Ginsberg's elegy for O'Hara is not one of his important poems, but it is a fascinating literary document, defining the relationship between two of the leading poets of the postwar era, poets united by their dislike of the Academic Establishment, their allegiance to Rimbaud, Whitman, Pound, and Williams, their search for open forms, and their homosexuality, but separated by their very different sensibilities and poetic aims. "City Midnight Junk Strains" begins:

> Switch on lights yellow as the sun
> > in the bedroom . . .
> The gaudy poet dead
>
> > > (*Planet News,* 134)

The image of Frank as "gaudy poet" dominates the elegy. Ginsberg has much affection for him, but one senses that he doesn't take him quite seriously. O'Hara is repeatedly referred to as "chattering Frank," mourned by his "Faithful drunken adorers," as the "Chatty prophet / of yr own loves, personal / memory feeling fellow," as the poet who wanders down Fifth Avenue "with your tie / flopped over your shoulder in the wind . . . off to a date with Martinis & a blond." Ginsberg recalls his "broken roman nose," his "wet mouth-smell of martinis / & a big artistic tipsy kiss"; he regrets the loss of "so many fine parties and evenings' / interesting drinks together with one / faded friend or new / understanding social cat." He concludes:

> Elegant insistency
> > on the honking self-prophetic Personal
> > as Curator of funny emotions to the mob,
> Trembling One, whenever possible. I see New York thru your eyes
> > and hear of one funeral a year nowadays—
> > > From Billie Holiday's time
> > appreciated more and more
> a common ear
> > > for our deep gossip.   (p. 137)

This is essentially the mythologized poet discussed in Chapter 1, the "gay" (in both senses of the word) "Curator of funny emotions," the celebrant of New York and purveyor of "deep gossip." The Fire Island accident turns this connoisseur of art into a piece of modern sculpture:

> ... dear Edwin Denby serious as Herbert Read
> with silvery hair   announcing your dead gift
> to the grave crowd   whose historic op art   frisson was
> the new sculpture your big blue wounded body made in the
> Universe
> when you went away   to Fire Island for the weekend
> tipsy with a family of decade-olden friends   (p. 136)

The melodrama of these lines (O'Hara did not, for instance, have a "big" body) looks ahead to Alfred Leslie's painting *The Killing of Frank O'Hara*. A more individual note is struck in Ginsberg's peculiarly candid appraisal of O'Hara's sexuality:

> Who were you, black suited, hurrying to meet,
> Unsatisfied one?
> Unmistakable,
> Darling date
> for the charming solitary   young poet with a big cock
> who could fuck you all night long
> till you never came
> (p. 135)

His own sexual capacities, Ginsberg asserts, are very different:

> I tried   your boys and found them ready
> sweet and amiable
> collected gentlemen
> with large sofa apartments
> lonesome to please   for pure language

The self-congratulatory note of this passage is, I think, out of key with the demands of the elegy form; it is as if, even though Frank's "bones" are "under cemetery grass," Allen still wants to compete with him for the favors of young men. And this competitive, aggressive note gives us some measure of the enormous difference between the two poets: the prophetic, expansive, religious Ginsberg, who wants his poetry to *change* the world, can only partially penetrate the consciousness of the urbane, witty, sophisticated, skeptical, agnostic O'Hara. The scattered references to Ginsberg in the *Collected Poems* suggest that the reverse was equally true: consider the following comically petulant response to Ginsberg's projected journey to India in 1961:

> Now that the Charles Theatre has opened
> it looks like we're going to have some wonderful times
> Allen and Peter, why are you going away
> our country's black and white past spread out
> before us is no time to spread over India. . . .   (*CP,* 399)

In this context, Ginsberg's declaration in the elegy that "I see New York thru your eyes" is inadvertently funny, for in fact Ginsberg sees New York through the most different eyes possible. His New York is a kind of urban hell, the city of cops and drug raids, of crime and ugliness and injustice; it is the opposite of O'Hara's companionable, exciting, and eternally entertaining Manhattan. Witness the following lines from Ginsberg's "Waking in New York":

> The giant stacks burn thick grey
>   smoke, Chrysler is lit with green,
> down Wall street islands of skyscraper
>   black jagged in Sabbath quietness—
> Oh fathers, how I am alone in this
>   vast human wilderness
> Houses uplifted like hives off
>   the stone floor of the world—
> the city too vast to know, too
>   myriad windowed to govern
>   from ancient halls—
> "O edifice of gas!"   (*Planet News,* p. 72)

Surely Frank O'Hara could never have written these lines which recall the visionary fervor of Hart Crane's *The Bridge.* O'Hara never felt "alone in this / vast human wilderness"; on the contrary, he felt at home only when he was participating in the life of "this hairy city," for he was convinced that "the country is no good for us / there's nothing / to bump into / or fall apart glassily / there's not enough / poured concrete" (*CP,* 476–77).

Near the end of "City Midnight Junk Strains," Ginsberg introduces a facet of O'Hara's character that the other elegists stress with equal conviction and of which I have already spoken—the poet's incredible generosity, his ability to make anyone he was with feel better:

> You're in a bad mood?
>> Take an Asprin.
>>> In the Dumps?
>>>> I'm falling asleep
>>>>> safe in your thoughtful arms.
>>>>>> (*Planet News,* p. 136)

It is O'Hara's marvelous capacity for friendship that Ginsberg most admires. As such, his portrait of the artist may be somewhat one-sided, but it is a testament of love. And we must remember that in 1966, when Ginsberg wrote this elegy, no one, not even Frank's closest friends, had an adequate idea of the magnitude of the poet's accomplishment, the number of still unknown poems whose publication would dispel the romantic image of O'Hara as "Chatty prophet" and "Curator of funny emotions."

It is interesting to turn from "City Midnight Junk Strains" to Patsy Southgate's elegy for O'Hara. Hers is a much more modest poem, the testimonial of a close friend:

> You said:
> "I love your house because my poems are always on the coffee table!"
> "I always have such fun with you!"
> "Oh really, don't be an ass!"
> "Just pull yourself together and sweep in!"
> "Now *stop* it!"
>
> An endless series of exclamation points
> has ended.
>
> Your voice
> ran across the lawn wearing nothing but a towel
> in the good old summertime.
> You always sounded so positive!
> What freedom!
> I'll get a flag! (I must!)

I loved your house too
with Grace Church looking in the window
and your imposingly empty ice-box;
all that work piled on the table
and lavished love on the walls and everywhere.
You would say, yacking away, shaving at the kitchen sink (*the* sink)
that we were going to be late again, for shit's sake, but
"You look perfectly gorgeous, /
my dear, would you mind feeding the cats?"
in those arrogant days
before your grave.

You said, during the intermissions, on the phones, at the lunches,
in the cabs:
"If you *want* to do it, just *do* it! What else is there?"
"My heart your heart" you wrote.
It all added up.
How flawless you were!

In focusing on Frank's own words and gestures, Patsy Southgate has saved her elegy from sentimentality. The repetitions "You said," "Your voice," "You would say," "You always sounded" unify the poem, and the expressions chosen give us an image of strength rather than the weakness of Ginsberg's charming child-poet. Despite his childlike abandon ("Your voice / ran across the lawn wearing nothing but a towel"), his candor ("'I love your house because my poems are always on the coffee table!'"), his insouciance ("your imposingly empty ice-box," "shaving at the kitchen sink [*the* sink]"), Frank's most memorable quality, according to Patsy Southgate, is his resilience, both for himself and for others: "'If you *want* to do it, just *do* it! What else is there?'" It is this peculiar courage ("You always sounded so positive!"), this unsentimental optimism that makes Patsy Southgate exclaim, "How flawless you were!"

A third elegy of a very different kind is James Schuyler's "Buried at Springs." Unlike Ginsberg's, this poem makes no attempt to recapture the immediate particulars of O'Hara's life; unlike Southgate's, it does not invoke his typical phrases and gestures. A more traditional elegy in the Romantic tradition, it begins:

There is a hornet in the room
and one of us will have to go

out of the window into the late
August mid-afternoon sun. I
won.

In the course of the poem, it becomes apparent that the "one of us" who "will have to go" is not just a hornet but Frank, and that the speaker has "won" nothing at all. Watching from his window, he sees "Rocks with rags / of shadow, washed dust clouts / that will never bleach." But then he pulls back and says laconically "It is not like this at all." The dust clouts *will* bleach for nothing remains the same:

> The rapid running of the
> lapping water a hollow knock
> of someone shipping oars:
> it's eleven years since
> Frank sat at this desk and
> saw and heard it all

This is not just the conventional opposition of the mortality of man to the eternal renewal of nature. For Schuyler's "nature," like that of such related painters as de Kooning, Motherwell, and Kline, is submitted to a series of "painterly" arrangements. He recomposes landscapes ("rock, trees, a stump") in various ways, finding new shapes and patterns:

> Sandy
> billows, or so they look,
> of feathery ripe heads of grass,
> an acid-yellow kind of
> goldenrod glowing or glowering
> in shade.
>
> Boats are light lumps on the bay
> stretching past erased islands
> to ocean and the terrible tumble

But because of Frank's absence, none of these painterly compositions is finally satisfying, and in the end, Schuyler gives it up. No more billows looking like "feathery ripe heads of grass"; no more boats resembling "light lumps on the bay," sailing past "erased islands." The pastoral landscape now gives way to a harsher reality:

> a faint clammy day, like wet silk
> stained by one dead branch
> the harsh russet of dried blood.

Within the earlier context of pretty seascapes with "great gold lichen" on "granite boulders," this oblique deathnote is arresting. "Buried at Springs" is a poem O'Hara himself would surely have admired; its modest tone, its unexpected line breaks ("I / won") and halting rhythms ("the incessant water the / immutable crickets"), its abstraction from natural forms—all these are reminiscent of O'Hara's own poetry, although O'Hara never possessed Schuyler's intrinsic reverence for the world of nature.

One poet who did *not* write an elegy for Frank O'Hara, even though he wrote the beautiful introduction to the *Collected Poems,* was John Ashbery. I mention this not because I think Ashbery should have written one, but because it tells us something about the essential difference between these two poets, who have so frequently been paired in critical commentary.[22] The personal elegy has never been an Ashbery genre; his is a poetic mode that absorbs personality into larger metaphysical structures.

Ashbery and O'Hara first became friends at Harvard, and when O'Hara moved to Manhattan in 1951, the two poets met regularly. In an interview with Richard Kostelanetz, Ashbery recalls:

> Frank got me interested in contemporary music . . . before much of this music had been recorded. He used to play it to me on the piano. He was also reading Beckett and Jean Rhys and Flann O'Brien before anybody heard of them. . . . We were all young and ambitious then. American painting seemed the most exciting art around, American poetry was very traditional at that time, and there was no modern poetry in the sense that there was modern painting. So one got one's inspiration and ideas from watching the experiments of others. Much of my feeling for Rothko and Pollock came through Frank.[23]

When *Some Trees* appeared in 1956, O'Hara gave it a perceptive review in *Poetry.* "Everywhere in the poems," he declared, "there is the difficult attention to calling things and events by their true qualities.

He establishes a relation between perception and articulateness." And he concluded: "Mr. Ashbery has written the most beautiful first book to appear in America since *Harmonium*."[24] In thus comparing Ashbery to Stevens, O'Hara was obviously on the right track; since then, most commentators, especially Ashbery's most famous advocate, Harold Bloom, have been at pains to demonstrate the Stevens connection. By the same token, however, O'Hara was suggesting that Ashbery's inspiration was unlike his own, for Stevens was never a central influence on O'Hara's work, nor was he himself particularly interested in "calling things and events by their true qualities."

It is important to note that since Ashbery lived in Paris from 1954 to 1965, he was absent from the New York scene during O'Hara's productive years. But the two poets corresponded regularly and copied out each others' poems in letters to friends. Writing to Mike Goldberg on 26 August 1957, Frank announced with great excitement: "JOHN ASHBERY IS ARRIVING SEPTEMBER 2d. I got a letter from him Saturday with some wonderful new poems. . . ." He proceeds to quote the funnier parts of Ashbery's letter and then the complete text of " 'They Dream Only Of America,' " followed by the comment, "Pretty snappy, eh?"[25] Or again, in 1961, when Ashbery asked O'Hara to contribute to the Reverdy issue he was preparing for the *Mercure de France,* Frank responded with a long letter (1 February 1961) saying, among other things: "I am still enthralled (literally) with *Europe* and love *America* too. . . . If I get up the energy after sending you some of the things I think are related to Reverdy . . . I'll try to include a couple of new things which are footnotes to *Europe,* and should be collected under the title *Little Verses for the Admirers of Ashbery's Europe.*"[26]

It is interesting that O'Hara was so enchanted by "Europe," that long disjointed poem made up of 111 fragments, which Ashbery himself now thinks of as a dead end.[27] Harold Bloom has called it "a fearful disaster," arguing that "The Ashbery of *The Tennis Court Oath* [the volume in which "Europe" appeared] may have been moved by de Kooning and Kline, Webern and Cage, but he was not moved to the writing of poems. . . . who can hope to find any necessity in this calculated incoherence?"[28] The point here is that Bloom, reading *The Tennis Court Oath* with the retrospective insight gained from his exposure to *The Double Dream of Spring* (1970) and *Three Poems* (1972), responds to Ashbery's early experimentation with Dada and Surrealist modes with "outrage and disbelief." O'Hara, on the other hand, was fascinated by these experiments because he himself was tapping the same springs, even if the results turned out to be very different. "Europe" is, in fact, an exercise in automatic writing; Ashbery recalls: "I'd get American magazines like *Esquire,* open the pages, get a phrase from it, and then start writing on my own. When I ran out, I'd go back to the magazine. It was pure experimentation." Several passages in the poem were taken intact from a British children's book, *Beryl of the Biplane* by William Le Queux, which Ashbery found in a Paris bookstall.[29] One is immediately reminded of Max Ernst's collage novels, currently being rediscovered.[30] In this context, Richard Kostelanetz calls "Europe" "one of the great long poems of recent years—a classic of coherent diffuseness." It can, he argues, "be characterized as 'acoherent,' much as certain early 20th-century music is called 'atonal'" (p. 23).

Ashbery's assimilation of French Surrealism complements O'Hara's, but it is remarkable how different their experiments are. Take "'They Dream Only of America'" (1957), which O'Hara cites so enthusiastically in his letter to Mike Goldberg. It begins:

> They dream only of America
> To be lost among the thirteen million pillars of grass:
> "This honey is delicious
> *Though it burns the throat.*"
>
> And hiding from darkness in barns
> They can be grownups now
> And the murderer's ash tray is more easily—
> The lake a lilac cube.[31]

Compare this to the opening of O'Hara's "Easter" (1952):

> The razzle dazzle maggots are summary
> tattooing my simplicity on the pitiable.
> The perforated mountains of my saliva leave cities awash
> more exclusively open and more pale than skirts.
> O the glassy towns are fucked by yaks
> slowly bleeding a quiet filigree on the leaves of that souvenir
> of a bird chastely crossing the boulevard of falling stars

cold in the dull heavens
drowned in flesh,
it's night like I love it all cruisy and nelly
fingered fan of boskage fronds the white smile of sleeps.

(*CP*, 96–97)

"'They Dream Only Of America'" is a much quieter, more reflective, more detached and abstract poem than "Easter," with its racy, slangy, concrete language, its nervous rhythms and purposely foolish alliteration, its exclamatory fervor and intimate, personal tone. Ashbery's language is more chaste, and his verse forms and sentence structure are more traditional than O'Hara's, the four-line stanzas providing an orderly frame for a series of complete sentences. But although a statement like "They dream only of America" offers no syntactic difficulties, semantically it is much more elusive than anything we find in "Easter." Who are the "They" of line 1 and line 6? The murderer of line 7? The link between one phrase and the next, between, say, the image of the "murderer's ash tray" and the "lake" as a "lilac cube," is even more tenuous than are O'Hara's typical connections. It is impossible to tell with any certainty what these two stanzas are saying; indeed Ashbery himself has always insisted that poems like this one aren't "saying" anything. By comparison, "Easter" is almost transparent; this first section, as I pointed out in Chapter 2, presents the poet's scatological vision of an unredeemed pre-Easter landscape with its absurd parade of bodily parts and other objects filing across the stage.

Interestingly, when both poets renounced "straight" Surrealism in the later fifties, the divergent stylistic traits I have just noted persisted—a situation that suggests to me that *The Tennis Court Oath* is not, as Bloom would have it, a total aberration from the Ashbery canon, a volume we can wish away in the interest of the later poetry. Here is a passage from "The Skaters," which is generally regarded as the finest poem in *Rivers and Mountains,* the volume Ashbery published in 1966, the year of O'Hara's death.

There was much to be said in favor of storms
But you seem to have abandoned them in favor of endless light.
I cannot say that I think the change much of an improvement.

> There is something fearful in these summer nights that go on
>   forever. . . .
>
> We are nearing the Moorish coast, I think, in a *bateau*.
> I wonder if I will have any friends there
> Whether the future will be kinder to me than the past, for example,
> And am all set to be put out, finding it to be not.
>
> Still, I am prepared for this voyage, and for anything else you
>   may care to mention.
> Not that I am not afraid, but there is very little time left.
> You have probably made travel arrangements, and know the feeling.
> Suddenly, one morning, the little train arrives in the station, but
>   oh, so big.
> It is! Much bigger and faster than anyone told you.
> A bewhiskered student in an old baggy overcoat is waiting to
>   take it.
> "Why do you want to go *there*," they all say. "It is better in the
>   other direction."
> And so it is. There people are free, at any rate. But where you
>   are going no one is.[32]

This is one of the more accessible parts of Ashbery's complex meditative poem about selfhood. Certainly its quest motif—the poet em-
barks on some sort of spiritual journey—is a familiar Romantic topos.
Lines like "I cannot say that I think the change much of an improvement" or "But where you / are going no one is" recall the Eliot of *Four
Quartets;* others, like "There is something fearful in these summer
nights that go on / forever" recall the Stevens of "An Ordinary Evening in New Haven." The text as a whole has affinities to Rilke's *Duino
Elegies.*

But the nature of the journey is shrouded in mystery. It begins "in
these summer nights" as the unspecified "We" near "the Moorish
coast, I think, in a *bateau*"—an obvious allusion to Rimbaud. But then
the *"bateau"* is replaced by "the little train," and it must be winter for
"A bewhiskered student in an old baggy overcoat is waiting to take it."
We do not know what the poet fears or why "there is very little time
left." "They"—whoever "They" are—warn him not to go *"there,"* and
he agrees that "in the other direction . . . people are free, at any rate."
But since we have no idea where *"there"* is, we cannot discriminate
between it and its opposite. And Ashbery obviously wants it that way.

The "travel arrangements" depicted in "The Skaters" are thus worlds apart from O'Hara's daily journeys through the streets of Manhattan:

> It's my lunch hour, so I go
> for a walk among the hum-colored
> cabs. First, down the sidewalk
> where laborers feed their dirty
> glistening torsos sandwiches
> and Coca-Cola, with yellow helmets
> on. They protect them from falling
> bricks, I guess. Then onto the
> avenue where skirts are flipping
> above heels and blow up over
> grates. The sun is hot but the
> cabs stir up the air. I look
> at bargains in wristwatches. There
> are cats playing in sawdust   (CP, 257)

O'Hara's "voyage" is a perfectly ordinary lunchtime stroll, but the poet's "phalanx of particulars" is carefully chosen to convey the peculiar animation that characterizes the city even on a hot day: the "hum-colored cabs" "stir up the air," the laborers' "dirty ... torsos" are "glistening"; their "yellow helmets" "protect them from falling / bricks"; "skirts are flipping / above heels and blow over grates." Everything is moving, changing, shifting ground, for the poem deals with the passage of time and eventually with death.[33] Ashbery's voyage "into the secret, vaporous night ... the unknown that loves us" (note the allusion to Baudelaire's "Le Voyage") is, by contrast, elusive, shadowy, archetypal. If his poetry lacks O'Hara's immediacy, it has, perhaps, a greater suggestiveness, a deeper resonance. If his voice is less genial and engaging, it compensates by its astonishing self-awareness, its fidelity to the mind's baffling encounter with the objects, whether real or imaginary, that it contemplates.

But we need not prefer one mode or one poet to the other. I have outlined some of the major differences between Ashbery and O'Hara only to make clear that the label "New York School," always something of a misnomer,[34] is no longer meaningful. Edwin Denby has put it beautifully:

Met these four boys Frank O'Hara, John Ashbery, Kenneth Koch, and Jimmy Schuyler ... at the Cedar Bar in '52 or '53. Met them through Bill (de Kooning) who was a friend of theirs and they admired Kline and all those people. The painters who went to the Cedar had more or less coined the phrase "New York School" in opposition to the School of Paris (which also originated as a joke in opposition to the School of Florence and the School of Venice). Great things started to happen in the Fifties—the point was the great effort in the Eighth Street Club . . . the brilliant discussions among painters which had broken through the provincialism of American painting. . . . So the poets adopted the expression "New York School" out of homage to the people who had de-provincialized American painting. It's a complicated double-joke. . . . So the New York School was a cluster of poets and it was through Frank O'Hara that the uptown poets and the downtown poets got together and eventually the West Coast too, plus the painters and Frank was at the center and joined them all together. After his death there was no center for that group.[35]

"After his death there was no center for that group." There we may, for the time being, let the matter rest. Today both Ashbery and O'Hara, like Allen Ginsberg, who was already famous in the early sixties, have an influence that transcends schools and geographic boundaries. Younger poets coming out of the O'Hara tradition no longer write direct imitations of his "personal poems" as did the first set of disciples who believed, in the words of Anne Waldman, that "Frank O'Hara gave a whole new generation of poets the freedom to put anything you want in a poem" and "showed that poems could be written on the run."[36]

It was, of course, never as simple as that. David Shapiro, a poet still under thirty, has observed that O'Hara's special forms of improvisation and speed must not be confused with "dashing things off" or putting anything you want in a poem. For at its best, "improvisation" becomes a way of discovering truth; in poems like "Memorial Day 1950," or "Joe's Jacket," or "The Day Lady Died," the fleeting "improvisatory" gestures ultimately become what Wallace Stevens called "Parts of a World." As in the great Abstract Expressionist paintings O'Hara loved, the "charged" poetic surface exemplifies the notion that "thinking *is* looking."[37]

"I remember," writes Joe Brainard, "Frank O'Hara's walk. Light and sassy. With a slight bounce and a slight twist. It was a beautiful walk. Confident. 'I don't care' and sometimes 'I know you are look-ing.'"[38] All his life, O'Hara refused to *care* in the conventional sense; he would not fight for publication or scramble for prizes. But perhaps he adopted this stance because he knew, all along, that sooner or later we would indeed be looking. As David Shapiro put it in the elegy he wrote for O'Hara when he was only twenty, we are now "lying against [the] cement to bring it back."[39]

NOTES

ABBREVIATIONS

CP   *The Collected Poems of Frank O'Hara.* Edited by Donald Allen. New York: Knopf, 1971.

PR   *Poems Retrieved.* Edited by Donald Allen. 240-page manuscript, in press. Bolinas, Calif.: Grey Fox Press. References are to typescript.

AC   *Art Chronicles 1954–1966.* New York: Braziller, 1975.

SS   *Standing Still and Walking in New York.* Edited by Donald Allen. Bolinas, Calif.: Grey Fox Press, 1975.

MS   All unpublished manuscripts, unless otherwise indicated, belong to the Frank O'Hara Estate. The numbers have been assigned by the executrix, Maureen Granville-Smith, and the literary editor, Donald Allen.

Chapter 1.: THE AESTHETIC OF ATTENTION

[1] Frank O'Hara speaking about David Smith in the NETA broadcast, "David Smith: Sculpting Master of Bolton Landing," *New York: The Continuity of Vision* series (New York: WNDT-TV, 1964).

[2] Alfred Leslie, preface to the catalogue of his solo exhibition, Allan Frumkin Gallery, 50 West 57th Street, New York (October 25–November 21, 1975). *The Killing of Frank O'Hara* is reproduced in the catalogue (Pl. 1) and in the following: *New York Times,* 9 November 1975, Section 2, p. 33; *Village Voice,* 10 November 1975, p. 112; and *Journal of Modern Literature,* 5, no. 3 (September 1976), 447.

[3] *Village Voice,* 10 November 1975, p. 113.

[4] *Soho Weekly News,* 13 November 1975, p. 24.

[5] Hilton Kramer comments: "It is a powerful painting, in which a great many pictorial tasks are handled with remarkable authority, and all of its dramatic effects serve to amplify a single, sustained idea. Yet I have to confess that I found something foolish in the notion, so clearly implied in the treatment here, that the poet's death, unbearably sad though it was for his friends and admirers, could legitimately be compared to Christ's descent from the cross. It is no disrespect to the memory of Frank O'Hara—quite the contrary, I think—to feel that the whole idea has been woefully misconceived." *New York Times,* 9 November 1975, Section 2, p. 33.

[6] The 1972 version was exhibited at the Whitney Biennial: see Jeanne Siegel, *Art News,* 72 (March 1973), 68–69. This version shows O'Hara lying flat on his back on the beach, while boys and girls in bathing suits are pushing the beach buggy away from the body. A young girl sits in front of the beach buggy, guarding the corpse. Stylistically, the 1972 version resembles the later one, but the death is not mythologized so thoroughly.

[7] Review of *CP* in *New York Times Book Review,* 28 November 1971, p. 7.

[8] Cf. O'Hara's "Ode on Causality" (*CP,* 302):
    make my lines thin as ice, then swell like pythons
    the color of Aurora when she first brought fire to the Arctic in a sled
    a sexual bliss inscribe upon the page of whatever energy I burn for art
    and do not watch over my life. . . .

[9] "Frank O'Hara Dead at 40," *East Village Other,* August 1966, p. 11.

[10] *Planet News* (San Francisco: City Lights Books, 1968), pp. 135–36.

[11] For a challenging but ultimately unconvincing presentation of the "myth" of the suicidal poet, see A. Alvarez, *The Savage God, A Study in Suicide* (New York: Random House, 1972).

[12] *The Advocate* (San Francisco), 2 June 1976, pp. 23–24, 31–33. Saslow draws much of his information from John Gruen's journalistic memoir, *The Party's Over Now, Reminiscences of the Fifties—New York's Artists, Writers, Musicians, and their Friends* (New York: Viking, 1972). Elaine de Kooning's comment, for example, is cited by Gruen on p. 212.

[13] See John Button, "Frank's Grace," *Panjandrum,* 2 & 3 (1973): Special Supplement, *Frank O'Hara (1926–1966),* edited by Bruce Boone, unpaginated. My sources for the information about the accident itself are: (1) the official transcript of the State of New York Department of Motor Vehicles hearing (Case No. 6-374190) held at Suffolk County Center, Riverhead, New York, February 15, 1967, before Roger Whelan, referee. Testifying were Kenneth L. Ruzicka, the driver of the jeep that hit O'Hara, and Patrolman Warren Chamberlain. (2) The deposition made on 15 January 1968 by J. J. Mitchell in the law offices of Sol Lefkowitz, 50 Broadway, New York, N.Y. I cite only those facts that are identical in both reports.

[14] "Frank O'Hara: Lost Times and Future Hopes," *Art in America,* 60 (March–April 1972), 53.

[15] *The New American Poetry,* ed. Donald Allen (New York: Grove, 1960). For an amusingly vituperative attack on *New American Poetry* and on O'Hara in particular, see Cecil Hemley, *Hudson Review,* 13 (Winter 1961), 626–30.

16 *New York Review of Books,* 31 March 1966, p. 20. For similar response, see Galway Kinnell, review of *Meditations in an Emergency* (1957) in *Poetry,* 92 (June 1958), 179; Kenneth Rexroth, review of *Meditations in an Emergency* in *New York Times,* 6 October 1957, p. 43; Raymond Roseliep, review of *Lunch Poems* (1964) in *Poetry,* 107 (February 1966), 326; Francis Hope, review of *Lunch Poems* in *New Statesman,* 69 (30 April 1965), 688.

Those who praised these books include Kenneth Koch, review of *Second Avenue* (1960) in *Partisan Review,* 28 (January–February 1961), 130–32; Ted Berrigan, review of *Lunch Poems* in *Kulchur,* 5, no. 17 (Spring 1965), 91–94.

17 *Hudson Review,* 25 (Summer 1972), 308. See also Pearl K. Bell, review of *CP* in *New Leader,* 55 (10 January 1972), 15–16. For more favorable reviews, see Ralph Mills, Jr., *Showcase/Chicago Sun-Times,* 13 February 1972, Section 16, p. 19; Walter Clemons, *Newsweek,* 20 December 1971, pp. 95–96.

18 "The Virtues of the Alterable," *Parnassus: Poetry in Review,* I(Fall/Winter 1972), 5.

19 *CP,* v. Since the publication of the *Collected Poems,* dozens of other O'Hara poems, especially from his earlier years, have surfaced and will fill two more volumes (see Bibliographical Note). We may, then, conceivably look forward to an even larger *Collected Poems* in the future.

20 "All the Imagination Can Hold" (review of *CP*), *New Republic,* 1 & 8 January 1972, p. 24.

21 Shapcott, *Poetry,* 122 (April 1973), 41; Rosenthal, *The New Poets, American and British Poetry Since World War II* (New York: Oxford, 1967). Cf. Monroe K. Spears, *Dionysus and the City, Modernism in Twentieth-Century Poetry* (New York: Oxford, 1970). Spears devotes twenty pages to Lowell, nine to James Dickey, two to Ginsberg, none to O'Hara.

22 *Salmagundi,* ed. Robert Boyers, No. 22–23 (Spring–Summer 1973); *The Norton Introduction to Literature: Poetry,* ed. J. Paul Hunter (New York: Norton, 1973). The most notable exception among anthologies is *Contemporary American Poetry,* ed. A. Poulin Jr., 2d ed. (Boston: Houghton Mifflin, 1975). Poulin covers thirty poets, representing the various contemporary schools. O'Hara is given nine pages—about the same number devoted to Denise Levertov or W. S. Merwin. In *The Norton Anthology of Modern Poetry* (New York: Norton, 1973), editors Richard Ellmann and Robert O'Clair adopt a very inclusive policy (more than 150 poets appear!); O'Hara is represented by nine poems.

23 The new interest in O'Hara among younger poet-critics may be exemplified by the following: Veronica Forrest-Thomson, "Dada, Unrealism and Contemporary Poetry," *20th Century Studies,* 12 (December 1974), 77–93; Charles Molesworth, "'The Clear Architecture of the Nerves': The Poetry of Frank O'Hara," *Iowa Review,* 6 (Summer–Fall 1975), 61–74; Anthony Libby, "O'Hara on the Silver Range," *Contemporary Literature,* 17 (Spring 1976), 240–62; Susan Holahan, "Frank O'Hara's Poetry," in *American Poetry Since 1960, Some Critical Perspectives,* ed. Robert B. Shaw (Cheadle Hulme: Carcanet Press, 1973), 109–22. A hopeful sign of things to come is the new edition of the well-known anthology, *Naked Poetry, Recent American Poetry in Open Forms* (New York: Bobbs–Merrill, 1976), edited by the poets Stephen Berg and Robert Mezey. The first edition (1969) did not include O'Hara among its nineteen poets. The new edition rectifies this omission.

[24] *The Poem in its Skin* (Chicago: Big Table, 1968), p. 204.

[25] See Fig. 3. This collaboration will be discussed fully in Chapter 3.

[26] Notes for a talk on "The Image in Poetry and Painting," The Club, 11 April 1952. Unpub. MS 467. In a second talk at The Club (14 May 1952), O'Hara criticizes younger poets like Richard Wilbur for creating an aesthetic "based on the memory of adolescent reading of Tennyson's *Idylls* and the dross of such important writers as T. S. Eliot." Even the California poets are criticized for "following the line Eliot discovered in his study of the English Metaphysical and French Symbolist poets. . . ." (unpub. MS 156).

[27] "The End of the Line: American Poetry, 1945-1955," Chapter 1 of a projected book; p. 23 of typescript.

In an unpublished letter to Mike Goldberg, 16 February 1956, O'Hara writes: "Did you read William Carlos Williams' autobiog? I love his poems, but the book is oddly crotchety and contentious and provincial. . . . I'm not sure that at the time things happened he didn't feel genuine admirations and thereby could advance and be stimulated, and then when he comes to right [*sic*] this book so many years later he forgets them. . . ." This comment would bear out Breslin's contention.

[28] See "T. S. Eliot as The International Hero," *Partisan Review,* 12 (Spring 1945); rpt. in *The Selected Essays of Delmore Schwartz,* eds. Donald A. Dike and David H. Zucker (Chicago: University of Chicago Press, 1970), pp. 120-28; "The Literary Dictatorship of T. S. Eliot," *Partisan Review,* 16 (February 1949); rpt. *Selected Essays,* pp. 312-31. On Williams's reputation, see Paul L. Mariani, *William Carlos Williams, the Poet and his Critics* (Chicago: American Library Association, 1975), esp. pp. 125-37.

[29] *Poetry and the Age* (New York: Knopf, 1953), p. 140.

[30] Phillip Cooper, *The Autobiographical Myth of Robert Lowell* (Chapel Hill: University of North Carolina Press, 1970), pp. 38-43.

[31] Breslin, "The End of the Line," p. 34.

[32] Frederick Seidel, "An Interview with Robert Lowell," *The Paris Review,* 25 (Winter–Spring 1961); rpt. in *Robert Lowell: A Portrait of the Artist in his Time,* eds. Michael London and Robert Boyers (New York: David Lewis, 1970), pp. 269-70.

[33] "A Poem's Becoming," *In Radical Pursuit* (New York: Harper & Row, 1975), p. 42.

[34] Boston: Little, Brown, 1964, p. 17.

[35] Paul Carroll's last chapter, "Faire, Foul and Full of Variations: The Generation of 1962," *Poem in its Skin,* pp. 202-59, is very helpful. See also Robert Creeley, *Contexts of Poetry: Interviews 1961-1971,* ed. Donald Allen (Bolinas: Four Seasons Foundation, 1973), especially Fred Wah's interview with Creeley and Ginsberg in Vancouver in 1963, pp. 29-43. Almost every essay in the special Charles Olson issue of *Boundary 2,* II (Fall 1973/Winter 1974) touches on the question of the Black Mountain revolt against tradition.

[36] "Frank O'Hara's Question," *Book Week,* 25 September 1966, p. 6.

[37] Edward Lucie-Smith, "An Interview with Frank O'Hara," *SS,* 13; first published in abbreviated form in *Studio International,* September 1966.

[38] Joseph LeSueur, "Four Apartments: A Memoir of Frank O'Hara," in *Another*

World, ed. Anne Waldman (New York: Bobbs-Merrill, 1971), p. 290. This important essay is hereafter cited as "Four Apartments." LeSueur added further detail to the anecdote and discussed O'Hara's reluctance to criticize other poets in an interview with the author on 30 July 1975, hereafter cited as "LeSueur Interview."

[39] In my opinion, O'Hara's judgment is less than fair here. "Skunk Hour," like the other poems in *Life Studies,* does represent a significant departure from neo-Symbolist poetics. See my *Poetic Art of Robert Lowell* (Ithaca, N.Y.: Cornell University Press, 1973), pp. 80–99.

[40] "Non-American Painting: Six Opinions of Abstract Art in Other Countries," *It is* (Winter–Spring 1959); rpt. as "American Art and Non-American Art" in *SS,* 98. In "Gregory Corso" (*SS,* 82–85), O'Hara talks of "the extraordinary beauties of Corso's poems."

[41] In an unpublished letter to Jasper Johns of 15 July 1959, O'Hara says, "Gary Snyder and Philip Whalen are both marvellous but you have to find them in EVERGREEN, MEASURE, BLACK MOUNTAIN, or YUGEN I think." He also praises Mike McClure.

[42] In the letter to Johns cited above, O'Hara writes: "Kerouac's DOCTOR SAX is his best work, I think, and after that the first sections of OLD ANGEL MIDNIGHT which are printed in the first issue of BIG TABLE." Joe LeSueur recalls an evening at the Cedar Bar in the Village, c. 1960, when Kerouac, very drunk, came up to O'Hara and said: "I thought you liked me." O'Hara replied: "It's not you I like, it's your work," a remark that pleased Kerouac very much.

[43] In the letter to Johns, Wieners heads O'Hara's list of poets that interest him.

[44] Letter to Johns. Of Robert Duncan, O'Hara writes to Johns: "I can't stand him myself, but he is their [the West Coast's] Charles Olson—to me he is quite flabby by comparison, but maybe because I'm on the East Coast."

[45] "Frank O'Hara and his Poems," *Art and Literature,* 12 (Spring 1967), 54.

[46] In the 1961 "Statement for Paterson Society" (*CP,* 510–11), O'Hara explains that "Personism" was intended for *New American Poetry,* but that "Allen thought it unwise to use it in relation to the earlier poems included, quite rightly, so I wrote another which he did use. This latter [*CP,* 500], it seems to me now, is even more mistaken, pompous, and quite untrue, as compared to the manifesto. But it is also, like the manifesto, a diary of a particular day." In "Four Apartments," Joe LeSueur describes the amusing genesis of "Personism," written in less than an hour (the zero hour because Don Allen was on his way over to pick it up!) to the tune of Rachmaninoff's Third blasting on the radio: Waldman, *Another World,* p. 296.

[47] O'Hara's familiarity with "Projective Verse" is made clear from the reference to "Charles Olson (whose theory of projective verse, among other things, recommends the use of the typewriter as an instrument, not just a recorder of thought)," in "Design Etc." (notes for a talk at The Club, 11 April 1952), *SS,* 34.

[48] *SS,* 33–34.

[49] See, for example, Bly, "On English and American Poetry," *The Fifties,* No. 2 (1959), pp. 45–47; and "The Dead World and the Live World," *The Sixties,* No. 8 (Spring 1966), pp. 2–7. LeRoi Jones attacks Bly's poetry and poetics in *Kulchur* 3 (Summer 1963), 83–84.

[50] L. S. Dembo, "George Oppen: An Interview," *Contemporary Literature,* 10 (Spring 1969), 161. Although this interview was made after O'Hara's death, it represents the kind of theorizing he disliked.

[51] Cited by John Ashbery in his review of *In Memory of My Feelings* in *Art News,* 66 (January 1968), 68.

[52] Unpub. letter to Bill Berkson, 12 August 1962.

[53] "Statement for *The New American Poetry* (1960)," *CP,* 500.

[54] "Art as Technique," in *Russian Formalist Criticism: Four Essays,* trans. and ed. Lee T. Lemon and Marion J. Reis (Lincoln, Neb.: University of Nebraska Press, 1965), pp. 12–13. For a fuller discussion of Shklovsky's aesthetic and a comparison of various translations of his key terms, see my "New Thresholds, Old Anatomies: Contemporary Poetry and the Limits of Exegesis," *Iowa Review,* 5 (Winter 1974), 88–89.

[55] "American Art and Non-American Art," *SS,* 98.

[56] There are a number of allusions to Rilke in the *Collected Poems,* for example: "Do you know young René Rilke?" in "Poem (To be idiomatic in a vacuum)," *CP,* 282; and "Aus Einem April" (*CP,* 186) is a loose adaptation of Rilke's poem. Albert Cook praises this poem for its ingenious way of "de-'poeticizing' the language" of the German poet. "His *Aus einem April,*" says Cook, "is a commentary on Rilke so full-throated that all the chaste ironies of Pound's commentaries on Propertius and Gautier, Waller or Homer, get lost in the Saturnalian shuffle...," "Frank O'Hara, We Are Listening," *Audit/Poetry,* 4, no. 1 (1964): Frank O'Hara Issue, 34.

[57] The German text is:
> Ja, die Frühlinge brauchten dich wohl. Es muteten manche
> Sterne dir zu, dass du sie spürtest. Es hob
> sich eine Woge heran im Vergangenen, oder
> da du vorüberkamst am geöffneten Fenster,
> gab eine Geige sich hin. Das alles war Auftrag.

The text used is Rainer Maria Rilke, *Duino Elegies, with English Translations* by C. F. MacIntyre (Berkeley and Los Angeles: Univ. of California Press, 1968), p. 4. The translation is my own since I disagree with some of MacIntyre's readings, but it is a very difficult passage to translate accurately: "die Frühlinge," for example, when translated literally as "the springs," loses its effect. On the poet's duty to be "attentive," see also Rilke, *Letters to a Young Poet,* trans. M. D. Herter Norton (New York: Norton, 1962), p. 65.

[58] "Larry Rivers: A Memoir," *CP,* 515.

[59] Larry Rivers, *Collage with O'Hara Poem,* exhibited in "Frank O'Hara, A Poet Among Painters," *Whitney Museum of American Art,* 12 February–17 March 1974. In "Post the Lake Poets Ballad" (*CP,* 336–37), O'Hara refers to "a letter from Larry":
> it's so hot out
> and I read the letter which says
> in your poems your gorgeous self-pity
> how do you like that
>
> that is odd I think of myself
> as a cheerful type who pretends to

> be hurt to get a little depth into
> things that interest me. . . .

> no more self-pity than Gertrude
> Stein before Lucey Church or Savonarola
> in the pulpit Allen Ginsberg at the
> Soviet Exposition am I Joe

[60] According to Donald Allen, this essay was written in 1953 or later, apparently as a letter to an editor of a literary magazine (*CP*, 495).

[61] "The Search for the Real in the Visual Arts," in *Search for the Real and Other Essays*, eds. Sara T. Weeks and Bartlett H. Hayes, Jr. (Cambridge, Mass.: M.I.T. Press, 1967), pp. 44–45.

[62] *Jackson Pollock* (New York: Braziller, 1959); rpt. *AC*, 34–35.

[63] "Growth and Guston," *Art News* (May 1962); rpt. *AC*, 141.

[64] "Art Chronicle I," *Kulchur*, 2 (Summer 1962); rpt. *SS*, 132; *AC*, 11.

[65] "Art Chronicle I," *SS*, 130; *AC*, 9.

[66] "Art Chronicle III," *Kulchur* 3 (Spring 1963), 56; rpt. *SS*, 141.

[67] "David Smith: The Color of Steel," *Art News*, 60 (December 1961); rpt. *SS*, 123.

[68] "The Sorrows of the Youngman, John Rechy's *City of Night*," *Kulchur* 3 (Winter 1963); rpt. *SS*, 162–63.

[69] In a letter to the author dated 13 July 1975, Donald Allen writes: "In conversation with me in 1958 and 1959 Frank spoke several times of WCW as being the only poet around that he could read in the late forties (when *Paterson* was appearing)." In the unpublished letter to Mike Goldberg of 16 February 1956 (see Note 27 above), O'Hara says: "If the long poem in his new book of poems JOURNEY TO LOVE isn't great, I'm going to take up knitting." The reference is to "Asphodel, that Greeney Flower." Williams's influence is discussed more fully in the next chapter.

[70] "About Zhivago and his Poems," commissioned by Donald Allen and first published in *Evergreen Review*, 2 (Winter 1959); rpt. *CP*, 503.

[71] "Abstraction in Poetry," *It Is*, 3 (Winter–Spring 1959), 75.

[72] On this point, see Charles Altieri, "The Significance of Frank O'Hara," *Iowa Review*, 4 (Winter 1973), 99. Altieri's essay is of central importance and I am indebted to it throughout this book.

[73] *Belgrade, November 19, 1963* (New York: Adventures in Poetry, n.d.), pp. 1–2.

[74] *CP*, 325–26. "515 is 'off' Madison on 53d; Frank would have passed it every day to and from the Museum. Its door facade is very beautiful" (Bill Berkson to Donald Allen, July 1969), *CP*, 543.

Chapter 2: THE EARLY YEARS (1946–53)

[1] Journal: October 8, 1948 to January 28, 1949. Unpub. MS 472, p. *n*. Hereafter cited as Harvard Journal.

[2] *A Portrait of the Artist as a Young Man* (New York: Viking/Compass, 1967), p. 168.

[3] "Lament and Chastisement: a Travelogue of War and Personality," Unpub. MS 631, pp. 7, 17–18.

[4] Unpub. Course Description, "Francis Russell O'Hara. Harvard College A.B. 1950," prepared by Marion C. Belliveau, Registrar, Harvard University, June 24, 1974.

[5] Notebook A, Unpub. MS, pp. 73–131.

[6] Harvard Journal, pp. *i–j.*

[7] "V. R. Lang: A Memoir," *Village Voice,* 23 October 1957; rpt. *SS,* 86.

[8] Dated 24 April 1947: Notebook A, p. 10.

[9] Unpub MS 146.

[10] In an interview conducted on 15 September 1975 in New York, John Ashbery told the author that he doubts O'Hara knew enough French to read these difficult texts. Donald Allen, in a letter to the author of 19 September 1975, writes: "Frank was not terribly confident of his French. He asked me to have John A. check his translations before publishing them because John had lived so long in France and perfected his knowledge. But Frank's knowledge must have been considerable; he read it with ease; and he did translate some very difficult French verse. He translates part of a Breton title in 'All that Gas,' another instance." Paul Schmidt, who says in the Preface to his translation of Rimbaud's *Complete Works* (New York: Harper & Row, 1975) that he owes a special debt "to the late Frank O'Hara, whose criticism and suggestions are reflected many times here" (p. xx), concurs with Allen's view in a letter to the author dated 16 September 1975.

[11] Lucie-Smith, "Interview with Frank O'Hara," *SS,* 10. Later in the interview, O'Hara tells Lucie-Smith, "There's a big gap in my thinking about English poetry, although for instance I admire very much Tomlinson and Thom Gunn" (p. 24).

[12] Notes for a talk on "The Image in Poetry and Painting," The Club, 11 April 1952, Unpub MS 467, p. 2.

[13] In the interview of 15 September 1975, Ashbery described how O'Hara tried to talk him into attending a Schoenberg concert at Harvard; Ashbery did not attend but later came round to O'Hara's high opinion of the composer.

[14] John Ciardi, undated letter to Donald Allen.

[15] Harvard Journal, pp. *g, t.*

[16] Aside from the Preface to the Collected Poems and the obituary essay in *Book Week,* 25 September 1966, p. 6, Ashbery wrote an important review of *In Memory of My Feelings* for *Art News,* 66 (January 1968), 50–51, 67–68.

[17] PR, 1.

[18] Dated 15 November 1946: Notebook A, pp. 1–4.

[19] *CP,* 12–13. O'Hara here weaves together lines and phrases from various poems by Baudelaire, especially "La Beauté," and Rimbaud's notorious prose poem, "H," which

is generally taken to be about masturbation or anal intercourse and ends with the enigmatic words, "trouvez Hortense." See Rimbaud, *Oeuvres,* ed. Suzanne Bernard (Paris: Garnier, 1960), pp. 531–32.

[20] Unpub. MS 296, "Pastorals," pp. *d–p.* Cf. *CP,* 519.

[21] One could make an interesting comparison between O'Hara's early poetry and that of Rimbaud. Both poets begin by trying to write—against the grain—conventional heterosexual love poems in keeping with the going convention and then later drop the mask. In both cases, the early poetry is full of blasphemous attacks on the Church and scatological imagery. See, for example, Rimbaud's "Les premières communions" and "Remembrances du vieillard idiot."

[22] Rilke's clearest statement about the doll as a death symbol is found in the essay "Puppen, Zu den Wachs-Puppen von Lotte Pritzel," *Sämtliche Werke,* Vol. 6 (Berlin: Insel Verlag, 1960, pp. 1063–73, and notes on pp. 1486–89).

[23] *Dada* (New York: Studio Vista/Dutton, 1970), pp. 37–38.

[24] Mary Ann Caws, *The Poetry of Dada and Surrealism* (Princeton: Princeton University Press, 1970), p. 14.

[25] In the First Manifesto (1924), Breton gives this definition: "SURREALISM, noun. Pure psychic automatism by means of which we propose to express either verbally, in writing, or in some other fashion what really goes on in the mind. Dictation by the mind, unhampered by conscious control and having no aesthetic or moral goals." Translation by Herbert S. Gershman, *The Surrealist Revolution in France* (Ann Arbor: University of Michigan Press, 1974), p. 35.

[26] *CP,* 10. Duchamp invented the word play "Rrose Sélavy" in 1920; Desnos then borrowed the name for his amusing series of poems of 1922–23. In the same poem O'Hara also refers to Duchamp's famous *Nude Descending a Staircase:*
> the next time I see you
> clattering down a flight of stairs like a
> ferris wheel jingling your earrings and feathers . . .

[27] *The Poetry of Surrealism, An Anthology* (Boston: Little, Brown, 1974). Hereafter cited as *Poetry of Surrealism.*

[28] Notes for a talk on "The Image in Poetry and Painting," The Club, 11 April 1952. Unpub. MS 467, p. 2.

[29] Notes for a talk on "The New Poets," The Club, 14 May 1952, Unpub MS 156, p. 3.

[30] Letter to Jasper Johns, 15 July 1959. O'Hara's allusion is to Williams's essay "Revelation," first published in *Yale Poetry Review* (1947) and reprinted in *Selected Essays of William Carlos Williams* (New York: New Directions, 1954), pp. 268–71. The essay begins: "The objective in writing is, to reveal. It is not to teach, not to advertise, not to sell, not even to communicate . . . but to reveal."

[31] Notes for a talk on "The New Poets," The Club, 14 May 1952, Unpub. MS 156, p. 3.

[32] *The Collected Earlier Poems of William Carlos Williams* (Norfolk, Conn.: New Directions, 1951), p. 105.

[33] John Ashbery, Joe LeSueur, and Donald Allen have all noted in conversation that O'Hara's selection of poems to be published tended to be arbitrary, and that he did not care to judge his own work.

[34] Ashbery, Preface to the *Collected Poems,* vii.

[35] It is interesting to compare O'Hara's reference to plane trees to Robert Lowell's well-known "As a Plane Tree by Water," in which Lowell alludes to Ecclesiastes 24:19: "As a plane tree by the water in the streets, I was exalted," implying that in the modern "Babel of Boston," "flies are on the plane trees"—nature is wholly corrupted. The plane tree, used as a central symbol by Lowell, is simply an item in the Cambridge landscape for O'Hara—another tree would do just as well.

[36] Again an allusion to Rilke; see Note 22 above.

[37] See Caws, *Poetry of Dada and Surrealism,* pp. 20, 47–48. The concept of *vertige* is particularly prominent in the poetry of Aragon, for whom "the term *vertige* implies both rapidity . . . and total involvement."

[38] John Ciardi, unpublished letter to Donald Allen, undated.

[39] Underneath the title, O'Hara wrote "A Pathetic Note to George Montgomery" and then crossed it out.

[40] *The Collected Poems of Dylan Thomas* (New York: New Directions, 1953), p. 142.

[41] "John Ashbery and Frank O'Hara: The Painterly Poets," *Journal of Modern Literature,* 5, no. 3 (September 1976), 442–43.

[42] *A Homemade World, The American Modernist Writers* (New York: Knopf, 1975), pp. 86, 59.

[43] *Williams, Collected Earlier Poems,* p. 173. For additional analogues, see "The Descent of Winter, 9/30" (p. 298), especially the last stanza: "there is no hope—if not a coral / island slowly forming / to wait for birds to drop / the seeds will make it habitable"; and "Night Rider," in *The Collected Later Poems of William Carlos Williams* (New York: New Directions, 1963), p. 71.

[44] Many other love poems from the Ann Arbor period are similarly written in the Williams mode. "A Proud Poem" (*CP,* 52–53), for example, recalls Williams's "Danse Russe" in its charming bravado: "I am hopelessly happily conceited / in all inventions / and divertissement. . . .and when I'm cornered at the final / minute by cries 'you've / murdered angels with toys' I'll go down / grinning into clever flames."

[45] "Frank O'Hara: A Poet Among Painters" (review of the Whitney show by that name), *Art News,* 73 (May 1974), 44–45.

[46] "The Club," *Artforum,* 4, no. 1 (September 1965) Special Issue: The New York School, 27–31.

[47] "Design Etc.," *SS,* 33–35.

[48] See Eliot, "Reflections on Vers Libre" (1917) in *To Criticize the Critic* (New York: Farrar, Straus & Giroux, 1965), p. 185.

[49] Notes for a talk on "The Image in Poetry and Painting," The Club, 11 April 1952, Unpub. MS 467, p. 4.

50 *A Homemade World,* Chapter 3. *passim.*

51 W. H. Auden, unpublished letter to Frank O'Hara, 3 June (1955?). The parody of Wyatt may be compared to the actual octave:

> My galley charged with forgetfulness
> Through sharp seas in winter nights doth pass
> 'Tween rock and rock and eke my foe, alas,
> That is my lord, steereth with cruelness.
> And every [oar] a thought in readiness.
> As though that death were light in such a case,
> An endless wind doth tear the sail apace
> of forced sighs and trusty fearfulness.

52 Caws, *Poetry of Dada and Surrealism,* pp. 33–35.

53 I owe this information to Donald Allen (letter to the author, 2 January 1976).

54 *The Collected Poems of Wallace Stevens* (New York: Knopf, 1961), pp. 3, 76.

55 Thomas Shapcott, *Poetry,* 122 (1973), 43–44. Charles Molesworth, in "'The Clear Architecture of the Nerves': The Poetry of Frank O'Hara," *Iowa Review,* 6 (Summer-Fall 1975), calls the mode of "Easter" that of "surreal serendipity. . . . It resembles very strongly the 'paranoical-critical' method enunciated by Salvador Dali, and in attributing occult and protean abilities to everyday objects, it has the same mixture of theatricalized terror and whimpering playfulness as Dali's paintings" (pp. 66–67).

56 Rimbaud, *Complete Works,* trans. Paul Schmidt, pp. 108–13. Schmidt freely translates the title as "Remarks to a Poet on the Subject of Flowers."

57 "A Note on Frank O'Hara in the Early Fifties," *Audit/Poetry,* 4, no. 1 (1964): Frank O'Hara Issue, 33; rpt. *CP,* 526.

58 "Poetry Chronicles," *Partisan Review,* 28 (January–February 1961), 130–32.

59 *CP,* 558.

60 Interview with Grace Hartigan, conducted in Baltimore, 25 November 1975.

61 In *Parnassus* (Fall/Winter 1972), Helen Vendler says: "The longest poems end up simply messy, endless secretions, with a nugget of poetry here and there, slices of life arbitrarily beginning, and ending for no particular reason. 'Dear Diary,' says O'Hara, and after that anything goes" (pp. 5–6). In his essay on O'Hara for *Alone with America* (New York: Atheneum, 1969), pp. 396–412, Richard Howard writes: "Each time I read *Second Avenue* I bear off a handful of glittering lines . . . but they are never the same lines, and never suggest anything converging, opposing or even subordinating in the kind of tension that makes for unity. . . ." (p. 404). Howard calls *Second Avenue* "a poem . . . of promiscuous agglomerations, a virtuoso *performance* in discourse without composition" (p. 403).

62 For another example of O'Hara's incorporation of the names of friends into the poetry of this period, see "Day and Night in 1952," *CP,* 93–94.

Chapter 3: POET AMONG PAINTERS

1 *Art in America,* 53 (October–November 1965), 24.

[2] Preface to *In Memory of My Feelings. A Selection of Poems by Frank O'Hara,* ed. Bill Berkson (New York: Museum of Modern Art, 1967), pages unnumbered.

[3] *Art News,* 66 (January 1968), 68. Cf. John Button, "Frank's Grace," *Panjandrum,* 2 & 3 (1973): "The job at MOMA gave him less and less leisure at precisely the time he could have been writing his best poetry."

[4] "Four Apartments," p. 291. Cf. James Schuyler, *Art News,* 73 (May 1974), 45: "Frank needed a job and he was in love with the museum and brooked no criticism of it. . . . And he was highly organized, with a phenomenal memory."

[5] In a letter to Bruce Boone, the editor of the special O'Hara supplement of *Panjandrum,* Grace Hartigan writes: "that Frank was a homosexual was very understandable to me—I love men, why shouldn't he? It never—what would?—interfered with our love for each other. I'm not the first person to say that sex isn't necessarily love and vice-versa." Grace Hartigan made the same point to the author in an interview conducted on 25 November 1975. Between 1951 and 1960, she and Frank saw each other or spoke on the phone almost every day. They frequently spent weeks—even months— together in the country. Thus they knew each other's projects intimately. In 1960, after a major quarrel with Frank, Grace left New York, married, and settled in Baltimore. She sent him a strongly worded letter breaking off all relations. They did not see each other again for five years, and then only briefly.

[6] *CP,* 486.

[7] In a letter to the author dated 10 February 1976, Grace Hartigan identifies the first painting as "Ocean Bathers" (1953), Collection of Mrs. Muriel Newman (Chicago), and the second as "Frank O'Hara and the Demons" (1952), Collection Grace Hartigan. Both paintings, Hartigan notes, seek to capture "Frank's body stance, his posture."

[8] In an unpublished letter of 8 April 1957, O'Hara wrote to Helen Frankenthaler:

> I'm enclosing a poem I wrote recently to find out if I can use your title on it [*Blue Territory*]. Now, please, if you don't like it or if the association bothers you in the slightest . . . please tell me and I can change it to "Boo Titulary" or something. . . . I can always call it tersely, "Poem" as in the past.

In a poetry reading at Buffalo on 25 September 1964, taped by Donald Allen, O'Hara remarked before reading "Blue Territory" that seeing Helen Frankenthaler's large abstract painting by that name in the Whitney gave him the idea for the poem, though he didn't quite know why.

[9] *Dada, Surrealism, and Their Heritage* (New York: Museum of Modern Art, 1968), p. 148. See also Diane Waldman, *Joseph Cornell* (New York: Braziller, 1977).

[10] See, for example, "Design Etc.," *SS,* 33; and "Apollinaire's Pornographic Novels," *SS,* 156–59. Grace Hartigan told me in the interview of 25 November 1975 that Frank often said he didn't want to live any longer than Apollinaire. The French poet died at the age of 40; so, by uncanny coincidence, did O'Hara.

[11] *Apollinaire on Art, Essays and Reviews 1901–1918,* The Documents of 20th Century Art (New York: Viking, 1971), p. xxix.

[12] *Kulchur,* 3, no. 9 (Spring 1963); rpt. *SS,* 140.

[13] John Canaday was the *Times* art critic; Emily Genauer wrote for the *Herald Tribune*. O'Hara writes:

> . . . each has devoted, at least one slack week in each season, a whole column to their difficulties in getting themselves physically to the galleries, Mr. Canaday notably in his lament over bus service on Madison Avenue column, and Miss Genauer in her candid appraisal of a safari as far south as Houston Street, with aid of cab driver and delicatessen clerk, in search of the Delancey Street Museum. Neither one of them has any better sense of geography of traffic than they do of art.
>
> Mr. Canaday's speciality along this line has been the wise-suspicion-of esthetic-hoax strategy, a strategy aimed exclusively at the abstract-expressionists with the equally simplistic belief, apparently, that no figurative artist has ever wanted to sell a painting. (*SS,* 144–45)

[14] "Watch Out for the Paint! The Salon des Indépendants. 6,000 Paintings are Exhibited" (1910), in *Apollinaire on Art,* pp. 64–65.

[15] See Amy Golden, *Art in America,* 63 (March–April 1975), 41; Eleonor Dickinson, *San Francisco Review of Books,* 1, no. 4 (August 1975), 6, 18–19. I take the opposite position in my review of *AC* in *The New Republic,* 1 March 1975, pp. 23–24.

[16] "Introduction," *New Spanish Painting and Sculpture* (New York: Museum of Modern Art, 1960), p. 10.

[17] *Art News,* 52 (December 1953), 42.

[18] *Art News,* 53 (January 1954), 64.

[19] *Art News,* 54 (February 1955), 53.

[20] *Art News,* 53 (April 1954), 47.

[21] See, for example, Allen Weller, *Art Journal,* 20 (Fall 1960), 52–56. Similar strictures can be made about O'Hara's short essay, "Jackson Pollock 1912–1956," in *New Images of Man,* ed. Peter Selz (New York: Museum of Modern Art, 1959), pp. 123–28. O'Hara calls Pollock's black-and-white paintings of 1951 "ideographs from a subjective world we do not know . . . the *Chants de Maldoror* of American art" (p. 123).

[22] *Horizon* (September 1959), rpt. *AC,* 106–20. Cf. O'Hara's television interview with David Smith (cited Chapter 1, Note 1). O'Hara calls Smith's life "the American tragedy in reverse," for Smith was "a Henry James hero who influenced Europe rather than being corrupted by it," a "Thomas Wolfe, whose dreams, strangely enough, came true." The interview suggests that Smith did not think of his sculptures as "abstract" at all. He calls them "females," saying, "I don't do males. I like the presence of these females." To which O'Hara responds: "They seem like friends who came to New York. They're relieved not to be in mid-air any more." O'Hara interviewed Barnett Newman for the same series.

[23] See Sam Hunter, *Larry Rivers,* with a Memoir by Frank O'Hara and a Statement by the Artist, Exhibition of the Poses Institute of Fine Arts, Brandeis University, Waltham, Mass., 1965. Hunter provides a brief chronology (pp. 45–46), and his introduction is very useful.

[24] Hunter, *Larry Rivers,* p. 20.

[25] Larry Rivers wrote: "His long marvelous poem *Second Avenue,* 1953, was written in my plaster garden studio overlooking that avenue. One night late I was working on a piece of sculpture of him. Between poses he was finishing his long poem. Three fat cops saw the light and made their way up to make the 'you call this art and what are you doing here' scene that every N.Y. artist must have experienced." "Life Among the Stones," *Location* (Spring 1963); rpt. *CP,* 529.

[26] See Roger Shattuck, *Guillaume Apollinaire* (New York: New Directions, 1971), pp. 18–20.

[27] Reproduced in Rubin, *Dada, Surrealism and their Heritage,* pp. 27–28.

[28] Motherwell, *The Dada Painters and Poets, An Anthology* (New York: Wittenborn, Schultz, Inc., 1951), p. 62. The translation is by Ralph Manheim.

[29] Ibid., pp. 56, 274. In "The Grand Manner of Motherwell" (1965), O'Hara writes: "I first met Motherwell in East Hampton in, probably, 1952. When we did talk later, it was almost always about poetry: Apollinaire, Baudelaire, Jacob, Reverdy, Rilke (not so much), and Lorca (lots), and we also got to Wallace Stevens and William Carlos Williams. I had been tremendously impressed by the Documents of Modern Art Series [*Dada Painters* was No. 8] which Motherwell had edited (indeed it was the Gospels for myself and many other poets)," *SS,* 176.

[30] Rubin, *Dada, Surrealism,* p. 96, Plate 129.

[31] "Max Ernst: Passed and Pressing Tensions," *Hudson Review,* 23 (Winter 1970–71); rpt. *Art Journal,* 33 (Fall 1973), 12.

[32] Quoted by Lippard, "Max Ernst," 12.

[33] Lippard, 14.

[34] *Location* (Spring 1963), 90–98.

[35] "The Skin of the Stone," *The Scene, Reports on Post-Modern Art* (New York: Viking, 1976), p. 58. Tompkins provides a very interesting biographical sketch of Tatyana Grossman and discusses *Stones* as well as the other collaborations made in her workshop. See also Cleve Gray, "Tatyana Grossman's Workshop," *Art in America,* 53 (December–January 1965–66), 83; Herbert Mitgang, "Tatyana Grossman, 'the inner light of 5 Skidmore Place,'" *Art News,* 73 (March 1974), 29–32.

[36] Quoted by Tompkins, *The Scene,* pp. 61–62.

[37] Rivers, *Location,* 92. Succeeding quotations from Rivers are from the same source.

[38] Sidney Tillin, *Arts Magazine,* 34 (December 1959), 62.

[39] See Gertrude Stein, *Everybody's Autobiography* (1937; rpt. New York: Vintage, 1973), p. 15.

[40] In the Lucie-Smith interview, O'Hara suggests that his only true collaboration was *Stones* (*SS,* 4–5). He quite rightly points out that his work with painters like Mike Goldberg and Grace Hartigan did not involve collaboration; rather they used his poems. But he seems to have forgotten *Poem-Paintings,* which was nothing if not a truly collaborative effort, the two artists working simultaneously throughout.

[41] Notes to Exhibition catalogue of *Poem-Paintings,* Loeb Student Center, New York University, January 9–February 5, 1967.

[42] *Art News,* 65 (February 1967), 11.

[43] Interview with Norman Bluhm, 2 December 1975, New York.

[44] *Art News,* 65 (February 1967), 11.

[45] The O'Hara–Brainard cartoons were originally made for *C Comics,* edited by Joe Brainard (New York, 1964–65). A series of these is reproduced in *Panjandrum,* 2 & 3 (1973).

[46] A related example may be found in the work of Franz Kline. Kline took O'Hara's "Poem (I will always love you . . .)," written in 1957, and incorporated it in O'Hara's own handwriting in an etching made for the portfolio *21 Etchings and Poems,* published by the Morris Gallery in 1960; see Notes to the *CP,* 539.

[47] "Poets and Painters and Painters and Poets." *New York Times,* 11 August 1968, Section II, 24.

[48] Berkson, Notes to catalogue of *Poem-Paintings.*

[49] Unpub. letter to Gregory Corso, 15 March 1968.

Chapter 4: IN FAVOR OF ONE'S TIME (1954–61)

[1] Unpub. letter to Fairfield Porter, 7 July 1955.

[2] The friendship with Grace Hartigan ended in 1960 when she left New York (see Chapter 3, Note 5). Patsy Southgate met O'Hara on Memorial Day 1958 when she gave a Bloody Mary party at Easthampton; Mike Kanemitsu, Donald Allen, and Mike Goldberg (later Patsy's husband) were also there. In an interview conducted in New York on 30 March 1976, Patsy Southgate told the author, "I was his closest woman friend during the last part of his life. We were in love."

[3] Unpub. letter to John Ashbery, 1 February 1961.

[4] LeSueur Interview, 30 July 1975.

[5] Lawrence Ferlinghetti, letter to Bruce Boone, 3 February 1973, in *Panjandrum,* 2 & 3 (1973), unpaginated.

[6] *Lunch Poems* (San Francisco: City Lights Books, 1964), back cover. Ferlinghetti estimates that seven years elapsed between his proposal that O'Hara "make a book" from the "poems he wrote on his lunch hour" and the publication of *Lunch Poems* (letter to Bruce Boone cited above). We know that the project was on O'Hara's mind in 1959, because when John Ashbery asked him for a group of poems possibly influenced by Reverdy, to be used in Ashbery's forthcoming essay on Reverdy's influence on American poets, O'Hara replied: "I had them [the poems] prepared to go into *Lunch Poems* which Ferlinghetti asked me for 2 years ago and has doubtless ceased to care about. But that's why I have copies to send," unpub. letter to John Ashbery, 1 February 1961.

[7] The others are "Now that I am in Madrid and Can Think," "Song (Did you see me walking by the Buick Repairs?)," "Cohasset," "Beer for Breakfast," "St. Paul and All

That," "Pistachio Tree at Château Noir," "Adventures in Living," and "Hôtel Particulier."

[8] Introduction to *The Floating Bear,* rpt. of the semimonthly newsletter 1961–69, eds. Diane di Prima and LeRoi Jones (New York: 1970), pp. viii–ix. Diane di Prima was quite right, as O'Hara's Harvard Notebook and the forthcoming *Poems Retrieved* make clear.

[9] Unpub. letter to Mike Goldberg, 16 February 1956. Courtesy Giorno Poetry Systems, The Archives, in which the letter is numbered 15,306. The story of the lost typewriter is told by Joe LeSueur in "Four Apartments," p. 290.

[10] In an interview conducted in New York on 30 March 1976, David Shapiro told the author that John Ashbery once expressed this feeling about using long lines. That O'Hara equated line length with strength and vitality is suggested by the prayer in "Ode on Causality": "make my lines thin as ice, then swell like pythons" (*CP,* 302).

[11] In the interview of 30 July 1975, LeSueur told the author that he preferred O'Hara's realistic, documentary poems—the "I do this, I do that" poems—to all others.

[12] Shapiro interview, 30 March 1976.

[13] "Art as Technique," in *Russian Formalist Criticism, Four Essays,* trans. and ed. Lee T. Lemon and Marion J. Reis (Lincoln, Neb.: University of Nebraska Press, 1965), p. 13.

[14] "The Significance of Frank O'Hara," *Iowa Review,* 4 (Winter 1973), 91.

[15] The phrase is David Shapiro's; interview of 30 March 1976. For an excellent account of O'Hara's ability to transcend "pure facts" and empiricism, see Shapiro's article on O'Hara in *Contemporary Poets,* ed. James Vinson, 2d ed. (New York: St. Martin's, 1975), pp. 1778–81.

[16] *The Poem in its Skin* (Chicago: Big Table, 1968), p. 164.

[17] *The Dada Painters and Poets, An Anthology,* ed. Robert Motherwell (New York: Wittenborn, Schultz, 1951), pp. xxxv–vi. The translation is by Dollie Pierre Carreau. See also Carroll, *The Poem in its Skin,* pp. 164–68.

[18] *The Cantos of Ezra Pound* (New York: New Directions, 1971), pp. 508–09.

[19] *Iowa Review,* 4 (Winter 1973), 93–94.

[20] Eric Sellin, "The Esthetics of Ambiguity: Reverdy's Use of Syntactic Simultaneity," in *About French Poetry from DADA to "Tel Quel," Text and Theory,* ed. Mary Ann Caws (Detroit, Mich.: Wayne State University Press, 1974), p. 117.

[21] *Art and Illusion: A Study of the Psychology of Pictorial Representation,* The A. W. Mellon Lectures in the Fine Arts, 1956 (New York: Pantheon, Bollingen Series XXXV.5, 1960), pp. 281–86.

[22] *Selected Writings of Guillaume Apollinaire,* trans. and ed. Roger Shattuck (New York: New Directions, 1971), p. 121.

[23] A whole essay could be written on O'Hara's allegiance to Reverdy, although the actual influence of the French poet is one of spirit rather than substance. In "A Step Away from Them," O'Hara writes: "My heart is in my / pocket, it is Poems by Pierre Reverdy" (*CP,* 258). When Ashbery asked O'Hara to contribute poems that might be

influenced by Reverdy for the special Reverdy issue of *Mercure de France,* O'Hara responded, half-jokingly: "I just couldn't stand the amount of work it [the Reverdy project] would seem to take, since the minute you mentioned it I decided that everything I've written except *In Memory of My Feelings* and *Dig my Grave with a Silver Spoon* has been under his influence." Later in the letter (1 Feb. 1961), he adds: "I think probably 'the eyelid has its storms' is somewhat influenced by *Une vague solitaire*" and then asks, "Do you think *Naphtha* is sort of Reverdian?" O'Hara did collaborate with Bill Berkson on a short prose-poem on Reverdy; see *Mercure de France,* 344 (1962), 97–98. Among other things, this piece contains the sentence: "In America there is only one other poet *beside* Reverdy: William Carlos Williams." The prose poem is reprinted in *The World,* Special Translations Issue (4 April 1973), 91–92. See also John Ashbery, "Reverdy en Amérique," *Mercure de France,* 344 (1962), 109–12.

[24] Translation by Eric Sellin, in Caws, ed., *About French Poetry,* p. 119.

[25] See Chapter 1. In the interview with Lucie-Smith, O'Hara says: "I think Lowell has . . . a confessional manner which lets him get away with things that are really just plain bad but you're supposed to be interested because he's supposed to be so upset" (*SS,* 13).

[26] See "About Zhivago and his Poems" (1950); rpt. *CP,* 501.

[27] "All the Imagination Can Hold," *New Republic,* January 1 & 8, 1972, 24; David Shapiro, in a letter to the author dated 20 July 1976, says: "The collected works is Frank O'Hara's best work and should be thought of (like Stevens) as the lyric as it attempts epic scale." Joe LeSueur, in a letter to the author dated 20 July 1976, mentions that James Merrill also read the *CP* cover to cover "as an autobiography."

[28] See James Schuyler's note to the poem "Mayakovsky" (1954) in *CP,* 532–33.

[29] *The Bedbug and Selected Poetry,* ed. Patricia Blake and trans. Max Hayward and George Reavey (Bloomington, Ind.: Midland Books, 1975), p. 159.

[30] *The Bedbug and Selected Poetry,* pp. 137–43.

[31] Another influence frequently cited is that of Rilke. My own view (see Chapter 1) is that Rilke had more influence on O'Hara's poetic than on his poetry, although O'Hara's "Aus Einem April" (*CP,* 186) is an important example of "Making it New" via parody-translation. There are also important thematic links—the treatment of the dolls in "Memorial Day 1950" (see Chapter 2) is a case in point. But O'Hara's style does not really resemble Rilke's.

[32] I owe this information to Patsy Southgate, interview of 30 March 1976.

[33] Unpub. letter to Bill Berkson, 12 August 1962.

[34] *Larry Rivers* (New York: Abrams, 1971), p. 24.

[35] Grace Hartigan, letter to the author dated 14 March 1976.

[36] Rimbaud, *Complete Works, Selected Letters,* ed. and trans. Wallace Fowlie (Chicago: Phoenix Books, 1966), pp. 217–18.
I am the saint in prayer on the terrace like the peaceful animals that graze as far as the sea of Palestine.
I am the scholar in his dark armchair. Branches and rain beat against the library window.

I am the wanderer along the main road running through the dwarfish woods . . .
I might be the child abandoned on the wharf. . . .

[37] See Chapter 3, Note 7.

[38] Unpub. letter to Fairfield Porter, 7 July 1955.

[39] Poetry Reading, Buffalo, New York, 25 September 1964, taped by Donald Allen.

[40] I think O'Hara is referring to Pollock's early painting *Bird* (1941; Collection Lee Krasner, New York), reproduced in Alberto Busignani, *Pollock* (New York: Crown, 1970), p. 20. The painting has a birdlike shape emerging from a white cloud near the top center of the canvas. Others have suggested that O'Hara was thinking of Brancusi's famous sculpture *Bird in Space* in the Museum of Modern Art. In either case, the implication is that the dead artist is reborn as a work of art.

[41] The fifteen poems in *Love Poems (Tentative Title)* (New York: Tibor de Nagy Gallery, 1965) are roughly equivalent to what I call the "Vincent Warren" poems although there are some exceptions like "Post the Lake Poets Ballad" and "Poem (Now the violets are all gone . . .)." In the *Collected Poems,* the Vincent Warren poems are found on the following pages: 331, 332, 338, 342, 345, 346, 349–56, 360–62, 366–69, 373–74, 376–78, 380, 382, 385, 387, 396, 400, 402, 405–06.

[42] "The Corn-Porn Lyric: Poetry 1972–73," *Contemporary Literature,* 16 (Winter 1975), 84–125.

[43] Vincent Warren, untitled memoir of Frank O'Hara (Montreal 1973) in *Panjandrum,* 2 & 3 (1973), unpaginated.

[44] Unpub. letter to John Ashbery, 1 February 1961.

Chapter 5: THE PILLAR OF OUR DEATHS

[1] In the *Collected Poems,* the period from July 1961 to June 1966 is covered by a scant 84 of the total 491 pages, and most of the poems in this section date from 1961–62. The year 1963 is represented by only eleven poems, 1964 by thirteen, 1965 by three. We have only one published poem for 1966: the "Little Elegy for Antonio Machado," written for the catalogue of John Bernard Myers's "Homage to Machado" Show (a benefit for refugees of the Spanish Civil War) at the Tibor de Nagy Gallery. *Poems Retrieved* adds eleven poems from 1961 (a number of which are "For Your Information" poems for Bill Berkson), nine for 1962, three for 1964, one for 1965. These are, on the whole, slight occasional poems.

[2] In an unpublished letter to John Ashbery, dated 1 February 1961, O'Hara writes: "I have been writing in desultory fashion a little play called THE GENERAL'S RETURN FROM ONE PLACE TO ANOTHER but am having quite a bit of trouble as to ending it (and how?) or letting it go on until it is the size of a Lope de Vega. . . . I believe it was inspired by a wonderful production of Brecht's wonderful *In the Jungle of Cities* which the Living Theatre has in repertory now and my dislike for General MacArthur, if inspired at all can be mentioned in 'connection' with it."

[3] *Art and Literature,* 10 (1965); rpt. in *Eight Plays from OFF-OFF Broadway,* eds. Nick Orzell and Michael Smith (New York: Bobbs Merrill, 1966), p. 21.

[4] Joe LeSueur Interview, 20 July 1975.

[5] Unpub. letter to Frank Lima, 6 February 1963.

[6] In advance commentary, John Ashbery writes: "The poems in Frank Lima's marvelous new collection are bright, corrosive, funny, terrifying—reflections in a surreal eye focused outward on life in today's city;" and David Shapiro says: "Frank Lima's work has developed into something as steely, menacing and fine as the welder's art of David Smith. It is a species of American linguistic sculpture" (*New York Review of Books,* 24 June 1976, p. 13).

[7] *In Public, In Private* was originally published in 1948 by James A. Decker Co., Prairie City, Illinois. It is reprinted in Edwin Denby's *Collected Poems* (New York: Full Court Press, 1975).

[8] "Paraphrase of Edwin Denby speaking on 'The New York School'," as recorded by Anne Waldman, *The World* (April 1974), 73.

[9] *Panjandrum,* 2 & 3 (1973), unpaginated.

[10] John Ashbery, Note appended to "Play," by John Ashbery, Kenneth Koch, and Frank O'Hara, *ZZZ* [*Z,* no. 3], ed. Kenward Elmslie (Calais, Vt.: Z Press, 1974), 122.

[11] Unpub. letter to Bill Berkson, 12 August 1962.

[12] *Hymns of St. Bridget* has been published in pamphlet form (New York: Adventures in Poetry, 1974). Two of these "Hymns," which are still very much in the tradition of O'Hara's "I do this, I do that" poems, were published in *Evergreen Review,* 6, no. 24 (May–June 1960), 107–09. "Us Looking up at St. Bridget," for example, begins:

> Let's see now where are we
> it is dust in New York about to be
> Christmas and next 1961 we are not
> detectives are we so we don't care
> what time it is

The "Letters of Angelicus & Fidelio Fobb" have recently been reprinted in *ZZZ* [*Z,* no. 4] (1975), 90–109. These letters seem to be modeled on the prose of Ronald Firbank or Evelyn Waugh. For example, one letter from Angelicus to Fidelio, dated 14 August 1961 from the "Alhambra Hotel, Secondary Bridge Road, Punselheim, Pa.," begins:

> Upon lighting my first cigarette of this morning, I found that I was excruciatingly bored, not to say sick unto death. Even the permissions which Prussy has placed and arranged so delicately on my breakfast plate could not assuage this terrible feeling which must have had something to do with the night before and the day (or days) ahead. (p. 92)

This is a fair example of the humor of the Fobb Letters.

[13] *CP,* 553–54. *M.L.F.Y.* evidently means "My Love For You." "Biotherm" was the one O'Hara poem included in Paris Leary and Robert Kelly's anthology, *A Controversy of Poets* (New York: Doubleday/Anchor, 1965), which also contains a brief biographical and bibliographical note on O'Hara (p. 544).

[14] This is the view of Charles Molesworth, who calls "Biotherm" a "collage which seldom rewards lingering attention or compels an energized response. Somehow the poem manages to bring the marvelous and the humdrum together, not so much as

fragments of heterogeneous values jostling together, but as an aleatory set of transcriptions, the recording of many merely different things," "The Clear Architecture of the Nerves: The Poetry of Frank O'Hara," *Iowa Review,* 6 (Summer–Fall 1975), 64.

[15] Ted Berrigan, *The Sonnets* (New York: Grove, 1964), p. 32.

[16] Ron Padgett, *Great Balls of Fire* (New York: Holt, Rinehart and Winston, 1969), p. 9.

[17] "Frank O'Hara Dead at 40," *East Village Other,* August 1966, p. 11.

[18] The four elegies are "To an Actor Who Died" (*CP,* 226); "For James Dean" (*CP,* 228); "Thinking of James Dean" (*CP,* 230); and "Four Little Elegies" (*CP,* 248)—all written in 1955–56.

[19] "The Significance of Frank O'Hara," *Iowa Review,* 4 (Winter 1973), 103. See also Paul Carroll, *The Poem in its Skin* (Chicago: Big Table, 1968), pp. 155–68.

[20] On this point, see Norman Holland, *Poems in Persons, An Introduction to the Psychoanalysis of Literature* (New York: Norton, 1973), p. 122.

[21] See the following: Allen Ginsberg, "City Midnight Junk Strains," *Planet News* (San Francisco: City Lights Books, 1969), pp. 134–37; Patsy Southgate, "Nobody Operates like an IBM Machine: For Frank O'Hara," *Evergreen Review,* 45 (February 1967), 50; Tony Towle, "Sunrise: Ode to Frank O'Hara," *Paris Review,* 11 (Fall 1967), 117; James Schuyler, "Buried at Springs," *Freely Espousing* (New York: Doubleday, 1969), rpt. *An Anthology of New York Poets,* ed. Ron Padgett and David Shapiro (New York: Random House, 1970), pp. 15–17; David Shapiro, "Ode," *Poems From Deal* (New York: Dutton, 1969), pp. 59–60; Gerard Malanga, "In Memory of the Poet Frank O'Hara 1926–1966," *The World Anthology,* ed. Anne Waldman (New York: Bobbs-Merrill, 1969), pp. 134–36; Ron Padgett, "Strawberries in Mexico," *Great Balls of Fire,* pp. 83–85; John Wieners, "After Reading *Second Avenue:* For Frank O'Hara," *Paris Review,* 13 (Winter 1971), 60–61; Diane di Prima, "From Kerhonson, July 28, 1966" and "Inverness, Cape Breton Island," *Panjandrum* 2 & 3 (1973), unpaginated.

[22] The trend for such pairing was probably first established by John Bernard Myers in his anthology *The Poets of the New York School* (Philadelphia: Falcon Press, 1969), pp. 1–29. See also Fred Moramarco, "John Ashbery and Frank O'Hara: The Painterly Poets," *Journal of Modern Literature* 5, no. 3 (September 1976), 436–62. Stephen Koch, "The New York School of Poets: The Serious at Play," *New York Times Book Review,* 11 February 1968, pp. 4–5.

[23] Richard Kostelanetz, "How to be a Difficult Poet," *New York Times Magazine,* 23 May 1976, pp. 19–20.

[24] "Rare Modern," *Poetry,* 89 (February 1957); rpt. *SS,* 77–78.

[25] Unpub. letter to Mike Goldberg, 26 August 1957.

[26] Unpub. letter to John Ashbery, 1 February 1961.

[27] Kostelanetz, *New York Times Magazine,* p. 22.

[28] "The Charity of Hard Moments," *Salmagundi,* 22–23 (Spring–Summer 1973), 103–31; rpt. *American Poetry Since 1960, Some Critical Perspectives,* ed. Robert B. Shaw (Cheadle Hulme: Carcanet Press, 1973), pp. 83–108. For the comments cited, see Shaw,

pp. 85–86. "Europe" appeared in *The Tennis Court Oath* (Middletown, Conn.: Wesleyan University Press, 1962), pp. 64–85.

29 Kostelanetz, *New York Times Magazine,* p. 22.

30 See, for example, John Russell, review of *Une Semaine de Bonté, A Surrealistic Novel in Collage* (1934; rpt. New York: Dover, 1976), in the *New York Times Book Review,* 4 July 1976, pp. 6–7.

31 *The Tennis Court Oath,* p. 13.

32 *Rivers and Mountains* (New York: Holt, Rinehart and Winston, 1966), p. 43. "The Skaters" first appeared in *Art and Literature,* 3 (Autumn/Winter 1964); O'Hara undoubtedly read it there.

33 I discuss "A Step Away from Them" more fully in "Poetry Chronicle 1970–71," *Contemporary Literature,* 14 (Winter 1973), 99–102.

34 At the time Donald Allen used the term in his *The New American Poetry* (1960), it did, of course, have validity in distinguishing O'Hara, Ashbery, Koch, Schuyler, Barbara Guest, and Edward Field from the Black Mountain Poets, the Beats, and the poets of the "San Francisco Renaissance." But Allen himself insists that his divisions are "somewhat arbitrary and cannot be taken as rigid categories" (p. xii). Of the New York group, he writes quite simply: "John Ashbery, Kenneth Koch, and Frank O'Hara, of the fourth group, the New York Poets, first met at Harvard where they were associated with the Poets' Theatre. They migrated to New York in the early fifties where they met Edward Field, Barbara Guest, and James Schuyler, and worked with the Living Theatre and the Artists' Theatre" (p. xiii).

35 *World,* 29 (April 1974), 73.

36 Lita Hornick, "Anne Waldman: A Myriad Woman," *The Poetry Project Newsletter,* 36 (1 June 1976), 1.

37 David Shapiro, letter to the author, 20 July 1976.

38 *I Remember* (New York: Full Court Press, 1975), p. 14.

39 "Ode," *Poems from Deal* (New York: Dutton, 1969), p. 60.

BIBLIOGRAPHICAL NOTE

PRIMARY SOURCES

Poetry

The Collected Poems of Frank O'Hara, edited by Donald Allen (New York: Knopf, 1971), is the definitive critical edition. Aside from the poems, it contains selected essays and statements by the poet as well as excellent notes by Donald Allen. The volume thus supercedes the following earlier collections: *A City Winter, and Other Poems* (New York: Tibor de Nagy Gallery, 1952); *Meditations in an Emergency* (New York: Grove Press, 1957; 2nd ed., 1967); *Second Avenue* (New York: Totem Press-Corinth Books, 1960); *Odes* (New York: Tiber Press, 1960); *Lunch Poems* (San Francisco: City Lights Books, 1964); *Love Poems* (*Tentative Title*) (New York: Tibor de Nagy Gallery, 1965).

In 1974, Alfred A. Knopf published *The Selected Poems of Frank O'Hara,* edited by Donald Allen. This generous selection contains 216 pages of poems. Allen is currently preparing for publication two more volumes to include those poems that have come to light since 1971 as well as juvenilia. They will be called *Early Writing* and *Poems Retrieved,* both to be published by Grey Fox Press, Bolinas, California.

With the appearance of these two volumes, publication of the poems will be largely complete.

In Memory of My Feelings, A Selection of Poems by Frank O'Hara, edited by Bill Berkson, with "original decorations" by thirty artists, a Preface by René d'Harnoncourt and an Afterword by Bill Berkson, is an important collector's item containing illustrations by Willem de Kooning, Jasper Johns, Grace Hartigan, Alfred Leslie, and others.

The following of O'Hara's collaborations have been published: *Hymns of St. Bridget,* with Bill Berkson (New York: Adventures in Poetry, 1974); "Letters of Angelicus and Fidelio Fobb," with Bill Berkson, *ZZZZ,* ed. Kenward Elmslie (Calais, Vt.: Z Press, 1975), pp. 90–109; "The Purest Heart in the Whole Wide World" and "Sam" (1964) with Tony Towle, *Panjandrum,* 2 & 3 (San Francisco, 1973): Special Supplement, *Frank O'Hara (1926–1966),* ed. Bruce Boone.

The World, 27 (April 1973; Special Translations Issue), 92–98, contains O'Hara's translations of poems by Hoelderlin, Rilke, Rimbaud, Mallarmé, and Char. O'Hara was very modest about these translations; Ron Padgett, editor of the special issue, points out that "the versions selected and presented in this issue must not be considered final ones," since the poet would have wished to check them. But some, like the translation of Rimbaud's "Le Coeur Volé," are remarkable, constituting a valuable adjunct to the *Collected Poems.*

Miscellaneous Prose

O'Hara published more than a hundred essays, reviews, notes, and introductions to books and catalogues. The most important of these are collected in *Art Chronicles 1954–1966* (New York: Braziller, 1975) and *Standing Still and Walking in New York,* ed. Donald Allen (Bolinas, Calif.: Grey Fox Press, 1975). Others—art criticism, literary criticism, reviews of friends' books, etc.—are cited in the Notes above. The bibliography at the back of *Art Chronicles* is helpful for the uncollected art criticism.

Plays

The following plays have been published: "Try! Try!," in *Artist's Theatre,* ed. Herbert Machiz (New York: Grove Press, 1960); "The General Returns from One Place to Another," in *Art and Literature,* 10

(1965), rpt. in *Eight Plays from OFF-OFF Broadway*, eds. Nick Orzell and Michael Smith (New York: Bobbs Merrill, 1966), pp. 21–52; "Surprising J.A.," with Larry Rivers, in *Tracks*, 1 (November 1974), 59–62.

Unpublished Manuscripts

The Frank O'Hara Estate has an important group of unpublished essays, journals, and miscellaneous papers. Notebook A, dating from the Harvard years, contains, aside from the poems to be published by Donald Allen in *Early Writing*, a Commonplace Book, outlining O'Hara's literary interests. This, together with MS 146, a French reading list, help the reader to track down O'Hara's sources. MS 296, "Pastorals," a group of nineteen poems, is the first version of the early sequences of "Oranges."

MS 472 ("Journal, October 8, 1948 to November 30, 1948, with an appendix, January 21, 1949 to January 28, 1949") is an important autobiographical source, providing background on the Harvard years. MS 656 ("False Positions"), MS 631 ("Lament and Chastisement: a Travelogue of War and Personality"), and MS 638 ("Eye at Argos") are undergraduate essays. MS 467 ("Notes for a talk on 'The Image in Poetry and Painting,' The Club, 11 April 1952") and MS 156 ("Notes for a talk on 'The New Poets,' The Club, 14 May 1952") provide invaluable information about O'Hara's aesthetic. These two lectures should be read in conjunction with "Design Etc.," in *Standing Still and Walking in New York*, pp. 33–36.

Manuscripts of unpublished plays include: "Change Your Bedding," produced by the Poets' Theatre in Cambridge, Mass., in 1951; "Love's Labor: An Eclogue" and "Awake in Spain," both produced by the American Theatre for Poets in New York in 1960; "The Moon Also Rises" (MS 245), 1957, unproduced.

Forthcoming Publications

Donald Allen's edition of *Early Writing* will include the following: "Notebook Poems, 1946–1949"; a second group of poems written between 1946 and 1950, some of which were included in the manuscript of *Poems Retrieved*, which is my source throughout; "Pastorals" (MS 296)"; and prose pieces MSS 472, 631, 638, 656.

Full Court Press in New York is currently preparing an edition of the *Selected Plays of Frank O'Hara*, with a Preface by Joe LeSueur. The Museum of Modern Art is planning to reissue the Frank O'Hara-Larry Rivers lithographs *Stones* in a portfolio. Twenty-two of the O'Hara-Norman Bluhm *Poem-Paintings* were included in the Autumn 1976 show of the Grey Art Gallery, New York University, where they are available for viewing.

Donald Allen is editing the *Collected Letters of Frank O'Hara*. This is a formidable undertaking: O'Hara was a brilliant and prolific correspondent, and his letters will provide an invaluable document on the art world of the fifties and sixties.

Alex Smith is now at work on a comprehensive bibliography of Frank O'Hara for Garland Publishing Company.

SECONDARY SOURCES

The following short list includes only the most important items, both biographical and critical. All but the most minor articles, reviews, and memoirs of O'Hara are included in the Notes above.

Altieri, Charles. "The Significance of Frank O'Hara," *Iowa Review,* 4 (Winter 1973), 90–104.

Ashbery, John. "Frank O'Hara's Question," *Book Week,* 25 September 1966, p. 6.

———. Review of *In Memory of My Feelings, Art News,* 66 (January 1968), 50–51, 67–68.

———. Preface to *The Collected Poems of Frank O'Hara.*

Berkson, Bill. "Frank O'Hara and his Poems," *Art and Literature,* 12 (Spring 1967), 50–64.

———. Afterword to *In Memory of My Feelings* by Frank O'Hara.

Carroll, Paul. *The Poem in Its Skin* (Chicago: Big Table, 1968).

Feldman, Morton. "Frank O'Hara: Lost Times and Future Hopes," *Art in America,* 60 (March–April 1972), 52–55.

Forrest-Thompson, Veronica. "Dada, Unrealism and Contemporary Poetry," *20th Century Studies,* 12 (December 1974), 77–93.

Holahan, Susan. "Frank O'Hara's Poetry," *American Poetry Since 1960, Some Critical Perspectives,* ed. Robert B. Shaw (Cheadle Hulme: Carcanet Press, 1973), pp. 109–22.

Koch, Kenneth. "All the Imagination Can Hold" (review of the *Collected Poems*), *New Republic*, 1 & 8 (January 1972), 23–24.

LeSueur, Joseph. "Four Apartments: A Memoir of Frank O'Hara," *Another World*, ed. Anne Waldman (New York: Bobbs-Merrill, 1971), pp. 287–300.

Libby, Anthony. "O'Hara on the Silver Range," *Contemporary Literature*, 17 (Spring 1976), 140–62.

Lucie-Smith, Edward. "An Interview with Frank O'Hara" (1965), *Standing Still and Walking in New York*, ed. Donald Allen (Bolinas, Calif.: Grey Fox Press, 1975), pp. 3–26.

Molesworth, Charles. "'The Clear Architecture of the Nerves': The Poetry of Frank O'Hara," *Iowa Review*, 6 (Summer–Fall 1975), 61–73.

Myers, John Bernard. *The Poets of the New York School*, selected and edited by John Bernard Myers (Philadelphia: Falcon Press, 1969).

Perloff, Marjorie. "Poetry Chronicle 1970–71," *Contemporary Literature*, 14 (Winter 1973), 99–102.

————. "New Thresholds, Old Anatomies: Contemporary Poetry and the Limits of Exegesis," *Iowa Review*, 5 (Winter 1974), 83–99.

Rivers, Larry. "Life Among the Stones," *Location* (Spring 1963), 90–98.

Schuyler, James. "Frank O'Hara: Poet among Painters," *Art News*, 73 (May 1974), 44–45.

Shapiro, David. "Frank O'Hara," *Contemporary Poets*, ed. James Vinson, 2d. ed. (New York: St. Martin's, 1975), pp. 1778–81.

Vendler, Helen. "The Virtues of the Alterable," *Parnassus: Poetry in Review*, 1 (Fall/Winter 1972), 5–20.

Special Journal Issues Devoted to O'Hara

Audit/Poetry, 4, no. 1 (Buffalo, 1964): "Featuring Frank O'Hara," eds. Michael Anania and Charles Doria. Contains essays by Kenneth Koch and Albert Cook.

Panjandrum, 2 & 3 (San Francisco, 1973): "Special Supplement, Frank O'Hara (1926–1966)," ed. Bruce Boone. Contains memoirs and essays by Virgil Thompson, Vincent Warren, Joe Brainard, and John Button.

GENERAL INDEX

Strindberg, Arthur, 33
Stroheim, Eric von, 130
Swenson, May, 11

Tate, Allen, 10, 34
Taylor, Elizabeth, 28
Taylor, Paul, 114
Tchaikowsky, Pyotr Ilich, 58
Tennyson, Alfred, Lord, 32, 202 n. 26
Thomas, Dylan, 34, 54, 60, 139
Thompson, Virgil, 114
Tillin, Sidney, 212 n. 38
Tobey, Mark, 87
Todd, Ruthven, 60
Tolstoy, Leo, 33
Tomlinson, Charles, 206 n. 11
Tompkins, Calvin, 100, 212 n. 35
Towle, Tony, 183
Tworkov, Jack, 60
Tzara, Tristan, 29, 40, 65, 74, 120, 126, 156

Van Dongen, Kees, 90
Van Gogh, Vincent, 52
Vega, Lope de, 216 n. 2
Velazquez, Diego, 130
Vendler, Helen, 6, 72, 209 n. 61
Verlaine, Paul, 103–104, 181–182
Villiers de l'Isle-Adam, 34
Voltaire, Francois, 33–34

Wah, Fred, 202 n. 35
Waldman, Anne, 196, 217 n. 8
Waldman, Diane, 210 n. 9

Warhol, Andy, 87
Warren, Robert Penn, 9–10
Warren, Vincent, 80, 114, 117, 148, 156–163, 171, 216 n. 41
Waugh, Evelyn, 217 n. 12
Weber, Ben, 114
Webern, Anton von, 191
Webster, John, 33
Weill, Kurt, 34
Weiss, Theodore, 8
Weller, Allen, 211 n. 21
Welles, Orson, 28
Whalen, Philip, 8, 14, 184, 203 n. 41
Whitehead, Alfred North, 56
Whitman, Walt, 18, 32, 67, 69, 184
Wieners, John, 15, 114, 183, 203 n. 43
Wilbur, Richard, 9, 11, 24, 202 n. 26
Williams, Tennessee, 114
Williams, William Carlos, xii, 9–10, 25, 38
    44–48, 54–56, 61, 63, 69, 76, 120, 125, 138,
    149, 173, 180, 182, 184, 202 n. 27, 205 n. 69,
    207 n. 30, 208 n. 43 and n. 44, 212 n. 29,
    214–215 n. 23
Wolfe, Thomas, 211 n. 22
Woolf, Virginia, 33
Wordsworth, William, 32, 45, 52, 139, 153,
    156
Wright, James, 8, 30
Wyatt, Thomas, 62, 175, 209 n. 51

Yeats, W. B., 34, 60, 62, 131, 136, 157, 181

Zukovsky, Louis, 61
Zweig, Paul, 8

INDEX
THE WRITINGS OF
FRANK O'HARA

of a typical general store, complete with all the goods stocking the shelves.

The research library at the museum is a historian's dream come true. Open to the public, it houses the largest collection of materials relating to the history of Nevada and the Great Basin. You can find long-lost relatives plus delve into the minutiae of the past in the library's books, newspaper files, maps, and photographs.

The society also sponsors a provocative variety of ongoing educational events throughout the year, such as lectures, trips, and gala exhibits. If you're looking for volunteer opportunities, it's a great place to investigate: Volunteers are used in many areas, including the expanded gift shop. You can also support the museum by buying an annual membership for about $35.

The museum and gift shop are open Monday through Saturday from 10:00 a.m. to 5:00 p.m., and the library is open Tuesday through Saturday from noon to 4:00 p.m. Admission to the museum is $3 for adults, $2 for seniors, and children are admitted free.

I recommend combining visits to the museum and the Fleischmann Planetarium since they're adjacent to each other (see the earlier entry for details on the planetarium).

i The winner of the 1929 contest that named Reno "The Biggest Little City in the World" walked away with $100 in prize money, even though he copied the slogan from one used for the Jeffries-Johnson boxing match that took place in 1910.

RENO ARCH NORTH
Virginia Street and
Commercial Row

If you're on North Virginia Street in downtown Reno, you simply can't miss the Reno Arch. Blazing with 800 feet of neon tubing and 1,600 lights, it welcomes visitors in grand style to "The Biggest Little City in the World." The slogan was the result of a 1929 contest conducted by the mayor to publicize the city.

The slogan stuck, and the Arch has been the identifying landmark for Reno ever since. It has been redesigned and replaced several times; the present structure was erected in 1987. An older arch constructed mainly of steel and lit with neon is at 10 Lake Street next to the National Automobile Museum.

SIERRA SAFARI ZOO
10200 North Virginia Street
(775) 677-1101
www.sierrasafarizoo.com

Animal lovers say they have died and gone to animal heaven when visiting this zoo nestled at the base of Peavine Mountain. It offers a rare up-close and personal opportunity to interact with more than 150 exotic animals. Distinct from the glitzy, big-city zoos of concrete cages and prolific souvenir stands, this zoo is just about animals in a natural setting.

Free to roam behind security fences, most of the animals have been born and hand-raised in captivity. Many are exceptionally gentle and tolerant of human touch. Visitors can view 40 different species from around the world, including ringtail lemurs (primates from the Malagasy Republic), audads (sheep from the Middle East), and servals (cats from the African savannas).

Children especially enjoy the petting section of the zoo, where they can wander among the animals to pet and feed them.

Dedicated to the propagation and preservation of animals, the zoo is nonprofit and staffed almost entirely by volunteers. Zoo workers have named all the animals, such as Elvira, the North American alligator who is affectionately known as "the lizard with an attitude," and Baby, an adorable sulfur crested cockatoo who enjoys saying "I love you."

To reach the zoo, take the Red Rock Road exit off US 395 about 8 miles north of Reno. Turn left and go underneath the underpass to the second road, and then turn left again. Don't be put off by the unpretentious appearance of the zoo. It's well worth the visit. The zoo is open daily April through October from 10:00 a.m. until 5:00

p.m., weather permitting. If the weather is questionable, you might want to call ahead. (See the Kidstuff chapter for more information.)

TRUCKEE RIVER WALK
Arlington and Island Avenues

On its route from Lake Tahoe to Pyramid Lake, the Truckee River flows through Reno, bringing much-needed water to the desert environment. The river provides a fertile habitat for a wide variety of wildlife as well as a delightful place for residents and visitors to enjoy the outdoors.

One of the easiest ways to enjoy the river is to take the Truckee River Walk in either direction from Wingfield Park on Arlington and Island Avenues. Heading west, the walk meanders past old Victorian homes shaded by huge elms and cottonwoods, and then enters Idlewild Park, with its rose garden, children's playland, and ponds full of waterfowl. From here it continues on for several miles past Oxbow Park to Chrissie Caughlin Park on West McCarran Boulevard.

Going east through the business section of downtown, the path wanders through a variety of other small parks to finally end near Vista Boulevard east of Sparks. The distance from Chrissie Caughlin Park to Vista Boulevard is about 10 miles. As you walk along, keep your eyes peeled for the many birds that live here, such as flycatchers, mallards, belted kingfishers, hawks, and Canada geese. And don't be surprised at the number of anglers trying their luck, as the Truckee is considered a premium fishing stream (see the Fishing and Hunting chapter).

Bikes and in-line skates are welcome on the path, but motorized vehicles are not. Dogs need to be leashed, and owners are expected to clean up after them. See the Parks chapter for more details about Wingfield and Idlewild Parks.

THE WILBUR MAY CENTER AT RANCHO SAN RAFAEL PARK
1595 North Sierra Street
(775) 785-5961
www.maycenter.com

The Wilbur May Center at Rancho San Rafael Park has something for everyone. It's a museum, an arboretum, and an adventure park. The son of David May, founder of the May Department Stores Company, Wilbur D. May lived in Reno from 1936 until his death in 1982. A philanthropist dedicated to the welfare of children, Wilbur D. May's legacy lives on through the foundation that built and maintains the center.

Designed as a comfortable ranch-style home, the Wilbur D. May Museum showcases May's eclectic collection of memorabilia gathered from his more than 40 trips around the world. An avid art and antiques collector, May acquired such treasures as rare T'ang Dynasty pottery, primitive African artwork, and Egyptian scarabs. His life as a rancher is chronicled in the tack room, with its elaborate array of Western artifacts. And his years as a big-game hunter are reflected in the trophy room, with dozens of animals from all over the world. Although the contents are professionally displayed and documented, the museum has the ambience of a home rather than a public building. Visitors almost feel as if May himself had invited them over for a private showing of his residence.

The Wilbur D. May Arboretum and Botanical Garden contains pools, waterfalls, and a xeriscape garden of plants indigenous to the high-desert climate. And designed especially for children ages 2 through 12, the Wilbur D. May Great Basin Adventure has a petting zoo, pony rides, and a log flume ride.

Hours and admission prices of the museum change, so call (775) 785-5961 for current information. The adventure park is open from 10:00 a.m. to 5:00 p.m. Tuesday through Saturday and from noon to 5:00 p.m. Sunday from Memorial Day through Labor Day. Admission is $5 for adults and $3.50 for seniors and children ages 3 though 12. Children younger than age 3 are admitted free. A children's birthday pavilion can be rented for three hours at $30. There is no charge to view the botanical garden. (See the Kidstuff chapter.)

SPARKS

SPARKS HERITAGE FOUNDATION AND MUSEUM

820 Victorian Avenue
(775) 355-1144
www.nevadamuseums.org

In 1904 Sparks was the busiest railroad terminal between Ogden, Utah, and Sacramento, California. Its location near the base of the Sierra Nevada mountains was strategic for the large steam engines that pulled trains over the mountain passes to the valleys in California. Much of the city's early history is tied to the railroad, including its nickname, Rail City.

The Sparks Heritage Foundation and Museum allows visitors to step back in time and experience those turn-of-the-20th-century railroad days. Much of the memorabilia is railroad oriented, such as the model train collection that begins with the DeWitt Clinton and ends with the last of the steam-driven engines. Other displays include a barber shop with a collection of 200 razors and a full-size Amish-type carriage, circa 1910. While the displays are not elaborate, history buffs will love the variety and attention to detail.

Hours are 11:00 a.m. to 4:00 p.m. Tuesday through Friday and 1:00 to 4:00 p.m. Saturday; closed Sunday and Monday. Although admission to the museum is free, donations are welcomed. (See also the Kidstuff chapter.)

VICTORIAN SQUARE

Victorian Avenue

When the citizens of Sparks decided to revitalize their downtown area some years ago, they selected a colorful turn-of-the-20th-century theme appropriate to the Rail City's history. The result was Victorian Square, a 4-block area featuring a bandstand gazebo, Victorian-style storefronts and streetlights, park benches, a fountain, and a 14-screen movie theater complex.

Also in keeping with the historical theme is the Glendale School at the east end of the square. Constructed in 1864 on a nearby ranch, it is the oldest remaining school building in Nevada. It was relocated to the square in 1993.

Victorian Square is the place to be for special events, such as the Best in the West Nugget Rib Cook-Off, Hot August Nights, and the Sparks Hometowne Christmas. (See the Annual Events chapter for details on these.) On Thursday from June through September, you can buy fresh produce and enjoy cooking demonstrations and musical events at the Sparks Hometowne Farmers' Market. Hours for the market are 4:00 to 9:00 p.m. June through late August.

To get to the square, take Interstate 80 east and exit on Rock Boulevard. Turn left onto Rock, and then right onto Victorian Avenue.

WILD ISLAND FAMILY ADVENTURE PARK

250 Wild Island Court
(775) 359-2927
www.wildisland.com

Wild Island Family Adventure Park has more than enough excitement to keep the family entertained all day. With eight exciting water adventures, two miniature golf courses, a 40-foot roller coaster, and a variety of racetracks in the Formula K Raceway, it's hard to decide which adventure to tackle first. (For more details see the write-up in the Kidstuff chapter.)

NORTH SHORE LAKE TAHOE

CABLE CAR AT SQUAW VALLEY USA

California Highway 89
6 miles north of Tahoe City, CA
(530) 583-6955, (800) 545-4350
www.squaw.com

Best known as the site of the 1960 Winter Olympics, Squaw Valley USA is one of America's premier year-round resorts. The Olympic flame still burns brightly as you make the turn into Olympic Valley, but other amenities of the games, such as the ski jump and Olympic ice rink, have been torn down.

Squaw Valley is a veritable paradise of recreation and activities, which are covered in more detail in the chapters on Resorts, Recreation, Golf, and Winter Sports. But whatever your choice of activity, winter or summer, a ride in the tram from the Base Village to High Camp Bath & Tennis Club is a must. From a base elevation of 6,200 feet, the tram rises 2,000 feet to a world-class playground perched high above Lake Tahoe. The unobstructed views are simply awe inspiring.

You can while away an entire day in this alpine Eden. Enjoy hiking, skiing, ice-skating, swimming, bungee jumping, playing tennis, and mountain biking. In the winter it's crowded with skiers, but in the summer it can be a quiet getaway undiscovered by most. If just relaxing in the sun is what you want, you won't find a better place than the decks around the swimming lagoon and spa. And you won't go hungry, as the bars and restaurants at High Camp offer everything from casual fare to fine dining.

During ski season, the tram operates from 9:00 a.m. until 9:00 p.m. weekdays and from 8:30 a.m. until 9:00 p.m. weekends. Daily hours during the summer are 9:40 a.m. to 4:00 p.m. Most services at the resort are unavailable from mid-October to mid-November. Tram-only tickets cost $22 for adults and $6 for children age 12 and younger. A variety of packages that combine activities such as skating and swimming with the cable-car ticket are also available.

In summer, I strongly suggest bringing along sunscreen and also a jacket, because the temperature is much cooler here than in the valley. If the weather is questionable, call (530) 583-6985 to check the cable-car operation schedule. (See also the Kid-stuff chapter.)

FANNY BRIDGE
Junction of California Highways 89 and 28, Tahoe City, CA

Fanny Bridge spans the Truckee River where it empties from Lake Tahoe on its journey toward Pyramid Lake. Also at this site is the concrete dam with 17 gates used to raise or lower the level of the lake. While this in itself may not be particularly interesting to visitors, the number of enormous rainbow trout living in the waters around the bridge merit your attention. Although catching fish is not permitted anywhere near the bridge, it's perfectly legal to feed them. Almost any day of the year, groups of people can be seen leaning over the edge of the bridge (fanniés sticking out) to feed the fish. (See also the Kidstuff chapter.)

GATEKEEPER'S MUSEUM
Junction of California Highways 89 and 28
Tahoe City, CA
(530) 583-1762
www.northtahoemuseums.org

The gatekeeper of Lake Tahoe was entrusted with the responsibility of monitoring the level of the lake, using a hand-turned winch system to keep the water at prescribed levels. He lived in the gatekeeper's cabin on the south side of Fanny Bridge. The original cabin, built sometime between 1910 and 1916, was destroyed by fire in 1978. The present cabin was built in 1981 with funds raised by the North Lake Tahoe Historical Society.

Since 1986 the Federal Watermaster's Office in Reno has regulated the level of the lake. Today the gatekeeper's cabin is a museum showcasing Lake Tahoe's past through natural history displays, stories of pioneers, and priceless artifacts. Of particular interest are exhibits showing the effects of growth and pollution on the Tahoe Basin.

Tucked away in a forest of ancient conifers, the handcarved, lodgepole pine structure is an exemplary specimen of Tahoe-style architecture. Its interior is cozy and warm, almost inviting you to curl up in front of the fire with a good historical novel. Be sure not to miss the Marion Steinbach Indian Basket Museum, a collection of more than 800 baskets from tribes all over the country, on display here.

The museum is open Wednesday through Sunday May 1 through June 15 and from Labor Day until October 1, and it's open every day from June 16 through Labor Day. The hours are 11:00 a.m. to 5:00 p.m. Admission is nominal, and donations are welcome.

i For information about scheduling a special event on the lakeshore near the Gatekeeper's Museum, call (530) 583-1762 or click on www.northtahoe museums.org.

WATSON CABIN LIVING MUSEUM
560 North Lake Boulevard
Tahoe City, CA
(530) 583-8717
www.northtahoemuseums.org

Built in 1909, the Watson Cabin Living Museum is the oldest building in Tahoe City. Listed on the National Register of Historic Homes, the cabin contains the first indoor private bathroom in Tahoe City, as well as antiques and collectibles from the turn of the 20th century. Currently the cabin is open Memorial Day through June 30 on weekends and from July 1 through Labor Day Wednesday through Monday. Hours are noon to 4:00 p.m.

SOUTH SHORE LAKE TAHOE

EMERALD BAY AND VIKINGSHOLM CASTLE
California Highway 89
5 miles from South Lake Tahoe, CA
(530) 541-3030 (summer only)
(530) 525-7277
www.comspark.com/eldorado
www.parks.ca.gov

If there is a signature view of Lake Tahoe, Emerald Bay with tiny Fannette Island would be the No. 1 choice. This narrow arm on the southwestern shore of the lake is especially picturesque with its emerald green water surrounded by sheer granite cliffs. The scenery alone is worth the drive, but the real jewel of this spot is Vikingsholm Castle.

The castle is not accessible by car; it's a 1-mile walk from the Emerald Bay parking lot. Built by Mrs. Lora Knight in 1929 as her summer residence, the home is one of the finest examples of Scandinavian architecture in the Western Hemisphere. Because the site of the house reminded her of fjords in Norway, Mrs. Knight decided that the house should also be Scandinavian.

Constructed of granite and timber found at the lake, the 38-room mansion is a replica of an 11th-century Viking castle. Although in some ways the interior seems dark and cold, the building can be appreciated for its workmanship and attention to detail. Tours are usually available 10:00 a.m. until 4:00 p.m. daily from mid-June

through Labor Day and on weekends after Labor Day until the end of September. The fee is $5 for adults and $3 for children ages 6 through 17.

From Vikingsholm the trail continues for about 2.5 miles along the shore of the bay to Emerald Point on the main body of the lake, and from there another 4.5 miles to D. L. Bliss State Park. The real trailblazers can hike another 1.5 miles to Eagle Point, on the newest leg of this trail system.

Another popular hike from this area is the 1-mile walk to Eagle Lake. The trail-head begins across the road from the Emerald Bay parking lot in the Eagle Falls Picnic Area.

Because this is probably the most visited site at Lake Tahoe, parking in the summer is always difficult. I recommend getting there early in the morning to avoid the crowds. This section of CA 89 is often closed in winter because of heavy snowfall, so be sure to call prior to your visit.

FALLEN LEAF LAKE
Junction of California Highway 89 and
Fallen Leaf Road
South Lake Tahoe, CA

The second-largest natural lake in the Lake Tahoe Basin, Fallen Leaf was an appendage of Lake Tahoe many years ago. Three miles long, Fallen Leaf Lake is considered by many scientists to be a microcosm of Lake Tahoe. Because it is smaller, researchers are studying the effects of pollution on the lake as they believe the same effects will appear in a similar way later in the larger Lake Tahoe.

A variety of easy hikes begin from the Fallen Leaf Campground about a half mile from CA 89. Other longer hikes begin from the parking lot just past the Fallen Leaf Marina at the end of the lake. The drive alone is worth the trip, though, because the lake is very scenic. Keep in mind that the going is slow—the road is one-way with few turnouts.

To reach the lake, take CA 89 northwest at its junction with US 50 in South Lake Tahoe (the "Y"). Look for Fallen Leaf Road about 3 miles on, turn left, and follow it to the lake. Fallen Leaf Lake is frequently not accessible during winter months because of heavy snowfall.

FANNETTE ISLAND
Emerald Bay
(530) 541-3030
www.comspark.com/eldorado

Fannette Island is the only island in Lake Tahoe. A granite island sparsely covered with timber and brush, it is located in Emerald Bay on the lake's west shore. Fannette Island was not always known by that name. During the past century it has been known as Coquette, Fannette, Baranoff, Dead Man's, Hermit's, and Emerald Isle. Fannette was the name that finally stuck. The only "structure" on the island is the stone shell remains of a miniature castle that was built around the same time that the Vikingsholm Castle was constructed and used as a "teahouse" by Mrs. Lora Knight and her guests when they boated over from the castle.

Visitors are welcome to use the island for day-use activities between 6:00 a.m. and 9:00 p.m. Camping is prohibited, and dogs are not allowed on the island. From February 1 through June 15, the island is closed to all visitors so that the up to 100 geese that come to the island to nest are afforded ample peace and privacy. Access to the island is by private boat only, unless you are a really strong swimmer. Given that the average temperature for Lake Tahoe is 40 degrees, however, I'd recommend you find a boat.

GONDOLA RIDE AT HEAVENLY SKI RESORT
Heavenly Ski Resort
Corner of Wildwood and Saddle
South Lake Tahoe, CA
(775) 586-7000
www.skiheavenly.com

For a million-dollar view of Lake Tahoe, it's hard to beat the 2.4-mile gondola ride that climbs over 6,200 feet from Stateline, providing skiers and hikers alike direct access to the ski resort from the downtown area of South Lake Tahoe/Stateline. From the top station at 9,156 feet, skiers can access the new intermediate trails, and hikers can embark on their journey to explore the resort's 4,800 acres. The gondola is California's longest ski gondola and, with 138 cabins, has the most uphill carrying capacity of any gondola in California. Because

Heavenly is a world-class ski resort, the winter amenities are covered in the chapter on Winter Sports. Sightseeing tickets for the gondola are $30 for adults, $26 for teens, and $20 for kids 5 to 12. The base of the gondola is just steps from shops and restaurants in The Shops at Heavenly Village.

TAHOE QUEEN
Marina Village, at the foot of Ski Run Boulevard
South Lake Tahoe, CA
(800) 238-2463
www.zephyrcove.com

Seeing Lake Tahoe from the deck of a boat is an unforgettable experience. The recently renovated *Tahoe Queen* sails from its pier in South Lake Tahoe across the lake and into Emerald Bay daily throughout the year. The cruises last from two to three hours and are available with options that include meals, drinks, and dancing. Departures are from 11:00 a.m. to 7:00 p.m. in the summer, but vary in other seasons. Prices for the cruise only are typically $46 for adults and $22 for children ages 3 through 12 (see the Kidstuff chapter for more details). Other cruise options are available, so call for specific prices and times. A second ship, the *M.S. Dixie II*, sails from Zephyr Cove on a similar schedule.

When Lake Tahoe was formed 3 million years ago, it was initially hundreds of feet higher than it is now.

TALLAC HISTORIC SITE
California Highway 89
South Lake Tahoe, CA
(530) 544-7383, (530) 541-5227
www.fs.fed.us/r5/ltbmu/recreation/tallac/

Following the discovery of silver in Nevada, Lake Tahoe became a popular summer retreat for wealthy people from San Francisco, Virginia City, and Sacramento. In 1880 Elias J. "Lucky" Baldwin built an opulent resort including a casino and two hotels on this site. For more than 30 years it was the place to be at Tahoe. But as the area became more accessible through the use of automobiles, those who could afford it were building their own lavish estates all around the lake.

The Tallac Resort was torn down in 1916, but the foundation is still visible. Visitors to the Tallac Historic Site can see several examples of luxurious old private estates. The Baldwin Estate, built in 1921 of handhewn logs, is now the Tallac Museum. The museum is free and is open daily from 10:00 a.m. to 5:00 p.m. from Memorial Day weekend through September and from 11:00 a.m. to 4:00 p.m. the last two weeks of September. The Pope Estate, the largest and most luxurious at the site, was constructed in 1894 and has art exhibits and a living-history program. The outbuildings have viewing screens that allow visitors to see the opulence of the interior furnishings. The Heller Estate, also known as Valhalla, is a community events center where concerts, art shows, and special events are held during the summer.

Aside from offering a peek into Tahoe's past, Tallac Historic Site is a lovely place to enjoy a beautiful white-sand beach bordered by large pine trees more than 400 years old. Taylor Creek Visitor Center is just a stone's throw away on the Tallac Historic Site Trail.

To reach the site, take CA 89 northwest for 3 miles past its junction with US 50 in South Lake Tahoe (the "Y"). Parking is available at either the Tallac Historic Site or the Taylor Creek Visitor Center.

TAYLOR CREEK VISITOR CENTER
California Highway 89
South Lake Tahoe, CA
(530) 543-2674
www.r5.fs.fed.us

Adjoining the Tallac Historic Site, the area around Taylor Creek Visitor Center, run by the USDA Forest Service, gives the visitor ample opportunities to experience the Taylor Creek ecosystem and to understand its relationship to Lake Tahoe. With Mt. Tallac rising 9,735 feet in the background, you can wander the paths through this meadow to view the native flora and fauna.

In spring and summer tiny wildflowers spring up everywhere, and in the fall much of the vegetation turns crimson and gold. Flowing from Fallen Leaf Lake to Lake Tahoe, Taylor Creek is a premier spawning ground for kokanee salmon in October. The creek becomes a ribbon of red during the spawning season as the fish leave Lake Tahoe to mate and die upstream. Taylor Creek is one of the few places outside Alaska where the salmon spawn can be seen so easily. Visitors can study a diverted section of Taylor Creek through aquarium-like windows at the Lake Tahoe Stream Profile Chamber in the visitor center.

Be sure to pick up brochures and trail maps inside the building; they'll direct you to special events and other hikes in the area. The center is open 8:00 a.m. to 5:30 p.m. June 15 to September 30 and 8:00 a.m. to 4:30 p.m. in October. Admission to the stream profile is free.

KIDSTUFF

E ven though the Reno/Tahoe area is normally thought of as an adult playground, you'll find plenty of things to do here as a family. One thing that Insiders will tell you is that local businesses are definitely kid-friendly.

So what does the area have to offer? A lot of activities, both indoor and outdoor, to keep you and your kids entertained.

You'll notice that most of the activities I recommend are outside—after all, the area is renowned for its scenic beauty, and I feel it imperative that you and your kids get away from your hotel or motel room. Some of my suggestions keep you inside, though, and some even include things to do in and around the casinos.

On the subject of kids and casinos, heed these words of warning: When traveling through the casinos with your children, don't dillydally. Kids are allowed to walk through casinos as long as they don't linger, especially near the slot machines or the table games. Also, parents are not allowed to make bets with their children in tow. The best way to traverse the gambling establishments is with your little ones firmly in hand. The hustle and bustle and the bright lights of the casino floor will mesmerize most kids, causing even the least interested to stop and stare unless parents are firm about moving along.

To help you locate the activities that best fit your interests, I have arranged this chapter by category, then I've further divided the activities by my four geographical areas (Reno, Sparks, North Shore Lake Tahoe, and South Shore Lake Tahoe). Although I do my best to give you up-to-date figures for hours and prices, they can vary somewhat by the time you read this book. It's a good idea to call and verify this information before setting out with the entire family, especially if you have a carload of little ones. For other things to do as a family, check out the Recreation, Winter Sports, Spectator Sports, Annual Events, and Day Trips chapters.

AMUSEMENT PARKS AND RIDES

Reno

BOOMTOWN FAMILY FUN CENTER
Interstate 80, 7 miles west of Reno
(775) 345-6000, (800) 648-3790 (casino)
(775) 345-8683 (fun center)
www.boomtownreno.com
Boomtown Casino & Hotel Reno has one of the best fun centers in Reno. The center is jammed with about 200 video and arcade games where kids can win tickets and turn them in for prizes. It

also has a nine-hole miniature golf course, a merry-go-round, an indoor Ferris wheel, a vertical bouncing Rodeo Rider, and the only Iwerks 3-D Motion Theater in town. The theater has hydraulically activated seats that react with the movie on the screen and special polarized 3-D glasses. The center is open Monday through Thursday from 11:00 a.m. to 9:00 p.m., Friday 11:00 a.m. to midnight, Saturday from 10:00 a.m. to midnight, and Sunday 10:00 a.m. to 10:00 p.m. Individual rides range from about $1.50 to $5, and passes range from $10 to $30. Instead of juggling tokens and tickets, players use game cards for the video games.

CIRCUS CIRCUS HOTEL/CASINO—RENO
500 North Sierra Street
(775) 329-0711, (800) 648-5010
www.circusreno.com
www.ultimaterushpark.com

Kids love this casino because it has a circus and a carnival on the second floor—a circus complete with clowns, trapeze artists, and tightrope walkers. It also has a large area that houses most carnival games, plus its fair share of video and arcade games. Kids can win standard carnival prizes like stuffed animals. The circus acts take place daily about every half hour. Hours can vary with the season, so it's best to call and verify the times first before bundling the family in the car.

THE ULTIMATE RUSH THRILL RIDE
Grand Sierra Resort and Casino
2500 East Second Street
(775) 786-7005
www.grandsierraresort.com

Insider kids say this is the best and most exciting ride in the Reno/Tahoe area. It is like hang gliding and skydiving rolled into one. Riders strap into the same kind of harness hang gliders use; up to three people can ride together. The harness is connected to two long poles by cables. Operators pull riders to the top of a 185-foot launch tower. Once riders are at the top, they are released and free-fall for 50 feet toward the ground, clearing it by 6 feet and accelerating to about 65 miles per hour. Riders then swing back and forth until slowed down.

Riders have to be at least 42 inches tall. Weight and age of the rider are not restricting factors—a 3-year-old has taken the plunge, as has an 87-year-old! Insiders say the best time to ride is at night. The cost is $25 per person for one ride. The ride opens year-round at 11:00 a.m., but if the weather looks iffy, call ahead because it shuts down in bad weather. This property (formerly the Reno Hilton) also offers bumper cars, a sling shot, race karts, and miniature golf.

Sparks

WILD ISLAND FAMILY ADVENTURE PARK
250 Wild Island Court
(775) 359-2927
www.wildisland.com

Wild Island offers a water park, miniature golf courses, a bowling alley, and a go-kart raceway. The water park is the favorite of most visitors.

This water park is a great place to go in the summer, no matter how old you are. There are five mini-slides in the Little Lagoon for small children, including the Dragon and Frog slides, and small ones also can float around in the Lazy River. Older children and some adults can get their thrills on the bigger slides, like the Sting-ray and Shark Bait, which twists and turns all the way down. But if you're looking for a more adventurous ride, try a drop down the Red Viper or slide through the dark on the Black Widow. If you think these two slides are too much for one person, you can rent a double-person tube and go down in tandem.

Wild Island also has a place called Hurricane Cove, where swimmers can get in water fights at the water gun stations or stand underneath a giant waterfall that dumps 650 gallons of water from a bucket at the top of a tree house. Hurricane Cove also has tube slides and rope climbs.

The best waves in northern Nevada can be found at the Montego Bay wave pool. Swimmers can bodysurf here or just float around in a tube. This place is fun for most everyone. Kokomo's 21 Club is a spa designed for adults.

The water park usually opens in May and stays open all summer until the weather gets cold again. Entrance fees begin at around $16 for children less than 48 inches tall, and season passes are available.

Wild Island also has two 18-hole miniature golf courses with waterfalls and little rivers run-

i Looking for other activities for children in the Reno/Tahoe area? The concierges at any resort will have contacts for area activities, and some resorts have activities of their own for the younger set.

ning through them, along with a 20-lane bowling alley. It's a fun place for families, and it is open all year. Inside they also have a game arcade and a booth to trade in tickets for prizes. Both inside and outside are open day and night. Call for the times, as they vary with the season.

The Formula K Raceway has two tracks, one for larger children and one for smaller. The big kids get to drive Indy cars, and the little ones get to drive Sprint cars.

Adding to the excitement of Wild Island's year-round activities, is its Wild Cat Roller Coaster. Two six-passenger trains provide thrills on a 40-foot Myler steel coaster that's available to riders at least 42 inches tall.

Wild Island can also cater birthday parties. Prices vary, so call for details.

South Shore Lake Tahoe

HEAVENLY FLYER
Heavenly Ski Resort
Corner of Wildwood and Saddle
South Lake Tahoe, CA
(775) 586-7000
www.skiheavenly.com

Thrill rides come in all sizes and shapes, but the Heavenly Flyer is especially exhilarating as it zooms riders down a 3,100-foot zip-line cable, barely skimming the treetops at Heavenly Mountain Resort. Strapped in chairs that hang from the cable, riders enjoy this high-speed jaunt along with gorgeous views of Lake Tahoe as it rushes up to meet them. The flyer operates summer and winter from 11:00 a.m. to 4:30 p.m. daily and for limited hours during off season. To be on the safe side, however, call first before heading to the mountain. The ride is not suitable for small children, but pre-teens and older kids love this ultra-cool experience. To ride you must be between 52 and 80 inches tall and weigh between 75 and 275 pounds. You'll need a gondola ticket (if not skiing) along with the flyer ticket, which is $30.

LAKE TAHOE BALLOONS
(530) 544-1221, (800) 872-9294
www.laketahoeballoons.com

This is among the most adventurous things to do at Lake Tahoe—float above the crystal blue water in a hot-air balloon. The company's balloons take off and land on a special launch boat on the lake. The only drawback is that it is expensive, $250 per person, but that's a small price to pay for an adventure not soon forgotten. For more information on ballooning, see the Recreation chapter.

TAHOE FAMILY ZONE AMUSEMENT PARK
2401 Lake Tahoe Boulevard
South Lake Tahoe, CA
(530) 541-1300

This is a good amusement park that has lots of rides and carnival games. You can buy a book of tickets that lets your kids ride on go-karts, a blow-up slide, a merry-go-round, a Tilt-A-Whirl, a variety of kiddie rides, and more. There is a snack bar, and the park is open from May through September from 11:00 a.m. to 7:00 p.m. Family packs of tickets and coupons are available.

ARCADES AND GAMES

Reno

GRAND SIERRA RESORT AND CASINO FUN QUEST
2500 East Second Street
(775) 789-1127
www.grandsierraresort.com

This video arcade is located inside a casino and is a favorite of Insider kids because it has more than 125 video and arcade games. Along with these, it has some of the best interactive games available. Kids can get into a great game of laser tag on the Q-2000 Laser Tag battlefield or, along with six other pilots, fly an X-Wing fighter in the Galaxian Theater. They can also take a virtual ride on the Max Flight Roller Coaster.

Fun Quest also runs the Tumble Town Playground, where tiny tots can jump and climb on playground equipment. The arcade is open noon to 10:00 p.m. Monday through Thursday, noon to 11:00 p.m. Friday, 10:00 a.m. to 11:00 p.m. Saturday, and 10:00 a.m. to 10:00 p.m. Sunday.

Sparks

NUGGET SKYWALK ARCADE

John Ascuaga's Nugget
1100 Nugget Avenue
(775) 356-3300, (800) 648-1177
www.janugget.com

The best arcade in Sparks, the Skywalk Arcade is located on the second floor above the casino and features two different rooms, one with video and arcade games for younger children, and one with up-to-date video and redemption games for older kids. Insider kids say the best thing about this arcade is that the prices are the cheapest around. It's a good place to take the kids in Sparks if the weather is bad.

North Shore Lake Tahoe

HYATT REGENCY LAKE TAHOE RESORT, SPA & CASINO

111 Country Club Drive
Incline Village, NV
(775) 832-1234, (800) 233-1234
www.laketahoehyatt.com

Children and teenagers staying at the hotel use this small arcade most of the time. It only has about 30 games, but they are all state-of-the-art video. The games start at 25 cents and go up to $1 for more advanced games. The arcade is open 24 hours per day, but the state's curfew does apply (10:00 p.m. for children age 18 and younger).

South Shore Lake Tahoe

HARVEYS LAKE TAHOE CASINO & RESORT

U.S. Highway 50
Stateline, NV
(775) 588-2411
www.harrahs.com

Harveys has more than 180 games for kids and teenagers in its Virtual Forest Arcade. Half of the games are interactive video, and the rest are redemption games. Games begin at 25 cents and climb to $1. The arcade is open 24 hours a day, but children age 16 and younger must be out of the arcade by 10:00 p.m. on weekdays and midnight on weekends. The ticket booth is open from 10:00 a.m. to 10:00 p.m.

BOATING AND WATER SPORTS

North Shore Lake Tahoe

NORTH TAHOE WATERSPORTS

700 North Lake Boulevard
Tahoe City, CA
(530) 583-7245 (Tahoe City)
(530) 546-9253 (Kings Beach)

If you're not afraid of heights, you can enjoy a spectacular view of Lake Tahoe literally below your feet as you parasail high above the water. Older kids love this adventure, since it's not something they can do every day. The height and length of the flight range from 450 feet of line for an 8-minute jaunt to 1,500 feet for a 15-minute thrill. Because takeoffs and landings are done on a launch pad on the back of a boat, you don't even have to worry about getting dunked in the frigid waters of the lake. North Tahoe Watersports can also outfit the family in other water-sports equipment. Call for rates.

NORTH SHORE PARASAIL

8290 North Lake Boulevard
Kings Beach, CA
(530) 546-7698

Like North Tahoe Watersports (the previous listing), North Shore Parasail offers riders the next thing to flying as it offers safe dry "flights" over the lake. Call for rates.

TAHOE SAILING CHARTERS

Tahoe City Marina
Tahoe City, CA
(530) 583-6200
www.tahoesail.com

If you ever wanted to try sailing, this is the place. This company rents sailboats and offers a variety of sailing cruises on the lake. They even give sailing lessons. This is a cool way to relax on Lake Tahoe on a hot day. (See the Recreation chapter for more boat-rental information.)

South Shore Lake Tahoe

Experiencing the beauty of Lake Tahoe from the

deck of a boat gives a totally different perspective of this gorgeous body of water and its environs.

MS DIXIE II
Zephyr Cove, NV
(800) 238-2463
www.zephyrcove.com

TAHOE QUEEN
Marina Village
South Lake Tahoe, CA
(800) 238-2463
www.zephyrcove.com

If you're not up to renting your own boat, a wonderful alternative for the whole family is a cruise on either the *Tahoe Queen* or *MS Dixie II*. You can leave the "driving" to the able captain while you lean back and just enjoy the spectacular views. Cruises last a couple of hours, with some including dinner, dancing, and/or lunch. The bars and restaurants are always open, however. The *Dixie* sails from Zephyr Cove and the newly renovated *Tahoe Queen* is berthed at Marina Village at South Shore. Cruise-only fares run around $22 for children and $49 for adults, but ask if they are running any specials.

LAKEVIEW SPORTS
3131 U.S. Highway 50
South Lake Tahoe, CA
(530) 544-0183

This is the place to go on the South Shore to rent just about any type of recreational toy you might need to have fun in the lake or around it. You can rent in-line skates, Jet Skis, and bikes. If you want to rent a boat, they run a shop nearby called Tahoe Key Boat Rentals, (530) 544-8888. Both of these establishments are kid-friendly. (See also the Recreation chapter.)

ZEPHYR COVE RESORT
U.S. Highway 50
Zephyr Cove, NV
(775) 589-4906, (800) 238-2463
www.zephyrcove.com

This is one of the best places on the South Shore

to take the family because you can do and rent just about everything here. You can swim, fish, sail, rent boats or Jet Skis, or go parasailing during the summer months. In winter you can rent snowmobiles, and you can ride the MS Dixie II paddle wheeler around the lake anytime. Or you can just relax on the beach. Prices vary depending upon the activity you plan, and an entrance fee of about $6 is charged to park your vehicle. This is a great place to spend the day.

i Children can walk through casinos but can't linger, and they must be accompanied by an adult.

DAY AND SUMMER CAMPS

Lake Tahoe's hotels and resorts have excellent reputations for being both kid-friendly and for taking great care of children. A few even have summer and day camps available to keep the kids occupied while you're off doing grown-up things. Most of these camps require that the children be at least three years old and toilet-trained; some have even stricter age guidelines.

The costs for the sessions vary depending upon the length of stay and time of day, but half-day programs start at about $30, and full-day programs begin at about $70, with meals included. The programs vary but can include supervised hikes, swimming, sledding, snowshoeing, arts and crafts, video arcade visits, games, sports, and beach play—all depending upon the time of year.

Here are a few that I think are tops.

North Shore Lake Tahoe

CAMP HYATT HYATT REGENCY LAKE TAHOE RESORT, SPA & CASINO
111 Country Club Drive
Incline Village, NV
(775) 832-1234, (800) 553-3288
(775) 886-6174
www.laketahoehyatt.com

Camp Hyatt will take meticulous care of your

children (if you're staying in the hotel) and provide a challenging variety of activities year-round that even the most well-rounded child will enjoy. During the summer, day sessions run from 9:00 a.m. to 4:00 p.m. and night sessions from 5:00 to 11:00 p.m.

The program operates on weekends only during the winter and is limited to children 3 to 12 years old. The cost is $75 per child per session, which also includes a meal. Reservations are required.

MOUNTAIN BUDDIES RESORT AT SQUAW CREEK
400 Squaw Creek Road
Olympic Valley, CA
(530) 581-6624, (530) 583-6300,
(800) 327-3353
www.squawcreek.com

Mountain Buddies is a year-round program for children 4 to 12 years old. Chaperones take the kids on hikes; supervise arts and crafts; take the kids swimming; and, during the winter months, take them sledding and ice-skating. This resort program always receives high praise from both parents and children.

The cost for an all-day stay with lunch is around $90, and for a half-day stay, the price is about $50. A full day begins at 9:00 a.m. and ends at 5:00 p.m. Half-day programs go from 9:00 a.m. to 12:30 p.m., 1:30 to 5:00 p.m., and 6:30 to 10:00 p.m.

South Shore Lake Tahoe

KIDS CAMP
Harveys Lake Tahoe Casino & Resort and
Harrah's Lake Tahoe
U.S. Highway 50
Stateline, NV
(775) 588-0752, (866) 454-3386
www.harrahs.com
www.tahoekids.com

Kids Camp is the perfect place to leave the children if you want a night out on the town. This camp offers both day and evening sessions, and it's open daily. Kids 6 to 13 years old are welcome, and they don't have to be guests of the hotel. Activities include trips to the movies, the video arcade, bowling, and other activities depending upon the time of year. The cost for the daytime session from 10:00 a.m. to 4:00 p.m. is $90, and the evening session from 6:00 p.m. to 10:00 p.m. costs $60. Reservations are required.

i If you're looking for a comprehensive adventure camp for kids in the Tahoe area, call (800) PRO-CAMP or click on www.800procamp.com.

FISHING

Reno

THE TRUCKEE RIVER
If you or your kids like to fish, you should try the stretch of the Truckee River that runs through Reno. It's a unique place for anglers because there's great trout fishing right downtown. Actually, any place in the river is good for fishing. Some people think that you have to go a long way up or down the river to catch fish, but that's not necessarily true. A lot of fish have been caught from Idlewild Park, Mayberry Park, and Fisherman's Park. The only problem with the Truckee River is that you have to have a fair amount of skill and experience to catch fish. Call the Nevada Division of Wildlife at (775) 688-1500 or log onto www.ndow.org. (See the Fishing and Hunting chapter for more information on these activities.)

Sparks

SPARKS MARINA PARK
East end of Nichols Boulevard
The City of Sparks Parks and Recreation Department
(775) 353-2376
www.ci.sparks.nv.us

The city of Sparks transformed a former gravel pit and community eyesore into one of the best fishing spots in the Reno/Sparks area, and now this lake provides outstanding fishing for both adults and children. The city has spent more than $35,000 stocking the lake with catchable and trophy-size trout. No boats with gas-powered engines are allowed on the water, keeping pollution at a minimum. Bank fishing is excellent, as is fishing from float tubes, and from self-propelled and boats with electric motors. All types of bait except live fish are permitted, including worms, salmon eggs, Power bait, spinners, and flies. There is no charge for fishing at the lake, but a valid Nevada fishing license is required (see the Fishing and Hunting chapter for details).

South Shore Lake Tahoe

SAW MILL POND
Saw Mill Road
South Lake Tahoe, CA
You'll find lots of places to take kids fishing on and around Lake Tahoe, but as we've said before, you have to be a fairly good angler to catch anything (besides, fishing with kids is not as much fun as *catching fish* with kids!). So, if you're looking for fishing spots that cater to the younger anglers on the South Shore, try Saw Mill Pond. You have to bring your own gear here, and only children younger than age 16 are allowed to fish in the pond. There is no charge. The pond is located about 1 mile south of South Lake Tahoe on US 50.

TAHOE TROUT FARM
1023 Blue Lake Avenue
South Lake Tahoe, CA
(530) 541-1491
Tahoe Trout Farm is the other place especially for kids to fish. They loan the young anglers rods and reels and even supply the bait. Prices vary. This farm usually opens in May and closes in September. Questions about other fishing in California can be answered by calling the California Department of Fish and Game at (916) 445-0411, or go to www.dfg.ca.gov.

HORSEBACK RIDING

Reno

RED ROCK STABLES
15670 Red Rock Road
Reno, NV
(775) 969-3315
www.ranchoredrock.com
For peaceful rides into the hills north of Reno contact Red Rock Stables; they can customize your riding experience to your ability and expectations. This full-service stable is open year-round. It's a bit of a drive out of town, but well worth the beauty and solitude once you are there.

VERDI TRAILS
175 Trelease, Verdi, NV
(775) 345-7600, (888) 345-7603
www.verditrailsranch.com
Verdi Trails is only 10 miles from Reno at the foot of the Sierra Nevada. This stable offers trail rides and hayrides and a full-service equestrian center open from 9:00 a.m. until sunset. Call for rates.

North Shore Lake Tahoe

For many people, riding a horse is an unusual experience that they can only enjoy while on vacation a few times a year. Several stables in the North Shore area offer riding lessons, guided trips, hay rides, and sleigh rides. Call for the latest information on the stable of your choice.

ALPINE MEADOWS
355 Alpine Meadows Road (south of Truckee, CA off of California Highway 89)
(530) 583-3905
www.gotahoenorth.com

SQUAW VALLEY STABLES
Squaw Valley exit off California Highway 89 between Tahoe City and Truckee, CA
(530) 583-7433
www.squaw.com

South Shore Lake Tahoe

Like the North Shore, the South Shore also offers opportunities to enjoy the great outdoors from the back of a horse. Rides vary in length, starting with an hour, and include the cost of a competent guide. If you're not up to riding, you can always enjoy a hayride that includes breakfast, lunch, or dinner. Call the individual stable for rates and schedules.

CAMP RICHARDSON
California Highway 89
South Lake Tahoe, CA
(530) 541-3113
www.camprich.com

CASCADE STABLES
California Highway 89 near Cascade Lake, CA
(530) 541-2055

ZEPHYR COVE STABLES
U.S. Highway 50
Zephyr Cove, NV
(775) 588-5664
www.zephyrcove.com

MINIATURE GOLF

Reno

MAGIC CARPET GOLF
6925 South Virginia Street
(775) 853-8837

This miniature-golf establishment has three different courses that kids find fun to play. The prices start at about $6 and go up, depending on how many holes you want to play. After you're finished with the miniature golf, you can try your skills on a special hole: If you score a hole-in-one here, you win a prize. The course also has a pizza parlor for those hungry golfers.

i **Both Nevada and California have 10:00 p.m. curfews for anyone younger than 18.**

North Shore Lake Tahoe

MAGIC CARPET GOLF
5167 North Lake Boulevard
Carnelian Bay, CA
(530) 546-4279

This big facility has three recently remodeled miniature golf courses. They're all fun, and prices are reasonable (about $6 for a round). But these courses are very popular, and they can be crowded. The courses open when the snow melts in April and close when the snow returns in October. Call for times.

South Shore Lake Tahoe

MAGIC CARPET GOLF
2455 Lake Tahoe Boulevard
South Lake Tahoe, CA
(530) 541-3787

Magic Carpet Golf is the place to play miniature golf on the South Shore. Their three big courses are not usually overcrowded and provide great entertainment for kids. The facility is closed during the winter months. The price per round is about $6.

MOVIES

No matter how many entertainment choices you have for the family, going to a movie is always a winner. The four Century complexes in Reno/Sparks are relatively new and boast stadium seating, expanded snack bars, video arcades, and the latest sound equipment. Grand Sierra Resort and Casino recently reopened its theater on the lower level of the casino, providing comfortable couch seating in an intimate setting, all at bargain prices. With the exception of the new state-of-the-art Heavenly Village Cinema, the theaters in the Lake Tahoe area in general are older and smaller, but they all show the same movies, and that's what it's all about, right? Following is a list of theaters with contact information. You'll also find movie listings in all local newspapers. So grab your popcorn, sit back, and enjoy the show.

Reno

CENTURY PARK LANE 16
210 East Plumb Lane
(775) 824-3300
www.centurytheaters.com

CENTURY RIVERSIDE 12
11 North Sierra Street
(775) 786-2753
www.centurytheaters.com

CENTURY SUMMIT SIERRA
13965 South Virginia Street
(Summit Sierra Mall)
(775) 851-4635
www.centurytheaters.com

GRAND SIERRA CINEMA
2500 East Second Street
(Grand Sierra Resort and Casino)
(775) 789-2093

Sparks

CENTURY SPARKS 14
1250 Victorian Avenue
(775) 353-7470
www.centurytheaters.com

COBBLESTONE CINEMA
465 North Lake Tahoe Boulevard
Tahoe City, CA
(530) 546-5951

INCLINE VILLAGE CINEMA
901 Tahoe Boulevard
Incline Village, NV
(530) 546-5951

North Shore Lake Tahoe

BROCKWAY TWIN THEATER
8707 North Lake Boulevard
Kings Beach, CA
(530) 546-5951

WEST WIND EL RANCHO DRIVE-IN 4
555 El Rancho Avenue at Oddie Boulevard
(775) 358-6920 (summer only)

South Shore Lake Tahoe

HEAVENLY VILLAGE CINEMA
1021 Heavenly Village Way
South Lake Tahoe, CA
(530) 544-1100
www.theshopsatheavenlyvillage.com

HOLLYWOOD HORIZON STADIUM CINEMAS/WALLACE THEATERS
50 U.S. Highway 50
Stateline, NV
(775) 589-6000
www.horizoncasino.com
www.hollywood.com (for online feature listings)

MUSEUMS

Reno

FLEISCHMANN PLANETARIUM
1650 North Virginia Street
(775) 784-4811
www.planetarium.unr.nevada.edu
This great family outing works on two levels—not only do you get to see a planetarium show with stars and planets, you also get to see a short movie on an educational subject. In the past the planetarium has shown movies on climbers ascending Mt. Everest and on the Antarctic and penguins in addition to its planetarium shows. Don't pass up this great place! The planetarium is open all year at 10:30 a.m. daily, closing at 8:00 p.m. weekdays during the summer and at 7:00 p.m. during the winter and at 9:00 p.m. weekends. Admission to the theater is $5 for adults and $4 for kids age 12 and younger, as well as seniors age 60 and over. (For more information see the Attractions chapter.)

NATIONAL AUTOMOBILE MUSEUM
10 Lake Street
(775) 333-9300
www.automuseum.org

If you're a car nut, this is the place for you. The old saying "They don't make cars like this anymore" really fits here. The museum displays a wide variety of vehicles, including the 1949 Mercury James Dean drove in the movie *Rebel Without a Cause* and an Indy 500 race car that most kids really like. The museum is set with four period street settings. You can also have your picture taken in an old car—the museum even lends you period clothes so the shot looks authentic. (The use of the clothes and the picture are free.) The museum has more than 200 cars in four different galleries, including two galleries with changing exhibits, so there's plenty to see. Hours are Monday through Saturday from 9:30 a.m. to 5:30 p.m. and Sunday from 10:00 a.m. to 4:00 p.m. Admission prices are $10 for adults, $8 for seniors, and $4 for children. (See the Attractions chapter for more details.)

WILBUR D. MAY GREAT BASIN ADVENTURE
Rancho San Rafael Park
(775) 785-5961
www.co.washoe.nv.us/Parks/great.htm
www.maycenter.com

Wilbur May, a department-store mogul, traveled around the world about 40 times, collecting odds and ends. He donated most of his collection to the city of Reno, and now it's housed in a replica of his ranch in Rancho San Rafael Park. Most visitors agree that the most interesting room in this museum is the one with his trophies from big-game hunting. Renovations completed in 2003 include a gift shop and a gallery for rotating exhibits of local artists.

The best thing about this park is that there is something to do for everyone. The park has a petting zoo, pony rides, an old-fashioned log ride, and a mine where kids can pan for gold. There's also a nature walk and a place where children can climb on one-third-size replicas of dinosaurs. Indoor gardens house two goldfish ponds, many kinds of flowers and plants, and a waterfall. This is an entire day trip. Hours change with the seasons. In the summer, the park is open from noon to 5:00 on Sunday and from 10:00 a.m. to 5:00 p.m. the rest of the week. The museum entrance fee is around $5, but it'll cost you more to take part in the other activities at the park. (See the Attractions chapter for more information.)

Sparks

SPARKS HERITAGE FOUNDATION AND MUSEUM
820 Victorian Avenue
(775) 355-1144
www.nevadamuseums.org

Sparks is nicknamed "Rail City" because it used to be a railroad town, so most of the pieces in this museum have to do with trains. There's a collection of old lanterns used by the trains' brakemen, and a stationary train across the street that visitors can walk through. The museum is free, but a donation of $1 or more per person is requested for the museum fund. (See the Attractions chapter for more details.)

North Shore Lake Tahoe

EMIGRANT TRAIL MUSEUM AT DONNER MEMORIAL PARK
Donner Pass Road, Truckee, CA
(530) 582-7892
www.parks.ca.gov

This park and museum is outside of North Shore Lake Tahoe proper, but it's a great place for the family to visit. The history portrayed in the museum is disturbing: It highlights the pioneers who tried to cross the Sierra Nevada in winter but were snowed in. After they ran out of food, they ate their horses and cows; eventually they had to eat their saddles and leather harnesses. Some of the pioneers also turned to cannibalism to survive.

The museum shows slides of drawings of the Donner Party's wagon train and their encampment. And in summer you can visit two of the original cabin sites. Museum hours are 9:00 a.m. to 4:00 p.m. daily. (See the Day Trips chapter for more to see and do in nearby Truckee.)

TAHOE MARITIME MUSEUM
5205 West Lake Boulevard
Homewood, CA
(530) 525-9253
www.tahoemaritimemuseum.org
Celebrating the maritime history of Lake Tahoe, the Tahoe Maritime Museum boasts a treasure trove of memorabilia dating from the late 19th century, when boats were the primary mode of transportation on the lake. Housed in a new 5,800-square-foot-facility next to Homewood Mountain Resort, the collection of 25 boats includes the *Shanghai*, an 1890s launch rescued from the bottom of the lake; the *Lemme Go First*, a 1929 Gar Wood boat once owned by Henry J. Kaiser; and the *Vent D'Ete*, a 1915 petite sailing vessel. Museum visitors will also find displays of aquaplanes, motors, and water skis. With a dedicated children's area for hands-on activities, the museum is especially kid-friendly. Hours are 10:00 a.m. to 5:00 p.m. Friday, Saturday, and Sunday during the winter and Thursday through Tuesday in the summer. Admission is $5, free for children under 12.

South Shore Lake Tahoe
VIKINGSHOLM CASTLE
Emerald Bay State Park
California Highway 89,
5 miles from South Lake Tahoe, CA
(530) 541-3030 (summer only)
(530) 525-7277
www.parks.ca.gov
www.comspark.com/eldorado
Around here we call it a castle, but it's really an elaborate stone home built at the water's edge. The home was designed with a Scandinavian look and resembles architecture associated with the Vikings, hence its name. The question most visitors ask is how the stones were transported here, since there are only two ways to get to the house: from the lake or down a steep dirt path about a mile long. (When you visit, the rangers will be glad to give you the answer.) Bear in mind that when you visit, you'll have to hike down—and then back up—that same steep trail.

Once at the bottom of the trail, you can swim at the beautiful beach or picnic at one of the many barbecue pits. Don't forget to ask the rangers about the little house the owner built on the island across the water from the main home. They say she had tea there every day. Tours of the main house are offered during the summer months, but call for times as they vary. (See the Attractions and Parks chapters for more information.)

i On the Nevada side, children are allowed in establishments that sell liquor as long as the establishments serve food as well. It is always a good idea to check the surroundings to prevent youngsters from being exposed to inappropriate or adult situations.

OUTDOOR FUN
Sparks
VICTORIAN SQUARE
Victorian Avenue
Victorian Square has remained the heart and soul of Sparks in spite of recent growth that has pushed the city north and east. To preserve its historic ambience and past, the city fathers have focused redevelopment efforts along Victorian Avenue. The result is an eclectic variety of shops, restaurants, and businesses that coexist with several casinos and the railroad. Victorian Square is also the site of a number of annual events, such as Hot August Nights, Sparks Hometowne Farmers' Market, and the Best in the West Nugget Rib Cook-Off. You can easily while away a few hours here with the kids by letting them play in the interactive fountain, catch a movie, or grab dinner at Great Basin Brewing Company.

North Shore Lake Tahoe
FANNY BRIDGE
Junction of California Highways 89 and 28
Tahoe City, CA
This bridge spans the Truckee River as it flows out of Lake Tahoe. The Truckee is the only river

that leaves the lake, and this bridge overlooks the charming dam that controls the water. When you lean over the rail, you can see huge trout swimming between the dam and the bridge. It's called Fanny Bridge because so many people lean over it to watch the trout that passersby can only see their rear ends. Drive to the "Y" (the intersection of CA 89 and CA 28) in Tahoe City and look for the fannies—you can't miss them or the bridge. (See the Attractions chapter for more information.)

SQUAW VALLEY USA
Squaw Valley, CA
(530) 583-6955
www.squaw.com
Squaw Valley is located just up the road from Lake Tahoe, and it's definitely worth the drive, not only to ride the cable car up the mountain but to try all the other activities in the area, too.

Near the entrance to the cable car, Squaw has a rock-climbing wall that's about 45 feet tall. It's set up for all kinds of climbers, from beginners to experts, so try it out before you hop on the cable-car ride. Once you are at the High Camp (prices vary for the ride), you can visit the Olympic Museum. Squaw Valley was home to the 1960 Winter Olympics. You can also go ice-skating, play tennis or golf, go horseback riding, take the ropes course, go mountain biking, take a swim, or hike. This is definitely an all-day trip. Prices for the different activities vary. For more information see the Attractions, Resorts, and Recreation chapters.

South Shore Lake Tahoe
GONDOLA RIDE AT HEAVENLY SKI RESORT
Heavenly Ski Resort
Corner of Wildwood and Saddle
South Lake Tahoe, CA
(775) 586-7000
www.skiheavenly.com
The gondola at Heavenly takes you up the mountain for about 3,000 feet, and the views of the Lake Tahoe Basin from the top are spectacular. Up high you'll find a huge deck where you'll be treated to more spectacular views. You can also take a hike from the gondola, basking in the high-altitude sun (don't forget the sunblock). The sightseeing gondola ride is $30 for adults, $26 for teens, $20 for children ages 5 to 12, and free for those younger than 5. See the Attractions chapter for more details.

LAKE TAHOE ADVENTURES
(800) 865-4679
www.laketahoeadventures.com
This company provides what some might call the second most adventurous activity on the South Shore—the first being, arguably, a ride in a hot-air balloon over Lake Tahoe. (See the Lake Tahoe Balloons entry in the "Amusement Parks and Rides" section of this chapter.)

Tahoe Adventures can arrange four-wheeling trips around the lake's rugged trails. You can opt to travel in an ATV, a jeep, or a Hummer to a variety of destinations. The off-road tours last from about one hour to all night—if you want to join one of the company's camping excursions. The trips are classified from "easy" to "difficult." One of the best rides is on Rubicon Trail. Prices vary, so call for rates.

PARKS AND PLAYGROUNDS

Reno
IDLEWILD PARK
1900 Idlewild Drive
(775) 334-2262
www.visitreno.com/parks
Although Reno has a large number of parks sprinkled around its neighborhoods, Idlewild remains one of the most popular because of its size and location along the Truckee River. There's plenty of room to run and play with fields for soccer, football, volleyball, softball, and baseball and a variety of play equipment. Skateboarders revel in the 13,000-square-foot skateboard facility. You'll also find a beautiful rose garden, picnic areas, and the Truckee River Walk that winds all the way through the park.

Sparks

THE CITY OF SPARKS PARKS AND RECREATION DEPARTMENT
98 Richard Way
(775) 353-2376
www.ci.sparks.nv.us/living/parks-rec/
The city has more than 50 different parks that have baseball and softball fields, swimming pools, and playgrounds. Plus, the rec department puts on numerous activities for kids throughout the year.

The department has programs in arts and crafts; swimming and other sports like tennis, soccer, and, of course, baseball and softball, gymnastics, dance, poetry, drawing, painting, theater, cheerleading, snowboard lessons, and self-defense classes, just to name a few. The department prints a catalog of activities, which is available at its office on Richard Way. The fees vary by activity and are very reasonable.

North Shore Lake Tahoe

LAKE TAHOE–NEVADA STATE PARK
2005 Nevada Highway 28
Incline Village, NV
(775) 831-0494
www.parks.nv.gov
This spectacular park offers wonderful recreational opportunities on its 13,000 acres. In fact, there are so many things in the park that a family could spend its entire vacation here, fishing, swimming, picnicking, hiking, camping, mountain biking, scuba diving, boating, and horseback riding. A phone call is a must to see what's going on when you arrive. (See also the Parks chapter.)

SAND HARBOR
Nevada Highway 28
Incline Village, NV
(775) 831-0494
Although the beaches of Sand Harbor are the best around the lake, don't come here if you're trying to get away from other people. These white-sand beaches are popular, and the water is so clear that you can see the bottom of the lake regardless of the depth. Besides swimming and boating, there are nature trails for hiking. Entrance fees are around $6.00 per carload in summer. (See the Parks and Recreation chapters for more details.)

South Shore Lake Tahoe

TAYLOR CREEK VISITOR CENTER
California Highway 89
South Lake Tahoe, CA
(530) 543-2674
www.fs.fed.us/r5/ltbmu/recreation/visitor-center/
This center is the starting point for a wonderful nature walk called "The Rainbow Trail," where hikers are introduced to the plants and animals that live and grow around the lake. The highlight of this trail is a viewing chamber below the level of the stream where you can see the trout and Kokanee salmon in their natural environment. You can also visit Taylor Creek Marsh, a protected wetlands. The visitor center and trail are great ways for youngsters to learn about the birds, fish, animals, and plants around Lake Tahoe. The rangers are really outstanding, and they love to answer youngsters' questions. (See the Attractions chapter for more information.)

i Interesting day trips from the Reno/ Tahoe area can include visits to the Sierra Nevada Childrens Museum in Truckee (11400 Donner Pass Road, 530-587-5437, www.kidzonemuseum.org) or to the Northern Nevada Children's Museum in Carson City (813 North Carson Street, 775-884-2226, www.cmnn.org).

ROCK HUNTING

RENO GEM & MINERAL SOCIETY
P.O. Box 2004
Reno, NV 89520
(775) 356-8820
Around the Reno/Tahoe area are numerous places to hunt for rocks and minerals. If you want to take the kids rock hunting, write to the address above, and the society will be glad to send you a

map showing you where to go and what kinds of rocks and minerals you'll find there. For more information, call between 7:00 and 9:00 p.m. on Monday or Tuesday.

SKATEBOARDING

Reno

IDLEWILD PARK SKATEBOARD PARK
Idlewild Park
1900 Idlewild Drive
(775) 334-2262
www.cityofreno.com
This 13,000-square-foot park gets heavy use, and it's free. Skateboards, in-line skates, and bikes can be used at the park. The Reno Parks and Rec Department recommends the use of safety equipment, but it doesn't require its use—if you don't use protective gear, you skate at your own risk. The park is open all year, from sunup until 10:00 p.m. in summer.

RATTLESNAKE MOUNTAIN SKATEBOARD PARK AT MIRA LOMA PARK
Mira Loma Drive and McCarran Boulevard
(775) 334-2262
www.cityofreno.com
The largest skate park west of the Rocky Mountains, Rattlesnake Mountain offers the latest in challenging terrain. Opened in 2002, the $1.25 million facility provides 38,000 square feet of adventure, with three bowls, ramps, bars, rails, and a mini half-pipe. No bikes are allowed.

i Two other skateboard parks north of Reno include Silver Lake Skate Park, 8855 Red Baron Boulevard and Panther Valley Skate Park on Link Lane in Sun Valley.

North Shore Lake Tahoe

INCLINE SKATE PARK
Tahoe and Southwood Boulevards
Incline Village, NV
(775) 832-1300
www.inclinerecreation.com/outdoor-recreation/parks
Incline Village welcomes skateboarders to its park from 8:00 a.m. to dusk daily, weather permitting. Only skateboards and in-line skates are allowed, and adventure seekers must wear helmets, knee pads, and elbow pads.

South Shore Lake Tahoe

SOUTH TAHOE SKATEBOARD PARK
Bijou Park
Al Tahoe Boulevard
South Lake Tahoe, CA
(530) 542-6055
www.recreationintahoe.com
This skateboard park is very well designed and popular. Helmets and pads are required, and you can use skateboards, in-line skates, and bikes. The park is open from sunup to sunset, weather permitting. There is no charge to use the park.

SKATING

Reno

ROLLER KINGDOM
515 East Seventh Street
(775) 329-3472
www.rollerkingdom.org
If your kids like to skate indoors, this is the place to be. It's open all year, and kids can use in-line skates if they prefer. The rink has special times for certain age groups, so I suggest you call the number above and check the automated messages. You can also schedule birthday parties and other events as roller-skating bashes. Plan to set aside about $7 per person for this skating adventure.

ZOOS AND ANIMALS

Reno

ANIMAL ARK ∖
1265 Deerlodge Road
(775) 970-3111
www.animalark.org
A great place to see wild animals, the Animal Ark is a wildlife sanctuary, taking care of animals that can't take care of themselves. The Ark has foxes, mountain lions, bobcats, wolves, bears, tigers, an arctic wolf, and a snow leopard. The best thing about the Ark is that kids can get a close-up look at all the animals. The Ark has animal demonstrations and picnic areas, and during October you can even howl with the wolves at night. Following a serious forest fire that swept through the Ark several years ago, it's back stronger than ever. Recent renovations include educational displays and newly constructed animal exhibits.

The Animal Ark is open from April through October 10:00 a.m. to 4:30 p.m., but it doesn't open if the weather is rainy. It's closed Monday except major holidays. The entrance fees are $7 for adults and $5 for kids ages 3 through 12.

The Ark is slightly off the beaten path. Drive north on U.S. Highway 395 to Red Rock Road (exit 78), turn right and drive about 11 miles to Deerlodge Road, then look for the ANIMAL ARK sign. (See the Attractions chapter for more information.)

SIERRA SAFARI ZOO
10200 North Virginia Street
(775) 677-1101
www.sierrasafarizoo.com
With more than 150 animals, Sierra Safari Zoo is Nevada's largest zoo. The zoo has a zebra, wallaby, buffalo, llamas, camels, and other wild animals. The best thing about this zoo is that children can pet, feed, and play with some of the animals. The people who run the zoo are very hospitable and will try to answer all your questions. This zoo is open daily from April 1 to October 31 from 10:00 a.m. to 5:00 p.m. (See the Attractions chapter for more details.)

ANNUAL EVENTS

The Reno/Tahoe area is a mecca of entertainment for visitors and locals alike, evident by the thousands of things to do, places to go, and sights to see detailed throughout this book. In this chapter, listed by month, are the events I feel are the biggest crowd-pleasers. But I also touch on the more time-honored events that we Insiders find just plain charming and down-homey.

The more flamboyant and highly visual celebrations that tend to be the norm on the Nevada side of the area are outlined, as well as the less dramatic but equally entertaining and fun festivals and celebrations that touch on the area's historical beginnings and cultural diversity.

Most of the events listed are for visitors, but some are aimed at getting locals involved in the community. No matter which, everyone is welcome.

If you're planning to be in the area for some of the major events, like Hot August Nights, the Great Reno Balloon Race, the Reno National Championship Air Races, or the Reno Rodeo, make sure you reserve your hotel or motel rooms early. And I do mean early: With attendance at Hot August Nights around 800,000, just about every room in the area is booked almost a year in advance.

Specific dates haven't been included because most events are associated with just the month, so the dates are fluid. Therefore it behooves you to call the contact number or check the Web site address to verify the event's actual date and location if you are planning to attend and want to set aside vacation time for the visit. (See the chapter on The Arts for more information on other cultural events.)

I've also included some events that are outside of the geographical area but that I think are definitely worth the time and effort to attend. Along with the major events described in this chapter, nonprofit organizations put on hundreds of cultural and athletic events each year to raise funds and to bring friends, family, and community together. Check local newspapers for specific happenings.

JANUARY

MARTIN LUTHER KING JR. BIRTHDAY CELEBRATION
(775) 329-8990
The event around the 15th of the month includes free entertainment and culminates with an awards dinner. Past guest speakers have included the Reverend Lewis Anthony. Call for location.

ℹ️ For an expanded list of events, visit www.renosparkschamber.org/calendar.htm.

FEBRUARY

BOWLING TOURNAMENTS
National Bowling Stadium
300 North Center Street
Reno, NV
(775) 334-2600
www.renobowlingtournaments.com
Thousands of bowlers flood into Reno throughout the year for different types of bowling tournaments, including those who participate in the American Bowling Congress (ABC) Championship Tournament. Even if you're not competing, it's fun to watch at this state-of-the-art facility. The schedule varies widely; consult the Web site for details.

NORTH TAHOE SNOW FESTIVAL

(530) 583-7167

www.tahoesnowfestival.com

This is a 10-day event in North Shore Lake Tahoe and Truckee. Most of the ski areas and businesses on the northern part of the lake participate in the 120 or more events including parades, snow sculpting, ski and snowboard races, fireworks, food events, and a Polar Bear swim. This is truly a family event and includes many spectator-involved activities. The carnival usually begins in late February. Even though some events are free, don't forget to bring money for food and drinks.

MARCH

POKER TOURNAMENTS

Grand Sierra Resort and Casino

2500 East Second Street

Reno, NV

(775) 789-2000, (775) 789-2313

www.grandsierraresort.com

Although the World Poker Challenge is no longer played in Reno, Grand Sierra was in the planning stages of booking several other world-class poker events at the time this book went to press. With pots in the thousands, the no-limit games provide plenty of heart-stopping action for players as well as spectators. You can watch it all for free from bleachers set up around the playing arena. Call or check the Web site for up-to-date details.

SPRING FESTIVAL

Reno Sports Complex

Intersection of North Virginia Street and North McCarran Boulevard

Reno, NV

(775) 334-2262

A low-key event for young families, the Spring Festival kicks off warm weather with a variety of kid-focused events such as carnival games, a bounce house, and an Easter egg hunt as well as various contests. Children must be accompanied by an adult. Admission is $4—an inexpensive way to spend a fun day with the family.

APRIL

EAGLE VALLEY MUZZLELOADERS' SPRING RENDEZVOUS

Carson City, NV

(775) 883-7736, (775) 887-1221

http://webpages.charter.net/twofalls/

The Eagle Valley Muzzloaders are a group of Nevadans trying to preserve America's heritage by reenacting the lives of the rugged mountain men who were among the first white men in the region. In late April these mountain men gather for a weekend at an encampment along Canyon Road in Carson City to participate in a survival hike, black-powder shoot, strongest-man contests, and other antics associated with these rough-and-tumble pioneers. This is a great, free event for the entire family. From Reno take U.S. Highway 395 south for 30 miles to Carson City.

MAY

ARTS IN BLOOM FESTIVAL

Sparks Marina Park

Sparks, NV

(775) 353-2991

Arts in Bloom honors mothers with an eclectic arts and crafts show on Mothers Day. With colorful exhibits artistically arranged along the waterfront, the festival is also a celebration of spring and all that it promises for the coming year. When the weather cooperates, this event can be a wonderful way for families to spend quality time together, especially treating moms to a special day. The event runs from 10:00 a.m. to 4:00 p.m.

CINCO DE MAYO

Victorian Square, Sparks, NV

(775) 826-1818

As the Hispanic population in the Reno/Lake Tahoe area grows (it has tripled in the past decade), Cinco de Mayo just keeps getting bigger and better. A colorful celebration of Hispanic culture that offers food, music, and art for three fun-filled days, this event is held annually on the weekend closest to May 5. Sponsored by Nevada

Hispanic Services, Cinco de Mayo activities take place from 11:00 a.m. to 5:00 p.m. Be prepared for crowds and weather, because most events are outside.

RENO FILM FESTIVAL
Downtown theaters
Reno, NV
(775) 334-6707
(800) 648-3560 (tickets)
www.renofilmfestival.com
You can step into the Hollywood of yesterday in a big way during the four-day Reno Film Festival. Highlighted by screenings, workshops, and social events, the festival goes all out to promote the appreciation of classic films. And what film event could possibly be complete without a sprinkling of bona fide celebrities? So get set to rub elbows with the likes of Elliott Gould, Piper Laurie, or Gary Busey.

RENO RIVER FESTIVAL
Truckee River Whitewater Park at
Wingfield Park
2 North Arlington Avenue
Reno, NV
(800) 367-7366
www.renoriverfestival.com
www.visitrenotahoe.com
The popularity of Nevada's first kayak slalom racing course in downtown Reno has given rise to this action-packed four-day event of white-water racing. Professionals and amateurs paddle it out in open freestyle, boater cross, and invitational freestyle events. The course consists of 11 drop pools over 2,600 feet of Class II and III rapids on a difficulty scale from 1 to 6. With lots of vantage points and picnic spots along the course, the event is especially spectator-friendly. You can also enjoy live music, exhibits, clinics, and a variety of foods for sale.

> **i** Crisis Call Center sponsors Run 4 Life each year at Hidden Valley Park. For details call (775) 784-8085 or click on www.crisiscallcenter.org.

JUNE

AMERICA'S MOST BEAUTIFUL BIKE RIDE
South Shore Lake Tahoe, NV
(800) 565-2704
www.bikethewest.com
For the conditioned recreational bicyclist, this 72-mile event with plenty of ups and downs is a worthwhile challenge. Beginning at South Shore Lake Tahoe, riders circumnavigate Lake Tahoe with rest stops, food, support, and a plethora of gorgeous scenery along the way. A 35-mile ride is also offered with a cruise on the lake, which can include family and friends. Amenities include an after-ride pool party in South Lake Tahoe. Limited to 3,000 participants, the event attracts riders from all over the country.

FALLON AIR SHOW
Naval Air Station Fallon
Fallon, NV
(775) 426-2550, (775) 423-4556
The U.S. Navy really rolls out the carpet at this annual event at NAS Fallon. It's such a great event for all ages that it just gets bigger and better every year. While it may seem strange to have such a naval presence in the middle of the desert, the Fallon air station has been a vital part of our nation's defense since the 1940s. (See the Day Trips chapter for more about the base.)

The air show features a variety of precision flying demonstrations, such as those put on by the Thunderbirds and Blue Angels, along with numerous static displays of aircraft and rescue equipment. One of the highlights of the show is the Wall of Fire, a simulated bombing run featuring impressive pyrotechnics. Parking and admission are free.

Fallon is 60 miles east of Reno/Sparks. Take Interstate 80 east to Fernley, take the second exit, and look for signs to Alt. U.S. Highway 50 and Fallon. To get to the base, take U.S. Highway 95 south for about 5 miles to Union Lane, and then follow the signs.

RENO RODEO
Reno Livestock Events Center
1350 North Wells Avenue, Reno, NV
(775) 329-3877
(800) 225-2277 (tickets)
www.renorodeo.com
The Reno Rodeo is considered by some to be
the best rodeo in America. World-class cowboys
compete for thousands of dollars in prize money
in the "wildest, richest rodeo in the West." The
nine-day event in late June includes not only
rodeo events every night but also a parade, a carnival, and craft booths. This is one of the premier
events in the Reno/Tahoe area. Don't miss this
one. (See also the Spectator Sports chapter.)

SPARKS HOMETOWNE FARMERS' MARKET
Victorian Square
Sparks, NV
(775) 353-2291
www.ci.sparks.nv.us
An old-fashioned farmers' market is held every
Thursday from 4:00 to 9:00 p.m. starting in the
middle of June and running until late August.
More than 120 vendors offer fresh-picked fruits
and vegetables, specialty foods, and breads. You
can also enjoy cooking demos, a children's play
area, homegrown music, and a friendly atmosphere. This farmers' market is a favorite hangout
for Insiders. Bring plenty of cash for the great
fruits and veggies.

VALHALLA ARTS AND MUSIC FESTIVAL
Tallac Historic Site
California Highway 89
South Lake Tahoe, CA
(530) 541-4975
www.valhallatahoe.com
This is a summer-long program that presents
Native American fine arts, reggae, folk, Latin,
jazz, and bluegrass concerts, as well as a classic
film series, theatrical performances for children
and adults, art gallery tours, and a variety of celebrations honoring the Tallac Historic Site. The
festival begins in early June and runs through

September. The concerts are usually held both
on weeknights and weekends. One of the best
events held around the lake, it makes money for
the historic site from small admission fees. The
site is located about 3 miles north of South Lake
Tahoe on California Highway 89.

JULY

AMERICAN CENTURY CHAMPIONSHIP GOLF TOURNAMENT
Edgewood Tahoe Golf Course
180 Lake Parkway
Stateline, NV
(775) 588-3566
www.tahoecelebritygolf.com
www.edgewood-tahoe.com
This early July golf tournament boasts some of
the biggest names in entertainment and sports
as its participants. This event has featured players the likes of Dan Marino, John Elway, Michael
Jordan, James Woods, Kevin Costner, and Randy
Quaid. The tournament is open to current and
former professional athletes and entertainers.
Spectators can buy tickets for one or more days at
the gate. Prices vary but usually start at $15.

ARTOWN
Various locations
Downtown Reno, NV
(775) 322-1538
www.renoisartown.com
This monthlong Reno summer arts festival features more than 200 different performers and
exhibits at different citywide locations. Highlights
include a touring Broadway musical, music concerts, ballet on the banks of the Truckee River,
and film and visual arts demonstrations. Children
are welcome and even have their own acting and
arts workshops. Most of the events are free. (See
the chapter on The Arts for more information.)

FOURTH OF JULY CELEBRATIONS
Many different celebrations are scattered around
the area to celebrate our Independence Day (see

the Skyfire listing for Reno's celebration). Call the following numbers for locations and starting times:

North Lake Tahoe, (800) 824-6348
South Lake Tahoe, (530) 544-5050
Sparks, (775) 353-2291
Squaw Valley USA, (530) 583-6985

GREAT ELDORADO BBQ, BREWS & BLUES FESTIVAL

Events Plaza
Fourth and North Virginia Streets
Reno, NV
(775) 786-5700, (800) 648-5966
www.eldoradoreno.com

You can wash down some of the hottest barbecue in town with cold microbrews and cool blues at this laid-back summertime event. With booths set up at the busiest corner in downtown Reno (just outside the Eldorado Hotel/Casino Reno), it's also a premier people-watching event.

LAKE TAHOE SHAKESPEARE FESTIVAL

Sand Harbor Beach
Incline Village, NV
(775) 832-1616, (800) 747-4697
www.laketahoeshakespeare.com

"The Bard Done Lakeside" or "The Bard on the Beach"—that's how Insiders describe this festival. For about five weeks beginning in July, the event features noted classical theater troupes performing some of Shakespeare's greatest plays. The magical backdrop of Lake Tahoe adds to the already perfect atmosphere—you'll see why the event is voted Lake Tahoe's best, year after year. Seating varies from general seats in the sand to assigned reserved seating complete with wait service. You can either bring your own picnic or purchase food at the site. Ticket prices run from about $22 to $67. Don't miss this event. (For more information see the chapter on The Arts.)

LAKE TAHOE SUMMER MUSIC FESTIVAL

Various locations
North Shore Lake Tahoe
(530) 583-3101
(530) 581-1184 (tickets)
www.tahoemusic.org

One of the lake's most ambitious undertakings and one of the best organized in the area, this festival consists of a series of outdoor concerts featuring classical, jazz, bluegrass, swing, blues, Broadway, and pops music. The festival begins in mid-July and runs through mid-August. Concert tickets range from $15 for lawn seating to $55 for preferred seating. Season tickets are also available. These concerts are always a good way to spend a family outing. (See also the chapter on The Arts.)

MASTERCRAFT PRO WAKEBOARD TOUR FINALS

Sparks Marina Park
Sparks, NV
(800) 367-7366, (407) 628-4802
www.visitrenotahoe.com
www.prowakeboardtour.com

The world's best wakeboarders compete during this two-day event at Sparks Marina Park. You can bring the whole family and enjoy a picnic and walk around the lake while viewing the acrobatics of the competitors. This area of Sparks has seen a lot of redevelopment in the past couple of years, with upscale condos and restaurants now lining the shore of the lake.

RENO BASQUE FESTIVAL

Wingfield Park
2 North Arlington Avenue
Reno, NV
(775) 762-3577, (800) 367-7366
www.visitrenotahoe.com

A great way to learn about the area's Basque heritage is to attend this festival. It includes traditional food, dancing, and games. The public is welcome to all of the events, which include a barbecue and a Basque Mass. Don't miss the "Irrinitzi" competition, in which contestants attempt the loudest and longest Basque yell. The events are free, but bring money for food and drinks.

SKYFIRE
Rancho San Rafael Park
1595 North Sierra Street
Reno, NV

Skyfire is a free Fourth of July fireworks display in the Truckee Meadows. Come and celebrate America's independence with entertainment and food in the park, working up to a spectacular fireworks display. You have to arrive early for this event if you want a parking spot. Insiders flock to the park and the surrounding area for the just-after-dark fireworks show. Admission to the park is free, but bring money for food and drinks.

AUGUST

BURNING MAN
Black Rock Desert,
about 100 miles north of Reno, NV
(415) 863-5263
www.burningman.com

From a tiny Summer Solstice celebration on a beach in San Francisco in 1986, Burning Man has evolved into a one-of-a-kind event that attracts some 25,000 people from around the globe every year. Attendees become part of an experimental community where they are encouraged to express themselves in some way that depicts the theme of that year. Typical expressions include large-scale artwork, costumes (or lack of clothing), and camps designed with a theme. The climax of the weeklong party is the burning of the statue of man, which rises around 40 feet above the desert. This event is definitely not for everyone. Before considering going, I strongly recommend that you read information provided on the Web site. In general the event has appealed to aging flower children and young laid-back adults. You'll find a fair amount of nudity and typical party behavior. Because no services are provided, other than emergency medical, participants must come equipped to be self-sufficient. Tickets begin at around $200 per person.

GREEK FESTIVAL
St. Anthony's Greek Orthodox Church
4795 Lakeside Drive
Reno, NV
(775) 825-5365

Greek-food lovers cannot miss this annual event, usually put on toward the end of August by the parishioners of St. Anthony's. Everything from baklava to gyros is on the menu, plus live Greek music and dances performed by award-winning dance groups. Admission is usually $4 and food tickets begin at $10. *Opah!*–come on by for a great Greek time.

HOT AUGUST NIGHTS
Various locations throughout Reno
and Sparks, NV
(775) 356-1956, (800) 367-7366
www.hotaugustnights.net

Hot nights, hot rods, hot times, and a great location to enjoy it—this describes the premier event in the Reno/Tahoe area. It's a celebration of America's love affair with hot cars and rock 'n' roll music. For a week in early August, thousands of pre-1970 autos cruise the streets, accompanied by good food and great live music. This is the largest event in northern Nevada, with 800,000 attendees enjoying the nostalgia of a bygone era. Hotels and motels are usually booked a year in advance, so make sure you plan way ahead for this spectacular event.

NEVADA STATE FAIR
Reno Livestock Events Center
1350 North Wells Avenue
Reno, NV
(775) 688-5767
www.nevadastatefair.org

This is a really fun, old-fashioned state fair usually held on the last weekend in August and featuring livestock exhibits, baking and cooking exhibits, special events, entertainment, rides, and midway games. If you ever wanted to visit a down-home country fair, this is the one.

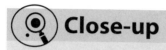 **Close-up**

Reno Rodeo Cattle Drive

When around 50 guests and 35 volunteers saddle up for the Reno Rodeo Cattle Drive each June, they become part of a tradition that has existed for centuries. Using the same methods and gear that generations of their ancestors employed, Great Basin buckaroos in northern Nevada help keep the culture of the Old West alive by herding cattle on horseback.

Driving a herd of 300 steers across the Nevada desert can go a long way toward fulfilling a city slicker's dream of becoming a cowboy or cowgirl. Each year the aspiring drovers come from all over the world to spend five days in the saddle, helping to drive the cattle 100 miles to the rodeo at the Reno Livestock Events Center. The drive is unique, as it ends by bringing the herd down city streets. The steers are used in the competition, which is the third largest and richest Professional Rodeo Cowboys Association event in the country.

During the drive, guests eat gourmet food around the campfire, sleep under the stars and, depending upon their riding ability, try to maintain their position in driving the herd. But perhaps the most meaningful part of the trip is the singular opportunity to experience first-hand the ranching culture of the American West.

The cost for guests includes the horse, meals, and ground transportation. Riders must be at least 18 years old, but they don't need to be experienced on horseback. For details, cost, and registration, go to www.renorodeo.com or call (775) 329-3877.

LEGENDS RENO-TAHOE OPEN
Montreux Golf and Country Club
2500 Spinnaker Drive
Reno, NV
(775) 849-9444, (775) 322-3900
(888) 848-7366
www.renotahoeopen.com

The newest golf tournament on the PGA Tour has quickly become a favorite with many of the world's finest golfers. Hosted by the Jack Nicklaus–designed Montreux Golf and Country Club, the weeklong event is played on one of the toughest but also most scenic courses in the Reno/Tahoe area. Tucked at the base of the Sierras along the meandering Galena Creek, Montreux simply flaunts the best of high-altitude golf. Because the tournament is still new, spectators have the advantage of watching all the action without the enormous crowds and hassles of many other PGA events. I strongly suggest you stop by before the mobs discover this fun event. A variety of ticket packages is offered, so be sure

to call to find out which best suits your needs. Shuttle transportation to the course is provided from various locations in the area.

SEPTEMBER

September is the Reno/Tahoe area's busiest month for annual events. If you're planning an extended trip here, this is the month to do it. Besides a plethora of things to do, the weather is perfect for outdoor activities.

THE BEST IN THE WEST NUGGET RIB COOK-OFF
Victorian Square
Sparks, NV
(775) 356-3428, (800) 648-1177
www.janugget.com
www.nuggetribcookoff.com

About 300,000 people crowd into Victorian Square in Sparks over the five-day Labor Day weekend each year to munch on some of the best barbecue ribs you'll find anywhere in the world. And along with consuming about 130,000 pounds of ribs during the event, spectators also enjoy free headliner entertainment and shop at 200 different crafts booths. Even though the cook-off is great fun and has fantastic food for spectators, the participants get down to serious business. About 25 barbecue cookers from all over the United States and the world compete for the title of "Best in the West" and the $7,500 Grand Prize. So for some cookers it's not all fun and games. But for those of us who like barbecue, it's a chance to taste a variety of finger-lickin'-good ribs.

THE GREAT RENO BALLOON RACE
Rancho San Rafael Park
Reno, NV
(775) 826-1181
www.renoballoon.com

The early-morning Reno sky is alive with color when the nation's top 100 balloonists compete in early September for cash and prizes in the Hare and the Hound and various target drops. The Dawn Patrol, at 5:30 a.m., offers a spectacular light show as the balloonists ascend in their multicolored balloons. Children especially like this event because of the variety of balloons, some in shapes as unusual as champagne bottles, frogs, panda bears, and giant hamburgers. It's a great way to spend an early morning in September, but be sure to dress warmly because temperatures in the desert before dawn are very cold this time of year. Both admission and parking are free. (See the Spectator Sports chapter for more.)

INTERNATIONAL CAMEL RACES
Virginia City, NV
(775) 847-4386, (800) 718-7587
www.virginiacity-nv.org
www.allcamels.com

This wild and crazy time began in 1960, when Hollywood director John Huston won the first race on a borrowed camel. The yearly event, held in mid-September, turned into an international event when the Australians jumped into the fray in 1987. The races are all in fun and have even included ostriches and water buffalo sprints. Other humorous events include a parade down C Street with the town's legal prostitutes dressed in 1880s fashions. Virginia City comes alive once again during this unforgettable weekend: a fun time for the entire family. An entrance fee, usually $10, is charged for the actual camel races. (See the Day Trips chapter for more on Virginia City and on the origin of the Camel Races.)

NATIONAL CHAMPIONSHIP AIR RACES
Reno Stead Airport
Reno, NV
(775) 972-6663
www.airrace.org

If you like airplanes, you won't want to miss this, the longest-running air race in the world. Hundreds of planes fill the sky during this five-day event, which features six classes of racing. Besides the air races, military jets are on hand to thrill the crowd, as well as planes doing aerobatics, skywriting, and the ever-popular daredevil wingwalkers. General admission entrance fees vary from $10 to $27 for adults, depending on the day. (See the Spectator Sports chapter for more.)

STREET VIBRATIONS
Downtown Reno, NV
(775) 329-7469, (800) 200-4557
www.road-shows.com

Reno is in hog heaven in late September. Reported to be the country's sixth largest motorcycle event, the five-day festivities include arts and crafts, parades, an auction, nightly entertainment, and a motorcycle poker run. These events are free to participants and spectators.

The World Championship Outhouse Races are held in Virginia City in October. Call (775) 847-0311 for information.

OCTOBER

GREAT ITALIAN FESTIVAL
Eldorado Hotel/Casino Reno
Fourth and Virginia Streets
Reno, NV
(775) 786-5700, (800) 648-5966
www.eldoradoreno.com

Celebrated along with Columbus Day, this event includes great Italian food, entertainment, a grape-stomping contest, and a parade. The highlight for most spectators is the spaghetti-eating contest. Admission is free. All you have to do is pay for your food and drinks. Insiders love this festival.

KOKANEE SALMON FESTIVAL
Taylor Creek
South Lake Tahoe, CA
(530) 543-2600
www.fs.fed.us/r5/ltbmu/recreation/visitor-center/

This event is held when the bright-red kokanee salmon make their annual spawning run up Taylor Creek, usually around mid-October. The salmon can be viewed from windows below water level at the Lake Tahoe Visitor Center's Stream Profile Chamber. Also included in this fun two-day festival are a kokanee cook-off, educational displays and programs, nature walks, and a children's fishing booth. All events are free to the public.

OKTOBERFEST AT CAMP RICHARDSON
Camp Richardson Resort
1900 Jameson Beach Road
South Lake Tahoe, CA
(877) 217-7407
www.camprich.com

With the leaves turning and a slight chill in the air, October is usually the most spectacular month of the year at Lake Tahoe. Because the Kokanee Salmon Festival (see previous listing) and Okto-berfest are held at the same time, you can easily attend both. They are literally side by side so parking is not much of an issue. Both events are wonderful family affairs that get everybody outside and aware of the changing seasons. Spread out over the beautiful grounds at Camp Richardson; Oktoberfest offers a variety of food, games, and arts and crafts—and a heavy dose of oompah music to entertain attendees in typical Bavarian style.

NEVADA DAY PARADE
Carson City, NV
(775) 882-2600, (866) 683-2948
www.nevadaday.com

Nevada joined the Union on October 31—yes, Halloween—in 1864. Nevadans celebrate their heritage the last weekend in October with a parade, live music, an art show, a best beard contest, and a 1860s period fancy ball at the Governor's Mansion (by invitation only). It's definitely an Insiders' event, but visitors also find the day entertaining. All of downtown Carson City is closed off for this celebration.

NOVEMBER

SPIRIT OF ARTOWN
Various locations
Downtown Reno, NV
(775) 322-1538
www.renoisartown.com

Expanding upon the phenomenal success of Artown, the Spirit of Artown showcases the fall in downtown Reno with more than 100 eclectic cultural events. You can soak up the sights and sounds of autumn by touring galleries, attending concerts, and perhaps just strolling along the river with a cup of hot chocolate in hand.

SPARKS TURKEY TROT
Sparks Marina Park
Sparks, NV
(775) 353-7898

For a guilt-free Thanksgiving feast, you can work off the calories before sitting down to dinner by participating in the Sparks Turkey Trot Thanksgiving morning. The popularity of this run/walk event that benefits local charities has continued to grow over the past few years. The action starts at 8:30 a.m. and is over in plenty of time to sit down to a turkey dinner. One note of caution: Be sure to dress for cold weather as the temperatures can be very chilly that early in the morning this time of year.

DECEMBER

SPARKS HOMETOWNE CHRISTMAS
Victorian Square
Sparks, NV
(775) 353-2291
www.ci.sparks.nv.us
This is the only Christmas event in Nevada that has a parade complete with all the local political figures and Santa Claus. This annual Christmas celebration is sponsored by the city of Sparks and includes a crafts fair, holiday music, and a spectacular tree-lighting ceremony in the evening followed by group caroling. This is a great way to get into the holiday spirit and is a wonderful time for the entire family. It's usually held in early December.

THE ARTS

Most people know the Reno/Tahoe area is absolutely tops for outdoor recreation and non-stop casino action—but they may not know that it's also rich in culture, with an appreciation of the arts that's deeply ingrained in its history. Far from a cultural wasteland, Reno has been dubbed "the Paris of Northern Nevada" by *VIA* magazine. And because a national survey of reading habits found Reno to be the most well-read city in the country, it could also be nick-named "The Biggest Little Literary City in the World."

In this chapter information about the arts is organized into six categories: support organizations, performing arts (theater, music, dance, and venues), visual arts, literary arts, educational institutions, and galleries. The regular geographical sequence has been used, except Reno and Sparks have been combined into one area because most of the arts offerings aren't restricted to either one community or the other. (Though it's been divided geographically, don't let that limit your options since the regions are close enough for day or afternoon trips. If you're staying in Reno, you might still enjoy some of the offerings in the Tahoe area and vice versa.) Also featured are the some of the ethnic and cultural organizations that celebrate the rich diversity of the area. (For performing arts associated with nightclubs and casinos, see the Casino Nightlife and Nightlife chapters.)

Although this treatment of the arts is designed to show the richness and diversity of offerings available, it's not intended to be exhaustive. It's impossible to list everything, but this representative sample should whet your appetite to find out more about your particular interests in the arts. For an all-inclusive listing, you can contact Sierra Arts at (775) 329-ARTS or www.sierra-arts.org. Ask for a copy of their monthly publication, *Encore*. You can also find updated information about arts events by reading *Artifacts*, a quarterly publication available free in newspaper racks in the Lake Tahoe Basin, and the *Reno News & Review*, a weekly publication distributed free in newspaper racks throughout the Reno/Tahoe area. The *Reno Gazette-Journal* publishes arts news in Best Bets on Thursday and Calendar on Friday. All of the Reno/Tahoe art galleries aren't listed, but instead examples that illustrate the richness and variety of artistic works available in the area. You'll find additional galleries listed in local telephone directories.

HISTORY

Since pioneer days, music and drama have been important to people living in this part of the West. The first entertainers wandered from mining camp to mining camp, performing in tents before audiences craving culture and amusement. Banjos, off-color jokes, and fleeting appearances by "real" women were the unsophisticated fare of the day (or night). As the mines prospered, the demand for quality live entertainment increased, ushering in a golden age of theater and music by the second half of the 19th century.

The first real theater in Nevada, The Howard Theater, was built in 1860 in Virginia City. With millions of dollars pouring out of the Comstock mines, the silver barons had plenty of money to indulge their appetites in cosmopolitan pleasures. Other mining towns followed suit (although not in quite so elaborate a fashion), with theaters springing up in such hamlets as Eureka, Gold Hill, and Carson City. While Virginia City was home to a number of theaters and tent shows, the most famous venue is Piper's Opera House, which is listed by the League of Historic

Theaters as the most significant vintage theater in the West. This "Grand Dame of the Comstock" is being renovated to its original splendor using a phased-in approach that allows for selected events to take place during the restoration. For details about the theater and upcoming events, call (775) 847-0433 or log onto their Web site at www.pipersoperahouse.com Be sure to read the Day Trips chapter to find out about other things to see and do in Virginia City.

As frontier entertainment moved to more elegant surroundings, it became more refined, with leading performers from the East eagerly heading to stages in the wild, wild West. Famous players and singers—such as Enrico Caruso, Edwin Booth, Lillie Langtry, and Joe Jefferson—presented Shakespearean drama and popular music to packed houses. A particular favorite was Adah Isaacs Menken, nicknamed "The Menken," who shocked audiences by riding across the stage while lashed to a horse and wearing only flesh-colored provocative tights. During its heyday Virginia City rivaled San Francisco as the cultural center of this part of the West.

But as the fortunes of the mines petered out, so did the ability to pay for top-notch entertainment. The focus of culture shifted to Reno, where its first playhouse, Dyer's Theater, was built in 1871. It was followed by Smith's Academy of Music, Hammond and Wilson's Theater, Wheelman's Theater, the McKissick Opera House, the Wigwam, and the Majestic Theater. By the time the Rialto (later renamed the Granada) opened in 1915, Reno was a major stopover for theater companies en route by train from New York to San Francisco, due to special privileges granted by the railroad. This was somewhat short-lived, however, as World War I put a damper on lavish stage productions and the railroad later rescinded its privileges. By about 1920, Reno's theaters had switched to the latest entertainment craze—movies.

Although films took the place of traveling road shows, art in its various forms continued to develop in the Reno/Tahoe area. The Latimer Art Club was organized in Reno in 1921 and remained the only organization of its kind in the state until other arts groups joined the scene in 1939. The Reno Municipal Band, founded in 1890, continued to perform (as it does today), and the Reno Little Theater opened to enthusiastic performing arts fans in 1935. Beginning in the 1960s the arts blossomed with the arrival of the Nevada Arts Council in 1967, Nevada Opera and the Pioneer Center for the Performing Arts in 1968, the Reno Philharmonic Association in 1969, the Sierra Arts foundation in 1971, the Reno Chamber Orchestra in 1974, the Lake Tahoe Shakespeare Festival in 1978, and the Nevada Motion Picture Division and the Nevada Festival Ballet in 1984. The strong support enjoyed by the arts in the Reno/Tahoe area is the envy of other communities; in fact, Reno boasts more arts organizations per capita than any other city of similar size in the country.

Far from an elitist "arts and furs" scene, the arts reach into every area of the community. Outreach is the name of the game, with a comprehensive variety of programs available to everyone regardless of age or income. The direction of the future is to increase this inclusive appeal, by continuing to cultivate new audiences and to develop more arenas for the celebration of the arts. In Reno the focus is directed in part toward developing an arts corridor downtown encompassing the area along the river between the National Automobile Museum and Oxbow Park. Sprinkled like a string of pearls along the Truckee River, the arts district includes the Lear and Brüka Theaters, the Riverside Artist Lofts, the Nevada Museum of Art, the Pioneer Center for the Performing Arts, and the Century Riverside movie theaters, along with a collection of galleries, boutiques, and restaurants. Much like pearls developing from grains of sand, the gems of downtown redevelopment haven't appeared overnight. A lot of work remains to be done as nonprofits join business and government to reenergize the entertainment, business, and arts districts of downtown.

The face of downtown Reno is changing not only because of an expanding arts community but also with increased efforts on the part of business and government leaders to attract residential projects where people will live full time. The demise of several casinos, such as the Golden Phoenix Hotel Casino, has given rise to condominium conversion projects. Other developments are planned or under construction new from the ground up on previously vacant land. These new upscale addresses include Sierra Vista Towers on West Fourth Street, The Montage on West Second Street, The Waterfront on First and Lake Streets, the Palladio on Sierra and First Streets, and the Village at Idlewild Park on Idlewild Drive. A number of other projects are still on the drawing boards. It is hoped that once these condominiums are fully occupied, residents will support not only the revitalized arts district but also a diverse downtown that is an attractive neighborhood to live in as well as to visit.

As the Reno/Tahoe area continues to grow, support for the arts is anticipated to increase. Many new residents who are transplants from larger cities expect sophisticated cultural choices in their new home and have stepped up to the plate in support of existing as well as future artistic endeavors. For many years artists have been attracted to the area because of its beauty and quality of life. This trend will undoubtedly continue, bringing more residents who embrace the arts as a part of their everyday life.

If you're looking for volunteer activities, there's a wealth of opportunities in myriad events and groups associated with the arts. Virtually every organization welcomes volunteer help with open arms. The entire arts movement in the Reno/Tahoe area owes its success in part to the thousands of devoted arts boosters who give unselfishly of their time, talent, and resources to make the area increasingly artistic and arts-friendly.

RENO/SPARKS

Support Organizations

ARTOWN RENO, NV
(775) 322-1538
www.renoisartown.com

Attracting more than 350,000 attendees, Artown celebrates the art and soul of Reno in sizzling style throughout the month of July. Founded in 1996 to bring Renoites back downtown, the phenomenal success of this event has put Reno on the national cultural map. Accolades range from "an awesome festival" by *Good Morning America* to "Reno Is Art Town" by *New York Newsday*.

At a dozen different indoor and outdoor venues in Reno, a smorgasbord of more than 350 performing and visual arts events is offered up to eager arts buffs. You can learn about history at the Great Basin Chautauqua in San Rafael Park, you can enjoy world-famous art exhibits at the Nevada Museum of Art, and you can experience fine music and dance along the banks of the Truckee River. The festival is unique not only because of the variety of activities but also because most functions are either free or very low-cost. Artown was recently expanded to include the Spirit of Artown, a celebration of more than 100 artistic events held in November and December. (See also the Annual Events chapter.)

CITY OF RENO ARTS AND CULTURAL DIVISION
925 Riverside Drive
Reno, NV
(775) 334-2417
www.cityofreno.com

As part of the City of Reno Parks, Recreation and Community Services Department, the Arts and Cultural Division promotes a full agenda of artistic events through the auspices of the city. It manages the amphitheater in Wingfield Park, where a large number of outdoor artistic performances are held, as well as the McKinley Arts and Culture Center (see separate listings later in this chapter). The division sponsors the Reno Municipal Band and the Public Art Program. The parks department also offers a variety of arts, crafts, and dance classes for all ages. You can pick up a catalog of specific programs at their office at 1301 Valley Road or have one mailed to you.

NEVADA ARTS COUNCIL
716 North Carson Street, Suite A
Carson City, NV
(775) 687-6680
www.nevadaculture.org
Since its creation as a state agency in 1967, the Nevada Arts Council has instituted a number of programs to enrich the cultural life of the people of Nevada. It supports the work of local artists through the Artists' Services Program, promotes art in the schools with its Arts in Education Program, and preserves the traditional arts of Nevada's many cultural groups in the Folklife Program. You can also learn about Nevada's arts scene by reading Nevada Arts News, a publication put out by the Nevada Arts Council.

NEVADA FILM OFFICE
108 East Proctor Street
Carson City, NV
(775) 687-1814, (800) 336-1600
www.nevadafilm.com
The history of Nevada and the movies goes back to 1897, when the state's first film, *The Corbett–Fitzsimmons World Champion Fight*, was filmed in Carson City. From then on, hundreds of movies have been shot in the state, using the picturesque desert/mountain landscapes and the miles of open road as realistic backdrops. The Nevada Film Office, a division of the State Commission on Economic Development, boasts a library of 45,000 photos of location sites in the state. And if producers don't find what they want from that inventory, the film office will customize a search for "locations less known." Favorite locations in Reno include the famous Reno Arch, proclaiming "The Biggest Little City in the World," and the campus at the University of Nevada, Reno, with its wooded Ivy League look. The gorgeous scenery anywhere around Lake Tahoe is a sure winner for any film needing an authentic mountain location. In addition to providing location assistance, the film office also offers production coordination for every aspect of a film project. The list of movies filmed in the Reno/Tahoe area parallels the history of film, and the roster of stars reads almost like a who's who in the industry.

In 1983 the state of Nevada acknowledged what moviemakers had known for years: Nevada is an extremely attractive location for shooting and casting films. To facilitate and attract more film ventures in the state, the Motion Picture Division of the Economic Development Commission was established. With the financial impact from films generating in excess of $100 million each year, movies continue to be big business in the Reno/Tahoe area.

SIERRA ARTS
17 South Virginia Street
Reno, NV
(775) 329-2787
www.sierra-arts.org
If you want to find out about the local arts scene, your first phone call should be to Sierra Arts (SA). Established in 1971 to assist artists and arts organizations, the foundation maintains a complete up-to-date list of all arts groups. It also keeps a master calendar of upcoming performances, exhibitions, and events and publishes a monthly arts magazine titled Encore. SA functions in many ways as a large clearinghouse of information for anything that has to do with the arts in the Reno/Tahoe area.

The foundation has an ambitious outreach program that brings the arts and arts appreciation to a wide audience in the community. It places professional artists in school classrooms and helps teach teachers how to use the arts across the curricula. It celebrates cultural diversity in the Sierra Folklife Festival and manages galleries at the Riverside Artist Lofts and the Northwest Reno Library. It also sponsors a variety of special events, such as movie festivals and storytelling presentations. The foundation is headquartered in the renovated Riverside Artist Lofts, in the heart of the arts district in downtown Reno.

THE THEATER COALITION
528 West First Street
Reno, NV
(775) 786-2278
www.theatercoalition.org
The Theater Coalition was founded in 1994 to

meet a growing need for more professional performance facilities for the regional arts community. More than 50 performing arts, educational, and cultural organizations joined the coalition to purchase the First Church of Christ, Scientist, and renovate it into the Lear Theater (see the description of the theater later in this chapter).

Although the coalition has been directly involved in a number of performing projects over the years, the recent focus has been directed at the continuing renovation of the theater. You can still consult the coalition Web site for news of the project and events held in the theatre.

VERY SPECIAL ARTS NEVADA
250 Court Street
Reno, NV
(775) 826-6100
www.lakemansion.com

Very Special Arts Nevada brings the arts to children and adults who are under-served because they are disadvantaged, disabled, or at risk. The organization conducts workshops in the visual and theater arts at a variety of events and in conjunction with other community programs. It also brings hands-on arts programs to nursing-home residents, conducts several arts festivals for children each year, and offers visual arts and drama workshops to the general public. After some years of moving around town, VSA has found a permanent home in the historic Lake Mansion, which was relocated to Court Street in downtown Reno.

i With 1 percent of the construction budget of public buildings mandated for art, Reno is enjoying an increase in the number of public art pieces being placed around town.

Performing Arts
Theater
AGELESS REPERTORY THEATRE
Reno, NV
(775) 345-7323

Ageless Repertory Theatre gathers local actors of all ages together to read plays, perform, and rehearse at local libraries.

BRÜKA THEATRE OF THE SIERRA
99 North Virginia Street
Reno, NV
(775) 323-3221
www.bruka.org

For bare-bones theater (minus high-tech bells and whistles), Brüka Theatre of the Sierra offers children's and avant-garde adult theater at its very best. Stripped of elaborate props, the emphasis is on the quality of acting, which local theater fans know is always top-notch. Its downtown venue is quintessential casual, with cozy couches tucked casually around the intimate stage. Right next to the Truckee River, it's also convenient to downtown casinos and restaurants. In case you're wondering what "Brüka" means, it was the name of a turn-of-the-20th-century German artistic group.

RENO LITTLE THEATER
Hug High School Little Theater
Sutro Street and North McCarren Boulevard
Reno, NV
(775) 329-0661
www.renolittletheater.org

In 1935 the population of Reno was only 19,000, and live entertainment was sparse, to say the least. But a small group of determined theater aficionados joined together to form the Reno Little Theater, which has played to enthusiastic supporters ever since. Call for dates and performance offerings.

Music
BELLA VOCE
(775) 359-1533
www.bellavocereno.com

One of the area's premier vocal groups, Bella Voce performs at many musical and special events throughout the year. You must audition to belong to this approximately 20-woman choir. For a schedule of the group's appearances, check the Web site.

MASTERWORKS CHORALE

(775) 324-1940

www.themasterworkschorale.org

With an appearance at Carnegie Hall in its résumé, the MasterWorks Chorale is one of the most outstanding performing arts groups in the Reno/Tahoe area. More than 80 trained and auditioned singers make up this volunteer-based choral group. You can enjoy their diverse repertoire, which includes opera, spirituals, Broadway musicals, and classics, in their performances around the area.

NEVADA OPERA

(775) 786-4046

www.nevadaopera.org

A nationally recognized regional opera company, Nevada Opera has been called the "grande dame" of Nevada's performing arts groups. It debuted in 1968 in the tiny 260-seat Reno Little Theater (which has since been torn down) with *The Barber of Seville* and *Rigoletto*. In just three years it outgrew this small venue and relocated to the Pioneer Center for the Performing Arts, where it's been performing since 1971.

Far from stuffy and boring, Nevada Opera performances are ambitious, exciting affairs. They are always fully staged with elaborate costumes, sets, and a full orchestra. And even though they are sung in the original language, opera buffs can easily follow the plot because the English translation is projected above the proscenium stage.

The company has performed a provocative variety of works over the years, ranging from the grand *Verdi Requiem* and the familiar classic *Swan Lake* to light operettas, such as *Showboat* and *Mame*. With more than 100 main-stage productions to its credit, the opera usually performs three separate works each season in addition to a variety of concerts and special events. In addition to Friday-evening performances, it offers Sunday matinees that appeal to opera fans from out of town and those who prefer not to drive at night.

The company offers emerging artists opportunities to perform with mature talents by showcasing guest performers from other opera companies in Europe and the United States. Many young talents whose careers began with Nevada Opera have gone on to national and world acclaim, including famous mezzo-soprano Dolora Zajick.

As part of the opera's extensive outreach and education program, the Nevada Opera Youth Chorus offers professional training and performing experience to talented school-age youngsters. The Nevada Opera Studio brings shortened versions of standard operas to more than 50,000 area students each year.

RENO CHAMBER ORCHESTRA

925 Riverside Drive, Suite 5 (office)

Reno, NV

(775) 348-9413

www.renochamberorchestra.org

Known as Reno/Tahoe's "intimate orchestra," the 30-some-member Reno Chamber Orchestra plays music designed specifically for small orchestras. Performances are classy but cozy affairs at the 615-seat Nightingale Concert Hall on the campus of the University of Nevada, Reno. In spite of some ups and downs weathered over the years, the group has enjoyed a growing audience of enthusiastic supporters since its founding in 1974. An impressive roll call of guest soloists and conductors have shared its stage along the way, including Daniel Heifetz, Itzhak Perlman, Scott Yoo, Pepe Romero, Bion Tsang, and Emil de Cou.

Part of the mission of the RCO is to assist the area's young musicians in developing their talents. It sends many promising musicians to summer camps each year and offers opportunities to perform with its Youth String Competition, the Reno Youth Symphony, and the RCO College Concerto Competition. It also reaches outlying areas in northern Nevada and California, where classical music is a rarity, through broadcasts on radio station KUNR-FM.

For your convenience you can order tickets through the Web site listed above.

RENO CONCERTS
(775) 786-7300
www.renoconcerts.org
If you're looking for quality entertainment at an affordable price, the events presented by Reno Concerts (formerly the Washoe County Concert Association) will certainly fill the bill with tickets for adults running around $20. Performances vary from the classics to popular music and include soloists and small groups. The association has sponsored first-rate touring musicians to the Reno/Tahoe area for more than half a century. Call or check the Web site for specific dates and offerings.

RENO MUNICIPAL BAND
(775) 334-2417, (775) 657-4630
www.cityofreno.com
Founded in 1890, the Reno Municipal Band is the oldest performing arts group in the Reno/Tahoe area. It's also one of only three municipal bands in the country that are professional, with funding provided equally by the city and various foundations. With a whopping 150 performances each year, funders don't need to worry about getting their money's worth from this group.

In addition to playing in the principal band, the 50-plus players perform in smaller groups, which include the swing bands, the banjo band, the barbershop group, the country band, the brass quintet, and the String Beings. Most members are professional musicians or music teachers. Although the bands play at special events throughout the year, the best place to catch a performance is during the band's Summer Concert Series in Wingfield Park in downtown Reno.

RENO PHILHARMONIC ASSOCIATION
925 Riverside Drive, Suite 3
Reno, NV
(775) 323-6393
www.renophilharmonic.com
Frequently voted Best Performing Arts Group in the *Reno Gazette-Journal*'s annual "Best of Reno" contest, the Reno Philharmonic Orchestra is a splendid mainstay to the Reno/Tahoe music scene. A professional symphony comprising the area's finest musicians, the Phil (as it's affectionately known by locals) has grown steadily in stature and popularity since its founding in 1969. In a typical year the group performs six MasterClassics subscription concerts and six Young People's Concerts for students plus a variety of special performances. A not-to-be-missed gala is Pops on the River, where music fans feast on gourmet picnics and pops music at festively decorated tables along the banks of the Truckee River. Over the years the Phil has also had the honor of performing with a number of well-known guest artists, including Luciano Pavarotti, Ray Charles, Jose Iturbi, George Shearing, and Jerry Lewis.

In keeping with its commitment to Reno/Tahoe's young people, the Reno Philharmonic Association sponsors the Reno Philharmonic Youth Orchestras, consisting of the brightest up-and-coming school-age musicians in the area. The youth orchestras usually perform about 15 concerts each year in various venues around the region. Through the youth and adult orchestras and the in-school Discover Music program of ensemble performances, more than 60,000 students enjoy first-rate live concerts every year.

The social and fund-raising arms of the association are the Reno Philharmonic Guild for the Reno/Sparks area, the Alliance for Philharmonic Youth, and the Sierra Philharmonic League for the Carson Valley. The groups sponsor events during the year that support the Philharmonic's programs while also enhancing the culture of the region.

RENO POPS ORCHESTRA
925 Riverside Drive
Reno, NV
(775) 673-1234
www.renopops.org
The love of music and performing motivates the 40-plus members of the Reno Pops Orchestra. Composed of players from all walks of life, it's truly a community group. With a mission to make music available to everyone, the group offers its six annual concerts free as gifts to the general public. The orchestra also brings its performances to area at-risk schools for no cost.

Although you might think all concerts are just "pops" music, the orchestra's repertoire is much broader. Beyond the basic criteria that selections have instant audience appeal, programs include overtures, well-known symphonies, and concertos.

If you've ever contemplated dusting off your old clarinet from high school band days, now might be the time: The orchestra is always looking for additional players. You can also join in the chorus at the orchestra's annual *Messiah* sing-along during the Christmas season.

TRINITY EPISCOPAL CHURCH
200 Island Avenue
Reno, NV
(775) 329-4279
www.trinityreno.org
One of the most glorious sounds in the Reno/Tahoe area is the Casavant pipe organ at Trinity Episcopal Church. Custom built in Quebec, Canada, the organ has 2,000 pipes and took 85 employees about six months to construct. Aside from hearing this magnificent instrument during church services, you can enjoy concerts and other musical events on a regular basis. Guest organists from all over the country are eager to perform because the acoustics and overall musical experience in the church are of such high quality. Call the church for a schedule of events.

Dance
A.V.A. BALLET THEATRE
73 West Plumb Lane
Reno, NV
(775) 762-5165
www.avaballet.com
Through its professional quality performances in northern California and Nevada, A.V.A. Ballet Theatre has given local dancers and artists opportunities to appear in high-caliber theater since its founding in 1994. The experienced faculty are especially equipped to guide and mentor talented performers who aspire to professional careers. Theatergoers are the beneficiaries of these efforts with their attendance at topnotch events, such as

Cinderella, Vortex, Tatu, and *Alice in Wonderland.* The group annually presents the *Nutcracker Ballet* with the Reno Philharmonic at the Pioneer Theater for the Performing Arts. Check the Web site for a schedule of performances.

BALLANTINE'S BALLROOM AND SCHOOL OF DANCE
2920 Mill Street, Reno, NV
(775) 324-1000
www.ballantinesballroom.com
Learning the basics of all types of ballroom dancing is fun and easy at Ballantine's. A favorite place to meet and greet for many older folks, the school offers lessons at all levels of proficiency along with open dancing. Call for rates and a schedule.

BALLET NEVADA
2920 Mill Street (Ballantine's)
Reno, NV
(775) 329-2026
www.balletnevada.com
Boasting an impressive roster of professional performers, Ballet Nevada Performing Arts School offers high-quality training in dancing, acting, and music. Their NPA North facility has four dance studios that comprise the largest studio space in northern Nevada. Dedicated to promoting excellence and diversity in the performing arts, the school teaches the basics, such as microphone technique, as well as advanced performance skills. Classes are open to all ages.

LET'S DANCE STUDIO
1151 North Rock Boulevard
Sparks, NV
(775) 351-1400
www.letsdancereno.com
You can let the experts help you swing into the increased popularity of ballroom dancing with lessons and practice sessions at Let's Dance Studio. Students can quickly become proficient in swing, Argentine tango, country, and hustle, to name a few. The studio is also the representative for the Nevada Tango Society. Classes are

offered at all levels and for all ages. Drop-ins are welcome, but call for a schedule.

RENO FOLKDANCERS
First Congregational Church
Reno, NV
(775) 677-2306

You can celebrate diversity with dances from around the world at the First Congregational Church. You don't need a partner to join in the fun of traditional dances from Greece, Israel, and Serbia. A small fee is charged, and beginners are welcome. Dances are usually scheduled on Tuesday at 7:00 p.m. and occasionally on Saturday, but call to verify the day and time.

SIERRA NEVADA BALLET
(775) 783-3223
www.sierranevadaballet.com

A relatively new professional ballet company in Northern Nevada, Sierra Nevada Ballet incorporates well-known classical creations with New Age contemporary pieces. It features principal dancers as well as apprentices. The company specializes in outreach lectures and performances. Summer intensive workshops are given in Reno at In Motion Studio on Prototype Drive. Call or check the Web site for the performance schedule and more information.

WING & A PRAYER DANCE COMPANY
925 Riverside Drive, Reno, NV
(775) 323-0766
www.wnpdance.org

With members ranging in age from 6 to 47, Wing & A Prayer Dance Company is one of the few intergenerational dance companies in the country. It was born in 1992 as a choreography project at the University of Nevada, Reno and now, as a mature company, offers lecture presentations, artist-in-residence programs, dance workshops, and master classes as well as a full schedule of exciting contemporary performances. Its Dance-in-Education Series provides free performances for students; its Master Dance Workshops offer classes taught by nationally acclaimed dancers;

its Loneliest Roads Tour brings quality dance to rural communities in Nevada and California.

The name of the group reflects the uplifting nature of its performances. To celebrate the joyful aspects of life and movement, catch this group in action at any of their appearances in the Reno/Tahoe area.

Venues
BREWERY ARTS CENTER
449 West King Street, Carson City, NV
(775) 883-1976
www.breweryarts.org

Even though Carson City is covered as a day trip in this book (see the Day Trips chapter), I'd be remiss by not telling you about the Brewery Arts Center in this chapter. Since its founding more than 20 years ago, it's been a veritable hotbed of artistic activity. The 140-seat black box theater hosts more than 50 dramatic and musical performances every year. Resident companies include the BAC Stage Kids and the Proscenium Players, the second-oldest local theater group in northern Nevada.

The visual arts are equally well represented in the center, with a full-service pottery studio, a full array of classes and workshops, receptions, exhibits, and the Artisans' Store, which features works from more than 70 local artisans.

Just as interesting as the events that take place here is the physical structure itself. Built originally as part of the Carson Brewery in 1864, the building is one of the most historic landmarks in downtown Carson City. It was listed on the National Register of Historic Places in 1977 and is easily identifiable by the mural of 11 pioneers on its front facade.

Because Carson City is within an hour's drive of most parts of the Reno/Tahoe area, it's easy to attend events at the Brewery Arts Center.

LAWLOR EVENTS CENTER
University of Nevada, Reno
North Virginia Street, Reno, NV
(775) 784-4444
(800) 225-2277 (tickets)
www.unr.edu/lawlor

Lawlor Events Center is a multipurpose arena that's the home address for many University of Nevada, Reno, athletic events. But when it's not busy hosting Wolf Pack basketball, it's available for ice shows, concerts, and other special events. With a seating capacity of about 12,000, the center is a large, no-frills venue. When attending events here, don't expect luxury since the ambience is strictly gymnasium. You can buy tickets at the box office or at www.tickets.com.

(I can't give you a physical address for the center because it doesn't have one. Just look for the large circular building perched on North Virginia Street on the north end of the UNR campus.)

LEAR THEATER
501 Riverside Drive
Reno, NV
(775) 786-2278
www.theatercoalition.org

Designed by internationally acclaimed architect Paul Revere Williams, the First Church of Christ, Scientist, has been a historic landmark in downtown Reno since it was constructed in 1939. Williams achieved fame during the Golden Age of Hollywood with such works as Chasen's and Perino's restaurants, the Fountain Coffee Shop at the Beverly Hills Hotel, and the Los Angeles Airport.

The Theater Coalition purchased the Reno church in 1998 and is in the process of converting the building into a state-of-the-art theater facility named for the late philanthropist Moya Olsen Lear. Renovations will preserve the historical integrity of the building while providing a 450-seat auditorium, a studio theater, a rehearsal hall, and dressing rooms. With its picturesque location on the banks of the Truckee River, the Lear Theater is part of a growing arts presence in the heart of downtown Reno, offering a variety of small productions during its renovation.

MCKINLEY ARTS AND CULTURE CENTER
925 Riverside Drive, Reno, NV
(775) 334-2417
www.cityofreno.com

Nestled in an old historic neighborhood along the banks of the Truckee River, the McKinley Arts and Culture Center was formerly the McKinley Park School. Constructed in 1910 in Spanish Mission style, the facility houses galleries, arts and crafts workshops, classrooms, an auditorium, and offices for nonprofit organizations. Although it was completely renovated recently, the building maintains its quiet integrity as a faithful example of this particular type of architecture. If you're strolling along the Truckee River Walk in downtown Reno, you can't miss it: Look for the circular steel sculpture in the front yard.

PIONEER CENTER FOR THE PERFORMING ARTS
100 South Virginia Street, Reno, NV
(775) 686-6600 (information)
(877) 840-0457 (tickets)
www.pioneercenter.com

The Pioneer Theater Auditorium was constructed in 1968 to meet the need for more convention and meeting facilities in downtown Reno. Later renamed the Pioneer Center for the Performing Arts, it has become the focal point and premier venue for many top-notch cultural events in the Reno/Tahoe area. Some of the groups that call it home include the Reno Philharmonic, the Nevada Opera, Reno Concerts, and the Sierra Nevada Master Chorale. With about 130 different cultural productions presented annually, the facility is busy with events approximately 240 days of the year. In addition to local and regional groups, it hosts a variety of touring performances. As part of the center's Broadway Comes to Reno series, theatergoers have enjoyed world-class presentations of *Les Miserables, Cats, 42nd Street, Tommy, Stomp,* and *She Loves Me.*

The theater's gold geodesic dome, considered an architectural masterpiece at the time it was constructed, is a standout among the mostly mundane banks and office buildings nearby. Its upscale interior is hushed and quiet, almost cathedral-like, which lends an air of expectation to most performances. Since the classy surroundings provide just the right background for formal attire, don't be surprised if you find yourself in a sea of fur coats, especially at the opera or philharmonic concerts.

But even a facility as lovely as this has downsides, mainly its small size and lack of parking. Although its 1,500-seat capacity gives an almost intimate feel to large productions, many shows are sold out early.

I recommend you reserve tickets as early as possible and that you allow plenty of time to park prior to performances. Parking is available in a large lot across the street. The box office is open weekdays from 11:00 a.m. to 6:00 p.m.

R. Z. HAWKINS CULTURAL AMPHITHEATER
Bartley Ranch Regional Park
6000 Bartley Ranch Road, Reno, NV
(775) 823-6526, (775) 823-6500
www.washoecountyparks.com
Tucked into a natural bowl in Bartley Ranch Regional Park, the R. Z. Hawkins Cultural Amphitheater is a 400-seat outdoor facility for drama and music productions. In keeping with the ranch theme of the park, the stage has a country look, with barn doors and a corrugated tin roof. You can picnic in the park and then attend evening performances under the stars when the weather permits. Remember this is an outdoor venue so it's important to layer your clothing because it can get very chilly by the end of the performance. See the Parks chapter for details about the park.

RIVERSIDE ARTIST LOFTS
17 South Virginia Street, Reno, NV
(775) 329-2787, (775) 786-8824
www.sierra-arts.org
Several years ago it was hard to believe the Riverside Hotel's guest list once read like a who's who in show business. Vacant and crumbling, it entertained migrating flocks of birds and groups of transients instead of glitzy celebrities and powerful politicians. Oozing of history of the early days of gaming in Reno, this historic old structure was designed by noted architect Frederic DeLongchamps and erected on the founding

cornerstone of Reno in 1927. But by 1987 it was shut down, its glory days long gone, eclipsed by larger, newer hotel/casinos.

Ten years later it was saved from further decay by an alliance between the city, Sierra Arts, and Artspace Projects, Inc., who completely renovated the building into live/work spaces for artists. In addition to the 35 lofts, the structure also houses retail space, an art gallery, and the offices of Sierra Arts. The outstanding success of the project is indicated by a number of awards it's received, including the 2001 Audrey Nelson Community Development Achievement Award and the 2000 Tourism Development Award.

ℹ️ The county library in Incline Village exhibits works by local artists.

WINGFIELD PARK AMPHITHEATER
2 North Arlington Avenue, Reno, NV
(775) 334-2262
www.cityofreno.com
In downtown Reno next to the Truckee River Walk, the Wingfield Park Amphitheater is a venue with a view: You can drink in the beauty of the river, with the city lights of downtown Reno as a bedazzling backdrop. It's the outdoor site of numerous concerts and special affairs, and it's a real treat to attend events here when the weather permits (see the description of Wingfield Park in the Parks chapter).

Visual Arts
GREAT BASIN BASKETMAKERS
(775) 626-8108
www.greatbasinbasketmakers.org
Baskets are a magical art form when created by artisans in the Great Basin Basket-makers group. Members gather each month to network, attend workshops, and sponsor exhibits. The yearly dues of $15 entitles these artists to the group newsletter and access to a large library.

NEVADA CASTING GROUP, INC.
5440 Louie Lane #108
Reno, NV
(775) 322-8187
www.nevadacasting.com

So you wanna be a star? Nevada Casting Group, Inc., gives many newcomers a start in the movies and television with its casting, training and models services You could be just a phone call away from seeing yourself on the screen.

SIERRA WATERCOLOR SOCIETY
www.sierrawatercolor.com
carenbe@hotmail.com

The Sierra Watercolor Society was organized in 1989 to help promote local artists' love of watercolors. With about 100 member artists from around the area, the group sponsors exhibits of members' works, gives demonstrations in the schools, and presents workshops by visiting artists. Members network through their bimonthly meetings and also keep in touch through a monthly newsletter.

Literary Arts

BARNES & NOBLE
5555 South Virginia Street
Reno, NV
(775) 826-8882
www.bn.com

The epitome of a super bookstore, Barnes & Noble is a one-stop cultural emporium. More than just a splendid shopping mart for books, music, and videos or a cozy place to enjoy a steaming cup of espresso, it's a vibrant center for special cultural events. Literary-minded Insiders will tell you it's also a great place for culturally inclined singles to meet and greet.

BORDERS BOOKS
4995 South Virginia Street
Reno, NV
(775) 448-9999
www.borders.com

It's not enough for megabookstores to simply sell books, videos, and music. They also sponsor special events, such as book signings, poetry readings, and concerts. As a mini cultural center with its own gourmet cafe, Borders is a comfortable hangout for literary fans. Check local newspapers or call the store for its upcoming events.

NEVADA POETRY SOCIETY
P.O. Box 7014, Reno, NV 89510
(775) 322-3619

As a member of the National Federation of State Poetry Societies, the Nevada group helps area poets hone their craft. At the monthly meetings, members critique one another's work and study different forms of writing poetry. It's literally a prize-winning group: With the encouragement of their peers, many members have won awards in national and state poetry contests.

UNNAMED WRITERS' GROUP
www.unnamedwriters.org
rewcrew@charter.net

Started by three writers in 1995, the Unnamed Writers' Group has about 150 members who are published and unpublished writers. With its mission of "helping writers write better," the group sponsors workshops and seminars on different forms of writing and presents guest speakers at its monthly meetings. Members also critique one another's work and participate in a community writing project that involves charity each year.

WASHOE COUNTY LIBRARY SYSTEM
301 South Center Street, Reno, NV
(775) 327-8300
www.washoe.lib.nv.us

When the Washoe County Library System tells you it "offers more than just books," you'd better believe it. Its 13 physical facilities are focal points for community activities as well as storehouses of information for every interest imaginable. The main branch on Center Street in Reno is a wonderful place for reading and browsing. With loads of leafy green plants and trees, its arboretum atmosphere is a delightful haven from the busy downtown streets outside. The branch on Robb Drive is especially user-friendly, with a latte cart, a drive-up window, and a used bookstore operated by the Friends of Washoe County Library.

Although libraries have been synonymous with the printed word for many years, today most of them are also high-tech, with all the bells and whistles needed for high-speed transmittal of electronic information. The Washoe system is no exception since its Internet Branch provides access to more than 1,000 information sources on the Internet.

Outreach is alive and well in this library system, with about 130 programs for adults and an amazing 1,737 for children and young adults. The variety of specific events is impressive to say the least and much too long to list in this chapter. You can call the library for its calendar of events and watch local newspapers for current happenings.

If you love to buy books (and what avid reader doesn't?), you won't want to miss the "Booksale Bonanza," sponsored by the Friends of Washoe County Library. It's northern Nevada's largest community-wide book sale, with more than 25 tons of books up for grabs.

Educational Institutions

TRUCKEE MEADOWS COMMUNITY COLLEGE
(Main Campus)
7000 Dandini Boulevard, Reno, NV
(775) 673-7000
www.tmcc.edu

TMCC offers a wide variety of classes in the performing, visual, and literary arts. I can't begin to describe them all: Consult the college catalog for a complete listing. The public frequently shares the work and accomplishments of TMCC's arts students and faculty through their theater productions and visual arts exhibits. The college does more than just teach the arts: it brings them to the community as a way of enriching life in the Truckee Meadows. (For more information on the school, see the Education and Child Care chapter.)

UNIVERSITY OF NEVADA, RENO (UNR)
North Virginia Street, Reno, NV
(775) 784-1110
www.unr.edu/arts

It's possible to estimate the economic impact of the University of Nevada, Reno, on the Reno/Tahoe area, but how do you begin to describe its influence on the local culture and quality of life? Since the answer to that question is quite subjective, I think it's enough to simply understand that a major university permeates every facet of life in a community, injecting intellectual choices and cultural contributions that the area might not have had otherwise.

Because it offers a wide variety of programs and degrees in various artistic disciplines, UNR has been a focal point for the local arts scene for many years. The university sponsors a veritable kaleidoscope of stimulating events throughout the year, presented by students and faculty as well as members of the community, guest artists, and speakers. In the university's Nightingale Concert Hall you can enjoy first-class performances by such talented resident groups as the Argenta Quartet, the UNR Orchestra, the UNR Mastersingers, and the Reno Jazz Orchestra. In the Redfield Proscenium Theatre and the Redfield Studio Theatre you can delight in exquisite dance and lively theater. And in the Lawlor Events Center (when not used for major athletic events), you can attend large productions, such as ice shows and rock concerts, in a typical arena-style venue.

As the only university repertory company in the country, the Nevada Repertory Company gives students, faculty, and community members the opportunity to work in a different show each night. With four distinct productions offered each season, the company provides a well-rounded theater experience to both cast and crew. Selections from previous seasons have included Into the Woods, Angels in America, A Clockwork Orange, and A Grand Night for Singing. For information call (775) 784-4444 or go to www.unr.edu/nevadarep. Be sure to ask about weekend dinner/theater options. For tickets call (800) 225-2277.

Aside from this tantalizing array of performing arts events, UNR is also a dynamic supporter of the visual and literary arts. You can always count on a top-notch exhibit in the Sheppard Art Gallery along with other displays in the Matheweson–IGT Knowledge Center and the Joe Crowley Student Union.. The university's Black Rock Press has been a mainstay for local writers for many years, publishing such well-known authors as Robert Laxalt and Gary Snyder.

Although parking on university campuses is often restrictive and challenging for visitors, UNR's parking garage just north of the Church Fine Arts building provides adequate parking for most events.

For updated information on all UNR arts events, call the University Arts Hotline at (775) 334-9696 or (775) 784-4278.

Galleries

ARTISTS CO-OP GALLERY
627 Mill Street, Reno, NV
(775) 322-8896
www.artistsco-opgalleryreno.com
Situated in a historic brick building at the corner of Wells Avenue and Mill Street, the Artists Co-op Gallery was the first art cooperative in Nevada when it opened in 1966. The 20 award-winning artist members offer original art at reasonable prices and with payment schedules. The works include oils, watercolors, pastels, mixed media, photography, and pottery. The gallery is open daily from 11:00 a.m. to 4:00 p.m.

ART SOURCE
Foothill Commerce Center
9748 South Virginia Street
Reno, NV
(775) 828-3525
www.artsourcereno.com
With 8,000 square feet of display space on two levels, Art Source has an eclectic array of art, prints, and sculpture. They also offer custom framing service. Hours are 10:00 a.m. to 6:00 p.m. Monday through Friday and 11:00 a.m. to 5:00 p.m. Saturday. The Foothill Commerce Center is next to Winco on South Virginia Street.

BOYCE ART IMAGES
4900 Charlotte Way
Reno, NV
(775) 857-6136
www.boyceart.com
Award-winning wildlife artist Fred Boyce is one of the best-known outdoor artists in the Reno/Tahoe area. For those who love "nature" art and Nevada landscapes, his gallery is truly a treasure. He has also published two coffee-table books with photos of his work, The Other Nevada and The Other Nevada II. You can view his originals, limited editions, and lithographs from 10:00 a.m. to 6:00 p.m. daily.

LA BUSSOLA
20 Cheney Street
Reno, NV
(775) 348-8858
www.2by2creations.com/labussola
La Bussola features original art and refurbished furniture. The focus is on emerging local artists in all types of media. If you're looking for affordable art, I recommend you check this place out, since prices are very reasonable. You can easily combine a jaunt along the Truckee River with a visit to the gallery. Hours are 10:00 a.m. to 6:00 p.m. Wednesday through Saturday and Monday and 11:00 a.m. to 4:00 p.m. Sunday. It's closed on Tuesday.

NEVADA MUSEUM OF ART
160 West Liberty Street, Reno, NV
(775) 329-3333
www.nevadaart.org
The only accredited fine-arts museum in Nevada, the Nevada Museum of Art is housed in an intriguing structure of black geometric shapes interspersed with glass. Once you've admired the building, I invite you to enjoy the delights inside. You'll find 55,000 square feet of experimental, rotating, and permanent works. The building

also boasts a theater, library, classrooms, and a rooftop sculpture garden. The museum gift shop is chock-full of unique artistic gifts you won't find anywhere else. It's almost impossible to browse without buying. A delightful place for lunch, the Cafe Musee is frequently the site of wine tastings, special events, and concerts. If you're an art lover, this museum is a must-see. Although smaller than many big city museums, the NMA is first-class in the quality of its exhibits and the events that are offered. Hours are 10:00 a.m. to 5:00 p.m. Tuesday through Sunday and until 8:00 p.m. on Thursday.

RICHARDSON GALLERY OF FINE ART
3670 South Virginia Street
Reno, NV
(775) 828-0888, (800) 628-0928
www.richardsonfineart.com
Showcasing a delightful variety of inspirational paintings and exquisite sculptures, Richardson Gallery of Fine Art is a great place for both art browsers and serious buyers. Conveniently located between the Peppermill and Atlantis casinos, at Richardson you'll find a large variety of works by today's most talented and well-known artists. The gallery is open 10:30 a.m. to 6:30 p.m. Monday through Saturday and 11:00 a.m. to 5:00 p.m. Sunday.

SHEPPARD GALLERY
Church Fine Arts Building
University of Nevada, Reno
(775) 784-6658
Sheppard Gallery showcases the wonderfully eclectic works of students and faculty at the University of Nevada, Reno as well as nationally known artists. Exhibits change every month and include all types of media. You can browse or buy from 9:00 a.m. to 5:00 p.m. Monday through Thursday and from 11:00 a.m. to 2:00 p.m. Friday. To park at the university, pick up a visitors parking pass from the information booth just off Ninth Street.

SIERRA ARTS GALLERY
17 South Virginia Street, Reno, NV
(775) 329-1324
www.sierra-arts.org
Showcasing the best of new and emerging contemporary artists, Sierra Arts Gallery is always full of surprises. Housed in the Riverside Artist Lofts, the gallery boasts 17-foot ceilings that accommodate large works and major sculptures. This historic building is also home to 35 resident artists, the offices of Sierra Arts, and Dreamer's Cafe (see separate listings in this chapter). Call for hours.

STREMMEL GALLERY
1400 South Virginia Street
Reno, NV
(775) 786-0558
www.stremmelgallery.com
Founded in 1969, Stremmel Gallery is one of the oldest galleries in the Reno/Tahoe area. Its modern, sleek exterior is a reflection of the contents within, mainly abstract and representative contemporary art. The gallery displays an interesting mix of two-and three-dimensional works, in such media as oils, pastels, bronzes, and marbles. The gallery recently was renovated to double its space. It's open from 9:00 a.m. to 5:30 p.m. Monday through Friday and 10:00 a.m. to 3:00 p.m. Saturday. It's closed on Sunday.

NORTH SHORE LAKE TAHOE

Support Organizations
ARTS FOR THE SCHOOLS
(530) 546-4602
Arts for the Schools is the only organization that provides year-round artistic multicultural programs in the North Shore Lake Tahoe area. Although it was founded to expand quality arts experiences in the schools, the group's accomplishments reach the entire community. Programs include arts outreach, cultural events, and artistic performances.

180

NORTH TAHOE ARTS
380 North Lake Boulevard, Tahoe City, CA
(530) 581-2787
www.northtahoearts.com
From its base at the North Tahoe Art Center, the North Tahoe Arts group supports the arts through exhibits, education and outreach. Membership includes invitations to all events, opportunities to network with the artistic community of North Tahoe and a subscription to the bi-monthly newsletter ARTalk. You don't have to be an artist to join, just a lover of the arts.

TAHOE ARTS AND MOUNTAIN CULTURE (TAMC)
www.tahoeculture.com
Created as a networking tool for Tahoe artists, TAMC seeks to unify those whose connection to the region has inspired artistic expression. It also promotes the healthy lifestyle that many residents and visitors enjoy in the Tahoe area. For more information, check the group's Web site.

Performing Arts
Theater
LAKE TAHOE SHAKESPEARE FESTIVAL
Sand Harbor
Incline Village, NV
(775) 832-1616, (800) 747-4697
www.laketahoeshakespeare.com
Shakespeare might be astonished to see his classic works performed on the shore of North America's largest alpine lake, but somehow the richness of productions like *Romeo and Juliet* and *Twelfth Night* is enhanced by the awesome beauty of the outdoor venue. The Lake Tahoe Shakespeare Festival has enjoyed robust success since its founding in 1978 and in 1999 was named one of the "Top 100 Festivals in North America" by *Destinations* magazine. Although the setting is laid-back and natural, a night at the festival offers much of the pageantry found in a traditional theater, from the call of the trumpets signaling the start of the performance to the colorful Shakespearean banners decorating the entrance.

The performances are further enhanced by the comprehensive new stage with state-of-the-art sound and lighting systems.

With a first-class setting and a first-rate performance, only fine wining and dining can complete the picture. You can bring your own gourmet picnic or choose from a wide variety of delicacies offered for sale at the park. For maximum comfort bring beach chairs (they must be the low-back, short-legged type) or consider renting them for $3. And because the temperature drops rapidly after the sun goes down, be sure to bring a sweater or jacket to avoid getting cold.

Performances begin at 7:30 p.m., but theatergoers begin arriving earlier to enjoy dining with a world-class view. Because it's dark when the performance ends around 10:00 p.m., remember to bring a flashlight to help you find your car afterward. The festival takes place the last five weeks of the summer before Labor Day. Reserved seating is $67 to $72 and guarantees comfortable wood-frame chairs directly in front of the stage. General admission is around $22 to $27 and is open seating. If you suspect a performance may be canceled because of rain, be sure to call on the day you plan to attend. (See also the Annual Events chapter.)

The cast for the festival is provided by The Foothill Theatre Company, which also hosts a Shakespeare Camp for children 8 to 16 years old. Students from all over the country learn set and costume design, acting, makeup, and character design at the one- and two-week sessions in August.

Music
INCLINE VILLAGE CHAMBER MUSIC SOCIETY
(775) 831-2298
Although I've often heard "there's no free lunch," the Incline Village Chamber Music Society proves that old aphorism wrong with its Sunday concerts. For six consecutive Sundays in July and August, you can attend live performances by top-quality classical artists—absolutely free. The series is made possible through the generous support of local patrons. Concerts are at 3:00 p.m.

at the Donald W. Reynolds Non Profit Community Center at 948 Incline Way in Incline Village. Call for specific dates and program details.

LAKE TAHOE SUMMER MUSIC FESTIVAL
(530) 583-3101
(530) 581-1184 (tickets)
www.tahoemusic.org
The Lake Tahoe Summer Music Festival is a magical marriage of fine classical music and nature at its most exquisite. Founded in 1986 by Edgar Braun, the longtime conductor of the San Francisco Chamber Orchestra, the festival offers an exciting feast of concerts from July through mid-August. Venues are at Alpine Meadows, Donner Lake Beach, Homewood, and Tahoe Donner.

If you enjoy high-quality music and gorgeous scenery (and who doesn't?), you simply can't go wrong in attending any of these events. The events are outdoors, so layer your clothing. Call for specific locations, programs, and times (see the Annual Events chapter for more information).

Visual Arts
SIERRA ARTISTS' NETWORK AND NORTH TAHOE ART CENTER
380 North Lake Boulevard
Tahoe City, CA
(530) 581-2787
www.northtahoearts.com
Since its founding in 1989, the Sierra Artists' Network has been the heartbeat of the arts scene in the North Shore Lake Tahoe area. With a membership of about 300 enthusiastic artists and art appreciators, the group sponsors art shows, receptions, guest speakers, and fund-raisers. SAN's Tahoe ARTour is mid-August, the oldest annual open studio tour and sale which showcases local artists in their own environment.

Since 1994 SAN has been headquartered in the North Tahoe Art Center, one of Tahoe City's historic lakeside buildings. The center serves as a focal point for artists, with its gallery exhibits, gift shop, and meeting rooms for workshops and classes.

Educational Institutions
SIERRA NEVADA COLLEGE
999 Tahoe Boulevard
Incline Village, NV
(775) 831-1314
www.sierranevada.edu
Although it's a small school by university standards (see the Education and Child Care chapter for details), Sierra Nevada College offers an interesting variety of classes in the arts, including art history, ceramics, drawing, painting, photography, printmaking, electronic arts, sculpture, music, and theater. It offers bachelor's degrees in art and music. For lifelong, non-degree learners it also has a continuing-education program that includes creative arts courses. SNC's summer Visiting Arts Workshops present an amazing potpourri of artists that span the spectrum of disciplines, such as high-fire porcelains, wheel-thrown ceramics, raku firing, conceptual sculpture, digital imaging, musical pet therapy, and modern poetry.

You can also enjoy performances and exhibits by SNC students and visiting artists in the Croom Theater and the Tahoe Gallery at the Mountain Campus. Call for schedules and details.

Ethnic and Cultural Groups
DAUGHTERS OF NORWAY
(775) 826-7751

DAUGHTERS OF PENELOPE (GREEK ORTHODOX)
(775) 825-5365

HELLENIC DANCERS OF ST. ANTHONY
(775) 825-5365

INTER-TRIBAL COUNCIL
(775) 355-0600
www.itcn.org

NAACP
(775) 322-2992
www.naacp.org

NEVADA HISPANIC SERVICES
(775) 826-1818
www.nhsreno.org

NEVADA SOCIETY OF SCOTTISH CLANS
(775) 996-7185
www.nvssc.org

NORTH AMERICAN BASQUE ORGANIZATION
(775) 784-4854
www.basque.unr.edu

NORTHERN NEVADA BLACK CULTURAL AWARENESS SOCIETY
(775) 329-8990

PHILOPTOCHAS SOCIETY (GREEK ORTHODOX)
(775) 825-5365

SCOTTISH AMERICAN MILITARY SOCIETY
www.nvssc.org

SIERRA NEVADA BALALAIKA SOCIETY
(775) 746-1809
www.bdaa.com

SIERRA NEVADA CELTIC SOCIETY
www.sncs.info/

SONS AND DAUGHTERS OF ERIN
www.irishnv.org

SONS OF NORWAY
www.sofn-district6.com

ZENBAT GARA BASQUE FOLK DANCE ENSEMBLE
zenbatgara@charter.net

Galleries

ART ATTACK GALLERY
Christmas Tree Village
868 Tahoe Boulevard
Incline Village, NV
(775) 832-7400, (800) 637-3183
www.tahoeartgallery.com
Browsing is a delight in this roomy gallery in the Christmas Tree Village shopping mall in Incline Village. (I tell you more about the picturesque mall in the Shopping chapter.) Art Attack Gallery hosts many well-advertised special exhibits throughout the year in addition to its ongoing displays of originals and limited-edition prints. You can visit the gallery daily from 10:00 a.m. to 6:00 p.m.

JAMES HAROLD GALLERIES BOATWORKS MALL
760 North Lake Boulevard, Tahoe City, CA
(530) 581-5111
www.jamesharoldgalleries.com
When you're browsing the Boatworks Mall in Tahoe City, be sure to stop by James Harold Galleries. It features a diverse collection of original paintings, *objets d'art*, sculptures, glass art, limited reproductions, and collectibles. The mall offers an interesting mix of stores and restaurants right on the shore of Lake Tahoe (see the Shopping chapter for details). The gallery opens at 10:00 a.m. daily and closes at 6:00 p.m. Monday through Friday, at 8:00 p.m. Saturday and at 5:00 p.m. Sunday. Hours are extended to 10:00 p.m. during the summer months. The gallery recently moved from the second floor to the first floor of the mall.

NORTH TAHOE ART CENTER
380 North Lake Boulevard
Tahoe City, CA
(530) 581-2787
www.northtahoearts.com
You can view a new exhibit and meet the artist who created it the first Friday of every month in

the North Tahoe Art Center. The gallery features an intriguing mix of artistic works throughout the year, mostly from artists who live and work in the Lake Tahoe area. You can also buy local artists' work in the gift shop. Hours are 11:00 a.m. to 4:00 p.m. Wednesday through Monday and 10:00 a.m. to 5:00 p.m. daily during the summer.

FRAMES BY RYRIE
Cobblestone Center
475 North Lake Boulevard
Tahoe City, CA
(530) 583-3043

In the picturesque Cobblestone Center Mall across the street from Lake Tahoe, Frames by Ryrie offers unique gifts, posters, and ready-made frames as well as a beautiful collection of ski prints by Cecile Johnson. The mall is great for browsing (see the Shopping chapter for details). The gallery is open 10:00 a.m. to 5:00 p.m. Monday through Saturday and 11:00 a.m. to 5:00 p.m. Sunday.

THE POTLATCH
930 Tahoe Boulevard
Incline Village, NV
(775) 833-2485
www.potlatchlaketahoe.com

Visiting The Potlatch is a visual delight: The variety of textures and hues in this vibrant collection of Native American and Southwestern art is colorful, to say the least. With a large selection of fine crafts and jewelry, it's a great place to purchase gifts at a reasonable price. It's open daily from 10:00 a.m. to 5:30 p.m.

THE POTTER'S WHEEL
8331 North Lake Boulevard
Kings Beach, CA
(530) 546-8400

If you're looking for fine pottery, this store is a must-stop. It offers a selection of weavings, watercolors, and woodworking. Hours are 9:30 a.m. to 5:30 p.m. daily in the summer. It's closed Monday through Wednesday in winter.

TAHOE GALLERY
800 College Drive
Incline Village, NV
(775) 831-1314
www.sierranevada.edu

Sierra Nevada College displays students' work as well as the works of visiting and local professional artists in the Tahoe Gallery.. Special exhibits with receptions for the artists are also held every few weeks throughout the school year. Regular gallery hours are 8:00 a.m. to 5:00 p.m. Monday through Friday. Call for specific exhibit information.

VISTA GALLERY
7081 North Lake Boulevard
Tahoe Vista, CA
(530) 546-7794
www.vistagallery.com

If you're looking for vintage Lake Tahoe photographs, check this gallery out: It has a collection of more than 600. It also features original antique memorabilia and prints of the lake and the Sierras. Other works displayed include wood sculptures, blown glass, paintings, and ceramics by about three dozen different artists. While many galleries don't encourage children to visit (for obvious reasons), this gallery is child-friendly, with a play area set aside especially for them. The gallery is located above the Old Range Steakhouse with a lovely view of the lake, and I recommend feasting on the artwork upstairs and then feasting on a mouthwatering steak downstairs. The gallery is open 10:00 a.m. to 5:30 p.m. Tuesday through Saturday.

SOUTH SHORE LAKE TAHOE

Support Organizations

TAHOE ARTS PROJECT (TAP)
(530) 542-3632
www.tahoeartsproject.org

Because Lake Tahoe is geographically isolated by mountainous terrain, exposure to performing arts is limited. The Tahoe Arts Project was established in 1987 in South Lake Tahoe, California, to bring fine arts to children in the schools and artistic performances to the general public. Since its founding, TAP has produced hundreds of lectures, master classes, and workshops in the South Shore Lake Tahoe area and annually reaches around 5,000 students. TAP helps fill an important void in the educational curriculum, since school budgets are often inadequate to provide quality arts-in-education.

Public events are a mixed bag and have included such offerings as a mystery dinner, Gamelan music from Indonesia, children's theater, An Evening with the Academy Awards, and musical ensembles. Call or access the Web site for the current schedule of events.

TAHOE TALLAC ASSOCIATION
(530)541-4975
www.vahallatahoe.com

The Tahoe Tallac Association was formed in 1979 to restore the historic estates in the Tallac Historic Site near South Lake Tahoe, California (see the description of the site in the Attractions chapter). The association also produces the annual Valhalla Arts,Theatre and Music Festival, a wildly diverse celebration of art, music, and theater that lasts throughout the year.

Some events have included the Valhalla Renaissance Festival, Celtic Sunday, the Brews & Blues Festival, Reggae Sunday, and the Classic Film Festival, to name a few. You can also attend plays in the historic Valhalla Boathouse Theatre, view local artists' work in the Dextra Baldwin Art Gallery and the Pope Fine Art Gallery, or test your acting or artistic wings in a theater or art workshop.

The festival is truly a feast of the sights and sounds of many cultures—a feast that can be relished in one of the most gorgeous natural settings in the world. Be sure to check the schedule of events if you're in the South Lake Tahoe area, especially in the summer. At almost any event, I guarantee you'll experience some of the unique magic of this extraordinary historical setting. (See the Annual Events chapter for more information.)

Educational Institutions
LAKE TAHOE COMMUNITY COLLEGE (LTCC)
1 College Drive, South Lake Tahoe, CA
(530) 541-4660
www.ltcc.cc.ca.us

Colleges and universities bring a wealth of culture to their home communities, and Lake Tahoe Community College is no exception. Besides its generous class offerings in the arts, the campus of LTCC is an artistic beehive of activity, promoting an array of cultural events for both students and the general public. You can enjoy performances and exhibitions by students as well as by guest performers and artists from around the region.

Drama, dance, music, and films are presented by the Performing Arts League in the LTCC New Theatre. Art exhibits can be viewed in the Haldan Art Gallery, which opens at 11:00 a.m. Tuesday through Saturday. Call for a complete schedule of activities throughout the year. See the Education and Child Care chapter for more information about LTCC.

Galleries
A FRAME OF MIND GALLERY
169 Shady Lane (off Kingsbury Grade)
Stateline, NV
(775) 588-8081
www.aframeofmind.com

A Frame of Mind Gallery showcases all natural landscape photography and has been voted the "Best of Tahoe" gallery by the *Tahoe Tribune*. You can drink in the beauty of Lake Tahoe and its surrounding environs in this luscious collection of local photos. It's open daily from 11:00 a.m. to 7:00 p.m.

LAKE TAHOE COMMUNITY COLLEGE (LTCC)
1 College Drive
South Lake Tahoe, CA
(530) 541-4660, ext. 711
www.ltcc.cc.ca.us

An appealing variety of art is exhibited at the new Haldan Art Gallery on the campus of LTCC. Gallery visitors not only view the art but also have the opportunity to learn more about the artists and art in general through interactive technology provided in the gallery's Discovery Center. The center is also a vibrant educational resource, offering a host of activities for visiting children. The gallery opens at 11:00 a.m. and closes at 4:00 p.m. Tuesday and Wednesday, at 6:00 p.m. on Thursday and at 2:00 p.m. on Friday and Saturday.

MARCUS ASHLEY GALLERIES
The Village Center
4000 Lake Tahoe Boulevard, #23
South Lake Tahoe, CA
(530) 544-4278
www.marcusashley.com
Specializing in original artwork, the gallery showcases a wide variety of oil and acrylic paintings, sculpture, art glass, jewelry, and limited edition prints. They also offer custom framing, private home shows within 60 miles, and worldwide shipping. The gallery has recently moved to a larger space across the parking lot in the Village Center shopping complex. Summer hours are

10:00 a.m. to 7:00 p.m. daily. Call for winter hours. Because art gallery hours frequently are flexible, call ahead to check.

WYLAND GALLERIES LAKE TAHOE
The Shops at Heavenly Village
1001 Park Avenue, Suite 7
South Lake Tahoe, CA
(530) 541-7099
www.wylandgalleries.com
Art lovers can indulge their passion for marine art to their heart's delight in this upscale gallery. Along with the works of Wyland, the gallery features a large collection of pieces by other international and locally acclaimed artists. James Coleman, Steven Power, Walfrado, John Pitre, and Treas Atkinson are just a few of those whose works are on display. The gallery also has a number of showings throughout the year where artists are present to meet potential buyers. Hours are 10:00 a.m. to 7:00 p.m. Sunday through Thursday and until 8:00 p.m. Friday and Saturday. Hours are extended in the summer and on holidays.

PARKS

With Mother Nature as the chief architect, the Reno/Tahoe area is blessed with all the natural ingredients for awesome parks. Managed by a variety of governmental agencies, the plethora of area parks goes a long way toward preserving the environment and making the great outdoors more accessible for everyone to enjoy. You can hike in rugged mountain terrain and sunbathe on pristine sandy beaches in Lake Tahoe Basin parks, bike along the Truckee River and attend cultural events in Reno/Sparks parks, and relax with family and friends over a gourmet picnic in any of the dozens of neighborhood parks scattered throughout the Reno/Tahoe area.

Using the four geographical areas, in this chapter I give you a sampling of the kinds of parks just waiting your exploration. Since descriptions aren't meant to be all-inclusive, I also tell you where to get complete lists of parks from the various parks departments and visitors bureaus. You can also let your fingers do the walking through area telephone directories for maps and parks listings. If you're interested in the myriad programs offered by the parks departments, be sure to request their program booklets. You'll be amazed at the variety of activities offered, from every sports adventure you can possibly imagine to a tantalizing array of arts, crafts, and self-improvement courses.

Many parks, especially the neighborhood variety, are free and accessible year-round. For others I tell you about fees, seasons, and hours as of press time. Be aware, however, that these specifics could change. Your visit to most any of the parks will be more enjoyable if you're informed about what's offered there. I strongly recommend getting information from one of the visitor centers or parks departments ahead of time or picking up maps and brochures when they're available at the parks themselves. Although I describe here some of the recreational opportunities you can enjoy in area parks, the Recreation chapter gives more details, such as additional beaches for swimming at Lake Tahoe and specifics of the area's not-to-be-missed hiking trails.

The Incline Village General Improvement District (IVGID) manages a variety of parks and recreational facilities in Incline Village largely for the benefit of local residents. The golf courses and ski resort are open to the public, but the recreation center is not. Access to Ski, Incline, and Burnt Cedar Beaches is restricted to residents during the summer but is available to the public the rest of the year. If you've booked accommodations in Incline Village, be sure to ask if it includes an IVGID recreation pass.

And last, but by no means least, before you head out to bask in nature's glory, take proper precautions to protect yourself against the elements and the environment. Be sure to use sunscreen and to carry food and water if you're planning to hike or cross-country ski for any distance. Be aware of the weather and wear proper clothing for the occasion. If you're planning to swim in Lake Tahoe, you need to know its frigid waters can be dangerous. Although it's extremely inviting, the lake's 60-degree temperature can cause hypothermia in just minutes: Be sure to take precautions. (For more outdoor safety tips, see the Winter Sports chapter.)

RENO/WASHOE COUNTY SOUTH OF RENO

BARTLEY RANCH REGIONAL PARK
6000 Bartley Ranch Road
(775) 828-6612
www.washoecountyparks.com

On the site of a former working ranch, Bartley Ranch Regional Park gives visitors a snapshot of Nevada's ranching heritage. Tucked in a quiet pastoral setting, the picturesque ranch house and surrounding 2-mile walking trail offer a chunk of quiet solitude on the edge of the city. You can spread a gourmet picnic in the shade, ride horses on the trail or in the arena, and attend cultural events in the amphitheater (see the chapter on The Arts for details). If you're curious about the huge white-fenced spread next door, I'll satisfy your curiosity right now: Once the home of Bill Harrah (founder of Harrah's Hotels/Casinos), it's now the residence of John Harrah, Bill's son.

BOWERS MANSION PARK
U.S. Highway 395
21 miles south of Reno
(775) 849-1825, (775) 828-6642
(775) 849-0644 (swimming pool)
www.washoecountyparks.com

The next best thing to a time machine, Bowers Mansion (in its namesake park) allows visitors to step back into the opulence enjoyed by Nevada's mining barons in the 1860s. Built by L. S. "Sandy" Bowers, the first Comstock Lode millionaire, the 16room mansion is completely restored and decked out with furnishings from around the world. Call for times of daily tours.

Surrounded by expansive lawns and huge shade trees, the mansion is a delightful playground for picnics and affords a lovely view of Washoe Valley. The park also has a swimming pool along with a children's playground. Daily summer hours usually run from 8:00 a.m. to 9:00 p.m. and winter hours from 8:00 a.m. to 5:00 p.m. No pets are allowed.

Park Information Contacts

California State Parks, (530) 525-7232, (800) 777-0369; www.cal-parks.ca.gov

City of Reno Parks & Recreation & Community Services, (775) 334-2262; www.cityofreno.com

City of South Lake Tahoe Parks and Recreation Department, (530) 542-6055; www.cityofslt.us/

City of Sparks Parks & Recreation, (775) 353-2376; www.ci.sparks.nv.us, www.sparksrec.com

Incline Village Parks & Recreation Department, (775) 832-1310; www.ivgid.org

Lake Tahoe Visitors Authority, (800) 288-2463, (775) 588-5900; www.bluelaketahoe.com

Nevada State Parks, (775) 687-4379; www.parks.nv.gov

North Lake Tahoe Chamber of Commerce, (530) 581-6900, (888) 434-1262; www.gotahoenorth.com

Tahoe-Douglas Chamber of Commerce, (775) 588-1728; www.tahoechamber.org

Truckee Donner Recreation and Park District, (530) 582-7720; www.tdrpd.com

USDA Forest Service, Lake Tahoe Basin Management Unit, (530) 543-2600; www.fs.fed.us/r5/ltbmu/

Washoe County Parks and Recreation Department, (775) 828-6642; www.co.washoe.nv.us, www.washoecountyparks.com

DAVIS CREEK PARK
U.S. Highway 395
20 miles south of Reno
(775) 849-0684
www.washoecountyparks.com

Tucked in tall Jeffrey pines on the eastern slope of the Sierra Nevada, Davis Creek Park offers hiking, picnicking, and overnight camping. You can take easy self-guided nature strolls around the park or head up the Ophir Creek Trail to Price Lake (about 3 miles) and on to Tahoe Meadows (about 6 miles). The campsites have water and showers but no trailer hookups. The park is open year-round, and camping facilities are on a first-come, first-served basis.

GALENA CREEK PARK
18350 Nevada Highway 431
(775) 849-2511
www.washoecountyparks.com

Nestled in the shadow of Mt. Rose, Galena Creek Park boasts a refreshing alpine environment just 25 minutes from downtown Reno. The recreational day-use area offers lovely picnic spots under immense pine trees, a self-guided nature trail, and evening campfire programs during the summer. The park is also the trailhead for hikes along Galena, Whites, and Jones Creeks. Because it's so close to Reno, it's a favorite with hikers and bikers who want a quick escape from the summer heat. In winter it's often the closest spot for cross-country skiing, sledding, and snowshoeing.

The park and creek are named for the town of Galena, a hamlet founded in 1860 just several miles away. Originally developed as a mining property, the settlement became more important as a lumbering center when the "galena" (lead sulfide in the gold float) made the mining operation unprofitable. The town boasted 11 sawmills, a school, saloons, and dozens of homes at its peak. Fires in 1865 and 1867 destroyed much of the town, and it was eventually abandoned.

IDLEWILD PARK
1900 Idlewild Drive
(775) 334-2262
www.cityofreno.com

Stretching along the Truckee River just minutes from downtown casinos, Idlewild Park is a popular oasis for walkers, in-line skaters, and picnickers. You'll find a paved path right alongside the river, meandering through the 49 acres of lush green grass and tall trees. There's also a large kiddie park with a variety of rides, a swimming pool, skate park, picnic areas, and a first-class rose garden sure to delight any horticulturist. If you're strolling west along the Truckee River Walk from downtown, you're sure to wander through Idlewild Park. The park is also home to dozens of Canada geese, who find the river and nearby ponds especially welcoming. (See also the Kidstuff chapter.)

OXBOW NATURE STUDY AREA
3100 Dickerson Road
(775) 334-2262
www.cityofreno.com

Tucked along the Truckee River in west Reno, Oxbow Nature Study Area offers the unhurried visitor a stellar opportunity to commune with nature. Take your time as you wander along the path and the viewing areas; there's a good chance you'll spot quail, falcon, golden eagle, beaver, muskrat, and deer up close. It's a great place for kids to learn about native habitats.

RANCHO SAN RAFAEL PARK
1595 North Sierra Street
(775) 785-4512
www.washoecountyparks.com

Rancho San Rafael Park is best known as the starting point of the Great Reno Balloon Race and the site of the Wilbur May Center (see the Annual Events and Attractions chapters for details). It's popular with picnickers, walkers, bikers, and kite flyers. You'll find lovely expanses of green grass, shaded picnic areas, and a 1.5-mile interpretive nature walk. It's open year-round and easily accessible off Sierra Street near the University of Nevada, Reno campus.

VIRGINIA LAKE
1980 Lakeside Drive
(775) 334-2262
www.cityofreno.com

With an inviting running path encircling it, Virginia Lake is one of Reno's most popular jogging/walking areas. Come rain or shine it's always a beehive of activity, with kids in strollers and dogs on leashes joining the pack of in-line skaters, walkers, and joggers. The course isn't long—about a mile—but nothing will prevent you from going round and round until you get enough exercise. If you're into bird-watching or feeding, bring a sack of bread crumbs: Virginia Lake is also a favorite hangout for hundreds of local birds.

Future plans for Virginia Lake include rehabilitation of the park along with new residential and retail development on the north and east sides. The resulting increase in traffic will undoubtedly impact the serene nature of the park.

WINGFIELD PARK
2 North Arlington Avenue
(775) 334-2262
www.cityofreno.com

A small oasis in busy downtown Reno, Wingfield Park is easy to spot if you're strolling along the Truckee River Walk. Just three acres in the middle of the river, it's a lovely spot to sit and watch the water rush by, often carrying kayakers on the white-water course. The amphitheater is the site of many outdoor cultural events (for details see the chapter on The Arts).

SPARKS

GOLDEN EAGLE REGIONAL PARK
6400 Vista Boulevard
(775) 353-2376
www.sparksrec.com

Situated on about 140 acres east of Wingfield Springs in Sparks, Golden Eagle Regional Park is the epitomy of municipal sports complexes. With more than 1.4 million square feet of artificial turf (the largest single installation in North America), this park is ready to accommodate any and all kinds of sports events, including softball, bocce ball, baseball, football, soccer, and volleyball. As the city of Sparks continues to grow, projects like Golden Eagle reflect the town's commitment to maintaining its quality of life. Newcomers never need worry about having a first-class facility for the kids and entire family to enjoy participating in sports.

PAH RAH PARK
1750 Shadow Lane
(775) 353-2376
www.sparksrec.com

Some years ago the city fathers in Sparks decided that every neighborhood should have a park. As the city has grown, they've kept up with this goal by building parks along with the new housing developments. The landscape of Sparks is splashed with the green of dozens of neighborhood parks that offer inviting spots for play and relaxation. They provide a variety of amenities that include tennis courts, swimming pools, picnic areas, and playgrounds. To find the park nearest you (and it can't be very far away), check the Web site listed above.

Typical of parks in Sparks, Pah Rah Park is a great place to bring the family for an outing right in town. Its huge grassy area provides plenty of room for the kids to run and play games. There's also several playground areas with a variety of equipment, a couple of covered picnic spots, tennis courts, and bathrooms. A big plus is the great view of downtown Reno and the Sierra Nevada to the west.

To get to the park from Sparks, take Interstate 80 east, exit on Vista Boulevard, and go north for about 2 miles. You'll see the sign for the park just after crossing Baring Boulevard.

SPARKS MARINA PARK
East end of Nichols Boulevard
(775) 353-2376
www.sparksrec.com

Not too long ago, the site of Sparks Marina Park was an eyesore and an embarrassment to the city. As part of an ambitious reclamation project, however, what was once a gaping gravel pit has become an 80-acre lake that's a source of pride and joy for the community. Stocked with trophy-size trout, the sparkling lake is a favorite fishing hole with Insiders. Other amenities include a jogging path that encircles the water, a dog park, a swimming lagoon, and shaded picnic areas.

Recent development has added upscale condominiums and retail establishments (see the Shopping chapter for a description of Scheels sporting goods store) on the north and east shores of the lake. Future plans include a full service casino resort along with additional retail as part of the Legends of Sparks Marina project. (See the Restaurants chapter for more information about Anchors Bar & Grill.) The park is the site of a variety of special events throughout the

year, such as the MasterCraft Pro Wakeboard Tour Finals and the Mutt Strut.

To get to the park from Reno or Sparks, head east on I-80, exit on McCarran Boulevard, and go north to the intersection of Nichols Boulevard. The park is about 1 block east, just behind the Western Village Inn/Casino.

NORTH SHORE LAKE TAHOE

KINGS BEACH STATE RECREATION AREA
North Lake Boulevard, Kings Beach, CA
(530) 546-4212
www.cal-parks.ca.gov

With more than 700 feet of lakeshore and ample shade beneath ponderosa pines, Kings Beach State Recreation Area offers yet another site from which you can bask in the beauty of Lake Tahoe. It's a nice spot for water sports with its pier and picnic tables. A parking fee of about $5 is levied.

Dog-friendly Parks

Parks that have designated play areas for dogs include:

Bijou Community Park, 1201 Al Tahoe Boulevard, South Shore Lake Tahoe, CA (530) 542-6055

Hidden Valley Regional Park, 4740 Parkway Drive, Reno, NV, (775) 828-6612

Incline Beach (near boat launch), Lakeshore Boulevard across from the Hyatt Regency Lake Tahoe Resort & Casino, Incline Village, NV, (775) 832-1310 (October to April)

Sparks Marina Park, east end of Nichols Boulevard, Sparks, NV, (775) 353-2376

Virginia Lake Park, 1980 Lakeside Drive, Reno, NV, (775) 334-2262

Whitaker Park, 550 University Terrace, Reno, NV, (775) 334-2262

LAKE TAHOE–NEVADA STATE PARK
2005 Nevada Highway 28
Incline Village, NV
(775) 831-0494
www.parks.nv.gov

One of the loveliest sections of shoreline and backcountry in the Lake Tahoe Basin is preserved for public use in Lake Tahoe–Nevada State Park. Extending along the east shore of Lake Tahoe south and east of Incline Village, the park encompasses miles of exquisite beach from Sand Harbor to Skunk Harbor, beautiful Spooner Lake at the junction of U.S. Highway 50 and NV 28, Cave Rock Marina about 7 miles north of Stateline, Nevada, and more than 13,000 acres of rugged forest in the Marlette/Hobart Backcountry near Spooner Summit. The variety of terrain offers limitless opportunities for outdoor fun.

The crystal white-sand beach and vivid turquoise water at Sand Harbor (about 3 miles south of Incline Village) make it one of the most popular and picturesque playgrounds at Lake Tahoe. You can swim, sunbathe, picnic, hike, launch your boat, or just sit under a spreading Jeffrey pine and drink in one of the most beautiful views on

Earth. The parking lot fills fast in the summer, so if you're planning to spend the day, be sure to arrive early. It's open daily from 8:00 a.m. to 9:00 p.m., and the parking fee is $8 during summer and $4 the rest of the year. Be sure to stop by park headquarters, where you can pick up information about the park. Sand Harbor is also the site of the Lake Tahoe Shakespeare Festival (see The Arts chapter for details).

About 2 miles north of Sand Harbor, you'll find additional beach access at Hidden Beach, and more beach access at Memorial Point, which is about 1 mile north of Sand Harbor. About 2.5 miles south of Sand Harbor, you can park in the paved parking lot above the lake or along the road and walk into Chimney Beach, Secret Harbor, and Whale Beach. Hidden among huge boulders and enormous trees, numerous tiny coves along this stretch of shoreline offer secluded hideaways perfect for nude sunbathing. Just watch the sun on those least-exposed parts.

About 2.5 miles farther south you can park along the highway and walk into Prey Meadows (ablaze with wildflowers in late spring and early summer) or plunge down to secluded and lovely Skunk Harbor. This unmarked trailhead is tucked off the lake side of the highway, and roadside parking is limited.

Even though several parking lots serve these beaches, parking is usually a challenge along this section of NV 28. There's limited parking along the road, but be sure to pay attention to the stretches with No Parking signs to avoid getting a ticket. To beat the crowds, try hitting the beach early in the morning or late in the afternoon.

Cupped beneath heavily forested peaks, Spooner Lake offers hiking, biking, and catch-and-release fishing in summer. You can take a leisurely 2-mile stroll around the lake, strike out into the Marlette/Hobart Backcountry to Marlette Lake, pick up north- or southbound portions of the scenic Tahoe Rim Trail, as well as head off to other wilderness destinations (see the Recreation chapter for hiking and biking details). Parking fees are about $6. In winter Spooner Lake is a prime cross-country ski resort, featuring more than 80 kilometers of groomed trails (see the Winter Sports chapter for details).

For more information on activities at Spooner Lake, visit www.spoonerlake.com.

i One of the top Sierra snowstorms dropped 11.75 feet of snow at Central Sierra Snow Lab near Donner Summit in January, 1952.

NORTH TAHOE REGIONAL PARK
875 National Avenue
Tahoe Vista, CA
(530) 546-5043, (530) 546-4212
www.ntpud.org

You can enjoy periodic glimpses of Lake Tahoe from about 5 miles of multiuse trails that loop through the tall pines at North Tahoe Regional Park. In summer it's popular with hikers, bikers, and picnickers (see the Recreation chapter for more information). In winter it's a vision of white, perfect for snowshoeing, cross-country skiing, and snowmobiling (see the Winter Sports chapter for details). You can contact North Tahoe Winter Adventures at (530) 546-0405 for information on renting sleds and purchasing tickets to the snowplay hill. You'll also find a softball field, tennis courts, disc golf, sand volleyball courts, playground, restrooms, and picnic areas.

To get to the park from Incline Village, go west on NV 28 to Tahoe Vista (just west of Kings Beach), turn right onto National Avenue, and follow the signs to the park. It's open from 6:00 a.m. to 10:00 p.m. in summer and from 7:00 a.m. to 7:00 p.m. in winter. Pay the $3 parking fee using the self-service box.

SOUTH SHORE LAKE TAHOE

BIJOU COMMUNITY PARK
1201 Al Tahoe Boulevard
South Lake Tahoe, CA
(530) 542-6055
www.cityofslt.us/

If you want to escape the crowds at the beaches on Lake Tahoe, you can spread your picnic at

Bijou Community Park. You'll find sand volleyball courts, horseshoe pits, basketball courts, a skateboard park, a world-class 27-hole disc golf course, playground equipment, group picnic areas, and picnic shelters. (For more information on disc golf, see the Recreation chapter.) The park is open from sunrise to sunset winter and summer. There are no fees. The park is located about 1 mile southeast of the intersection of Al Tahoe Boulevard and US 50.

D. L. BLISS STATE PARK
California Highway 89, 9 miles north of South Lake Tahoe, CA
(530) 525-7277 (summer)
(530) 525-9529 (winter)
www.cal-parks.ca.gov
Boasting 3.5 miles of shoreline along the west side of Lake Tahoe, D. L. Bliss State Park is paradise for anyone who loves the outdoors. Two sundrenched beaches beckon sunbathers to warm sands—Calawee Cove Beach, a protected cove ringed by boulders and trees, and Lester Beach, a wide-open expanse of white sand with maximum exposure to the sun.

When you get tired of catching rays, you can take a hike in the area. I highly recommend the spectacular Rubicon Trail, which takes you south along the lakeshore to Emerald Point, the entrance to Emerald Bay. (Learn more about this splendid hike in the Recreation chapter.) The Balancing Rock Interpretive Trail is another favorite, as is the relatively short trek to the lighthouse overlooking Rubicon Point.

The park also has one of the best campgrounds in the area (see the Camping and RVing chapter for details), but it fills fast, so be sure to reserve ahead. Call for day parking rates. To get a place during the busy summer months, especially during July and August, arrive before 10:00 a.m. You can inquire about parking within the park, as well as other park facilities, at the visitor center. The park is open from 8:00 a.m. to dusk, Memorial Day to mid-September.

Bliss is just a few short miles from Emerald Bay State Park (see next entry), Vikingsholm Castle (see the Attractions and Kidstuff chapters), and Sugar Pine Point State Park (also described in this chapter). Together, Bliss and Emerald Bay State Parks preserve more than 1,800 acres of prime Tahoe scenery. Whether you are visiting or planning to stay in the area, these parks are well worth extensive exploration.

ED Z'BERG SUGAR PINE POINT STATE PARK
California Highway 89
1 mile south of Tahoma, CA
(530) 525-7982
www.parks.ca.gov
You can soak up a chunk of Lake Tahoe's history while enjoying its incredible natural beauty at Ed Z'berg Sugar Pine Point State Park. With more than 2,000 acres stretching along 1.75 miles of shoreline, the park offers a lovely swimming beach and choice hiking trails, along with the historic Ehrman Mansion, a nature center, and a 19th-century log cabin.

Finished in 1903, the mansion is an elegant example of Queen Anne architecture, with about 12,000 square feet of period extravagance. I suggest taking the tour to learn about the turn-of-thecentury heydays of the wealthy who spent their summers at the lake. Tours are held every hour from 11:00 a.m. to 4:00 p.m. from July to Labor Day, and a small fee is charged. Also be sure to see the log cabin that was built in 1860 by Gen. William Phipps, a trapper believed to be the first permanent settler of record in this area of the Lake Tahoe Basin. If you're interested in the wildlife of the area, stop in at the nature center and view its bird and animal exhibits; the admission cost is covered by the park's $5 parking fee.

You'll find hiking trails suitable for almost everyone at Sugar Pine Point, from the easy Dolder Nature Trail, which meanders along the lakeshore, to the moderate General Creek Trail, which you can take for a 6.5-mile round-trip hike to Lily Pond. From Lily Pond you can continue on to a large variety of alpine lakes and meadows in the Desolation Wilderness. If a laid-back picnic is more your style, the beautifully manicured lawn in front of the Ehrman Mansion is the perfect place.

Open all year, the park is a favorite place for cross-country skiing and snowshoeing in winter. Be sure to pick up a Sno-Park permit for winter parking at the Lake Tahoe Basin Management Unit of the USDA Forest Service, which is located at 870 Emerald Bay Road in South Lake Tahoe. (For a description of the park's camping opportunities—there are 175 sites for tents and RVs—see the Camping and RVing chapter.)

EMERALD BAY STATE PARK
California Highway 89,
about 8 miles north of South Lake Tahoe, CA
(530) 525-7277 (summer)
(530) 525-9529 (winter)
www.cal-parks.ca.gov

Lake Tahoe's Emerald Bay is easily the most photographed site in the entire Lake Tahoe Basin. Its emerald green waters edge into the feet of the snow-capped granite peaks of the Desolation Wilderness—a spectacular sight by any standard.

Attractions in Emerald Bay State Park include the shoreline around the bay, Vikingsholm Castle, and Eagle Falls, a string of waterfalls that tumble out of the Desolation Wilderness into the bay. Created in 1969 to preserve more than 60,000 acres of unique mountain environment, the wilderness is a wonderland of alpine lakes sprinkled among velvety meadows and rugged peaks.

You'll find lovely spots to picnic, swim, and sunbathe along the stretches of Tahoe's shore within the park. You can take a level 1.5-mile hike to Emerald Point, where there are gorgeous views of the rugged mouth of the bay. From the point you can turn north and follow the Rubicon Trail along the lakeshore toward D. L. Bliss State Park.

If you're feeling very ambitious, I recommend following Eagle Creek up to Eagle Lake in the Desolation Wilderness. Although it's a somewhat steep climb, it's only a mile long and affords luscious panoramic views along the way. Once you've made it to Eagle Lake, the grandeur of

the Desolation Wilderness unfolds before you, with more than 100 additional lakes that can be explored. The Eagle Lake trailhead is in Eagle Falls Picnic Area, across CA 89 from the parking lot at Emerald Bay State Park. You'll need a permit to enter the Desolation Wilderness: You can either get a permit at the trail-head or at the Taylor Creek Visitor Center, located 3 miles north of South Lake Tahoe at 870 Emerald Bay Road. More information is also available on the Forest Service's Lake Tahoe Basin Management Unit Web site at www.fs.fed.us/r5/ltbmu.

Because this area of Lake Tahoe is extremely congested during the summer, parking is difficult. My advice is to get there as early in the day as possible during July and August. (For more information about Emerald Bay and Vikingsholm, see the Attractions chapter. For hiking and wilderness outings within and around the park, see the Recreation chapter.)

i The Lake Tahoe Basin averages 273 days of sunshine every year, each one an opportunity to enjoy the unlimited outdoor activities available in area parks.

SOUTH LAKE TAHOE RECREATION AREA
U.S. Highway 50 and Rufus Allen Boulevard
South Lake Tahoe, CA
(530) 542-6055
www.cityofslt.us

Close to all the casino action in Stateline, the South Lake Tahoe Recreation Area offers access to several Lake Tahoe beaches, along with picnic areas and facilities for horseshoes, basketball, and volleyball. Other amenities include a children's playground, jogging trails, a swimming pool, fitness center, and boat ramp. The campground by the lake (open in summer only) has 172 sites for tents and RVs and provides piped water, fire rings, and flush toilets.

RECREATION

Dubbed "America's Adventure Place," the Reno/Tahoe area serves up a mind-blowing menu of activities guaranteed to challenge your wildest expectations. The variety is huge—so huge I devote entire chapters to Winter Sports, Golf, and Fishing and Hunting. I describe other recreation in this chapter, organized alphabetically by activity rather than by geographical area.

With so much recreation to choose from, locals take it seriously. Laden with recreational goodies like bikes, skis, kayaks, or hang gliders, sport utility vehicles reign. You'll see a higher percentage of them here than in most communities. But unlike sparkling showroom models, local SUVs are more likely to be frosted with snow or coated with mud from recent four-wheel-drive treks into the mountains.

If gambling's your game, you can enjoy it to your heart's content here. But don't forget that one of the most magnificent destinations on the planet is just outside. You can best see it, feel it, smell it, and taste it from a hot-air balloon hovering over the tops of tall Jeffrey pines or from a kayak sliding silently through crystal-clear waters, or from a forest trail meandering through a meadow hip-high with wildflowers.

This chapter is chock-full of suggestions to help you make the very most out of your time in the Reno/Tahoe area. But whatever activities you choose, remember the most important thing is to relax and have fun.

AUTO RACING

The Reno/Tahoe area is devoid of auto-racing facilities, but if you're a die-hard enthusiast of the "fastest sport in America," I have listed two oval tracks and a drag strip that are close enough to make the drive worthwhile.

RATTLESNAKE RACEWAY
2000 Airport Road Fallon, NV
(775) 423-7483
http://rattlesnakeraceway.tripod.com
Rattlesnake Raceway, located at Rattlesnake Hill in Fallon, offers mud-slinging action Saturday nights and occasional Sunday afternoons April through November. It's the oldest operating oval dirt track in Nevada. The schedule varies, so call or visit their Web site for specifics. Racing fans can expect to pay about $8 for a night of racing that can include street stocks, bombers, and Gen X cars. Track modifications in 2005 increased the length, making the track run faster.

To get to Fallon from Reno, take Interstate 80 east to exit 48 (East Fernley). Continue over the railroad overpass and turn left onto Alternate U.S. Highway 50 and follow the signs to Fallon. (For other activities in Fallon, see the Day Trips chapter.)

RENO-FERNLEY RACEWAY
Alternate U.S. Highway 95
Fernley, NV
(775) 575-7217
www.reno-fernleyraceway.com
Reno-Fernley Raceway's oval is called the "Racing Field of Dreams" and is located about 36 miles from Reno. Boasting 15 configurations and more than 30 turns, this 4-mile-plus facility has it all: clay oval racing, motocross tracks, off-road racing, sand drags, BMX, and go-kart racing. Usually oval track racing is presented every Saturday during the summer months, with racing action in IMCA & Outlaw modifieds, street stocks, hobby stocks, modified minis, and pure stock minis. Admis-

sion ranges from $5 to $15. The track also offers a special pit pass for $10 to $20. Although this roadcourse appeals to hardcore racing fans of all types, it has much broader appeal with its special events such as Hot August Nights Street Drags and the Annual Reno Historic Races. You might never make it to Indy, but you can see many of the same cars burning up the track here when high-profile racing teams arrive from all over the country with their historic multimillion-dollar race cars. The historic races allow spectators to see well-known cars and drivers up close and personal in a visitor-friendly raceway. Call the track or check its Web site for a detailed schedule and prices of events. Overnight campers are welcome. To help keep kids amused throughout the race day, Herbie's Paintball Games is open from 10:00 a.m. to 4:00 p.m. on Saturday. For information go to www.herbiespaintball.com or call (775) 575-6946.

To get to the raceway, take I-80 east from Reno to exit 46 (West Fernley). Follow Main Street until the intersection of Alternate US 95. Take Alternate US 95 about 6 miles until you see the signs for the raceway on the right-hand side of the highway.

TOP GUN RACEWAY
U.S. Highway 95, Fallon, NV
(775) 423-0223, (800) 325-7448
www.topgunraceway.com
The only sanctioned NHRA drag strip in Northern Nevada, this 0.25-mile drag strip is located just 10 miles south of Fallon on US 95 and features drag racing in several different classes on Saturday and Sunday from March through NovemberTickets run from $8 to $15, depending on the type of drags. The schedule varies so it's best to call or consult the Web site for times and events.

To get to Fallon from Reno, take I-80 east to exit 48 (East Fernley). Continue over the railroad overpass and turn left onto Alternate US 50 and follow the signs to Fallon. Once in Fallon, pick up US 95 south and follow signs to the raceway. (For more things to do in Fallon, see the Day Trips chapter.)

BACKPACKING

If you can't get enough of nature with a simple day hike, rest assured that most area hiking destinations are also suitable for overnight camping. With its huge variety of lakes, the Desolation Wilderness is one of the most popular backpacking areas (see the "Hiking" section later in this chapter). Once in the wilderness, you can spend days backpacking from lake to lake.

You can split up longer hikes to any destination by overnight stays, or you can hike into a single site and stay for a day or two. I suggest stopping at visitor centers (see the Attractions chapter for locations) or the USDA Forest Service office at 870 Emerald Bay Road in South Lake Tahoe for more information. Be sure to have maps and proper equipment if you're backpacking, and remember you'll need a permit for the Desolation Wilderness. See the "Hiking" section in this chapter for some suggested destinations.

BALLOONING

LAKE TAHOE BALLOONS
South Lake Tahoe, CA
(530) 544-1221, (800) 872-9294
www.laketahoeballoons.com
When you book a flight with Lake Tahoe Balloons, you can marvel at the majesty of the lake from two vantage points: floating over it in a hot-air balloon and floating on it in a 40-foot catamaran. After flying over verdant mountain meadows and hovering above the crystal-clear waters of the lake, the balloon lands on the boat, where you can indulge in a delicious champagne brunch while cruising back to shore. The cost of the three-hour trip is $250 per person, and reservations are required. The company offers free shuttle transportation within the South Lake Tahoe area and customized wedding services, too. All flights begin at sunrise and are seasonal.

MOUNTAIN HIGH BALLOONS
Truckee, CA
(530) 587-6922
The oldest balloon company in the Reno/Tahoe

area, Mountain High Balloons will take you up, up, and away on half-hour and one-hour trips in the Truckee area. The balloons lift off from nearby Prosser Reservoir and then drift lazily over the Martis Valley south of downtown Truckee. You can see gorgeous views of Lake Tahoe to the south and pick pinecones from the tops of huge trees. Floating through the peace and quiet as the sun rises to the east is an incredibly special way to greet a summer day.

The cost per person is around $110 for a half hour and $175 for one hour. Kids younger than 10 years old can fly free when accompanied by an adult (limit of one child per adult). Children 10 to 16 years old are half price. Flights are available at 7:00 a.m. daily from May through November, but reservations are necessary. (For more to do and see in Truckee, see the Day Trips chapter.)

BIKING

Due to the hundreds of miles of dirt roads and paved paths that give ready access to the great outdoors, biking in the Reno/Tahoe area is very popular. You'll see cyclists everywhere, zipping along city streets and huffing up rocky mountain paths. Whether you're an experienced rider or first-time-ever cyclist, you'll find terrain and paths just right for you. You can enjoy biking on paved streets and paths, on dirt roads and trails, and in mountain bike parks complete with chair-lifts. It's not possible to list all the opportunities and adventures that await you, since it's simply too exhaustive, but I will tell you about some of the favorite rides around the area to give you an idea of the variety of biking fun that's available.

Be aware that many of the paths and trails I describe in the "Walking/Running" and "Hiking" sections of this chapter are also suitable for biking. For maps and other routes, I suggest you stop at area visitor centers (see the Attractions chapter for locations) and also inquire at local bike shops. Also see the Parks chapter for information about walking/biking paths in local parks.

Before heading out, it's important to be aware of a few basic safety rules for biking in the Reno/Tahoe area. Always plan ahead by knowing where you're going and whether the skills of everyone in the group are suited to the expected terrain. Some strenuous routes are not advisable for children, for example. If you're not familiar with a particular trail, find out from appropriate authorities what it's like. Dress for the weather, and be prepared for the sudden storms that frequently come up in the mountains. Use sunscreen and carry plenty of water and snacks. And last, but not least, know the courteous rules of the trail and practice them. Since many trails are shared with others—walkers, joggers, hunters, anglers, animals, and four-wheeldrive vehicles—be ready to yield the trail and ride under control at all times.

If you're interested in biking clubs in Reno, you can contact the Procrastinating Pedalers at president@pedalers.org, www.pedalers.org, P.O. Box 9897, Reno, NV 89507; or the Reno Wheelmen at (775) 690-7385, www.renowheelmen .org, P.O. Box 12832, Reno, NV 89510.

ANGORA RIDGE
Fallen Leaf Campground, 2 miles north of South Lake Tahoe, CA, off California Highway 89
For spectacular views of Fallen Leaf Lake and Mt. Tallac, you can take this moderate 8-mile round-trip jaunt to lovely Angora Lakes. Starting at Fallen Leaf Campground, where you can park your car, pedal along Fallen Leaf Lake Road. Take the first left, continue for about 0.5 mile to Angora Ridge Road, and then turn right. Be prepared for a veritable Kodak moment when you reach the abandoned Angora Lookout—the panoramic view from the saddle of this glacial moraine is stunning, to say the least. Just down the road you'll find a dirt parking lot where you can lock up your bike to follow the last 0.5 mile of the route on foot. Your reward at the end of the trail is two sparkling alpine lakes, with a rustic resort tucked on the shore of the second lake. Be sure to save time for a refreshing swim and lunch.

GENERAL CREEK LOOP RIDE
Ed Z'berg Sugar Pine Point State Park
California Highway 89
1 mile south of Tahoma, CA
(530) 525-7982
www.parks.ca.gov
You don't have to have legs of steel for the General Creek Loop Ride. In fact, you can be a first-time mountain biker and get along just fine. Snaking through the forest for about 6 miles, the trail is mostly level and easy to navigate. Look for the trailhead in Sugar Pine Point State Park (see the Parks chapter for more about this lovely park).

HIDDEN VALLEY REGIONAL PARK
4740 Parkway Drive, Reno, NV
(775) 828-6642
www.washoecountyparks.com
With 480 acres, Hidden Valley Regional Park boasts an interesting variety of paved and dirt trails for both hiking and biking. Tucked at the base of mountains on the east side of Reno, it offers great views of the city and the Sierra Nevada mountains to the west. It's one of the few places close to town where outdoor enthusiasts can wander for long distances just exploring the natural landscape. A large herd of wild horses inhabits the range above the park, and the animals are often in view. The park also provides a riding arena, children's playground, dog park, rest-rooms, and a picnic area. This scenic park with a view is the perfect site for the annual Crisis Call Center Run4Life each spring. Check www.crisiscallcenter.org for the date.

MARLETTE LAKE/FLUME TRAIL
Trailhead at Spooner Lake
Junction of U.S. Highway 50 and Nevada Highway 28
(775) 831-0494, (775) 749-5349
www.parks.nv.gov
A heart-stopping ride for intermediate bikers and above, the Flume Trail will thrill you with challenging terrain and awesome views of Lake Tahoe. The trail follows an old water flume line, climbing about 5 miles to Marlette Lake, and then continuing another 7 miles to Tunnel Creek Road.

For information about shuttle service back to the Spooner Lake parking area, call (775) 749-5349 or check www.theflumetrail.com. I don't recommend a round-trip of 24 miles, since the first 12 are rugged enough for most bikers.

The most difficult part of this ride is the 7 miles past Marlette Lake, where the narrow trail hugs a ledge with sheer dropoffs toward Lake Tahoe far below. You should be in good physical shape and not be afraid of heights to ride this trail. It's not for families and not for children. You might want to try a trial run to test your stamina by riding the 10-mile round-trip to Marlette Lake and back first.

NORTH TAHOE REGIONAL PARK
875 National Avenue
Tahoe Vista, CA
(530) 546-5043
www.ntpud.org
With 5 miles of dirt paths winding through the trees, the trail system at North Tahoe Regional Park offers gentle runs for beginners and steeper terrain for more-advanced riders. Never crowded and close to residential areas, it's a favorite with locals year-round. See the Winter Sports and Parks chapters for more details on this fun-filled spot in Tahoe Vista.

NORTHSTAR-AT-TAHOE
California Highway 267
6 miles north of Lake Tahoe
(530) 562-1010
www.skinorthstar.com
With more than 100 miles of forested trails to explore, Northstar-at-Tahoe offers Lake Tahoe's most extensive mountain bike park. You can enjoy everything from gentle leisurely loops to stiff uphill climbs, including jaunts to Watson Lake and Northstar Reservoir. There's something for everyone, and best of all, you can conserve your stamina by taking advantage of Northstar chairlifts. Northstar skiers especially like to bike their favorite ski runs, because the terrain appears so much different when it's devoid of snow. When you're ready for a refreshing lunch break, you can head down to the village at the base of

the mountain, where you'll find a variety of restaurants along with special events on weekends. (I tell you more about this first-class resort in the Resorts and Winter Sports chapters.)

TOM COOK TRAIL
Woodland Avenue
4 miles west of Reno, NV
(775) 828-6642
www.washoecountyparks.com
You may have to get off and push part of the way, but the Tom Cook Trail gives access to the Steamboat Ditch Trail along with a bona fide maze of other trails to explore west of Reno. Follow West Fourth Street west of town and turn left onto Woodland Avenue at the sign for Mayberry Park. After parking at the park, cross the footbridge over the Truckee River on the west end of the park (near Patagonia's building). The Tom Cook Trail starts here, and your biking adventure can unfold as you see fit. Because this terrain is fragile, it's important to stay on the trails to minimize your impact.

BILLIARD PARLORS

Though you won't be overwhelmed with options for billiards in the Reno/Tahoe area, here are my favorites if eight-ball is your game.

CLASSIC CUE
1965 Lake Tahoe Boulevard
South Lake Tahoe, CA
(530) 541-8704
Classic Cue calls itself the best billiard room and burger joint on the lake. Besides its 10 pool tables, there's also indoor hoops, Foosball, and darts. This pool hall also provides patrons with a satellite TV. Mostly frequented by a younger crowd, Classic Cue also repairs and sells pool cues. The hours of operation are daily from noon to midnight.

DIAMOND BILLIARDS
5890 South Virginia Street
Reno, NV
(775) 828-0616
With 13 4-foot by 9-foot, top-of-the-line Robertson Black Max pool tables, Diamond Billiards is a classy place. The equipment is meticulously maintained, and players appreciate the attention to detail. Formerly Breaktime Billiards, the parlor now sports a separate cigar lounge along with a full bar and poker machines. Action starts daily at 10:00 a.m.; closing is at 2:00 a.m. on weekdays and at 4:00 a.m. on weekends. Rates are around $11 per hour, with the second hour free except Friday and Saturday nights.

Q'S BILLIARD CLUB
3350 South Virginia Street
Reno, NV
(775) 825-2337
www.poolbargrillreno.com
The largest and most modern pool parlor in the area, this over-21 club likes to call itself the coolest pool hall in Reno. Featuring a rotation of 17 draught beers, it's also the only parlor in the area with a bar and grill on the premises. The going rate for shooting a game of pool on any of its 15 tables is around $10 per hour. You can rack them up here from 11:00 a.m. to 3:00 a.m. daily.

BOATING

Nowhere is boating more popular than on the sapphire-blue water of Lake Tahoe. Just imagine gliding across the ripple-free water in the morning with the sun's rays glancing off the mirrorlike surface and soaking up some of the most spectacular scenery in the United States. On any given day, especially during the warmer months, you can see every type of watercraft imaginable navigating the lake from before sunrise to well after sunset. Here, I list the ramps available for launching your private boat, as well as facilities that will rent you just about any type of watercraft to fit your fancy: speedboats, fishing boats, sailboats, pontoon boats, paddle-boats, canoes, kayaks, Jet Skis, WaveRunners, sailboards, and float tubes.

Boat Ramps

All the boat ramps listed charge a fee for launching except Kings Beach, which charges a $5 parking fee. The launch fees range from around $13 each way for the little boats to $35 each way for the bigger boats. All the launch facilities listed have paved ramps.

CAVE ROCK
Near Zephyr Cove, NV
(775) 831-0494

EL DORADO
South Lake Tahoe, CA
(530) 542-6056

HOMEWOOD MARINA
Near Homewood, CA
(530) 525-5966

KINGS BEACH
North Tahoe Public Utility District
Kings Beach, CA
(530) 546-4212

LAKE FOREST BEACH
Between Tahoe City and Carnelian Bay, CA
(530) 583-3796

MEEKS BAY RESORT
Meeks Bay, CA
(530) 525-6946, (530) 525-5588

NORTH TAHOE MARINA
Tahoe Vista, CA
(530) 546-8248

OBEXER'S
Between Meeks Bay and Homewood, CA
(530) 525-7962

SAND HARBOR
Incline Village, NV
(775) 831-0494

SIERRA BOAT COMPANY
Carnelian Bay, CA
(530) 546-2551

SUNNYSIDE MARINA
Near Tahoe City, CA
(530) 583-7201

TAHOE KEYS MARINA
South Lake Tahoe, CA
(530) 541-2155

ZEPHYR COVE MARINA
Zephyr Cove, NV
(775) 589-4901

Boat and Watercraft Rentals

You can find all kinds of watercraft on Lake Tahoe. At last count, about 25 water-sports rental businesses encircle the lake, where you can rent just about anything that floats. Although you'll see boats on the lake almost all year, water-sports rentals are seasonal, with most of these establishments operating during summer and early fall only.

Sailing the translucent water of Lake Tahoe has been a longtime recreational activity, and when the wind kicks up in the afternoon, you'll see why. Sailboarding has also become a popular sport on the lake, and every afternoon brave souls can be seen whipping over the waves, seemingly hanging on for their lives. And if powerboats are more to your liking, speedboat rentals are available for the novice to the advanced boater.

Prices for the rentals seem to change every season and are dependent on the size of the watercraft, the time of the year, and the time of day. Generally, hourly rental rates are close to these prices: powerboats, $125 to $200; sailboats, $40 to $60; pedal boats, $20; fishing and pontoon boats, $35 to $60; canoes and kayaks, $20 to $30; Jet Skis and WaveRunners, $100 to $125; and water-ski tows, $40 to $50.

ACTION WATERSPORTS OF TAHOE
3411 U.S. Highway 50
South Lake Tahoe, CA
(530) 544-5387
www.action-watersports.com
Action Watersports is located at Timber Cove Marina and rents just about anything that floats.

From powerboats to floating lounge chairs, this concession rents them out at some of the most reasonable rates around the lake. Hours are 9:00 a.m. to 6:00 p.m. during the summer months only.

CAMP RICHARDSON MARINA
1900 Jameson Beach Road
South Lake Tahoe, CA
(530) 542-6570
www.camprichardson.com
This marina is open from May through the end of September from 8:00 a.m. to 8:00 p.m. and offers a wide selection of powerboats, bowriders, two-person WaveRunners, pontoon boats, kayaks, canoes, and pedal boats. Its location at Camp Richardson makes it a popular and sometimes crowded place. This is one of the only rental concessions that accepts reservations.

CAPTAIN KIRK'S BEACH CLUB
Zephyr Cove, NV
(775) 589-4901
www.zephyrcove.com
The Captain's is located at Zephyr Cove Marina and offers almost every type of watercraft for rent. It specializes in powerboats and Jet Skis. It also offers parasailing (see the "Parasailing" section in this chapter). It's open during the summer from 8:00 a.m. to 5:00 p.m. You can write to Captain Kirk's at P.O. Box 481, Zephyr Cove, NV.

H2O SPORTS
Stateline, NV
(775) 588-4155
www.rhpbeach.com
This shop guarantees the lowest rental prices at the lake. H2O has a full line of water-sports rental equipment. It's located 2 miles north of Stateline at Round Hill Pines Beach. It also provides a daily tour of Emerald Bay by SeaDoos.

TAHOE CITY MARINA
700 North Lake Boulevard
Tahoe City, CA
(530) 583-1039
www.tahoecitymarina.com

Tahoe City Marina specializes in powerboat rentals but also has a 21-foot sailboat. It's also a full-service marina that offers fuel and docking and is close to two shopping centers. The marina is open from 8:00 a.m. to 6:00 p.m. during the summer.

TAHOE SAILING CHARTERS
700 North Lake Boulevard
Tahoe City, CA
(530) 583-6200
www.tahoesail.com
If you'd like to set sail on Lake Tahoe, this center has it all—skippered sailing cruises, yacht charters, sailing lessons, and regatta racing. Here you can enjoy sailing by yourself or sit back and let someone else do all the work while you enjoy the lake's spectacular scenery. Tahoe Sailing Charters is the ultimate sailing rental business on the lake.

BOWLING

The Reno/Tahoe area is usually known around the United States because of its outdoor recreation, but if indoor sports are more to your liking, you have to try the bowling alleys scattered around the area. Remember, too, that if watching professionals hit the lanes is your thing, Reno's National Bowling Stadium has top-ranked tournaments (see the Spectator Sports chapter for more details). If you're relocating here and would like to join a league, contact the individual bowling alleys for more details on league play. Most alleys offer open bowling, but because league schedules vary, you should call for availability.

AMF STARLITE BOWL
1201 Stardust Street
Reno, NV
(775) 747-3522
www.amf.com/starlitelanes
This bowling alley is the oldest in Reno and a favorite hangout of Insiders. It has 32 lanes, a snack bar, and video poker machines. Hours are Monday through Thursday noon to 11:00 p.m., Friday noon to 1:00 a.m., Saturday 9:00 a.m. to 1:00 p.m. and Sunday 9:00 a.m. to 11:00 p.m.

BOWL INCLINE
920 Southwood Boulevard
Incline Village, NV
(775) 831-1900

This bowling alley bills itself as the North Shore's only complete family recreation center. Bowl Incline has 16 lanes with automatic scoring, bumper bowling, a pool table, a video arcade, video poker machines, darts, a bar, and a full-swing golf simulator. Sundays are designated smoke-free. The alley is open from 11:00 a.m. to midnight every day. Open bowling prices are $4 per game and $3 for shoes.

GRAND SIERRA RESORT AND CASINO
2500 East Second Street
Reno, NV
(775) 789-2296
www.grandsierraresort.com

The Grand Sierra has a 50-lane bowling alley that is one of the most popular in the Reno/Tahoe area. Bowling is on a first-come, first-served basis from 8:00 a.m. to 2:00 a.m. Sunday through Thursday and around the clock on weekends. The best times to find an open lane are early afternoon or late evening. Rates depend upon the time of day, topping out at $3.75 per game and $3.50 for shoes. The most expensive time to bowl is between 6:00 p.m. and midnight and on all holidays. Lower rates are available for children and seniors during the week.

TAHOE BOWL
1030 Fremont Avenue
South Lake Tahoe, CA
(530) 544-3700

This bowling alley has 16 synthetic lanes and features lighted bumper bowling and a video arcade. It's open from 9:00 a.m. to 1:00 p.m. Sunday, from 2:00 p.m. to 11:00 p.m. Monday, and from 11:00 a.m. to 1:00 a.m. Tuesday through Saturday. It's relatively quiet during the summer months, so open bowling is no problem. During winter, show up before 6:00 p.m. to get a lane. Rates vary but are in line with other bowling facilities.

i AMF Starlite Bowl offers Xtreme Bowling, an adventure with lights and music Friday and Saturday.

CANOEING

If canoeing is your aquatic preference, Lake Tahoe is the perfect spot to take to the paddle. The scenery is magnificent and the water is crystal clear, making a trip by canoe a tranquil adventure. Most canoers cruise close to the shoreline because once the wind picks up, often with no warning, staying upright can be a big challenge. You don't see canoes on the Truckee River because of its swift current and because of the many hazardous boulders poking out from beneath the water. The Truckee River is preferred by rafting and kayaking enthusiasts. Canoes can be rented from the many water-sport companies around the lake (see the "Boat and Watercraft Rentals" section under "Boating" earlier in this chapter).

DISC GOLF

With the cost of playing a round of golf going up, up, up, it's refreshing to find a course that's absolutely free. But you won't be teeing off with a Big Bertha driver, and you won't be chipping out of sand traps. Instead you'll be throwing golf discs (similar to Frisbees) into a series of baskets that are laid out in a golf course format. Played in several area parks, disc golf has been growing in popularity by about 15 percent a year since 1996. It's far less structured than traditional golf and offers a great way for families to get out and have fun in the sun together. You can buy equipment at Scheels in Sparks (see the Shopping chapter) and at Bicycle Bananas at 2005 Sierra Highlands Drive in Reno. For more information, go to www.northtahoediscgolf.org and www.renodiscgolf.com.

You can try your skill at this up-and-coming sport at Bijou Community Park in South Lake Tahoe, where you'll find an interesting 27-hole layout that's been challenging local golfers since 1994. The park is on Al Tahoe Boulevard, about

1 mile southeast of the boulevard's intersection with US 50. For information call (530) 542-6055 (see the Parks chapter for more details about the park).

You can also tee off at Zephyr Cove Park in Zephyr Cove. To reach the park, drive about 6 miles north of Stateline on US 50, turn right onto Warrior Way, and follow the drive in the park to the end. For information call (775) 586-7271.

Attesting to the growing interest in this sport, several new facilities have recently sprung up. You'll find a very challenging course snaking through the heavy timber at North Tahoe Regional Park, (530-546-5043), providing wonderful peaks of Lake Tahoe as you hunt for your disc in the brush. The newest course in the area, The Ranch, provides a wide open, more forgiving layout at 2975 North Virginia Street in Reno, in the north end of Rancho San Rafael Park. You can also hook up with the Reno Disc Golf Association, which meets regularly and schedules tournaments and events at The Ranch. For information, visit www.renodiscgolf.com or e-mail rdga@charter.net.

If you're in the mood for a drive, try the 18-hole Disc-wood course at Kirkwood Mountain Resort, (209-258-6000), about 90 minutes from Reno, or Truckee Regional Park in Truckee, CA (530-582-7720). (See the Winter Sports chapter for details about Kirkwood Mountain.)

DIVING

Although you won't see coral reefs and schools of tropical fish, diving in Lake Tahoe is a spectacular experience because the water is so clear. Due to visibility from 45 to 90 feet in the summer, you'll feel as if you can reach out and touch the native fish swimming by, including rainbow, brown, and cutthroat trout. But remember the temperature of the water is anything but warm: You'll need drysuits to protect yourself against the frigid water. If you're inexperienced in high-altitude diving, I suggest you contact a dive school for proper training.

SIERRA DIVING CENTER
104 East Grove Street
Reno, NV
(775) 825-2147
www.sierradive.com

With more than 30 years of experience in Lake Tahoe diving, Sierra Diving Center can certainly claim to be experts on the subject. The company offers a full range of dive services, including PADI-certified classes, instructor certification, technical training, equipment sales and rentals, and tours. If you've ever had a yen to scuba dive, the professionals here will make it easy for you with short evening and weekend sessions.

To dive safely in Lake Tahoe, you can take the one-day Altitude Specialty Course, which includes two open dives in the lake plus training in all the high-altitude changes that affect divers. For up-to-date schedules and prices, call the number above or access their Web page.

TROPICAL PENGUINS SCUBA & WATER SPORTS
961 Matley Lane #130
Reno, NV
(775) 828-3483
www.tropicalpenguinscuba.com

Whether you're a first-timer or an experienced diver just needing a refresher course, the professional staff at Tropical Penguins Scuba & Water Sports will help you splash into the underwater world of adventure. Classes at this complete dive facility include basic and advanced open-water certification, rescue diver, divemaster, instructor development, scuba tune-up, and specialty courses such as altitude diving. The shop features all levels of PADI and ANDI certification plus equipment sales and rentals.

Before you decide to explore the hidden treasures of Lake Tahoe (or other dive sites included in their travel packages), I suggest you stop by and assess your readiness to dive with their trained staff. Call for schedules and prices on travel and classes.

FOUR-WHEELING/OFF-ROAD ADVENTURES

You'll definitely want to bring your camera or camcorder if you decide to strike out on an off-road tour in the Reno/Tahoe area. One visitor called his four-wheeling trip near Lake Tahoe "the best half-day of my life." If off-roading has been something you've always wanted to try, Lake Tahoe has the premier company to hook up with.

LAKE TAHOE ADVENTURES
South Lake Tahoe, CA
(530) 577-2940, (800) 865-4679
www.laketahoeadventures.com
This company offers off-road tours ranging from easy to rugged and challenging. Tours include riding the trails in ATVs, Jeeps, and Hummers, for varying amounts of time, such as. a six-hour tour on the Rubicon Trail or a two-hour trip to Genoa Peak. Call for prices.

Other tours are available, such as the historic desert tour and tours by snowmobile in winter. A yacht is available for touring on Lake Tahoe as well. This company also provides custom tours, so if you have something special in mind, just ask. Reservations are required.

FRISBEE

A growing sport among young men and women, ultimate Frisbee combines the nonstop motion of soccer with the passing of football. The Reno Ultimate Frisbee League meets regularly during summer and fall at Idlewild Park and includes teams with eclectic names such as Slackjaw Dance Squad and How Do You Tune a Taco?. For information go to www.renoultimate.org.

GO-KARTS

WILD ISLAND
250 Wild Island Court, Sparks, NV
(775) 359-2927
www.wildisland.com

Wild Island has a wonderful go-kart racing facility. The raceway has two tracks, one for larger children and one for smaller. The big kids get to drive gas-powered Indy cars, and the little ones drive gas-powered Sprint cars. .In addition to the go-karts, Wild Island has a water park, miniature golf courses, and an assortment of other attractions for kids of all ages.

HANG GLIDING

NEVADA SPORTS FLYERS
(775) 883-7070
www.serioussports.com
In summer, hang gliders are a common sight around Mt. Rose and other peaks along the eastern escarpment as they launch from the high peaks and flirt with the warm currents of air rising from the high desert.

If you've ever wanted to "fly," you should consider learning in the Reno/Tahoe area: The Sierra Nevada offers one of the premier soaring sites in the country. I recommend you contact Nevada Sports Flyers before launching into this exhiliarating sport. This group of dedicated professionals, which functions more like a club than a business, can get you started in a safe, dependable way whether you choose a large hang glider or a smaller paraglider.

HIKING

Although you can appreciate the beauty of the Reno/Tahoe area driving through it in your car, the very best way to experience this wonderland is to grab your backpack and hit the trail. Fields of wildflowers, rushing mountain streams, and the crunch of pine needles underfoot await explorers of one of the most gorgeous natural habitats in the world. These hikes are not necessarily extreme: The Reno/Tahoe area encompasses treks for hikers of all abilities. You don't have to scale Mt. Tallac to be a hiker. You can take a leisurely stroll in Tahoe Meadows (one of my very favorite outings any time of the year) and still enjoy nature at its very finest.

In this section I describe some of the not-to-be-missed hikes in the area, which I'm sure you'll enjoy. But with hundreds of miles of trails, I can't list all the magical destinations awaiting your discovery. I leave those for you to find with the aid of maps you can pick up at visitor centers (see the Attractions chapter for locations). Be sure to check out the large variety of hikes in area parks and historical sites. You can take easy jaunts at Spooner Lake and Sand Harbor (see the Parks chapter) and also at the Taylor Creek Visitor Center and the Tallac Historic Site (see the Attractions chapter).

Because this lovely mountain environment is so very fragile, it's important that every visitor minimize his or her impact on the area. Hikers should be especially careful to not disturb the surrounding areas of their wilderness destinations. Zero impact guidelines include:

- Pack it in, pack it out: Don't leave any trash on the trail. Whether it's biodegradable or not, human discards are not part of the natural environment and may prove harmful to both the flora and fauna of the wilderness.
- Use restroom facilities at the trailheads. If you must "go" on the trail, pack out your waste and toilet paper. Even if human waste is buried, animals can dig it up. Carry a plastic zip-locked bag, and add a little baking soda to absorb odor.
- Don't pollute streams or lakes.
- Stay on the trails to reduce damage to the fragile environment. Shortcutting causes erosion.
- Enjoy the wildflowers, but never pick them; similarly, don't remove artifacts from the trails. Leave them for the next hiker to enjoy.

For more information about responsible hiking, you can call Leave No Trace, Inc., at (800) 332-4100.

For your safety and comfort, always dress properly and be prepared for sudden changes in the weather. All trails around Lake Tahoe are at high altitude; familiarize yourself with the symptoms of altitude sickness, and retreat to a lower elevation if you or one of your party should exhibit signs of this serious illness. The sun is more intense at high altitude, so be sure to wear sunscreen and carry a hat and clothing to protect yourself from harmful rays. Carry a map so you know exactly where you're going and about how long it will take to get there. Be sure to take food, water, and first-aid items in your backpack. Don't drink the water in the wild unless you have water purification tablets or a good portable filter. Many hikers have learned the hard way that even though the water in mountain streams looks crystal clear, it contains *Giardia lamblia,* an organism that can cause severe intestinal disease.

Also be aware that no fires are allowed in the wild. If you're hiking with dogs, keep them under control and don't let them wander too far from you. For more tips about dos and don'ts in the backcountry, see the Winter Sports chapter.

Miles and miles of hiking trails in the Tahoe area are described on the Internet. You can visit generic outdoor sites like www.gorp.com for more information; or log on to your favorite browser, search for hiking in Tahoe, and explore.

DESOLATION WILDERNESS
Southwest of South Lake Tahoe, CA
(530) 543-2600
www.fs.fed.us/r5/ltbmu/
Spanning about 100 square miles high above Lake Tahoe, the Desolation Wilderness is a veritable Shangri-la for hikers and backpackers. Tucked into the backcountry are more than 100 shimmering alpine lakes and 20 majestic peaks towering more than 9,000 feet above sea level. Exploring this entire wonderland would take months: I can't possibly describe in detail all of the hikes you'll find here. I suggest you pick up maps from area visitor centers (see the Attractions chapter for directions) or from the USDA Forest Service office at 870 Emerald Bay Road in South Lake Tahoe. You'll also need a free permit to day hike in the wilderness and a backcountry permit to spend the night. Permits can be obtained from the Forest Service or at the trailheads. Since the number

of overnight permits is limited, you should call (530) 644-6048 for reservations.

You can access the wilderness from these major trailheads: Eagle Falls, Glen Alpine, and Echo Lakes. Eagle Falls is 5 miles northwest of South Lake Tahoe on CA 89, directly across from the parking lot at Emerald Bay. Glen Alpine is at the southwest end of Fallen Leaf Lake. To reach the lake from South Lake Tahoe, take CA 89 northwest from its junction with US 50 for about 3 miles. Turn left (west) onto Fallen Leaf Road; continue on Fallen Leaf Road for about 5 miles to a junction, then follow the signs to Lily Lake. To reach Lower Echo Lake, take US 50 southwest from South Lake Tahoe past Echo Summit, and turn right onto Johnson Pass Road. Continue through this residential area to the parking lots at the lake.

One of the most popular hikes in the wilderness is to Eagle Lake, a 1-mile jaunt from the Eagle Falls trailhead that climbs through huge stands of trees. Stunning views of Lake Tahoe are behind you; you can enjoy these more easily on the descent. Eagle Lake is a tiny azure jewel, perfect for a cold dip and picnicking. If you continue on this trail another 4 or 5 miles, you'll reach Middle Velma, Upper Velma, and Fontanillis Lakes. Be prepared for a trail that's steep and rocky in places.

Starting from the Glen Alpine trail-head, you can make an uphill climb of about 6 miles, past Grass, Suzie, and Heather Lakes, to Lake Aloha, perched in a glacial area on top of the Sierra Crest. Return as you came, or make any of several long loops back to Fallen Leaf Lake.

An outing perfect for families begins at the marina on Lower Echo Lake. You can take a 15-minute water taxi across the lake and through the channel connecting to Upper Echo Lake. From the dock at the west end of Upper Echo Lake, you can take a leisurely 3-mile stroll back to the marina at Lower Echo Lake or continue west to a variety of lakes in the Desolation Wilderness, including Ralston, Tamarack, Lake of the Woods, and Lake Aloha.

FIVE LAKES
Trailhead 2.2 miles west of California Highway 89 on Alpine Meadows Road, 6 miles north of Tahoe City, CA

Snuggled in alpine country on the back side of Squaw Peak, Five Lakes (none of which are named) is a popular destination for hikers, anglers, and dogwalkers. The round-trip jaunt is only about 5 miles, with an elevation gain of about 1,000 feet. The well-marked trail is rocky in spots but very easy to follow.

From the trailhead on Alpine Meadows Road, the path climbs sharply through forest sprinkled with an eclectic variety of wildflowers (if you're hiking in spring or summer). After about a mile, the trail breaks into the open and you're treated to breathtaking views of the granite peaks around Alpine Meadows ski resort.

Approaching the lakes, you enter the forest again, and if you look up to the north you can see the ski lifts on top of Squaw Peak and KT-22 at Squaw Valley USA. You can wander around from lake to lake and find your own little Eden for swimming and relaxing. Although this area gets heavy use during high season, it's still possible to find a niche of privacy to enjoy the day. But if you're looking for a total wilderness experience, this probably won't fit the bill, unless you hike after Labor Day.

To reach the trailhead from Tahoe City, go north on CA 89 about 6 miles to Alpine Meadows Road and follow it for about 2.2 miles. The trailhead is on the right side of the road in a residential area and is marked by a GRANITE CHIEF WILDERNESS sign. You'll need to park along the road.

MARLETTE LAKE
Trailhead at Spooner Lake, junction of U.S. Highway 50 and Nevada, Highway 28

With an elevation gain of 1,157 feet, the 5-mile hike to Marlette Lake is a bit of a challenge but well worth the effort. The dirt path is wide and easy to follow, but it's aerobic for most hikers, given its steady ascent. As you hike through North Canyon to the lake, you'll climb past thick aspen groves, velvety alpine meadows, and tumbling mountain creeks. In spring and summer you'll see wildflowers ablaze with color everywhere, and in fall you can enjoy the reds, golds, and yellows of the mountain landscape.

When you arrive at the lake, be sure to take time to picnic in this special alpine hideaway. Anglers can try their luck at catching the large trout that are usually quite close to shore. But don't expect to have a fish dinner—it's catch-and-release only. You can continue on toward the Flume Trail, a harrowing 7-mile plunge down the ridge to Incline Village. Drink in the great views of Lake Tahoe from the start of the Flume Trail, but don't go farther, since it's mainly for hard-core mountain bikers (see the "Biking" section in this chapter for more details). Be on the lookout for cyclists throughout this hike, particularly those on the downhill run from the lake.

Marlette Lake is not only scenic but historic as well. A system of flumes (including the one along the Flume Trail) used water from the lake to float timber to the silver mines in Virginia City back in its heyday.

MT. ROSE (PEAK)
Trailhead 0.5 mile south of summit on Nevada Highway 431

Because so many things have the name "Mt. Rose," I think a brief explanation might head off any confusion you might have. The Mt. Rose Highway (NV 431) connects Reno and Incline Village, passing between the summit of Mt. Rose and Slide Mountain. The highest point of the highway is called the Mt. Rose summit. Mt. Rose–Ski Tahoe ski resort is on Slide Mountain (not on Mt. Rose), and Mt. Rose Peak (the mountain described in this hike) is located northwest of Slide Mountain.

At 10,776 feet, Mt. Rose is the third highest peak in the Reno/Tahoe area and a challenge worth exploring. The view from its barren summit is truly breathtaking, and in spring and summer the trek offers up an explosion of wildflowers that's hard to beat. With an elevation gain of

about 2,000 feet, you should be in good shape to take this hike. Proper clothing is also important: Dress in layers to protect yourself from the winds on exposed ridges, and wear comfortable hiking boots suitable for rocky terrain. Be sure to bring plenty of water and snacks, and don't forget your camera to commemorate your summiting the peak.

Hikers have a choice of two routes to the Mt. Rose summit, both from trailheads off NV 431. The first route follows a closed dirt road, which can be accessed from the summit parking lot on the west side of the highway or from the intersection of the road and highway near an old maintenance building southwest of the lot. You can either use the paved parking lot or park along the road near the building. The round-trip to the top using this route is about 12 miles from the building and about 0.5 mile farther from the parking lot.

The first several miles of this route are a steady climb affording views of Lake Tahoe cupped below the peaks of the Desolation Wilderness. The trail passes through radiant fields of wildflowers, including blue lupine, crimson evening primrose, and yellow mule ears. At a small snowmelt pond the path forks: The right-hand path takes you to the top of Mt. Rose and the left to a relay station that also has great views. If you're not up to going to the top, consider hiking to the pond: It's a great 5-mile round-trip outing, with spectacular views and the aforementioned wildflowers. You can also take time to explore the tiny mountain meadow around the pond and see how many wildflowers you can identify.

If you're continuing on to the summit, the path begins a steep rocky ascent from the pond through a series of switchbacks. Breaking through the trees at the top of the mountain, you enter a special environment indeed—an exhilarating alpine habitat awash in the dazzling colors of hardy wildflowers.

A second route to the summit can be accessed from the trailhead sign near the parking lot. Climb up the steps at the sign for a slightly more direct, forested route to the top of the mountain. You won't have views of Lake Tahoe, at least until you begin the final push to the top, but you'll hike through a quiet forest environment with streams and a waterfall.

To reach the trailheads from Reno/Sparks, take U.S. Highway 395 southwest to NV 431. Follow to the parking lot on the right at the summit, or continue just around the corner to the old maintenance building. From Incline Village take NV 431 northeast just past Tahoe Meadows. Look for the building on the left, or keep going to the summit to the parking lot, also on the left.

PREY MEADOWS/SKUNK HARBOR

Trailhead on Nevada Highway 28, 2 miles north of intersection with U.S. Highway 50
You can stroll through a lovely sun-washed meadow brimming with wildflowers and swim and sun in private coves tucked deep in the forest on this hike to the east shore of Lake Tahoe. From NV 28 the trail descends along a sandy road through stands of Jeffrey pine, white fir, and cedar. Along the way you'll see the remains of a railroad grade used in the 1870s as part of a system to supply timber for the mines in Virginia City, Nevada. About 0.5 mile down, the trail forks, with the left branch going to Prey Meadows and the right to Skunk Harbor.

If you choose the left branch in spring and summer, you'll enjoy it all the way down. You'll likely see pink buckwheats, red snowplants, yellow Sierra wallflowers, and purplish-brown spotted mountain bells. Once in the meadow you can wander along the creek and marvel at the tiny flowers clinging to life along its banks. It's a wonderful place to sit back, relax, and enjoy a picnic lunch.

If you choose the right branch of the trail, you'll have a winding descent to the shore of Lake Tahoe, enjoying teasing peeks of the lake as you go. A prominent San Francisco family built the large gray stone structure that sits near the lakeshore in the 1920s as a secluded picnic spot. The tiny beaches along this section of the lake are perfect for private sunbathing and swim-

ming. Just wander along the path and find the perfect spot.

You can visit both Skunk Harbor and Prey Meadows if you allow enough time. The round-trip hike to the harbor is approximately 3 miles, and the hike to Prey Meadows is about the same distance. With an elevation gain of only about 600 feet, the outing is considered moderate and is suitable for most hikers.

To find the trailhead, look for a green gate on the west side of NV 28 about 2 miles north of the intersection with US 50. There are several parking pullouts right near the trailhead. See the Parks chapter for more information about the surrounding Lake Tahoe–Nevada State Park.

 Lake Tahoe contains 39 trillion gallons of water.

RUBICON TRAIL

D. L. Bliss State Park
California Highway 89
9 miles north of South Lake Tahoe, CA
(530) 525-7277
www.cal-parks.ca.gov
Winding along a heavily wooded rocky section of Lake Tahoe shoreline, the Rubicon Trail is a splendid example of the best Tahoe has to offer. With stunning views of deep turquoise water lapping at huge granite boulders, the trail begins in the campground of D. L. Bliss State Park and ends 4.4 miles later at Vikingsholm Castle on Emerald Bay. You can hike the 9-mile round-trip or leave a car in the parking lot above Emerald Bay, about 1 mile up from Vikingsholm.

The only downside to this hike is the difficult parking situation. If you're planning to hike during July or August, it's a good idea to arrive very early in the day. The trailhead is 2.5 miles past the park entrance, and parking near it is very limited. If you're hiking after Labor Day, call ahead to be sure you can drive to the trailhead. Dogs aren't allowed on the trail but are okay in the park if they're leashed. For more information about Bliss and Emerald Bay, see the Parks chapter.

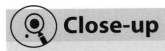 **Close-up**

Tahoe Rim Trail

After 20 years of dedicated volunteer efforts, the Tahoe Rim Trail welcomed hikers, bikers, and horseback riders for the first time in 2001. Fulfilling the dreams of local outdoor enthusiasts, the 165-mile trail encircles the Lake Tahoe Basin as it snakes along the ridge tops surrounding the lake. Although you won't be strolling the beaches that line the shore of the lake as you enjoy this alpine wonderland, you'll pass through a mind-blowing variety of mountain terrain including meadows of hip-high wildflowers, magnificent forests of Jeffrey pines, and a plethora of cool mountain streams that tumble toward the lake. As you enjoy spectacular views of the lake along the way, you'll meander through six counties, three national forests, and two states. Hundreds of people proudly claim membership in the Tahoe Rim Trail 150-Mile Club, indicating they've hiked or biked the entire route. If you have about a week and a half to devote all at once, you can earn your club stripes quite quickly. If not, the route can be covered systematically in sections—the method most people prefer. Although you're sure to encounter serious hikers everywhere along the trail, you'll find even more people simply out for a great day hike communing with nature. You can begin your journey at trailheads located at Big Meadow, Echo Summit, Echo Lake, Barker Pass, Tahoe City, Brockway Summit, Tahoe Meadows, Spooner Summit, Kingsbury North, or Kingsbury South. I highly recommend picking up the book *The Tahoe Rim Trail* by Tim Hauserman, which gives a mile-by-mile description of the terrain along with invaluable tips on how to plan your hike. It's especially critical for those who plan to backpack the entire route. For more trail information, visit www.tahoe rimtrail.org or call (775) 298-0012.

TAHOE MEADOWS

West of the Mt. Rose summit on Nevada Highway 431

An enchanting carpet spread beneath imposing granite peaks, Tahoe Meadows is an intriguing escape to another world any time of the year (see the Winter Sports chapter for more on fun in the snow at the meadow). But in spring and summer, when the meandering Ophir Creek becomes a series of streams overflowing with snowmelt, the meadow explodes with color as an amazing variety of wildflowers bursts into bloom.

In late spring this alpine paradise becomes a sea of gold with masses of buttercups flowering among the verdant grass. As the season progresses the meadow becomes an ever-changing kaleidoscope of color—the purples of the larkspurs, the oranges and reds of the giant paintbrushes, the whites of the marigolds, and the blues of the alpine veronicas. The colors are stunning and brilliant, almost seeming to shout at you as you stroll along the bubbling streams. But take the time to look closer: Some of the real treasures in this alpine garden are tiny blooms almost hidden from view. Look for delicate alpine shooting stars, clinging in solitary splashes of pinkish-purple along the banks of the streams, or little elephant head flowers, with their miniature pink trunks nodding in the gentle wind.

You can follow the meandering water and variety of paths to the back of the meadow, where the main trail enters the trees and descends to Price Lake and eventually to Davis Creek Park south of Reno on US 395. If you're planning to go all the way to Davis Creek, I suggest you leave a car there, since the round-trip back to NV 431 is about 12 miles. Recent environmental work in the meadow resulted in the installation of sections of wooden bridges to protect the fragile stream banks; please stay on the walks where they are provided. Hikers were also discouraged from going to the extreme back of the meadow during the summer of 2008, but it's expected that the work will be finished in 2009 when new trails will be open.

Tahoe Meadows is really not about long-distance hiking for most locals, however. It's more of a touchstone with nature, a place to sink into the magic of a mountain meadow all year. The real joy is taking the time to smell the flowers (literally) and viewing this special environment as it changes with the seasons. Tahoe Meadows is very dog-friendly (just be careful of the occasional coyote), so be sure to bring Fido along. You'll find the Whole Access section of the trail at the northeast end of the meadow, where a wide, smooth path that is a little more than a mile long is suitable for wheelchairs. Look for the parking lot and trail access just west of the summit.

To reach the meadow from Reno/Sparks, take US 395 southwest to NV 431 (the Mt. Rose Highway) and follow it south to just past the summit. From Incline Village take NV 431 northeast to where it levels out just before the summit. You can park along the road or in the parking lot just west of the summit.

TAHOE RIM TRAIL
Various access points around Lake Tahoe
Encircling the ridges around Lake Tahoe, the Tahoe Rim Trail offers more than 150 miles of adventure for hikers, bikers, and equestrians. See the Close-up on Tahoe Rim Trail in this chapter.

HORSEBACK RIDING

VERDI TRAILS
175 Trelease Lane, Verdi, NV
(775) 345-7600, (888) 345-7603
www.verditrailsranch.com
Horseback riding is an old tradition on the east side of the Sierra Nevada, and at Verdi Trails, the wranglers help keep this tradition alive. This outfit caters to families but suggests that the younger riders be at least six years old unless they are experienced. This stable is located at the foot of the mountains, and the rides provide outstanding

scenery. Verdi Trails specializes in trail rides, but this is a full-service equestrian center that also offers hayrides, barbecues, and other fun services. The stables open at 9:00 a.m. and close at sunset. The stables are located off I–80 west of Boomtown.

North Shore Riding Stables
Around the North Shore of Lake Tahoe stables offer horseback riding by the hour (starting at about $27 per hour) along with guides. These stables also offer riding lessons, hayrides during summer, and sleigh rides during winter. For the latest information, call: **Alpine Meadows Stables** (California Highway 89, between Tahoe City and Truckee, CA; 530-583-3905) or **Squaw Valley Stables** (Squaw Valley exit, California Highway 89, between Tahoe City and Truckee, CA; 530-583-7433; www.squaw.com).

South Shore Riding Stables
Like the North Shore, the south part of the lake is home to several outfits that rent horses. At most of them, you can take lessons, go on trail rides, go on hayrides, and in winter go on sleigh rides. Contact each stable for current information.

CAMP RICHARDSON CORRAL
California Highway 89
South Lake Tahoe, CA
(530) 541-3113
www.camprichardson.com

CASCADE STABLES
California Highway 89, near Cascade Lake, CA
(530) 541-2055

ZEPHYR COVE STABLES
U.S. Highway 50
Zephyr Cove, NV
(775) 588-5664
www.zephyrcove.com

KAYAKING

Kayaking is wonderful fun and very easy to learn, but if you've never been in a kayak before, I recommend taking a guided tour on which you can learn the basics. Hugging the shoreline of Lake Tahoe, guided tours for first-timers provide a good introduction to the sport without the rough water sometimes found in rivers. If you're an experienced paddler, however, you can rent a kayak and do your own thing, either on the lake or in nearby rivers. It's important to follow safety instructions, whichever way you choose, and to remember that the water of Lake Tahoe is beautiful but can be deadly if you tip over and can't right yourself.

More experienced kayakers should drop their crafts into the Truckee River Whitewater Park in downtown Reno, where river runners can test their skill on its 11 drop pools year-round. See the Annual Events chapter for more information about the Reno River Festival, which showcases slalom racing on this course.

KAYAKS ETC.
2505 Sutro Street, Reno, NV
(775) 849-2714
www.kayaksetc.net
With more than 150 boats in stock, Kayaks Etc. is sure to have the perfect paddle craft just for you. You can choose from expedition, touring, white-water, and recreational kayaks from tried-and-true brands. Because of the plethora of choices, owner Bob Krause recommends taking advantage of the free personalized demos before investing in a kayak. If you're not in the business of buying, you can rent a craft for $40 to $55 a day, including life preserver and paddle. Krause also offers half-day lessons for $50 and full-day for $100. Summer store hours are 1:00 to 6:00 p.m. weekdays, 10:00 a.m. to 5:00 p.m. Saturday, and 10:00 a.m. to 3:00 p.m. Sunday. Hours are shortened November to May, so call before heading to the store.

KAYAK TAHOE
3411 U.S. Highway 50 and Ski Run Boulevard
South Lake Tahoe, CA
(530) 544-2011
www.kayaktahoe.com
For just $30 per person, you can enjoy the splendor of sunset on Lake Tahoe as you take a guided tour along the shore with the experts from Kayak Tahoe. This outfit also offers wildlife tours on the Upper Truckee River for $45 and trips to Emerald Bay for $65. The company rents kayaks for $15 per person (with a 10 percent discount for early birds) and gives lessons. Kayak Tahoe has several locations, including Timber Cove Marina and on El Dorado Beach.

SIERRA ADVENTURES
Silver Legacy Resort Casino Adventure Desk
(866) 323-8928
www.wildsierra.com
You can't get much closer to the kayak action on the Truckee River than Sierra Adventures. Tucked just steps from the water's edge, the shop is a full-service outfitter with rentals, tours, retail sales, and lessons. You can book a series of four lessons for $199, including gear, or rent a kayak for $19 an hour. Sierra Adventures also rents equipment and provides tours that include other modes of transport, such as bikes, rafts, and ATVs. You'll find the helpful staff on duty from 10:00 a.m. to 6:00 p.m. daily, usually March through November. Winter hours are shortened, with the shop closed on Tuesday and Wednesday.

TAHOE PADDLE & OAR
8299 North Lake Boulevard
Kings Beach, CA
(530) 581-3029
www.tahoepaddle.com
You can explore the picturesque boulder fields and hidden coves of Crystal Bay on a guided tour hosted by Tahoe Paddle & Oar. The cost is $90 per person, with a minimum of two people, and reservations are required. For a longer trip the guides will take you out to Sand Harbor, where you'll paddle your own kayak along the dramatic granite boulders and turquoise waters between Sand Harbor and Secret Harbor. This trip will run you $100, and there is a two-person minimum. If you're a free spirit and want to go it on your own, you can rent a kayak and explore; the cost is about $20 per hour.

MARTIAL ARTS

From young children to retired seniors, interest in martial arts is growing in the Reno/Tahoe area. When you check local telephone directories, you'll find a somewhat bewildering array of self-defense classes listed under the umbrella of martial arts. The various types include karate, kodenkan jujitsu, taekwondo, judo, and tai chi.

Academies in the Reno/Sparks area include Bushidokan Martial Arts Temple, 311 Ninth Street, Sparks (775-358-1518); Aikido of Reno, 135 South Wells Avenue, Reno, (775) 337-8030; and United Studios of Self Defense, 4792 Caughlin Parkway, Reno, (775) 852-3383. In the South Shore Lake Tahoe area, call the School of Tao Martial Arts, (530) 577-4515. For a complete listing of locations and types of classes, check the most recent telephone directory.

MINIATURE GOLF

MAGIC CARPET GOLF (RENO)
6925 South Virginia Street
Reno, NV
(775) 853-8837

Located on Virginia Street heading out of town toward Carson City, this establishment has two 19-hole courses and one 28hole course. It's open daily from 10:00 a.m. to 6:00 p.m. during winter, weather permitting, and from 10:00 a.m. to 10:00 p.m. during the warmer months. The company offers birthday parties and discounts for groups of more than 20. After your round of golf, you can also enjoy the Magic Carpet's pizza parlor and arcade.

MAGIC CARPET GOLF (CARNELIAN BAY)
5167 North Lake Boulevard
Carnelian Bay, CA
(530) 546-4279

Magic Carpet Golf has a 19-hole course and a 28-hole course. It's open from 10:00 a.m. to 10:00 p.m., April through October, weather permitting. It's usually crowded.

MAGIC CARPET GOLF (SOUTH LAKE TAHOE)
2455 Lake Tahoe Boulevard
South Lake Tahoe, CA
(530) 541-3787

The South Shore of Lake Tahoe also has a Magic Carpet, also with 19- and 28-hole courses. It's open daily from 10:00 a.m. to 11:00 p.m. during summer and 10:00 a.m. to 7:00 p.m. on weekends during spring and fall. It's closed during winter.

WILD ISLAND FAMILY ADVENTURE PARK
250 Wild Island Court, Sparks, NV
(775) 359-2927
www.wildisland.com

Part of the Wild Island water park complex, this newly renovated miniature golf course has two 18-hole courses, which feature piped-in music on all of the holes. It's open all year with winter hours Monday through Thursday from 2:00 to 7:00 p.m., Friday from 2:00 to 9:00 p.m., Saturday from 11:00 a.m. to 9:00 p.m., and Sunday from 11:00 a.m. to 7:00 p.m. Hours may be extended during the summer.

PAINTBALL

Playing paintball is an excellent way to test your mettle as a warrior without the possibility of dying in battle. At worst, you'll end up with paint splattered all over your clothes.

HERBIE'S PAINTBALL GAMES INC.
Alternate U.S. Highway 95, about 6 miles outside of Fernley, NV
(775) 575-6946
www.herbiespaintball.com

Herbie's catch phase is "just show up and squeeze the trigger." The 14 outdoor battlefields are open on Saturday from 10:00 a.m. to 4:00 p.m. Herbie's welcomes walk-ons and single players but suggests calling ahead to see if a game is on. The course can be rented for private wars or parties for half days and full days, and Herbie's hosts tournaments, too. There are themed battlefields, one of which is a simulated ghost town.

Rates depend on the package you purchase. The deluxe Package #1 at $35 per person includes a semiautomatic paintball gun, 200 paintballs, a camo suit, gloves, goggles, and a mask.

To get to Herbie's from Reno, take I–80 east to the West Fernley exit, number46. Turn right from the interstate and follow Main Street through town to Alternate US 95. Take Alternate US 95 for 6 miles. The battlefield is on the right-hand side of the road near the Reno-Fernley Raceway. The mailing address is P.O. Box 2434, Fernley, NV 89408.

PARASAILING

If you prefer sailing over Lake Tahoe rather than on it, there are several companies that offer parasailing. Imagine flying high over the water under a multicolored parachute, towed behind a fast-moving speedboat skippered by U.S. Coast Guard–approved captains. Flying high above the shoreline lets you check out the fabulous scenery and the gorgeous lake-front estates. You'll really appreciate the phrase "bird's-eye view" after a parasailing adventure.

Flights last anywhere from 8 to 20 minutes and cost between $45 and $180, depending upon number of flyers and height of the parachute over the lake.

Besides renting water-sports equipment (see listings under the "Boating" and "Boat and Water-craft Rentals" sections earlier in this chapter), the following companies also offer parasailing.

ACTION WATERSPORTS OF TAHOE
3411 U.S. Highway 50, South Lake Tahoe, CA
(530) 544-5387

CAPTAIN KIRK'S BEACH CLUB
Zephyr Cove, NV
(775) 589-4901

NORTH TAHOE WATERSPORTS
700 North Lake Boulevard
Tahoe City, CA
(530) 583-7245

RACQUETBALL

In Reno you'll find racquetball courts at Double Diamond Athletic Club, (775) 851-7171; Sports West Athletic Club, (775) 348-6666; and South Reno Athletic Club, (775) 853-4050. Because the cost of club membership and court availability varies, I recommend you call ahead.

RAFTING

TAHOE WHITEWATER TOURS
303 Alpine Meadows Road
Tahoe City, CA
(530) 581-2441, (800) 442-7238

400 Island Avenue, Reno, NV
(775) 787-5000
www.gowhitewater.com
Trips with Tahoe Whitewater Tours offer fun and excitement for first-time rafters as well as experienced paddlers. In the immediate Reno/Lake Tahoe area, you can choose from two-hour or full-day runs on the Truckee River and half-day and full-day outings on the East Carson River. Both these rivers provide a fair amount of pristine solitude and placid water coupled with sections of exciting white water. The company also provides several day trips on the South Fork of the American River and overnighters on the Middle and North Forks. The 21-mile white-water section of this river from Chili Bar (near Placerville, California) to Salmon Falls (near Folsom Reservoir) is one of the most popular river runs in the West. Prices range from about $48 to $135, and longer trips include lunch. The company also offers guided kayak tours to the Truckee River Whitewater Park in Reno.

TRUCKEE RIVER RAFT COMPANY
Fanny Bridge Raft Rentals
California Highway 89 at Fanny Bridge
Tahoe City, CA
(530) 583-0123
www.truckeeriverraft.com
Due to its location at Fanny Bridge, you won't have any trouble finding this raft company: Just

look for their trademark red bus. The first 5 miles of the Truckee River, as it empties out of Lake Tahoe at Fanny Bridge to the River Ranch near Alpine Meadows ski resort, is the most popular rafting run in the Reno/Tahoe area. Meandering lazily through the huge trees along CA 89, this self-guided float takes most rafters two or three hours to complete. The turquoise water found along this route makes it easily one of the most beautiful sections of the Truckee River. After taking your raft out at River Ranch Pond, be sure to head up to the River Ranch deck for drinks and lunch before catching the free shuttle bus back to your car at Tahoe City.

Although this outing is convenient, safe, and scenic, most of the time it's quite crowded. If you're looking for solitude, you probably won't find it here unless you go after Labor Day. Weather and water permitting, the rafts operate daily May through October from 8:30 a.m. to 3:30 p.m. The last shuttle from the River Ranch back to Tahoe City runs at 6:00 p.m. Rates are $35 for those 13 and older, $30 for 6 to 12 years, and $5 for 5 and under. Group discounts are also available.

ROCK CLIMBING

Insiders who thrive on the excitement of scaling the face of solid rock cliffs will tell you the secret to great rock climbing: Find a place with perfect rocks and perfect weather. I've tried to make it even easier for you by listing some of the Reno/Tahoe area's best indoor and outdoor rock-climbing centers with instructors just waiting to help you take that first step. Today the wall, tomorrow Mt. Everest.

In addition to the locations below, you can also learn to belay in Reno at Sports West Athletic Club, 1575 South Virginia Street, (775) 348-6666; and in summer only at REI, 2225 Harvard Way, (775) 828-9090.

ADVENTURE PARK
Northstar-at-Tahoe
U.S. Highway 267 (6 miles north of Lake Tahoe), Truckee, CA
(530) 562-1010

Northstar provides climbers of all ages and abilities a 25-foot-high, granitelike, multi-faced outdoor climbing wall to practice on. It's located in the Adventure Park behind Northstar Village. The friendly and talented staff teaches belaying and supervises the climbs. The wall is open for climbs from 10:00 a.m. to 6:00 p.m. Wednesday through Sunday from mid-June until early September. All ages may climb, but belayers must be at least 14 years old or have staff approval. An hour pass runs about $10, but they do offer discounts for three or more climbers in the group. All-day passes are available for around $20. Groups are welcome to schedule events.

HEADWALL CAFE AND CLIMBING
The Cable Car Building
Squaw Valley, CA
(530) 583-7673
www.squawadventure.com

This climbing center is located in the Cable Car Building at the base of Squaw Valley USA. The wall is 30 feet high and has 25 different routes, ranging in difficulty from beginner to expert. The center supplies harnesses and ropes that must be used when climbing. Unlimited climbing is around $12, with climbing shoes costing $4 extra to rent. It's open from noon to 6:00 p.m. in winter and from 11:00 a.m. to 6:00 p.m. in summer. It's a low-key, fun climbing facility.

ROCKSPORT INDOOR CLIMBING CENTER
1901 Silverado Boulevard, Sparks, NV
(775) 352-7673
www.rocksportreno.com

RockSport's climbing wall is the biggest in the Reno/Tahoe area. It's 32 feet high and spans the entire length of this warehouse's wall. The center offers several workshops during the week, ranging from belaying lessons to kid's climb night. It also offers monthly memberships. If you just want to climb, it's open from 10:00 a.m. to 10:00 p.m. during the week, 10:00 a.m. to 8:00 p.m. on Saturday, and 10:00 a.m. to 6:00 p.m. on Sunday. RockSport offers day passes for $12 and a variety of special pricing throughout the week for activities such as Monday Night Madness, ladies and youth nights, and kids climb time. The center provides all the necessary equipment, which you can rent for $5 per day.

SHOOTING

SAGE HILL CLAY SPORTS
7370 Desert Way, Reno, NV
(775) 851-1123
www.sagehillclays.com

Practice makes perfect on the trap fields and skeet ranges at Sage Hill Clay Sports. The club is also home to several leagues and hosts tournaments throughout the year. Tucked in the foothills south of Reno on the way to Virginia City, it's a little tricky to find, so call the number above for recorded directions.

SKATEBOARDING

With the rising popularity of skateboarding, boarders are deserting the sidewalks for sophisticated parks that challenge their abilities. In addition to the parks below, you can also twist and turn at the Incline Skate Park on Tahoe and South-wood Boulevards in Incline Village, the Silver Lake Skate Park at 8855 Red Baron Boulevard and the Panther Valley Skate Park on Link Lane in Reno. See the Kidstuff chapter for more information.

IDLEWILD PARK SKATEBOARD PARK
Idlewild Park
1900 Idlewild Drive, Reno, NV
(775) 334-2262
www.cityofreno.com

This is a 13,000-square-foot park located at Idlewild that is open to the public. Although recommended, safety equipment is not required, so it's skate-at-your-own-risk. The park is open year-round, weather permitting, during daylight hours.

RATTLESNAKE MOUNTAIN SKATEBOARD PARK AT MIRA LOMA PARK
Mira Loma Drive and McCarran Boulevard
Reno, NV
(775) 334-2262
www.cityofreno.com

One of the newest and largest skateboard parks in the area, Rattlesnake Mountain has quickly become the place to be for the skateboard crowd. Its 38,000 square feet has enough ramps, bowls, and pipes to satisfy even the most ardent boarders.

SOUTH TAHOE SKATEBOARD PARK
Bijou Park
Al Tahoe Boulevard
South Lake Tahoe, CA
(530) 542-6055
www.recreationintahoe.com

This city-run park requires helmets and pads. It's located in Bijou Park on Al Tahoe Boulevard, 1 mile from US 50. The park is open from dawn to dusk during the non-snow months.

SOARING

One of the most spectacular and serene ways to view the grandeur of the Reno/Tahoe area is from 10,000 feet in the cockpit of a glider. If you think that the excitement of flying motorless high above the Sierra might be your thing, check out these area companies that provide glider rides and lessons. And don't forget your camera!

SOAR MINDEN
Minden-Tahoe Airport, Minden, NV
(775) 782-7627, (800) 345-7627
www.soarminden.com

Soar Minden provides year-round glider flights from the Minden-Tahoe Airport. It charges $110 to $225 for a one-person ride and $175 to $290 for a two-person flight. The cost depends on the time aloft. This company soars over the Carson Valley but high enough to catch a great view of Lake Tahoe. It also provides private pilot lessons. Ardent fliers can take advantage of package rates that include hotel and unlimited flying.

To get to the Minden-Tahoe Airport from Reno, take US 395 south to Airport Road, just south of Carson City. Follow Airport Road for about 1 mile to the large paved parking area. From Lake Tahoe take US 50 to US 395 and go south on US 50 to Airport Road. Turn left onto Airport Road and drive down the road to the airport.

SOAR TRUCKEE
Martis Creek Dam Road
Near Truckee-Tahoe Airport, Truckee, CA
(530) 587-6702, (866) 762-7875
www.soartruckee.com
Soar Truckee is located at the Truckee-Tahoe Airport, just a few miles north of Lake Tahoe on CA 267 (see the Getting Here, Getting Around chapter for details on the airport). This soaring center has everything to keep you entertained—lessons, scenic rides, towing services, rental gliders, and a campground for pilots and passengers. The sightseeing flights are usually flown a little north of the airport, but Lake Tahoe is still visible. (See the Day Trips chapter for more to see and do in Truckee.) Soar Truckee is open mid-May to mid-November.

TROPIC BIRD SOARING
Minden-Tahoe Airport, Minden, NV
(775) 783-1817
www.tropicbirdsoaring.com
If you're a glider pilot and want to sharpen your skills, Tropic Bird Soaring has a state-of-the-art Schempp-Hirth Duo Discus available for hire and instruction. The daily rental rate of $340 includes all equipment but not the tows. Reservations are required.

SOFTBALL

No one in Nevada or California will dispute the fact that softball is the "King of Sports" in the Reno/Tahoe area. The cities of Reno and Sparks are home to most of the teams because of the cooperative weather, but leagues do exist around the lake as soon as the snow melts. In Sparks alone, parks and recreation figures estimate that about 8,700 people (out of a population of 65,000) play softball. Between Reno, Sparks, and Lake Tahoe, you can hook up with one of hundreds of teams in a number of different leagues depending upon your age, skill level, and gender. The leagues consist of 18 and older fastpitch, modified pitch, church co-ed, adult slow-pitch, senior, 65-plus senior, youth slow-pitch, youth fastpitch, and ponytail. So you can see that there's a league and an ability level for anyone who wants to "chuck that white pill around."

For more information on softball leagues near you, contact the following organizations:

- **City of Sparks Parks and Recreation,** (775) 353-2376; www.ci.sparks.nv.us
- **Incline Village Parks and Recreation,** (775) 832-1322, (775) 832-1310; www.ivgid.org/recreation Reno Recreation Department, (775) 334-2262; cityofreno.com
- **South Tahoe Parks and Recreation,** (530) 542-6056, www.ci.south-lake-tahoe.ca.us
- **Tahoe City Park & Recreation Department,** Public Utility District, (530) 583-3796; www.tahoecitypud.com

ℹ **Sparks is one of the largest softball communities per capita in the nation.**

SWIMMING

If your accommodations in the Reno/Tahoe area offer a swimming pool, you won't have far to go to beat the heat or to get some exercise. You can also head to one of the glorious beaches at Lake Tahoe or to one of the area's public swimming pools to swim your laps. Remember, however, to take precautions in the frigid waters of the lake: You might consider wearing a wetsuit if you're a serious swimmer.

I describe several popular swimming beaches here and also tell you where to find some local swimming pools (see the Parks chapter for additional swimming holes). For exotic dips I suggest you try the soothing waters at Steamboat Villa Hot Springs Spa at 16010 South Virginia Street in Reno (775-853-6600; www.steamboatsprings .org) or David Walley's Resort, Hot Springs & Spa in Genoa, Nevada (775-782-8155; www.david walleys.com). (See the Day Trips chapter for more about Genoa.) You'll also find swimming pools and spas at area health and fitness clubs. Weather permitting, I highly recommend a leisurely day at the spa and swimming lagoon at High Camp Bath & Tennis Club at Squaw Valley USA (see the description under "Tennis" in this chapter).

Swimming Pools

ALF SORENSON COMMUNITY CENTER
1400 Baring Boulevard, Sparks, NV
(775) 353-2385 (indoor)

CITY OF SOUTH LAKE TAHOE POOL
1180 Rufus Allen Boulevard
South Lake Tahoe, CA
(530) 542-6056 (indoor/outdoor)

DEER PARK POOL
1700 Prater Way, Sparks, NV
(775) 353-2385 (outdoor)

IDLEWILD POOL
1805 Idlewild Drive, Reno, NV
(775) 334-2267 (outdoor)

NORTHEAST POOL
1301 Valley Road, Reno, NV
(775) 324-2262 (outdoor)

NORTHWEST POOL
2925 Apollo Way, Reno, NV
(775) 334-2203 (indoor)

OPPIO PARK POOL
2355 Eighteenth Street, Sparks, NV
(775) 353-2385 (outdoor)

TRANER POOL
1600 Carville Drive, Reno, NV
(775) 334-2269 (outdoor)

i Tahoe swimmers win bragging rights competing in the 200-yard Polar Bear Swim near Garwoods restaurant each winter.

Beaches

BALDWIN BEACH
California Highway 89
4 miles north of the "Y" intersection
South Lake Tahoe, CA
This lovely stretch of white sand is tucked along the lakeshore near the Tallac Historic Site. After swimming and enjoying a picnic near the lake, you can take in the cultural events at Tallac (see the chapters on The Arts and Attractions for details). No dogs are allowed.

KINGS BEACH STATE RECREATION AREA
North Lake Boulevard
Kings Beach, CA
(530) 546-4212
www.cal-parks.ca.gov
If you like lots of activity while you swim and sunbathe, this just might be the spot for you. You'll find all the usual water sports at Kings Beach State Recreation Area, along with a day-use park. It's a very busy place, with easy access to shops and restaurants in Kings Beach. Dogs are not allowed.

NEVADA BEACH
Elk Point Road near Zephyr Cove, NV
Next to a popular campground, Nevada Beach offers a large expanse of sand along with amenities such as picnic facilities and restrooms. It's close to the action at Stateline but worlds away when you're lazing on the beach. Come early in the day: The parking lot and picnic spots fill up fast during high season. No dogs allowed.

POPE BEACH
California Highway 89
2 miles north of the "Y" South Lake Tahoe, CA
Pope Beach offers a picturesque oasis of sun and sand close to all the action in South Lake Tahoe. The unobstructed access to the water is great for

families, but leave the family pets at home, since they're not allowed here. You'll find picnic facilities and restrooms on the beach.

SAND HARBOR

Nevada Highway 28
3 miles south of Incline Village, NV
(775) 831-0494
www.parks.nv.gov

With sparkling turquoise water lapping at a mile of white-sand beach, Sand Harbor is considered by many to be the most beautiful beach at Lake Tahoe. You can take nature walks, launch your boat, swim, or just laze on the sand. In the evening, stick around for culture since Sand Harbor is the site of the Lake Tahoe Shakespeare Festival. (For more information on Sand Harbor, see The Arts chapter and the description of Lake Tahoe–Nevada State Park in the Parks chapter.)

SECRET HARBOR

Nevada Highway 28
2.5 miles south of Sand Harbor, NV

Although Secret Harbor is no secret to Insiders, its tiny beaches are completely hidden from sightseers on NV 28. Clothing is optional here, which is known locally as the Nude Beaches. You won't find groups of naked people standing along stretches of sand staring at one another, however. Access to the water is found in a series of coves, each secluded from the next. It's also a great place for dogs. To reach the lake from the parking lot above requires a walk of between a half mile and a mile, but the beauty and seclusion at the end of it is well worth every step. (For more information on Secret Harbor and nearby beaches, see the description of Lake Tahoe–Nevada State Park in the Parks chapter.)

TENNIS

You'll find tennis courts in public parks, on school grounds, and at resorts and hotels in the Reno/Tahoe area. If you're used to playing at or near sea level, don't be surprised if you're gasping in the thin mountain air after just a few games. You can take heart knowing your stamina and game should return to normal after a few days of getting used to the higher elevation, however.

Tennis facilities in the area are too numerous to list. As an Insider I suggest several places guaranteed to be winners if tennis is part of your vacation. I also direct you to some public courts sprinkled around the area. For more locations you can call parks departments (see the Parks chapter) or inquire about tennis facilities when booking your accommodations.

INCLINE VILLAGE TENNIS COMPLEX

964 Incline Way
Incline Village, NV
(775) 832-1235
www.ivgid.org

In a lovely mountain setting, the Incline Village Tennis Complex is sure to meet all of your tennis needs and expectations. Awarded a National Facility Award by the United States Tennis Association, marking it as one of the top 10 facilities in the country, the facility includes a pro shop, viewing deck, backboard, and 24-hour stringing service, along with 11 outdoor courts. You can participate in tournaments, take lessons and clinics, and just play for enjoyment. Fees are lower for Incline Village residents and their guests or for those staying in accommodations that include IVGID recreation passes. Because of heavy demand, I strongly suggest you call ahead to reserve your court. The courts are generally open mid-April through September, depending on snowfall.

LAKERIDGE TENNIS CLUB

6000 Plumas Street
Reno, NV
(775) 827-3300
www.ltcreno.com

A members-only club, Lakeridge Tennis Club has 14 outdoor and 4 indoor courts. Along with playing tennis year-round, you can also enjoy all the amenities of a full-service health club. For dedicated players living in the Reno area, it's the best place to immerse yourself in the game.

NORTH TAHOE REGIONAL PARK
875 National Avenue
Tahoe Vista, CA
(530) 546-5043
www.ntpud.org

You can volley long after the sun goes down on the five lighted tennis courts at North Tahoe Regional Park. It's first-come, first-served, so pack a picnic lunch or enjoy a short hike in the park if you need to wait for a court (see the Parks chapter for more information on the park).

NORTHSTAR-AT-TAHOE
California Highway 267
6 miles north of Lake Tahoe
(530) 562-1010
www.skinorthstar.com/summer/tennis.html

Northstar-at-Tahoe offers tennis lessons, camps, and leisure play for residents and guests only. If you're looking for an all-inclusive resort experience that includes tennis, Northstar is a great choice. Ask about specific packages when booking accommodations. (See the Winter Sports and Resorts chapters for more details about this fun-filled family resort.)

RENO TENNIS CENTER
2601 Plumas Street, Reno, NV
(775) 689-2975
www.cityofreno.com

Owned and managed by the city of Reno, the 16 outdoor courts at the Reno Tennis Center are busy all year. It's a popular site for tournaments and group events, which can be arranged for reasonable fees. The city also sponsors a variety of tennis events here, including junior clinics and lessons. For a listing of neighborhood courts, consult the Web site.

SQUAW VALLEY USA
California Highway 89
6 miles north of Tahoe City, CA
(530) 581-7255
www.squaw.com

It might be hard to keep your eye on the ball when playing at Squaw Valley USA: The scenery is absolutely first-rate, even if your game isn't. You can play at an elevation of 6,200 feet at the Resort at Squaw Creek or huff and puff your way through a set at High Camp Bath & Tennis Club at 8,200 feet (obviously, this is summer-only playing). A variety of packages, lessons, clinics, and leisure-play options are available, so I suggest you call to find what suits you best.

Indisputably a world-class resort, Squaw is a winner year-round, with activities galore and a natural setting guaranteed to take your breath away. (I tell you more about this very special resort in the Winter Sports chapter.)

WALKING/RUNNING

You can run and walk almost anywhere, but let's face it, some terrain is more scenic and suitable for outings than others. I assume most walkers and runners prefer fairly level courses that are well defined (even though a few super jocks sprint up steep mountain trails designed for hiking), so keeping in mind this average walker/runner, I tell you about some paved and some dirt paths that are free of obstacles and easy to navigate in running or walking shoes.

INCLINE VILLAGE/LAKESHORE BOULEVARD
Incline Village, NV

For scenic Lake Tahoe views and peeks at luxurious gated estates, you can run, walk, or bike the 2.5-mile paved path along Lakeshore Boulevard in Incline Village. For your first visit to Lake Tahoe, it's a great way to get oriented and to ease into the laid-back tempo of mountain life. The level course parallels the shore of the lake, winding through huge trees and past gorgeous beaches. You can access the path easily all along the way, but it's convenient to park at the Hyatt Regency Lake Tahoe Resort & Casino and begin your outing there. Don't forget the family dog (leashed): The route is a veritable dog show, with every breed imaginable on display by proud owners. At the end of your walk, I suggest enjoying your favorite drink by the firepit on the beach in front of the Hyatt (see the Resorts chapter for details).

POPE-BALDWIN BIKE PATH
California Highway 89
0.5 mile north of the "Y" to Camp Richardson
South Lake Tahoe, CA

Drinking in the gorgeous South Shore Lake Tahoe landscape from this 3.4-mile paved path is entertainment in itself. But you can also take in cultural events at Tallac Historic Site, enjoy a wide variety of outdoor sports at Camp Richardson, and stop for refreshments at picnic spots and restaurants along the way (see the Attractions and Vacation Rentals chapters for more details).

STEAMBOAT DITCH TRAIL
Reno, NV

Beginning at the California–Nevada border near Verdi, Steamboat Ditch carries irrigation water for 48 miles through ranches and housing developments to its endpoint near Rhodes Road south of Reno. Although its main purpose for many years has been to water thirsty ranchlands and farmlands, the trail used for maintaining the ditch has become one of the most popular walking, running, and biking routes in Reno.

The ecosystem supported along the banks of the ditch is a kaleidoscope of nature, changing with the seasons to offer up delightful surprises for the unsuspecting outdoor enthusiast. In spring and summer you see an amazing array of flowers bursting with color against the beige desert landscape—the regal purple of hardy thistles, the brilliant pink of dainty wild roses, and the soft gray of fuzzy pussy willows. In fall you enjoy the bright oranges and golds of leaves as they drop lazily into the flowing water, and in winter you see the delicate white patterns of crusty snow and ice as they freeze along the ditch banks and the trail.

You can access the trail from a variety of spots as it wanders through Reno, but I suggest trying Horsemans Park at the corner of Skyline and Pioneer Drives.

The trail is bisected by roads as it courses through Reno, so occasionally you need to cross streets and pick up the trail on the other side.

It's also an easement through private land, so remember to respect the property rights and privacy of those living along the trail. The trail is one of the most popular areas for exercising dogs, and dogs can run free if they're well behaved. One last note—don't be surprised if the ditch is dry in winter: The water runs only April through October.

TRUCKEE RIVER RECREATION TRAIL
Along California Highway 89
1.5 miles north of the River Ranch
Tahoe City, CA

Hugging the banks of the Truckee River as it flows from its source at Fanny Bridge, the Truckee River Recreation Trail is a relatively flat, paved path that meanders for about 4.5 miles next to CA 89. Along the trail you'll meet lots of joggers, walkers, and bikers, and in the river you'll see rafters, tubers, and anglers. It's a strikingly beautiful section of the river, with enormous trees shading the crystal-clear water. You can also stop at the River Ranch for people-watching and refreshments as part of your outing (see the description of the River Ranch in the "Rafting" section of this chapter and in the Winter Sports chapter).

TRUCKEE RIVER WALK
Arlington and Island Avenues
Reno, NV

Strolling along the Truckee River Walk, you can trace the route of the river as it flows from west to east through various neighborhoods in Reno. (For details about what you'll see along this paved path, see the Attractions chapter.) Dogs must be leashed.

VIRGINIA LAKE
1980 Lakeside Drive, Reno, NV
(775) 334-2262

In a busy urban neighborhood, Virginia Lake is a mecca for runners and walkers. It's a great people-watching and bird-feeding spot but won't offer much in the way of solitude (see the Parks chapter for more details).

WEST SHORE BIKE PATH
Along California Highway 89 between Tahoe City, CA, and Sugar Pine Point State Park
The West Shore Bike Path winds for about 9 miles between Tahoe City and Sugar Pine Point State Park, passing beaches, picnic areas, and the small towns of Tahoma and Homewood. You can walk or run any section along the way, stopping for sightseeing and meals. The paved route crosses CA 89 several times, so you need to be alert to traffic. If you're looking for a quiet walk, this popular path may be too busy for you, especially during high season. You can access the path in Tahoe City or farther along the way by parking at Kaspian Campground, about 4 miles south of Tahoe City on CA 89, or at Ed Z'berg Sugar Pine Point State Park.

WATERCRAFT RENTAL

See "Boat and Watercraft Rentals" under "Boating" earlier in this chapter.

WATERSKIING

Only water-skiers truly understand that special thrill of skimming effortlessly across the surface of a sparkling body of water. With a number of lakes nearby, you can indulge in this sport to your heart's content in the Reno/Tahoe area.

If you have your own boat and equipment, you can launch at a number of sites on Lake Tahoe, such as Cave Rock Marina, about 7 miles north of Stateline on US 50; Sand Harbor, about 4 miles south of Incline Village on NV 28; and Captain Jon's at 7220 North Lake Boulevard in Tahoe Vista. You can also head out to neighboring lakes, such as Pyramid and Lahontan or Donner Lake, on I-80 near Truckee, California, and Boca Reservoir, about 9 miles east of Truckee on I-80.

If you're looking for lessons or a tow, you can try one of the water-ski schools at Lake Tahoe: They'll furnish everything you need (including the all-important wetsuit) to guarantee a great time on the water.

ACTION WATERSPORTS OF TAHOE
3411 U.S. Highway 50
South Lake Tahoe, CA
(530) 544-5387
www.action-watersports.com
Action Watersports of Tahoe can outfit you with almost any equipment you could want for fun on the water. You can rent Jet Skis, SeaDoos, WaveRunners, and a variety of boats. They also offer water-ski lessons. If all this isn't enough excitement for you, ask them to hook you into a parachute for an aerial view of the shoreline from their parasailing rig. (See also the previous listing under "Boating" in this chapter.)

LAKE TAHOE WATER-SKI SCHOOL
Camp Richardson Resort
1900 Jameson Beach Road
South Lake Tahoe, CA
(530) 544-7747, (530) 577-7928
(530) 542-6570
www.camprich.com
For a great time on water skis, at Camp Richardson Resort all you need is to show up with a camera and a smile. For about $150 an hour Lake Tahoe Water-Ski School provides everything you need—wetsuits and skis, plus a boat with an experienced driver. The company also offers 2-mile tows for around $50. A full-service resort on a gorgeous stretch of Lake Tahoe frontage, Camp Richardson has all the amenities needed to keep you entertained all day long (for details see the chapters on Camping and RVing and Vacation Rentals).

PYRAMID LAKE
Nevada Highway 445
33 miles northeast of Reno, NV
(775) 476-1155, (775) 574-1000
On a calm sunny day, Pyramid Lake is an absolutely prime choice for waterskiing. Its huge expanse of pristine water and miles of isolated beaches ensure quality fun in the sun without being on top of other outdoor enthusiasts. You need to be mindful of the wind, however: Skiing

on this placid playground can quickly become a risky venture when the wind churns the surface into a sea of dangerous whitecaps. (See the Day Trips chapter for a detailed description of this lovely desert oasis.)

YOGA

In their pursuit of good health and fitness, an increasing number of people in the Reno/Tahoe area are looking to the ancient art of yoga for exercise and healing. For some aficionados it offers another health practice in addition to other exercise forms, while for others it becomes a total conditioning program and even a way of life. Space doesn't permit me to discuss all the various forms of yoga, but classes on all levels are available in the area.

First Class at The Yoga Center, 720 Tahoe Street #C in Reno (775-881-7848; www.tycreno .com), is designed to demystify yoga and inform first-timers of the many benefits of this form of discipline. The center also has a full schedule of classes for varying abilities and includes prenatal and children's sessions. Many health and fitness clubs include yoga in their class schedules. You can find classes in Reno at Sports West Athletic Club, 1575 South Virginia Street (775-348-6666), and in the North Shore Lake Tahoe area at High Altitude Fitness, 880 Northwood Boulevard, Incline Village, Nevada (775-831-4212).

GOLF

If golf is your game, you'll be delighted to know that the Reno/Tahoe area has enough luscious layouts to last you your golfing lifetime. With the increase in population over the past decade or so, the demand for more golf courses has been intense. The result has been a plethora of links to keep even the most hard-core players swinging. The variety of terrain can be mind-boggling, from ribbons of green snaking through enormous stands of Jeffrey pines to wide-open fairways laid flat along the desert sands. Whatever best matches your game, you're sure to find it somewhere in the area.

Most courses in the flatlands (Reno, Sparks, and surrounding rural areas) are open year-round, weather depending. So if you've got the stamina, it's possible to ski and golf all in the same day. The mountain courses, however, are seasonal from about April to November. Call or consult Web sites to check if you're in doubt. I'll tell you about the public and semiprivate courses that are open for play, but if you're looking for a private course to join, you can choose from the following: Arrowcreek Country Club, Reno, (775) 850-4653; Hidden Valley Country Club, Reno, (775) 857-4742; Montreux Golf Club Ltd., Reno, (775) 849-1090; the Private Club at Red Hawk, Sparks (775) 626-6000; Somersett Country Club, Reno, (775) 787-1800; and Thunder Canyon Golf & Country Club, Washoe Valley, (775) 884-4597.

Nearby Truckee, California, has become a destination for affluent golfers. Three posh courses have recently opened with all the bells and whistles of luxury living and golfing: Lahontan Golf Club, (530) 550-2400, www.lahontan.com; Old Greenwood, (800) 754-3070, www.old greenwood.com; and The Golf Club at Gray's Crossing, www.grayscrossing.com. If you're interested in golf course living, keep in mind that you don't have to be on a private course. Most public courses have homes lining the fairways, and the most recently built courses are still selling lots for new construction.

In acquainting you with the public courses, I've included the kinds of information that'll help you choose the one to fit your game and style: the yardage (from the men's white tees), pars, U.S. Golfing Association (USGA) ratings and slopes, 18-hole greens fees with cart included (summer rates), reservation policy, and a brief description of each course. Unless stated otherwise, each course has a driving range, putting green, pro shop, and restaurant.

To help orient you to the location of the courses, the chapter is divided into the four standard geographical areas—Reno, Sparks, North Shore Lake Tahoe, and South Shore Lake Tahoe. Some of the courses I mentioned fall outside these areas, but I think they are close enough and worth the drive to play. Consequently, these courses are designated "Worth the Drive" (big pun intended) and are included at the end of the geographical section closest to the course.

So let's tee it up and get started. But remember one other thing: The views from all of the golf courses in the area are so magnificent that you won't mind hooking the occasional ball into the sagebrush or slicing one into that sapphire-blue lake crowned with Canada geese. Honest.

RENO

LAKE RIDGE GOLF COURSE
1218 Golf Club Drive
(775) 825-2200, (800) 815-6966
www.lakeridgegolf.com

This Robert Trent Jones Jr.–designed course built in 1969 has large greens, large tee boxes, large bunkers, and lots of water. Most visitors know the course because of its signature hole—the 15th, a 230-yard par 3, which features a tee box 360 feet above Lake Stanley, requiring a tee shot to an island green. This is probably the most talked-about and most photographed hole in the Reno/Tahoe area. Access to the green is by a footbridge. During winter you are only allowed to walk on this course. The course is located in a prestigious neighborhood and sports a country-club atmosphere with upscale homes lining the fairways. It's closed for several months during winter. Reservations for a group of 20 or more may be made a year in advance. Tee times can be scheduled online. Lake Ridge has been voted the No. 1 course in the Reno/Sparks area for many years.

Yardage: 6,140
Par: 71 USGA rating: 69.1
Slope: 132
Greens fees: $45 to $100
Reservations: 7 days in advance

ROSEWOOD LAKES GOLF COURSE
6800 Pembroke Drive
(775) 857-2892
www.rosewoodlakes.com

This is not a long course, but it is difficult because it plays like a links-style course. Rosewood was built around 60 acres of protected wetlands preserve, and if you don't hit the ball straight, it will end up in the tules. Once the ball enters the wetlands, you are not allowed to retrieve it, so it's important to bring plenty of balls when you play this course. The fairways are flat and open, and the greens are medium size and on the slow side. Water comes into play on every hole, making this a challenging course. The greens fees are some of the cheapest in the area, and it's popular with the locals. The signature eighth hole is a treacherous par 4, with a bunker and lake lining the entire right side and a lake lining the left. An accurate drive is a must, making the second shot to the large, elevated green easy. One par 3 is a blind tee shot because the tules have grown so tall that they completely block the view to the green. This course, designed by Brad Benz and built in 1991, is one of the top-conditioned municipal courses in the West because of its easy access to year-round water.

Yardage: 6,104
Par: 72
USGA rating: 68
Slope: 115
Greens fees: $33, excluding cart
Reservations: 7 days in advance; weekends, the previous Monday

> **i** You can save money at Rosewood Lakes Golf Course by using the City of Reno Discount Card that comes with membership in the course's men's and women's clubs.

WASHOE COUNTY GOLF COURSE
2601 South Arlington Avenue
(775) 828-6640
www.washoegolf.org

Washoe County is the oldest golf course in Nevada. Built in 1936, this course is well established, close to downtown Reno, and popular among locals, especially the seniors (greens fees are cheap for residents in comparison to other courses around the area). The first hole has a great view from an elevated tee box, overlooking a dogleg left par 4. A good drive here sets you up for an easy shot to the green, but trees lining both sides of the fairway can intimidate the best hitters. In fact, trees line the fairways on the entire front nine. Don't let the flat and wide fairways on the front fool you into thinking the entire course is flat: The back nine is extremely hilly and tight, and you still have to contend with some trees. The course has small bent-grass greens, well protected by sand bunkers. The course is always in good shape. Try to do your best scoring on the relatively easy front nine, because you'll need all the strokes you can get for the back.

Yardage: 6,468
Par: 72
USGA rating: 68.8
Slope: 124
Greens fees: $20 to $30, excluding cart
Reservations: 10 days in advance

WOLF RUN GOLF CLUB
1400 Wolf Run Road
(775) 851-3301
www.wolfrungolfclub.com

The Wolf Run golf course winds its way through rolling desert terrain southwest of Reno and offers great views of the valley, downtown, and Mt. Rose. Named for the University of Nevada, Reno, athletic teams, it's also home to their golf teams. The course was designed by John Fleming, Steve Van Meter, and Lou Eiguren, and the three made sure that the high desert and loads of sagebrush come into play on almost every hole. The signature hole, No. 15, is a long par 5 with a large green surrounded by Thomas Creek, creating an island-green effect and making it a great three-shot hole. The course has a no-kidding 19th hole. This short hole is designed in the shape of a wolf's paw and can be used to settle any carryover bets or can be used as a play-off hole. The course is extremely enjoyable and very playable. You can book reservations online.

Yardage: 6,086
Par: 71
USGA rating: 67.9
Slope: 122
Greens fees: $45 to $75
Reservations: 14 days in advance

SPARKS

D'ANDREA GOLF CLUB
2900 South D'Andrea Parkway
(775) 331-6363
www.dandreagolf.com

Designed by renowned golf course architect Keith Foster, D'Andrea was opened to the public in 2000. This is the course for those who love the high desert. The back nine offers especially spectacular views as elevation gains offer ever-expanding vistas. The signature hole here is the 162-yard par 3 No. 6, with a green that is almost completely surrounded by water. A rock wall in front of the hole makes the distances quite deceiving. Even if you're unable to ace the hole, however, you'll be sure to enjoy the breathtaking view of Reno and Sparks and the surrounding mountains.

Because it's on the high plateaus in the desert and has no trees, folks should try to get out in the early morning or late afternoon.

Yardage: 6,501
Par: 71
USGA rating: 68.5
Slope: 121
Greens fees: $45 to $100
Reservations: 7 days in advance

THE LINKS AT KILEY RANCH
5800 Kiley Links Drive
(775) 354-2100
www.golf.travelnevada.com

Designed by local LPGA Hall of Fame golfer Patty Sheehan, along with Mark Miller, The Links at Kiley Ranch is the newest course to debut in the Reno/Sparks area. As part of the burgeoning new community of Kiley Ranch, this executive nine-hole course adds a welcome inexpensive alternative for golfers who want to practice their short game and for those who are just learning the sport. It's open to the public year-round, weather permitting. The course is about 7 miles north of I-80 in Sparks off Sparks and Henry Orr boulevards.

Yardage: 1,391
Par: 27
Slope: 55.9/79
Green fees: $25 to $30, excluding cart

RED HAWK GOLF CLUB
6600 North Wingfield Parkway
(775) 626-6000
www.theresortatredhawk.com

The Lakes Course at Red Hawk Golf Club offers magnificent views of the Truckee Meadows and the surrounding mountains. Robert Trent Jones designed this course around the marshlands and lakes of an old hunting club, so water comes into play on several holes. The fairways are so plush that you almost hate taking a divot, and the bent-grass greens are extremely well manicured and fast. The course is lengthy with wide-open fairways, but beware when the wind kicks up.

This is one of the examples of the scenic backdrop being so magnificent that you really don't mind playing a lousy game of golf. The golf carts are equipped with state-of-the-art measuring devices. Red Hawk features a Golf Learning Center, a program designed to teach every part of the game for every level of play. Red Hawk also has the Hills Course, a private layout designed by Hale Irwin.

Yardage: 6,138
Par: 72
USGA rating: 68.4
Slope: 119
Greens fees: $50 to $100
Reservations: 14 days in advance

WILDCREEK GOLF COURSE
3500 Sullivan Lane
(775) 673-3100
www.wildcreekgc.com
This club has two courses—an 18-hole regulation course and a 9-hole executive par 3 course.

Course One—The 18-hole design features rolling fairways, lots of water, bunkers, and sagebrush. The course was carved from a hillside, making the fairways uneven and leading Insiders to nickname the course "Wild Bounce." Besides the undulating fairways, the course has six lakes and a creek running through it to make your game extremely challenging. The bent-grass greens are big and well protected by lots of sand. Some of the holes feature elevated tees and terraced greens, making the course one of the toughest to play in the area. It hosted three Senior Tour events in the 1980s.

Yardage: 6,244
Par: 72
USGA rating: 69.4
Slope: 127
Greens fees: $35 to $59
Reservations: 14 days in advance

Course Two—The nine-hole executive par 3 features tiny greens and tight fairways. Several water hazards are sprinkled in among the holes, making shot placement a priority. The course is always crowded, but it is an excellent place to come to hone your short-game skills or to teach a new golfer.

Yardage: 1,300
Par: 27
Greens fees: $13 for nine holes
Reservations: Walk-on

Worth the Drive

CRYSTAL PEAK GOLF COURSE
444 River Pines Drive, Verdi, NV
(775) 345-1551
www.verdi.us
Just 10 miles west of Reno on Interstate 80, Crystal Peak Golf Course is the newest to join the growing ranks of links in the Reno/Tahoe area. Created by Love Golf Design, it boasts several distinctions: It's the only championship nine-hole course in the Reno/Sparks area and the only course that uses an island in the Truckee River. The island houses the green for the second hole along with the par 3 third hole. Meandering through a spectacular forest of Jeffrey pines, the course takes full advantage of its mile of riverfront property. A nature lover's delight, it also challenges even the best golfers with its demand for accuracy. The interesting array of bunkers and the fairways lined with tall trees and sagebrush demand thoughtful shots in order to score well. It's a family-owned enterprise, so don't expect the glitz of full-service courses with restaurants and pro shops. Playing a round of golf here is also communing with nature. You can golf here from April to November, weather permitting.

Yardage: 2,520 to 3,253 for nine holes
Par: 71.2
Slope: 131
Greens fees: $30 for 9 holes, excluding cart
Reservations: Call anytime

GOLF CLUB AT FERNLEY

4000 Farm District Road, Fernley, NV
(775) 835-6933
www.fernleygolfclub.com

This 18-hole bent-grass course, opened in 1996, is located in Fernley, Nevada, about 35 miles east of Sparks. It was built among the sagebrush of the high desert, but just to add a little more of a challenge, designer Bob Bingham laced 30 lakes around the 18 holes. It plays easily, though, if you can control your shots. It's almost a guarantee that errant shots will find water or the sagebrush. Most greens are moderately fast and protected by white-sand bunkers. The course plays fast and is never crowded during the week. The only drawback is the fact that during summer, temperatures in Fernley can reach or even exceed the 100-degree mark. The course features a 605-yard par 5 that doglegs around the sagebrush and a lake. The signature hole is a short par 3 called "The Hanging Tree," which features water in the front and the back and a 100-year-old cotton-wood tree looming next to the green. The course is wide open with only a few trees, so when the wind kicks up, usually during the afternoon, it can wreak havoc with your game.

Yardage: 6,085
Par: 72
USGA rating: 68
Slope: 120
Greens fees: $25 to $40
Reservations: 7 days in advance

NORTH SHORE LAKE TAHOE

COYOTE MOON GOLF COURSE

10685 Northwoods Boulevard
Truckee, CA
(530) 587-0886
www.coyotemoongolf.com

If you're torn between hiking through the incredibly beautiful Sierra Nevada and wanting to get in a great game of golf, your dilemma has been solved. Coyote Moon Golf Course offers players unbelievable views and vistas on its 250 acres of rolling fairways through the mountainsides and secluded pines of Tahoe-Donner. Designer Brad Bell took full advantage of the natural setting, incorporating the towering pines, enormous granite outcroppings, and beautiful Trout Creek to add dramatic elements of risk to the course. The signature 13th hole, a 227-yard par 3, is a 100-plus-foot elevation drop over Trout Creek. According to *Golf Today* magazine, "the front 9 is captivating, and the back 9 spectacular."

Yardage: 6,211
Par: 72
USGA rating: 69.1
Slope: 130
Greens fees: $100 to $160
Reservations: 30 days in advance

i Technology gives players a big boost at Coyote Moon Golf Course, where carts come equipped with GPS and computer yardage systems.

INCLINE VILLAGE GOLF RESORT

690 Wilson Way (mountain course)
(775) 832-1150
955 Fairway Boulevard (championship course)
(775) 832-1146

Incline Village, NV
(866) 925-4653 (reservations only)
www.golfincline.com

Owned and managed by the Incline Village General Improvement District (IVGID), Incline Village Golf Resort boasts both an 18-hole championship course and an 18-hole mountain course. The championship course was closed for two years for renovation but welcomed players back in 2005.

The Championship Course—Consistently rated four stars by *Golf Digest* magazine, this course has tight, rolling fairways bordered by towering pines. A mountain creek snakes its way through the course and provides for strategically placed water hazards on 13 of the 18 holes. Robert Trent Jones Sr. called this course "an example of an ideal mountain course," and he should know because he designed it. His layout demands accuracy as well as distance. Golfers are faced with heavily bunkered greens on almost every hole (more than 50 sand traps are scattered around the course). The greens are large, undulating, and fast. Almost every shot here poses a challenge to the most experienced golfer. The signature hole, No. 16, is a 406-yard par 4 with a dogleg-right fairway and a spectacular view of Lake Tahoe in the distance. The second shot on this magnificent hole requires you to hit over a ravine to an isolated green. Golf Digest always rates this course as one of the best in the West. It lives up to Jones's philosophy that every hole should be a tough par but an easy bogey.

Yardage: 6,447
Par: 72
USGA rating: 70.2
Slope: 129
Greens fees: $99 to $174
Reservations: 14 days in advance

The Mountain Course—This par 58, 3,500-yard course was designed by Robert Trent Jones Jr. and is rated as one of the top five executive courses in the United States. It is also cut out of the gigantic pines and has outstanding views of Lake Tahoe. The course is hilly and has all the hazards of the championship course with the exception of length. The mountain course features 14 par 3 holes, averaging more than 170 yards in length. This course has played host to the National Executive Course Championship.

Yardage: 3,513
Par: 58
USGA rating: 56.6
Slope: 94
Greens fees: $44–$64
Reservations: 14 days in advance

NORTHSTAR-AT-TAHOE GOLF COURSE
129 Basque Drive at Northstar-at-Tahoe
Truckee, CA
(530) 562-2490, (530) 562-3290 for tee times
www.skinorthstar.com

Spectacular scenery of the mountains near Lake Tahoe add to this course's appeal. Its 18 holes are intertwined among woods and fields, and golfers like to call this kind of course "two-faced" because the front and back nine are totally different. The front nine is played through a valley with rolling, wide-open fairways, and the back nine changes looks as it climbs into the tall pines. These holes have skinny fairways, numerous doglegs, and require tricky, target golf shots. The course has plenty of water and sand bunkers, and its par 3s are gorgeous. The greens are medium size and fast. The course has a habit of eating golf balls, so bring plenty. It's usually open May through October. The course is located in the Northstar-at-Tahoe resort (see the Resorts chapter).

Yardage: 6,015
Par: 72
USGA rating: 67.5
Slope: 125
Greens fees: $45 to $99
Reservations: 14 days in advance

OLD BROCKWAY GOLF CLUB
7900 North Lake Boulevard
Corner of California Highways 267 and 28
Kings Beach, CA
(530) 546-9909
www.oldbrockway.com

This nine-hole course is located a block from Lake Tahoe and features rolling hills, a meandering creek, tall pines, and excellent views. Built in 1924 and home of the first Bing Crosby Tournament, Brockway is one of the oldest courses at Lake Tahoe. It was also a favorite of the Rat Pack (Frank Sinatra, Dean Martin, Sammy Davis Jr., and crew). Extremely challenging because of its narrow fairways and wooded roughs, it is usually the first to open and the last to close at the lake. Reminiscent of its colorful history, the clubhouse showcases the Old Tahoe style of architecture, with massive logs and soaring ceilings. I suggest lunch or an after-round drink on the lovely patio that faces the lake. The following information is based on 18 holes of play.

Yardage: 6,054
Par: 72
USGA rating: 67.6
Slope: 125
Greens fees: $35 to $75, excluding cart
Reservations: 7 days in advance

For news, events, and more detailed information concerning the golf courses in the Reno/Tahoe area, visit www .golf thehighsierra.com.

PONDEROSA GOLF CLUB
10040 Reynold Way
Truckee, CA
(530) 587-3501
www.ponderosagolfcourse.com
This is one of the easiest courses at Lake Tahoe and is ideal for the beginning golfer. The nine-hole course is mostly flat and nestled beneath towering pines, but it is forgiving. The course has no water hazards, and the greens are in excellent condition. Don't play this course unless you like to wait while playing. The course is open from May through October. The following information is based on 18 holes of play.

Yardage: 5,800
Par: 70
USGA rating: 66.6
Slope: 111
Greens fees: $50, excluding cart (call or check Web site to verify)
Reservations: 10 days in advance

RESORT AT SQUAW CREEK
400 Squaw Creek Road
Olympic Valley, CA
(530) 583-6300, (530) 581-6637
(800) 327-3353 (reservations only)
www.squawcreek.com/lake-tahoe-golf.php
This Robert Trent Jones Jr.–designed course is everything you would expect from both the prolific designer and a Lake Tahoe resort course: beautiful mountain and meadow views and a challenging course set among existing wetlands and forested hills. The course has been honored by *Golf* magazine as one of the "Top 10 Courses You Can Play," and by Golf Today as one of the top resort courses in northern California. It's lush and plays like a links course, with tees, landing areas, and greens strategically placed to take advantage of the natural hazards. The front nine has narrow fairways and rows and rows of towering pines. The back nine has elevated wooden cart paths built over the wetlands and has a propensity for eating golf balls, so bring an extra supply. The signature hole is the par 5 13th, which is 500 yards long and requires at least a 200-yard drive off the tee to carry the wetlands. See the Winter Sports, Recreation, and Resorts chapters for more information on Squaw Valley. The course is usually open from April through October.

Yardage: 6,010
Par: 71
USGA rating: 69.3
Slope: 125
Greens fees: $60 to $115
Reservations: 30 days in advance for nonguests; 3 months in advance for guests

TAHOE CITY GOLF COURSE
251 North Lake Boulevard
Tahoe City, CA
(530) 583-1516
Located behind a commercial block off the main thoroughfare in Tahoe City and easily spotted from Fanny Bridge, this nine-hole course is hilly, wooded, and well bunkered. Built in 1917 and designed by May "Queenie" Dunn Hupfel, it is the oldest course in the Tahoe Basin and has some spectacular views of Lake Tahoe, which is right across the street. Its claim to fame is that it drew Hollywood stars like Frank Sinatra, Bing Crosby, and Bob Hope regularly during the 1940s and 1950s, and it has remained a locals' hangout to this day. It is the shortest course at the lake and is open from April through October. The following information is based on 18 holes of play.

Yardage: 5,261
Par: 66
USGA rating: 65.1
Slope: 111
Greens fees: $25 to $75, excluding cart
Reservations: 14 days in advance

TAHOE DONNER GOLF CLUB

11509 Northwoods Boulevard
Truckee, CA
(530) 587-9440
(530)587-9443 (pro shop)
www.tahoedonner.com

This course is located in a residential/resort development and features narrow, tight fairways through the pines. Here, accuracy is more important than power. The first hole is an example of the kind of play needed on the entire course. The hole is a straight-ahead, 450-yard par 5 lined with pines requiring straight hitting. A slice or a hook here is real trouble. A creek comes into play on eight holes, and the course is hilly, with many drops from tee to fairway to green. This course is extremely well maintained and difficult to play. But it may be even more difficult to get a tee time, because residents get first pick during the season that lasts from May through October.

Yardage: 6,587
Par: 72
USGA rating: 71.2
Slope: 128
Greens fees: $150
Reservations: 10 days in advance for weekdays; Friday before for weekends

Worth the Drive

The following golf courses are located in and around the Graeagle area of California adjacent to California Highway 89 and California Highway 70. (See the Day Trips chapter for more information about Graeagle.) This section of the Sierra has been dubbed "The Pebble Beach of the North" because of the many excellent and scenic golf courses in the area that are open for seasonal play. The driving time is about 40 minutes from the North Shore of Lake Tahoe and one hour from Reno.

FEATHER RIVER PARK RESORT

8339 California Highway 89
Blairsden, CA
(530) 836-2328
www.featherriverparkresort.com

Because the holes are short and not intimidating, this course is ideal for senior and junior golfers. Located along the Feather River, this nine-hole course is flat and relatively open. A few pine trees are sprinkled around the course, but they pose little problem and mostly just add to the great scenery. The two par 5 holes on the course are less than 450 yards, making them reachable in two. This course is part of a resort with small cabins and other recreational activities. It has no driving range. The following information is based on 18 holes of play.

Yardage: 5,164
Par: 70
Greens fees: $18 to $22, excluding cart
Reservations: Walk-on

i A 240-yard golf shot at sea level would be a 280-yard shot at Tahoe because of the 6,000-foot elevation.

GOLF CLUB AT WHITEHAWK RANCH

768 Whitehawk Drive, Clio, CA
(530) 836-0394, (800) 332-4295
www.golfwhitehawk.com

Resting against the eastern slope of the Sierra in the Mohawk Valley, this championship course is located in the middle of a housing development. But don't panic: The development only has 200 homes, and the developers have maintained the rustic, rural charm of the mountain atmosphere. They hired Dick Bailey to design the course (a first for this architect), and he did such a good job that the California Golf Writers' Association awarded White-hawk its 1997 Environmental Award for protecting the environment while furthering the game of golf. The course was built in 1996 and includes plenty of pines, water, and 45 acres of native grasses and wildflowers bordering the fairways. Some people think this course is on even par with the prestigious Edgewood at South Shore Lake Tahoe. The course has four signature holes, but the prettiest may be the 10th, which has a magnificent view of the Mohawk Valley. Most of the holes have streamlined fairways and multitiered greens. The course is well maintained, and once again the views will almost make you forget your golf game. Don't come here unless you like a challenge. The Northern California Golf Association added White-hawk to its championship rotation, which includes such renowned courses as Pebble Beach, Spyglass, and the Olympic Club.

Yardage: 6,422
Par: 71
USGA rating: 70.2
Slope: 122
Greens fees: $85 to $140
Reservations: 6 months in advance

GRAEAGLE MEADOWS GOLF COURSE

18 California Highway 89
Graeagle, CA
(530) 836-2323
www.playgraeagle.com

Graeagle Meadows weaves its way through the Mohawk Valley, straddles the Feather River, and makes good use of the towering pines. This course is always in excellent shape and, like so many others in the Sierra, has spectacular scenery. The most renowned landmark is Chief Graeagle, a rock formation to the west of the sixth tee. Ask any Insider to point out his headdress and moccasins at either end of the 2-mile-long formation. Great scenes like this can almost make you forget about the flat, narrow fairways and well-protected greens. The most intimidating hole is the short par 3 16th, with a pine tree blocking the center of the green. The course is usually open from late March through October.

Yardage: 6,345
Par: 72
USGA rating: 70.1
Slope: 128
Greens fees: $30 to $60
Reservations: Anytime during season

PLUMAS PINES GOLF CLUB

402 Poplar Valley Road
Blairsden, CA
(530) 836-1420
www.plumaspinesgolf.com

This golf resort is open to the public and is one of the most popular around if you are a low-handicap player. Another "twofaced" course (distinctively different front and back nines), it has a front nine that lies in a valley surrounded by lots of water and a narrow, hilly back nine that climbs into the pines. One of the best-manicured courses in the Sierra, it demands a high level of play. Water exists on 11 holes, and it has several blind doglegs. The greens are heavily bunkered, and houses parallel many of the holes, making accuracy your prime objective. The signature hole is the 395-yard par 4 No. 9 with its view across a small lake to the clubhouse, which sits on a hill overlooking the course. The most difficult hole may be the 18th, with a double dogleg, an uphill approach, and a tiered green. Some of the holes on this course are the most difficult of all the courses in the area. This golf club is usually open from May through October.

Yardage: 5,894
Par: 72
USGA rating: 68.5
Slope: 123
Greens fees: $55 to $95
Reservations: No limitations

SOUTH SHORE LAKE TAHOE

BIJOU GOLF COURSE

3464 Fairway Boulevard off Johnson Boulevard
South Lake Tahoe, CA
(530) 542-6097
www.ci.south-lake-tahoe.ca.us/

A historic nine-hole executive course built in 1920 in the center of South Lake Tahoe, this course is perfect for all level of players. Bijou Creek winds through the course, providing the water hazards, and of course pine trees add to golfers' frustration. It has a great view of Heavenly Ski Resort and Freal Peak. The course allows only pull carts and doesn't take advance reservations, but it is usually easy to get on. The following information is based on 18 holes of play for a nonresident (pull carts are $3).

Yardage: 4,056
Par: 64
Greens fees: $33, excluding cart
Reservations: None taken in advance

EDGEWOOD TAHOE GOLF COURSE
180 Lake Parkway Stateline, NV
(775) 588-3566
(888) 881-8659 (reservations)
www.edgewood-tahoe.com

This course is *it*—the premier golfing experience in the Reno/Tahoe area. Built along the lush shoreline of Lake Tahoe, Edgewood features both wide-open fairways and narrow ones laced through the pines with both rolling and flat terrain. It is rated by *Golf Digest* as one of the top 25 courses in the country. Edgewood has more than 80 sand traps, many of which protect the large, undulating, and terraced greens that are pro caliber and super fast. Many strategically placed trees come into play; water is a factor on 11 holes. This course is the most difficult to score well on in Nevada. The Crown Jewel of the Sierra, Edgewood has the distinction of having the only holes on the shore of Lake Tahoe: the signature 17th, a 207-yard par 3, and the 574-yard par 5 18th.

This course is a must-play for the true golf aficionado, but its popularity makes it difficult to get a tee time. The course has played host to many professional events and is currently home to the American Century Championship Golf tournament every July (see the Spectator Sports and Annual Events chapters). Do yourself a big golfing favor, and don't leave the area without playing this George Fazio–designed masterpiece.

Yardage: 6,365
Par: 72
USGA rating: 70.2
Slope: 127
Greens fees: $170 to $240
Reservations: 90 days in advance

LAKE TAHOE GOLF COURSE
2500 Emerald Bay Road
South Lake Tahoe, CA
(530) 577-0788
www.laketahoegc.com

This course used to be called the Lake Tahoe Country Club, to give you an idea of the quality of play here. Conveniently located in an alpine meadow surrounded by tall Sierra peaks, the course is just minutes from the glitter of Stateline, Nevada. It's flat to slightly rolling, with the Upper Truckee River and artificial lakes coming into play on 16 holes. The greens are in excellent condition. This layout isn't long, but it is treacherous, making good ball placement a top priority. Over the last decade or so, the course has gone through extensive renovations.

Yardage: 6,160
Par: 71
USGA rating: 68.8
Slope: 120
Greens fees: $60 to $80
Reservations: 60 days in advance

TAHOE PARADISE GOLF COURSE
3021 U.S. Highway 50
South Lake Tahoe, CA
(530) 577-2121
www.tahoeparadisegc.com

This executive course was South Lake Tahoe's first 18-holer. The course is short but once again has all the nasty quirks of a mountain course— narrow fairways, tree-lined roughs, and small greens. But thankfully, water comes into play on only two holes. The most difficult hole is a 377-yard par 4 that requires a tee shot through a gap only 50 yards across. The signature hole is the fifth, a 110-yard par 3 with a lake in front and a view of the surrounding mountain peaks.

Yardage: 4,034
Par: 66
USGA rating: 60.9
Slope: 103
Greens fees: $42 to $60
Reservations: 7 days in advance

Worth the Drive

Carson City, Nevada's capital, and the surrounding Carson Valley sit just over the mountain from Lake Tahoe and are 30 miles down U.S. Highway 395 from Reno. Here, excellent golf courses wait for you to tee one up. All of these courses are definitely worth the drive because they are some of the best maintained in Nevada and are a lot of fun to play.

CARSON VALLEY GOLF COURSE
1027 Riverview Drive
Gardnerville, NV
(775) 265-3181
www.carsonvalleygolf.com
Just by the address, you can guess the biggest hazard on this course: water. The East Fork of the Carson River snakes its way through this 18-hole course, creating a natural water hazard on all but two holes, so bring plenty of extra golf balls. Even though it's not in the mountains, its fairways are still narrow with a lot of rough and out of bounds, but at least you won't have to worry about pine trees—here, it's towering cottonwoods that line the fairways. Although it's a joy to play, it can be quite frustrating if you can't hit a straight shot. Carson Valley has a real rustic feel to it and is located on the outskirts of one of the prettiest small towns in Nevada. (Check out the Day Trips chapter for more to see and do in Gardnerville.)

Yardage: 6,003
Par: 71
USGA rating: 66.8
Slope: 111
Greens fees: $40 to $46
Reservations: 7 days in advance; beyond 7 days, a credit card is required

DAYTON VALLEY GOLF CLUB
51 Palmer Drive, Dayton, NV
(775) 246-7888, (800) 644-3822
www.daytonvalley.com
This is a magnificent Arnold Palmer–designed course located 11 miles east of Carson City in the high desert. The course has been open since 1991, and it ranks among Golf Today's list of top 20 daily-fee courses in northern California and Nevada, which means it is in the same company as Pebble Beach, Spyglass, and Spanish Bay.

Palmer designed a beautiful layout that combines the natural beauty of the high desert with rolling fairways sculpted in a links style. Rolling hills are dotted with sand traps that surround the fairways that must be mastered before reaching the huge, sloping greens. The course has few trees, but strategically placed water hazards come into play on 12 holes. The course is superbly maintained and is known for its plush, velvetlike fairways and immaculate greens. The first par 3 on the front nine is dubbed the "Moon Crater" because the green sits below the tee box in a small glade surrounded by steep hills and sand traps, giving the hole a surreal feel.

The number-one handicapped hole is the par 4 No. 9, which requires you to hit over and around two water hazards. After a good tee shot (more than 230 yards), you still have at least 160 yards, all over water, to carry the green. As with the No. 6, a par on this hole is an accomplishment.

Yardage: 5,897
Par: 72
USGA rating: 68.2
Slope: 128 Greens fees: $35 to $105
Reservations: 2 weeks in advance

EAGLE VALLEY GOLF COURSES
3999 Centennial Park Drive
Carson City, NV
(775) 887-2380
www.eaglevalleygolf.com
This golf facility has two regulation 18-hole courses—The West and The East—which offer two distinctively different modes of play. The West Course has lots of water, trees, sand bunkers, and sagebrush. The East Course is wide open.

The West Course—This links-style course is hilly and requires you to hit the ball straight, since almost every hole is lined with water or sagebrush. It was designed by Jack Snyder in 1977 to challenge you on every hole, and it does that and more. Playing well requires correct club selection and good course management. This course has great views of Carson City as it winds its way up, down, and around the foothills on the northeastern side of town. The 14th tee offers spectacular views of the eastern side of the Sierra. Changes in course elevation and strategically located water and bunkers add to its challenging layout. A round here isn't for the fainthearted golfer. If your game isn't top drawer, you'll no doubt be frustrated.

Yardage: 5,819
Par: 72
USGA rating: 67.3
Slope: 127
Greens fees: $25 to $45
Reservations: 10 days in advance

The East Course—This 18 is wide open and offers a good game for all styles of play. A great course for couples, seniors, juniors, and beginning to intermediate golfers, it features manicured fairways and quick greens. Rambling throughout the flat valley beneath the foothills, it was made for the big hitters who like to go for broke. A wayward shot will usually find another fairway, so trouble is at a minimum here. The East Course is great for walking a quick 9 or riding a leisurely 18.

Yardage: 6,314 **Par:** 72
USGA rating: 68
Slope: 117
Greens fees: $25 to $35
Reservations: 10 days in advance

EMPIRE RANCH GOLF COURSE

1875 Fair Way Drive
Carson City, NV
(775) 885-2100, (888) 227-1335
www.empireranchgolf.com

This course opened in 1997 and is set among the wetlands overlooking the Carson River. Its 27 holes are squeezed between high bluffs and include 46 acres of wetlands and six lakes. You can see that water hazards are plentiful, so bring a lot of golf balls. You can start on any nine holes, so you really have a choice of playing three courses here. Once again, several shots must carry the wetlands, but course designer Cary Beckler was thoughtful of the high handicappers. He designed a bailout option on almost every hole for those who need the help.

Yardage: 6,207
Par: 72
USGA rating: 69
Slope: 124
Greens fees: $20 to $40
Reservations: 7 days in advance

GENOA LAKES GOLF CLUB

1 Genoa Lakes Drive
Genoa, NV
(775) 782-4653, (866) 795-2709
www.genoalakes.com

A semiprivate club with the amenities of a private one, Genoa Lakes is located in Nevada's oldest town. This Peter Jacobson/John Harbottle–designed course is spectacular and rests against the slopes of the eastern Sierra with miles and miles of valley and mountain views. Built around a large wetlands, this links-style course is long and extremely challenging. Water comes into play on 13 holes, and its huge sand traps have a propensity for reaching out and grabbing even the best golf shots. Home of the 1998 U.S. Open Qualifying Tournament, this course will definitely test every part of your game—but again, the views are so magnificent you won't mind shooting a mediocre game of golf. The signature hole is the 13th, a 652-yard par 5, the longest in Nevada. The trick to this course is a well-placed tee shot. Any other type of tee shot is trouble with a capital "T." Partnered with Genoa Lakes Golf Resort (formerly Sierra Nevada Golf Ranch), this course is also known as the Lakes Course.

Yardage: 5,969
Par: 72
USGA rating: 67.0
Slope: 122
Greens fees: $60 to $120
Reservations: 7 days in advance

GENOA LAKES GOLF RESORT
2901 Jacks Valley Road
Genoa, NV
(775) 782-7700, (866) 795-2709
www.genoalakes.com

Formerly Sierra Nevada Golf Ranch, Genoa Lakes Golf Resort (nicknamed the Resort Course) was acquired by Genoa Lakes Golf Club in 2005. Because the two courses are paired, you can schedule tee times for both at the same number and Web site. It was designed in what golf architects call a nonparallel format, meaning holes don't run next to one another. This gives the effect that you and your foursome are the only golfers on the course, because you can't peek over onto the next fairway to see anyone else. The holes are laid out with a sense of solitude in mind.

The front nine begins on the valley floor and climbs 300 feet up the eastern slope of the Sierra. The back nine snakes its way through desert terrain. Water comes into play on four holes, including a spectacular waterfall on No. 17. The course also has 114 sand bunkers and several grass ones lining the greens and fairways. The 10th hole is one of the prettiest, with the entire right side framed by a cascading creek. The signature hole is No. 17, a 165-yard par 3 with a huge island green surrounded on three sides by a lake with a waterfall located in back. The hole with the best view from the tee is the 478-yard sixth. The green on this hole seems to float above the purple-hued valley with the Sierra looming in the background. This is also the number-one-handicapped hole, so don't let the wonderful view distract you.

The facility offers 10 acres of practice area, which the club calls "The Shooting Range" instead of the driving range. It also has the largest clubhouse in Nevada, a 20,000-square-foot wood-and-stone building that used to be a hunting lodge.

Yardage: 6,207
Par: 72
USGA rating: 69.7
Slope: 129
Greens fees: $50 to $90
Reservations: 1 week in advance

SILVER OAK GOLF CLUB
1251 Country Club Drive
Carson City, NV
(775) 841-7000
www.silveroakgolf.com

Silver Oak is the newest golf course in Carson City. It opened in the summer of 1999 and provides middle- to high-handicappers a great course that is quite forgiving. It's located behind the Kmart store in northwest Carson City and winds its way through the Silver Oak development and the Sierra foothills. The course is relatively short, even from the tournament tees (6,564 yards long), and it offers five tee boxes on every hole (tournament, championship, regular, silver, and oaks).

Designed by Tom Duncan and Sid Salomon, Silver Oak is a fun but challenging golf experience. The golf pro here won't say what the signature hole is because, according to him, all of them are unique and wonderfully laid out. But most golfers who have tested the course say they like the middle-length par 5s, especially No. 12, except when the wind picks up. The 18-hole course stretches over 150 acres, and it has a beautiful practice facility with a driving range, a bunker, and a putting green.

Annika Sorenstam of the LPGA and Scott McCarron, Kirk Triplett, and Dan Forsman have maintained homes in the Reno/Tahoe area.

Yardage: 5,716
Par: 71
USGA rating: 66.6
Slope: 118
Greens fees: $25 to $50
Reservations: 2 weeks in advance

SUNRIDGE GOLF CLUB
1000 Long Drive
Carson City, NV
(775)267-4448
(775)884-2110 (toll-free from Reno)
www.sunridgegolfclub.com

Sunridge was carved from the steep hills on the

southern edge of Carson City. Its entrance is through a development just off US 395, and after rounding the last corner of the development, you can see the course cut from the hills and nestled on the valley floor. The front nine opens with a tough par 5 that is almost impossible to reach in two. The rest of the holes require good club selection and course management. The uphill No. 7 is a par 3 that will scare the daylights out of you. You have to hit a 150-yard shot over a gully to an elevated green surrounded by sand traps. Once there, you have to contend with a big swale that cuts through the huge green. Sunridge could become one of the most challenging courses in the area.

Yardage: 5,947

Par: 72

USGA rating: 68.1

Slope: 128

Greens fees: $35 to $60

Reservations: 14 days in advance

WINTER SPORTS

When you ask winter-sports enthusiasts to describe winter in the Reno/Tahoe area, one word comes up over and over again—awesome! In some years the heavy storm fronts begin arriving from the Pacific Ocean as early as October, dumping huge amounts of that wonderful white stuff that turns the Sierra Nevada mountains into a winter wonderland. Snow is often measured in feet, not inches, and a normal winter will see accumulations of 30 to 40 feet in the higher elevations. Winter can last up to six months in the mountains, so there's plenty of time to indulge in your favorite outdoor activity. But in spite of massive amounts of snow, the temperatures stay relatively mild, usually above freezing during the day and dipping into the 20s at night. When it's not snowing, you can count on plenty of sunshine, making most days absolutely glorious for outdoor recreation.

Because Reno and Sparks get much less snow than the Lake Tahoe Basin (usually not more than a total of 2 feet), you can live in the banana belt but be on the ski slope in less than an hour. If you wanted to, you could play a round of golf in Reno or Sparks in the morning and ski in the nearby mountains that afternoon.

During normal snow years, many ski resorts are open by Thanksgiving, but when Mother Nature doesn't cooperate, ski resorts compensate by making snow. Occasional droughts have caused most resorts to install sophisticated snow-making equipment on a large percentage of their terrain. Often the diehards, like Squaw Valley USA and Alpine Meadows, operate through July 4. As the ski season extends into the summer months, you can combine skiing in the morning with river rafting in the afternoon for an especially invigorating day. The first skiers in the Reno/Tahoe area were gold miners from Scandinavia who introduced the long, wooden boards as a means of transportation in the mid-1800s. With deep snow blocking roads and trails during winter, even the mail was carried on skis in those early pioneer days. Between 1856 and 1876, the legendary Snowshoe Thompson made the trip from Placerville, California, to Genoa, Nevada, twice a month, lugging about 100 pounds of mail. During the winter months, Thompson was able to get through the rugged mountainous terrain by strapping on hefty 10-foot-long skis that weighed about 25 pounds. Although skiing was simply utilitarian in the beginning, it wasn't long before it evolved into a recreational sport with lifts, competitions, and established resorts. To find out more about the history of skiing in the West, you can visit the Western SkiSport Museum at Boreal Mountain Resort near Truckee, California. (See the description of Truckee in the Day Trips chapter.)

Today the Reno/Tahoe area has the largest concentration of ski resorts in North America, with 15 alpine resorts and 11 cross-country resorts. Because these resorts offer such a diverse variety of terrain and amenities, it's a good idea to acquaint yourself with them before you decide where to ski or snowboard. For the ultimate in vertical, you can dive off the heart-stopping chutes at Squaw Valley. For all-out cruising you can burn down the meticulously groomed slopes at Northstar-at-Tahoe. For a fun first time on skis, you can snowplow without fear on the gentle runs at Tahoe Donner. To help you decide where it's best for you to ski or board, I give you vital statistics about area alpine and cross-country ski resorts in this chapter. I also give you Insiders' tips, such as where you can find the deepest ungroomed powder, which resorts have the most exciting snowboard terrain, what mountains offer the greatest views, which trail systems are the most interesting, and much more.

Since the weather influences the quality of your ski experience, you need to consider it when choosing where to go. To avoid the wind on stormy days, one of the best places to go is Northstar, because its tree-lined runs will shield you from the gusts. Resorts with high wind exposure include Mt. Rose, Squaw, Alpine, and Sugar Bowl, where it's not unusual to have upper lifts on wind-hold on windy days. If it's raining and you still want to ski, try resorts at the higher elevations, such as Mt. Rose or Boreal, since it may be snowing rather than raining there. For maximum sun exposure you can ski the open bowls at Squaw and Alpine and the upper runs at Diamond Peak Ski Resort and Heavenly Ski Resort, where you're sure to get a winter tan (or burn) after just a few trips down the mountain.

If you're a first-time or novice skier or snowboarder, I strongly recommend you take lessons at one of the resorts. Although your friends may be well-meaning in volunteering to teach you, learning the basics from a professional instructor is the fastest and best way to go. All the resorts offer packages that include rental equipment, lift tickets, or trail passes along with lessons. You can choose from individual or group instruction. If you plan to be at the resort for a full day, try to get a lesson first thing so you can use the rest of the day to practice your new skills.

If you're unfamiliar with a resort, be sure to carry a trail map. It's very easy to become disoriented on the mountain, especially if the weather turns stormy. Many resorts also have large trail maps at the tops of chairlifts, so you can get your bearings without fumbling for the map you've stashed in the inside pocket of your parka. To avoid injury, it's a good idea to stretch before hopping on the lift and to make your first runs easy warm-ups to get the feel of the snow. Also be sure to follow the Skier Responsibility Code that is printed on most trail maps and lift tickets.

To beat the crowds, Insiders ski the major alpine resorts like Squaw, Alpine, Heavenly, Northstar, Diamond Peak, and Kirkwood during the week rather than on weekends. You can try smaller alpine resorts and cross-country locations on the weekends. To avoid being shut out, consider buying your lift tickets online at the resort Web sites. Many offer that option along with special rates for teens, seniors, and small children.

But winter isn't just about skiing and snowboarding; it's also the jingle of sleigh bells on horse-drawn sleighs, the swoosh of skates skimming on ice, the zooming of snowmobiles zigzagging through the forest, the plopping of snowshoes in deep powder snow, and the barking of dogs pulling fur-laden sleds. In this chapter I tell you where and how you can enjoy these other winter activities as well.

Now let's get back to skiing and boarding and take a look at the eclectic variety of resorts you can choose from. The ski resorts in the Reno/Tahoe area are scattered in and around the Lake Tahoe Basin, so they're listed by the two geographic areas at the lake. Prices are quoted as of press time for all-day adult lift tickets and trail passes, but keep in mind that they could be slightly higher because some resorts raise them each ski season.

ALPINE SKIING AND SNOWBOARDING

North Shore Lake Tahoe

ALPINE MEADOWS
2600 Alpine Meadows Road
Tahoe City, CA
(530) 583-4232, (800) 441-4423
www.skialpine.com
Base elevation: 6,835 feet
Top elevation: 8,637 feet
Vertical drop: 1,802 feet
Number of runs: 100-plus
Capacity: 16,500 skiers per hour
Terrain: 25 percent beginner, 40 percent intermediate, 35 percent advanced
Skiable acres: 2,400

Longest run: 2.5 miles
Number of lifts: 13
Average snowfall: 495 inches
Lift tickets: $64
Terrain parks: 2
Snowphone: (530) 581-8374
Getting there: To get to Alpine Meadows, take California Highway 89 north 6 miles from Tahoe City or CA 89 south 13 miles from Interstate 80 in Truckee to Alpine Meadows Road.

From plunging chutes to gentle trails and from open bowls to tree-lined runs, Alpine Meadows has it all. Because of the diversity of terrain for all levels of skiers and boarders, it's a great favorite with locals. The resort includes both sides of Ward and Scott Peaks, with ungroomed advanced territory sprinkled among the groomed beginner and intermediate runs. Novice skiers can feel comfortable with two chairlifts servicing several gentle runs that are out of the way of more advanced skiing terrain. Fearless young boarders and skiers especially like Alpine's adventure zones, which are similar to backcountry areas, along with its terrain parks that feature jumps, spines, halfpipes, and table tops.

The resort has several restaurants on the mountain as well as the usual bars and cafes in the lodge at the base. For the best après-ski action, be sure to stop at the River Ranch Lodge at the intersection of CA 89 and Alpine Meadows Road. Jutting out over the Truckee River, this old lodge, with its huge rock fireplace, is warm and cozy after an invigorating day on the mountain. Check out the trout swimming by while you enjoy your favorite drink, and then stay for a lovely continental dinner in the inviting dining room. During summer the outdoor patio is a great people-watching hangout since it's the termination point for rafters coming down the Truckee River.

Because it's so popular, Alpine can be very crowded. The parking lot fills up fast, so try to arrive early to minimize your walk from the car to the base of the mountain. Shuttle buses will take you from outlying parking lots to the base once the close-in lots fill up.

BOREAL MOUNTAIN RESORT

Interstate 80, 45 miles west of Reno, NV
(530) 426-3666
www.borealski.com
www.jibassicpark.com
Base elevation: 7,200 feet
Top elevation: 7,800 feet
Vertical drop: 500 feet
Number of runs: 41
Capacity: 8,000 skiers per hour
Terrain: 30 percent beginner, 55 percent intermediate, 15 percent advanced
Skiable acres: 380
Longest run: 1 mile
Number of lifts: 10
Average snowfall: 420 inches
Lift tickets: $47
Terrain park: Jibassic Park
Snowphone: (530) 426-3666
Getting there: Boreal Mountain Resort has easy access from I-80, 45 miles west of Reno off the Castle Peak exit.

With short runs on mostly beginner to intermediate terrain, Boreal appeals to those who are learning to ski. You don't have to spend a fortune to learn at Boreal; lift tickets and lessons are cheaper than at some other resorts. It boasts a variety of children's programs, and because of the resort's small size, it's easy for parents to observe their children's learning progress. New in 2005 is Jibassic Park, a state-of-the-art terrain park featuring a 450-foot superpipe along with 50 rails and 50 fun boxes.

Boreal's high elevation and comprehensive snowmaking allow it to be one of the first resorts to open every year. It offers night skiing until 9:00 p.m. and bar and restaurant service in its base lodge. Rooms are also available in the Boreal Inn, just steps from the lifts. While at Boreal, be sure to visit the Western SkiSport Museum (for more information see the Day Trips chapter).

DIAMOND PEAK SKI RESORT

1210 Ski Way Drive
Incline Village, NV
(775) 832-1177
www.diamondpeak.com

Base elevation: 6,700 feet
Top elevation: 8,540 feet
Vertical drop: 1,840
Number of runs: 30
Capacity: 7,700 skiers per hour
Terrain: 18 percent beginner, 46 percent intermediate, 36 percent advanced
Skiable acres: 655
Longest run: 2.5 miles
Number of lifts: 6
Average snowfall: 300 inches
Lift tickets: $49
Terrain park: Snowbomb Terrain Park
Snowphone: (775) 831-3211
Getting there: To reach Diamond Peak from Reno/Sparks, take Nevada Highway 431 to Incline Village, turn left onto Country Club Drive, and then look for Ski Way Drive, and follow it to the top. From Incline Village take Nevada Highway 28 to Country Club Drive, and then turn onto Ski Way Drive and continue to the top. For information on free local ski shuttles, call (775) 832-1177 or check www.laketahoetransit.com or www .diamondpeak.com. The Hyatt Regency Lake Tahoe Resort, Spa & Casino also provides free transportation for its guests.

Not very many communities own and manage their very own ski resorts, but Incline Village isn't your average town. Operated by the Incline Village General Improvement District (IVGID), the governing body of the town, Diamond Peak Ski Resort emphasizes family fun. The resort offers a variety of passes that make family skiing a little more affordable, such as teen tickets and interchangeable parent passes. Skiers between ages 6 and 12 and 60 and 79 can ski for only $17. Residents of Incline Village are also eligible for special discounts. You don't have to worry about keeping track of your children at Diamond Peak; all of the runs funnel into one base area, making it a very secure environment for families.

Along with its intimate atmosphere and short lift lines, Diamond Peak offers some of the most spectacular views of any ski resort in the area. For a stunning panorama of Lake Tahoe, ride the Crystal Quad chair to the top and take a lei-

surely run down the ridge. With an unobstructed all-around view, it will seem as though the lake engulfs you as you cruise to the base. For lunch with a view, nothing beats a big juicy hamburger at the Snowflake Lodge, perched high above the lake at the top of the Lakeview Quad chair. If lunch at the base is more to your taste, you'll find a newly renovated base lodge with expanded deck areas that enhance lake and mountain views, along with an updated menu and decor.

Because many of the upper runs here are exposed to the wind and sun, conditions may be icy, especially if no snow has fallen recently. Also, the parking lot at Diamond Peak fills up fast on weekends, so try to arrive early. At the end of your ski day, I highly recommend an après-ski drink at the Big Water Grille, which is just across the lower end of the resort parking lot. The sunset view of Lake Tahoe from this tasteful bar/restaurant is absolutely stunning (see the review in the Restaurants chapter).

DONNER SKI RANCH
19320 Donner Pass Road, off Interstate 80
Norden, CA
(530) 426-3635
www.donnerskiranch.com
Base elevation: 7,031 feet
Top elevation: 7,781 feet
Vertical drop: 750 feet
Number of runs: 45
Capacity: 7,200 skiers per hour
Terrain: 25 percent beginner, 50 percent intermediate, 25 percent advanced
Skiable acres: 460
Longest run: 1.5 miles
Number of lifts: 6
Average snowfall: 396 inches
Lift tickets: $30 to $40 depending upon day of week
Snowphone: (530) 426-3635
Getting there: To get to Donner Ski Ranch, take I–80 west about 45 miles from Reno and exit at the Soda Springs/Norden exit onto Donner Pass Road. The resort is 3.5 miles east.

Perched at the top of Donner Summit, Donner Ski Ranch is one of Reno/Tahoe's best-kept ski and snowboard secrets. It's not the Ritz, but it offers a back-to-basics mountain experience for half the price of major resorts. One of the oldest ski resorts in the West, it boasts the distinction of being one of California's last family-owned ski resorts. Its setting is simply spectacular, with gorgeous views of Donner Lake and the surrounding Sierra Nevada. Because the runs are wide open, you can enjoy the panorama all the way from the top to the bottom.

Donner Ski Ranch can provide welcome relief from the hassles found at major ski resorts. If you don't need dozens of watering holes, world-class cornices, and multi-mile runs, you can kick back here and just commune with the unspoiled mountain environment. Insiders know it's a great place for beginners: The small size and uncrowded slopes give novice skiers and snowboarders a feeling of comfort and security. Donner Ski Ranch offers the essential amenities found at most resorts, including a ski school, a base lodge with bar, a cafeteria, and a ski shop.

My only word of caution about this resort is that it can get very windy when winter storms are coming into the area.

GRANLIBAKKEN SKI RESORT
725 Granlibakken Road
Tahoe City, CA
(800) 543-3221, (877) 552-6301
www.granlibakken.com
Base elevation: 6,310 feet
Top elevation: 6,610 feet
Vertical drop: 300 feet
Number of runs: 1
Terrain: 25 percent beginner, 75 percent intermediate
Skiable acres: 10
Number of lifts: 2
Average snowfall: 325 inches
Lift tickets: $21
Getting there: Granlibakken is about 0.5 mile south of Tahoe City, just off CA 89.

Tiny Granlibakken is the oldest, the smallest, and one of the least expensive ski resorts at Lake Tahoe. Built in 1927 by Tahoe Tavern Resort and the Southern Pacific Railroad, Granlibakken was founded primarily as a training hill for Olympic ski jumpers. While much of the early history of Lake Tahoe skiing took place here, the resort has been eclipsed for many years by the larger, more comprehensive resorts in the Reno/Tahoe area.

The nearby Granlibakken Resort is an upscale conference center with modern condominium accommodations, seminar rooms, and a restaurant. Resort guests can use the ski hill at half price, and family packages are available.

If you're a total novice skier, Granlibakken (which means "hill sheltered by fir trees" in Norwegian) might provide enough challenge for you. Amenities include equipment rentals, lessons, a snack bar in the warming hut, lodging packages, a snow play area, and children's programs. The resort is open Friday, weekends, and holidays.

MT. ROSE–SKI TAHOE
22222 Mt. Rose Highway (Nevada Highway 431)
Reno, NV
(775) 849-0704
(800) 754-7673 (outside Nevada only)
www.skirose.com
Base elevation: 7,900 feet
Top elevation: 9,700 feet
Vertical drop: 1,800 feet
Number of runs: 60
Capacity: 13,400 skiers per hour
Terrain: 20 percent beginner, 30 percent intermediate, 40 percent advanced, 10 percent expert
Skiable acres: 1,200
Longest run: 2.5 miles
Number of lifts: 8
Average snowfall: 400 inches
Lift tickets: $64
Terrain parks: Badlands, Doubledown
Snowphone: (775) 849-0704
Getting there: To get to Mt. Rose, take NV 431 east for about 11 miles from Incline Village or go west for 22 miles from Reno.

With the highest base in the Reno/Tahoe area, Mt. Rose often enjoys snow while resorts lower in elevation may be drenched with rain. And when spring has sprung at other resorts, Mt. Rose's high altitude keeps the snow longer, blessing the resort with some of the best late-season skiing in the area. Although Mt. Rose is the closest major ski resort to an international airport in the world (25 minutes from Reno/Tahoe International Airport), it's always been a locals' resort rather than a tourist destination. When you ski here, you run into all your neighbors and friends. If your attorney wasn't in his office that morning, don't be surprised if you see him whizzing by you on Northwest Passage.

One lift ticket gives access to both the open bowls on the east, or Slide, side and the tree-lined runs on the Rose side. You can ski either side from the top, but I recommend skiing the Slide side in the morning when it's the sunniest and working your way over to the runs on Mt. Rose in the afternoon. The terrain here is varied enough to challenge skiers and boarders of all abilities. New in 2004, The Chutes offer 200 acres of heart-stopping ungroomed vertical between the Slide and Mt. Rose sides of the resort. And when Mother Nature dumps a foot or so of new snow on this peak, the powderhounds rejoice because it's one of the best spots for ungroomed powder in the area.

Both sides of the mountain have parking, ticket sales, food service, and rest-rooms, but the Mt. Rose side has a ski school, equipment rentals, and a ski shop. The restaurant on the Mt. Rose side is much larger, with a lovely deck for outdoor eating and a bar that really hops when the lifts close down. For really affordable skiing Mt. Rose offers a variety of weekday specials, such as Two-fer Tuesdays, Over the Hill Wednesdays, and Ladies' Day Thursdays.

From the summit of this resort, you can see forever, with Reno and Sparks glinting like tiny toy towns far in the distance. But this mountain catches the wind and the weather in a pretty brutal way, so don't be surprised if the resort is closed due to high winds or if the road is impassable because of heavy snow. If the weather looks dicey at all, call ahead or check current conditions at the resort Web site to avoid having to turn around.

i Check out the Web site for whichever ski resort you plan to ski—you'll find up-to-date information on snow depths and road conditions, and some areas even have resort cams that offer timely views of conditions on the mountain.

NORTHSTAR-AT-TAHOE

California Highway 267 North
6 miles north of Lake Tahoe
(530) 562-1010, (800) GO-NORTH
www.skinorthstar.com
Base elevation: 6,330 feet
Top elevation: 8,600 feet
Vertical drop: 2,270 feet
Number of runs: 73
Capacity: 32,500 skiers per hour
Terrain: 25 percent beginner, 50 percent intermediate, 25 percent advanced
Skiable acres: 2,904
Longest run: 1.3 miles
Number of lifts: 18
Average snowfall: 350 inches
Lift tickets: $79
Terrain parks: Superpipe, halfpipe, 8 terrain parks, 1 fun park, 4 adventure parks
Snowphone: (530) 562-1330
Getting there: To get to Northstar, take I-80 west from Reno about 30 miles to Truckee, and then CA 267 south for 6 miles. From Kings Beach, California, take CA 267 north about 6 miles. For information about shuttle transportation to Northstar from the Lake Tahoe area, call (775) 883-2100. For information on ride sharing, call (800) GO-NORTH, and for free shuttle service from Reno, call (877) 274-7366. You can also visit www.laketahoetransit.com.

Northstar-at-Tahoe calls itself the "Mountain of Fun," and as a major year-round destination resort, it's definitely a toss-up whether it's more fun in winter or in summer. I tell you more about

North-star, including warm-weather activities, in the Vacation Rentals, Resorts, and Recreation chapters, but for now, let's talk skiing, snowboarding, and tubing.

Because Northstar is one of the most comprehensive and best-maintained resorts in the Reno/Tahoe area, you can always have a great time here. The north-facing slope of Mt. Pluto is sheltered and tree-lined, providing ample protection from wintry weather. Many runs on this side of the mountain are long intermediate cruisers, impeccably groomed for maximum running speed. But powder seekers and extreme skiers can find chutes and short shots of ungroomed tree skiing scattered among the more gentle slopes.

The back side of Pluto is for more advanced skiers, with 1,860 vertical feet of groomed, ungroomed, and mogul skiing and boarding. Because this side of the mountain faces west (you get a gorgeous view of nearby Squaw Valley when riding the lift), it catches the brunt of storms as they approach from that direction. If the wind kicks up when you're skiing back here, you can find plenty of protected runs on the other side of the hill. North-star also offers 200 acres of steep and deep on Lookout Mountain. Serviced by a high-speed quad, the five black-diamond runs are named for reservoirs that can be seen from the mountain: Boca, Gooseneck, Martis, Prosser, and Stampede. When it's time for the last run of the day, I recommend a leisurely looping run of about 3 miles starting at the top of Mt. Pluto and heading down East Ridge, Loggers Loop, and The Woods. As you glide on down to the village below, enjoy the spectacular view as the sinking sun paints the surrounding mountains and Martis Valley an intense golden hue. For a meaningful experience with the great outdoors, nothing beats this run for the gold.

As a major destination resort, North-star is lacking in nothing when it comes to services that enhance your overall mountain experience. The charming Village Mall has a wide variety of shops, restaurants, and bars surrounding a picturesque ice-skating facility. Skating is complimentary, and rentals are available. Expansion of the mall started in 2004 and will continue to add upscale amenities over the next few years. When hunger pangs hit, you can head into the Lodge at Big Springs, which is midmountain, and enjoy hearty skier food while you people-watch from the expansive outdoor deck. Or if you'd rather have lunch with a gorgeous Lake Tahoe view, you can indulge your appetite at the Summit Deck & Grill perched at the very top of Mt. Pluto.

To minimize hassles and maximize the time skiers and boarders have on the snow, Northstar has a large electronic board at the top of Mt. Pluto showing the exact wait times for all lifts and restaurants on the mountain. It also runs a trolley from the parking lot and a free shuttle from all its resort accommodations to get you to the base of the mountain quicker and easier. (For details on accommodations see the Vacation Rentals and Resorts chapters.)

Frequent skiers and boarders at Northstar can save money plus keep track of the number of vertical feet they rack up by joining the Vertical Plus program. You can buy a personal electronic bracelet that logs in your vertical feet each time you board a lift. Vertical Plus members have their own lift access, plus they can receive discounts and rewards based upon the number of vertical feet they ski. For additional details call (530) 562-2267 or visit www.doublewhammypass.com. The program is interchangeable with Sierra-at-Tahoe Snowsport Resort.

You simply can't go wrong spending a day (or days) at Northstar, since this resort has been delivering quality mountain adventures to outdoor enthusiasts for years. Because the number of skiers and boarders allowed on the mountain is cut off once the parking facilities are full, be sure to arrive early on weekends and holidays. If you're planning to stay at Northstar, you can choose from a huge variety of accommodations, including condos, rental homes, and hotel-type units. For the ultimate in luxury, the Ritz-Carlton Club (new in 2009) offers a plethora of mid-mountain luxuries to make your stay as hassle free as possible. For lodging info, call (800) 466-6784 or book online at the Northstar Web site.

i Northstar-at-Tahoe and Sierra-at-Tahoe sell a Double Whammy Pass, which is good for skiing at both resorts. For details call (530) 562-2267.

SODA SPRINGS

Interstate 80 at Donner Summit
Norden, CA
(530) 426-3901
www.skisodasprings.com
Base elevation: 6,700 feet
Top elevation: 7,352 feet
Vertical drop: 652 feet
Number of runs: 16
Terrain: 30 percent beginner, 50 percent intermediate, 20 percent advanced
Skiable acres: 200
Longest run: 1 mile
Number of lifts: 4
Average snowfall: 420 inches
Lift tickets: $30 to $35
Terrain parks: Kids X Park
Snowphone: (530) 426-3901
Getting there: To get to Soda Springs, take I–80 west from Reno for about 45 miles to the Soda Springs/Norden exit, and follow the signs to Soda (about 1 mile). From Tahoe City take CA 89 north to Truckee, and then I–80 west to the Soda Springs/Norden exit.

One of the oldest ski resorts in the Lake Tahoe area, Soda Springs is a great beginner hill. You can count on uncrowded runs, even on weekends and holidays, and the prices can't be beat. It's easy for novice skiers to feel comfortable here, since the runs are comparatively gentle and wide open. Soda's location at the top of Donner Summit affords breathtaking views of the surrounding mountains on clear days. Amenities include a full-service rental shop, snowtubing, sledding, snowshoeing, ski lessons, and a cafeteria.

With an emphasis on family fun, Soda offers a variety of affordable lesson packages plus a moving carpet for first-time skiers and boarders age 8 and under. Kids ages 6 through 12 can also try out mini-snowmobiles on weekends and holidays.

SQUAW VALLEY USA

1960 Squaw Valley Road
Olympic Valley, CA
(530) 583-6985, (800) 545-4350
(800) 403-0206
www.squaw.com
Base elevation: 6,200 feet
Top elevation: 9,050 feet
Vertical drop: 2,850 feet
Number of runs: 150
Capacity: 50,000 skiers per hour
Terrain: 25 percent beginner, 45 percent intermediate, 30 percent advanced
Skiable acres: 4,200
Longest run: 3.2 miles
Number of lifts: 32
Average snowfall: 450 inches
Lift tickets: $79
Terrain parks: Belmont, Riviera/Central Park, Ford Freestyle Superpipe Snowphone: (530) 583-6955
Getting there: To get to Squaw Valley USA, take CA 89 north for 6 miles from Tahoe City. From Reno head west on I–80 for about 30 miles to Truckee, and then go south for about 13 miles on CA 89. For information on shuttle service from South Shore or North Shore Lake Tahoe and Reno, call (866) 769-4653; from North Shore or West Shore Lake Tahoe, contact (530) 581-7181; from Truckee and Tahoe City, call (530) 550-1212.

In February 1960 the greatest winter athletes in the world, representing 34 different nations, gathered in Squaw Valley to compete in the VIII Winter Olympics. A relatively unknown ski resort with four double chairlifts and one rope tow, Squaw Valley USA was catapulted into the world limelight by the resulting media coverage. Since that time Squaw has blossomed expansively, along with the growing popularity of winter sports in general. Big, bold, and beautiful, today it's a world-class resort in every way. The aura of the Olympics still abounds at Squaw, with the Olympic Flame still burning brightly in front of The Tower of Nations at the entrance to the resort. Sporting the five Olympic rings that represent the continents that compete (the Americas get one ring), the tower stands 79 feet high and 29 feet wide.

Spread out over six spectacular peaks, the amount of skiable terrain is absolutely daunting. It's divided into three sections: the base level at 6,200 feet, the upper level at 8,200 feet, and the Snow King area on the resort's eastern side. Some of the best beginner runs are on the upper elevation, which gives novices the same full mountain experience as more advanced skiers and snowboarders. Intermediates find comfortable runs in all sections, and advanced skiers are challenged by the spine-tingling chutes off Squaw Peak and KT-22, so named for the 22 kick-turns needed by most skiers to get to the bottom. Snowboarders are not forgotten: Squaw also has a variety of terrain parks with a challenging array of jumps, boxes, rails, and pipes designed especially for them. Squaw especially caters to new skiers at the Papoose Learning Area at the base. Dedicated to beginners, this expansive terrain allows novices to learn without worrying about being hit by or running into more advanced skiers and riders.

Because Squaw is so large, it's important to study the trail map to find your way around. Most of the skiable terrain is open and treeless, a disadvantage during windy weather. The state-of-the-art funitel transport system reduces upper mountain wind closures during high winds, but it doesn't diminish the wind on you once you get up to the higher elevation. But even if you decide to confine your skiing and boarding to the lower elevations, be sure to go to the top to enjoy the view. You can literally see for miles in every direction, with gorgeous Lake Tahoe shimmering to the south and magnificent snowcapped mountains all around you.

Squaw is a major destination resort by anyone's standards, so the list of its amenities goes on and on. (See the Resorts, Vacation Rentals, and Recreation chapters for information about accommodations and warm-weather activities.) You can find dining and entertainment mid-mountain at High Camp and Gold Coast, with a plethora of eating and watering holes to choose from. In the base village you'll find an eclectic variety of more than 20 pubs and restaurants sprinkled among the upscale boutiques and sports shops. You can learn about the 1960 Winter Olympics at the Olympic Winter Games Museum or just continue skiing and boarding until 9:00 p.m., since Squaw also offers night skiing.

For a total mountain experience with all the glitz and glamour you read about in ski magazines, you can't go wrong at Squaw. It has everything any skier or snowboarder could conceivably imagine, including the new Axess Smart Gates system, which allows skiers and boarders to keep their pass or lift ticket in their pockets as it is electronically scanned by sensors at the lifts. But because it has so much to offer, it's usually extremely crowded. Even though its highly sophisticated lift system has been successful in eliminating long lift lines, you still have to contend with crowds at the base. The word to the wise is to arrive early to find a place to park your car in the free lots. Then with so many restaurants to choose from mid-mountain, consider having breakfast with a view before you start your skiing day. Squaw offers a season parking pass in the structure adjacent to Squaw Kids Children's Center. For information call (530) 581-7123. For the ultimate in convenience you can utilize the valet parking service that is available near the entrance to the cable car. Just drive up and look for the valet parking employees.

i You can start your ski day on the water by taking the *Tahoe Queen* winter ski shuttle, a paddle wheeler that will pick you up at Ski Run Marina at South Shore and drop you off in Tahoe City at the north end of the lake. A quick shuttle ride will deliver you to the lifts at Squaw Valley USA. For details call (800) 238-2463.

SUGAR BOWL
Interstate 80 at Donner Summit
Norden, CA
(530) 426-9000
www.sugarbowl.com
Base elevation: 6,883 feet
Top elevation: 8,383 feet

Vertical drop: 1,500 feet
Number of runs: 84
Capacity: 21,740 skiers per hour
Terrain: 17 percent beginner, 45 percent intermediate, 38 percent advanced
Skiable acres: 1,500
Longest run: 3 miles
Number of lifts: 12
Average snowfall: 500 inches
Lift tickets: $46
Snowphone: (530) 426-1111
Getting there: To get to Sugar Bowl, take I–80 west about 45 miles from Reno and exit at the Soda Springs/Norden exit onto Donner Pass Road. The resort is about 3 miles east. From Tahoe City take CA 89 north to Truckee, and then I–80 west about 10 miles to the Soda Springs/Norden exit.

If you've always wanted to ski in Europe but never quite made it, come to Sugar Bowl, where the ambience is decidedly old-world Austrian. Built in 1939 by wealthy families from San Francisco (who continue to own and operate it), Sugar Bowl has a colorful history that includes the rich and famous. It was the winter playground for celebrities like Walt Disney (he even had a mountain named for him), Errol Flynn, and Janet Leigh, who would arrive on the train and cozy up in the charming Sugar Bowl Lodge or in one of the picturesque cabins scattered among the pine trees. Home to the first chairlift in northern California and the first gondola in the country, Sugar Bowl offers a peek into the past with a dash of high-tech. Today it maintains its quintessential classic flavor amid the sophisticated technology of a modern-day ski resort.

Skiing here is on four mountains: Mt. Judah, Mt. Lincoln, Mt. Disney, and Crows Peak. Beginner terrain may be found at both entrances, and intermediate terrain is found on the west side of Disney, the east side of Lincoln, and also on Judah. Because Sugar Bowl is often the snowiest of all Reno/Tahoe resorts, expert skiers absolutely revel in its deep ungroomed powder. Insider shredheads (ardent snow-boarders) know that Sugar Bowl is one of the best boarding resorts in the area: It offers an abundance of natural chutes along with terrain parks with pipes, jumps, and rails. With magnificent views from almost any run, Sugar Bowl delivers a quality mountain high for skiers and boarders of all abilities.

Parking is somewhat limited at the Magic Carpet gondola, which you reach first on Donner Pass Road, but if you arrive early enough, I recommend taking the gondola for a picturesque ride to the base of the mountain. Other parking and base facilities are found just a short way down the road at Mt. Judah. Amenities include bars and restaurants midmountain and at both bases, but the most colorful is the original Sugar Bowl Lodge near the gondola. For a truly romantic ski getaway, the lodge offers a classic alpine experience, with comfortable rooms and gourmet dining. A 14,000-square-foot addition to Mount Judah Day Lodge includes a new bar and restaurant.

TAHOE DONNER
11509 Northwoods Boulevard
Truckee, CA
(530) 587-9444
www.tahoedonner.com
Base elevation: 6,750 feet
Top elevation: 7,350 feet
Vertical drop: 600 feet
Number of runs: 14
Capacity: 1,000 skiers per hour
Terrain: 40 percent beginner, 60 percent intermediate
Skiable acres: 120
Longest run: 1 mile
Number of lifts: 4
Average snowfall: 300 inches
Lift tickets: $36
Snowphone: (530) 587-9444
Getting there: To get to Tahoe Donner from Reno, take I–80 west about 30 miles to Truckee and exit at the Central Truckee exit, which puts you on Donner Pass Road. About 0.5 mile down the road, turn right onto Northwoods Boulevard and follow the signs for about 5 miles to the ski area. From Tahoe City head north on CA 89 to Truckee and turn left onto Donner Pass Road. Sev-

eral blocks farther on, turn right onto Northwoods Boulevard and follow the signs to Tahoe Donner.

Tucked away in the Tahoe Donner residential area in Truckee, this resort is a great learn-to-ski hill, especially for children. The terrain is a relatively gentle open bowl with few obstacles for beginners to worry about. Meticulous grooming makes the snow very forgiving, even for the very novice skiers and snowboarders. And since there are no crowds and no lift lines, you can ski till you drop. Amenities include a full-service ski shop and a comfortable alpine ski lodge at the base of the hill. Strong intermediates and expert skiers and boarders won't be challenged here, but I recommend that beginners give it a try—the price is right, and it offers a quality mountain experience with none of the hassles encountered at larger resorts. There's a children's snowplay area next to the Trout Creek Recreation Center at 12790 Northwoods Boulevard.

After a fun day on the snow, try dinner or drinks at the Lodge, an upscale restaurant at 12850 Northwoods Boulevard.

South Shore Lake Tahoe

HEAVENLY MOUNTAIN RESORT
End of Ski Run Boulevard, off U.S. Highway 50
South Lake Tahoe, CA
(530) 541-1330, (775) 586-7000,
(800) 243-2836
www.skiheavenly.com
Base elevation: 6,540 feet
Top elevation: 10, 067 feet
Vertical drop: 3,500 feet
Number of runs: 95
Capacity: 52,000 skiers per hour
Terrain: 20 percent beginner, 45 percent intermediate, 35 percent advanced
Skiable acres: 4,800
Longest run: 5.5 miles
Number of lifts: 30
Average snowfall: 360 inches
Lift tickets: $70
Terrain parks: 4 high roller parks
Snowphone: (775) 586-7000
Getting there: Because this resort is often very

congested at the base, it's a good idea to take advantage of the free shuttle transportation that's available on both sides of the mountain. For shuttle information call (530) 541-7548. To reach the California side of Heavenly from the Reno/Sparks area, head south on U.S. Highway 395 through Carson City, and then take US 50 west to South Lake Tahoe. The base of the mountain is at the east end of Ski Run Boulevard. To get to the Nevada side from Reno/Sparks, continue south on US 395 past Carson City to Jacks Valley Road, where you turn west and then south through the tiny town of Genoa. Just past Genoa, turn west onto Nevada Highway 207 (Kingsbury Grade) and follow the signs for the resort at the top of the summit.

From Incline Village take NV 28 south to the intersection with US 50. Continue south on US 50 to NV 207, turn east, and follow the signs at the summit to the Nevada side of the resort. To reach the California side, continue south on US 50 to Ski Run Boulevard in South Lake Tahoe, and follow the signs to the east end.

With a name like "Heavenly," how can your ski experience here be anything but out of this world? Sprawling across the California–Nevada border, Heavenly Ski Resort has more skiable acres than any other Reno/Tahoe ski resort. The variety of terrain is awesome to say the least, from the hip-high, knee-burning moguls on Gunbarrel, to the immaculately groomed cruiser snow on Orion, to the deep and steep untracked powder in Mott Canyon. Although there's a smattering of beginner runs sprinkled around the mountain, Heavenly appeals largely to intermediate and expert skiers and snowboarders. Because of its daunting size, it's hard to sample it all in one day. With the highest elevation at Lake Tahoe and the most comprehensive snowmaking capacity, Heavenly is usually able to open early in the season and to maintain quality snow until its late closure.

Along with the mind-boggling variety of runs to choose from, Heavenly offers spectacular views of Lake Tahoe to the west and the Carson Valley to the east. True to its name, the mountain experience here is divine, giving you a feeling you are skiing at the top of the world. If you want an even bigger thrill than hip-high mogols on Gunbarrel, check out the Heavenly Flyer, a ziprider accessed via the gondola and Tamarack Express lift. See the Kidstuff chapter for details. Amenities include on-mountain lodges, perched on the edge of the mountain on the California side, tubing at the top of the gondola (see the Attractions chapter for more information about the gondola), and licensed day-care facilities for children ages six weeks through six years old. The opening of the The Shops at Heavenly Village added upscale boutiques, lodging, and dining to the California side of the resort. You can start your skiing day from the two lifts on the Nevada side of the resort or at the base on the California side. Because the Nevada side of the mountain is usually less crowded than the California side, I suggest you try to escape the crowds by parking there if you're driving.

Heavenly is the closest ski resort to all the casino nightlife at South Lake Tahoe. You can book packages that include lodging, skiing, shows, meals, and tours to local sights by calling (800) 243-2836.

HOMEWOOD MOUNTAIN RESORT
California Highway 89
Homewood, CA
(530) 525-2992
www.skihomewood.com
Base elevation: 6,320 feet
Top elevation: 7,880 feet
Vertical drop: 1,650 feet
Number of runs: 59
Capacity: 8,500 skiers per hour
Terrain: 15 percent beginner, 50 percent intermediate, 35 percent advanced
Skiable acres: 1,260
Longest run: 2 miles
Number of lifts: 8
Average snowfall: 350 inches
Lift tickets: $39 to $58
Terrain parks: 2
Snowphone: (530) 525-2900

Getting there: To reach Homewood from the Reno/Sparks area, take I–80 west about 30 miles to Truckee, and then CA 89 south for about 6 miles past Tahoe City. From South Lake Tahoe it's about 19 miles west on CA 89. You can also ride Tahoe Area Regional Transit (TART) in the North Shore Lake Tahoe region. For the schedule and fares, call (530) 550-1212 or (800) 736-6365, or visit www.laketahoetransit.com.

Far from the crowds but with magnificent lake views, Homewood is very popular with locals. Spread over two slopes, the terrain is diverse and challenging enough to keep skiers and boarders of all abilities busy for the entire day. Since the resort has two separate bases, skiers can start their day at either the South Lodge or the North Lodge. Parking is readily available on both sides. On windy days Homewood is especially attractive because many of its runs are protected; but be careful during spring skiing as its relatively low elevation causes the snow to melt early. If you're looking for glitz, this probably isn't the place for you. This resort offers just the essential amenities in a back-to-basics style. But if maximum time on the snow, spectacular views, and hassle-free skiing and boarding interest you at all, give Homewood a try. It's a great place to kick back and sink into a quality mountain experience.

KIRKWOOD MOUNTAIN RESORT
Off California Highway 88 at Carson Pass
Kirkwood, CA
(209) 258-6000
www.kirkwood.com
Base elevation: 7,800 feet
Top elevation: 9,800 feet
Vertical drop: 2,000 feet
Number of runs: 65
Capacity: 17,905 skiers per hour
Terrain: 15 percent beginner, 50 percent intermediate, and 35 percent advanced
Skiable acres: 2,300
Longest run: 2.5 miles
Number of lifts: 12
Average snowfall: 500 inches

Lift tickets: $72
Terrain parks: 3
Snowphone: (209) 258-3000, (877) 547-5966
Getting there: To reach Kirkwood from the Reno/Sparks area, take US 395 south to Minden, and then CA 88 west. It's about a 90-minute drive when the roads are clear. From South Shore Lake Tahoe, take US 50 southwest to Myers, and then turn left onto CA 89. Go south for about 12 miles, then turn onto CA 88 west for another 14 miles. For shuttle information call (530) 541-7548 .

Nestled in a box canyon ringed by jagged pinnacles at the end of gorgeous Hope Valley, Kirkwood is an impressive sight, even for the nonskier. Although it's tricky to get to (over winding hairpin mountain passes), it's well worth the effort. This resort is a skier's and snowboarder's joy. The diverse terrain presents challenges for all abilities, with heart-stopping chutes and cornices for advanced skiers and boarders, wide sweeping bowls for intermediates, and easy, gentle slopes for beginners. Kirkwood frequently has the distinction of having America's deepest snow. During the 2004–2005 season it boasted 804 inches. With such awesome snow and scenery, you can't go wrong at Kirkwood.

One of the most appealing aspects of this resort is its isolation from crowds and traffic. Tucked away in a world of its own, it offers a total mountain experience, remote from the hustle and bustle of everyday life. Even though the après-ski activities are sedate compared to some other resorts, the recently renovated Kirkwood Village has an interesting mix of watering holes, eateries, shops, and accommodations. Its picturesque alpine style is absolutely perfect in this pristine mountain setting. If you're planning to settle down and stay for a few days in one resort, I highly recommend Kirkwood as an ideal escape for any skier or snowboarder.

SIERRA-AT-TAHOE SNOWSPORT RESORT
1111 Sierra-at-Tahoe Road
Twin Bridges, CA
(530) 659-7453
www.sierratahoe.com

Base elevation: 6,640 feet
Top elevation: 8,852 feet
Vertical drop: 2,212 feet
Number of runs: 46
Capacity: 14,870 skiers per hour
Terrain: 25 percent beginner, 50 percent intermediate, 25 percent advanced
Skiable acres: 2,000
Longest run: 2.5 miles
Number of lifts: 12
Average snowfall: 420 inches
Lift tickets: $69 to $72
Terrain parks: 6 Snowphone: (530) 659-7475
Getting there: To reach Sierra-at-Tahoe from South Shore Lake Tahoe, take US 50 southwest for about 12 miles and turn onto Sierra-at-Tahoe Road. From North Shore Lake Tahoe, take CA 89 south from Tahoe City to US 50 and continue southwest for about 12 miles. From the Reno/Sparks area, take US 395 south to Carson City, and then follow US 50 through South Lake Tahoe to Sierra-at-Tahoe Road, about 12 miles farther. For information on the free shuttle from South Shore Lake Tahoe, call (530) 541-7548.

Although Sierra-at-Tahoe provides great terrain for skiers and boarders of all abilities, beginners especially love it because it has such a wide variety of slopes they can feel perfectly comfortable on. You won't find sharp cornices and steep chutes here, but there's plenty of thrilling cruiser runs cutting through the tall timber. Boarders can choose from six award-winning terrain parks, which are impeccably groomed for the latest thrills.

A sister resort to Northstar-at-Tahoe, Sierra offers the Vertical Plus frequent skier program also available at Northstar (see the previous description of Northstar for details). Listed in *Snow Country* magazine as the best resort in the far West for on-mountain food, the eight eateries at this resort are certainly a cut above the average. For a tasty lunch with a world-class view of Lake Tahoe, drop into the Grandview Bar & Grill at the top of the mountain.

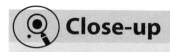

Close-up

Winter Safety

In winter the Sierra Nevada mountains offer a glorious playground with unlimited opportunities to enjoy the great outdoors. But without proper precautions, this winter wonderland can be unpleasant and sometimes it can be downright deadly. Extreme weather conditions and high altitude present challenges and dangers if you're not adequately prepared. Being "winter aware" and following recommended mountain safety practices will make your outings safer and more enjoyable.

Anyone who spends time outside in these high altitudes should know about altitude sickness, frostbite, hypothermia, and sunburn. But with proper precautions these mountain health hazards shouldn't present problems for most people. If you have health conditions that could be more hazardous in the mountains, especially heart disease or high blood pressure, you should check with your doctor before planning trips to high elevations.

Because most winter sports in the Reno/Tahoe area are enjoyed at altitudes between 6,000 and 9,000 feet, you are breathing air with less oxygen in it than the air at sea level. This lack of oxygen causes what's known as altitude sickness—chemical changes in the bloodstream that can cause headaches, fatigue, decreased appetite, nausea, shortness of breath, and restless sleep in some people. Although the body will usually adjust within a couple of days, you should avoid overexertion, get plenty of rest, drink lots of fluids, eat lightly, and avoid alcohol, particularly if you experience any of these symptoms.

Frostbite occurs when the water in cells freezes and is indicated by a burning, tingling, numbness, or whitish discoloration of the skin. Fingertips, toes, ears, cheeks, and the nose are especially vulnerable. To prevent frostbite, it's important to cover all areas of your body, especially on cold, windy days. Hats and masks are essential for warmth because a large percentage of body heat is lost through the head. You should dress in layers and even overdress. You can always peel off a jacket or vest if you get too warm. If your toes or fingers start to get cold, keep wiggling them until you can get out of the cold. If you start to feel chilled, keep moving and get inside as soon as possible.

When your body is not able to generate enough heat to keep its core temperature at its normal 98.6 degrees, hypothermia can occur. Your organs can malfunction with this loss of heat, causing shivering, fatigue, distorted thinking, impaired motor skills, and changes in mood. One of the most dangerous aspects of hypothermia is that often those affected don't realize they have it because they are unable to think clearly. It's important that everyone on an outing together monitor each other for any symptoms and help any affected persons get dry and out of the cold right away. To protect yourself against hypothermia, you should wear warm, layered clothing; take periodic indoor breaks on cold days; stay dry; and refrain from drinking alcoholic beverages.

Sunburn is a risk anytime you're outdoors, but in the mountains it's an even greater risk because at high elevations you receive five times the amount of ultraviolet rays that you would receive at sea level. It's pretty easy to protect yourself by using a sunscreen with a minimum of SPF 15 on any exposed areas of your body. Also, because ultraviolet rays are very harmful to your eyes, it's important to wear sunglasses or goggles to protect them. Eyewear also protects your eyes from tree branches when you're skiing or snowshoeing in wooded terrain.

While you should follow these health tips wherever you are in the mountains, I recommend additional safety precautions for venturing into the backcountry: Don't even pack the car until you've checked the weather forecast. With reliable and accurate weather forecasts readily available now (such as on www.weather.com), there's really no excuse for claiming ignorance of what the weather might be. If it's snowing or if a storm is on the way, it's wise to play it safe and wait for clear weather. Because blowing snow can greatly reduce your visibility, it's easy to become disoriented in a storm, even in terrain with which you are familiar. If you decide it's okay to go, check your equipment to make sure everything is in working order. If you have a problem with your skis or snowmobile, it's better to fix it before you go when you're in a safe environment. Besides your sporting gear, you should also bring along a backpack or fanny pack containing basic survival items, including waterproof matches, water, dried fruit or granola bars, a whistle, a candle, a metal cup for melting snow, a cellular phone or change for emergency phone calls, two large plastic bags for emergency shelter, a map, a compass, and a first-aid kit. Make sure you're well fed and hydrated and not overly tired before setting out. And also practice the buddy system by going with at least one other person. It's not only safer but also more fun to share your outdoor experience with a friend. Last but not least, tell a friend or family member where you're going and when you expect to be back.

When you get to your destination, leave a note on the dashboard in your car detailing where you're going, when you'll return, and who is in the group. As you strike out into the backcountry, pay attention to weather and snow conditions, especially in areas that may be avalanche prone. Because these deadly slides are more likely to be triggered on slopes 30 degrees or steeper, stay away from steep-sided ravines and the bottoms of narrow gullies, particularly just after a heavy snowfall. Also avoid terrain where vegetation has obviously been cleared away by avalanches in the past. For updated information about local avalanche danger, you can call the Tahoe National Forest Avalanche Hotline at (530) 587-2158 or access their Web site at www.avalanche.org.

Be sure to drink water often to remain hydrated and eat snacks to keep your energy level up. If you're a newcomer to the backcountry, it's wise to experience it at a leisurely pace that won't exhaust anyone in your group. Leave the macho spirit at home and be willing to finish the outing when others are ready to.

Of course, first you have to get to your mountain destination. Winter driving in the mountains can be a fun-filled adventure or a frustrating and hazardous challenge, depending upon how well prepared you are. Before heading into snow country, make sure your car is in good running condition and that you have the proper-size chains. You should also start with a full tank of gas and carry basic survival items, such as a windshield scraper or de-icer, a broom, a shovel, sand, food, water, blankets, and warm clothing. Because traffic delays are not uncommon, allow plenty of time to get to where you're going. If you encounter ice or snow on the road, slow down and give other cars around you plenty of room. Because your car needs at least three times more distance to stop on slick roads, remember to maintain a minimum distance of four to eight seconds between your vehicle and the one in front of you. If you need to pull off the road to brush off the windshield or put on chains, be sure to get completely off the pavement and to turn on your hazard lights. When you see the CHAINS REQUIRED signs, you'll have about a mile to install them before the checkpoint. Be sure to comply; you can be cited and fined if you don't. If you have a four-wheel-drive vehicle, you can usually proceed right to the checkpoint because chains are usually not required for them.

If you're properly prepared for your mountain experience, it will be safer and more comfortable. Although you can't anticipate everything that may happen, you can reduce the potential danger by using common sense and being "winter aware."

CROSS-COUNTRY SKIING

North Shore Lake Tahoe

CLAIR TAPPAAN LODGE

Donner Pass Road, off Interstate 80
Norden, CA
(530) 426-3632, (800) 679-6775
www.ctlsierraclub.org

Tucked deep into the forest on top of Donner Summit, this rustic old lodge is owned by the Sierra Club. It operates its own track system consisting of 13 kilometers of machine-groomed trails, with about 60 percent beginner and 40 percent intermediate terrain. Wandering through stands of magnificent pines, the striding and skating lanes provide a great workout and spectacular scenery. Instruction and rental equipment are available. Trail passes are $7. Accommodations in the lodge are open to both members and nonmembers of the Sierra Club, but because it's a very popular place, I recommend you reserve as far in advance as possible.

To reach Clair Tappaan from the Reno/Sparks area, take I–80 west about 45 miles to the Norden/Soda Springs exit, and then travel east for 2.4 miles on Donner Pass Road. From Tahoe City take CA 89 north to Truckee, and then I–80 west about 10 miles to the Soda Springs/Norden exit. The lodge is on the left, partially hidden in the trees above the road; you need to look carefully so as not to miss it.

GRANLIBAKKEN SKI RESORT

725 Granlibakken Road
Tahoe City, CA
(800) 543-3221
www.granlibakken.com

You can ski free here, but you're pretty much on your own as most of the 7kilometer trail is not maintained or machine set. For a lovely view of Lake Tahoe, ride the poma lift up and then follow the road to Lookout Point. If you're really ambitious, keep going for about 2 miles and you'll reach Page Meadows. Rental equipment is available, but there are no other amenities.

To get to Granlibakken from the Reno area, head west on I–80 about 30 miles to Truckee, and then south on CA 89 to Tahoe City. The resort is about 0.5 mile south of Tahoe City on CA 89.

ℹ Be sure to ask about special deals when buying your lift ticket or trail pass. Every resort has packages that may save you significant amounts of money. If you're also booking accommodations, find out if tickets and passes are included in your rental rate.

NORTHSTAR-AT-TAHOE

California Highway 267 North
6 miles north of Lake Tahoe
(530) 562-2475, (530) 562-1010
www.skinorthstar.com

Because the 50 kilometers of machine-groomed track at this major destination resort are near the alpine ski runs, you can enjoy many of the amenities offered to alpine skiers and snowboarders. Scenic trails that wind through the trees are groomed for striding and skating. Northstar is also a great telemark and snowshoe area. Rental equipment and lessons are available, and warming huts and picnic tables are scattered throughout the trail system. You can purchase trail passes at the ticketing and season pass office in the village, and then ride the gondola to the Cross-Country Ski & Snowshoe Center midmountain (next to Vista Express lift) for equipment and lessons. Trail passes are $25 for both skiers and snowshoers.

If you cross-country ski to escape the hassles found at many alpine resorts, this may not be the place for you. Although the trail system provides the quiet solitude of a backcountry outing, you're integrated with the alpine skiers in the base area and on the gondola. For more details about Northstar, see the previous description under "Alpine Skiing and Snowboarding" and read the Resorts chapter listing.

To get to Northstar, take I–80 west from Reno for about 30 miles to Truckee, and then take CA 267 south for 6 miles. From Kings Beach,

California, take CA 267 north for about 6 miles. For information about shuttle transportation to Northstar from the Lake Tahoe area, call (800) GO-NORTH, (800) 736-6365, (530) 562-3559 or (877) 274-7366. You can also visit www.lake tahoetransit.com.

RESORT AT SQUAW CREEK
Cross-Country Ski Center
400 Squaw Creek Road
Olympic Valley, CA
(530) 583-6300, ext. 6631, (800) 327-3353
www.squawcreek.com

Tucked in gorgeous Olympic Valley with the towering peaks of Squaw Valley as a backdrop, the 18 kilometers of trail at the Resort at Squaw Creek are scenic to say the very least. Although it's one of the smaller cross-country resorts in the area, it gives you a chance to soak in the awesome beauty of this very special place without the hassles of alpine skiing at Squaw Valley USA. The trails are groomed for striding and skating, and you can also try snowshoeing. Because much of the terrain is open and relatively level, it's perfect for novices. More-advanced skiers can also find some ups and downs, including several trails that wind up the mountain behind the hotel. Amenities include rentals, instruction, a ski shop, and twilight skiing. The trail pass is around $14. Since the Resort at Squaw Creek is easily one of the most exquisite resorts in the Reno/Tahoe area, I suggest you have dinner or an après-ski drink in the hotel after your day on the snow. (For more details about this resort, see the Resorts chapter. For more information on Squaw Valley, see the description of Squaw Valley USA in this chapter.)

To reach the resort from Reno/Sparks, take I–80 west for about 30 miles to Truckee, and then CA 89 south about 10 miles. After turning into Squaw Valley at the main entrance, look for Squaw Creek Road and turn left. You can either have valets park your car at the resort or use the parking lot. From Tahoe City take CA 89 north about 6 miles. For information on shuttle service to Squaw Valley USA, call (800) 327-3353, (866) 769-4653, (530) 581-7181, or (530) 550-1212.

When surfing the Web for Tahoe ski information, try these Web sites: www.virtualtahoe.com, www.tahoe.com, and www.tahoeinfo.com.

ROYAL GORGE
Interstate 80 at Donner Pass
Soda Springs, CA
(800) 500-3871
(800) 666-3871 (from northern California)
(530) 426-3661 (Rainbow Lodge)
www.royalgorge.com

Ranked the No. 1 cross-country ski resort in North America by *Snow Country* magazine, Royal Gorge has absolutely everything you could want for a perfect Nordic ski vacation. With 330 kilometers of groomed track and more than 9,000 acres of skiing terrain, it's also the largest cross-country ski resort in North America. The 90 trails range in elevation from 5,800 feet to 7,538 feet and are ranked 28 for beginners, 44 for intermediates, and 16 for experts. The resort also has four surface lifts for telemark skiing. Because of its immense size and diversity, Royal Gorge is a world unto itself. You could ski here for a week and still not explore it all. Beginners especially enjoy the Van Norden Track System, a large open meadow ringed by magnificent jagged peaks. Intermediates have a mind-boggling array of trails to choose from, including the Palisade Peak and Devil's Peak systems for awesome views of the surrounding country. Experts have more than their share of challenging terrain, including the 22.6-kilometer track to the edge of the Royal Gorge of the American River.

The resort has warming huts, trailside cafes, and several overnight lodges, such as Ice Lakes Lodge, which is tucked deep in the trees on the edge of a pine-rimmed lake For a traditionally elegant stay, you can choose Rainbow Lodge, which is also owned by Royal Gorge. At this old stagecoach stop along the Mormon-Emigrant Trail, Western history seems to ooze from its heavy rock walls. Insiders have long known that a continental dinner at the lodge's Engadine Cafe, served with just the right wine, is the ideal ending to a day of skiing at Royal Gorge.

With trail pass fees of $29 on weekends and holidays and $25 during the week, Royal Gorge is more expensive than other cross-country ski resorts, but you get what you pay for here since Royal Gorge offers the ultimate cross-country ski experience. With a recent change in ownership, the resort has reduced operating days to Thursday through Sunday except over holidays when it is open daily.

To reach Royal Gorge from Reno/Sparks, head west on I–80 about 45 miles to the Norden/Soda Springs exit and follow the signs to Summit Station. From Tahoe City take CA 89 north to Truckee, and then I–80 west about 10 miles to the Soda Springs/Norden exit.

SPOONER LAKE CROSS-COUNTRY SKI AREA
Nevada Highway 28, near the junction with U.S. Highway 50
(775) 749-5349
(888) 858-8844
www.spoonerlake.com
With 80 kilometers of groomed track, Spooner Lake is best known for the marvelous lake and mountain views skiers can enjoy from the intermediate and expert trails. The terrain is divided between the high-country trails and the meadow trails, with beginners enjoying scenic loops around frozen Spooner Lake and Spooner Meadow and more-advanced skiers climbing the surrounding slopes toward Marlette Lake, Snow Valley Peak, and Hobart Reservoir. For the ultimate backcountry experience, you can rent a beautiful hand-hewn wilderness cabin right at Spooner. Nothing beats being the first skier to hit the trails in the morning, For reservations call (775) 749-5349. Amenities include lessons, equipment rental, a day lodge, and a warming hut. The carefully groomed tracks have both striding and skating lanes, and snowshoeing is also allowed. In summer Spooner is a popular hiking/biking area and is the access point for the renowned Flume Trail mountain bike ride. Spooner has recently changed its policy about allowing dogs on its trails. If you want to bring Fido along, call to ask when dogs are allowed. The trail pass is $21.

To get to Spooner Lake from the Reno/Sparks area, head south on US 395 through Carson City, and then take US 50 west for about 15 miles toward South Lake Tahoe. The parking lot is just north of the intersection of US 50 and NV 28 on NV 28. From South Shore Lake Tahoe, take US 50 east for about 15 miles toward Carson City. From Incline Village take NV 28 south for about 12 miles. Shuttle services are available from the major casinos and hotels in Reno and from the Hyatt in Incline Village. Call (775) 749-5349 for information.

TAHOE CROSS-COUNTRY SKI AREA
Country Club Drive, Tahoe City, CA
(530) 583-5475
www.tahoexc.org
With 65 kilometers of set skating and striding track, Tahoe Cross-Country (Tahoe XC) has something for every skier. Beginners can enjoy the lower trails that wander through the pristine forest, intermediates can climb higher for peeks at Lake Tahoe, and experts can test their stamina by skiing all the way to Truckee if they wish. Even dogs especially enjoy this resort, since they can cavort off-leash (except in the parking lot and around the lodge) Monday through Friday all day and from 3:00 to 5:00 p.m. on weekends and holidays. The facility is meticulously maintained and offers instruction, equipment rental, moonlight tours, and two restaurants. Trail passes are $21.

To reach Tahoe XC from Tahoe City, head northeast on California Highway 28 for about 2 miles to the Shell service station at Dollar Hill. Turn left onto Fabian Way, then right onto Village Drive. Go up and around the corner to Country Club Drive and turn left. From the Reno/Sparks area, take I–80 west about 30 miles to Truckee, head south on CA 89 to Tahoe City, and then follow the directions above.

TAHOE DONNER CROSS-COUNTRY SKI AREA
Alder Creek Road, Truckee, CA
(530) 587-9484
www.tahoedonner.com

Stretching over 4,800 acres of terrain, Tahoe Donner Cross-Country Ski Area offers 115 kilometers of machine-groomed trails over three scenic track systems. Of the total trails, 16 are rated beginner, 24 intermediate, 5 advanced, and 1 expert. There are two wilderness trails and two for snowshoers only. The diversity of terrain includes open meadows, gentle bowls, and tree-lined trails. One of the most pristine track systems in the Reno/Tahoe area, delightful Euer Valley offers trails that meander along picturesque Prosser Creek. Just 4 kilometers from the day lodge, much of this track system is rated for beginners. You can spend the whole day here, stopping just to enjoy the views, and to refuel in the Euer Valley Cookhouse.

Amenities at this resort include snowshoeing, equipment rental, instruction, a retail shop, and four warming huts. Tahoe Donner is also the only cross-country ski area to offer night skiing (Wednesday from 5:00 to 7:00 p.m.). The trail pass is $23.

To reach Tahoe Donner from Reno/Sparks, take I–80 west for 30 miles to Truckee, and then CA 89 north for 2.2 miles. Turn left onto Alder Creek Road and travel about another 7 miles. Coming from Tahoe City, take CA 89 north to Truckee, turn left onto Donner Pass Road, and then right onto Northwoods Boulevard. Follow the signs to the ski area, about 5 miles farther on.

South Shore Lake Tahoe

CAMP RICHARDSON CROSS-COUNTRY SKI CENTER
1900 Jameson Beach Road
South Lake Tahoe, CA
(530) 542-6584, (800) 544-1801
www.camprich.com

For skiing with drop-dead-gorgeous views along the shore of Lake Tahoe, head to Camp Richardson, which offers 18 kilometers of groomed track and 20 kilometers of skier-packed track, with routes to nearby Fallen Leaf Lake and Taylor Creek. Amenities include lodging, rentals, and a restaurant. Most of the groomed trail is geared to beginners since it's fairly level, but skiers of all abilities can certainly appreciate the gorgeous environment. Since most of the skiing is at lake level, the snowpack is less than at higher elevations. It's wise to call ahead to make sure there's enough snow for skiing. Call for trail pass rates.

To get to the resort from South Lake Tahoe, take US 50 west to the "Y" (the intersection of US 50 and CA 89 in South Lake Tahoe), and then turn right and follow CA 89 north for about 2.5 miles. (For more information about Camp Richardson, see the Vacation Rentals chapter.)

HOPE VALLEY CROSS-COUNTRY
14255 California Highway 88
Hope Valley, CA
(530) 694-2266, (800) 423-9949
www.sorensensresort.com
www.hopevalleyoutdoors.com

Nestled in exquisite Hope Valley, this ski area offers an unspoiled mountain experience that's hard to beat. Environmentalists, including the folks at Sorensen's Resort just down the road, have worked successfully for years to preserve the pristine nature of this valley. It's also blessedly tranquil since snowmobiles and other vehicles are prohibited. There's very little set track, but that's part of the charm, since you can just head out on your own to explore the marked terrain. Amenities include rental equipment, instruction, and guided tours, including one that traces part of Snowshoe Thompson's famous route delivering mail to snowbound residents in the 1800s. Dogs are welcome on the trails and there is no fee, but donations are welcome.

Sorensen's offers cozy overnight lodging in unique alpine cabins with names like Dancehall, Tanglewood, and Saint Nick's. You can even bring the family dog along—pets are welcome in some of the units. A hearty meal near the fire in the country cafe here is a delight after an invigorating day on skis or snowshoes. The resort also sponsors periodic cultural events that showcase the history and natural beauty of the area. Kirkwood ski center is just 20 minutes away, so you can also take advantage of all the amenities offered there.

To reach Hope Valley Cross-Country from the Reno/Sparks area, take US 395 south to Minden, and then CA 88 west. It's about a 90-minute drive when the roads are clear. From South Shore Lake Tahoe, take US 50 west to Myers, and then turn left onto CA 89. Go south for about 12 miles, and turn left again onto CA 88. The cross-country facility is about 0.25 mile past Sorensen's Resort.

KIRKWOOD CROSS-COUNTRY & SNOWSHOE CENTER

California Highway 88, Kirkwood, CA
(209) 258-7248
www.kirkwood.com

Kirkwood Cross-Country is the largest, most-comprehensive cross-country ski area in the South Shore Lake Tahoe area, with more than 4,000 acres of exceptional terrain. The 80 kilometers of groomed track are rated 20 percent beginner, 60 percent intermediate, and 20 percent advanced. The center welcomes dogs on the High Trail behind Kirkwood Inn and the Inner Loop in the meadow. Kirkwood is easily one of the most picturesque regions outside the Lake Tahoe Basin, where you can ski through lovely meadows and along scenic ridgelines in the shadow of jagged volcanic peaks. Because Kirkwood is higher in elevation than many other cross-country ski areas, the snow here is deeper and drier, and the season is longer. A trail pass costs $22.

The resort offers a full array of amenities, including equipment rental, lessons, a retail shop, three warming huts, a restaurant, and trackside lodging. Kirkwood's ski resort is just down the road, so you can also take advantage of all the activities in Kirkwood Village at the base of the ski mountain. (See the description under "Alpine Skiing and Snowboarding" in this chapter.)

To reach Kirkwood from the Reno/Sparks area, take US 395 south to Minden, and then CA 88 west. It's about a 90-minute drive when the roads are clear. From South Shore Lake Tahoe, take US 50 southwest to Myers, and then turn left onto CA 89. Go south for about 12 miles, then turn right onto CA 88, and go west for another 14 miles.

BACKCOUNTRY AND PUBLIC CROSS-COUNTRY SKI AREAS

You don't have to go to a ski resort to enjoy the great outdoors: There's a large variety of backcountry and public areas where you can play in the snow. You're pretty much on your own at these areas, however, since most don't have any facilities. But if you're on a budget, the price is right—many are free, and some require only a few dollars for a Sno-Park permit. If there's no set track for skiers, it's usually okay to bring your dog, but consider the depth of the snow before you do; smaller animals have a difficult time in very deep snow. When snowmobilers are in the area, it's also necessary to keep a close watch on your pets. In any of these areas you'll find people enjoying the great outdoors in a variety of ways—tubing, sledding, snowshoeing, skiing, and snowmobiling. However you choose to play in the snow, the main thing is to have a good time.

I describe a few of my favorite spots below, but you can find out about others by picking up information at the Tahoe-Douglas Visitor Center at 195 US 50 in Stateline, Nevada. Trail maps and Sno-Park permits are available during business hours at the Lake Tahoe Basin Management Unit of the USDA Forest Service at 870 Emerald Bay Road in South Lake Tahoe. You can call for information at (916) 324-1222. On weekends and evenings, permits can be purchased at the Shell station at the "Y" in South Lake Tahoe (the intersection of US 50 and CA 89), and the Shell station in Myers, California. Many retail businesses near Sno-Parks sell permits, including Alpenglow Sports in Tahoe City, California; Mountain Hardware in Truckee, California; Longs Drug Store in South Lake Tahoe, California; and Homewood Hardware in Homewood, California. You can also buy permits online at www.ohv.parks.ca.gov.

DONNER MEMORIAL STATE PARK

Donner Pass Road, Truckee, CA
(530) 582-7892
www.parks.ca.gov

Operated by the California Department of Parks and Recreation, Donner Memorial State Park has a very scenic 2.5-mile set track that meanders through the trees and along the shore of Donner Lake. The terrain is relatively level and perfect for beginning skiers. It's a great area for skiing and snowshoeing, but snowmobiling and sledding are not allowed.

To get there from Reno/Sparks, take I–80 west for about 30 miles to Truckee, take the Squaw Valley exit, and turn right. At the stoplight, turn left at Donner Pass Road and follow it for 0.5 mile. From Tahoe City take CA 89 north to Truckee, and turn left onto Donner Pass Road at the second stoplight.

MARTIS LOOKOUT TRAIL
Martis Lookout Road just north of Brockway Summit, California Highway 267

Like many Forest Service roads that aren't plowed in winter, Martis Lookout Road becomes a popular access route to the backcountry when it's covered with snow. If you're really ambitious, you can follow the 8-mile loop that climbs about 1,400 feet to the top of Martis Peak. Once on the summit, you're rewarded with top-of-theworld vistas—both Lake Tahoe and the Martis Valley spread out in all their splendor directly below. The trek up is something of a challenge, but the exciting run back down makes it all worthwhile. You'll find cross-country skiers, snowshoers, and snowmobilers, with pets, kids, and the rest of the family enjoying the area. Parking is limited to a small area at the turnoff and along the road, so it's best to go early or late in the day to find a spot. When snowplows are working to clear CA 267, access may be limited even further.

To get to Martis Lookout Road from Kings Beach, take CA 267 north to the turnoff, which is about 0.25 mile past Brockway Summit and on the right. From the Reno/Sparks area, head west on I–80 about 30 miles to Truckee, and then south for about 10 miles on CA 267.

MT. WATSON ROAD
Brockway Summit, California Highway 267

At more than 7,000 feet in elevation, Mt. Watson Road is often covered with snow when areas lower down are completely bare. The road winds through deep forest for more than 20 miles, giving periodic peeks at Lake Tahoe along the way. If you keep to the right when the road forks, the climb is gradual and suitable for most levels of skiers. Going to the left puts you on a narrower, steeper path more appropriate for intermediate skiers. This is also a wonderful area for snowshoeing because you can stick to the beaten path or head off into the trees for a first-rate day in the forest. You need to watch out for snowmobiles, however, since snowmobile tour operators frequently bring groups into the area.

To get to Mt. Watson Road from Kings Beach, take CA 267 north to Brockway Summit and either park along the road or use the parking lot at the top. From the Reno/Sparks area, take I–80 west about 30 miles to Truckee, and then CA 267 south for about 10 miles to Brockway Summit.

NEVADA HIGHWAY 431
Across from Mt. Rose–Ski Tahoe

You can ski, snowshoe, sled, and tube on a little-used tract of heavily wooded land along the northwest side of NV 431 just past the entrance to Mt. Rose–Ski Tahoe ski resort. A Forest Service road winds through the trees, providing a packed surface with a gentle incline. For more ups and downs, especially for tubes and sleds, try the slopes alongside the more level surface of the road. You'll find parking at a pullout on the right side of the road as you're traveling from Reno to Incline Village, about a mile from the ski resort. I

i If you plan to go backcountry skiing, make sure you are prepared for emergencies. Though the wet "maritime" snowpack of the Sierra doesn't slide as often as drier snows in the Rocky Mountains, you should still carry avalanche beacons, probe poles, and snow shovels. Other important items for any back-country skier's pack include additional layers of clothing, food, water, a first-aid kit, flashlight, waterproof matches, and a utility knife.

don't recommend snowmobiling here, however.

To reach the area, take NV 431 east for about 11 miles from Incline Village, or west for 22 miles from Reno.

NORTH TAHOE REGIONAL PARK
875 National Avenue, Tahoe Vista, CA
(530) 546-5043, (530) 546-4212
www.ntpud.org

Insiders know if the wind is gusting over the upper mountain elevations, you can still have a great day in the snow sheltered by the dense forest at North Tahoe Regional Park. With approximately 5 miles of meandering trails, the park offers enough variety to entertain beginning as well as more-advanced skiers. But don't expect impeccable tracks, since grooming is best described as sporadic. You can rent sleds and snowmobiles, but you're on your own for any other sporting equipment. With a lot of room to roam, It's a great place to bring dogs and also a bargain—a trail pass is only $3 and is available at the self-pay system near the restrooms at the entrance to the park. Be aware, however, that the park is at relatively low elevation (around 6,000 feet), so check on snow coverage before heading out to ski here.

To get to the park from Incline Village, go west on NV 28, just past Kings Beach, to Tahoe Vista, and turn right onto National Avenue and follow the signs to the park.

TAHOE MEADOWS
West of the Mt. Rose summit on Nevada Highway 431

An exquisite alpine meadow cupped below Mt. Rose and Slide Mountain, Tahoe Meadows is one of the most popular backcountry playgrounds in the Reno/Tahoe area. You can stick to the flats by staying in the meadow proper, or you can find plenty of up-and-down by venturing through the trees on the surrounding mountains. Climbing up the ridges on the southwest side of the meadow affords gorgeous views of Lake Tahoe and lovely spots to stop for a snowy picnic. If you venture to the end of the main meadow, you also get

views of Washoe Lake and Washoe Valley. NV 431 bisects the meadow, with the largest part on the left as you approach from Reno. The smaller area on the other side of the road has less level terrain, providing open slopes popular with sledders. Snowmobilers are also restricted to this side.

Tahoe Meadows is great for family outings (including the family dog), and you'll find people doing just about everything you can do on the snow—skiing, snowmobiling, snowshoeing, tubing, and sledding. There are no facilities, so you need to bring your own food and drinks. Because of its high elevation, the meadow gets snow early in the year and keeps it well into late spring. When other mountain areas are devoid of the white stuff, you can usually find enough to ski on here. But the high elevation means that the weather can get pretty wild, so check on the forecast before you head up the mountain. The snow really piles up here, so don't be surprised if it's over the top of your car when you park along the road. Look for cuts in the snowbanks that you can use to get access to the meadow. Those tall poles with reflectors you see along the road will give you an idea of how high the snow gets; they're used as guides for the snowplows that clear the road.

For a convenient place to get on the snow (it's just minutes from either Reno or North Shore Lake Tahoe), I highly recommend Tahoe Meadows. If you're there at sundown, listening to the swish of your skis on the snow as it turns golden, you'll agree that it's a very special place to be.

To reach the meadow from Reno/Sparks, take US 395 south to NV 431 (the Mt. Rose Highway) and follow it to just past the summit. From Incline Village take NV 431 to where it levels out just before the summit.

TALLAC HISTORIC SITE TRAIL
California Highway 89
South Lake Tahoe, CA

When the snow level drops to the shores of Lake Tahoe, the 2-mile loop that winds through the Tallac Historic Site is perfect for novice cross-country skiers. You're treated to scenic views of

Lake Tahoe, Mt. Tallac, and some grand old estates dating from the 1800s. (See the Attractions chapter for a complete description of this area.)

The site is about 3 miles north of the "Y" (the intersection of US 50 and CA 89 in South Lake Tahoe) on CA 89. Be sure to pick up a Sno-Park permit before you go. Snowmobiles are not allowed here.

ICE SKATING

CITY OF SOUTH LAKE TAHOE ICE ARENA
1176 Rufus Allen Boulevard
South Lake Tahoe, CA
(530) 542-6262
www.cityofslt.us
Operated by the city, the ice arena in South Lake Tahoe offers relatively inexpensive skate sessions from about 11:00 a.m. to 9:00 p.m. during the season. Call for exact schedule. Adults can hit the ice for around $9. Skates are available for rental for just $2.

HEAVENLY VILLAGE ICE RINK
Heavenly Village Way
South Lake Tahoe, CA
(530) 542-4230, during season
www.theshopsatheavenly.com
Adding to the fun and excitement of the Shops at Heavenly Village, the outdoor ice rink offers skating from 10:00 a.m. to 10:00 P.M (weather permitting) during winter months. Adults can buy an all day pass for $20 and children 12 and under for $15, including skates. You can ride the gondola, browse the shops, check out the eateries, and skate in between for a full day of winter fun. Be sure to bundle up if you're skating after dark.

NORTHSTAR-AT-TAHOE
California Highway 267 North
6 miles north of Lake Tahoe
(530) 562-1010
Tucked among the quaint shops at the expanded village at Northstar, the ice rink offers complimentary skating and rentals. Call for hours.

RESORT AT SQUAW CREEK
400 Squaw Creek Road
Olympic Valley, CA
(530) 583-6300, ext. 6802, (530) 581-6624, (800) 327-3353
www.squawcreek.com
The outdoor skating rink at this elegant luxury resort has a classic Christmas-card view of Olympic Valley and the surrounding snowclad peaks. You don't have to be a guest to enjoy all the top-of-the-line amenities here, so lace up those skates and luxuriate in the ambience of one of the country's top winter resorts. (For a detailed description of Squaw Valley USA and the Resort at Squaw Creek, see previous sections of this chapter, along with the Resorts chapter.) The rink is open for daily sessions during winter from 10:00 a.m. to 10:00 p.m. for $10 per session for adults and $8 for those 16 and younger who have their own skates. Equipment can be rented for an additional $5. Instruction is available if you make reservations in advance.

To reach the resort from Reno/Sparks, take I–80 west for about 30 miles to Truckee, and then CA 89 south for about 13 miles. From Tahoe City take CA 89 north about 6 miles. After turning into Squaw Valley at the main entrance, look for Squaw Creek Road, and turn left. You can either take advantage of valet parking at the resort or use the parking lot.

> **i** Efforts are under way to attract the 2014 Winter Olympic Games to the Reno/Tahoe area.

RINK ON THE RIVER
10 North Virginia Street
Reno, NV
(775) 334-2262
www.cityofreno.com/res/com_service/icerink/
Almost resembling a progressive dinner, the skating rink in downtown Reno has been moved from location to location over the past several years. It seems finally to have found a permanent

home, however, on the site of where the historic Mapes Hotel once stood in downtown Reno. As an entertainment option, it's relatively cheap, with admission of $6 for skaters age 13 and older and $4.00 for those ages 3 through 12 and 55 and older. Skate rental is $2. The rink also offers season passes, group rates, and lessons. If you're into skating, it's worth checking out. After all, where else can you do triple lutzes under the glare of all that casino neon? The rink is open daily during the winter. Check the Web site or call for the schedule of skating sessions.

SQUAW VALLEY USA OLYMPIC ICE PAVILION
1960 Squaw Valley Road
Olympic Valley, CA
(530) 583-6985, (800) 545-4350
www.squaw.com

Perched midmountain, high above exquisite Olympic Valley, the outdoor Olympic Ice Pavilion at Squaw Valley USA gives you a one-of-a-kind skating experience with a breathtaking view. Adults can buy a transport/skate ticket year-round (which includes two hours of skate rental) for $27 beginning at 11:00 a.m. Termination hours vary with the season. Once on the mountain you can enjoy all the restaurants, shops, and watering holes provided at High Camp. (For more details about all the amenities offered at this world-class resort, see the description earlier in this chapter under "Alpine Skiing and Snowboarding.") Because this part of Squaw Valley can get very windy at times, it's wise to call ahead and get a weather report for the mountain. Also be sure to dress warmly, since you'll be skating outside at 8,200 feet in elevation.

To get to Squaw Valley USA, take CA 89 north from Tahoe City for about 6 miles. From Reno head west on I–80 about 30 miles to Truckee, and then go south for about 13 miles on CA 89.

TRUCKEE RIVER REGIONAL PARK
California Highway 267, south of Truckee, CA
(530) 587-6172
www.tdrpd.com

A new ice rink with all the comforts and ambience of a first-class skating experience has outclassed the natural pond that residents of Truckee skated on for years. Set among the pines along the Truckee River, the rink has an ice chilling system to create ice that even Dorothy Hamill would approve of. You can skate daily for just $6 a day (all day), in addition to $2 for skate rental. Call (530) 587-6172 or visit the Web site to find out when it opens for the season and for hours of operation.

DOGSLED RIDES

SIERRA SKI TOURING
Gardnerville, NV
(775) 782-3047
www.highsierra.com/sst

It's the only way to get around in a few corners in the world, but in Hope Valley, just 30 minutes from South Shore Lake Tahoe, riding in a dogsled is a winter experience that's uniquely entertaining. You can drive through this beautiful valley, and you can also cross-country ski and snowshoe in it, but skimming across the snow, bundled in blankets, behind eight highly trained dogs, offers a different perspective altogether. A one-hour ride is $100 for adults and $50 for children, with a minimum charge of $185. The sled can accommodate up to 375 pounds. Moonlight, picnic, and special-event rides are also offered, but you need to reserve in advance.

WILDERNESS ADVENTURES DOG SLED TOURS
(530) 550-8133
www.dogsledadventure.com

In business for more than a decade, Wilderness Adventures has introduced hundreds of winter enthusiasts to the gorgeous terrain around Sugar Bowl and Squaw Valley. One-hour daytime and sunset tours are available for $95 to $110 for adults and $45 to $55 for kids under 60 pounds. On weekdays, Wilderness Expedition trips of around two hours are also offered, covering 15 to 20 miles of majestic mountain country. The business owner takes pride in having made his own sleds by hand. Tours operate daily during winter and spring, weather permitting. Reservations advised.

SLEIGH RIDES

What's more in keeping with a winter wonderland vacation than dashing through the snow in a one-horse open sleigh? For details and reservations in the South Shore Lake Tahoe area, call Borges Sleigh Rides Stateline at (775) 588-2953 or (800) 726-7433, or click on www.sleigh ride.com; or Camp Richardson Corral at (530) 541-3113. In the North Shore Lake Tahoe area, call Borges Sleigh Rides at (800) 726-7433.

SNOWMOBILE TOURS

When the mountains and backcountry roads around Lake Tahoe are covered with a deep blanket of snow, one of the most thrilling ways to experience the great outdoors is on a snowmobile. Don't worry if you've never ridden or driven one before—it's easy to learn, and the tour operators make sure you know the basics before heading out.

You can take guided tours out to wild areas for gorgeous views, or you can race around groomed tracks in open meadows and on golf courses. Eagle Ridge Snowmobile Outfitters also offers all-day outings and overnight trips, which include stays in cozy mountain lodges. If you don't have proper clothing, don't spend a fortune buying it, because most operators will also rent you whatever gear you might need.

For details and reservations in the North Shore Lake Tahoe area, call Eagle Ridge Snowmobile Outfitters at (530) 546-8667, www.tahoe snowmobiling.com; Northstar-at-Tahoe at (530) 562-1010, www.skinorthstar.com; Lake Tahoe Snowmobile Tours at (530) 546-4280, www.lake tahoesnowmobiling.com, or High Sierra Snowmobiling at (530) 546-9909. In the South Shore Lake Tahoe area, call Lake Tahoe Winter Sports Center at (530) 577-2940 or Zephyr Cove Snowmobile Center at (775) 589-4908, www.zephyr cove.com.

FISHING AND HUNTING

Fishing and hunting inspire almost religious devotion among Insiders here in the Reno/
Tahoe area. Hang around any of the sports bars, and you can't help but overhear folks talking about the four-pound trout that got away or the huge mule deer that bounded into the
shelter of the woods before they could fire a shot. As a testament to the importance that sports
play in the area, Scheels and Cabela's invested millions in developing huge retail stores in the
Reno/Sparks area. See the Shopping chapter for details.

In this chapter, I'll give you a quick overview of the fishing and hunting scenes in the Reno/
Tahoe area. I'm not going to make you experts, but I will give you a few tips and hints to get you
started and help you have an enjoyable time. In addition to everything else the area offers, it is
a rare paradise that includes many opportunities for anglers and hunters.

FISHING

The Reno/Tahoe area is renowned for its trout
fishing—unsurpassed by many other spots in
the contiguous 48 states. Within 60 miles of Lake
Tahoe, anglers have more than 400 lakes, reservoirs, rivers, creeks, and streams to fish, all set in
spectacular, scenic country. Whether you're fly
fishing on the cool, swift waters of the Truckee
River, have a hankering to land a big Mackinaw
from Lake Tahoe, or are out for a day trip to Pyramid Lake, you'll find fishing in the area thrilling
and challenging.

Both the Nevada Division of Wildlife and the
California Department of Fish and Game operate stocking programs in the Reno/Tahoe area,
but which species of fish they plant, where the
fish are planted, and when they are planted are
subject to change annually, depending on the
recommendations of wildlife biologists, angler
surveys, and stocking and management plans
for specific fisheries. You can find out which
fish have been planted where by accessing the
weekly reports given on these agencies' Web
sites. Also, because water levels in streams and
lakes can vary considerably depending upon the
amount of snow that fell the previous winter, I
recommend checking on the status of your fishing hole before heading out to catch the big one.
In addition to fish and game Web sites, some of

the best information can be found at local tackle
stores. For California click on www.dfg.ca.gov,
and for Nevada www.ndow.org.

In Lake Tahoe you can fish year-round
because the lake never freezes over. In addition
to the game fish that naturally inhabit the lake,
the California Department of Fish and Game
closely monitors the number of kokanee salmon
that spawn in Taylor Creek every year and, when
necessary, boosts the stocks of these popular fish
that end up in the lake by planting fingerlings.

In the Desolation Wilderness (see the Area
Overview and Recreation chapters for a description), some 130 lakes await the trout angler,
and all of these lakes teem with fish, including
the elusive and scarce golden trout, found only
in the highest lakes in the wilderness. Though
Desolation Wilderness is among the most used
wilderness areas in the United States, most hikers don't head into the high country expressly to
fish, leaving an abundance of opportunity for the
avid angler.

Pyramid Lake, a high-desert lake just 35 miles
north of Reno, is home to the legendary cutthroat
trout, which fascinated John Frémont and his
group (see the History section for a brief description of Frémont's expedition, and the Day Trips
chapter for more about Pyramid Lake). The record
size of a cutthroat trout (caught in 2005) was 33.5

inches and weighed 24 pounds 12 ounces. For other record trophy fish caught in Nevada, visit www.ndow.org. Pyramid Lake sits on an Indian reservation, so you don't need a Nevada fishing license to cast your line here, but you will have to purchase a permit on the reservation.

The fishing in Lake Tahoe and Pyramid Lake alone is good enough to qualify the area as a trout angler's mecca. There are more opportunities in other lakes and streams, but the limitations of this guide make it impossible to cover every creek, stream, and lake within the 60-mile radius. Instead I'm going to concentrate on the Lake Tahoe–Truckee River–Pyramid Lake water system—the major system in the Reno/Tahoe area. It's easily accessible and will provide more fishing action than the average visitor to the area can handle, as well as plenty of opportunities for the resident angler. (If you're itching for more, you might also want to check out Dave Stanley's No Nonsense Guide to Fly Fishing in Nevada, by Dave Stanley, and The Nevada Angler's Guide, by Richard Dickerson.)

The Truckee River connects Lake Tahoe and Pyramid Lake, and together they make up what's known as a closed water system—in other words, their waters never reach the ocean. At one time, fish could swim from one lake to the other by way of the Truckee River. Today that's not so, and the system is treated as three different fisheries, each requiring different fishing techniques.

This chapter provides basic information about these three exceptional fisheries, which should enable you to catch more trout and have more fun doing it. Remember that trout fishing, especially in the Reno/Tahoe area, is both a recreational sport and an art. Trout grow big and wily because anglers underestimate them. They're smart, but I hope to make you smarter by giving you a few Insiders' tricks to help you fill your creel. If that creel, by chance or plan, remains empty, keep in mind that you don't have to catch fish to have fun, especially in this area. You will be out in the fresh air, enjoying the scenery, far from the worries and cares of crowded city life, and that is reward enough. Go fishing, and give your mind a chance to relax.

Lake Tahoe

When anglers first get a look at Lake Tahoe, they usually scratch their heads and ask, "Where do I begin?" After all, the lake is 22 miles long and 12 miles wide, and most experienced Lake Tahoe guides will tell you that successfully fishing this lake takes more skill and finesse than many other American lakes. It ranks 5th in the world in mean depth (1,027 feet), and 10th in the world in maximum depth (1,636 feet), and its mirrorlike conditions make for some real spooky trout.

Most first-time anglers have a difficult time landing game fish in Lake Tahoe. In fact, I know one experienced angler who fished the lake for five years and only netted two lake, or Mackinaw, trout. But then, he was a stubborn fellow who wouldn't ask the experts for help; thus my first bit of advice for new anglers on Lake Tahoe is to hire a guide. I understand that to some this is akin to stopping your car at a gas station to ask for directions, but you'll have more fun if you heed this advice.

More than 25 guides make a living on Lake Tahoe (see the end of this chapter for an abbreviated listing), and hiring one to show you the ins and outs of Tahoe's fishing scene is money well spent. A guide can show you the techniques needed to land the "big one"; once you've learned from a professional, catching fish on your own should be a lot easier.

Because Lake Tahoe is located both in California and Nevada, the states have agreed to honor a fishing license from either state when fishing the lake. Any person 16 years of age or older must have a license to fish. Limits are five game fish, of which no more than two may be Mackinaw.

Lake Tahoe is open year-round, and fishing is permitted on a daily basis beginning one hour before sunrise and ending two hours after sunset. Fishing is not permitted in the following areas:

- Within 300 feet of Tahoe's tributaries and upstream to the first lake from October 1 to June 30 on the California side
- Within a 200-yard radius of the mouths

of Third, Incline, and Wood Creeks on the Nevada side

- Within a 500-yard radius of Sand Harbor boat ramp
- Within the boat-launch area in the jetty at Cave Rock

ℹ️ Disabled anglers delight in the barrier-free fishing platforms on the West Fork of the Carson River. You'll find them in Hope Valley, one of the most beautiful sections of the river, at the intersection of California Highways 88 and 89, 15 miles south of South Lake Tahoe.

BOAT FISHING

The first thing to remember about fishing Lake Tahoe is that a boat with a fish-finder is mandatory if you expect to catch "the big one." Lake Tahoe has a lot of water and several species of game fish (kokanee salmon; brook, brown, rainbow, and Mackinaw trout; and the native, endangered, and extremely rare cutthroat trout), making trolling the most popular method used by anglers on this lake.

The theory behind trolling is that you can cover a lot of territory in a short amount of time, and you can bring the bait to the fish rather than waiting for the fish to come to the bait. On Lake Tahoe, anglers usually use two trolling methods for the prized Mackinaw—downrigging and lead lining.

Downriggers are fishing devices fixed to the boat that enable you to use heavy weights on a separate reel. These weights are attached to your fishing line by clips. Once a fish strikes, the weights are released and reeled in, and it's just you and the monster Mackinaw on the other end of the line. The weights help you troll with lures and live bait at varying depths, depending on where the fish are. The fish-finders help determine the depth of the fish, too.

Lead lining is a technique used to go deep—sometimes as much as 200 feet—for the big Macks. The technique is to use flashy lures like wobbling spoons, Rebels, and Rapalas behind a lead-core nylon line or metal line. You run the line out—sometimes as far as 300 yards, depending on how deep the fish are—and wait for a strike.

Jigging is another method anglers use to catch Mackinaws in Lake Tahoe. Jigging usually consists of using a live minnow on a treble hook combined with a jig. Jigging lures resemble wounded fish. The idea is to work the rod with small tugs to give the impression that the minnow is wounded, with the hope of drawing the Mack in for the strike.

To go for the feisty rainbows in Lake Tahoe, the preferred method is to top line, trolling a lure just below the surface near the lake's shore. Some anglers find fighting a rainbow on light line a lot more fun than dragging in a half-drowned Mackinaw and 300 yards of lead line. The rainbows fight like crazy, leaping out of the water and making long runs trying to spit the hook. The best place to top-line troll for rainbows is along the rocky shoal areas using Flatfish and Hot Shot plugs, or Rebel and Rapala lures.

During summer and early fall, fishing for kokanee salmon is extremely popular. The salmon spawn up Taylor Creek, and during the migrating run, thousands head to the spawning grounds. They can be caught by trolling with downriggers and, according to one local guide, make a tasty meal.

PIER AND SHORE FISHING

Don't fret if you don't have access to a boat, because pier and shore fishing around Lake Tahoe can be fun and productive, too. You just have to remember a few things—avoid fishing when the lake is mirrorlike calm, and try to make long casts from both pier and the shore so the fish don't see you. Remember, the fish in this lake are already spooky.

The best time to fish from a pier or the shore is when a healthy breeze blows waves on the water. Large trout will cruise into shore looking for minnows, crawfish, or any other food kicked up by the rough water. Spinners and lures work best, but bait anglers using worms, salmon eggs, and Power Bait have been known to pull in a few lunkers. Always use light monofilament line to hide the leaders. You can find trout close to shore at Rubicon Point, Dollar Point, Crystal Bay Point, Sand Harbor, Cave Rock, and south of Tahoe City, but don't restrict your fishing to these points, as trout can be found everywhere around the lake.

The Truckee River

The Truckee River, Lake Tahoe's only outlet, begins its trek from the dam at Tahoe City, California, and continues along California Highway 89 through the town of Truckee, California, then along Interstate 80 through Reno and Sparks, eventually emptying into Pyramid Lake. The 115 miles of river used to be the breeding ground of the monstrous Lahontan cutthroat trout. In autumns long gone, these fish would make spawning runs from Pyramid Lake back toward Lake Tahoe. The days of seeing so many fish you could almost walk on the Truckee River are gone, but thanks to several consecutive wet years, trout fishing in the river is amply rewarding, and attempts are being made to bring back the native Lahontan cutthroat.

The Truckee River is split into three separate lengths for purposes of fishing. The upper section runs from Lake Tahoe to the town of Truckee, California, the middle section from Truckee to the Nevada state line, and the lower section from the Nevada state line to Pyramid Lake.

The upper section is heavily fished because CA 89 runs parallel to the river, and several public campgrounds sit on its banks, making access to great fishing easy. The floods of 1997 and 2006 altered some of the characteristics of this upper section, but big pools of slow-moving water still exist, hiding some monstrous trout. During the summer, many people enjoy rafting and tubing this section of the river, so the best times to fish are usually early morning or late evening. Normally, the river has slowed from late June to early September, making these the best months to fish.

The season lasts from the last Saturday in April to November 15, but fishing is prohibited from Fanny Bridge at Lake Tahoe to 1,000 feet downstream. Just about any trout-fishing technique will work on the upper section of the river—lures, especially Mepps and Panther Martins; salmon eggs and worms bounced along the bottom; and for the fly-fishing enthusiast, caddis flies, streamers, and nymphs presented just before dark. The limit is five trout per day, but a local guide suggests you catch and release all fish along this stretch.

The middle section of the Truckee River is wild trout country, and legal restrictions vary depending on where you fish. A copy of the California Department of Fish and Game regulations is mandatory to stay out of legal trouble with the game wardens and to enjoy fishing this section; you can acquire this guide at any sporting-goods store that sells fishing licenses. From Trout Creek to Glenshire Bridge and from Prosser Creek to Boca Bridge, only artificial lures with barbless hooks are allowed. From Glenshire Bridge to Prosser Creek, only artificial flies with barbless hooks are allowed. From Boca Bridge to the state line, any type of fishing gear is permissible. A 2-mile stretch of the river, from the Glenshire Bridge to the first I-80 bridge downstream, is private property and off-limits. Obviously, close attention to the regulations is mandatory—but the rewards are sweet here.

The middle section is inhabited by rainbows, browns, and possibly some cutthroat. You'll find some of the most challenging fishing on the river in this section. But watch out near the state line: If you fish on it or cross it, you will need a license from both California and Nevada.

The season for this section is open from the last Saturday in April to November 15. The catch limit varies on this stretch, so consult the regulations.

The lower section of the Truckee River, which is entirely in Nevada, may offer opportunities for some trophy trout. And for the first time in many, many years, Lahontan cutthroat trout comprise 50 percent of the catchable trout on this section of the Truckee. The best fishing here will be associated with lower-flow conditions following the winter runoff—usually July through October.

The trophy section of the river, where trout grow big and smart, runs from the California border downstream to the I–80 bridge near Crystal Peak Park in Verdi. Only artificial lures with single, barbless hooks may be used, and the limit is 2 trout and 10 mountain whitefish, with the minimum size for the trout set at 14 inches. The remaining 75 miles of the river in Nevada have no gear limitations. The river in this section is easily accessed from Crystal Peak Park, Dog Valley Road bridge, and both bridges on Third Street.

This section of river often boggles experienced anglers' minds because they can enjoy some of the best trout fishing in the state only a few hundred yards from the glitter of Reno's downtown casinos. And fly fishing on this little river rivals many of the rivers in neighboring states, because the Truckee is home to most of the insects fly anglers like to imitate—stone flies, mayflies, caddis flies, and others. The trout fishing is simply great all along this section.

Bouncing salmon eggs and worms along the bottom is always a good technique in this section of the river, and using lures like Mepps, Panther Martins, Rapalas, and Rebels always works, too. Some of the more popular areas in Reno to fish the Truckee are Mayberry Park, Idlewild Park, and any of the three Fisherman's parks.

You can fish this section year-round, any hour of the day or night, except for the portion 1,000 feet downstream of Derby Dam, which is closed to all fishing. The limit is 5 trout and 10 mountain whitefish.

Pyramid Lake

Pyramid Lake is located 35 miles north of Reno by way of Nevada Highway 445 (the Pyramid Highway). It is located on the Pyramid Lake Paiute Indian Reservation. While a Nevada fishing license is not required, you must purchase a permit to fish on the reservation. Permits are available at the reservation store, at the lake's ranger station, and from most bait and tackle shops in Reno and Sparks.

The lake received its name from a pyramid-shaped tufa mound (calcium deposit) rising out of the water. It is a starkly beautiful lake, flanked by rugged mountains on the east and west. No trees grow here, but the lake is home to monstrous cutthroat trout. The average trout pulled is about 2 feet long and weighs around five pounds.

Fishing Pyramid Lake is great either from shore or from a boat. The cutthroat trout is very active in its search for food and often swims into shallow water. Trolling is the preferred method of catching fish at Pyramid, using lures that imitate minnows, and downriggers to get the lures to the correct depth. Boat anglers use Tor-p-Dos, Apex lures, U20 Flatfish, Pink Ladies, and flashers. Shore anglers stick to using Tor-p-Dos, Rapalas, Daredevils, and Maribu jigs.

Fly fishing is also popular at Pyramid Lake and probably the most exciting method of catching fish here. Cutthroats strike flies with a vengeance. Fly anglers use six- to nine-pound leaders with fast-sinking fly line (shooting heads) when fishing the drop-offs and a slow-sinking line at the shallow beaches. Black and purple Woolly Worms and Woolly Buggers are their favorite flies. And anglers will usually use two sizes of flies, one as a dropper, to find out what the fish are biting on. One of the most peculiar things that you'll see at the lake are anglers standing on small stepladders in the waist-deep water while casting. The added height can help increase an angler's casting distance but also makes for an unusual picture.

The fishing season at Pyramid Lake runs from October 1 through June 30. The keeper size for the cutthroat is 16 to 19 inches and any cutthroat more than 24 inches. The daily limit is two, with only one that is more than 24 inches. One rod and two hooks per angler are allowed, and fishing is permitted with artificial lures only. For more information about the lake, visit www .pyramidlakefisheries.org.

Fishing Licenses

All license fees are subject to change. These annual rates were current for the 2009 season. More details are available on the state wildlife services' Web sites: For Nevada: www.ndow.org; for California: www.dfg.ca.gov.

California

Everyone 16 years of age and older must have a valid fishing license. These rates were current at press time.
Annual resident: $40.20
Annual nonresident: $110.80
One-day resident or nonresident: $13.40
Ten-day nonresident: $41.20

Nevada

Everyone 12 years of age and older must have a valid fishing license.
Resident:
   16 years of age and older: $29
   12 to 15 years of age: $13
   Younger than 12 years old: Free
Nonresident:
   16 years of age and older: $69
   12 to 15 years of age: $21
   One-day license: $18

Pyramid Lake

Everyone must have a valid fishing permit to fish Pyramid Lake.
One-day permit: $9
Season permit: $74

Fishing Guides

Most fishing guides have morning and afternoon trips that include all the gear along with a meal or snacks and drinks. Call for rates and schedules.

Lake Tahoe

FIRST STRIKE SPORTFISHING
Tahoe Keys Marina South
Lake Tahoe, CA
(530) 577-5065
www.sportfishing.com
First Strike specializes in year-round charters for trout and salmon using the latest in electronic equipment and lightweight tackle. They have a morning and afternoon charter that includes bait, tackle, and snacks—and they'll even clean your

fish. Write P.O. Box 13107, South Lake Tahoe, CA 96157 for more information.

KINGFISH GUIDE SERVICE
5110 West Lake Boulevard
Homewood, CA
(530) 525-5360
www.kingfishtahoe.com
This outfit runs charters year-round on the lake from a 43-foot boat named the Kingfish. All equipment—tackle, rods, and reels—is included. Trips leave early in the morning from the pier across from Homewood Mountain Resort. The mailing address is P.O. Box 5955, Tahoe City, CA.

MICKEY'S BIG MACK CHARTERS
Carnelian Bay, CA
(530) 546-4444, (800) 877-1462
www.mickeysbigmack.com
Fish year-round with master guide Mickey Daniels. He has been fishing Lake Tahoe for more than 30 years and guarantees he will find you fish. Call the number above or write for more information: P.O. Box 488, Carnelian Bay, CA 96140.

TAHOE SPORTSFISHING
900 Ski Run Boulevard, Suite 102
South Lake Tahoe, CA
(530) 541-5448, (800) 696-7797

Zephyr Cove Marina
Zephyr Cove, NV
(775) 586-9338
www.tahoesportfishing.com
Fishing the lake since 1953, Tahoe Sportfishing offers four-, five- and seven-hour trips that include all gear, tackle, and bait. Boats leave in the morning and in the afternoon. These guides also clean and wrap your catch. Fishing licenses are available here as well.

Pyramid Lake

CUTTHROAT CHARTERS
29555 Pyramid Highway
Sutcliff, NV
(775) 476-0555
www.fishpyramid.com

This family-owned and -operated business, which runs out of the Pyramid Lake Store, guarantees anglers will catch cutthroat trout. Cutthroat Charters is only 30 minutes from Reno and Sparks, and it operates seven days a week during the season. A four-hour trip is $125 per person; a six-hour outing is $175 per person.

Fly Fishing

Avid anglers in the area know that one of the best ways to keep informed about local fly fishing conditions is to associate with the Truckee River Flyfishers. Organized in the 1970s to promote and encourage the conservation of game fish, the group has regular get togethers, educational seminars and fishouts. For more information on membership, which also includes a regular newsletter, visit their Web site at www.truckeeriver flyfishers.org. Most meetings take place in Reno. You can also rely on local fly shops for equipment and education. The following establishments will supply you with all your fly-fishing needs, including licenses, lessons, fly-tying classes, equipment, and local knowledge.

Fly Fishing Retailers

CABELA'S
8650 Garson Road
Reno, NV
(775) 829-4100
www.cabelas.com
For a detailed description of this enormous retail sporting goods store, see the Shopping chapter.

MARK FORE AND STRIKE SPORTING GOODS
490 Kietzke Lane, Reno, NV
(775) 322-9559

ORVIS
13945 South Virginia Street
(Summit Sierra Mall)
Reno, NV
(775) 850-2272
www.orvis.com

RENO FLY SHOP
294 East Moana Lane #14
Reno, NV
(775) 825-3474
www.renoflyshop.com
The Reno Fly Shop has a sister store, Truckee River Outfitters, that is open from late April through September and offers all the services mentioned above, as well as guide services. The address is 10200 Donner Pass Road, Truckee, CA 96161; (530) 582-0900.

SCHEEL'S
1455 East Lincoln Way
(Legends at Sparks Marina)
(775) 331-2700
www.scheels.com
The world's largest collection of sporting goods merchandise under one roof. If that doesn't say it all, you'll find details in the Shopping chapter.

Fly Fishing Guide Services

JOHNSON TACKLE & GUIDE SERVICE
P.O. Box 26, Tahoma, CA 96142
(530) 525-6575 (summer)
(415) 453-9831 (winter)
www.flyfishingtahoe.com
Randy Johnson is not only a master guide but also a well-known fly-tier with more than 150 designs to his credit.

STILLWATER GUIDE SERVICE
Reno, NV
(775) 851-1558
www.out4trout.com
Specializing in fly fishing for trophy trout, Stillwater Guide Services offers trips in the Reno/Tahoe area along with lakes and reservoirs in northeast California. Call for rates and specifics.

TAHOE FLY FISHING OUTFITTERS
2705 Lake Tahoe Boulevard
South Lake Tahoe, CA
(530) 541-8208, (877) 541-8208
www.tahoeflyfishing.com
In addition to retail services including fly-fishing

equipment, bait and tackle, and fishing licenses, this company offers expert guide service for the entire length of the Truckee River, as well as the Carson Valley, Tahoe, and Truckee areas.

> **i** A great source for hunting and fishing information is Dave Rice's Friday column in the *Reno Gazette-Journal*.

HUNTING

Everything you've heard about the top quality of hunting in California and Nevada is true. Game abounds in these two states. Big animals like deer, bear, mountain lion, bighorn sheep, elk, antelope, and mountain goat roam open country in both states, along with migratory fowl, quail, grouse, dove, turkey, chukar, pheasant, rabbit, squirrel, and furbearing animals. Most species have specific hunting seasons, which vary from year to year, and differ depending on whether you are hunting with a conventional weapon, muzzleloader, or longbow.

While you can hunt for game birds, mule deer, and antelope near Reno and Lake Tahoe, the sport is relatively limited in the area. According to one local guide, development in the region has resulted in a reduction of the habitat necessary to support a large population of big game. Because of the relatively limited opportunities, I have limited the hunting section of this guide to just a few paragraphs, which will let you know where to find more detailed information.

In the Reno/Tahoe area, places to hunt small game and birds can be found outside of the cities of Reno and Sparks; for more abundant opportunities and bigger game, you might want to head north toward the Black Rock Desert. Prime hunting for ducks and geese is found around Fallon, about 60 miles east of Reno (see the Day Trips chapter). For information contact Greenhead Hunting Club at 9165 Pasture Road, Fallon; (775) 423-3071 during hunting season. For upland game birds Insiders head to the mountain ranges around Lovelock and Winnemucca, north

of Reno, or to central Nevada near the tiny town of Austin. On the California side of Lake Tahoe, hunting for deer, quail, and bear is allowed in some parts of the El Dorado National Forest and in the Desolation Wilderness.

Hunting regulations are stringent and detailed—the regulations for Nevada alone fill a large booklet and cover everything from use or possession of a firearm by a child to sunrise and sunset tables, application and tag regulations, and hunting season dates and quotas. The best way to educate yourself is to acquire the regulations for the state you plan to hunt in. Both states require a hunting license and have an established application process for obtaining big-game hunting tags. To hunt in the Reno/Tahoe area, you must apply for a tag specific to that area well in advance of the first day of the season.

Nevada

For detailed information on hunting regulations in Nevada, you should read the Nevada Hunt Book, which is updated annually and available in spring. This will provide you with everything you need to know, including information about regulations and fees and how to obtain the license and tag necessary to hunt the game of your choice. You can access it online or obtain a hard copy by calling or writing:

Nevada Division of Wildlife
1100 Valley Road
Reno, NV 89512
(775) 688-1500
(800) 576-1020 for information about tags
www.ndow.org

California

The California Department of Fish and Game publishes the California Hunting Regulations for Mammals and Furbearers and Resident and Migratory Upland Game Bird Hunting Regulations on an annual basis. The fees and regulations are in effect from each July to June of the following year. You can obtain this information online or by calling or writing:

California Department of Fish and Game
P.O. Box 944209
Sacramento, CA 94244-2090
(916) 653-4899
www.dfg.ca.gov

Hunting Guides

Sometimes the best plan of action is to hire a hunting guide, an Insider who knows the regulations, the game, and the lay of the land.

BLACK ROCK OUTFITTERS
P.O. Box 1192
Winnemucca, NV 89446
(775) 623-5926

A lifelong resident of Winnemucca and a guide since 1985, Michael Hornbarger of Black Rock Outfitters knows the back-country of northern Nevada intimately. Since learning to trap as a child, he's explored every inch of this wild land, guiding friends and clients on hunting and photo trips for years. He'll personalize a tour or hunt just for you, whether you're out to bag a mountain lion, want to go fishing, take a tour of the Black Rock Desert, or capture the wonders of the back-country in the lens of your camera.

NEVADA TROPHY HUNTS
P.O. Box 10, Gerlach, NV 89412
(775) 557-2238
www.nevadatrophyhunts.com

A former wildlife photographer whose work has appeared in *National Geographic* magazine, Tony Diebold of Nevada Trophy Hunts is the consummate outdoorsman. His personalized trophy hunts for mule deer, desert sheep, antelope, and elk are well known throughout Nevada, and he also leads guided fishing and sightseeing trips. If you shoot with a camera and not a gun, you can take wildlife photo trips with him to some of the most unspoiled animal habitats in the area.

TAHOE FLY FISHING OUTFITTERS
2705 Lake Tahoe Boulevard
South Lake Tahoe, CA
(530) 541-8208, (877) 541-8208
www.tahoeflyfishing.com

Mentioned in the fishing section, this outfit also offers guided hunts for migratory waterfowl in Nevada. The season varies but generally runs from October through January, depending on the type of game.

Hunting Licenses
Nevada

As with fishing licenses, fees are subject to change annually. Consult the Nevada Hunt Book or the Nevada Division of Wildlife for current rates.
Resident:
    16 years and older: $33
    12 to 15 years old: $13
Nonresident:
    General: $142

California

Fees are subject to change annually. Refer to the California Department of Fish and Game, the California Hunting Regulations for Mammals and Furbearers, or the Resident and Migratory Upland Game Bird Hunting Regulations for the most current rates.
Resident:
    General: $38.85
    Junior, 16 years or younger: $10.25
    Lifetime licenses are available.
Nonresident:
    General: $134.95

SPECTATOR SPORTS

Over the years, the Reno/Sparks area has seen a succession of professional and semiprofessional sports teams come and go as the area struggled to support them along with the sports programs at the University of Nevada, Reno. Recent growth in the area has made some local sports fans' dreams come true, however, with the arrival of the Reno Aces minor league baseball team and the Reno Bighorns, a D-League NBA Development team. The Aces occupy a new state-of-the-art stadium built especially for them in downtown Reno, and the Bighorns shoot it out at the Reno Events Center. Although the shaky economy makes the success of these teams perhaps harder to achieve, many local fans are hopeful that the Reno/Sparks area finally has enough financial clout to adequately support them well into the future. The teams were new in 2008 and 2009, and only time will tell what their ultimate successes will be. Local fans have always had other outlets for watching spectator sports, which is obvious if you visit a sports book at any casino over the weekend or wander into any of the numerous sports bar scattered all over. You'll also notice that community sports programs are well supported, with large numbers of participants and fans making good use of both indoor and outdoor sports venues throughout the year.

Also the Wolf Pack sports program at UNR does a fine job in providing high quality and variety for spectators throughout the year. Fans can choose from baseball, football, basketball, soccer, and volleyball. Once a very winning member of the Big West Conference, the university was moved to a higher level of competition in the Western Athletic Conference several years ago. Support for university sports is strong, with the fund-raising organization hosting a variety of lucrative events throughout the year. To find out how to become an active Wolf Pack booster, call (775) 784-6900. The Reno/Tahoe area is also home to two unique sporting events that attract spectators from all over the country—the annual National Championship Air Races and The Great Reno Balloon Race.

Furthermore, Reno's National Bowling Stadium is one of the largest and best in the country, hosting numerous bowling tournaments throughout the year. And there's always that favorite Western sports event, the rodeo, along with ski and snowboard events around Lake Tahoe.

Read on to see what the Reno/Tahoe area has to offer for those of you who like to be knee-deep in the sports action. I haven't used the usual geographical organization in this chapter, since most of the sports action happens in the Truckee Meadows—but don't let the drive from Lake Tahoe deter you from enjoying some great sports options.

AIR RACES

NATIONAL CHAMPIONSHIP AIR RACES
Reno Stead Airport
4895 Texas Avenue Reno, NV
(775) 972-6663
www.airrace.org

Bill Stead was a World War II ace, a Nevada rancher, and a dreamer. In 1964 he realized his biggest dream when he convinced local businessmen to bring Midwestern-style air racing to the Reno/Tahoe area. Today the National Championship Air Races are the biggest in the United States, with around 200,000 spectators watching six different classes of racing during the five-day event.

Every September, racers gather from all corners of the United States to participate in the fastest motor sport in the world. In addition to the on-hand, modern military aircraft, unlimiteds, AT-6s, biplanes, Formula Ones, jets, and sport-class kit aircraft swarm to the Stead Airport to race against the forces of nature, gravity, and one another. This spectacle is so amazing and so unbelievable, Insiders say that "the show needs the heavens as its stage." (See also the Annual Events chapter.)

Daily general admission tickets for adults for the Wednesday through Sunday event range around $10 to $27 and may be purchased over the phone by calling Ticketmaster at (775) 787-8497 or accessing www.ticketmaster.com.

BALLOON RACES

THE GREAT RENO BALLOON RACE
Rancho San Rafael Park
330 East Liberty Street, #200 (office)
Reno, NV
(775) 826-1181
www.renoballoon.com

More than 100 hot-air balloons in all shapes and sizes, including panda bears, whiskey bottles, D-cell batteries, and Burger King Whoppers, fill the predawn skies over Reno's Rancho San Rafael Park during The Great Reno Balloon Race. The event, usually held in September, draws a crowd of more than 130,000 over its four days. This free (both admission and parking) spectacular includes two types of balloon flying competition—a Hare and Hound race and various target drops.

In the Hare and Hound race, one balloon launches early (the hare), and the other balloons (the hounds) try to follow the path of the first balloon. The hare lands in a safe area and plants a target. The hounds try to drop a marker closest to the center of the target from the air.

The target drop–style of race has the pilots launching their balloons from a 1-mile radius outside the park. The balloonists navigate into the park where a target has been placed on the ground and attempt to place their markers closest to the center of the target from the air.

On Saturday and Sunday of the event, balloonists launch the Dawn Patrol, a pre-sunrise liftoff. The balloons' ascensions are usually choreographed to music, and it is a spectacular sight, with the balloons lighting up the dark sky. Only a few pilots worldwide are qualified to fly a Dawn Patrol, making the feat extra-special for spectators.

During the events, spectators are welcome to walk through the park and to talk with flight crews and pilots as they fill their balloons with air. Most spectators bring picnic breakfasts, but an extensive concession area is always set up ready to cater to everyone's needs.

BASEBALL

RENO ACES
Stadium at corner of East Second Street and Evans Avenue
Reno, NV
(775) 334-4700
www.renoaces.com

Formerly the Tucson Sidewinders, an affiliate of the Arizona Diamondbacks, the Reno Aces took up residence in their new $50 million ballpark in downtown Reno just in time for the opening season of 2009. The design-build stadium (not named as of press time) seats about 6,500 people with room for another 2,500 on the grass hill in right field. Local fans are very enthusiastic about the first-time arrival of a Triple-A minor league team of their very own. Team owners, SKBaseball, plan to keep ticket prices low enough to encourage families to attend games, with prices for single game adult seats starting at $9 and going up to $25 for box seats behind home plate. Consult the Web site for a schedule of games. Future plans for the stadium site include restaurants, retail shopping, and nightlife venues.

RENO ASTROS

Moana Stadium,
300 West Moana Lane Reno, NV
(775) 851-0937
www.renoastros.com

Although the Reno Astros are a semiprofessional team, many of the players have paid their dues playing professional ball. You can see all the action several days a week during the season, which runs from April through October. And, unlike the pros, the admission prices are very affordable for the whole family.

UNR BASEBALL

William Peccole Park
University of Nevada, Reno
(775)784-6900
(775)348-PACK (tickets)
www.nevadawolfpack.com

The Wolf Pack's baseball schedule begins in late January and ends in May. A perennial NCAA regional qualifier, the team has a very loyal following. The quality of the program over the years is shown by the number of players that move on to pro teams. Since 1990 more than 40 UNR players have signed professional baseball contracts. As with most college baseball venues, William Peccole Park is outdoors, so check the weather and be prepared to bundle up at the beginning of the season.

i You can show your support for University of Nevada, Reno, sports by purchasing Wolf Pack logo merchandise at www.nevadawolfpack.com.

BASKETBALL

RENO BIGHORNS

Reno Events Center
400 North Center Street
Reno, NV
(775) 284-2622
www.renobighorns.com

The Reno Bighorns began their inaugural season as a D-League NBA Development team in the 2008-2009 season. The 24-game schedule of home appearances is played at the Reno Events Center, which holds about 4,700 fans when configured for a basketball team. Intent on attracting families and filling the space, the league is committed to offering affordable entertainment, with general admission tickets beginning at $10. Visit ticketmaster.com or tickets@nbareno.com to purchase them.

UNR BASKETBALL

Lawlor Events Center
University of Nevada, Reno
(775) 348-PACK (tickets)
www.nevadawolfpack.com

Both men's and women's basketball programs at UNR provide exciting action for hoops fans each season. The men play about 15 home games, which attract an average of 6,000 spectators each. The men played in the Sweet Sixteen in 2005 and won the WAC championship in 2006.

Average attendance for the women is around 1,000 per game. Both teams play at Lawlor Events Center, a typical college arena with about 11,500 seats.

BOWLING

NATIONAL BOWLING STADIUM

300 North Center Street, Reno, NV
(775) 334-2600, (800) 304-2695
www.visitrenotahoe.com

This bowling stadium is the world's largest and most advanced. Built in 1995, this block-long masterpiece has 80 championship lanes, a circular theater, and a 450-foot-long video scoring system. The facility cost the Reno-Sparks Convention and Visitor's Authority (RSCVA) about $45 million to complete.

Although only professional tournaments were held in the stadium for the first years of its operation, the stadium hosts amateur tournaments and events of all kinds. When the pros are in town (which happens every year or so), visitors are welcome to watch all the action from the 1,200 spectator seats. Because dates of the tournaments vary, contact the stadium for specific days and times. (See the Attractions and Annual Events chapters for more information.)

FOOTBALL

UNR FOOTBALL MACKAY STADIUM
University of Nevada, Reno
(775) 348-PACK (tickets)
www.nevadawolfpack.com
To die-hard football fans, autumn leaves mean one thing—Wolf Pack action at Mackay Stadium. Although most spectators come for the activity inside the stadium, some come for the events outside, where you'll find elaborate tailgate parties sprinkled around the asphalt parking lot. The six home games are well supported, with an average attendance of around 20,000 per game. The season lasts from September through November.

ℹ️ The winner of the annual University of Nevada, Reno, and University of Nevada, Las Vegas, football game takes home the Fremont Cannon, a replica of the mountain howitzer that accompanied Lt. John C. Frémont on his expedition through Nevada in 1843-1844.

GOLF

AMERICAN CENTURY CHAMPIONSHIP GOLF TOURNAMENT
Edgewood Tahoe Golf Course
180 Lake Parkway, Stateline, NV
(775) 588-3566
(775) 588-5900 for ticket information
www.edgewood-tahoe.com
www.tahoecelebritygolf.com
See more than 70 sports and entertainment stars including the likes of Michael Jordan, Charles Barkley, Dan Marino, Jerry Rice, John Elway, Oscar De La Hoya, and many, many more compete for a $600,000 purse. Not only do these sports legends and movie stars provide a fun-filled week for spectators, they actually play three rounds of some intense golf.

The six-day event includes two days of practice rounds, a one-day celebrity/amateur tournament where Insiders get to play alongside their favorite stars, and the 72-hole tournament. The weeklong event has plenty of opportunities built in for spectators to hobnob with the stars at one of the most beautiful golf courses in the United States (see the Golf chapter for details on the Edgewood Tahoe Golf Course). The event is usually scheduled in early July, with daily tickets costing between $15 and $25, depending on the day.

LEGENDS RENO-TAHOE OPEN
Montreux Golf and Country Club
2500 Spinnaker Drive, Reno, NV
(775) 849-9444, (775) 322-3900
www.legendsrenotahoeopen.com
One of the newest tournaments on the PGA Tour, the Legends Reno-Tahoe Open (formerly Reno/Tahoe Open) drew rave reviews from players and spectators alike at its debut in 1999. Now, as a more seasoned event, it draws a large percentage of the top money winners on the tour and offers an attractive $3 million purse. Following the usual tour format, the tournament consists of a Pro/Am on Wednesday, followed by four days of golf for the pros only.

Along with the warm hospitality the tournament extends, the event provides a memorable outdoor experience for anyone who attends. Meandering through huge stands of ponderosa pines at the base of Slide Mountain, the course at Montreux Golf and Country Club is vintage Jack Nicklaus—bad, but oh, so beautiful. Because it's also very private, the tournament offers non-members a rare opportunity to see the layout up close and personal. And since the event is still relatively new to the PGA schedule, it's not as packed with spectators as some other more established tournaments. This event is a marvelous opportunity to not only see some of the best golf in the world but also to enjoy a hassle-free day in a beautiful mountain setting.

MOTOR SPORTS

RENO HISTORIC RACES
Reno-Fernley Raceway
Fernley, NV, 35 miles east of Sparks, NV
(775) 575-7217
www.automuseum.org
www.hmsausa.com
www.reno-fernleyraceway.com
Vintage cars such as Ferraris, Jaguars, and Porches race on Fernley's 4.3-mile course, one of the nation's longest. Sponsored by the National Automobile Museum and the Historic Motor Sports Association, the event also features guided tours of the staging area. About 150 participants enter the race. The raceway is a quick 25-minute drive east of Sparks on Interstate 80 and then 5 miles south on Alternate U.S. Highway 95.

RODEO

RENO RODEO
Reno Livestock Events Center
1350 North Wells Avenue, Reno, NV
(775) 329-3877
(800) 225-2277 (tickets)
www.renorodeo.com
This rodeo is billed as "The Wildest, Richest Rodeo in the West," and it's not hard to see why. The nine-day event has more than $41 million in prize money waiting for the top cowboys and cowgirls. The event usually kicks off on a Friday in mid-June with a party and a concert featuring a big name in country and western music. From Saturday through the next Sunday, cowboys and cowgirls compete for the prize money by team roping, barrel racing, bareback riding, bull riding, steer wrestling, saddle bronc riding, and calf roping. The event culminates at 1:00 p.m. Sunday with the championship rodeo performance.

Other attractions at the rodeo include a carnival, cowboy country shops and a Western exhibit hall, and a behind-the-scenes chute tour. General admission ticket prices range from $10 to $18 depending on performance, day, and seating.

i Children with special needs are paired with rodeo cowboys to perform in the Special Kids Rodeo on Sunday during the Reno Rodeo.

SNAFFLE BIT FUTURITY
Reno Livestock Events Center
1350 North Wells Avenue, Reno, NV
(775) 688-5750
(775) 787-8497 (tickets)
www.nrcha.com
www.ticketmaster.com (tickets)
Though not exactly a rodeo in the classic sense, the National Reined Cow Horse Association's Snaffle Bit Futurity matches three-year-old horses from around the world against one another in contests of steer cutting. Riders and horses are judged on how well they can cut a steer from a herd, and control the steer's movement along the fence and then into the center of the arena. Points are awarded for how well the horses respond to commands to turn and maneuver. The event is held in Reno during the last week in September and brings more than 700 horses and 750 riders to the area. The participants compete for more than $900,000 in prize money.

ROLLER DERBY

RENO ROLLER GIRLS
Roller Kingdom
515 East Seventh Street
Reno, NV
(775) 329-3472
www.rollerkingdom.org
www.renorollergirls.com
If you're a fan of roller derby, you'll be glad to know that Reno has a colorful team that competes as well as skates exhibition events, such as nonprofit fundraisers. To see the gals in action in a competitive match, contact the Roller Kingdom for their scheduled appearances.

SOCCER

UNR SOCCER
Mackay Stadium
University of Nevada, Reno
(775) 348-PACK (tickets)
www.nevadawolfpack.com

A relatively new sport to the University of Nevada, Reno, women's soccer pioneered in 2000. Although the win-loss record has not been impressive so far, the team is winning a few more games each year. Players have an extensive travel schedule but play eight games on their home turf each season.

VOLLEYBALL

UNR VOLLEYBALL
The Old Gym
University of Nevada, Reno
(775) 348-PACK (tickets)
www.nevadawolfpack.com

With a history of more than 30 years behind it, the women's volleyball program at the University of Nevada, Reno, is one of the more established ladies' sports programs at the school. As the popularity of female sports has increased over the years, the level of competition has also risen. The action at the 15 home games in The Old Gym is fast paced and intense. Tickets are available at the door and are reasonably priced.

DAY TRIPS

When you're surrounded by majestic mountains, dramatic deserts, and verdant valleys, it's impossible not to wonder what's just down the road or over the next hill. Although the Reno/Tahoe area itself is certainly captivating enough for even the most discriminating visitor, when it comes to nearby day trips, the immediate area is most assuredly not "all she wrote."

In this chapter we'll venture out to explore the wonder and magic that lie just two or three hours' drive away. We'll drift lazily in a hot-air balloon over cattle standing knee-deep in the Carson Valley's velvety green grass. We'll sink blissfully into the same soothing hot springs once enjoyed by Clark Gable and Mark Twain at David Walley's Resort, Hot Springs & Spa. In the historic town of Truckee, we'll visit the site of the most highly publicized acts of cannibalism in America. We'll immerse ourselves in the rowdiness of a Victorian-era mining settlement in colorful Virginia City. And we'll drink in the primal beauty of an enormous mosaic of moving sand at Churchill County's Sand Mountain. These experiences and more are guaranteed to pique your intellectual curiosity, overwhelm your physical senses, and, at the very least, keep you fully entertained for the better part of a day.

But before we head down the road, a word to the wise about the weather in this part of the world. If you're traveling into the desert during the summer months, you should be aware that temperatures during daylight hours often exceed 100 degrees. To beat the heat once you get where you're going, you can't always count on cooling off in the shade of a tree, since some desert regions are completely devoid of large vegetation. If you're expecting to picnic or to set up a day camp, you'll need an umbrella or tarp to provide shade. To be on the safe side, carry plenty of water and be sure to drink frequently to avoid dehydration, even if you're in the car. If you're tramping around in the desert, you should wear comfortable shoes, loose clothing, a sun hat, and sunscreen. Since temperatures can plummet 60 or more degrees in the desert when the sun goes down, it's also a good idea to have a jacket or light sweater handy if you're out after dark.

In the winter months, the enemy is not the sun but winter storms that can create blizzard conditions and make driving hazardous, especially in mountain areas. Insiders know the best rig for winter driving is a four-wheel-drive car, sport utility vehicle, or truck. In the absence of these, you can usually get around pretty well with chains or snow tires when conditions demand them. It's a good idea to keep some warm clothing, water, dehydrated food, and other emergency supplies in the car during winter months, since it's not unusual to get delayed, even on heavily trafficked roads, during winter storms. I don't want to discourage you from venturing out, but you should know that sometimes hazardous conditions do exist. If you're enamored with TV ads showing Hummers racing through deep snow and fording deep rivers, don't rent an SUV as a novice four-wheel driver and expect to do the same. Life-threatening conditions that even Hummers won't get you out of do exist. Be prudent and be safe. The best advice I can give you is to make sure you check the weather report and fill your tank with gas before heading into the mountains or out into the desert. For updated road information in Nevada, call (877) 687-6237 or go to www .nevada dot.com. In California call (800) 427-ROAD (7623) or click on www.dot.ca.gov.

ℹ️ You can rope and ride with real cowboys on the edge of the Black Rock Desert at Soldier Meadows Guest Ranch & Lodge. For information contact them at www.soldiermeadows.com, (775) 849-1666 or soldier@hughes.net. Allow two weeks for a response because of the ranch's isolation.

THE BLACK ROCK DESERT AND GERLACH, NEVADA

The magnificent, barren playa called the Black Rock Desert lies about 105 miles northeast of the Truckee Meadows. Once the bed of ancient Lake Lahontan, it rested some 500 feet underwater. The desert now stretches more than 100 miles through three counties (Washoe, Pershing, and Humboldt) surrounded by jagged peaks of rugged mountains. A dark rock about 400 feet tall, which served as a landmark for pioneers and rises above the paler background of the mountains, gave the desert its name. It sits almost in the middle of the stark plain.

Thousands of pioneers passed through this desert on their way to California via the Lassen-Applegate Trail, which branched off the California Emigrant Trail at Lassen Meadows in Nevada. The Lassen-Applegate Trail cut through the heart of the Black Rock Desert, followed High Rock Canyon, and popped the travelers out into northern California. This section of the trail became known as "The Death Route" for obvious reasons. John Frémont and Kit Carson (see the History chapter for more about these trailblazers) navigated straight down the desert on their expedition through Nevada, eventually running into Pyramid Lake and the Truckee Meadows. Not much has changed in the desert since then, and today a trip to the gateway of this historic locale, one of the major deserts in the world, is well worth the drive.

The day trip should begin in Sparks, where you pick up Nevada Highway 445, called the Pyramid Highway by Insiders. Drive north about 30 miles to its intersection with Nevada Highway 446 near Nixon on the Paiute Indian Reservation at Pyramid Lake (see the day trip to Pyramid Lake later in this chapter). Follow NV 446 to its intersection with Nevada Highway 447, then turn left and head north on NV 447 to the town of Gerlach. Between Pyramid Lake and Gerlach, you will see some of the most beautiful desert scenery in Nevada, but you will not find any place to get gas or pick up food or cold drinks except in the little town of Empire, which is about 5 miles from Gerlach. Stock up and fill up before you leave the Truckee Meadows.

The drive between Nixon and Gerlach is about 60 miles, and for 30 miles you will be traveling through the Indian reservation. On the way you will pass through the little town of Empire, noted for its garlic fields and owned by United States Gypsum Co., a mining company. One of the most interesting sights in Empire is the Burning Sands Golf Course. The mining company employees built this nine-hole course over the years, winding it through town and across several streets. It's free to play, but a donation is requested. No one takes credit for designing the course; locals just say it happened. If you're dying to play this unique golf course, the town's post office has score cards. Call (775) 557-2341, ext. 224, for more information.

Gerlach, a little town of 700 people 5 miles north of Empire, is considered the gateway to the Black Rock Desert. The town originally served as a depot stop for the Western Pacific Railroad; now it provides a jumping-off point to the desert and to northern California. While in Gerlach, stop by Bruno's Country Club (775-557-2220), which is really a coffee shop, for lunch or dinner. The house specialty is the overstuffed ravioli, which are renowned throughout northern Nevada.

A word of warning about the Black Rock Desert: If you get the urge to take a drive out into the desert, don't. It is an extremely hazardous place unless you know what you are doing and where you are going, have the correct mode of transportation and the right gear, or ride with an Insider who does. So please heed this warning.

Besides its obvious historical and natural wonders, the Black Rock Desert has several other claims to fame. In 1992 scientists uncovered America's largest complete skeleton of an Imperial mammoth in this desert. The skeleton is on display in the Nevada State Museum in Carson City (see the day trip to Carson City later in this chapter).

On October 15, 1997, Royal Air Force fighter pilot Andy Green made the record books as the first person to drive a car past the speed of sound. He did it in the supersonic Thrust SSC on the Black Rock Desert; his speed: 763 mph.

But recently the Black Rock Desert's number-one attraction has been the free-spirited romp called Burning Man. Some people call it naked fun in the sun. Others call it an abomination. Whatever it may be, the event draws more than 45,000 participants who flock to the desert for this weeklong party over the Labor Day weekend and momentarily convert the barren place into a small town dubbed Black Rock City. If you're not planning to attend Burning Man, I advise avoiding the area while it's going on (around Labor Day every year). See the Annual Events chapter for more information.

Whatever your motivation, the Black Rock Desert and Gerlach make a magnificent day trip. Buck Wheeler described it best in his book The Black Rock Desert when he wrote:

"It is a land of mystery where ancient man left evidence of his visits thousands of years ago. It is a place of history where Indian warriors fought for their way of life and where legends of the Old West were born."

For a faster return trip to the Truckee Meadows, once you leave Gerlach, head south on NV 447. Take the highway all the way to Wadsworth, pick up Interstate 80 West, and follow the signs to Reno/Sparks. The total trip length is about 210 miles.

i The Pony Express route, which traced the route of present-day US 50 and included a stop in Carson City, was in existence for a brief 18 months. One of the best preserved Pony Express sites is in Sand Springs, 25 miles east of Fallon.

For more information on the desert, contact the Bureau of Land Management at (775) 623-1500.

CARSON CITY, NEVADA

A day trip to Carson City, Nevada's historic state capital, should have history buffs tingling with anticipation: Visiting is like sliding back in time. The city sits just 30 minutes down U.S. Highway 395 from Reno and 14 miles from Lake Tahoe via U.S. Highway 50.

The Carson City Freeway, which branches off US 395 between South Reno and Carson City, provides faster and more comfortable access to the capital city. Routing traffic away from congested streets and the heart of downtown, the freeway allows drivers to avoid much of the stop-and-go traffic that has frustrated them for years. Residents are delighted that, with less traffic, much of the historic downtown will be quieter and more attractive. The first phase of the freeway opened in 2006, and the project is scheduled for completion in 2010.

Settled as a trading post in 1851 on Indian land, Carson City came to life after silver was discovered on the Comstock. This quaint city became the capital of the Nevada Territory in 1861 and remained the state capital when Nevada entered the Union in 1864. Most people think the city was named for legendary frontiersman Kit Carson, who accompanied John Frémont on his expedition through Nevada (see the History chapter), and in a roundabout way, they're right. The city was actually named for the Carson River, which Frémont named in honor of his good friend and scout—so indirectly, the town is a tribute to Kit Carson.

Carson City gained fame around the United States as a town built by the silver barons of the Comstock mines. Among their many accomplishments, these men built the Virginia & Truckee Railroad, one of the most productive small railroads in the United States, to supply their mines with goods from Carson City. These entrepreneurs also constructed mills along the Carson River to process the silver ore, and they convinced the federal government to erect a U.S. Mint in Carson City to pound out silver coins right in their own backyards. They also erected some of the most magnificent mansions west of the Mississippi; and the residential area west of the State Capitol on North Carson Street is one of the largest historical districts in the state and one of the best self-guided tours in Nevada.

If you visit Carson City, whether you are a history buff or not, you must explore this residential district. The best way to do that is to walk the blue-lined Kit Carson Trail. The trail, with blue lines painted on the sidewalks to point the way, is a 2.5 mile walking tour of Carson City that encompasses some 60 points of interest. Maps for the tour are available at the visitor center at 1900 South Carson Street (775-687-7410, (800) 638-2321; www.carson-city.org); the center is open weekdays from 8:00 a.m. to 5:00 p.m. The tour starts at the Nevada State Museum, formerly the U.S. Mint, at 600 North Carson Street (775-687-4810; www.nevadaculture.org). The museum is open year-round from 8:30 a.m. to 4:30 p.m. and features Nevada's silver-rich history. Considered by some visitors and historians to be one of the best museums in the West, the Nevada State Museum houses a full-scale model of a silver mine and a reconstructed ghost town, along with numerous other displays. A visit here costs $5 for adults and $3 for seniors; children younger than age 18 are free.

On the blue-lined trail, you will also find 24 "talking" homes that broadcast their histories on special radio frequencies. Their locations are listed in a booklet with a map for two self-guided tours. This booklet can be picked up at the visitor center. Included on the tour is the Krebs-Peterson House, featured in John Wayne's last movie, The Shootist. For more information on this walking tour, telephone (800) NEVADA–1 or visit www .carson-city.org.

Other points of interest to while away the day in this charming city include the State Capitol at 101 North Carson Street. It's the second-oldest capitol building west of the Mississippi, and its Alaskan marble and polished wood hallways are magnificent. The Governor's Mansion at 606

Mountain Street is another must-stop on the tour. This colonial-style home was built in 1908 and is still used by Nevada's top government official.

Another must-see exhibit is the Carson Nugget Casino's gold display. Located at 507 North Carson Street, this collection is valued at $1 million and contains examples of raw gold in leaf, ribbon, wire, thread, and crystallized forms—just as they were taken from the ground. Call the Carson Nugget Casino at (800) 426-5239, or visit www.ccnugget.com.

For train aficionados, Carson City has a wonderful railroad museum located south of town on US 395. The Nevada State Railroad Museum (775-687-6953; www.nsrm-friends.org) is home to tons of railroad equipment mostly acquired from the Virginia & Truckee Railroad, one of the most famous short lines in the United States. Volunteers offer guided tours of the various pieces of equipment, including steam engines, coaches, and freight cars. Don't forget to ask for a look at the storage warehouse in back, where you'll find more equipment waiting to be refurbished. The museum is open daily from 8:30 a.m. to 4:30 p.m. The admission is $4 for adults; free for children 18 years old and younger.

Other points of interest, depending on your tastes, include: the Brewery Arts Center at 449 West King Street (775-883-1976; www.brewery arts.org), an old brewery that features art exhibits and concerts and offers arts and crafts classes; and the Roberts House at 1207 Carson Street, the oldest Victorian home in Carson City, with tours offered May through October. For more information call (775) 887-2174 or visit www .robertshousemuseum.org.

Carson City's main drag is also crammed with restaurants, bars, markets, and shopping centers, as well as the state's Supreme Court and Legislature buildings. Ask for a Calendar of Events at the visitor center. If you can, visit during some of the more popular events, like the old-fashioned Nevada Day Parade at the end of October or the Fourth of July picnic and fireworks display. Allow at least a full day to explore this historic city and enjoy a leisurely lunch or dinner at one of the many excellent restaurants around town. I suggest you try Glen Eagles Restaurant, 3700 North Carson Street (775-884-4414; www .gleneaglesrestaurant.com) or Adele's in Carson City, at 1112 North Carson Street (775-882-3353; www.adelesrestaurantandlounge.com).

Carson City, along with many other northern Nevada communities, has become a retirement haven in recent years. With nine golf courses nearby, the new high-tech Carson-Tahoe Medical Center, and a burgeoning variety of shopping options, the capital city is an attractive place to live for many retirees.

i A host of Winter Olympians have hailed from the area around Truckee/ Tahoe, including Tamara McKinney, Daron Rahlves, Julia Mancuso, Eva Twardokens, and Kristin Krone, to name a few.

CARSON VALLEY, NEVADA

Tucked between the Sierra Nevada to the west and the Pine Nut Mountains to the east, the Carson Valley spreads out like a giant carpet of fertile farms and rich ranchlands surrounding the small towns of Genoa, Minden, and Gardnerville. In spring and summer the valley boasts verdant fields of thick alfalfa bisected by the meandering Carson River. In fall it's a profusion of color as poplars and aspens dress in their vivid autumn hues. In winter it's a vintage Christmas-card scene, with snow sometimes reaching from the nearby jagged peaks down to the valley floor.

You can get to the valley from Reno by taking US 395 south about 14 miles beyond Carson City. I recommend starting your tour of the valley in Genoa, so turn right onto Jacks Valley Road just after you enter the valley.

To reach the valley from Lake Tahoe, you can take Nevada Highway 207 (Kingsbury Grade) east from Stateline to Foothill Road, which is just south of Genoa. NV 207 was part of the historic Pony Express and Overland Stage routes during pioneer days. Turn left, and go north on Foothill Road. You'll reach David Walley's Resort, Hot Springs & Spa just before getting to Genoa.

Built as an elegant spa in 1862, Walley's has been a welcome retreat for the rich and famous for many years. (Coming from Reno, you can visit the resort after touring downtown Genoa.) Historic personalities such as General Grant, Clark Gable, Mark Twain, and Ida Lupino have soothed their souls and bodies in these hot mineral baths. Renovated periodically to keep up with the times, the resort is now a sparkling oasis with a swimming pool, fitness center, and tennis facility in addition to the mineral spas. Much to the chagrin of some locals, recent expansion added a multi-story hotel complex to the resort. Although the additional services were welcomed by some, others believe that high-rise modern development is not in keeping with the image of the oldest town in Nevada. The resort is open daily from 7:00 a.m. to 10:00 p.m., and you can bask in its pleasures all day for $20. The optimum time to sink into Walley's might be after an invigorating day of sightseeing, golfing, or skiing in the Carson Valley and its nearby mountains. For more information on Walley's, call (775) 782-8155 or visit www .davidwalleys.com.

Settled by Mormons in 1851 as a trading station for early pioneers, Genoa was known first as Mormon Station and later renamed Genoa for the Italian birthplace of Christopher Columbus. If you like history, you'll love Genoa, since this tiny town still has the look and feel of early frontier days. The best way to experience it is to park your car and just wander through the many well-preserved historic buildings.

For an introduction to the area, stop at the Genoa Courthouse Museum on Main Street, where eclectic exhibits showcase every facet of pioneer life. The museum is open daily May through October from 10:00 a.m. to 4:30 p.m. For details call (775) 782-4325 or visit www.genoanv.com.

Just across the road you can visit another museum at Mormon Station State Historic Park and also view a replica of an early stockade used by pioneers to enclose their livestock. This museum is open daily May through October from 10:00 a.m. to 4:00 p.m. For details call (775) 782-2590 or go to www.parks.nv.gov.

Continuing down Main Street, you can quench your thirst at the same saloon frequented by early settlers, the Genoa Bar, well known as Nevada's Oldest Thirst Parlor. Other historic buildings along the street include the Masonic Hall, built in 1862; the Genoa Country Store, dating from 1879; and the Genoa Town Hall, dedicated in 1886.

The most famous event in Genoa is the annual Candy Dance, held the last full weekend of September. Started in 1919 to raise funds for downtown streetlights, the fair has been so successful that today it raises enough money to pay for all the town's basic services. It's a candy lover's dream, since local residents sell pounds and pounds of their prized homemade fudge, divinity, almond roca, and turtles to eager buyers every year. More than 75,000 people pack the town during the two-day event, enjoying the dinner dance, arts and crafts show, and musical events that are part of the festivities. If you'd like to try the prize-winning recipes yourself, you can buy a copy of the Genoa Candy Book at the fair.

If you're in town around dinnertime, I highly recommend dining at La Ferme. Tucked in a historic building across the street from the Genoa Bar, this elegant eatery seems totally out of place in laid-back Genoa. The ambience is Victorian/French Country, and the cuisine is French. For reservations call (775) 783-1004 or visit www.la-ferme.genoa.com.

From Genoa you can continue your tour of the Carson Valley by heading east on Genoa Lane to US 395, where a right (south) turn will bring you to Minden. When the Virginia & Truckee Railroad extended its service to the Carson Valley in 1905, the town of Minden was founded around the train depot. Named for the Prussian birthplace of early pioneer Henry Fredrick Dangberg, Minden is an orderly little town of quiet streets and historic brick buildings. As you enter town, you pass the Carson Valley Inn, a full-service casino where you can enjoy fine dining and Nevada-style entertainment 24 hours a day. Farther down the street, you can see the old Minden Creamery buildings, and then on Esmeralda Street is the C.O.D. Garage, the oldest continually operating car dealership in the state, founded in 1910 to sell Model Ts. Minden Park and the courthouse lie farther north along this street.

Back on US 395, continue south to Gardnerville, which blends almost unnoticed into Minden. While Minden's roots are traced to the railroad, Gardnerville's beginnings are linked with agriculture. Founded in the 1860s as a convenient settlement for valley farmers, Gardnerville has been a ranching center since Basque sheepherders from Europe's Pyrenees Mountains arrived in the 1890s. Because of its high quality of life and business-friendly environment, the Carson Valley has become a burgeoning tech center and retirement community during the past decade. To get a taste of valley history and a sample of its art, stop off at the Carson Valley Museum and Cultural Center, which is right on US 395 as you go through town. Located in the old renovated high school that dates from 1915, the museum is open Monday through Saturday from 10:00 a.m. to 4:00 p.m. year-round. For more information call (775) 782-2555 or visit www.historicnevada.org.

If you continue on US 395 south of Gardnerville for about 5 miles, you can visit the Lahontan National Fish Hatchery, which raises Lahontan cutthroat trout for stocking Pyramid Lake. Visiting hours are daily from 8:00 a.m. to 3:00 p.m. Call (775) 265-2425 or click on www.fws.gov/lahontannfhc/ for more information.

About 13 miles beyond the fishery, you come to lovely Topaz Lake. Like Lake Tahoe, it's ringed by mountains and bisected by the California–Nevada state line. But unlike Tahoe, it's an artificial lake created by storage from the West Walker River. Although Topaz is much smaller and less dramatic than Tahoe, its appeal lies in its natural beauty, relatively uncluttered by homes and businesses. It's a pleasant place to fish, swim, and go boating away from the crowds. For picnicking and camping try Topaz Lake Park, which has a mile of beachfront with 140 campsites and picnic spots. To reach the park, look for its sign on US 395 and follow the access road about a mile down to the park on the lake. For information call

(775) 266-3343. Topaz Lake Lodge and RV Park, located on the north end of the lake, also has camping facilities, plus lodge accommodations, a 24-hour casino, and a restaurant with a beautiful view of the lake. For details call (775) 266-3338 or visit www.topazlake.com or www.topazlodge .com. For a reasonably priced meal, I highly recommend a lunch stop here where the food is pretty basic but guaranteed to please.

While visiting the Carson Valley, you may want to try a round of golf at the Carson Valley Golf Course, which is just off US 395 in Gardnerville (775-265-3181; www.carsonvalleygolf.com) or at either of the courses at Genoa Lakes Golf on Jacks Valley Road (775-782-7700). With the Carson River carving a picturesque ribbon through many fairways, these courses are extremely scenic as well as challenging. (For details see the Golf chapter.)

If you want a bird's-eye perspective of the valley, nothing beats a glider ride. Soar Minden (775-782-7627, www.soarminden.com) will give you a breathtaking, memorable vista from a glider soaring high above the valley floor. (See the Recreation chapter for more information on these activities.)

When it's time to eat, try sampling Basque cuisine at the Overland Hotel at 691 Main Street in Gardnerville (775-782-2138) or at the J&T Bar and Restaurant at 1426 US 395 in Gardnerville (775-782-2074). For steaks and seafood, Fiona's, in the Carson Valley Inn in Minden (775-783-6650), is a good choice. Weather permitting, you might want to picnic at Topaz Lake or Mormon Station State Historic Park.

For more information about the Carson Valley, you can stop by the Carson Valley Chamber of Commerce and Visitors Authority at 1477 US 395, Suite A, in Gardnerville. Call them at (800) 727-7677 or visit www.carsonvalleynv.org.

i Genoa is well known for the large herd of deer that roams freely around town.

FALLON, NEVADA

If you spend any time at all in the Reno/Tahoe area, you're sure to hear about "the other side of Nevada." An expression coined by the Nevada Commission on Tourism some years ago to increase overall knowledge about the state, "the other side" encompasses almost everything not directly related to gaming. Most visitors know you can drink, gamble, and enjoy live entertainment 24 hours a day in Nevada, but few are acquainted with the state's colorful Wild West history, the laid-back lifestyle of its rural ranch communities, or the breathtaking beauty of its unspoiled landscape. If you're curious about what Nevada is like—outside the bright lights of the casinos—head east from Reno on I–80 to Fallon, the seat of Churchill County, just an hour's drive away.

Leaving Reno, you follow the Truckee River as it meanders through the scenic Truckee River Canyon, bordering ranches and farms, to the small town of Fernley. Follow the signs to Fallon, taking exit 48 to connect with Alternate US 50, where you will continue southeast. For an affordable game of golf along the way, you can stop at the Golf Club at Fernley. Winding through the sand and sagebrush, the emerald-green fairways are almost startling to the eye, like an artist's brilliant brush strokes splashed on an enormous beige canvas. The course is open year-round, and greens fees range from about $25 to $40 for 18 holes, including cart. For tee times call (775) 835-6933 or visit www.fernleygolfclub.com. (See the Golf chapter for more information about the course.)

From the golf course you continue down Alternate US 50 to Leeteville Junction, where the road joins US 50 about 8 miles from Fallon. The junction was known to early pioneers as Ragtown, where they would wash and hang their clothes to dry after crossing the desert and before the trek over the Sierra Nevada. From Leeteville you travel on US 50, dubbed by *Life* magazine "The Loneliest Road in America," as it crosses the state of Nevada. Far from being just lonely, this ribbon of road bisects a fascinating land of awesome scenery and intriguing history.

With the pinkish Stillwater Mountains as a backdrop, you pass through lush fields of alfalfa as you approach Fallon, which you can see is aptly nicknamed "The Oasis of Nevada." The overused term "family values" is what makes the world go round in this rural farming town. Spectator sports include Little League baseball and watching the high school's "Greenwave" (so called for the fields of green alfalfa that wave in the desert winds) take on other football teams. The social events of the year are fund-raisers for the Churchill Arts Council or the Ducks Unlimited waterfowl habitats in the Pacific Flyway. Small businesses are passed down from parent to child, and local politicians know everyone by their first names. Boring and mundane? Not at all: Churchill County is an interesting mixture of past and present, where supersonic Navy jets zoom over remnants of the Pony Express route, and a state-of-the-art electronic warfare range shares the desert with ancient petroglyphs.

As an introduction to the rich history of the area, you must stop at the Churchill County Museum at 1050 South Maine Street. Bursting with artfully designed exhibits and displays, this free facility immerses you in the heritage of the area from the prehistoric to the pioneer days. It's open daily all year, but call (775) 423-3677 for specific hours or visit www.ccmuseum.org for more information.. At the museum be sure to look for information about Hidden Cave, an archaeological dig east of town, where ancient civilizations lived more than 8,000 years ago. Although you can find the cave on your own by continuing east on US 50 for about 10 miles, the best way to see it is with a group from the museum. Guided tours leave the museum the second and fourth Saturdays of the month at 9:30 a.m. Close to the cave is Grimes Point, where you can stroll along the mile-long path among petroglyphs considered to be thousands of years old.

About 15 miles farther down the road is Sand Mountain, a 600-foot-high sand dune more than 2 miles long. Formed by windblown sand from an ancient prehistoric sea, the mountain booms and moans as the ever-present wind continues to move the fine particles. If you want to enjoy this geological phenomenon in quiet solitude, it's best to visit during the week, since it becomes a lively playground for dune buggies and sand skiers on weekends and holidays. The trek to the top can be treacherous, especially in the summer since the surface is hot, and the deep sand makes the going very difficult. At the base of the mountain, you can learn about the geology and history of the area by walking the short trail through the Sand Springs Desert Study Area. And at the nearby Sand Springs Station you can visit a well-preserved Pony Express station that formed part of the legendary route that passed through the area in 1860. For more information call the Fallon Convention and Tourism Authority at (775) 423-4556 or the Bureau of Land Management at (775) 885-6000. The Web site is www.nv.blm.gov/carson. You can also visit www.fallontourism.com.

Other sights around Fallon include the Stillwater National Wildlife Refuge. In wet years as many as 700,000 ducks, ibises, snow plovers, and herons—along with other shorebirds and raptors—come to visit or nest in this refuge. To view this relatively unspoiled natural habitat, follow US 50 east of town for several miles and turn left onto Stillwater Road. Continue on Stillwater Road until you reach the large serene marsh stretching toward the Stillwater Mountains. Be sure to take insect repellent, since it's a rich breeding ground for bugs as well as birds. For more information on the refuge, you can call (775) 428-6452, visit stillwater.fws.gov, or visit the office at 1000 Auction Road in Fallon.

Heading west out of Fallon, you can visit the Lahontan State Recreation Area, a popular playground for camping, fishing, boating, and waterskiing. Lahontan Reservoir is a 17-mile-long lake completed in 1915 as part of the Newlands Irrigation Project. Water from the Truckee and Carson Rivers is held in the lake behind Lahontan Dam and then used to irrigate the fields of alfalfa, corn, sugar beets, and Heart O' Gold cantaloupes around Fallon. To reach Lahontan, go west on US 50 from Fallon for about 16 miles.

With more than 300 days of clear flying weather each year, the U.S. Navy hasn't found a more suitable training ground for its pilots than

Naval Air Station (NAS) Fallon. Home of the Naval Strike and Air Warfare Center (NSAWC), with its prestigious TOPGUN division (remember the movie *Top Gun* with Tom Cruise?), NAS Fallon is the only naval facility that can train an entire carrier air wing in the strike tactics used in combat. The F-18 Hornets and F-14 Tomcats scream off the Navy's longest runway (14,000 feet) and engage in mock dogfights and electronic warfare over the training area east of the Stillwater Mountains. If you want an up-close and personal view of these supersonic flying machines, you can watch them land and take off through a security fence at the base. To get to the base, take U.S. Highway 95 south for about 5 miles until you see the sign for the facility at Union Lane. Follow Union Lane to Pasture Road, where a left turn will give you a view of the runway. The Navy opens its gates to thousands of visitors each spring during the Fallon Air Show, when you can see free flying demonstrations and static displays of aircraft (see the Annual Events chapter for details). For more information call (775) 426-2880 or visit www .fallontourism.com.

Aside from the naval air show, Fallon plays host to a large variety of special events and ongoing entertainment throughout the year. You can see professional and amateur race car drivers speed around the track at the state-of-the-art Top Gun Raceway, about 15 miles south of town on US 95. See the Recreation chapter for more information. Call (775) 423-0223 or (800) 325-7448 for race times and dates, or access www.topgunraceway.com. You can watch barrel racers and bull riders from all over the country compete in Wild West action at the Silver State International Rodeo. You can enjoy the sweet, juicy taste of local Heart O' Gold cantaloupes at the Heart O' Gold Cantaloupe Festival. You can experience local Native American culture at the Nevada Indian Days All Indian Rodeo & Powwow for a taste of the arts and music, you can choose from a large variety of events sponsored by the Churchill Arts Council all during the year; for details call (775) 423-1440 or visit www.churchill arts.org. The Fallon Convention and Tourism Authority at 100 Campus Way (just off US 50 as you enter town from the west) is a good source of information about events in Churchill County. You can call them at (775) 423-4556 or click on www.fallon tourism.com.

If all this activity gives you an appetite, you don't need to leave town on an empty stomach. For good food at reasonable prices, try the Bonanza Inn (775-423-0558) or Stockman's Casino (775-423-2117) on US 50 on the west side of town.

i If you visit Fallon between August and October, you can challenge your navigational skills at the five-acre living corn maze at Lattin Farms, 1955 McLean Road. For more information call (775) 867-3750 or (866) 638-6293, or go to www .lattinfarms.com.

GHOST TOWNS, NEVADA

Old-timers here will tell you that 10 ghost towns exist for every living town in Nevada. Most of the ruins are difficult to find, however, because they are hidden in the hills and tucked away in the gullies overgrown with sagebrush and tumbleweed. Their only inhabitants now are desert creatures and the memories of past glory days. But they're out there, ready for those who wish to explore them. Rummaging through these ruins is more exciting than reading about them in dusty old history books, and they make for a worthwhile day trip if you wish to step way off the beaten path of the Reno/Tahoe area.

Most of these towns sprang up during Nevada's two great mining periods before World War I, and most lasted only as long as the silver and gold in their mines. These towns are sprinkled all over the state, but my suggestion is to explore the ghost towns nestled near the foot of the Shoshone Mountain Range in the Toiyabe National Forest just east of Gabbs, Nevada, a two-and-a-half-hour drive from Reno. To get to Gabbs from Reno, take I-80 east to the east Fernley exit. Pick up Alternate US 50 to Fallon. After Fallon, follow US 50, The Loneliest Road in America, to

Middlegate, about 47 miles. Turn right (south) onto Nevada Highway 361 to Gabbs. Most of the ghost towns suggested here are located off Nevada Highway 844, 2 miles north of Gabbs.

The ghost town of Ione sits 24 miles east of Gabbs at the end of State Route 91. This town prospered in 1863 after the discovery of a vein of silver. Ione became the seat of Nye County in 1864, but by 1880 only a few hard-core prospectors remained. Several collapsed and dilapidated buildings can be found at the site.

Ellsworth rests about 10 miles west of Ione via an unmarked graded road. In 1871, at its peak, this town pumped silver out from its mines and boasted about 200 citizens, and several businesses and homes were made from rocks. Some rock walls and a cemetery remain.

Berlin, perhaps the most renowned ghost town in Nevada, owes much of its fame to dinosaurs and the Berlin-Ichthyosaur State Park. This park is home to significant fossil finds of gigantic ichthyosaurs, marine reptiles that inhabited the state more than 200 million years ago. The word ichthyosaur means "lizard fish," but these dinosaurs are more closely related to the modern-day whale. The tumbled-down mining town sits close to the park and was abandoned about 100 years ago. Several buildings still stand in what preservationists call "arrested decay." In other words, the buildings aren't restored, but they are not allowed to decay any further, either. Berlin and the state park are located 19 miles east of Gabbs, about 2 miles south of SR 91. Visit the Web site at www.parks.nv.gov or call (775) 964-2440 for information.

The ghost town of Union is about 1.25 miles southeast of Berlin. This town sprang up in 1863, about the same time as Ione. Several stone buildings remain in Union. In Grantsville (located about 5 miles southeast of SR 91, 18 miles east of Gabbs), you can see a few building foundations, as well as a small cemetery. But the high points of a visit to Grantsville are its incredible views and its magnificent setting in the mountains. This town was also established in 1863.

On the way back to Reno, stop by Quartz Mountain, about 13 miles north of Gabbs just off NV 361. This town sprang up in 1920 and withered by 1926. The remains of several wooden buildings still lie scattered about.

I suggest a picnic lunch for this day trip. Be aware that beyond Fallon, gas stations and restaurants are scarce, so it's a good idea to fill up your gas tank and cooler before you leave Fallon.

If you wish to learn more about Nevada ghost towns, find a copy of *Nevada Ghost Town* by Lambert Florin or *Nevada Ghost Towns and Mining Camps* by Stanley W. Paher.

GRAEAGLE, CALIFORNIA

If you already live in a mountain paradise, where do you go to "get away from it all"? Insiders escape to the tiny hamlet of Graeagle (pronounced gray eagle), the ultimate getaway, tucked deep in the towering pines of the Plumas National Forest about 60 miles northwest of Reno. Named for Gray Eagle Creek, which runs nearby, this quaint little community began as a lumber town in 1916. The historic red and white frame buildings that line the main drag were brought in by rail and used as housing for workers in the mill. Today these structures are retail establishments that form the picturesque core of the downtown area. After the mill shut down in 1956, Graeagle was purchased in 1958 for $450,000 by a developer who saw its potential as a planned vacation community. Since then it has thrived primarily as a summer/fall retreat for hikers, golfers, and anglers. But in spite of modern development, it retains its historic charm. Quiet and peaceful, Graeagle is worlds apart from the hustle and bustle of many resort communities. And best of all, it's smack in the middle of some of the most gorgeous mountain scenery on the planet.

To get to Graeagle from Reno, take US 395 north about 24 miles to Hallelujah Junction, and then take California Highway 70 west to Blairsden. Finally, turn south on California Highway 89. About 8 miles before Graeagle on CA 70, you'll go through the lumber town of Portola, where you can climb on train cars and locomotives at the Western Pacific Railroad Museum. Follow the signs through Old Town Portola to the museum, which is at 700 Western Pacific Way. It's open daily March through November from 11:00 a.m. to 5:00 p.m. and in the winter from 11:00 a.m. to 4:00 p.m. For details call (530) 832-4131 or visit www.wplives.org.

Coming from Lake Tahoe to Graeagle, take California Highway 267 north from Kings Beach or CA 89 north from Tahoe City to Truckee, and then continue north on CA 89 for about 50 miles. This route takes you through some of the loveliest, most unspoiled forest in the Reno/Tahoe area.

With a variety of interesting golf courses to play, Graeagle has been called the "Pebble Beach of the Sierra." But even if your game isn't up to par, you can't go wrong on any of these layouts, since just enjoying the magnificent scenery can make your round worthwhile. About 5 miles south of Graeagle on CA 89, you can test your skills at the Golf Club at Whitehawk Ranch; call (800) 332-4295 or click on www.golfwhitehawk.com to book tee times. Other championship 18-hole courses include Graeagle Meadows, which is right downtown off CA 89 (530-836-2323; www .playgraeagle.com), and Plumas Pines Golf Resort, at 402 Poplar Valley Road in Blairsden (530-836-1420; www.plumaspinesgolf.com). The Feather River Park Resort on CA 89 (530-836-2328; www .featherriverparkresort.com) offers a more forgiving nine-hole layout. For a more detailed description of these courses, see the Golf chapter.

Bisected by the pristine Middle Fork of the Feather River and dotted with a multitude of crystal-clear alpine lakes, the mountainous terrain around Graeagle is a hiker's dream come true. With literally hundreds of trails to choose from, you'll probably want to get a map by calling the Plumas County Visitors Bureau at (800) 326-2247 (www.plumascounty.org) or the Plumas National Forest at (530) 283-2050 (www .fs.fed.us/r5/plumas). Another good Web resource is www.graeagle.com.

My favorite hike, which takes you to six different lakes, is the Round Lake Loop Trail in the Lakes Basin Recreation Area. With spectacular views and a modest elevation gain, this approximately 4-mile outing offers a fantastic diversity of scenery compressed in a relatively small geographic area. It's best done at a leisurely pace so you can enjoy the landscape as it spreads out before you. You can swim, fish, and picnic along the way— just pick your favorite lake. To get to the trailhead, look for the sign directing you to the Lakes Basin Recreation Area on the Gold Lake Highway just south of Graeagle and travel west for about 7 miles. Then look for the sign for Gold Lake Lodge and the Round Lake Trail at the crest of a hill and park in the lodge parking lot. The Round Lake Loop Trail begins at the end of this lot.

About 0.25 mile down the trail, it forks, with the trail to the right reaching Big Bear Lake in about 0.5 mile and taking you counterclockwise around the loop. I recommend going in this direction, since you arrive at the first lake sooner and because the overall climb is gentler. As the trail meanders through granite boulders and stately pines, it takes you from Big Bear Lake to Little Bear, Cub, Silver, Long, and Round Lakes. In the shadow of rocky Mt. Elwell, the hike is verdant green with splotches of wildflower color in summer, and in fall an explosion of reds, oranges, and golds. At Round Lake be sure to take a look at the abandoned gold mine at the southern end where miners hoped to strike it rich more than 100 years ago. This hike is an absolute jewel, not to be missed by anyone who enjoys the solitude and beauty of the mountains.

If you're curious what life was like for early gold seekers, you can find out at the mining museum in Plumas Eureka State Park. Steeped in history and surrounded by gorgeous scenery, this 6,700-acre park encompasses the old mining settlement of Johnsville, just 5 miles west of Graeagle on Johnsville Road (Plumas County Road A14). The indoor-outdoor museum features a restored miner's home, a blacksmith shop, and exhibits of early mining equipment. On Living History Day, once a month during the summer, costumed docents recreate the daily life of a miner searching for the big bonanza. For details call (530) 836-2380 or visit www.parks.ca.gov. You can also try your own luck at gold panning in nearby Jamison Creek. Crisscrossed by myriad trails leading to a number of lakes, Plumas Eureka State Park is also popular with hikers.

The more than 100 lakes of the Feather River watershed offer a large variety of fishing spots for anglers. In addition, dozens of small streams and the Middle Fork of the Feather River provide rich habitats for rainbow, brown, and brook trout. For details on seasons and regulations, contact the Plumas National Forest at (530) 283-2050.

For a picture-perfect ending to your day in the mountains, I suggest stopping at the Long Boards restaurant at Plumas Pines Golf Club for a drink or dinner. You can sit on the deck, high above the 18th fairway, and watch the last golfers play in as the sun sinks golden behind the emerald-green mountains. If you've hiked the Round Lake Loop, a wonderful stop for dinner is the Firewoods dining room at Gray Eagle Lodge right along the Gold Lake Highway as you head back to Graeagle. Call (800) 635-8778 for reservations. Other good dinner spots include the Grizzly Grill at 250 Banta Street in Blairsden (530-836-1300), and Olsen's Cabin on Johnsville Road (530-836-2801).

i Any good road trip requires preparation. Before setting off, make sure your vehicle is in good working order. Carry emergency equipment, including a flare, blankets, water and some food, and a first-aid kit. A cellular telephone is a nice addition to any road trip, but be aware that you may not have coverage in some locations.

PYRAMID LAKE, NEVADA

In 1844 explorer John C. Frémont was searching for a legendary river that supposedly emptied into the San Francisco Bay. Instead he was astonished to discover one of the most beautiful desert lakes in the world. Shimmering turquoise green against a pinkish-beige desert background, the lake seemed out of place, like a magical mirage in a harsh, barren environment. Frémont named this large landlocked body of water Pyramid Lake for the giant pyramid-shaped rock that juts 475 feet from the surface of the lake near its southern

end. (See the History chapter for more about Frémont's explorations.)

The Paiute Indians and their ancestors have made their home at Pyramid Lake for more than 4,000 years, well before Frémont arrived in the area. The oldest anthropological site in the area dates back 9,200 years, according to one local expert. Because fish from the lake was an important staple in their diet, the tribe became known as "Cui-ui Ticutta" or Cuiui Eaters. Since 1874 the lake and its environs have been owned and managed by the tribe as the Pyramid Lake Paiute Indian Reservation.

As a remnant of a large inland sea that used to cover most of northwestern Nevada, the lake is the terminal point for the Truckee River's 105-mile journey from Lake Tahoe. Stretching for 27 miles against the changing desert hues of the nearby mountains, the lake has a unique beauty and mystery. Adding an intriguing contrast to the sparkling water and naked rocks are the odd-shaped tufa formations, which are white calcium carbonate deposits piled up all along the shoreline. Next to the signature pyramid is one of the most prominent tufas, which is aptly named "Stone Mother and her Basket." But aside from its beauty, the history and geology of Pyramid Lake provide a fascinating lesson about the relationship between humans and their environment.

Two roads lead to Pyramid Lake from I-80: NV 445 from Sparks to Sutcliffe, and NV 447 from Wadsworth (about 30 miles east of Reno) to Nixon. NV 446 runs between these two roads along the south shore of the lake. You can make a loop of this route going either way, but I recommend starting on NV 445, since it's a quicker route to the lake and you will need to stop at the ranger station in Sutcliffe to buy a day-use permit.

Traveling east on I-80 in Reno, exit onto Pyramid Way in Sparks, which becomes NV 445. Travel north about 33 miles to the lake. About 20 miles north of Sparks, you'll pass the Wild Horse and Burro Placement Center, which is operated by the Bureau of Land Management. The animals are captured from large herds that roam free in Nevada, cared for in this facility, and then adopted out to qualified people all over the country. For more information on the wild horse program, visit www.wildhorseandburro.blm.gov.

After continuing north to the lake, you can keep to the left on NV 445 or turn right onto NV 446. If you stay on NV 445, you'll travel past several beaches on the way to Sutcliffe; the paved road turns to gravel a few miles farther on. Turning right onto NV 446, you will round the southern end of the lake to the intersection with NV 447, which travels north to Nixon and the tribal headquarters. The Truckee River empties into the lake here. To get a better idea of the lay of the land around the lake, pick up a map, preferably in Sutcliffe when you first arrive at the lake.

The waters of the lake provide a rich habitat for Lahontan cutthroat trout and the endangered cui-ui fish. The lake is one of the best trophy-trout fisheries in the world, with the average keeper weighing between 5 and 16 pounds. The prime time to fish is between October and May, when cooler surface temperatures lure the fish up from the 300-foot depths of the lake. (See also the Fishing and Hunting chapter.)

The lake also provides one of only eight nesting grounds for white pelicans in North America. Each spring rocky Anaho Island, just southwest of the pyramid, swarms with thousands of pelicans, double-crested cormorants, California gulls, great blue herons, and Caspian terns as they set up housekeeping and raise their young. And while the surrounding landscape may seem harsh and sterile, it's anything but, in terms of the wildlife it supports. It's not unusual to see herds of deer, antelope, and bighorn sheep quietly grazing on the steep hillsides around the water.

When you visit the lake, you'll find ample opportunities to learn about the area's culture and heritage by visiting its museums and visitor centers. Just off NV 447 between the towns of Wadsworth and Nixon, there's the Numana Hatchery and Visitors Center (775-574-0290, www.pyramid lakefisheries.org), with its wetlands nature trail. On NV 446 near Nixon you can visit the Scenic Byway Visitors Center and Tribal Museum (775-574-1088, www.byways.org), which offers tribal history and cultural exhibits as well as permits for fishing, boat-

ing, and camping. And in Sutcliffe, on NV 445, you can stop by the visitor center and museum near the Pyramid Lake Marina.

For a fascinating look at one of the most efficient and innovative fishery restoration programs in the country, be sure to stop in at the Dunn Hatchery, which is just south of the marina in Sutcliffe. Since its establishment in 1974, the program has planted about

2.8 million cutthroat and 10 to 18 million cui-ui fish every year. Overcoming the problem of raising cold-water fish in a desert lake, the hatchery program has helped guarantee the continued propagation of these species of fish. For hours and more information on these points of interest, call the Pyramid Lake Fisheries at (775) 476-0500, the Pyramid Lake Marina at (775) 476-1156, or the Pyramid Lake Paiute Tribal Offices at (775) 574-1000.

Pyramid Lake is a prime spot to enjoy everything the great outdoors has to offer without the crowds found at some other area lakes. As you drive along the shore of the lake, you can choose from a large variety of sandy beaches for swimming and picnicking. You'll need an umbrella or tarp for shade, however, since the shoreline doesn't have trees or shrubs.

On windless summer days, the tepid waters of the lake are a water-skier's dream come true, silky smooth and free of crowds. For the optimum skiing experience, try it at sundown, when you can skim across the glassy surface as the sinking sun turns the water a gorgeous pink and gold underneath your skis. You can launch your own boat or rent one for the day at the Pyramid Lake Marina in Sutcliffe. But if you're out on the lake when the wind comes up, be sure to head for shore right away, since dangerous whitecaps can appear in minutes.

Because the facilities all around the lake are pretty sparse, I don't have a list of recommended restaurants and watering holes. The best dining experience in this natural wonderland is the picnic lunch or barbecue you bring yourself. Head down to one of the beaches and enjoy your own gourmet cuisine along with an unobstructed view of this prehistoric phenomenon.

SACRAMENTO, CALIFORNIA

Sacramento is the first "big city" you come to as you go west over the Sierra Nevada from the Reno/Tahoe area. Most visitors know it as the birthplace of the greatest gold rush in American history. Not many know that it was also the last stop on the Pony Express route and the nation's telegraph system, and the western terminus of the Transcontinental Railroad. About two hours from Reno along I–80, California's state capital sits in a broad valley on the banks of two of the state's biggest rivers and is often described as the "Historic Capital of the West."

John Sutter, a German-Swiss immigrant, founded the first white settlement in Sacramento in 1839 after the Mexican government granted him 50,000 acres of land. He built an outpost known as Sutter's Fort and began ranching. His ranch prospered until an employee discovered gold at Sutter's Mill in Coloma, California, east of the outpost. The find put Sacramento on the map and decimated Sutter's ranch: Within the next five years, 500,000 people flooded into the Sacramento area.

The city became California's capital in 1854 and over the years grew in importance as an agricultural center. During World War II it grew as a military support center when the federal government built several defense plants and two airbases here (these bases are now closed). Today, Sacramento is crammed with attractions like the State Capitol Building, Old Sacramento, Sutter's Fort, the California State Railroad Museum, and the Governor's Mansion. It also has its share of historic buildings, art galleries, serene parks, rivers, and the 23-mile-long American River Parkway.

Like the entire town of Virginia City, Nevada (see the description of the day trip to Virginia City later in this chapter), Old Sacramento is designated a state historic park and national landmark. Located off Interstate 5 and bordering the Sacramento River, the old part of the city was the main riverboat landing for Sutter's Fort. Today, the 28-acre area has more than 60 buildings that have been restored to the 1850–1870 period. Specialty shops, restaurants, bars, and other busi-

nesses now partake of the 19th-century feel of this part of the city by operating out of the historical buildings. Don't miss the California State Railroad Museum, 125 I Street (916-445-6645; www.californiastaterail roadmuseum.org), which includes the Central Pacific Depot and the Eagle Theater. This museum houses one of the world's largest railroad locomotive and relics collections. Admission is $8 for adults, $3 for youths ages 6 to 17, and free for children 5 and younger.

The railroad museum isn't the only bastion of history and culture awaiting you in Sacramento. You can also visit the Discovery Museum, featuring history, science, and technology, at 101 I Street (www.thediscovery.org), the Crocker Art Museum at 216 O Street (www.crockerart museum.org), and a plethora of others. The Web site at www.sacmuseums.org is a good source for more information.

Sutter's Fort State Historic Park (916-445-4422) shares space with the California State Indian Museum (916-324-0971) on 27th and L Streets. Sutter's Fort provides visitors a living history of the gold rush era, presented by volunteers dressed in period costumes demonstrating examples of pioneer and Indian living and skills. Self-guided audio tours of Sutter's Fort are available and explain the exhibits, which include a blacksmith shop, bakery, prison, living quarters, and a livestock area. The fort is open daily from 10:00 a.m. to 5:00 p.m. ; closed Christmas, Thanksgiving, and New Year's Day. There is a nominal entrance fee for adults. The Indian Museum, located behind the fort, displays arts and crafts made by California Indians. It's open from 10:00 a.m. to 5:00 p.m. and charges a nominal admission fee for adults. Visit www.parks.ca.gov for more information.

While exploring this section of the city, don't forget to jump onboard one of the sightseeing boats and cruise the Sacramento River alongside Old Sacramento. Contact the Visitors Information Center, 1608 I Street (916-808-7777), or click on www.oldsacramento.com.

Capitol Park sits about 1 mile east of Old Sacramento. This park contains more than 40,000 trees and flowers in an area stretching from L to N Streets and 9th to 15th Streets. The California State Capitol building (916-324-0333) is the main attraction in this park, with its golden dome providing an unforgettable landmark. Construction of the capitol began in 1860 and continued for more than 14 years before finally being completed in 1874. The California Legislature voted to renovate the building in 1972 at the cost of $70 million, and the tour of this well-preserved building is well worth the time. Guided tours run from 9:00 a.m. to 4:00 p.m. daily except Christmas, Thanksgiving, and New Year's Day. There is no admission fee. Visit www.parks.ca.gov for more information.

The Vietnam Veteran's Memorial, located at the east end of the park, provides a sober reminder of California's military personnel who sacrificed their lives during the war. This memorial is one of the finest examples of bronze statuary in the West and contains the names of the war dead etched on granite panels arranged by hometown.

The 1877 Governor's Mansion at 16th and H Streets (916-323-3047) sits close to the park and provides another enjoyable guided tour. The cost of tours is nominal, with children younger than age 16 admitted free, and run daily from 10:00 a.m. to 4:00 p.m.

Located just south of downtown on South Land Park Drive between 13th Avenue and Sutterville Road, William Land Park spreads out over 161 acres. The park has more than 3,000 trees of 50 different varieties, but its main attraction is the Sacramento Zoo (916-808-5885; www.sac zoo.com). This enclosure is considered to be one of the best small zoos in the country, with more than 400 animals representing 130 species, including some rare and endangered species. The park also features a children's theme park, a fishing pond, a wading pool, amusement rides, and a nine-hole golf course. A family can make a day of visiting this park and enjoying its amenities: You'll find baseball, softball, soccer, and basketball facilities; picnic tables; barbecues; and an amphitheater. The park also has a 2-mile jogging and walking path with sit-up and push-up stands. For more information about this park, call (916) 808-6060 or visit www.cityofsacramento .org/parksandrecreation /parks/landpark.htm.

If real outdoor fun is your family's wish, the 5,000-acre American River Parkway should be your destination when visiting Sacramento. This magnificent park winds its way about 23 miles through the center of the city from the confluence of the Sacramento and American Rivers at Discovery Park to just below Folsom Lake. It has more than 20 major recreation areas, including a scenic, two-lane bike path; miles of equestrian trails; hundreds of fishing spots along the river; and several put-in spots to launch a craft for some exciting white-water rafting. For more information and maps, contact the County of Sacramento Parks and Recreation Department at (916) 875-6961 or visit www.msa2.saccounty .net/parks.

Sacramento has plenty to do and to see. The difficult task is deciding your game plan. I recommend that you spend the night in the city to break up the excursion into two leisurely days instead of a hectic one. The Visitors Bureau, 1608 I Street (916-808-7777, (800) 292-2334; www .sacramento cvb.org), publishes brochures listing many of the attractions, restaurants, accommodations, and tour information. Such a brochure is a handy guide for planning your trip.

TRUCKEE, CALIFORNIA

Sitting astride the original trail used by pioneers who traveled overland from Missouri to California in the 1840s, the bustling tourist town of Truckee, about 30 miles west of Reno, stands as a modern-day reminder of just how formidable those trips were. After crossing thousands of miles of blistering deserts and tortuous mountains, the final test for early emigrants came just west of Truckee, where the rugged pass through the Sierra Nevada presented a formidable obstacle to the fertile valleys of California on the other side. Because heavy snow made the route impassable once winter set in, travelers had to cross before the storms arrived, and cutting it close sometimes meant getting trapped in the high country or on the eastern side of the mountains. Even today, the section of I–80 that crosses the pass is frequently closed during winter months because of blizzard conditions.

In the winter of 1846–1847, the dreaded storms not only showed up early—they blew in with a vengeance, dumping record amounts of heavy snow on a group of 91 emigrants who attempted to cross the pass late in October. Named the Donner Party for their leader, George Donner, this group of families became stranded at a small lake near present-day Truckee. As the winter progressed and the snow piled up to more than 20 feet, the party's food supplies dwindled, then disappeared. The 49 who survived were forced to subsist off the bodies of those who died of starvation during the long, arduous winter. The lake and mountain pass were later named Donner Lake and Donner Pass for these ill-fated settlers. You can visit the site of the Donner Party's ordeal at Donner Memorial State Park, on the east end of Donner Lake, just west of downtown Truckee.

To get to Truckee from Reno, follow I–80 west and exit at any of the three Truckee exits. Coming from Lake Tahoe, you can take CA 267 north from Kings Beach, passing Northstar-at-Tahoe along the way. If you take CA 89 north from Tahoe City, you'll pass Alpine Meadows ski resort and Squaw Valley USA before reaching Truckee at the 12-mile mark. For a description of activities at these resorts, see the Winter Sports, Resorts, and Vacation Resorts chapters.

Donner Memorial State Park is at the west end of Truckee, just off I–80 on Donner Pass Road. To learn more about the Donner tragedy and the area's natural history, you can visit the Emigrant Trail Museum in the park. The large bronze Pioneer Monument behind the museum depicts a typical emigrant family and honors all those who made the difficult trek to the West. On the lighter side of things, the park has several miles of hiking trails, sites for camping and picnicking, and lovely beaches for swimming. It's also a popular area for cross-country skiing in the winter. For more information call (530) 582-7892 or visit www .parks.ca.gov.

Just as it was in the 1800s, Truckee's geographical location continues to be the root of its prosperity. Nestled along the banks of the Truckee River in the heavily wooded mountains, it profits from the many tourists who arrive on I–80 or on Amtrak. Its historic downtown is crowded with colorful shops and funky restaurants, most within easy walking distance of each other along Commercial Row. You can browse the boutiques for several hours, then enjoy gourmet dining at a variety of eateries right downtown. You can sample a sushi bar along with Pan-Asian cooking with a view of the main drag at Dragonfly (530-587-0557). For a panoramic view of the river and the downtown area, try the Cottonwood on the edge of town on CA 267 (530-587-5711). While wandering around downtown, be sure to take a look at the historic bronze eagle in front of the train station. Mounted on a granite base and with a 7-foot wingspan, the Victory Monument commemorates U.S. soldiers killed in World War I.

At 6,000-plus feet in elevation, the golf courses around Truckee are a great place to find out if your drive really does go farther at high altitude. You can tee it up at Tahoe Donner, with its daunting array of undulating fairways carved out of rugged mountain terrain. The course is located north of town at 12850 Northwoods Boulevard. Call (530) 587-9440 for rates and tee times, or visit www.tahoedonner.com. Just down the road from Tahoe Donner is Coyote Moon Golf Course, an equally challenging course (530-587-0886; www.coyotemoongolf.com). Located 6 miles south of town, just off CA 267, the narrow fairways and winding creek at Northstar-at-Tahoe will challenge even the best players' games. Call (530) 562-2490 for details, or visit www.skinorth star.com. And for a quick nine holes right in town, the Ponderosa Golf Course, just off CA 267, is an absolute delight at a reasonable price. Call (530) 587-3501 for information, or visit www.ponderosa golfcourse.com. If you've just hit Megabucks in Reno, however, you might want to try a round at Lahontan Golf Club. It will cost you the price of a membership and a multimillion-dollar home, however. As one of the most recent displays of Truckee's growing affluence, Lahontan is a private 27-hole layout tucked deep in the pines south of town. For information call (800) 582-9919 or visit www.lahontan.com. (See the Golf chapter for more details on area courses.)

If you visit Truckee during the summer, you can enjoy watching the gliders that soar and swoop like enormous birds high over the mountainous terrain. If you want to do more than watch, hang onto your hat (and your stomach): Soar Truckee will give you the ride and the view of your life. The natural geography of the area creates the thermal lifts that are absolutely ideal for soaring. Needless to say, the aerial view of Lake Tahoe and the surrounding Sierra Nevada from one of these big birds is simply breathtaking. Rides can be booked daily May through October from 9:00 a.m. to 5:00 p.m. by calling (530) 587-6702. The Web site is www.soartruckee.com. The Truckee Tahoe Airport, where glider flights originate, is just several miles south of town off CA 267. (See the Recreation chapter for more information.)

The lakes and streams around Truckee are especially inviting to those who like to fish, since they provide a variety of natural conditions along with wonderfully challenging species of fish. Martis Creek Lake, just south of town off CA 267, is a premier habitat for brown and rainbow trout. Don't bring your frying pan, however: It's catch-and-release only with barbless hooks. You can also try your luck in Donner Lake, known for its large Mackinaws, or the Truckee River on either side of town.

If your idea of a mountain experience is hiking through the natural beauty of a pristine forest, a trek along a stretch of the Pacific Crest Trail (PCT) will more than satisfy this need. To get to the trailhead, go west on I–80 from Truckee for about 8 miles to the rest stops at the summit, where you'll find a sign directing you to the trailhead. Hiking north on the PCT will take you through dense forest toward Castle Peak, where you can enjoy splendid views of Donner Lake and the surrounding mountains. Heading south will also give you marvelous views of the lake, but from a closer perspective.

For a unique view of area history from the perspective of snow skiing, the Western SkiSport Museum is a must-stop for both skiers and non-skiers. Take I–80 west from Truckee about 8 miles and exit on the Castle Peak exit at Boreal Mountain Resort. A visit to this one-of-a-kind showcase of the area's most popular sport is well worth the drive out of Truckee. While we think of skiing as merely a recreational activity today, it was introduced to the area as a far more utilitarian occupation: For the early gold seekers, skiing was the only way to get around in heavy winter snow. The fascinating exhibits show early, antiquated equipment, such as the 10foot-long, 25-pound skis used by the legendary Snowshoe Thompson when he delivered mail to snowbound settlers from 1856 to 1876. You can also see the Western Ski Hall of Fame, which honors individuals who contributed to the development of the sport in the West, along with numerous displays of Olympic medals, clothing, and vintage pictures. The museum is free and open from 10:00 a.m. to 4:00 p.m. Friday through Sunday during the ski season and by appointment the rest of the year. For more information call the Auburn Ski Club at (530) 426-3313, ext. 113, or go to www.auburnskiclub.org.

If you arrived in Reno by air and don't have a car, you can easily get to Truckee by bus or train. Greyhound has a number of departures daily; call (800) 231-2222 for exact times or visit www.greyhound.com. For details about Amtrak trains, which will drop you right downtown at the restored railroad depot, call (800) 872-7245 or visit www.amtrak.com (see also the Getting Here, Getting Around chapter). You can pick up a walking tour brochure and other information about Truckee at the visitor center at 10065 Donner Pass Road in the historic railroad station downtown, or call (530) 587-8808. The Web site is www.truckee.com.

i **Virginia City becomes a real ghost town during its Ghost Town Halloween Spectacular.**

VIRGINIA CITY, NEVADA

At the height of its glory, Virginia City, the "Queen of the Comstock," was the hellraisingest town in the United States. Touring actors put on Shakespearean plays, prostitutes plied their trade in a thriving red-light district, and the town boasted gunfights, murders, opium dens, rival newspapers, and competing fire companies. All of this activity was born of two drunken Irish prospectors and a con man named Henry Comstock (see the History chapter). Today, most people remember Virginia City as the place that Ben, Adam, Hoss, and Little Joe Cartwright visited when they needed supplies or a night on the town in the old hit TV show Bonanza.

Miners squeezed more than $300 million in silver from the surrounding lode during Virginia City's heyday, which ended in 1898 with the virtual abandonment of the mines. Today the entire city stands as a national landmark and the largest federally designated historical district in America maintained in its original condition. Boardwalks line the streets, and the shops and museums are located in original buildings dating from the 1860s and 1870s. The city, once called the "Richest Place on Earth," offers you a great day trip and a glimpse at the town's glorious past.

Even though Virginia City is only 20 minutes from Reno via US 395 and Nevada Highway 341, and 40 minutes from Lake Tahoe via Nevada Highways 431 and 341, you should set aside an entire day for your visit. After all, this is the city that's been "Live & Kickin' Since 1859."

Virginia City offers visitors a rare peek into American history—indeed, its third motto, "Adventure Back In Time," harkens to this theme. Most of us learn about our past through books. In Virginia City, you can relive it. The city features underground tours of mines, as well as tours of churches and cemeteries, plus tours of some of the most opulent mansions in the West. It still has bawdy saloons where you can get "two fingers of redeye," and you can buy keepsakes and souvenirs from the gift and specialty shops that dot every block. You can take a walking tour of the liveliest ghost town in the West or ride the trolley with a guide narrating the history of the buildings it passes.

Not much has changed since the bonanza days of the silver mines except that now, instead of catering to miners, the city takes care of tourists. The city is open all year with several events, celebrations, and attractions for your enjoyment. A few of the attractions include: the Castle Mansion tour, 10:00 a.m. to 5:00 p.m., which gives you an opportunity to visit a mansion built in 1868 still in its original state and not restored; the Chollar Mine tour, open 1:00 to 5:00 p.m. in summer, which gives you a glimpse of original square-set lumbering, tools, and equipment from the fifth largest producing mine on the Comstock; the Julia Bulette Red Light Museum (775-847-9394), open 10:00 a.m. to 9:00 p.m., which includes displays of contraceptives, medical instruments, and medical cure-alls (Julia Bulette, most famous of the Virginia City prostitutes, was murdered by one of her customers); and the Mackay Mansion (775-847-0173), open daily from 11:00 a.m. to 6:00 p.m., which was built in 1860 as the mining office and superintendent's residence by the Gould & Curry Mining Company and is completely furnished with period pieces. And don't forget to pop in and look around the Territorial Enterprise, the original 1876 building where Mark Twain began his literary career.

From May through November there is a narrated, 35-minute ride from Virginia City to Gold Hill on the historic Virginia & Truckee Railroad. This ride lets you view the mining district from the original 128year-old train. Tickets can be purchased at the train depot in the middle of Virginia City near the train tracks. The trains operate daily from 10:30 a.m. to 4:00 p.m. Memorial Day to Halloween.

Also, don't forget to visit the Comstock Fireman's Museum, Piper's Opera House, the Fourth Ward School, the First Presbyterian Church, St. Mary's in the Mountains Catholic Church, the Bucket of Blood and The Delta saloons, the Marshall Mint and Museum, and ask where you can view the 100-mile canyon. Come to think about it, you may need two days to totally enjoy Virginia City. If you wish to stay overnight in Virginia City, I suggest The Gold Hill Hotel (775-847-0111), which has been operating since 1859. The newest accommodation is the Ramada Inn (775-847-4484) 1 mile south of Virginia City on Nevada Highway 342. Virginia City has numerous cafes and restaurants, and all are about equal in price and value.

For more information about Virginia City visit www.virginiacity-nv.org or www.virginiacity-nv .com or call (800) 718-7587 or (775) 847-4386.

The International Camel Races

If we Insiders had to suggest a time of year to visit Virginia City, it would be in September, when the hilarious and raucous International Camel Races are held. Traditionally run on the weekend following Labor Day, these races were the brainchild of a *Territorial Enterprise* editor with a slow news week and a sense of humor.

Originally, the U.S. Army introduced camels into the West in 1856, reasoning that the animals would fare well in the desert here. In 1861 camel-train operators used the animals to carry salt from Nevada's marshes to miners on the Comstock. Prospectors used salt in a process called amalgamation, which reclaims gold and silver ore. These pack camels also hauled supplies and firewood

to Virginia City residents. But in the mid-1870s, with mining declining, most camel-train operators went bankrupt and released their animals to roam the high desert. The last wild camel in Nevada was spotted in 1936.

In 1957, in order to fill space in his newspaper, the editor of the Territorial Enterprise invented the fictitious camel race. The race never occurred—supposedly the camels became ill. For the next two years, the editor made up more phony excuses to postpone the nonexistent races. In 1960, however, Clark Gable, Marilyn Monroe, and director John Huston were in Virginia City filming *The Misfits* during camel race time. John Huston had heard about the fictitious event and decided to make it a reality. Riding camels that came to town with the San Francisco Chronicle, he and other Hollywood celebrities made the yearly tradition real.

These days, the camel races are the most popular event in Virginia City—and since 1962 they also include ostrich races. City fathers added "International" to the title in 1987 when they challenged officials from Virginia City's sister city, Alice Springs, Australia, to come over and join in the races. (Australia also used camels as pack animals during its expansion and exploration.)

RELOCATION

If you're thinking about relocating to the Reno/Tahoe area, it's not surprising. The quality of life here is enough to make many people consider pulling up stakes wherever they are. Nevada has boasted (or suffered from) the highest growth rate in the country for a number of years now, so it goes without saying that there must be something attractive about living here. As far as Reno/Tahoe goes, how about unlimited outdoor recreation with four mild seasons to enjoy it in? Or a tax-friendly environment that's more affordable than many comparable communities? Or nonstop nightlife along with a plethora of arts and cultural activities? But before you schedule the moving van, I suggest you read a little more about what life is like in this area. In addition to this chapter, I suggest reading the Health Care and Wellness, Retirement, Education and Child Care, Media, and Worship chapters, which also have information relevant to relocation.

Since choosing where to live is one of the major decisions you'll have to make when relocating, in this chapter I help you walk that minefield with a discussion of neighborhoods, real estate companies, and information about the housing market in general. But along with that I also tell you where you can register your car, enroll your children in school, and get a free relocation packet. Because not all neighborhoods are the same, let's begin this adventure in moving with a whirlwind look at them, broken down by the four geographic areas: Reno, Sparks, North Shore Lake Tahoe, and South Shore Lake Tahoe.

NEIGHBORHOODS

Reno

I have divided the Reno area into five neighborhoods: North Reno, Verdi/Mogul, the North Valleys, Southwest Reno, and Southeast Reno. Some of the neighborhoods are part of the incorporated city of Reno and some are in unincorporated Washoe County, but because the services and atmosphere are generally the same, this chapter does not separate the two.

North Reno

I have dubbed the area north of the Truckee River within the city limits "North Reno." This part of town contains just about everything that makes a city like Reno tick. Here you have hospitals, casinos, churches, stores, businesses, condos, apartments, and houses dating from the 1940s to the 1990s. There are three basic sections to this area: the Northeastern, the Northwestern, and the Northwest Suburban.

The Northeastern section contains the University of Nevada, Reno; Truckee Meadows Community College; and a plethora of housing ranging from low-income to upper middle class. Most of the older homes border Interstate 80, with the newer models built farther north.

The Northwestern section of this neighborhood stretches from the university (North Virginia Street) to North McCarran Boulevard. This area is crowded with private homes, apartments, duplexes, and multifamily complexes, and it contains most of the university's fraternity and sorority houses. This section is about 60 years old, with most of the dwellings rented out to students and university personnel. Some of the old homes are in fantastic shape, while others show the wear of being rentals.

The Northwest Suburban section of this neighborhood begins at North McCarran Boulevard and continues west to the former Northgate Golf Club. This area is mostly residential, with established commercial properties along North McCarran Boulevard. Realtors warn new buyers in this area, which sits on the slopes of Peavine Peak, that mature trees are a rare commodity and the area is extremely windy. From east to west the different developments represent the decades of growth in the northwest. The older homes, circa 1940, are closer in toward the university, and the newer 1990s models border the golf course. From east to west you will pass through developments built in the '60s, '70s, '80s, and '90s.

Realtors call North Reno an "area in transition" where first-time buyers can find older affordable homes and more affluent buyers can find new, upscale developments to trade up to.

i When relocating it's a good idea to consider renting for a while first. After you are familiar with the new area, you can make better-informed decisions about where to buy property.

Verdi/Mogul

These two rural areas sit just northwest of Reno along I–80. The Truckee River winds its way through them, and the Toiyabe National Forest butts up against their southern borders.

The splendor of the wide-open spaces dotted with trees and the rural feel make up Verdi's personality. Residents say they like the country atmosphere of the area and also like the idea that Reno and its amenities are only 10 miles away.

Some of the bigger, one-of-a-kind houses are situated in the west Verdi area in neighborhoods surrounding Crystal Peak Park and Dog Valley Road. The most popular areas to live include Lakeview Estates, Belli Ranch subdivision, and Donner Trail Ranch. Most of the homes are custom-built, and you'll find houses that are modestly priced as well as those that cost several million dollars.

Mogul, although rural like Verdi but without the trees, sports a different feel. Closer in toward Reno (only about 5 miles out), Mogul is a large development with similar-looking houses. The area remains popular because, like Verdi, it appears remote but is close enough to Reno to enjoy all the big city has to offer. Because many people live here to enjoy the rural environment, proposed annexation of some land by the city of Reno is a hotbed of controversy. The city's less-restrictive growth guidelines could open the floodgates to more growth and dense housing. This neighborhood also boasts Somersett, a master-planned golf community adjacent to Mogul and Verdi. Although I don't want to alarm you, Verdi/Mogul has been the center of periodic earthquake swarms since 2008. No major property damage has resulted, but it has jangled residents' nerves. However, because the incidents come and go at will, most people have learned to accept it when it happens. As of the time of this writing, it has been more of an annoyance than a serious problem.

The North Valleys

The North Valley communities include Stead, Lemmon Valley, Silver Knolls, Panther Valley, Raleigh Heights, Golden Valley, and Sun Valley. They are located just north of Reno along U.S. Highway 395. Generally these communities are perfect for people who like the wide-open spaces and want to live away from the busy city but close enough to commute.

Stead evolved during World War II when the government built a training base for the U.S. Army/Air Force. Now it is considered a bedroom community of Reno with an ever-expanding manufacturing and warehouse sector. Most people come here to work in the warehouses or industrial centers and to live close to work. Stead remains a manufacturing community, and its airport is home to the annual National Championship Air Races (see the Annual Events chapter).

Lemmon Valley and Golden Valley are ideal for people who want a large block of land but who also want to live close to Reno. Like Stead, these neighborhoods are north of Reno and border US 395. Lemmon Valley is the farthest out and offers the cheapest, easily accessible property. Golden Valley is closer in, is a little more expensive, and affords easy access to Reno and Sparks. Both of these neighborhoods offer large horse properties. Closer in toward US 395, mobile (manufactured) homes and older houses dominate the landscape. These valleys have a rural flavor but are only 10 to 20 minutes from downtown Reno.

Sun Valley sits on top of the northern border between Reno and Sparks, with mobile homes making up most of this neighborhood. Even though a few single-family homes dot the area and one new housing development sits in the northeastern corner, the neighborhood is still considered to be a manufactured-home haven. Citizen volunteers have been trying to combat the underdeveloped stigma attached to the neighborhood, but it still lacks the amenities of other Reno locations. Sun Valley has few streetlights and even fewer sidewalks, and a large portion of the streets remain unpaved dirt and gravel.

i **Property taxes in Nevada are assessed at 35 percent of the appraised or market value.**

Southwest Reno

The Southwest area of Reno has it all—businesses, older neighborhoods, newer housing developments, several upper-class custom home sites, and large country plots of land. As growth continues its steady march south, this area of town has experienced a large percentage of the upscale retail and business expansion. Dozens of new office complexes have sprung up interspersed with big box and boutique shopping. The area also boasts the new lifestyle shopping center, the Summit Sierra, along with the highest concentration of restaurants in the Reno/Tahoe area.

This neighborhood gives any buyer a wide variety of locations and home styles from sprawling country living to downtown togetherness. Realtors break the expansive Southwest down

into three real estate sections: the Old Southwest, the Southwest, and Southwest Suburban.

The Old Southwest is bordered by the Truckee River to the north, Plumb Lane to the south, South Virginia Street to the east, and South McCarran Boulevard to the west. This section is smack in the middle of downtown Reno and contains several city-maintained parks. The architecture here is the oldest in Reno, and brick is the dominant building material. Mature trees envelop the area, which has housing ranging from modest single-story homes to gigantic mansions.

The Southwest section of Reno sits directly underneath the Old Southwest, bordered by Plumb Lane to the north, South McCarran Boulevard to the south and west, and South Virginia Street to the east. This area has dozens of housing developments both old and new, four city parks, two golf courses, and a lake. Some of the more grandiose and older homes are situated around Washoe County Golf Course in the middle of the Southwest section, and many lower-priced homes and apartments sit south of Virginia Lake just 3 blocks east of the golf course. This area began its growth spurt in the 1980s when Reno expanded southward.

Lakeridge, one of the most upscale developments in Reno, sits in this Southwest section. Lakeridge community is on the golf course, with a montage of houses, condos, and apartments built around it and a tennis center. Insiders recognize the area as one of the most highbrow in the city.

But perhaps the most popular and luxurious development in the Southwest is Caughlin Ranch (pronounced Collin, without the "gh" sound). This development is one of the first planned communities in Reno; it contains luxury houses and condos but no apartments. The first development began in 1984, and, according to Realtors, it has added a development a year since then. The developments all use a wide-open-space design, with plenty of winding trails for jogging and hiking.

The Southwest Suburban section is the largest area of any real estate section in Reno and

Sparks. This area stretches from South McCarran Boulevard south along US 395 to Nevada Highway 431 (the Mt. Rose Highway), up the highway to the Mt. Rose–Ski Tahoe ski resort. Most of this section is in unincorporated Washoe County, and, like Verdi and Mogul, the expansive space gives the feel of country living.

Huffaker development sits at the extreme north of this section and includes a subdivision of larger, upscale houses with its own park, lake, and tennis courts. Working southward, most of the developments in the area feature the more expensive custom-built homes, but the dedicated buyer can find a subdivision to fit any lifestyle with varied price ranges. This area has four new golf courses and plenty of wide-open spaces.

Among the most popular of the newer subdivisions is Saddlehorn, just northwest of the Mt. Rose Highway. People buying here like the idea that their homes are unique and are located on the edge of Reno as well as close to Lake Tahoe.

Along the Mt. Rose Highway, subdivisions are gobbling up every inch of available vacant land. New buyers looking here have several price ranges and styles to choose from. For the more discriminating buyer, two new gated communities have sprung up around the area's three newest golf courses. Old European–style houses surround the Jack Nicklaus–designed Montreux Golf Course. Realtors like to say that these houses give homeowners a feeling of "private country-club living in an alpine setting."

Arrowcreek's two golf courses, designed by Arnold Palmer and Fuzzy Zoeller, are neighbors to Montreux. The gated community surrounding these two golf courses provides 1,500 acres of open land, large custom homes, semicustom homes, and a 12-acre swim and tennis center. A little farther up the highway, Galena Forest Estates and St. James's Village offer luxurious custom homes tucked deep into the forest.

Southeast Reno

For this guide I include the neighborhoods of Hidden Valley, Donner Springs, Damonte Ranch, Virginia Foothills, Steamboat, and the Virginia

City Highlands in the area I call Reno's Southeast. This section stretches from the Truckee River southeast along US 395 to Tahoe Junction (the intersection of US 395 and the Mt. Rose Highway). This large area contains the Reno/Tahoe International Airport, Meadowood Mall and an extensive commercial sector along US 395.

Hidden Valley and Donner Springs housing developments lie to the east and southeast of the airport and provide quality homes for the more upscale buyer. Homes in the older, more established Hidden Valley are sprinkled in and around the Hidden Valley Country Club. This neighborhood also has a large county park and includes Rosewood Lakes Golf Course, just east of the country club.

The newer Donner Springs neighborhood southeast of South McCarran Boulevard has more moderately priced homes in the neighborhoods east of Longley Lane. Modestly priced homes also can be found in Huffaker Hills on East Huffaker Lane and Double Diamond Ranch along South Meadows Parkway off US 395.

Just east of Tahoe Junction on either side of Nevada Highway 341 (the Comstock Highway), which winds its way up to Virginia City, sit the communities of Virginia Foothills (north of NV 341) and Steamboat (south of NV 341). Some of the older homes were built in the 1960s, but full-scale development here began in the 1970s. This area is more rural than the rest of the Southeast.

The last neighborhood in the Southeast is the Virginia City Highlands, located up the Comstock Highway just off Geiger Grade, which snakes its way to Virginia City. Houses here are scattered along the mountainside and have an outdoorsy feel and spectacular valley and mountain views. A big problem in this neighborhood is the fact that the Comstock Highway is a two-lane road that gets lots of snow during the winter months.

One of the drawbacks to living in the Southeast is that during the floods of 1997 and in 2006, parts of this area found themselves underwater, including the airport, and the city is still struggling with a comprehensive flood plan. Another issue to be aware of is the planned Southeast

Connector road that will pass through this area near Rosewood Lakes and Hidden Valley as it links Sparks Boulevard to Veterans Parkway. Before buying or leasing a home here, I strongly recommend you look at the route and what properties it will affect. Construction is scheduled to begin in 2009. I also caution you about the high crime rate in the neighborhood surrounding Neil Road just north and east of Meadowood Mall.

Sparks

I have divided Sparks into four neighborhoods: Old Sparks, East Sparks, Sparks Suburban, and Spanish Springs. Once again, some of the neighborhoods fall within the city limits and some are within the unincorporated confines of Washoe County. I do not make a distinction between the two.

Generally, Sparks is considered by most residents to be a family-friendly area with a high concentration of single-family homes. Despite recent growth that has ballooned the population to more than 90,000, residents of Sparks say it's still a small town with a laid-back lifestyle overall. One reason the Rail City has been able to maintain most of its original ambience is the attention paid by the Sparks City Council to make sure that the warehouse areas of the city stay separated from the residential neighborhoods.

Old Sparks

This is the oldest section of the city, and it lies north of I-80 between El Rancho Drive and North McCarran Boulevard. This is the original railroad settlement and contains City Hall, the casino area, and Victorian Square, Sparks's redevelopment project (see the Area Overview and Attractions chapters). The area is clustered with older, single-family homes that are very modestly priced. The housing has the late 1940s, early 1950s look and feel, with small, crackerbox designs and mostly single-story homes. Even though this section is old, the Sparks Police Department says the neighborhoods are safe.

East Sparks

East Sparks is bordered by I-80 to the south, Pah Rah Park to the north, North McCarran Boulevard to the west, and Vista Boulevard to the east. Most of Sparks's industrial sector is south of I-80 and along the first few miles of Vista Boulevard. The rest of East Sparks is made up of newer housing developments, such as the D'Andrea Golf Club complex. This area of Sparks houses the largest concentration of single-family residences in the city. The development began in the 1970s and continues today. East Sparks is also the home to Sparks Marina Park, a recreational area built around an artificial lake that was once a gravel pit (see the Parks chapter). As the core of Sparks is built out, the land to the east is destined for increased development.

Sparks Suburban

The Sparks Suburban area is bordered by Nevada Highway 445 (the Pyramid Highway) to the west, Red Hawk Golf Club to the north, and Pah Rah Park to the south. The east is wide-open, hilly space with tons of room for growth. This area is home to the newest housing developments, including Wingfield Springs, a community surrounding Red Hawk Golf Club. The enormous growth in this area required developers to construct the Galleria Sparks, a shopping complex at the intersection of Disc Drive and Vista Boulevard to accommodate the suburban residents. See the Shopping chapter for details. Depending upon which development you're looking at, you'll find homes that are modestly priced along with much more expensive property. Wingfield Springs, for example, is a very upscale housing development.

Spanish Springs

This area stretches north along the eastern side of the Pyramid Highway and is an area where most of the new construction is happening. The feel in this section is definitely rural, with houses built among the sagebrush of northern Nevada's high desert. Most of the residents here say they like the country feel and the fact that the city is only

8 to 10 miles away. As development continues to push north of Sparks, however, increased traffic will be a problem. The challenge is to maintain the quality of life, including the rural flavor, while welcoming new development. When considering relocation here or in Sparks Suburban, it would be wise to picture how future growth will affect the area. Also, because few jobs are located here and the development of some infrastructure has been lagging, many residents find they are faced with long commute times to their work.

Lake Tahoe

The 72 miles around Lake Tahoe take you on an inspirational tour of some of the most magnificent homes in the United States, from those resting on the shore of this pristine lake to those tucked away in the pine trees. Less expensive homes are available for the motivated buyer, but let's face the facts: Property around Lake Tahoe is expensive. The overall real estate picture in the Lake Tahoe basin is actually somewhat schizophrenic. You'll find a significant number of properties, owned by very wealthy people, that are priced in the millions. But you'll also occasionally find run-down ski cabins that are very overvalued because of their location. As time goes on, more and more of these cheaper properties will become teardowns. Because so little vacant buildable land is left in the basin, new construction relies on demolishing existing buildings.

Here I give a brief description of various areas around the lake; for more details read the Area Overview chapter.

North Shore Lake Tahoe

From Meeks Bay, California, on the western side of North Shore, to Incline Village, Nevada, on the eastern border of the area, many of the houses and condos are upscale residences. The notable exception is Kings Beach, which has more run-down real estate than any other area at the lake. The architecture of most of the homes fits into the Old Tahoe look—wood exteriors and interiors, rock fireplaces, some houses tucked away beneath majestic Jeffrey pine trees and some

with lake frontage amid natural boulders and glistening white sand. Property values are based not only upon the physical structure itself but also on its all-important view and proximity to the lake. So a house that may seem like nothing more than a fixer-upper in most markets may actually have a hefty price tag if it has any kind of view (but watch out for the Realtor's phrase "filtered view of the lake," which could mean a peek from a window in the upstairs closet). Any property actually on the lakeshore is obviously worth millions, regardless of what kind of structure is on it. In fact, older homes with views or lake frontage are considered teardowns and are frequently bulldozed to make way for new spectacular estates.

No fewer than 50 neighborhoods line the lake on the North Shore where prospective buyers can search for their one-of-a-kind homes, but one of the most populated is Incline Village. This unique village once attracted retired people and those looking for second homes. Now, more than 70 percent of the 9,000 citizens are permanent residents less than 50 years old. Lakeshore Boulevard and the steep slopes overlooking the lake showcase the luxurious estates of many of the country's rich and famous. Incline Village is also home to Sierra Nevada College, a four-year liberal-arts school.

South Shore Lake Tahoe

Real estate doesn't get any cheaper as you travel south around the lake from Incline Village. The first community in the northeastern corner of the area I call South Shore is Glenbrook, an upscale gated neighborhood nestled in and around Glenbrook Golf Course, a private layout.

Between Glenbrook and Stateline, Nevada, about 12 residential areas line the lake. From Uppaway, Logan Creek, and Lakeridge in the northern part to Zephyr Heights, Roundhill and Lake Village in the southern part of the area, buyers can find a variety of unique mountain and lake homes.

Perhaps the best buys around the lake are located in South Lake Tahoe, California. This city is the most populated around Lake Tahoe and contains amenities expected of a larger community—shopping, fast-food restaurants, an airport, and three golf courses. Here a buyer can find almost any type of residential property, some offered at prices lower than other locales around the lake. South Lake Tahoe has single-family residences, condos, town-homes, and apartments, with some properties, in neighborhoods away from the lake, actually modestly priced. Keep in mind that there's an enormous discrepancy among properties and in the prices listed for them.

 Residents who move away from Incline Village are known as "decliners."

REAL ESTATE

You'll find a tantalizing variety of homes awaiting you in the Reno/Sparks area, from ranchettes with plenty of room for horses and dogs to starter homes perfect for newlyweds or small families to apartments and condos with hassle-free maintenance. Although many real estate listings are of older properties, growth in the last decade has caused an explosion of new housing developments that fan out in every direction from the urban core. As in many other areas of the country, however, the economic downturn at press time has resulted in a buyers market in general in the Reno/Tahoe area, with a large inventory of homes for sale, but fewer buyers lined up to purchase. Because the prices have become very volatile, it's irrelevant to even give examples of them at this time. The best way to take advantage of this market, if you're able to buy, is to work with a reputable Realtor and to peruse the large number of listings you can choose from. While there's certainly enough gorgeous homes at Lake Tahoe that most people would love to own, the big question has always been affordability. You will definitely not get the same bang for your buck at the lake as you will in the Reno/Sparks area. Stringent building restrictions coupled with high demand have caused prices at the lake to skyrocket. Sales of houses in the millions of dollars is the norm, with fixer-uppers selling for hundreds

of thousands. If the price of a home is out of your league, consider buying a condo, which could be less expensive. And if you find that you just can't afford anything at all at the lake, take heart: Many people are surprised to learn that they don't have to live there to enjoy all its amenities. Keep in mind it's just a short drive away from Reno/Sparks and surrounding communities.

REAL ESTATE COMPANIES

The following associations of Realtors in the Reno/Tahoe area maintain lists of more than 350 real estate firms with more than 2,500 registered Realtors. The lists are free and can be obtained by contacting one of these five associations:

RENO/SPARKS ASSOCIATION OF REALTORS
(775) 823-8800
www.rsar.net

INCLINE VILLAGE ASSOCIATION OF REALTORS
(775) 831-3777
www.inclinerealtors.com

TAHOE SIERRA BOARD OF REALTORS
(530) 583-0275
www.tahoemls.com

SOUTH TAHOE ASSOCIATION OF REALTORS
(530) 541-7007
www.staor.org

SIERRA NEVADA ASSOCIATION OF REALTORS
(775) 885-7200
www.sierranvar.com

These associations will answer most of your questions about the real estate market in their particular areas, but they will not specifically recommend one of their member Realtors over another. One way to obtain a Realtor is to choose the area you would most like to live in and see which realty firm is most active there; another is to solicit referrals from friends or coworkers.

My list of Realtors, broken down into two general areas (Reno/Sparks and Lake Tahoe), just touches on a cross-section of the many real estate firms in the Reno/Tahoe area. All of my choices have access to the MLS (Multiple Listing Service). Some of the firms are affiliated with nationwide chains, and some are smaller firms with good local references and reputations. Because of the complex nature of real estate deals I highly recommend you use a qualified firm to help you navigate the minefields of buying and selling. The following list of Realtors is by no means exhaustive.

Reno/Sparks

COLDWELL BANKER–PLUMMER & ASSOCIATES

16500 Wedge Parkway, Reno, NV
(775) 336-6100
www.coldwellbankerreno.com
One of the largest real estate firms in the area, with more than 100 Realtors, this locally owned franchise specializes in relocation. It has a team of Realtors who specialize in making moving into the area easy. Realtors for this firm work in all aspects of real estate, from residential to commercial, including land and lot sales. In business since 1978, this firm also offers concierge service.

DICKSON REALTY

1030 Caughlin Crossing, Reno, NV
(775) 746-7000

500 Damonte Ranch Parkway, Suite 625
Reno, NV
(775) 850-7001

4870 Vista Boulevard, Sparks, NV
(775) 685-8800
www.dicksonrealty.com
Founded in 1973, this firm is a member of RELO, the largest network of independent brokers in the world. It's also the largest independently owned real estate firm in Reno, with more than 350 Realtors and 12 offices. The company only hires Realtors with proven track records.

FERRARI-LUND REAL ESTATE

3700 Lakeside Drive, Suite 100
Reno, NV
(775) 688-4000

690 Queen Way, Sparks, NV
(775) 685-7788, (800) 622-1777

500 Damonte Ranch Parkway, Suite 804
Reno, NV
(775) 850-7033 www.ferrari-lund.com
The Ferrari-Lund Real Estate firm has been operating in Reno since 1988 and specializes in relocation. It handles mostly residential listings but also has a good supply of commercial properties. The firm is one of the 50 top producers in the United States and hires only veteran Realtors. The firm has a relocation division and has more than 140 Realtors to attend to your needs.

HELP-U-SELL DRAKULICH REALTY

2205 North McCarran Boulevard
Sparks, NV
(775) 685-8585
www.helpusellnevada.com
Drakulich Realty specializes in residential properties and charges a flat fee instead of the normal 6 percent of the sale price. The firm has about 20 Realtors. It offers a free, weekly list of properties complete with prices, descriptions, and addresses. Drakulich is a full-service firm that shows both its own listings and listings of other brokers.

LANDFINDER COUNTRY PROPERTIES

1010 12th Street, Sparks, NV
(775) 358-0555
www.landfindercp.com
A small firm that specializes in out-of-town properties, this office concentrates on horse properties, ranches, and land away from the hustle and bustle of city life. Landfinder has been selling ranches for a number of years and has a good selection of rural properties for sale. Its Realtors are licensed in both Nevada and California. The owner says she is not a "city girl" and points out that she lives on a ranch 20 miles north of Reno.

PRUDENTIAL NEVADA REALTY, INC.

5370 Kietzke Lane, Reno, NV
(775) 829-3131
www.prurealty.com

Prudential Nevada Realty is associated with more than 3,500 Realtors in 150 offices in Nevada and northern California for relocation services. That's one of the reasons its owner says, "Relocating is our forte." Residential property sales make up the majority of the firm's business, and it boasts about its 88 percent success rate in sales of all its listings. The firm also provides each of its Realtors with 12 weeks of intensive training. The office has been around for more than 20 years and has more than 170 Realtors working for it.

i For a guide on how to avoid paying too much for a home in the Reno/Tahoe area, call (775) 829-3131 or click on www.renohomeseller.com.

RE/MAX REALTY PROFESSIONALS

6121 Lakeside Drive, Reno, NV
(775) 828-3200
www.remax-renonv.com

This office of RE/MAX has been in business since 1990. It recently changed hands but has maintained a staff of about 70 Realtors. The firm handles both residential and commercial properties and uses a worldwide network for relocating.

Lake Tahoe

ANN NICHOLS AND COMPANY

201 Stateline Road, Crystal Bay, NV
(775) 831-0625
www.annnichols.com

This small, independently owned office specializes in luxury second homes on the North Shore of Lake Tahoe. Its four Realtors are licensed in both California and Nevada, and they handle properties from Tahoma, California, to Incline Village, Nevada. The firm likes to boast that it has Realtors who specialize in personalized service and who really know the area. The office has been selling property since 1956.

BETTER HOMES REALTY

3000 North Lake Boulevard
Tahoe City, CA
(530) 583-0199
www.betterhomestahoe.com

Better Homes is a small office with a great reputation around Lake Tahoe. This firm handles single-family homes, condos, and townhomes all over the California side of the North Shore. It has Realtors spread out in Tahoe City, Soda Springs, Truckee, and North Lake Tahoe.

CHASE INTERNATIONAL

190 U.S. Highway 50, Zephyr Cove, NV
(775) 588-6130, (866) 233-7111

2070 Pray Meadow Road, Glenbrook, NV
(775) 749-5663

917 Tahoe Boulevard #100, Incline Village, NV
(775) 831-7300

775 North Lake Boulevard, Tahoe City, CA
(530) 581-0722

985 Damonte Ranch Parkway, Reno, NV
(775) 850-5900, (877) 922-5900
www.chaseinternational.com

With an office in London, England, Chase isn't kidding about having an international reputation. The firm's global presence speaks to the worldwide appeal of real estate in the Reno/Tahoe area. Founded at Lake Tahoe in 1986 by CEO Shari Chase, the firm specializes in high-end properties. The real estate boom in this area is reflected in the growth of this company to eight offices in the area.

COLDWELL BANKER NORTHERN CALIFORNIA

475 North Lake Boulevard
Tahoe City, CA
(530) 546-5924

Formerly Hauserman Real Estate, this firm has been dealing with buyers and sellers on the North Shore of Lake Tahoe since 1966. The 80-plus Realtors specialize in residential sales from Tahoe City to Incline Village and operate out of four offices in Tahoe City and Truckee, California.

RE/MAX SCENIC PROPERTIES
8611 North Lake Tahoe Boulevard
Kings Beach, CA
(530) 546-3356
www.scenicproperties.net
This RE/MAX location handles residential properties, condos, and lots on the extreme northern shore of Lake Tahoe. It has a solid reputation among Insiders and offers very specialized services.

WINDERMERE DISTINCTIVE HOMES INTERNATIONAL
212 Elks Point Road, Zephyr Cove, NV
(775)588-7710, (800) 878-1066

153 Country Club Drive #2, Incline Village, NV
(775)832-5111
www.windermeretahoe.com
Although you'll find a wide range of listings at this firm, most of them are high-end. Windermere is also a local affiliate for Christies Great Estates. With 12 experienced Realtors on board, the emphasis is on personalized boutique service. And when you're dealing in sales in the millions, it's probably expected. Most listings are in the Lake Tahoe basin but can range as far as Sacramento or Carson Valley.

HOME BUYING AND RENTAL GUIDES

Several real estate guides are available for the new-home buyer or renter in the Reno/Tahoe area. Almost every grocery and convenience store carries these free publications. Reno's daily newspaper, the *Reno Gazette-Journal,* also prints a weekly tabloid dealing with home sales. Look for real estate news in other newspapers as well, such as the Tahoe Daily Tribune and the North Lake Tahoe Bonanza.

FOR RENT MAGAZINE
3550 Barron Way, Reno, NV
(775) 829-7368
www.forrent.com
This free magazine is published every two weeks and contains about 100 pages of the area's mul-
tifamily rental properties. The guide includes university and student housing, senior living, and apartment complexes all throughout Reno and Sparks. The magazine includes a map of the area's apartment complexes, a quick-check guide of all properties listed with amenities, a reader's inquiry service to mail in for more information on individual apartments, and a national relocation service.

HOMEFINDER
Reno Gazette-Journal
955 Kuenzli Street Reno, NV
(775) 788-6200
www.rgj.com
HomeFinder is a weekly tabloid insert to the *Reno Gazette-Journal* that is billed as "Your weekly real estate guide." The tab is paid for by advertising from local real estate companies and is chock-a-block full of properties for sale, rentals, mobile homes, land, and information on real estate loans and mortgage rates. The tabloid averages about 50 pages and is an excellent reference guide to the Reno/Tahoe area. The tab is loaded with articles on how to obtain loans, relocation tips, local mortgage company rates, and how-to tips. It has a special section that focuses on one local neighborhood and one apartment complex each week.

HOMES & LAND MAGAZINE
(775) 831-8991
www.homesandland.com
This free weekly magazine is a nationwide realty guide with zoned editions for Reno, Sparks, North Shore, and South Shore Lake Tahoe. Homes & Land averages about 65 pages and is loaded with properties offered by local real estate companies. It has no narrative but lists about 250 residences per issue with a brief description and price. Real estate companies pay to advertise in this guide.

PREMIER PROPERTIES
(775) 833-3333
www.premierehomes.net
A small publication that features properties on the North Shore of Lake Tahoe and is paid for by real estate companies advertising their listings,

this once-a-month magazine averages about 25 pages per issue and has zoned editions for the Nevada and California sides of the North Shore. The magazine can be found at most grocery and convenience stores along the North Shore.

REALTORS REAL ESTATE DIRECTORY
5650 Riggins Court, Reno, NV
(775) 823-8838
Printed every other week by the Reno/Sparks Association of Realtors, this magazine averages about 85 pages and is bursting with properties for sale. It is a scaled-down version of the Multiple Listings Guide. This publication offers one to two pages of narrative; the rest of the pages are devoted to homes for sale. The write-ups include price, house and lot dimensions, and photographs. This magazine is free and can be found at all grocery and convenience stores.

RENO APARTMENT GUIDE
102 Vine Street, Reno, NV
(775) 329-1442
www.apartmentguide.com
A monthly publication that features about 200 pages of apartments for rent throughout the Reno and Sparks areas, this magazine groups the apartment complexes by neighborhoods and contains a detailed list of prices plus the amenities associated with each complex. This free publication can be picked up at most grocery stores.

APARTMENT LIVING

Many new residents to the area prefer apartment living. You'll find a huge selection to choose from in the Reno/Sparks area, with monthly rents ranging anywhere from $400 to $1,000 and more. The choices are too numerous to list, so I suggest picking up the apartment guides previously mentioned or visiting their Web sites for specific rates and property descriptions. You can find executive transition housing in Reno at Tanamera Apartment Homes (775-852-8989) or at Marriott Residence Inn (775-853-8800).

Apartments in the Lake Tahoe area are more plentiful in Incline Village and South Shore Lake Tahoe.

SCHOOLS

For information on area schools, check the Education and Child Care chapter. To enroll your children in public school, you can consult the appropriate school district below:

WASHOE COUNTY SCHOOL DISTRICT
425 East Ninth Street, Reno, NV
(775) 348-0200
www.washoe.k12.nv.us

TAHOE-TRUCKEE UNIFIED SCHOOL DISTRICT
11839 Donner Pass Road, Truckee, CA
(530) 582-2500
www.ttusd.org

DOUGLAS COUNTY SCHOOL DISTRICT
1638 Mono Avenue, Minden, NV
(775) 782-5134
www.dcsd.k12.nv.us

LAKE TAHOE UNIFIED SCHOOL DISTRICT
1021 Al Tahoe Boulevard
South Lake Tahoe, CA
(530) 541-2850
www.ltusd.org

DEPARTMENT OF MOTOR VEHICLE INFORMATION

Within 30 days of relocating to Nevada, you must register your vehicles and renew your driver's license. And in California you need to register your vehicles within 20 days and renew your driver's license within 10. I strongly advise you to visit the DMV Web sites to be completely informed before you set out on these tasks. You can also register to vote at DMV locations in both states. Click on www.dmvstat.com for Nevada and www.dmv.ca.gov for California. You'll find full-service DMV offices at 305 Galleti Way, Sparks, NV; 555 Wright Way, Carson City, NV; and 3344 B Lake Tahoe Boulevard, South Lake Tahoe, CA. You can call their offices at (800) 777-0133 for California and (775) 684-4368 for Nevada.

TOURIST BUREAUS AND CHAMBERS OF COMMERCE

Some of the best sources of relocation information, aside from real estate agencies, are chambers of commerce and tourist bureaus. Most have prepackaged materials they are eager to send to prospective new residents. To help make your decision to relocate as informed as possible, I suggest you contact the following:

SPARKS CHAMBER OF COMMERCE
831 Victorian Avenue, Sparks, NV
(775)358-1976
www.sparkschamber.org

TAHOE DOUGLAS CHAMBER OF COMMERCE AND VISITORS CENTER
195 U.S. Highway 50, Stateline, NV
(775)588-4591
www.tahoechamber.org

NORTH LAKE TAHOE CHAMBER OF COMMERCE
380 North Lake Boulevard
Tahoe City, CA
(530) 581-6900
www.northlaketahoechamber.com

LAKE TAHOE INCLINE VILLAGE/CRYSTAL BAY VISITORS BUREAU VISITORS AUTHORITY
969 Tahoe Boulevard, Incline Village, NV
(775) 832-1606, (800) 468-2463
www.gotahoenorth.com

GREATER RENO/SPARKS CHAMBER OF COMMERCE
1 East First Street, 16th floor, Reno, NV
(775) 337-3030
www.reno-sparkschamber.org

RENO SPARKS CONVENTION AND VISITORS AUTHORITY
(775) 827-7600
(800) 367-7366
www.visitrenotahoe.com

RETIREMENT

Silver is once again playing a hand in the economy and lifestyle of the Reno/Tahoe area. But instead of coming from the mines in Virginia City, it's arriving as a silver wave of retirees who've discovered that the area is the perfect place for their retirement. After spending their working years fighting traffic and breathing smog, they think they've died and gone to heaven in this natural mountain/desert environment. Washoe County, which includes Reno, Sparks, and Incline Village, has seen more than 23 percent growth in seniors in recent years. And as more baby boomers retire in the near future, demographers say Reno/Tahoe can expect an even greater number of retirees to make their homes here.

It's not hard to understand why so many people choose to relocate here. If they've visited before (which most have), they've probably fallen in love with the gorgeous scenery and the unlimited opportunities for recreation. And then there's the weather: four distinct seasons, all of which are relatively mild. The average high temperatures in the Reno/Sparks area range from around 90 degrees in July to 45 degrees in January. Average lows range from about 18 degrees in January to 47 degrees in July. Because they are located on the leeward side of the Sierra Nevada range, Reno and Sparks have very low humidity in summer and moderate humidity in winter. Snowfall usually runs around 27 inches a year. Lake Tahoe, however, has a colder and much wetter climate. Unless Reno experiences a winter inversion, temperatures around the lake are usually 5 to 10 degrees colder than in the leeward valleys. And even though the sun shines 274 days out of the year at the lake, annual snowfall at lake level averages 125 inches, with 300 to 500 inches falling in the surrounding mountains.

Many retirees are attracted to Nevada for financial reasons because the state has no income tax and no inheritance tax. They also find they can buy more house for their money in Nevada than in some other states, such as California. Last but not least, Reno/Tahoe is senior-friendly and welcomes newcomers with open arms.

Because they lead such busy lives, the word "retirement" is a misnomer to most Reno/Tahoe retirees. They've traded their three-piece suits for jogging outfits and are just as likely to leave home each morning with a pair of skis as a briefcase. When they're not pursuing their favorite outdoor sports or hobbies, you can find them volunteering, taking classes, or even developing new careers. They live life with gusto and seem bent on making the most of their golden years. If retirement to you means a life full of new challenges and adventures, Reno/Tahoe offers a plethora of options. In this chapter I tell you about the enriching opportunities you'll find for education, employment, entertainment, and volunteering.

If you're considering retiring in the Reno/Tahoe area, it's important to know the differences between living in the small mountain towns at Lake Tahoe and living in urban Reno or Sparks. While the small communities at the lake offer a comfortable laid-back lifestyle, they aren't large enough to provide the variety of services that are found in the Reno/Sparks area. But because Reno/Sparks are less than an hour drive away, even if you live at the lake, you can take advantage of some of the senior services in Reno/Sparks. Your best sources of information about what's offered at the lake are the senior centers I tell you about in this chapter.

In addition to having fewer services, full-time residence at Lake Tahoe can present problems in the winter because of snow removal. You should also know that some financial advantages available in Nevada are not offered by California and that housing at Lake Tahoe is usually more expensive than in Reno or Sparks. In general, the people who retire successfully at Lake Tahoe tend to be self-reliant and financially independent individuals.

To find out about senior issues and events, you can read the Senior Spectrum newspaper, which is available free at newsracks in the area.

i Many senior centers provide either free or low-cost transportation services. Check with the senior center closest to you to see if this service is available.

SENIOR CENTERS

Aging ultimately means significant life changes for most people. When they move or retire or suffer the loss of a spouse, they are often faced with having to build new lives and to make new social connections. Senior centers provide a touchstone for many by offering opportunities to socialize and to learn with people their own age. You can enjoy a nutritious meal with newfound friends, stretch your intellectual awareness in a class or seminar, get in touch with your emotional side in a support group, find out about services designed with seniors in mind, and forget all your worries and woes with musical entertainment at Reno/Tahoe senior centers. Most businesses or organizations say they can't be all things to all people, but senior centers give it a try, with arrays of services that seem to fulfill seniors' every need. If you're new to town, there's no reason to feel disconnected. Just drop in at one of the following centers, and you'll find a whole new world of friends and activities. Reno and Sparks each have a center, and South Shore Lake Tahoe has two. The North Shore Lake Tahoe area doesn't have a center, but people living there are always welcome at any of the centers listed below.

SOUTH LAKE TAHOE SENIOR CENTER
3050 Lake Tahoe Boulevard
South Lake Tahoe, CA
(530) 542-6094
www.recreationintahoe.com/senior-center
You can take classes, stop by for lunch, get help with senior resources, or just drop in to socialize at the South Lake Tahoe Senior Center. Owned by the city of South Lake Tahoe, the center is the focal point for senior activities in this area of South Shore Lake Tahoe. The welcome mat is always out for those who want to volunteer, and the center provides a variety of opportunities for getting involved. Recreational programs and activities include art workshops, quilting, water exercise, bridge, bingo, dancing, billiards, the writing club, stretch and tone classes, and Jazzercise. The center also sponsors day trips and parties, including Big Band dances. Support services include health screenings, the mature driving program, tax assistance programs, senior peer counseling, and home-delivered meals. Hours are 8:00 a.m. to 4:30 p.m. weekdays, with lunch served at noon. Call the center for information about transportation.

SPARKS SENIOR CENTER
97 Richards Way, Sparks, NV
(775) 353-3110
www.co.washoe.nv.us/seniorsrv
Like its sister center in Reno, the Sparks Senior Center is a beehive of activity. Regular events include arts and crafts, card games, pool and billiards, exercise classes, and dancing. Many of the same programs that are offered at the Reno facility are also available here (see the description below). Lunch is served weekdays at 11:30 a.m., and reservations must be made by 9:30 a.m. the same day in order to eat. The center doesn't provide transportation, but it's easily reached by Citifare bus. The hours for this comfortable, modern facility are 8:00 a.m. to 5:00 p.m. weekdays.

TAHOE-DOUGLAS SENIOR CENTER
U.S. Highway 50
Zephyr Cove, NV
(775) 588-5140

With a primary focus on social and recreational activities, Douglas County offers a limited senior program at the Tahoe-Douglas Senior Center. Because it's an all-volunteer facility, you're more than welcome to help out. Activities include arts and crafts, picnics, potlucks, day trips around the area, card games, and bingo. Hours depend upon the activities offered, so be sure to call ahead for the schedule. For a small donation, the center also offers area transportation for doctor appointments and shopping.

WASHOE COUNTY SENIOR SERVICES CENTER
1155 East Ninth Street Reno, NV
(775) 328-2575
www.co.washoe.nv.us/seniorsrv
A multipurpose facility sponsored by Washoe County, the Washoe County Senior Services Center is a focal point where people can obtain information, services, and access to community resources designed for older persons. When you visit the center, you're immediately aware of the high level of purposeful activity all around, from the enthusiastic exercise class in the multipurpose room to the quiet game of pool in the billiards room. The overall ambience of this large, comfortable facility is that of a club or resort, where people gather to pursue a large variety of pleasurable activities. The ongoing programs include arts and crafts, creative writing, card games, exercise classes, support groups, and a readers circle. Lunch is served weekdays from 11:30 a.m. to 12:30 p.m.

The Washoe County Library System maintains a full branch in the center, with a large selection of books (including large-print editions), paperbacks, videotapes, and newspapers. The Assistance League of Reno-Sparks sponsors the Senior Sampler Gift Shop, which sells items made by local senior crafters. And the American Association of Retired Persons (AARP) staffs an information booth in the lobby to help inform seniors of AARP programs. Other programs that are managed from the center include Benefit Assistance, Daybreak, the Homemaker Program,

Home Delivered Meals, and the Senior Law Program. I tell you more about these in the "Senior Services" section of this chapter.

The center is open weekdays from 8:00 a.m. to 5:00 p.m. Programs that are federally subsidized are free, but there are charges for meals, Daybreak, and some recreational activities. The center doesn't provide transportation, but it's easily accessible by Citifare bus routes. If you're driving your own car, there's ample free parking right in front of the building.

i If you're looking for an opportunity to make a difference in the community, contact Crisis Call Center at (775) 784-8085 about training to become a volunteer on their lines. Training sessions take place every other month.

EDUCATIONAL OPPORTUNITIES

LAKE TAHOE COMMUNITY COLLEGE
1 College Drive
South Lake Tahoe, CA
(530) 541-4660
www.ltcc.cc.ca.us
One does not live by physical activity alone—most of us need opportunities to explore our intellectual side as well. Retirement offers the chance for enriching educational experiences through classes and activities we probably didn't have time for during our working years. With its large variety of programs and classes, Lake Tahoe Community College is a great place to get in touch with your cerebral self. As part of the California Community College System, the school makes it affordable and easy to enroll. California residents pay just $13 per unit, and through its Good Neighbor Policy, people who've been residents of Nevada for at least one year pay $28 per unit. Enrollment is open to everyone, and courses are offered in art, business, culinary arts, computer science, health, humanities, and social sciences. (See the Education and Child Care chapter for a more detailed description of this school.)

Helpful Organizations

American Association of Retired Persons (AARP), (775) 328-2506

American Cancer Society, (775) 329-0609

American Lung Association, (775) 829-5864

El Dorado County Senior Information and Referral, (530) 621-6150

Eldercare Locator, (800) 677-1116

Lend-a-Hand Senior Services, (775) 322-8414

Meals on Wheels South Lake Tahoe, (530) 573-3130

Nevada Bureau of Services to the Blind and Visually Impaired, (775) 823-8140

Nevada Division for Aging Services, (775) 688-2964

Northern Nevada Center for Independent Living, (775) 353-3599

Placer County Senior Information and Referral, (530) 889-9500, (800) 878-9222

Renown Health Senior Options, (775) 982-5400

Senior Connection, (775) 784-8090

Senior Nutrition Program El Dorado County, (530) 621-6160

Senior Nutrition Program Placer County, (530) 888-7137

SIERRA NEVADA COLLEGE
999 Tahoe Boulevard
Incline Village, NV
(775) 831-1314, (866) 412-4636
www.sierranevada.edu
At a cost of around $20,000 for tuition per year for full-time students, it's pricey and posh, but

Sierra Nevada College (SNC) gives residents of North Shore Lake Tahoe enriching opportunities for expanding their intellectual horizons. About two-thirds of the students receive some kind of financial aid, however. There's no break for seniors (although they're welcome in all classes), but you can audit courses for no credit and pay by the credit. The only accredited four-year private liberal-arts college in Nevada, SNC offers courses in business, computer sciences, ski business and resort management, hotel management, humanities, environmental science, international studies, fine arts, and teacher education. It also sponsors The Tahoe Forum, a program that brings well-known speakers to the area. (See the Education and Child Care chapter for more details on the school.)

TRUCKEE MEADOWS COMMUNITY COLLEGE
7000 Dandini Boulevard (main campus)
Reno, NV
(775) 673-7000 (information)
www.tmcc.edu
You can pursue a degree or just take classes for enrichment through Truckee Meadows Community College (TMCC). (See the Education and Child Care chapter for a full description of courses and programs.) But TMCC goes above and beyond for seniors in its Silver College by offering classes to Nevada residents who are age 62 years or older for just $8. Classes are designed especially for seniors.

For more information on classes or to register at Silver College, call (775) 829-9010.

UNIVERSITY OF NEVADA, RENO
1664 North Virginia Street, Reno, NV
(775) 784-1110 (information)
www.unr.edu, www.olli.unr.edu
The best things in life are free for people age 62 and older at the University of Nevada, Reno (UNR): They don't have to pay tuition for regular university courses. If you've put off getting that first degree (or even second or third) because you didn't have the money for it, the university makes it easy for you by charging only for books and lab fees. Let your fingers do the walking through the catalog and pick from a large variety

of degree and nondegree programs. (Check out the Education and Child Care chapter for more specific information.)

UNR also offers free and minimal-fee classes through its Osher Lifelong Learning Institute (OLLI) . Targeted to older lifelong learners, OLLI provides interactive educational opportunities, with members planning and conducting classes as well as simply taking them. The annual $45 membership in OLLI also entitles you to university library privileges and a discount at the Lombardi Recreation facilities. For information call (775) 784-8053 or visit their Web site.

SENIOR SERVICES

Nonprofit organizations and governmental agencies in the Reno/Tahoe area offer a wealth of services designed specifically for seniors. I can't begin to list them all, but in this section I give you an overview of the kinds of programs older persons can take advantage of to enrich their retirement years.

ADVOCATE FOR ELDERS
445 Apple Street, Suite 104, Reno, NV
(775) 688-2964
www.nvaging.net
Managed by the Nevada Division for Aging Services, the Advocate for Elders gives homebound seniors an advocate for voicing their concerns and complaints. The services are free and confidential to those who are age 60 or older. The advocates investigate allegations of elder abuse, exploitation, and neglect within care homes and nursing facilities.

COMMUNITY HOME-BASED INITIATIVES PROGRAM (CHIP)
445 Apple Street, Suite 104, Reno, NV
(775) 688-2964
www.nvaging.net
As an alternative to nursing-home care, CHIP helps older persons maintain independence in their homes by providing nonmedical assistance. Attendants offer companionship in addition to help with personal care, shopping, and housekeeping.

DAYBREAK
1155 East Ninth Street, Reno, NV
(775) 328-2591
www.co.washoe.nv.us/seniorsrv
Operating every day but Sunday, Daybreak is essentially an adult day-care facility. In addition to giving caregiving families a break, it helps participants overcome the social isolation that often accompanies illness. While fees are $6 per hour, no one is denied participation because they are unable to pay.

HOME DELIVERED MEAL AND NUTRITION PROGRAMS
1155 East Ninth Street, Reno, NV
(775) 328-2575
www.co.washoe.nv.us/seniorsrv
For older persons unable to take care of their own nutritional needs, the Home Delivered Meal Program is literally a lifesaver. To qualify, a person must be age 60 or older and unable to cook and prepare food or to eat at a group location. Meals are delivered weekdays at no cost, but contributions are encouraged. Washoe County Senior Services also offers meals at its two senior centers and at five additional satellite locations in the county.

RENOWN HEALTH SENIOR OPTIONS
850 Mill Street, Reno, NV
(775) 982-5420
www.renownhealth.com
Renown Health (formerly Washoe Medical Center) offers a comprehensive wellness program for seniors which includes educational and preventive information along with social opportunities such as get togethers and trips. The emphasis is on leading a healthy lifestyle by being fit and engaged in the community and activities.
For information call (775) 982-5400.

SANFORD CENTER FOR AGING
800 Haskell Street, Reno, NV
(775) 784-4774
www.unr.edu/sanford
Exploring innovative ideas for successful aging, the Sanford Center for Aging pursues programs

in education, research, community outreach, and service. Major outreach includes the Retired and Senior Volunteer Program, wellness workshops for seniors, and the Nevada Care Connection information referral system.

SENIOR LAW CENTER
1155 East Ninth Street, Reno, NV
(775) 328-2592
www.co.washoe.nv.us/seniorsrv
It's hard to imagine you can get the expertise of an attorney for free, but the Senior Law Program provides consultation and representation at no cost for residents of Washoe County who are age 60 or older. Services are limited to elder-rights law, government benefits and entitlements, consumer matters, real property and housing issues, and lifetime planning. Although clients are expected to pay only for court costs and filing fees, donations are requested.

SENIOR SOCIAL SERVICES
1155 East Ninth Street, Reno, NV
(775) 328-2590
www.co.washoe.nv.us/seniorsrv
When seniors need a little extra help with their bills each month, Washoe County Senior Social Services can help. Based upon income and age criteria, older persons are eligible for rebates on property taxes, local telephone service, sewer fees, heating costs, and TV cable fees. The program also distributes free food.

WORKING AND VOLUNTEERING

AMERICAN ASSOCIATION OF RETIRED PERSONS (AARP)
Senior Community Service Employment Program
(775) 328-2506
AARP's employment program can launch you on a second career with its counseling, training, and information and referral service. The program is free for those who are age 55 or older who also have limited income.

FOSTER GRANDPARENT PROGRAM
406 Pyramid Way
Sparks, NV
(775) 358-2768
You can profoundly enrich your life as well as that of your foster grandchild in the Foster Grandparent Program. Volunteers provide one-on-one daily attention to at-risk youth in schools, hospitals, drug treatment centers, day-care centers, and correctional institutions. You can apply if you're age 60 or older, love children, meet certain income requirements, and can volunteer 20 hours a week. Benefits include a small stipend, reimbursement of expenses, insurance, and an annual physical.

GOLDEN OPPORTUNITY
1005 Terminal Way #202, Reno, NV
(775) 785-6106
www.join.org
If "retirement" means continued involvement in the world of work, Golden Opportunity can help you develop your talents, learn new skills, and find the right job to use them in. To qualify for the program, you must be age 55 or older, meet financial guidelines, and be seriously interested in working.

RETIRED & SENIOR VOLUNTEER PROGRAM OF WASHOE COUNTY
401 West Second Street, Suite 101
Reno, NV
(775) 784-1807
www.unr.edu/sanford
Volunteering where you can really make a difference is one of the most rewarding experiences many older persons discover in their retirement. The Retired & Senior Volunteer Program of Washoe County (RSVP) actively recruits seniors age 55 and older for a large number of local nonprofit and public agencies. With so many to choose from, you're sure to find the position that's just right for you. The program places volunteers in schools, museums, cultural events, hospitals, social agencies, parks, and senior services. If you're newly retired and/or new to town, there's no better way to meet people with similar interests.

SENIOR AUXILIARY VOLUNTEER EFFORT (S.A.V.E.)

455 East Second Street
Reno, NV
(775) 321-8312

If you've ever wanted to be a police officer, here's your chance. Sponsored by the Reno Police Department and the Retired & Senior Volunteer Program, S.A.V.E. is open to people age 50 and older who want to help make their community a better place to live. Duties of the uniformed volunteers include checking on the vacant houses of people who are on vacation, patrolling schools and parks, visiting housebound seniors, and patrolling during daylight hours in specially marked police cars. The role of the volunteers is limited to observing and reporting.

SENIOR COMPANION PROGRAM

406 Pyramid Way
Sparks, NV
(775) 358-2322

Many older persons delay or avoid living in nursing homes by using help provided by volunteers in the Senior Companion Program. Volunteers provide assistance to frail seniors by providing transportation, escorting seniors to doctor's appointments, running errands, and simply being a friend. Volunteers are reimbursed for their expenses and receive insurance and an annual physical as a benefit. To qualify for volunteering, you must meet certain age and income requirements and agree to work 20 hours a week.

 A quick way to find resources is to dial 211 on your telephone.

FUN AND FITNESS

BALLANTINE'S BALLROOM

2920 Mill Street Reno, NV
(775) 324-1000

If you like to dance for fun and fitness, you're sure to find your comfort zone at Ballantine's Ballroom. A popular dance hangout with the older crowd, Ballantine's offers ballroom, swing, jazz, and tap lessons as well as public dancing.

INCLINERS

Incline Village, NV
(775) 831-1310

With a whopping 800 members (almost 10 percent of the population of Incline Village, Nevada), the Incliners is the indisputable center of social activity for many older people living in Incline. Members meet twice a month for dinners and social events but also avidly pursue sports and hobbies together, such as tennis, golf, bike riding, and bridge. Members must be age 49 or older and be able to pay $10 in annual dues.

INCLINE VILLAGE RECREATION CENTER

893 Southwood Boulevard
Incline Village, NV
(775) 832-1324
www.ivgid.org

Although Incline Village doesn't have a senior center, the recreation center provides a large variety of services especially for older residents. Seniors can stay fit, happy, and healthy by participating in activities that include the senior book club, the craft cafe, ballroom dancing, yoga, conversation cafe, and the arthritis aquacise class.

NEWCOMERS CLUB OF RENO/SPARKS

P.O. Box 50044, Sparks, NV 89435
(775) 881-2040
www.newcomersclubofreno-sparks.org

Although it's not restricted to retired people, the Newcomers Club of Reno/Sparks certainly attracts large numbers of them. With more than 800 members, the group offers an enormous variety of activities to help people adjust to a move or a transition in their lives. The club breaks down into dozens of special interest groups, including photography, hiking, pursuing adventure, volunteering, and arts and crafts. If you want to join the fun, you must apply for membership within two years of moving to the area. Exceptions are for those who have gone through a life change, such as retirement, divorce, or widowhood. Its motto, "There are no strangers here, only friends we have not met," seems to say it all about this popular group.

PARADISE PARK ACTIVITY CENTER
2745 Elementary Drive, Reno, NV
(775) 356-3176
www.cityofreno.com
The city of Reno offers a veritable smorgasbord of activities for seniors at the Paradise Park Activity Center, including exercise classes, quilting bees, dance workshops, and card games. The parks and recreation department also welcomes suggestions for additional activities of interest to area seniors.

RENO SINGLES
(775) 747-2275, (775) 826-0654
www.renosingles.net
A casually organized group for people age 50-plus, Reno Singles gets together once a week for picnics, potlucks, cards, and games. The location and activities vary, so call for specific information.

i Another group of singles in the Tahoe/ Carson area can be reached by visiting their Web site at www.tahoesingles.com.

SPARKS RECREATION DEPARTMENT SENIOR SOFTBALL LEAGUES
(775) 353-2376
www.ci.sparks.nv.us
You may love watching your grandchildren play ball, but how about playing yourself? Dust off your mitt and join in the fun with the Senior Softball Leagues. With names like Reno Rowdies and Super Seniors, the 18 teams make up a large enthusiastic group of players that competes year-round. Sponsored by the Sparks Recreation Department, most league games take place on the Rail City's ball fields.

WHERE TO LIVE

The choices of retirement or senior housing in

Reno/Tahoe run the gamut, from private residences to apartments to full-service retirement homes with assisted living and nursing care. (See the Relocation chapter for an overview of housing and locales.)

As one of the fastest growing areas in the country, it's hard to keep up with the increasing number of options. Although I can't list them all, in this chapter I give you examples of residential choices geared specifically to older persons: retirement communities and assisted-living facilities. Rates are based upon single occupancy; facilities will charge several hundred additional dollars for a second occupant. For the assisted-living facilities, rates may vary depending on individual needs. For a complete listing of retirement living options, check in local telephone books under "Retirement."

Retirement Homes
CASCADES OF THE SIERRA
275 Neighborhood Way
Spanish Springs, NV (just north of Reno)
(775) 629-4562
www.cascadeliving.com
New in 2009, Cascades of the Sierra offers resort-style amenities and panoramic views of the surrounding foothills in its state-of-the-art facility. Units include 120 independent living spaces, 96 assisted living, and 24 memory care apartments. The quasi-rural setting 10 miles north of downtown Reno provides serenity (at least for now), but is somewhat distant from some kinds of services. Call for rates.

CLASSIC RESIDENCE BY HYATT
3201 Plumas Street, Reno, NV
(775) 825-1105
www.hyattclassic.com
True to its name, Classic Residence by Hyatt is classic in every sense of the word. For retirees age 55 or older who can afford the best, it combines the ambience of an exclusive country club with the warmth of a private home. If you've stayed at Hyatt resorts or hotels, you know the level of service and the elegant accoutrements Hyatt provides.

Classic offers studio and one- and two-bedroom apartments, many with patio or balcony views of the Sierra Nevada mountains and the Washoe County Golf Course. Monthly fees include meals, weekly housekeeping, scheduled transportation, apartment maintenance, and concierge assistance, with assisted living available at additional cost. Classic even provides a moving coordinator to help with relocation details.

Amenities of the facility include the Wintergarden Lounge, library, arts and crafts studio, exercise room, beauty/barber shop, outdoor walking paths, free laundry facilities, parking, computer center, private dining room, billiards lounge, and club room. Geared to active retirees, this facility goes out of its way to offer a large variety of cultural, educational, social, and recreational outlets for residents. The facility has recently been remodeled. Call for rates.

THE FOUNTAINS SENIOR CARE, INC.
1920 Harvard Way, Reno, NV
(775) 825-2044
www.fountainsal.com

Designed for carefree retirement living, the Fountains includes all the necessities for quality living in the rental payment. The rent for studio apartments and one-bedroom units includes weekly housekeeping and linen service, three daily meals, transportation, scheduled activities, and cable television. Residents can also take advantage of the on-site beauty and barber shop and the community visiting area. Since the Fountains is strictly a rental facility, residents are not required to sign leases or pay buy-in fees. Its location is especially convenient for shopping as it's right across from a large mall that has stores such as Costco and Office Depot along with many other small retail establishments. The facility has just been completely renovated. Call for rates.

LAKESIDE MANOR
855 Brinkby Avenue, Reno, NV
(775) 827-3606
www.quiltedcare.com

Within easy walking distance of lovely Virginia Lake in southwest Reno, the studio apartments at Lakeside Manor include housekeeping, laundry, transportation, utilities (other than phone and cable), and meals. Residents of the manor have a full array of activities to choose from, including arts and crafts, exercise classes, local trips, social events and parties, discussion groups, card games, and billiards. The facility also has a library, a beauty salon, and free transportation service. If you're a pet owner, you'll be delighted to know the welcome mat is out for Fido or Fluffy also. Call for rates.

ODD FELLOWS RETIREMENT MANOR
1155 Beech Street, Reno, NV
(775) 323-1911

In a picturesque parklike setting near the University of Nevada, Reno, the Odd Fellows Retirement Manor has 118 private rooms that rent for about $900 per month. Housekeeping, meals, activities, and transportation are included. The university campus and nearby Dick Taylor Memorial Park offer enjoyable routes for daily walks.

PROMENADE ON THE RIVER
525 Court Street, Reno, NV
(775) 786-8853
www.promenadereno.com

It would be hard to find a more elegant retirement facility than Promenade on the River. Resembling a lovely Roman villa of warm stone and tile, the building hugs a bluff overlooking the Truckee River in downtown Reno. Originally designed as upscale condominiums back in the 1980s, the facility has been remodeled to include six floors of 84 luxury apartments designed around an old-world European-style atrium. In addition to all the usual bells and whistles offered by senior living communities, Promenade also boasts a rooftop swimming pool and spa, underground parking, and concierge service. Its location in a quiet historic neighborhood close to downtown theaters and galleries is also a plus. You would think that all of this might put them in a class by themselves pricewise; however, all-inclusive monthly fees are competitive with other senior living facilities in the area.

TAHOE SENIOR PLAZA
1109 Third Street
South Lake Tahoe, CA
(530) 542-7048
Opened in the spring of 1999, Tahoe Senior Plaza is a lovely mountain chalet with 44 one-bedroom apartments, four of which are wheelchair accessible. Because the complex is federally subsidized housing for the elderly, residents must be at least age 62 and meet certain income guidelines. Those accepted will pay rent equal to about 30 percent of their adjusted annual income. Because demand is high, it's necessary to place your name on a waiting list.

VILLAS OF SPARKS
1900 East Prater Way, Sparks, NV
(775) 359-7700
www.assisted.com
Spacious and impressive, Villas of Sparks feels just like home. Comfortable seating and lush green plants in the public areas create a cozy environment perfect for stimulating conversation or quiet reading. The rental fee includes scheduled transportation, meals, utilities, weekly housekeeping, linen service, and cable television. A full-time activities director is in charge of the large variety of outings and events offered daily to residents. There's also a library, beauty shop, and even an ice-cream parlor. Call for rates.

Assisted Living
ATRIA SUMMIT RIDGE
4880 Summit Ridge Drive, Reno, NV
(775) 787-3000
www.arvi.com
Atria at Summit Ridge enables residents to age in place since it offers several levels of care depending upon individual needs. Monthly fees include meals, housekeeping and linen, basic utilities, scheduled transportation, and assistance with daily activities. Residents can enjoy the beautifully landscaped courtyard, the library with its cozy fireplace, an elegant private dining room, and the activities room with a big-screen TV. Call for rates.

WYNWOOD OF SPARKS
2000 East Prater Way, Sparks, NV
(775) 359-7733
www.assisted.com
Personalized service is the trademark at Wynwood of Sparks since residents' preferences are an integral part of their care. Assistance with unscheduled needs is provided 24 hours a day by professional staff. All of the apartments in this bright, modern facility have wall-to-wall carpeting and kitchenettes. Housekeeping and laundry service plus a full array of educational and social opportunities are included. Call for rates.

HEALTH CARE AND WELLNESS

ecause Reno/Tahoe is such an attractive place to live, it's not hard to understand why many doctors choose to live here. After all, if you can choose where to practice medicine, why not select a beautiful area with unlimited opportunities for recreation? Just a glance in local telephone books will show more than 800 physicians and surgeons practicing in every field of medical specialization. Almost any medical procedure you might need is available locally except organ transplants, which are routinely done in Sacramento, California, about two hours away by car.

In addition to the hundreds of medical doctors, about 100 podiatrists and doctors of osteopathy and more than 300 dentists have hung out their shingles here. Although most of these medical personnel practice traditional medicine, alternative care, such as acupuncture and homeopathy, is also available.

But despite the large numbers of medical people who live and work here, it can sometimes be difficult to find a doctor. If you're considering relocating to Reno/Lake Tahoe I strongly recommend finding a primary care physician before you actually move here. The physician referral services listed further on in this chapter is a good place to start. Because of the strong population growth the area has experienced in recent years, the demand for doctors in some areas has exceeded the supply.

Since the Reno/Sparks area is the largest center of population, it serves the medical needs of not only its own residents but also of people living in nearby rural communities in Nevada and California. And while Lake Tahoe has a high number of doctors per person and two small hospitals, the variety of medical care available in Reno and Sparks and nearby Carson City is much greater. Although the good news is the high quality and diversity of care available, the bad news is that it costs about 20 percent more than the national average.

You might not think that an area well known for its 24-hour lifestyle would be especially conscious of health care and wellness. Statistics also paint a rather grim picture, showing high rates for suicide, smoking, and alcohol abuse, particularly in Reno and Sparks. But in spite of this, a healthy lifestyle is a priority for an increasing number of residents because they want to participate fully in the outdoor activities available in the area. Insiders also know that many people living at Lake Tahoe are sports enthusiasts who spend as much time as possible hiking, biking, and skiing.

When not exercising outside, many people stay in shape at one of the more than 30 health clubs in the area. While some clubs are fitness studios emphasizing exercise machines and individual workouts, others are full-service health centers, with lap pools, child-care facilities, racquetball and tennis courts, tanning salons, massage therapy, clothing shops, restaurants, personalized training, and a large variety of classes. And because Reno is a 24-hour city, you can work out around the clock in many of its health clubs. Before joining a club, it's a good idea to shop around, since membership packages and prices vary a lot. Check local phone books under "Health Clubs" for complete listings.

But even athletes who are in good condition occasionally have accidents and get hurt. If that happens to you, you can take some comfort in knowing that the Reno/Tahoe area has attracted a number of athletically inclined physicians who specialize in sports medicine. They understand not only the clinical aspects of sports injuries but the practical side as well, since it's likely they spend a lot of their free time hiking, biking, and skiing. If you're looking for knee reconstruction or joint replacement, just let your fingers do the walking through the Yellow Pages, where you'll find a variety of highly qualified orthopedic surgeons listed. After all, with more than 20 ski resorts in the area, they have plenty of ski-related injuries to practice on.

While the variety of available medical care reflects in part the lifestyle of area residents and visitors, the medical community is further enriched by the University of Nevada School of Medicine in Reno. Established in 1969 by the Nevada State Legislature and funded in part by the late eccentric billionaire Howard Hughes, the School of Medicine is integrated with local hospitals, clinics, and physicians. More than 900 community physicians throughout the state are involved in its mission to provide medical education and training for Nevadans. The school is also an important center of medical research, focusing on problems that affect Nevada in particular. The University of Nevada, Reno, also trains registered nurses in its Orvis School of Nursing; Truckee Meadows Community College, also in Reno, trains registered nurses as well as certified nursing assistants. The Reno/Tahoe area is also home to a number of licensed schools of massage.

In this chapter I give you a general overview of the kinds of health care offered in the Reno/Tahoe area. I tell you about the major hospitals, which are comprehensive health-care delivery systems, as well as the smaller specialty hospitals and clinics. I tell you how to find a doctor, where to get emergency care, what support groups are available, and where to get alternative medical care. And last, but not least, I tell you how to get medical attention for the family pet.

HOSPITALS

Reno

IOANNIS A. LOUGARIS VETERANS AFFAIRS MEDICAL CENTER
1000 Locust Street
(775) 786-7200
(888) 838-6256 (outpatient clinic in Minden, NV)
www2.va.gov/directory/guide/home
Serving veterans in northern Nevada and northeastern California, the Reno Veterans Affairs Medical Center is a 62-bed general medical and surgical hospital with a 60-bed nursing-home-care unit. The VA is well known for its innovative geriatric health programs as well as research into diseases and geriatric rehabilitation. With more than 60 projects ongoing at any given time, the center conducts more research than all other hospitals in Nevada combined. The center has studied Alzheimer's, Parkinson's, kidney and cardiovascular diseases, hypertension, diabetes, and breathing disorders. The VA also offers Home Based Primary Care to veterans needing care in their home environment and Contract Adult Day Health Care, which helps delay admission to a residential care facility. Specific programs include telemedicine, a sleep apnea clinic, and treatment for Agent Orange exposure.

RENOWN REGIONAL MEDICAL CENTER
77 Pringle Way
(775) 982-4100, (775) 982-5757

RENOWN SOUTH MEADOWS MEDICAL CENTER
10101 Double R Boulevard
(775) 982-7000
www.renown.org
Formerly Washoe Medical Center, Renown Regional Medical Center is northern Nevada's oldest health-care facility. It is also Reno/Tahoe's largest and most comprehensive acute-care hospital, with the only Level II trauma center, bone-marrow transplant unit,

pediatric intensive care unit, and radiation therapy program in the area. It also has centers to treat diabetes, heart disease, cancer, and substance abuse as well as dialysis, surgical, and poison centers.

Recognizing that healing has emotional as well as physical aspects, Renown encourages loved ones to become part of the health-care team with its Very Important Partners program and provides interaction with dogs through its Pet Therapy with K-9 Kare. The annual Healing Arts Festival introduces patients, visitors, and staff to a variety of healing arts, including massage therapy, visual and musical arts, and humor. The public is invited to the keynote address, usually held at the Pioneer Center for the Performing Arts. Past speakers have included best-selling spiritual authors Deepak Chopra and James Van Praagh.

Because it's a large regional complex that serves people from outlying areas as well as locals, Renown has amenities not found in all hospitals. You can rent a hotel room at the inn, enjoy tasty meals in several restaurants, and shop in the boutique, all within the medical campus. There's also covered parking, a chapel, a pharmacy, and a dry cleaners. The health resource center provides a wealth of information about health care and wellness, with 400 books and periodicals and access to computers.

If you're more comfortable in a small hospital, Renown may seem too large for you. And if you prefer a private room, Renown does not always provide one, but Saint Mary's Regional Medical Center and Northern Nevada Medical Center will. In response to the growth south of Reno, Renown opened a second acute-care hospital on Double R Boulevard with 155 beds and a full complement of medical services.

Recent renovations to this medical complex include the 10-story Tahoe Tower, which added 200 ultra-user-friendly patient rooms and 18 more surgical suites, as well as additional ERs and ICU beds. As part of the hospital's commitment to healing arts it has gathered together 567 major works of art (with the help of local gallery owner Turkey Stremmel) which are tastefully displayed throughout the complex. In many respects, Renown resembles an upscale resort more than a medical center (and probably costs more).

SAINT MARY'S REGIONAL MEDICAL CENTER
235 West Sixth Street
(775) 770-3000
www.saintmarysreno.com

The legacy of Saint Mary's Regional Medical Center was born when a group of Dominican nuns arrived in Reno in 1877 to open a school for local children. The sisters soon learned that early Reno not only lacked educational structures but needed health-care facilities as well. To help address this need they built Sisters' Hospital in 1908, which was the forerunner of Saint Mary's.

The medical center is part of Saint Mary's Health Network, a large integrated delivery system encompassing 10 health care facilities, including Saint Mary's Galena, Hospice of Northern Nevada, and Saint Mary's Family Walk-in Health Center. The network consists of 800 physicians, 2,300 employees, and more than 300 volunteers. A recent $160 million expansion at the medical center doubled its size, adding office and parking space, emergency beds, and expanded services such as a wellness center along with critical care and rehabilitation services. Because Saint Mary's is still operated by Catholic sisters, the spiritual well-being of patients is part of the healing process. The inpatient hospital rooms at the center are especially appealing, because all of them are spacious and private.

TAHOE PACIFIC HOSPITALS–MEADOWS
10101 Double R Boulevard
Adjacent to Renown Regional Medical Center at South Meadows
(775)331-1044

TAHOE PACIFIC HOSPITALS–WEST
235 West Sixth Street, Fifth Floor
Saint Mary's Regional Medical Center
(775)770-7980
www.lifecare-hospitals.com

Tahoe Pacific Hospitals treat highly acute patients

who come directly from traditional hospitals. Specializing in long-term rehabilitative care, they provide speech, occupational, physical, and recreational therapy. The two Reno facilities work closely with Saint Mary's Regional Medical Center and Renown Regional Medical Center.

WEST HILLS HOSPITAL
1240 East Ninth Street
(775) 323-0478, (800) 242-0478
www.psysolutions.com/facilities/westhills
A 95-bed private psychiatric facility, West Hills Hospital offers inpatient hospitalization and a variety of outpatient programs for people of all ages who have mental health problems. Patients work with a treatment team, consisting of a psychiatrist, social worker or counselor, psychiatric nurses, and mental health technicians. The hospital has an extensive substance abuse program that is available on either an inpatient or outpatient basis.

WILLOW SPRINGS CENTER
690 Edison Way
(775) 858-3303
www.psysolutions.com/facilities/
willowsprings
Willow Springs Center is a 74-bed residential treatment center for children and adolescents ages 5 through 17. Established in 1988, Willow Springs provides a long-term therapeutic environment for young people experiencing emotional and behavioral problems. It's affiliated with West Hills Hospital, a mental health facility also in Reno.

i Although it's outside the immediate Reno/Sparks/Lake Tahoe area, the new $118 million Carson Tahoe Regional Medical Center in Carson City offers a plethora of high-tech medical care to people living just south of Reno. For information click on www.carsontahoe.com.

Sparks
NORTHERN NEVADA ADULT MENTAL HEALTH SERVICES
480 Galletti Way
(775) 688-2078
www.mhds.state.nv.us
Operated by the state of Nevada, the Northern Nevada Adult Mental Health Services offers psychiatric services, day treatment, and case management. Treatment in its 74-bed adult psychiatric hospital includes diagnostic and therapeutic services. Program fees are on a sliding scale, depending upon eligibility.

NORTHERN NEVADA MEDICAL CENTER
2375 East Prater Way
(775) 331-7000
www.northernnvmed.com
It's large enough to offer comprehensive medical services but small enough to add a personal touch to healing. Originally Sparks Family Hospital when it opened in 1983, Northern Nevada Medical Center (NNMC) is a 100-bed acute-care hospital on 23 acres in Sparks. It has a 24-hour emergency room and complete surgical and diagnostic services, including a comprehensive same-day surgery program.

Although it sounds like a pizza delivery system, it's the only hospital that has a "15-minute ER Guarantee," which means your emergency room visit is free if you're not seen within 15 minutes by a nurse and 60 minutes by a doctor. The center also follows up almost all cases that come through the ER with a phone call home after the patient is released from the hospital. NNMC also boasts a pre-admission program designed to familiarize patients with staff and hospital procedures before treatment. Owned and operated by Universal Health Services (the third largest hospital management company in the country), NNMC is dedicated to providing quality medical care in a comfortable, accessible environment. This philosophy begins with providing all private rooms at no additional cost. Its mission also includes a long history of special events and services that promote wellness in the community. The Senior Bridges program is nationally recognized and offers complete inpatient and outpatient psychological care for people age 65 and older.

North Shore Lake Tahoe

INCLINE VILLAGE COMMUNITY HOSPITAL
880 Alder Avenue Incline Village, NV
(775) 833-4100
www.tfhd.com

A division of Tahoe Forest Hospital District (which is based in Truckee, California), Incline Village Community Hospital is an eight-bed acute-care hospital. It offers 24-hour emergency care, diagnostic services, outpatient surgery, and inpatient observation. Because of its small size, the emphasis is on outpatient services.

South Shore Lake Tahoe

BARTON MEMORIAL HOSPITAL
2170 South Avenue
South Lake Tahoe, CA
(530) 541-3420
www.bartonmemorial.org

Barton Memorial Hospital is living testimony to what a small community can do when it works together to meet a critical need. Prior to the hospital's opening in 1963, medical care was provided by a small number of local physicians. The nearest hospitals in Reno and Carson City, Nevada, were nearly an hour away when the roads were clear and frequently were all but unreachable during periods of heavy snow. Realizing the necessity of having more accessible medical care, local residents worked to raise funds for the original 38-bed medical facility. Celebrities who regularly performed in the area even joined the effort, with the profits from Elvis Presley's benefit concert used to build the intensive care unit.

Since those first frantic fund-raising days, Barton Memorial has expanded to an 81-bed acute-care facility with a medical staff of more than 100 and a support staff of about 200. The medical complex also includes a Skilled Nursing

& Rehabilitation Center with 48 beds. Services include 24-hour emergency care with a trauma room, surgery, hospice care, home health, and diagnostics. As part of its commitment to health care and wellness in the community, Barton offers a variety of special events, support groups, and health-related classes.

Barton Memorial is an attractive, modern medical facility that is a source of great pride to those living in South Shore Lake Tahoe. It continues to be a not-for-profit hospital that is owned by the community and also affiliated with Carson Valley Medical Center in Gardnerville, Nevada.

REFERRAL SERVICES

If you're new to the Reno/Tahoe area or just visiting, the easiest way to find out about local doctors is to use the referral organizations below. Also note that most hospitals keep referral lists of physicians.

DIRECT DOCTORS PLUS
(800) 874-5775

NORTHERN NEVADA MEDICAL CENTER
www.northernnvmed.com

SAINT MARY'S HEALTH NETWORK
(775) 770-7100

WALK-IN CLINICS

The following clinics operate with extended hours and will accept patients with no appointments.

FASTER CARE
3967 South McCarran Boulevard Reno, NV
25 McCabe Drive Reno, NV
(775) 826-9111

INCLINE VILLAGE URGENT CARE & FAMILY PRACTICE
955 Tahoe Boulevard
Incline Village, NV
(775) 833-2929

SAINT MARY'S FAMILY AND URGENT CARE SERVICES
18653 Wedge Parkway, Reno, NV
(775)770-7210

6770 South McCarran Boulevard
Reno, NV
(775) 770-3254

5975 Los Altos Parkway #100
Sparks, NV
(775) 354-0200

SPECIALTY HEALTH CLINIC
350 West Sixth Street
Reno, NV
(775) 322-2122

STATELINE MEDICAL CENTER
155 U.S. Highway 50
Stateline, NV
(775) 589-8900

SOUTH VIRGINIA WALK-IN CLINIC
6580 South Virginia Street
Reno, NV
(775) 853-9959

SUMMIT RIDGE URGENT CARE
4791 Summit Ridge Drive
Reno, NV
(775) 624-2200

TAHOE URGENT CARE MEDICAL CLINIC
2130 Lake Tahoe Boulevard
South Lake Tahoe, CA
(530) 541-3277

TRUCKEE-TAHOE MEDICAL GROUP
925 North Lake Boulevard
Tahoe City, CA
(530) 581-8864

ALTERNATIVE MEDICAL CARE

It wasn't that long ago that alternative medicine, such as acupuncture and homeopathy, was viewed by many people as nothing more than treatments of last resort, used when all traditional methods of treatment had failed. But today a growing number of people rely on alternative medicine for ongoing and preventive medical care.

The Reno/Tahoe area has a number of clinics and doctors that integrate scientific and natural medicine. Some services available include homeopathy, herbology, neural therapy, chelation, hormone management, Chinese herbal medicine, sclerotherapy, trigger point therapy, and acupuncture. To find a listing of doctors and clinics, look under the subheading "Homeopathy" in the Physicians section of the SBC telephone book. You can also call the National Center for Homeopathy at (703) 548-7790 for referral and general information.

As a starting place, the following clinics and physicians offer some type of alternative medicine.

DAVID EDWARDS, M.D.
615 Sierra Rose Drive, Reno, NV
(775) 828-4055

GERBER MEDICAL CLINIC
1225 Westfield Avenue, Reno, NV
(775) 826-1900

SPECIAL SERVICES AND SUPPORT GROUPS

If you need a helping hand or simply moral support, it's just a phone call away since several hundred organizations offer support services in the Reno/Tahoe area. I can't list them all, but I'll give you a sampling of what's available. If you don't find what you need, call the Crisis Call Center at (775) 784-8090; they keep a complete list of community resources.

ALZHEIMER'S ASSOCIATION NORTHERN NEVADA CHAPTER
705 South Wells Avenue, Reno, NV
(775) 786-8061
www.alznornev.org
This association provides information, referral, support groups, and free respite care for families affected by Alzheimer's.

AMERICAN RED CROSS

1190 Corporate Boulevard, Reno, NV
(775) 856-1000
www.nevada.redcross.org
In addition to emergency disaster relief, the American Red Cross offers a variety of community education programs about AIDS, first aid, safety, and babysitting.

CARE CHEST OF SIERRA NEVADA

7910 North Virginia Street, Reno, NV
(775) 829-2273
www.carechest.com
People who have no insurance benefits or adequate financial resources for medications and medical equipment can obtain them at no cost through this program.

CATHOLIC COMMUNITY SERVICES OF NORTHERN NEVADA

500 East Fourth Street, Reno, NV
(775) 322-7073
This nonprofit organization offers emergency assistance on a variety of levels: clothing, housing, transportation, and food.

CHILDREN'S CABINET, INC.

1090 South Rock Boulevard, Reno, NV
(775) 856-6200
www.childrenscabinet.org
A highly successful organization with a large umbrella of services for children and families, Children's Cabinet is well respected for its counseling, tutoring, parenting, and substance abuse programs.

CHILDREN'S CABINET AT INCLINE VILLAGE

948 Incline Way, Incline Village, NV
(775) 298-0004
www.cciv.org
Through a variety of programs, this nonprofit is a centralized clearinghouse of information and services for children and families in North Shore Lake Tahoe.

CRISIS CALL CENTER

(775) 784-8090, (800) 992-5757
(775) 784-8085 (business)
www.crisiscallcenter.org
Established in 1966 as a suicide prevention hotline, Crisis Call Center is the longest continuously operating crisis line in the country. Highly trained volunteers answer more than 2,000 calls each month from those in need. The crisis line is staffed 24 hours a day and serves all of Nevada as well as the California area around Lake Tahoe.

FOSTER GRANDPARENT PROGRAM

406 Pyramid Way, Sparks, NV
(775) 358-2768
Children and seniors lend each other a helping hand through this program. Older persons receive a stipend, transportation, and meals in exchange for providing services to children with special needs.

GAMBLERS ANONYMOUS–RENO/SPARKS

(775) 356-8070
Individuals with gambling problems are offered support and counseling through this program.

GAMBLERS ANONYMOUS–SOUTH LAKE TAHOE

(530) 573-2423
The program offers help to those addicted to gambling.

GRIEF RECOVERY OUTREACH WORKSHOP (G.R.O.W.)

St. John's Presbyterian Church
1070 West Plumb Lane
Reno, NV
(775) 826-0990
www.stjohnschurch.org
Grief Recovery Outreach Workshop offers guidance, friendship, and support for those beginning the healing journey of grief. Programs are available at various times throughout fall, winter, and spring at St. John's Presbyterian Church,

Renown Regional Medical Center, and Saint Mary's Regional Medical Center. Call for specific times and dates.

HEALTH ACCESS WASHOE COUNTY (H.A.W.C.)

1055 South Wells Avenue (main clinic)
Reno, NV
(775) 329-6300
www.gbpca.org/hawc

This community health clinic provides low-cost medical services to Medicare, Medicaid, and uninsured patients. H.A.W.C. also operates outreach locations in Reno at 335 Record Street, (775) 324-2599; and 6490 South McCarran Boulevard A-9, (775) 825-6702.

I CAN COPE

6490 South McCarran Boulevard, Suite 40
Reno, NV
(775) 329-0609
www.cancer.org

Offered by the American Cancer Society, the program offers support and counseling for individuals and families affected by cancer.

NEVADA HISPANIC SERVICES, INC.

3905 Neil Road, Reno, NV
(775) 826-1818
www.nhsreno.org

For the growing Spanish-speaking population, this agency provides interpretation and translation services, immigration assistance, job placement, and youth programs.

PROJECT RESTART

490 Mill Street, Reno, NV
(775) 324-5166

As its name suggests, Project Restart has a variety of programs to help at-risk people start over with training and job placement.

RENO/SPARKS GOSPEL MISSION, INC.

145 West Third Street, Reno, NV
(775) 323-0386
www.rsgm.org

The Gospel Mission offers emergency food, cloth-ing, and shelter to anyone who has identification and is sober. Counseling is also available through their Christian Addiction Recovery and Education (C.A.R.E.) program.

RONALD MCDONALD HOUSE

323 Maine Street, Reno, NV
(775) 322-4663
www.thehousethatlovebuilt.org

The house provides a home away from home for families of children who are patients in any Reno hospital.

SAINT MARY'S HOSPICE OF NORTHERN NEVADA

3605 Grant Drive, Reno, NV
(775) 770-3081
www.saintmarysreno.com

Operated as part of Saint Mary's Health Network, the hospice provides medical and spiritual care for terminally ill patients and their loved ones.

SENIOR DAYBREAK

1155 East Ninth Street, Reno, NV
(775) 328-2591
www.co.washoe.nv.us/seniorsrv

This program provides day care for adults age 18 or older as an alternative to institutionalization. It offers caregivers daytime relief with nursing and social opportunities for those with disabilities.

SEXUAL ASSAULT SUPPORT SERVICES (SASS)

(775) 784-8085
www.crisiscallcenter.org

The program is a support group for survivors of sexual assault.

SOUTH LAKE TAHOE WOMEN'S CENTER

2941 Lake Tahoe Boulevard
South Lake Tahoe, CA
(530) 544-2118
(530) 544-4444 (hotline)
www.sltwc.org

Directed at women and families in crisis, South Lake Tahoe Women's Center offers counseling, emergency services, and educational outreach.

SURVIVORS OF SUICIDE (SOS)
(775) 784-8085
www.crisiscallcenter.org
Individuals who have survived the suicide of a significant other can join this self-help group.

TAHOE YOUTH AND FAMILY SERVICES
1021 Fremont Avenue
South Lake Tahoe, CA
(530) 541-2445
(800) 870-8937 (hotline)
www.tahoeyouth.org
Programs provided by this nonprofit include youth and family counseling, a 24-hour runaway hotline, and substance abuse counseling.

WASHOE ARC
790 Sutro Street, Reno, NV
(775) 333-9272
www.washoearc.org
Formerly known as Washoe Association for Retarded Citizens (WARC), Washoe ARC evaluates, trains, and provides work opportunities for retarded persons in its thrift stores. As a highly successful advocate for the mentally retarded, it also offers family counseling and community education programs.

WASHOE COUNTY SENIOR LAW PROJECT
1155 East Ninth Street, Reno, NV
(775) 328-2592
www.co.washoe.nv.us/seniorsrv
This project gives free legal help to those age 60 and older who are residents of Washoe County in the areas of Social Security, government benefits, Medicare, Medicaid, and landlord/tenant disputes.

PET CARE

If your pet needs medical attention, don't panic: State-of-the-art medical care is available at the many veterinary hospitals in the Reno/Tahoe area. Some clinics offer 24-hour emergency care, house calls, surgery, boarding, and even acupuncture. Some veterinarians specialize in just horses, cats, or small animals; others treat all types of pets.

Animals (like people) don't get sick at the most convenient times, so it's a good idea to have a couple of emergency numbers handy. Klaich Animal Hospital Ltd., 1990 South Virginia Street (775-826-1212), and The Animal Emergency Center, 6427 South Virginia Street (775-851-3600), provide on-call emergency care in Reno. In Incline Village, Nevada, you can call Incline Veterinary Hospital, 880 Tanager (775-831-0433), for emergency care. Also in North Lake Tahoe, Agate Bay Animal Hospital, 8428 Trout Avenue, Kings Beach, California (530-883-8238) offers emergency treatment until 10:00 p.m. In the South Shore Lake Tahoe area, most veterinarians rotate emergency duty, so the answering service at any of their offices will refer you to the doctor on call. Carson-Tahoe Veterinary Hospital (3389 Carson Street; 775-883-8238) in Carson City also has 24-hour emergency service.

PetMedic LLC is the Reno area's only emergency domestic animal ambulance service that provides rapid response, stabilization/first-aid, and transport for cats and dogs to an available emergency veterinary clinic. Owned and operated by a highly experienced EMT, PetMedic is one of the few services of its kind in Nevada and Northern California. For specific information, including rates, call (775) 827-9123 or visit www .petmedic.us.

If you need non-emergency transportation for your pet, call Pet Taxi in Reno at (775) 787-2222.

EDUCATION AND CHILD CARE

We take education seriously here in the Reno/Tahoe area, from our children in preschools to our graduate students at universities. Both California and Nevada are committed to providing each resident the opportunity to obtain a quality education, whether that student is starting kindergarten or entering a doctoral program.

Both Nevada and California have mandated high-school exit examinations, which all seniors must pass to obtain a high-school diploma. And, at the K through 8 levels, standardized tests are used by both states to evaluate student performance.

While schools in both states strive for excellence, each must cope with annual influxes of new students. Though the number of new students varies from year to year, all increases strain the already overcrowded hallways of school facilities. To help alleviate this problem, Nevada voters periodically pass bond issues to construct new schools.

As the number of students in the Reno/Tahoe area continues to grow, private educational facilities as well as charter schools become educational options for an increasing number of students. Private schools in the area serve kindergarteners, elementary, middle, and high-school students. A complete list of private schools in the state of Nevada is available through the state's education Web site, listed below.

Some families prefer to homeschool their children, which is permissible as long as the curriculum is approved by the local school district.

Students moving on to the local university continue to receive wonderful educational opportunities because the University of Nevada, Reno, is ranked as one of the top 100 colleges and universities in the United States by *U.S. News and World Report.*

This chapter begins with an overview of the public and private schools throughout the Reno/Tahoe area. Then I discuss the topic of child-care options in the area and give you a range of places to begin your search for those services that best suit you.

For more information on public and private schools in Nevada, you can visit www.doe .nv.gov or call (775) 687-9200. California's education Web site is www.cde.ca.gov; the telephone number is (916) 319-0800.

EDUCATION

Public Schools

Reno/Sparks and the Nevada Side of North Shore Lake Tahoe

WASHOE COUNTY SCHOOL DISTRICT
425 East Ninth Street, Reno, NV
(775) 348-0200
www.washoe.k12.nv.us

The Washoe County School District (WCSD) serves more than 63,000 students. Within the Reno/ Tahoe area, around 7,400 teachers, administrators, counselors, and others work in more than 90 schools. The average student/teacher ratio is 22.5 to 1 in the elementary grades, except first and second grades, where a state-mandated 16-to-1 ratio is maintained. To help remain in compliance with this state law, some first- and second-grade classrooms employ a team-teaching situation where two teachers are assigned to a class of 32 students. The middle-grade classrooms average a 26.2-to-1 student/teacher ratio, and the high schools maintain a slightly higher ratio.

WCSD is the second largest district in Nevada, with overcrowding a continual issue. To meet the challenge of maintaining a reasonable student/teacher ratio, some elementary schools have volunteered to go on a year-round singletrack or multitrack schedule.

All elementary school students are required by state law to take the Terra-Nova standardized test. In high school, seniors must pass state-mandated reading, writing, and math examinations to receive a high-school diploma, no matter what the student's overall grade point average is.

At the high-school level, WCSD oversees the Regional Technical Institute, which includes the Glenn Hare Occupational Center. The institute offers occupational and technical training to high-school students, including classes in electronics, computer-aided design, business systems, advanced child development, and many other occupational specialties. The WCSD also offers a magnet high-school program for juniors and seniors at a campus located at Truckee Meadows Community College (TMCC) in Reno. At TMCC, high-school students earn college credits while they finish their high-school graduation requirements.

Even though the majority of WCSD's schools are located in the Truckee Meadows, the district is responsible for one high school, one middle school, and one elementary school in Incline Village on the North Shore of Lake Tahoe.

To enroll a student in the WCSD, first contact the WCSD administration at the number listed to find out which school your home is zoned for. Then proceed to that school with the following documentation: your child's immunization record, proof of residency, and proof of the child's identity. A utility bill, a rental agreement, or a mortgage contract is acceptable as proof of residency. For child identification a birth certificate, a passport, or a baptismal certificate is sufficient. Another helpful document is a student's most recent report card to help place the student in the proper class or classes.

The WCSD provides bus service for K–12 if an elementary-aged student lives 1 mile or farther from his or her school; for middle-school students the distance stretches to 2 miles, and for high-school students it's 3 miles.

Nevada law requires that every child between the ages of 7 and 17 attend school. Kindergarten is not mandatory, but a student who does not attend kindergarten must be tested before entering the first grade.

i The annual budget for Washoe County School District has run around $425 million in recent years. However, shortfalls in revenue at both the state and federal levels have forced cuts for the near future.

California Side of North Shore Lake Tahoe

TAHOE-TRUCKEE UNIFIED SCHOOL DISTRICT
11839 Donner Pass Road
Truckee, CA
(530) 582-2500
www.ttusd.org

The Tahoe-Truckee Unified School District (TTUSD) is responsible for schools located on the California side of North Shore Lake Tahoe, including one elementary school, one alternative school, one middle school, and one high school located in Tahoe City, California. The district is also responsible for one elementary school in Kings Beach, California. The total population of these schools is around 2,000 students. California mandates a 20-to-1 student/teacher ratio in its K–3 classrooms, and all elementary school students must take a standardized achievement test. High-school students, in order to graduate, must take an exit examination.

To enroll a student in the TTUSD, first contact the district's administration at the number listed to find out which school your home is zoned for. Then proceed to that school with the following documentation: your child's immunization record, proof of residency, and proof of the child's identity. Required immunizations may be obtained from the county's health department or from a private physician. A utility bill, a rental agreement, or a mortgage contract is acceptable proof of residency. For child identification a birth certificate or a passport is preferred. Another helpful document is a student's most recent report card to help place the student in the proper class or classes.

The TTUSD provides bus service for K–12 if a student lives within the boundaries marked for his or her school, no matter the distance from the school. California law requires that children must attend school between first grade and their 18th birthday. Kindergarten is not mandatory.

South Shore Lake Tahoe
DOUGLAS COUNTY SCHOOL DISTRICT
1638 Mono Avenue
Minden, NV
(775) 782-5134
www.dcsd.k12.nv.us
The Douglas County School District (DCSD) is responsible for three schools on the South Shore of Lake Tahoe on the Nevada side. The district's administrative offices are located over the mountains in the tiny Nevada town of Minden, so at times students, teachers, and parents feel isolated from the rest of the school district, especially during the snow season.

The district maintains a high school, middle school, and one elementary school in Zephyr Cove, Nevada, along with 10 schools in the Carson Valley.

To enroll a student in the county's schools at the lake, proceed to your school with the following documentation: your child's immunization record, proof of residency, and proof of the child's identity. A utility bill, a rental agreement, or a mortgage contract is acceptable as proof of residency. For child identification a birth certificate, a passport, or a baptismal certificate is sufficient. Another helpful document is a student's most recent report card to help place the student in the proper class or classes.

The DCSD provides bus service for K–12 if a student lives 2 miles or farther from his or her school. Nevada law requires that every child

between the ages of 7 and 17 attend school. Kindergarten is not mandatory, but a student who does not attend kindergarten must be tested before entering the first grade.

LAKE TAHOE UNIFIED SCHOOL DISTRICT
1021 Al Tahoe Boulevard
South Lake Tahoe, CA
(530) 541-2850
www.ltusd.org
The fourth school district with jurisdiction around Lake Tahoe is the Lake Tahoe Unified School District (LTUSD) of South Lake Tahoe, California. This district has the responsibility of overseeing three elementary schools, one middle school, and three high schools. The students number about 5,000, and the district employs about 200 teachers.

By California state law, the elementary schools must maintain a 20-to-1 student/teacher ratio in grades K–3, but district officials say this ratio is maintained throughout all the elementary grades.

The district's high school options are intriguing. In addition to a traditional high school, students who don't speak English can attend a Transitional Learning Center, where they are placed in small classes and given more individual time with teachers. The third school is Mt. Tallac, a continuation high school attended by a small number of students, including teen parents, who would like to obtain an alternative to a high school diploma. All three high schools are on the same campus.

To enroll a student in the LTUSD, first contact the district's administration at the number listed to find out which school your home is zoned for. Then proceed to that school with the following documentation: your child's immunization record, proof of residency, and proof of the child's identity. Required immunizations and health exams may be obtained from the county's health department or from a private physician. A utility bill, a rental agreement, or a mortgage contract is acceptable proof of residency. For child identification a birth certificate or a passport is preferred. Another helpful document is a student's most recent report card to help place the student in the proper class or classes.

The LTUSD provides bus service for K–12 if a student lives within the boundaries marked for his or her school, no matter the distance from the school. California law requires that children must attend school between first grade and their 18th birthday. Kindergarten is not mandatory.

i The first Catholic school in the area was established in Virginia City, Nevada, in 1864.

Private Schools

About 40 private schools operate in the Reno/Tahoe area. The range of grades served by the institutions varies widely; you can find schools that only serve kindergartners, others that educate K–12, and others serving almost any grade combination between. Most of these educational facilities have religious affiliations, and only a few are large facilities. Most are smaller schools that boast low student/teacher ratios. With annual tuition ranging in the thousands of dollars, most of these schools are located in the Reno/Sparks area.

The following is an alphabetical sampling of some of the leading private schools in the Reno/Tahoe area. To locate schools not listed here, refer to the Yellow Pages under "Schools/Private," or, for Nevada, visit the Web site at www.doe.nv.gov.

BISHOP MANOGUE CATHOLIC HIGH SCHOOL
110 Bishop Manogue Drive, Reno, NV
(775) 336-6000
www.bishopmanogue.org
This is the only Catholic high school in the Reno/Tahoe area. It was established in 1948 and has always had an outstanding reputation in both academics and athletics. About 675 students attend Manogue. The school employs about 67 staff members teachers and is also known for its honors classes in English, science, math, and U.S. history. A dress code is enforced, and an entrance examination for freshmen is required. The school relocated to a new campus in south Reno in fall

2004. The new facility will initially accommodate 800 students, with eventual enrollment expected to be 1,200.

BROOKFIELD SCHOOL
6800 South McCarran Boulevard, Reno, NV
(775) 825-0257
www.brookfieldschool.com
Brookfield School is an independent private school with classes from preschool through eighth grade. The school is academically oriented and teaches French starting in first grade and Latin in grades 6, 7, and 8. It uses the LearnStar interactive learning method, the Spectra art program, and the Suzuki violin method. The school was founded in 1962 and requires an entrance examination. Accredited by the National Independent Private School Association, Brookfield maintains a 12-to-1 student to teacher ratio.

CHURCH ACADEMY
1205 North McCarran Boulevard, Reno, NV
(775) 329-5848
Established in 1979 and affiliated with the Church of Christ, Church Academy provides religious education to about 50 students in grades K–12. The school employs three teachers who instruct in multiage classrooms.

LAKE TAHOE SCHOOL
995 Tahoe Boulevard, Incline Village, NV
(775) 831-5828
Situated in a three-story building with 22 classrooms, Lake Tahoe School provides opportunities for students to explore technology, computers, science, and performing arts. Enrollment runs around 100 students, with a student-to-teacher ratio of 6 to 1. The schedule consists of four quarters, each averaging 45 days. LTS is fully accredited for students that are prekindergarten through grade 8.

LEGACY CHRISTIAN ELEMENTARY SCHOOL
6255 Pyramid Highway, Sparks, NV
(775) 424-1777 (elementary school)
(775) 358-1112 (middle school)
www.legacychristianschool.com

One of the newest Christian schools in the area, Legacy is nondenominational and offers K–12 classes on two campuses. The curriculum includes religious evangelical education, art, and athletics. About 300 students attend the two schools; 16 teachers work at the elementary site, and 12 teachers work at the middle and high school site. The school was founded in 1997. The Pyramid Highway campus serves the elementary levels; the middle and high school campus is located at 816 Holman Way in Sparks.

LITTLE FLOWER SCHOOL
1300 Casazza Drive, Reno, NV
(775) 323-2931

Little Flower is one of four Catholic elementary schools in the Reno/Tahoe area. The school teaches grades K–8 and has an enrollment of about 315. The students receive computer training in grades 1–5, and they receive instruction in health and nutrition from nursing majors at the local university.

MOUNTAIN VIEW MONTESSORI SCHOOL
565 Zolezzi Lane, Reno, NV
(775) 852-6162
www.mountainviewmontessori.com

This nondenominational school is affiliated with the Association Montessori International. The school teaches the self-paced Montessori curriculum to preschoolers through ninth grade, and it has mixed-aged classes. Courses include music, art, dance, drama, chess, skiing, computers, science club, Japanese, and Spanish. Its student population of around 130 is served by 10 teachers.

OUR LADY OF THE SNOWS SCHOOL
1125 Lander Street, Reno, NV
(775) 322-2773
www.ourladyofthesnows.com

This is one of the four Catholic elementary schools in the area. The school teaches grades K–8 and has an enrollment of 300. Our Lady of the Snows (OLS) boasts a hands-on science curriculum and an athletic program. And, as at most Catholic grade schools, uniforms are mandatory.

OLS has a waiting list, with preference given to its parishioners.

RENO CHRISTIAN ACADEMY
2100 El Rancho Drive
Sparks, NV
(775) 331-0909
www.renochristianacademy.net

This K–10 nondenominational Christian school uses the Abeka Christ-centered, accelerated curriculum, which includes traditional classes, religion, athletics, and extracurricular activities. The school provides before- and after-school care. It was founded in 1990 and has about 145 students and 18 teachers.

LAMPLIGHT CHRISTIAN SCHOOL
780 Lincoln Way
Sparks, NV
(775) 329-7775
www.lcsreno.com

This Baptist-affiliated school provides religious education to students in grades K–8. The school is equipped with a computer lab and boasts low student/teacher ratios.

SAGE RIDGE SCHOOL
2515 Crossbow Court Reno, NV
(775) 852-6222
www.sageridge.org

This school opened in the fall of 1998 and is the most expensive school in the area. It serves students in grades 6 through 12. Classes are taught using an integrated, universal curriculum that stresses liberal arts combined with technology. Every student is provided with a laptop computer. Core classes at the school are 80 minutes long. The school is attended by 170 students, and more than half its teachers have master's degrees.

ST. ALBERT THE GREAT CATHOLIC SCHOOL
1255 St. Albert's Drive, Reno, NV
(775) 747-3392
www.stalbertcatholicschool.org

This is the oldest and largest Catholic elementary school in the area. It was founded in 1955 and teaches 310 students in grades K–8. The school teaches the standard Catholic curriculum and boasts that, in addition to its state-of-the-art computer lab, every classroom is equipped with a computer. It has full-day kindergarten, prekindergarten, and day care. Uniforms are mandatory.

SQUAW VALLEY ACADEMY (SVA)
235 Squaw Valley Road
Olympic Valley, CA
(530) 583-9393
www.sva.org

The most prestigious school at Lake Tahoe, SVA is a boarding and day school that "provides a college preparatory curriculum in a structured environment" to students in grades 6 through 12. It boasts small classes and advanced placement courses. The coeducational school, which has 35 students and 13 teachers, administrators, and administrative staff, offers soccer, skiing, snowboarding, hiking, and tennis as its extracurricular activities. It was founded in 1978 and is fully accredited. Although not a ski academy, the school attracts a lot of competitive skiers and boarders.

TAHOE MONTESSORI SCHOOL
848 Glorene Avenue
South Lake Tahoe, CA
(530) 544-1818

This is one of only two schools at Lake Tahoe that uses the Montessori curriculum. The other is a preschool. This preschool through fifth-grade school offers year-round full- and part-time child care. It uses an individualized learning method and boasts a low student/teacher ratio. Summer programs are available at this nonsectarian, state-registered private school.

Charter Schools

Along with public and private schools, the Reno/Sparks area has a variety of charter schools. With smaller classes and more narrowly focused curriculums, charters often appeal to students who have not had a lot of success in traditional school settings. The schools listed below operate as autonomous educational entities that have received charters from the Washoe County School District or the state department of education.

ACADEMY FOR CAREER EDUCATION
(775) 324-3900
www.acehighschool.org

BAILEY CHARTER ELEMENTARY SCHOOL
(775) 323-6767
www.baileycharter.org

CORAL ACADEMY OF SCIENCE
(775) 323-2332 (secondary school)
(775) 322-0274 (elementary school)
www.coralacademy.org

FOREST CHARTER SCHOOL
Truckee, CA
(530) 550-7205
www.forestcharter.com

HIGH DESERT MONTESSORI SCHOOL
(775) 624-2800
www.highdesertmontessori.org

I CAN DO ANYTHING CHARTER HIGH SCHOOL
(775) 857-1544

MARIPOSA ACADEMY OF LANGUAGE AND LEARNING
(775) 826-4040
www.mariposaacademy.net

RAINSHADOW COMMUNITY CHARTER HIGH SCHOOL
(775) 322-5566
www.rainshadowcchs.org

SIERRA NEVADA ACADEMY
(775) 677-4500
www.snacsonline.org

Colleges and Universities

The state-run University and Community College System of Nevada comprises two doctoral-granting universities, four community colleges, and one environmental research facility. Of those, one university, one community college, and the research facility are located in the Reno/Tahoe area on the Nevada side. On the California side of Lake Tahoe, one community college affords students a chance at higher education.

In the private sector, five colleges offer accredited degree programs in the Reno/Tahoe area. These private colleges offer degree programs ranging from a BA in liberal arts to an MS in business administration.

Public Colleges and Universities
LAKE TAHOE COMMUNITY COLLEGE (LTCC)
1 College Drive, South Lake Tahoe, CA
(530) 541-4660
www.ltcc.cc.ca.us
LTCC is one of California's 106 public community colleges. Founded in 1974, the college is Lake Tahoe's only two-year college. LTCC offers 21 majors and 15 courses resulting in certificates of achievement. The majors include art, English, fine arts, physical education, humanities, natural science, culinary arts, fire science, Spanish, and criminal justice.

About 4,000 students attend the college, seeking either an associate's degree or certificates of achievement. Like most community colleges in California, LTCC offers transfer, career education, and occupational technologies programs.

The college has a child development center that is used as a lab for its Early Childhood Education programs, a theater, and a technology center. It participates in California's Golden Valley Conference in men's and women's cross-country running and women's volleyball.

LTCC recently expanded its vocational offerings by adding a nursing assistant program and a dental assistant program. It also opened a physical education facility and a culinary arts facility recently.

The college employs about 50 full-time faculty and numerous part-timers and offers both night and weekend classes to accommodate students who work (which is the majority of those who attend).

High school graduates are eligible for admission, as well as people 18 years old or older who are legal residents of the LTCC district. On special occasions, LTCC will admit students enrolled in grades 9–12 if their high school counselors recommend them.

TRUCKEE MEADOWS COMMUNITY COLLEGE (TMCC)
7000 Dandini Boulevard, Reno, NV
(775) 673-7000 (information)
www.tmcc.edu
TMCC provides the Reno/Tahoe area with more than 50 accredited occupational and university transfer degree and certificate programs, and it has offered two-year programs ranging from casino operations to electronics technology since 1971. Enrollment at the college has grown more than 46 percent in the last five years and totals nearly 11,000 credit and noncredit students.

The oldest schoolhouse in Nevada is the Glendale School in Sparks, built in 1864. The building was used until 1958. It is now part of the Heritage Park and Museum in downtown Sparks.

In addition to the 63-acre main campus on Dandini Boulevard, TMCC classes take place at the High Tech Center at Redfield on Wedge Parkway (a collaborative with UNR), the IGT Applied Technology Center on Edison Way, and the Meadowood Center on Neil Road. Performing arts classes are taught at the Nell J. Redfield Foundation Performing Arts Center on Keystone Avenue. Courses are also available at satellite centers, giving students more than 40 different places to take TMCC classes.

The college includes English as a Second Language program, Reentry and Women's Center, distance learning facilities, state-of-the-art computer labs, Veteran's Upward Bound Program, and Community Services Offices. The Institute of Business and Industry is part of TMCC's occupational education and business partnering mission.

The average TMCC student is 31 years old, employed, and in school part-time. TMCC conducts several courses at night and on the weekends to accommodate working students.

If you are at least 18 years old and a high school graduate, you may attend TMCC, but the school's admission policies are flexible, allowing some students to attend if they are younger than 18 or to earn a GED. Juniors and seniors in high school may also apply to TMCC High School, which is a combination high school and community college.

UNIVERSITY OF NEVADA, RENO (UNR)
1664 North Virginia Street, Reno, NV
(775) 784-1110 (information)
www.unr.edu

UNR is the oldest of Nevada's two universities and the only research institution. The campus was opened in 1885 as a land-grant institution and has grown from one building and 56 students to 200 acres and more than 15,000 students. Located within walking distance of downtown but secluded on a tree-covered campus, the university is supported by 10 schools and colleges offering 72 undergraduate majors, 64 master's degree programs, 33 doctoral programs, a four-year medical school, and a nationally recognized honors program.

UNR is fully accredited by the Northwest Association of Schools and Colleges and since 1991 has been ranked in the top 15 percent of America's public and private colleges. U.S. News and World Report always places UNR in the Top 100 schools (including Harvard and Yale) in its yearly "America's Best Colleges" issue. UNR's athletic teams receive regular regional and national attention.

UNR emphasizes a core curriculum of social sciences, natural sciences, mathematics, English, fine arts, and diversity, with additional requirements according to students' majors. The number of credits needed for graduation ranges from 124 to 134. The academic year is composed of two 15-week semesters beginning in August and ending in May. The university also offers three summer sessions. More than 96 percent of the 650 full-time faculty hold the highest degree available in their fields. Some of the colleges include College of Arts and Sciences, Business Administration, Education, Engineering, Mines, the Reynolds School of Journalism, graduate school, medical school, and continuing education. UNR is also the home of the National Judicial College and the National College of Juvenile and Family Court Justices.

Applications for admission should be received by UNR's Admissions and Records by February 1 for the fall semester and by November 1 for the spring semester. You can obtain an application packet from the Office of Admissions by calling (775) 784-4700.

Private Colleges and Universities

CAREER COLLEGE OF NORTHERN NEVADA
1195 Corporate Boulevard, Reno, NV
(775) 856-2266
www.ccnn4u.com

This trade and technical college has 250 students and provides training in electronics, data processing, word processing, medical and legal office management, and microcomputers. It is accredited by the Accrediting Commission of Career Schools and Colleges of Technology. The college offers associate's degrees in occupational studies in electronics engineering technology and occupational studies in computerized business management.

MORRISON UNIVERSITY
10315 Professional Circle, Reno, NV
(775) 850-0700
www.morrison.neumont.edu

Morrison is a senior college, founded in 1902, which specializes in business education. The college offers undergraduate programs in accounting, computer accounting, medical, legal assistant/paralegal, office administration, computer information systems, and business management. A master's program in business administration is also available.

The school boasts that its students can earn a specialized diploma in 6 to 9 months, an associate's degree in 15 months, and a bachelor's degree in 2 to 3 years. The college is accredited by the Accrediting Council for Independent Colleges and Schools.

SIERRA NEVADA COLLEGE
999 Tahoe Boulevard, Incline Village, NV
(775) 831-1314
www.sierranevada.edu

Sierra Nevada College (SNC) is a four-year, non-profit, independent liberal-arts college. The coeducational college is located on the North Shore of Lake Tahoe and offers programs in more than 15 different fields from its departments of business administration, visual and performing arts, humanities and science, and teacher education.

Sierra Nevada College is best known in the area for its fifth-year teacher education program. This program prepares students for teacher certification or recertification in California and Nevada.

Though no master's program for teachers is currently in place, the college is exploring this option.

The student/faculty ratio is 15 to 1. More than 95 percent of the classes have fewer than 20 students. The college is accredited by the Commission on Colleges and Northwest Association of Colleges and Schools. Its ski business and hotel, restaurant, and resort management major is one of the best in the United States.

Although SNC emphasizes academics, its alpine sports teams (the college's only athletic teams) are consistently the best in the nation. And why not, with so many ski resorts just down the road? Since 1989 the SNC men's and women's Eagles have won the U.S. Collegiate Ski and Snowboard Association Nationals almost every year.

UNIVERSITY OF PHOENIX
10345 Professional Circle #200, Reno, NV
(775) 828-7999, (866) 766-0766
www.phoenix.edu

The University of Phoenix is a private bachelor's and master's degree granting institution with programs in business, management, education, computer information systems, and counseling. Calling itself "a university created just for working adults," it offers undergraduate and graduate degrees in business management, business information systems, human services, business administration, organizational management, and education supervision.

The university's mission is to meet the higher educational needs of working adults. According to its plan, students attend classes one night a week and finish a course every five to six weeks. The university is accredited by the Commission on Institutions of Higher Education of the North Central Association of Colleges and Schools.

CHILD CARE

The Reno/Tahoe area is jam-packed with things to do, places to go, and people to meet, and moms and dads sometimes must do these things without the wee ones along. An abundance of day centers provide child-care services to meet the needs of working or busy parents, however, in addition to agencies that provide babysitter referrals and handle nannies and au pairs.

Even though Nevada's business is generally a 24-hour operation, there are no child-care centers that are open all night, and only a handful of home-care facilities offer overnight care. Casinos do not have child-care facilities for visitors, but most will recommend babysitting services. The phone books for each of the geographical locations (Reno, Sparks, North Shore Lake Tahoe, and South Shore Lake Tahoe) list child-care facilities, preschools, babysitters, and nannies. But just because they are listed in the Yellow Pages doesn't mean they are licensed. So how do Insiders pick their child-care providers? Carefully, and with an emphasis on the word licensed.

Choosing Quality Child Care

To choose a child-care facility wisely, you must first know what distinguishes a quality program from others. According to the National Association for the Education of Young Children (www.naeyc.org), the nation's largest organization of early childhood professionals, look for these characteristics in a child-care facility:

1. Children in the program are generally comfortable, relaxed, happy, and involved in play and other activities.
2. Small groups of children are supervised by a sufficient number of adults with specialized training in first aid and early childhood development and education.
3. Adult expectations are varied appropriately for children of different ages.
4. All areas of a child's development are stressed equally.
5. The staff meets regularly to plan and evaluate the program.
6. Parents are welcome to observe, discuss policies, make suggestions, and participate in the work of the program.

Also, the association recommends asking these questions when you visit a childcare setting to help make up your mind on the facility:
1. Are they licensed?
2. Do they charge for overtime when you are late?
3. Do they provide meals and snacks?
4. What kind of disciplinary methods are used?
5. How much training and experience does the caregiver have working with children?
6. What kind of turnover does the child-care program have?
7. What will your child be doing throughout the day?
8. Can you visit your child at any time?
9. Does the caregiver have a parent contract or written policies about fees, hours, holidays, illness, and other considerations?

Finding the right caregiver can be challenging, but it is also one of the most important decisions you'll make. Be as well educated about the facilities and caregivers as possible, and visit several child-care settings before choosing one. Also, never leave a child in a setting that you haven't personally visited, and always contact your local licensing agency to ask about the complaint history of the childcare provider that you are considering.

Child Care Facilities
Rules, Regulations, and Resources

On the Nevada side of the area, child-care facilities are licensed and regulated by the county upon recommendation of the state's Child Care Advisory Board and approval of the State of Nevada Division of Child and Family Services (775-684-4400; www.dcfs.state.nv.us). The Washoe County Department of Social Services (775-337-4470) is the licensing agent for the Reno area. On the California side, policies and procedures are regulated by the state's Health and Welfare Agency, Department of Social Services, Community Care Licensing Division (916-229-4530; www.ccld.ca.gov).

NEVADA

On the Nevada side of the Reno/Tahoe area, state law requires that all child-care providers be licensed, and it divides private caregiving operations into two categories. The first group is the family child-care home where a provider cares for up to six children. The second is a group child-care home where a provider cares for more than 6 but no more than 12 children. Each caregiver employee must obtain a work permit especially for childcare work from the appropriate sheriff's department. These employees must also be trained in CPR; policies, procedures, and programs of the facility; and the recognition of the symptoms of illnesses. Caregivers are also required to continue their training every year with a minimum of 12 hours related to courses in the field of developmentally appropriate practices for young children.

Several nonprofit agencies on the Nevada side of the Reno/Tahoe area provide free referral services for parents looking for child-care facilities. The Children's Cabinet (775-856-6210, (800) 753-5500; www.childrenscabinet.org) provides resource and referral services to help parents in their search for child-care services. The Community Services Agency (775-786-6023; www.csareno.org); The Division of Child and Family Services, Bureau of Services for Child Care (775-

684-4421); and The Washoe County Department of Social Services (775-337-4470) will also provide you with a list of licensed child-care providers and will advise you if any complaints have been filed against a particular facility.

CALIFORNIA

Private-family child-care homes in California are divided into two categories: small family child-care homes with up to 8 children and large family child-care homes with up to 14 children. Each child-care facility must be in strict compliance with staffing ratios and capacity restrictions. While not mandated by law, staff at these facilities are advised to get training in preventive health practices, CPR, pediatric first aid, sanitary food handling, child nutrition, caring for children with special needs, and reporting signs of child abuse. State statute requires that child-care providers receive training in prevention of infectious disease and childhood injuries. In addition to these training suggestions and requirements, all employees who have frequent and routine contact with the children must also be fingerprinted for a thorough background check. Furthermore, the facilities are under strict fire-safety rules, and the state has the right to send inspectors to large, licensed facilities at any time without notice.

The state of California's Community Care Licensing Division (916-229-4530; www.ccld .ca.gov) can tell you about any complaints lodged against day-care facilities. Several nonprofit consumer assistance groups provide information about child-care facilities on the California side of the Reno/Tahoe area. The Choices for Children Resource Agency (530-541-5848), in South Lake Tahoe, California, provides child-care referrals, parent and provider training, a resource library, and a child-care food program. In the North Shore Lake Tahoe area, the Tahoe-Truckee Community Collaborative (530-587-8322) is a free community resource for parents. Serving North Lake Tahoe and Truckee, California, as well as Incline Village, Nevada, the network provides child-care refer-

rals, parenting support, and recreation such as after-school sports. The Sierra Nevada Children's Service (530-587-5960) also serves the North Lake and Truckee area. The Children's Cabinet in Incline Village (775-298-0004; www.cciv.org) is a centralized clearinghouse of information and direct services for children and families in the North Shore Lake Tahoe area.

Nannies and Babysitters

Local governments in the Reno/Tahoe area don't regulate nannies, nor will they refer you to any. For information on nannies and au pairs you can contact Nanny Services of Nevada (775-334-4725; www.nannyservicesnv.com), The Nanny Club (775-333-6777; www.renonannyclub.com) and AuPairCare (800-428-7247). In addition to their nanny services, they also advertise babysitting.

Nannies generally are contracted for the traditional live-in arrangement. Even though not required by law, the more reputable nannies will be CPR-certified and licensed.Babysitting agencies in the Reno/Tahoe area are listed in the regional Yellow Pages, but like nannies, the local governments don't regulate or refer babysitters. The laws in both California and Nevada say that a license is required when caring for more than one unrelated family's child in the sitter's home, but if a sitter goes to the child's location, no license is required.

Your ideal babysitter could be your 13-year-old next-door neighbor or a 60-year-old professional. Either way, parents should always verify qualifications and check references. Babysitting rates vary, and a small deposit may be required. It's a good idea to discuss fees and arrangements with the sitter before you commit to hiring that person for the night or day.

The Nevada Discovery Museum, a learning center for children and their families, will open in 2009 in downtown Reno. For information visit www.nvdm.org.

Latchkey and After-School Programs

The problem of finding child-care services for working parents with school-age children has been eased by a local youth watch program coordinated by various parks and recreation departments in towns and cities in the Reno/Tahoe area. These youth watch programs include: before- and after-school care for kindergartners through sixth-graders, summer programs for students in schools with traditional academic year schedules, and year-round break programs for those students in year-round schools.

Before- and after-school programs are designed to provide a fun and safe environment for children when parents have to be at work before school starts or after school ends. These latchkey programs generally give children time to do their homework, provide arts and crafts training, and include special activities such as indoor and outdoor games. Program costs and requirements vary, but generally, before- and after-school care at park and rec departments in the Reno/Tahoe area are offered on a daily basis for very reasonable rates. In Reno, for example, a child can attend the park and recreation department's before-school program for about $6 per day, and the after-school program for about $10 per day. The rates for the park and rec program in Sparks are around the same. The South Lake Tahoe and Truckee Donner parks departments both offer after-school programs.

The summer program hours vary, but most begin at 7:00 a.m. and go until 6:00 p.m. These programs also vary in cost, and some require contracts on a week-to-week basis. The South Lake Tahoe district's program offers a very affordable drop-in rate—along with a wonderful variety of activities for the kids—which makes it a great choice for residents and tourists alike. The activities offered in each summer camp are diverse but can include field trips, arts and crafts, educational programs, and special activities like bike rodeos.

Because some of the elementary schools in the Washoe County School District have gone to a year-round schedule, the parks and recreation departments of Reno and Sparks have added year-round school break programs to their services. These full-day programs are for K–6 youth in year-round schools.

For more information on the programs mentioned here, contact the City of Reno Parks and Recreation Department, (775) 334-2262, www.cityofreno.com; the City of Sparks Parks and Recreation Department, (775) 353-2376, www.ci.sparks.nv.us; the City of South Lake Tahoe Parks and Recreation District (530) 542-6056, www.cityofslt.us; or the Truckee Donner Recreation and Parks District, (530) 582-7720, www.tdrpd.com.

Most of the private schools in the Reno/Tahoe area (see the "Education" section earlier in this chapter) have preschool or prekindergarten programs, and the majority offer before- and after-school child-care programs. Consult the individual school for specific information on programs and availability.

Also, the local YMCA can provide some services in the area of child care. (Be aware, however, that students and/or families must be members.) Contact the Sparks YMCA (775-323-9622, www.ymcasierra.org) for further details.

Another agency that can provide after-school programs is the Boys and Girls Club. These clubs are scattered around the area, and some have programs similar to the park and recreation department programs, offering games, arts and crafts, and study hours. Contact these Boys and Girls Clubs for more information: Reno/Sparks, (775) 331-3605, www.bgctm.org; North Shore Lake Tahoe, (530) 546-4324, www.bgcnlt.org; and South Shore Lake Tahoe, (530) 542-0838.

WORSHIP

Some locals say there's more praying in Reno/Tahoe casinos than in churches, but that's anybody's guess. What is clear is that the area has boasted rich religious diversity since the first pastors preached in mining camps, trading stations, and farming communities in the 1800s.

Bringing spiritual leadership to the pioneers of Reno and Lake Tahoe presented unique challenges, however. In addition to contending with the expected hardships of frontier life, the first clergy had to travel many miles to reach flocks scattered in the tiny far-flung settlements. Conditions were often less than ideal for conducting church services, since the early "towns" were sometimes nothing more than collections of tents or temporary structures. But the early preachers persevered, even offering sermons from pulpits in local saloons if necessary. When the population boomed, particularly after the discovery of silver in Virginia City, Nevada, in 1859, the first churches were constructed. And as Reno/Tahoe became more settled, representatives from a variety of denominations arrived to help "civilize" the area.

The Mormons first arrived in 1849, when a group was dispatched from Salt Lake City to develop a settlement in the Carson Valley south of Reno. Known originally as Mormon Station, the community was later renamed Genoa after the Italian town where Christopher Columbus was born. The oldest town in Nevada, Genoa was the site of the first government in what would later become the state of Nevada. (For details about the sights in this charming historic town, see the Day Trips chapter.) With more than 20 congregations, the Mormons continue to be a well-established religious group in the area.

The first Catholic church in the region was built after Father H. P. Gallagher arrived in Genoa in 1860. With around 40 parishes in the Diocese of Reno today, the Catholic church is an important part of the religious scene in Reno/Tahoe.

With about 4,000 families as members, the largest congregation is at St. Therese Church of the Little Flower at 875 East Plumb Lane in Reno. A modern circular structure completed in 1978, the church is open and spacious, with lovely faceted stained-glass windows.

St. Thomas Aquinas Cathedral in Reno had humble beginnings as St. Mary's Washoe Mission. Established in 1871 as an independent parish, it was elevated to the status of cathedral in 1931 by Pope Pius XI. After fires destroyed earlier buildings, the church settled into its present home at 310 West Second Street in 1910. Constructed in Italian Renaissance style, the cathedral showcases exquisite stained-glass windows created by Hungarian artists Isabel and Edith Piczek.

The Episcopalians arrived in the area in 1859, and though less numerous than some other denominations, six churches thrive today. If you're looking for churches with a view, none is lovelier than St. John's in the Wilderness Episcopal Church at 1776 U.S. Highway 50 in Glenbrook, Nevada. Overlooking the eastern shore of Lake Tahoe, the window behind the pulpit presents an inspirational panorama of snow-dusted mountains and azure water. Trinity Episcopal Church at 200 Island Avenue in Reno also boasts a delightful setting right on the Truckee River. After services, parishioners can enjoy refreshments on the front lawn of the church while watching the river flow by, weather permitting.

The First United Methodist Church in Reno, another intriguing church on the Truckee River, dates from 1868 and has been in its present building at First and West Streets since 1926. A charming ivy-covered stone building, its lighted tower is a well-known landmark in downtown. Like many churches, First United Methodist has beautiful stained-glass windows in its sanctuary. But unlike any other church, the windows are framed by the Hosanna Arch, which contains the delicate sculptured faces of infants and children in the parish.

Along with Protestants and Catholics, people of the Jewish faith also established early religious communities. The first B'nai B'rith lodge was founded in 1862 in Virginia City, and the Chevrah B'rith Sholom in Reno in 1878. The first Jewish temple, Temple Emanu-El, was built in Reno in 1921. Today Jewish services are held in Reno at conservative Temple Emanu-El (1031 Manzanita Lane, (775-825-5600, www.reno emanuel.org), reform Temple Sinai (3405 Gulling Road, 775-747-5508, www.templesinai-reno .org), and orthodox Chabad (3600 Clover Way, 775)-825-8928, www.chabadnorthernnevada .com). Services are also held at Temple Bat Yam (3260 Pioneer Trail, 775-588-4503, www.temple batyamtahoe.org) in Stateline, Nevada. The North Tahoe Hebrew Congregation meets at 7000 Latone Avenue in Tahoe Vista, California (530-546-0895, www.tahoetemple.org).

Bethel African Methodist Episcopal Church is the oldest African-American congregation in Nevada. Founded in Reno in 1907, it moved to its present building at 2655 North Rock Boulevard in Sparks, Nevada, in 1993. Tracing its roots to the Free African Society Church founded in 1787, Bethel AME has experienced strong growth in recent years.

With more than 200 churches and synagogues, Reno/Tahoe is diverse in religious options. Just a glance at a local phone book will show listings for every well-known denomination, such as Protestant, Catholic, and Jewish congregations, as well as some not so well known, including Baha'i, Buddhist, Eckankar, and Muslim groups. Diversity does not stop with the variety of religious communities but also extends to the languages used in the services. An increasing number of churches offer services in Spanish because of the significant number of Spanish-speaking people living in the Reno/Tahoe area. With the overall growth in population, the demand for more and larger churches has also increased. New churches are springing up to accommodate the growing number of people who want to affiliate with a religious community.

To find specific information about church services, look up "Churches" or "Synagogues" in the local telephone books, and give the congregation of your choice a call. If you don't connect with a person, most churches provide recorded messages about the times of services and activities. Church news is also printed in the Saturday edition of the Reno Gazette-Journal and periodically in the Tahoe Daily Tribune, the North Lake Tahoe Bonanza, and the Tahoe World.

RELIGIOUS UNITY AND OUTREACH

While significant differences exist among the eclectic religious groups in Reno/Tahoe, in recent years unity has become a goal for many. Some churches foster cooperation by sharing facilities, trading clergy, and holding services together.

While charity begins at home, with many religious groups reaching out to touch each other, it doesn't end there. The well-established tradition of helping those in need has expanded to include comprehensive outreach programs that fill the gaps left by governmental and nonprofit agencies. Reno/Tahoe religious congregations are involved in myriad good works, extending helping hands to the young and old, the disabled, the homeless, the hungry, and almost anyone with special needs. Virtually every religious group has organized programs that aid others in the community. They run shelters for the homeless, distribute food and clothing to the needy, offer support groups for those in crisis, and provide spiritual counseling for those in prison. If you're looking for meaningful charity work in the Reno/Tahoe area, any one of the many churches can employ you in a rewarding way.

TYING THE KNOT

Weddings have been big business in Reno/Tahoe for many years (see the History chapter for more details). Because of the exquisite scenery and the plethora of romantic locales for both the ceremony and the honeymoon, thousands of couples come to the area every year to tie the knot. And because no waiting periods or blood tests are required, it's easy to get married on the spur of the moment.

Full-service wedding chapels provide everything you need to make your wedding both romantic and legal, including the flowers, music, witnesses, minister, pictures—even a limousine to whisk you away to your wedding-night hideaway. Some chapels are small and utilitarian, while others are large and elaborate. Many resorts in the area specialize in weddings. Check with John Ascuaga's Nugget, (775) 356-3300, www .janugget.com; the Cal Neva Resort Hotel and Casino, (775) 832-4000 and (800) 233-5551., www.calnevaresort.com; the Hyatt Regency Lake Tahoe Resort, Spa & Casino, (775) 832-1234, www .laketahoehyatt.com; or Harrahs' Lake Tahoe, (775) 588-6611, www.harrahs.com. See the Resorts chapter for details on these properties.

Most churches will also perform wedding ceremonies, but keep in mind that, unlike some wedding chapels, a church service can't be organized at a moment's notice.

There are plenty of choices for wedding locales, but some offer truly exceptional settings. These include:

St. John's in the Wilderness Episcopal Church (1776 U.S. Highway 50, Glenbrook, NV, 775-586-2535), featuring lovely views of Lake Tahoe; The Lake-front Wedding Chapel (3351 Lake Tahoe Boulevard, South Lake Tahoe, CA, 530-544-6119; www.lakefrontwedding.com), the only chapel right on the shore of Lake Tahoe; and the North Tahoe Conference Center (8318 North Tahoe Boulevard, Kings Beach, CA, 530-546-7249). Public parks also provide excellent facilities with romantic ambience, such as a charming garden setting at Rancho San Rafael, a white sand beach at Sand Harbor, or a renovated stone fish hatchery perched on the edge of Galena Creek as it tumbles down from Mt. Rose at Galena Creek Park. See the Parks chapter for more information.

If you're looking for a more exotic locale than a church or chapel, that can be arranged, too. You can get married on a yacht through Woodwind Sailing Cruises (888-867-6394 or 775-588-3000; www.sailwoodwind.com) or on the paddle wheeler *M.S. Dixie* (775-543-6113, 888-896-3830, www.zephyrcove.com).

The possibilities for a perfect wedding are endless. Check local telephone books under "Wedding Chapels," "Churches," and "Wedding Consultants" for more information. You can also log onto www.tahoeweddings.com or www .tahoesbest.com for details.

MEDIA

The roots of the media in the Reno/Tahoe area go as deep as some of the silver veins did on the Comstock Lode. At one time, more than 80 newspapers dotted the scene from Virginia City to Lake Tahoe. These newspapers constituted the first written record of the area's flamboyant history and date from 1859.

Dan De Quille and Joe Goodman are recognized as pioneer journalists on Virginia City's *Territorial Enterprise*, the same newspaper that gave Mark Twain his literary start. Alf Doten and Wells Drury gave these pioneer writers on the old *Enterprise* all the competition they could handle as rival journalists for Gold Hill's *Daily News*. Now, with only three dailies and a sprinkling of nondailies remaining, head-to-head competition in mainstream English-language newspapers is a thing of the past. But with the exploding Hispanic population in the area, competition has heated up among Spanish-language publications. In recent years several new papers have sprung up to challenge the mainstay publication *Ahora* for room on local racks.

Radio seems to be thriving in the area: 30 radio outlets crowd the airwaves between Reno and Lake Tahoe. Listeners have choices ranging from alternative rock to conservative talk and everything in between. Listeners also have the opportunity to tune in, somewhere on the AM or FM dial, almost every nationally syndicated program that's almost guaranteed to appeal to almost everyone's listening tastes.

The area's television market boasts affiliates for all the big broadcasting companies, including NBC, CBS, ABC, CW, PBS, and Fox. The local news-broadcasting stations have very competent personnel who provide the area with spirited news competition.

NEWSPAPERS

In bygone days, the Reno/Tahoe area was legendary because of its intense newspaper rivalries. Today Reno finds itself a one-paper town. The Gannett-owned *Reno Gazette-Journal* is the regional daily; it zones its local sections for the rural counties and Carson City. Even though Sparks has its own daily, the *Daily Sparks Tribune*, the small-circulation newspaper cannot compete with the much larger Gannett newspaper and doesn't try to.

South Lake Tahoe's *Tahoe Daily Tribune* is the lake's only daily newspaper, but several well-written weeklies help keep the local communities informed.

The area has only one alternative newspaper, the *Reno News & Review*, but readers can find a good assortment of out-of-area newspapers in stock at most local book and convenience stores.

Newspapers appeared to rule the communication roost some years ago, but they are finding themselves increasingly challenged by the plethora of information that is available (independent of the papers) on the Internet. As the papers gamely attempt to repackage and restructure themselves to rise to the test, it's obvious that change is in the wind. The newspapers themselves operate Web sites in addition to their usual printed paper product so you have a choice of which (or both) versions to read. Only time will tell how the printed paper product will fare alongside the electronic edition of these publications.

The following section of this chapter is divided into daily and nondaily newspapers, with a subheading for specialty magazines and peri-

odicals. Most of the publications can be purchased through subscriptions or at newsstands.
Many of the smaller papers are free.

Dailies

DAILY SPARKS TRIBUNE
1002 C Street, Sparks, NV
(775) 358-8061
www.dailysparkstribune.com
The *Daily Sparks Tribune* has brought all the news
that's fit to print to residents of Sparks everyday
since 1910.. In no way does anyone see it as a rival to
the bigger, more powerful *Reno Gazette-Journal;* its
niche is its exhaustive coverage of Sparks.

Its small circulation (about 6,000) attests to
the fact that the only readers who give a hoot
about the paper are those living in Sparks's
neighborhoods. The newspaper gives its readers
balanced coverage of Sparks's politics, police,
courts, and education, and it has a great sports
section that includes good coverage of high-
school athletics.

The paper has been called the stepchild of
the Tribune Publishing Company, which owns
several other newspapers throughout the West.
Its advertising staff will tell you that the only thing
that keeps the *Sparks Tribune* afloat is the *Big
Nickel,* a free tabloid consisting of classified ads,
published Thursday for about 50,000 readers.

RENO GAZETTE-JOURNAL
955 Kuenzli Street, Reno, NV
(775) 788-6200
www.rgj.com
Reno's only daily newspaper, the *Gazette-Journal,*
reaches about 145,000 readers Monday through
Saturday and about 185,000 on Sunday. One of
about 100 newspapers owned by the Gannett
Co., Inc., it constantly wins awards in its parent
company's yearly in-house competitions and also
takes home its share of awards from the Nevada
Press Association.

Most criticism of the newspaper stems from
the fact that it is a Gannett-owned product.
Gazette-Journal critics condemn the newspaper
for putting profit above good journalism and ridi-

cule it for taking the path of least resistance with its
editorials. Proponents of the newspaper say they
like its community-oriented tradition and the way
the *Gazette-Journal* concentrates on local news.

The newspaper prints a *Best Bets* tabloid
insert every Thursday, covering the casino, entertainment, and nightlife scenes. On Friday it produces a guide to arts and entertainment outside
the casinos, including movies and the local music
scene, and on Saturday it distributes a real estate
guide to the area.

TAHOE DAILY TRIBUNE
3079 Harrison Avenue
South Lake Tahoe, CA
(530) 541-3880
www.tahoedailytribune.com
This newspaper, printed Monday through Friday,
is Lake Tahoe's only daily. It is a member of the
Swift Newspaper Group, which also owns all the
weekly newspapers scattered around the lake
communities. The paper is printed in the mornings, with a circulation of 9,600 Monday through
Thursday and 10,500 on Friday.

In keeping with company policy, the *Daily
Tribune* carries mostly local and community
news. The *Daily Tribune* serves the Lake Tahoe
area in El Dorado, Placer, and Alpine Counties
in California and Carson, Douglas, and Washoe
Counties in Nevada.

On a typical news day, the newspaper runs
about five local stories on the front page and
devotes one page to regional, one page to
national, and one page to international news.
The sports section runs Bay Area professional
sports news and national sports stories but tries
to cover Lake Tahoe high-school and local sports
as well. The newspaper is served by the Associated Press.

Over the years, the *Daily Tribune* has become
the media powerhouse of Lake Tahoe. Established in 1958, the newspaper aggressively promotes tourism to the area.

The *Daily Tribune* also publishes *Lake Tahoe
Action* (listed in the Weeklies section of this chapter).

Weeklies

AHORA
743 South Virginia Street, Reno, NV
(775) 323-6811
www.ahoranews.com
Founded in 1983, this newspaper provides Reno/Tahoe's growing Spanish-speaking community with local, national, and international news printed in both Spanish and English. The oldest Spanish-language newspaper in the area, it serves more than 200,000 Hispanics in communities all over northern Nevada and California. The paper features two sections and is distributed on Friday.

COMSTOCK CHRONICLE
66 North B Street, Virginia City, NV
(775) 847-0765
Recently purchased by seasoned journalists, the "Voice of the Comstock" brings news of Virginia City and its environs to around several thousand readers every Friday. The straight-arrow traditions of journalism that began in the early days of the *Comstock* are alive and well in this feisty little publication under the watchful eyes of a husband-and-wife team that boasts 40 years in the business. Reporting the news in a fair and balanced way is more than just talk in this well-written weekly.

LAKE TAHOE ACTION
3079 Harrison Avenue
South Lake Tahoe, CA
(530) 541-3880
The *Tahoe Daily Tribune* publishes *Lake Tahoe Action*, a weekly tabloid that serves as Lake Tahoe's entertainment guide. This tab comes out on Friday and covers the entertainment happenings around the lake. Its sections include music, sports, theater, hot spots, and casino shows. It is a must-have for visitors and locals alike. *Lake Tahoe Action* has been voted the best entertainment guide in California many times by the California Newspaper Publishers Association. Circulation is about 22,000 for the free guide.

LA VOZ HISPANA
677 Casazza Drive, Reno, NV
(775) 827-8787
www.lavozhispanadenevada.com
La Voz Hispana (The Spanish Voice) is widely distributed throughout the Reno and Lake Tahoe area. Founded in 1999, the paper is all in Spanish and is printed every two weeks. Its circulation is about 17,000.

NORTH LAKE TAHOE BONANZA
925 Tahoe Boulevard, Incline Village, NV
(775) 831-4666
www.tahoebonanza.com
One of the four newspapers in the Lake Tahoe area owned by the Swift Newspaper Group, this newspaper reflects the community it serves and is published three times a week.

Founded in 1970, the Bonanza concentrates on local news, local sports, and local politics in the northern part of the basin, covering Incline Village, Crystal Bay, Kings Beach, and Tahoe Vista. The front page is more likely to have a spread on the Incline High School graduation than a hard news story of a local burglary. The opinion page is lively with Letters to the Editor, tirades on local politics, and explanations of local happenings. The newspaper has a circulation of around 7,000.

NORTHERN NEVADA BUSINESS WEEKLY
780 Smithridge, Suite 200, Reno, NV
(775) 770-1173
www.nnbw.biz
Although *Northern Nevada Business Weekly* takes business very seriously, its style is far from stuffy. It strives to be readable as well as informative. It's read by about 28,000 business movers and shakers each week.

RENO NEWS & REVIEW
708 North Center Street, Reno, NV
(775) 324-4440
www.newsreview.com
The only alternative weekly in the Reno/Tahoe area, the *Reno News & Review* likes to take on the

establishment and especially likes to badger the *Reno Gazette-Journal*. The staff maintains that its alternative voice is not beholden to the powers that be, and it covers everything, including stories that the mainstream media won't touch.

This every-Wednesday publication began in 1993 as the *Nevada Weekly* and was founded by former *Reno Gazette-Journal* reporters as an alternative source of news to the Gannett-owned Reno daily. They soon found they were not financially equipped to go up against the Gannett Company. The founders sold the weekly to Chico Community Publishing, Inc., in 1995, and it became the *Reno News & Review*, joining the publishing company's two other alternative weeklies in Chico and Sacramento, California.

The weekly tabloid is progressive, spirited, and targeted at the young-adult crowd. Stories often rake local politicians over the coals, take potshots at the establishment, and wreak havoc on corporate America. It also devotes a lot of space to the local entertainment scene.

The newspaper prints about 35,000 copies each week and has an estimated readership of 95,000. It can be found all over the Reno/Tahoe area in bright-red street racks at convenience and grocery stores, malls, gas stations, restaurants, and just about anywhere else the Generation X crowd hangs out.

THE SIERRA SUN
12315 Deerfield Drive, Truckee, CA
(530) 587-6061
www.tahoe.com/sun
Another Swift Newspaper Group product, the *Sierra Sun* concentrates on local and community news. The paper has a circulation of 6,000 and reaches about two-thirds of the population of Truckee. Stories range from the Boy Scouts' annual Pinewood Derby to opinion pieces on year-round education in local schools. It has won a number of awards from the California Newspaper Publishers Association and the Nevada Press Association for its editorial pages.

TAHOE WORLD
395 North Lake Boulevard
Tahoe City, CA
(530) 583-3487
www.swift.com
The *Tahoe World* has the smallest circulation of the Swift Newspaper Group's weekly Lake Tahoe newspapers, but that doesn't prevent it from winning awards from the California Press Association.

The *Tahoe World* covers community and local news in Tahoe City, Kings Beach, and on the western side of the lake. Started in 1963, it reaches about 5,800 readers. Like its sister weeklies around the lake, this newspaper concentrates on keeping its readers informed of all the local happenings.

MAGAZINES AND OTHER PRINT MEDIA

CLEVER!
105 Cal Lane
Sparks, NV
(775) 358-8822
www.clevermagazine.net
If you're looking for inspiration on where to spend your money, look no further than *Clever!* magazine. Chock-full of pretty pictures of clothes, jewelry, and gift goodies, it's short on text but long on the very latest in fashion, beauty, and, best of all, where to buy it. You'll find *Clever!* at publication racks around town as well as at salons and a variety of waiting rooms where women kill time.

FAIRWAYS & GREENS MAGAZINE
527 Humboldt Street
Reno, NV
(775) 852-5845, (877) 399-4733
www.fgmagazine.com
A testament to the immense popularity of golf in the Reno/Tahoe area, *Fairways & Greens Magazine* keeps ardent golfers up to date with six issues a year full of travel and general golf news. You'll

never have to wonder what it might be like to play the newest courses; the magazine features detailed descriptions from a player's point of view. And what golfer doesn't simply relish travel that offers superb golf for a great discount? *FG* magazine ferrets out these deals to share with its readers. For your own copy, call the number above.

FAMILY PULSE
1000 Caughlin Crossing, Suite 15
Reno, NV
(775) 329-4331
familypulsemag.com

Moms, dads, and grandparents in the Reno/Tahoe area have embraced *Family Pulse* magazine for its invaluable information on every aspect of parenting. Profiling the reality of today's family life, the publication covers such things as health, education, activities, travel, and nutrition along with heartwarming stories and photos of real families. With a decidedly upbeat tone, Family Pulse gently reminds readers just how important their families are.

GENERATION BOOMER
1105 Terminal Way
Reno, NV
(775) 324-3705
www.generation4boomers.com

Published by *Senior Spectrum* newspaper, *Generation Boomer* is targeted at up-and-coming baby boomers who will soon be interested in aging issues. With stories on travel, leisure, health, fitness, and finances, the magazine seeks to educate as well as entertain its readers about leading a quality life that enables people to age gracefully. In contrast with many senior-oriented publications, *Generation Boomer* is colorful, slick and, upbeat. You'll find it in newspaper racks all around the area.

NEVADA FARM BUREAU AGRICULTURE & LIVESTOCK JOURNAL
2165 Green Vista Drive, Suite 205
Sparks, NV
(775) 674-4000
www.nvfb.fb.org

This monthly tabloid provides readers with news about Nevada's agriculture and farming. Produced by the Nevada Farm Bureau and circulated to farm bureau families, the newspaper's motto is "All the News Farmers Can Use." Its circulation is about 2,100, and copies are available by subscription or from the farm bureau.

NEVADA MAGAZINE
401 North Carson Street, Suite 100
Carson City, NV
(775) 687-5416
(800) 495-3281 (subscriptions)
www.nevadamagazine.com

Nevada Magazine is published by the Nevada Department of Tourism and reaches about 80,000 readers every other month. Even though the magazine is not published in Reno or Lake Tahoe, it devotes many articles and stories to the region. The publication is the state's official guide to recreation, travel, people, history, and events in the Silver State. The best magazine for learning about the state's history, it has been published since 1936 and is available by subscription; it can also be found at magazine racks around the area. You can buy Nevada memorabilia, such as slot machines and clothing, from the magazines's online stores.

THE NEVADA RANCHER
1022 South Grass Valley Road,
Winnemucca, NV
(775) 623-5011
www.nevadarancher.com

Reno is at the western edge of the vast ranchlands of the Great Basin, and this tabloid covers ranching and agricultural interests in Nevada and the West. It includes livestock events, a local calendar of events, feature stories, ranching news briefs, research articles, sales reports, 4-H happenings, and high school rodeo news. Founded in 1970, this monthly publication has a paid subscription of about 2,300 and reaches about 4,000 readers. It is available by subscription and can be picked up in Sparks at Rogers Cowboy Supply at 2252 Oddie Boulevard.

PET FOLIO
1605 Del Monte Lane, Reno, NV
(775) 722-9914
www.petfoliomagazine.com
For all the latest events and products concerning pets, pick up a free copy of bi-monthly *Pet Folio* in newspaper/magazine racks in the area. You'll find interesting stories written by pet psychics, veterinarians, dedicated pet owners, and retailers of pet products. If you like to get out and socialize with your pet, you won't want to miss the many activities offered especially for pets, such as the Mutt Strut at Sparks Marina Park and the free doggie swim day at Idlewild Park swimming pool.

RANGE
106 East Adams, Suite 201
Carson City, NV
(775) 884-2200
www.rangemagazine.com
Celebrating the cowboy spirit, *Range* magazine is an award-winning forum for issues that affect the American West. If you want to know about the people, lifestyles, lands, and wildlife of the "outback," you'll find plenty to pique your interest in this well-written publication. It's controversial, it's passionate, but it's never boring.

RENO MAGAZINE
955 Kuenzli Street, Reno, NV
(775) 788-6443 (subscriptions)
www.renomagazine.biz
Typical of many resort and city magazines, *Reno Magazine* is a feel-good publication loaded with pretty pictures of beautiful people living in beautiful houses and eating beautiful food. Published by the *Reno Gazette-Journal* people, it first hit magazine racks in 2002. You won't find any hard-hitting journalism here, but you'll probably enjoy wallowing in the "Reno Lifestyle."

RENOOUT
P.O. Box 70366
Reno, NV 89570
(800) 409-5112
www.renooutmag.com

The voice of the lesbian, gay, bisexual, and transgender (LGBT) community in Northern Nevada, *RenoOut* addresses issues of interest from a classy viewpoint. With a focus on families, heroes, celebrations, and LGBT community contributions, stories are upbeat and informative. This monthly mag can be picked up in racks around the area or purchased by subscription.

RLIFE
1000 Caughlin Crossing, Suite 15
Reno, NV
(775) 324-4332
www.rlifemagazine.com
Although *RLife* has some of the characteristics of a typical city magazine, such as photos of beautiful people doing beautiful things in beautiful homes, it also goes much deeper to explore the unique quality of life in the Reno/Tahoe area. Along with the glitz you'll find in-depth stories about the real people (as the name suggests) who live, work, and play in the Truckee Meadows. Each issue is a delight that can be enjoyed fully from cover to cover.

SENIOR SPECTRUM
1105 Terminal Way, Reno, NV
(775) 348-0717, (800) 253-3713
www.seniorspectrumnewspaper.com
Devoted to the senior population in the Reno/Tahoe area, this free monthly newspaper is dedicated to information and entertainment for the senior community and can be found in racks around the area. The *Spectrum* has carried articles dealing with retirement, financial and legal advice, health and fitness, nutrition, and columns by local doctors, lawyers, and investment counselors. The newspaper also has included restaurant reviews and has featured advertisements by some companies that give seniors discounts. A monthly calendar of events is included, as well as a classified ads section and feature stories about local seniors. The newspaper began publishing in 1985.

SIERRA NEVADA GLOW
580 Mallory Way
Carson City, NV
(775) 882-2111
www.sierranevadaglow.com
Launched in 2008, *Sierra Nevada Glow* dishes out stories on such subjects as self-improvement, managing finances, fashion trends, fun getaways, and cooking. Written for women from 20 to 45 years old, it's a classy resource sure to please. You can find it in racks in Carson City as well as in the Reno/Sparks and Tahoe area.

SUNNY DAY GUIDE TO LAKE TAHOE
(775) 833-4311
www.sunnydayguide.com
This publication is printed for the Incline Village/Crystal Bay, North Lake Tahoe, and Tahoe/Douglas Chambers of Commerce. The small magazine is filled with feature stories about both the North Shore and the South Shore of Lake Tahoe and includes maps of the entire lake. It has a calendar of events, a casino chart, a beach chart, and a list of almost every restaurant around the lake. It also includes special sections on shopping, lake activities, fishing, and golfing. Almost every page offers a discount coupon to one of the many businesses around the area. The *Sunny Day Guide* is published in June and December.

TAHOE QUARTERLY
770 Northwood Boulevard, Suite 10
Incline Village, NV
(775) 832-3700
www.tahoequarterly.com
Like *Reno Magazine*, *Tahoe Quarterly* oozes a luxurious lifestyle that many people can only dream about. Filled with gorgeous photos of lovely scenery and to-die-for homes, it showcases a world of luxury and wealth. Although there is much more to Tahoe than what is shown here, the magazine does occasionally cover environmental and social issues. You'll find a new issue of this slick publication at newsstands every quarter, plus several special issues throughout the year.

THE WEEKLY
200 Center Street
Carnelian Bay, CA
(530) 546-5995
www.tahoethisweek.com
This weekly magazine contains current events, entertainment, recreation, and sightseeing information for Truckee and the North Shore of Lake Tahoe. Visitors and residents alike find this guide useful in planning weekends or vacations around the northern part of the lake. The circulation is about 20,000, and copies can be found at various business locations around the North Shore.

THE WOLF PACK EDGE
105 Cal Lane, Sparks, NV 89432
(775) 787-3343
www.packedge.com
This newspaper is published monthly from September through June and is devoted to articles about athletics at the University of Nevada, Reno, and Northern Nevada High School. The publication is independently owned and is not affiliated with the university. It derives its name from a play on words using UNR's mascot and team name—the Wolf Pack. The newspaper does an outstanding job covering revenue-generating sports (football, basketball, and baseball) but also devotes a lot of ink to non-revenue–generating sports such as skiing, swimming, tennis, and golf. The 1997–1998 school year was its first year of publication, and it garnered a good readership; these days the paper has a print run of 25,000 copies. The paper can be found all over the area and often shares the news racks with the *Reno News & Review*.

RADIO

The first radio station hit the Reno/Tahoe airwaves in 1928, and since then radio has grown to offer every type of programming, from conservative talk to alternative rock. About 30 stations on both the AM and FM dials broadcast from Reno to the South Shore of Lake Tahoe.

The most popular stations, according to Arbitron ratings, are those with either country or news/talk formats. Following is a sampling of area stations categorized by format, but this roster is not chiseled in stone. Reno/Tahoe radio stations seem to change format and frequencies as often as two cherries pop up on the pay line of a slot machine.

Adult Contemporary

KRNO 106.9 FM

Alternative/Classic Rock

KDOT 104.5 FM; www.kdot.com
KLCA 96.5 FM (Alice)
KNEV 95.5 FM (Magic 95)
KODS 103.7 FM
KOZZ 105.7 FM; www.kozzradio.com
KRZQ 100.9 FM
KTHX 100.1 FM (The X)
KURK 92.9 FM
KZTQ 97.3 FM (K-Wins)

Christian

KIHM 920 AM
KLRH 88.3 FM; www.klove.com
KRNG 101.3 FM (The Renegade)

Country

KBUL 98.1 FM; www.kbul.com
KHIT 1450 AM
KUUB 94.5 FM; www.cubcountry945.com

Jazz

KJZS 92.1 FM; www.smoothjazzreno.com
KUNR 88.7 FM (Public radio from the UNR campus); www.kunr.org

News-Talk

KBZZ 1270 AM; www.kbzzradio.com
KKOH 780 AM; www.kkoh.com
KOWL 1490 AM
KRNV 101.7 FM

Oldies

KBDB 1400 AM KPTL 1300 AM

Spanish

KQLO 1590 AM
KRNV 102.1 FM
KXEQ 1340 AM (La Super Q)
KXTO 1550 AM

Sports

KPLY 1230 AM
KPTT 630 AM

TELEVISION

Reno/Tahoe television offers a variety of choices for viewers. Local TV stations that currently broadcast in the area are affiliated with ABC, CBS, Fox, NBC, PBS, CW, My TV, a public-access channel, and a Spanish-language station.

The ABC, CBS, and NBC affiliates provide news broadcasts at least four times per day, usually beginning at 6:00 a.m. This competition has been good for viewers. Each station has a bevy of reporters and camera technicians, minivans, and satellite trucks that constantly roam the area, providing excellent on-the-spot news coverage.

Azteca America provides a growing Latino population with national and local news. The addition of Sierra Nevada Cable Access Television (SNCAT) in 1997 gives the general community a place to go to produce hometown programs.

Although the choices in television stations and programming can be quite mind-boggling, the options for signing up for the programming are pretty limited. Charter Communications (formerly AT&T Cable Services) is the only game in town if you want to hook up directly to a television cable provided by them. They'll sell you Charter cable and Charter digital cable. But because the complaints about Charter's poor service are legendary, many viewers have opted for Dish Network satellite dishes. You can contact Charter at (877) 728-3814 or www.charter.com. Charter will also be eager to sell you a bundle of services that includes TV, Internet access, and phone. For Dish, call (800) 280-4388 or visit www .directv.com. Although most newspapers have some sort of printed TV guide, you can find a complete listing of programming in the guide that's on your TV screen.

The following local television stations are listed in alphabetical order by station call letters.

KAME-MY, Channel 21; (775) 322-5304, www.foxreno.com

KNPB-PBS, Channel 5; (775) 784-4555, www.knpb.org

KOLO-ABC, Channel 8; (775) 858-8888, www.kolotv.com

KREN-CW, Channel 27; (775) 333-2727 KRNV-NBC, Channel 4; (775) 785-1210, www.krnv.com

KRXI-FOX, Channel 11; (775) 856-1100, www.foxreno.com

KTVN-CBS, Channel 2; (775) 858-2222, www.ktvn.com

KUVR 46 (Spanish) Azteca America, 5250 South Virginia Street, Reno, NV; (775) 327-6800

SNCAT-SIERRA NEVADA CABLE ACCESS TELEVISION
4024 Kietzke Lane Reno, NV
(775)828-1211
www.sncat.org
This is Reno's community-access television station, which receives its revenue from local cable franchise fees and uses the money to help the general public produce TV programs. It offers editing, video, and producing classes, then helps students produce hometown programs. The station broadcasts city and county government meetings and also helps the local university and community college by transmitting distant learning classes, which enables students in the rural counties to attend classes by video conferencing. Programming runs 24 hours a day.

INTERNET ACCESS

Connecting to the Internet is a no-brainer; you'll find pages of listings for Internet service providers in local telephone books. High-speed access is just a phone call away by contacting Charter Communications (877-728-3814, www.charter .com), AT&T (800-288-2020, www.att.com), Clearwire (775-828-9600, www.clearwire.com), or High Desert Internet Services (775-322-5330, www .hdiss.net). Just let your fingers do the walking as you shop around.

INDEX

ABOUT THE AUTHOR

Born and raised in northwestern Montana, Jeanne Lauf Walpole first moved to Nevada after graduating from Washington State University in Pullman, Washington. She taught high school Spanish and geography and, together with her husband, established several family-owned casinos in Fallon, 60 miles east of Reno. After some years, the pressure of this 24-hour-a-day enterprise became grueling. They sold the business and moved to Sun Valley, Idaho, with their three sons, Chris, Scott, and Kevin. In this mountain paradise the family was able to fully indulge in their love of the outdoors. But after four years, Jeanne longed for the "real world" again.

She moved to Memphis, Tennessee, where she received her master's degree in journalism from the University of Memphis. She then returned to Reno to build a career in publishing and freelance writing.

Jeanne has written for a variety of publications and was editor of *Active Times*, a regional senior publication in Memphis, and editor/publisher of *Golden Gateways*, a travel newsletter for mature travelers. She was also a contributing writer for the book *Reno & Tahoe Country: An Illustrated History of Western Nevada*. She regularly writes for a variety of magazines that include *Nevada Business Journal, RLife*, and *Family Pulse*.

Community service has played an important role in her life, and she has served on numerous boards and been elected to public office. In the past several years, her commitment to those in need drew her to Crisis Call Center, where she answers calls of those in crisis and has served as president of its board of directors.

Her passion for travel began before she could read, as some of her earliest childhood memories are of looking at pictures in *National Geographic* magazine. She has traveled extensively abroad and lived in Bogotá, Colómbia, as a Fulbright Scholar and in Mexico City as a summer school student.

When not facing deadline, she can be found hiking or backcountry skiing with James and their Chesapeake Bay Retriever, Shelby.